ETHICS AND RHETORIC

Ethics and Rhetoric

Classical Essays for Donald Russell
on his Seventy-Fifth Birthday

Edited by
DOREEN INNES
HARRY HINE
and
CHRISTOPHER PELLING

CLARENDON PRESS · OXFORD
1995

Oxford University Press, Walton Street, Oxford OX2 6DP

Oxford New York
Athens Auckland Bangkok Bombay
Calcutta Cape Town Dar es Salaam Delhi
Florence Hong Kong Istanbul Karachi
Kuala Lumpur Madras Madrid Melbourne
Mexico City Nairobi Paris Singapore
Taipei Tokyo Toronto
and associated companies in
Berlin Ibadan

Oxford is a trade mark of Oxford University Press

Published in the United States
by Oxford University Press Inc., New York

British Library Cataloguing in Publication Data
Data available

Library of Congress Cataloging in Publication Data
Ethics and rhetoric: classical essays for Donald Russell on his
seventy-fifth birthday / edited by Doreen Innes, Harry Hine, and
Christopher Pelling.
Includes bibliographical references and index.
1. Classical philology. 2. Rhetoric, Ancient. 3. Ethics,
Ancient. I. Innes, Doreen. II. Hine, Harry M. III. Pelling, C. B. R.
IV. Russell, D. A. (Donald Andrew)
PA26.E84 1995 880'.09–dc20 95–14536
ISBN 0–19–814962–X

1 3 5 7 9 10 8 6 4 2

Typeset by Joshua Associates Limited, Oxford
Printed in Great Britain on acid-free paper by
Biddles Ltd., Guildford and King's Lynn

PREFACE

The contributors to this volume are indebted to Donald Russell in various ways. All have worked closely with him: most were his under-graduate or graduate pupils, some are or have been St John's col-leagues, one is a co-author. We have all learnt from him of the importance of both moral values and persuasion in the ancient world, of Ethics and Rhetoric.

The editors are most grateful to Madeline Littlewood for preparing the bibliography, and to Desmond Costa for welcome assistance with proof-reading. Our biggest debt, like that of the contributors, is to Donald Russell himself.

While these essays were being written, the contributors were sad-dened to hear of the death of Joy Russell. The marriage of Donald and Joy radiated such happiness that it brought pleasure to all who knew them. These essays are for Donald; but, with his permission, they are dedicated to Joy's memory.

D.C.I.
H.M.H.
C.B.R.P.

CONTENTS

Envoi: Valedictory on Donald Russell's retirement.
ROBIN NISBET *Corpus Christi College, Oxford* xi

Dedicatory Epigram xvii

A. LATIN, FROM THE CICERONIAN AGE ONWARDS

1. From Epos to Cosmos: Lucretius, Ovid, and the Poetics of Segmentation
DON FOWLER *Jesus College, Oxford* 3

2. Authorial Rhetoric in Virgil's *Georgics*
RICHARD RUTHERFORD *Christ Church, Oxford* 19

3. Friendship and its Problems in Greek and Roman Thought
JONATHAN POWELL *University of Newcastle upon Tyne* 31

4. Poetry, Philosophy, and Letter-Writing in Horace, *Epistles* 1
STEPHEN HARRISON *Corpus Christi College, Oxford* 47

5. Ovid and the Failure of Rhetoric
RICHARD TARRANT *Harvard University* 63

6. *Ut ornatius et uberius dici posset*: Morals into Epigram in the Elder Seneca
GRAHAM ANDERSON *University of Kent at Canterbury* 75

7. Seneca, Stoicism, and the Problem of Moral Evil
HARRY HINE *University of St Andrews* 93

8. Rhetoric as a Protreptic Force in Seneca's Prose Works
DESMOND COSTA *University of Birmingham* 107

9. Burning the Brambles: Rhetoric and Ideology in Pliny, *Natural History* 18 (1–24)
MARY BEAGON *University of Manchester* 117

10. On the Sacking of Carthage and Corinth
NICHOLAS PURCELL *St John's College, Oxford* 133

11. Reflections on Ekphrasis in Ausonius and Prudentius
ANNA WILSON *University of Birmingham* 149

B. LATER GREEK LITERATURE

12. Sense of Place in the Orations of Dio Chrysostom
    MICHAEL TRAPP *King's College, London*   163

13. Dio Chrysostom, Greece, and Rome
    JOHN MOLES *University of Durham*   177

14. The Poetics of the *Paraphthegma*: Aelius Aristides and the
    Decorum of Self-Praise
    IAN RUTHERFORD *Harvard University*   193

15. The Moralism of Plutarch's *Lives*
    CHRISTOPHER PELLING *University College, Oxford*   205

16. 'Subject to the Erotic': Male Sexual Behaviour in Plutarch
    PHILIP STADTER *University of North Carolina*   221

17. Lucian's Choice: *Somnium* 6–16
    DEBORAH LEVINE GERA *Hebrew University of Jerusalem*   237

18. Apollonius in Wonderland
    SIMON SWAIN *All Souls College, Oxford*   251

19. Female Characterization in Greek Declamation
    RICHARD HAWLEY *Royal Holloway, University of London*   255

20. Names and a Gem: Aspects of Allusion in Heliodorus'
    Aethiopica
    EWEN BOWIE *Corpus Christi College, Oxford*   269

21. περιγίνεσθαι as a Medical Term and a Conjecture in the
    Cyranides
    DAVID BAIN *University of Manchester*   281

22. Julian and Marcus Aurelius
    DAVID HUNT *University of Durham*   287

C. ANCIENT LITERARY CRITICISM

23. Criticism Ancient and Modern
    DENIS FEENEY *University of Wisconsin*   301

24. On Impulse
    MICHAEL WINTERBOTTOM *Corpus Christi College,
    Oxford*   313

25. Longinus, Sublimity, and the Low Emotions
    DOREEN INNES *St Hilda's College, Oxford*   323

Contents

26. 'Longinus' and the Grandeur of God
   MARTIN WEST *All Souls College, Oxford*   335

27. *Phantasia* and *Analogia* in Proclus
   ANNE SHEPPARD *Royal Holloway, University of London*   343

Bibliography   352

Index of Names   369

Index of Ethical, Rhetorical, and Critical Concepts   377

ENVOI

Valedictory on Donald Russell's retirement, Oxford, 3 June 1988

ROBIN NISBET

When I was asked to deliver an encomium on Donald, I was utterly at a loss, not knowing how to discover words adequate to my theme. But help came to me from where I least expected it, as I shall now relate. For the other night, as I lay pondering the matter, somebody larger than life seemed to stand by my head after midnight; he wore a cloak the colour of hyacinths, his brow was garlanded with a prickly garland, and in his left hand I thought he carried a card-index. 'Be not afraid,' said the apparition, 'I am Menander—not the comic poet of the same name but somebody very different in all respects, the so-called Rhetor himself. And behold I have written for you a treatise, *How one ought to praise a sophist on his retirement*, not in general terms, as is my custom, but praising this particular sophist, who now for the first time has made my treatises intelligible for the most part.' When Menander told me this, I tried to voice my thanks, but could not utter even a squeak; and he proceeded.

'First you will say that the sophist was educated in a fine *phrontis-terion*, or as you now would call it a think-tank, where he learned to write Attic Greek so gracefully that he seemed to drip pure Hymettus. And after that he turned to philosophy, not for ever splitting hairs and chopping logic, as the clever young people did at that time, but drawing inspiration from the inmost groves of the Academy, and revealing himself as truly a lover of wisdom, a thing rare among philosophers at that or any other time. And he did everything so effortlessly that his tutors marvelled greatly, as they were afterwards wont to relate. In this the disciple seemed to foreshadow the sophist; for truly *ethos* is something inborn and indelible, so as not to be corrupted totally even by education. For when our sophist discourses on a passage, the difficulties all disappear like the darkness before the shining shafts of day, as some poet says, so that his auditors think they have understood the passage all along, in which for the most part they are greatly mistaken.

'Next you will say that he migrated from the *phrontisterion* to a neighbouring city, adorned with even fairer gardens, and inhabited by citizens virtually as intelligent, though to be sure they pride themselves on it less. And such was his learning and the clarity of his discourse, that young men and young women kept coming to hear him from all the cities for a mile around. And what was strangest and most paradoxical of all, he made even rhetoric seem interesting and significant from time to time, a thing that happens to few. And many were so inflamed with love of the rhetorical art that they wrote subtle dissertations on the subject, and some of them in the end became sophists themselves also.

'You will go on to praise the many-sidedness of his learning, which he has carried to such an extreme of oddity as to discourse even on the poetry of the Romans, though as is to be expected he does not deign to write about such-like things. And he is well-versed not only in rhetoric and criticism but in biographies and declamations and diatribes, as they are called by some, knowing that worth-while writers lived after Aristotle, a thing that few once realized. And if it is right to crown a general with bay-leaves because he has extended by a few stades the boundaries of his city, then surely we ought to bedeck with many and all sorts of flowers one who has extended the knowledge of his pupils by many generations of men, not suffering the discourses of the sophists to languish in oblivion, but expounding and illuminating them, himself proving a wiser sophist than most of them.

'You will add that he gave much thought to the training of his disciples, and was present at many long colloquies on the subject, considering from which books especially they might derive some benefit. And in particular he was zealous that they should all write Attic Greek, and know the force of the word σφι and many other such-like things that it is unprofitable to enumerate. But even in berating them for their ignorance, he showed himself so mild and philanthropic that nobody took offence or bore it hard in any way, though to be sure they continued writing a kind of Greek that was no more Attic than previously.

'Finally you will say that the true sophist never hangs up his gown, or stands up out of his chair, for on the one hand as he grows older he rids himself of many banausic tasks, and on the other hand he continues as before both writing and learning; and his contemporaries delight in his conversation, and the young also, if at any rate they have any sense. And you will add a wish that he may continue the tranquil and contented course of his life.'

Menander was now in full flow and seemed likely to say even more, but at that moment a cock crowed and he was gone, holding tight to his card-index. And I have set down the bare headings of his discourse so far as I could remember them, but I fear that many things have escaped me.

PUBLICATIONS OF
DONALD RUSSELL

'Notes on Plutarch's *de genio Socratis*', *CQ* 4 (1954), 61–3.

Review of R. Westman, *Plutarch gegen Colotes*, *CR* 6 (1956), 305–6.

Review of Loeb *Moralia* xii, *CR* 9 (1959), 246–7.

Review of G. M. A. Grube, *A Greek Critic: Demetrius on Style*, *CR* 12 (1962), 207–9.

Review of G. R. Morrow, *Plato's Cretan City*, *CR* 12 (1962), 40–2.

'Plutarch's Life of Coriolanus', *JRS* 53 (1963), 21–8.

Review of A. Dihle, *Die goldene Regel*, *Gnomon*, 35 (1963), 213–15.

'Longinus' On the Sublime, edited with introduction and commentary (Oxford, 1964).

'Longinus' On Sublimity (translation) (Oxford, 1965).

Review of H. S. Long, *Diogenes Laertius*, *CR* 15 (1965), 174–6.

Review of Winifried Bühler, *Beiträge zur Erklärung der Schrift vom Erhabenen*, *CR* 15 (1965), 172–4.

Review of Loeb *Moralia* ix, *CR* 16 (1966), 180–2.

'On Reading Plutarch's Lives', *G&R* 13 (1966), 139–54.

'Plutarch, *Alcibiades* 1–16', *PCPS* 12 (1966), 37–47.

'Rhetoric and Criticism', *G&R* 14 (1967), 130–44.

'On Reading Plutarch's *Moralia*', *G&R* 15 (1968), 130–46.

Articles in *OCD*², e.g. Plutarch, Literary Criticism in Antiquity, Rhetoric (Greek) (1970).

Ancient Literary Criticism: The Principal Texts in New Translations (Oxford, 1972), written in conjunction with M. Winterbottom.

Review of C. P. Jones, *Plutarch and Rome*, *JRS* 62 (1972), 226–7.

Plutarch (London and New York, 1972).

'Remarks on Plutarch's *de vitando aere alieno*', *JHS* 93 (1973), 163–71.

Review of C. O. Brink, *Horace on Poetry II: Ars Poetica*, *Gnomon*, 45 (1973), 659–63.

Ars Poetica, in C. D. N. Costa (ed.), *Horace* (London, 1973), 113–34.

'Letters to Lucilius', in C. D. N. Costa (ed.), *Seneca* (London, 1974), 70–95.

'Rhetors at the Wedding', *PCPS* 205 (1979), 104–71.

'Donald James Allan', *P. Brit. Ac.* 65 (1979), 565–71.

'Classicizing Rhetoric and Criticism: The Pseudo-Dionysian *Exetasis* and *Mistakes in Declamation*', *Entretiens Hardt*, 25 (Geneva, 1979), 113–34.

'*De Imitatione*', in D. West and T. Woodman (edd.), *Creative Imitation and Latin Literature* (Cambridge, 1979), 1–16.

'Eric Robertson Dodds', *P. Brit. Ac.* 67 (1981), 357–70.

Criticism in Antiquity (London, 1981).

'Longinus Revisited', *Mnemosyne*, 34 (1981), 143–55.

Menander Rhetor (Oxford, 1981), written in conjunction with N. G. Wilson.

Review of Janet Fairweather, *Seneca the Elder*, *CR* 32 (1982), 28–30.

Greek Declamation (Cambridge, 1983).

Review of C. O. Brink, *Horace on Poetry: Epistles Book II*, *CR* 33 (1983), 198–201.

Review of L. Håkanson, *Declamationes XXIX Maiores Quintilio falso ascriptae*, *CR* 35 (1985), 43–5.

'Richard Rudolf Walzer', *P. Brit. Ac.* 73 (1987), 705–10.

Review of Kathy Eden, *Poetic and Legal Fiction in the Aristotelian Tradition*, *CR* 37 (1987), 203–5.

'The Ass in the Lion's Skin: Thoughts on the Letters of Phalaris', *JHS* 108 (1988), 94–106.

The Place of Poetry in Ancient Literature: A Valedictory Lecture (Oxford, 1989).

'Greek Criticism of the Empire', in G. A. Kennedy (ed.), *Cambridge History of Literary Criticism*, i (1989), 299–329.

'Arts and Sciences in Ancient Education', *G&R* 36 (1989), 210–25.

'Πρόλογος' and 'Only the Other Day', in E. M. Craik (ed.), *'Owls to Athens': Essays on Classical Subjects presented to Sir Kenneth Dover* (Oxford, 1990), 1–2 and 293–4.

An Anthology of Latin Prose (Oxford, 1990).

'Greek and Latin Literature' and 'Aristides and the Prose Hymn', in D. A. Russell (ed.), *Antonine Literature* (Oxford, 1990), 1–17 and 199–219.

'*Ethos* in Oratory and Rhetoric', in C. B. R. Pelling (ed.), *Characterization and Individuality in Greek Literature* (Oxford, 1990), 197–212.

An Anthology of Greek Prose (Oxford, 1991).

Review of A. Dihle, *Die griechische und lateinische Literatur der Kaiserzeit*, *JRS* 81 (1991), 203–4.

'Ἦθος nei dialoghi di Plutarco', *Ann. Sc. norm. di Pisa*, 32 (1992), 399–429.

Dio Chrysostom: Orations VII, XII, XXXVI (Cambridge, 1992).

Review of T. Cole, *The Origins of Rhetoric in Ancient Greece*, *JHS* 102 (1992), 185–6.

Review of S. V. Teodorsson, *A Commentary on Plutarch's Table Talk*, vols. i and ii (Books 1–6), *AJPh* 113 (1992), 309–12.

Plutarch, Selected Essays and Dialogues (Oxford, 1993).

'Self-Disclosure in Plutarch and Horace', in G. W. Most, H. Petersmann, and A. M. Ritter (edd.), *Philanthropia kai Eusebeia*, Festschrift für A. Dihle (Göttingen, 1993), 426–37.

ὦ φίλος, ἕπτ᾽ ἐτέων δεκάδας καὶ πεντάδα πρὸς ταῖς
ἐκτελέσας, χαίρων τάσδε δέχου σελίδας.
ἢν μὲν γὰρ ποθέεις, οὔ τοι δυνάμεσθ᾽ ἀποδοῦναι,
ἢν δ᾽ ἔχομεν δίδομεν τήνδε λάλον Χάριτα.

M.L.W.

A

LATIN, FROM THE CICERONIAN AGE ONWARDS

I

From Epos to Cosmos: Lucretius, Ovid, and the Poetics of Segmentation

DON FOWLER

Again, what after all is the power which explores what is hidden, which is called discovery and research? Do you think it was compounded from this earthy, mortal, and transitory nature, for example, the man who first gave names to things, a feat which Pythagoras thought required outstanding wisdom, or who first gathered together mankind, hitherto dispersed, and called it to a communal way of life, or who brought within the limits of only a few written signs the sounds of speech which seemed infinite, or who marked the courses, advances, and pauses of the wandering stars?

(Cicero, *Tusc.* I. 61–2, trans. Douglas)

Die Sprache ist im Äusserlichsten und im Innerlichsten, im Grössten wie im Kleinsten selbst gegliedert, und sie ist gleichzeitig auf allen diesen Stufen Mittel zur Gliederung der Wirklichkeit. Dies unterscheidet die menschliche Sprache von allen Lautäusserungen der Tiere, dies ist Grundlage und Voraussetzung für alle ihre Leistungen im Dienste des Geistes und der Kultur.

(W. Porzig, quoted in Lämmli (1961), 88)

An important means for the informational activization of a structure is *its violation*. An artistic text does not merely represent the implementation of structural norms, but their violation as well. It functions in a dual structural field consisting of the tendency to establish order and to violate it. Although each tendency tries to dominate and destroy the opposing one, the victory of either would prove fatal to art. The life of an artistic text depends on their mutual tension.

(Lotman (1977), 299)

> To-day we have naming of parts. Yesterday
> We had daily cleaning. And tomorrow morning,
> We shall have what to do after firing. But to-day,
> To-day we have naming of parts.
>
> (Henry Reed)

One of the features of Latin poetry most familiar to critics is the oppo-sition between the narrative and the neoteric hexameter. The unit of sense in the narrative hexameter is the verse paragraph, consisting of several lines with colon-breaks distributed across the paragraph: the 'art' of the form lies in the variation of the placing of these colon divi-sions so that there is a dialectic between the cola and the stichic struc-turing of the hexameter line. Here, for example, is the opening of the boat-race in *Aeneid* 5. 151–8, with some possible colon-divisions[1] marked with ‖:

> Effugit ante alios ‖ primisque elabitur undis ‖
> turbam inter fremitumque ‖ Gyas; ‖ quem deinde Cloanthus
> consequitur, ‖ melior remis, ‖ sed pondere pinus
> tarda tenet. ‖ post hos aequo discrimine ‖ Pristis
> Centaurusque ‖ locum tendunt superare priorem; ‖
> et nunc Pristis habet, ‖ nunc victam praeterit ingens ‖
> Centaurus, ‖ nunc una ambae iunctisque feruntur
> frontibus ‖ et longa sulcant vada salsa carina. ‖

By contrast, in the neoteric hexameter sense-pauses come at the end of individual lines, and the dialectic between line and paragraph is replaced with an emphasis on the patterning of words within the line. Here, for instance, is the opening of the ekphrasis in Catullus 64. 52–9:

> namque fluentisono prospectans litore Diae ‖
> Thesea cedentem celeri cum classe tuetur ‖
> indomitos in corde gerens Ariadna furores, ‖
> necdum etiam sese quae visit visere credit, ‖
> utpote fallaci quae tum primum excita somno ‖
> desertam in sola miseram se cernat harena. ‖
> immemor at iuvenis ‖ fugiens pellit vada remis, ‖
> irrita ventosae linquens promissa procellae. ‖

---

[1] I have been generous with admitting short cola: since colon-division is a matter of rhetoric rather than syntax, there is no single correct analysis of the structure of a Latin period. For the notion of the 'colon', see of course Fraenkel (1964, 1965) and Habinek (1985). On the use made of the various possible metrical locations for sense-pauses in the hexameter, Winbolt (1903) remains invaluable.

Colon-division coincides with line-end, and division within the line is usually prevented by 'Sperrung', the separation of grammatically related words, with a tendency for the word that is less complete in sense to come first: so adjectives tend to precede the nouns they modify, particularly when the *Sperrung* is between the main caesura and the line end (*ventosae . . . procellae*).

These two forms of the hexameter are rarely, of course, kept quite as separate as this: 'neoteric' line-patterning is a familiar feature of Virgil and Ovid as well as of Catullus, and enjambement is by no means absent from epyllia. But the two approaches to the hexameter represent much more than a formal polarity. The verse paragraph is a marker of *epic*, of the continuous narration of substantial events with an emphasis on plot: the patterned line is a marker of a Callimachean poetics of syncopation, with an emphasis on description rather than narration. As with the similarly end-stopped elegiac couplet with which it associates itself, the neoteric line tends to fragment the continuity of the narrative voice into a succession of partial views of a situation. The opposition between the two forms of the hexameter thus becomes also a bearer of an ideological contrast between a unifying master narrative and a mosaic of partial glimpses of reality.[2]

Although this opposition is, as I say, a familiar one, it is less commonly observed that the *didactic* verse of Lucretius offers a third alternative to these approaches to the Latin hexameter. In the *De Rerum Natura*, the unit tends to be neither the individual line nor the verse paragraph, but the block of two, three, four, or more lines, with extensive internal patterning on the neoteric model, but within the block rather than the line. Here is an example from Book Five, 762–7:

> Et cur terra queat ‖ lunam spoliare vicissim
> lumine ‖ et oppressum solem super ipsa tenere, ‖
> menstrua dum rigidas coni perlabitur umbras, ‖
>
> tempore eodem ‖ aliud nequeat succurrere lunae
> corpus ‖ vel supra solis perlabier orbem, ‖
> quod radios interrumpat lumenque profusum?

Each of the two three-line sections in this passage divides into two lines followed by a third containing a separate clause, introduced by *dum* and *quod* respectively. Each two-line section consists of a verb of possibility in the subjunctive (*queat*, *nequeat*) with two infinitives dependent upon it (*spoliare*, *tenere*; *succurrere*, *perlabier*). The word for

---

[2] Cf. Conte (1986) and the image of Virgil's 'broken mirror'.

'moon' occurs in the first line of each section and the word for 'sun' in the second, *super* in 763, *supra* in 766. And once we have begun to project the principle of equivalence onto the axis of combination in this way, we may detect other parallels between the lines at the phonetic or graphemic level: and as with similar correspondences in strophic verse, such as the choral odes of Greek tragedy, the phonetic equivalencies may be either at the same point in the verse (762 *et cur terra*, 765 *tempore*, etc.) or displaced (763 *oppressum*, 767 *profusum*).

In the case of these lines from Book Five, there is a particular point to the equivalence between the two blocks, since Lucretius is arguing for the equipollence of the two possible explanations for lunar eclipse, in accordance with the Epicurean principle that in the case of 'unclear things' such as astronomical phenomena we should admit the (possible or actual) truth of multiple explanations.[3] Such special motivations for block structuring may be constructed in other instances also. In 1. 867–74, for instance, Lucretius is attempting to reduce to paradoxical absurdity the Anaxagorean view that to explain chemical change it is necessary to suppose that all compound substances contain elements of other substances. He gives two examples, and it is to his point that these examples are parallel:

> praeterea quaecumque e terra corpora crescunt
> si sunt in terris, terram constare necesse est
> ex alienigenis, quae terris exoriuntur.
>
> transfer item, totidem verbis utare licebit.
>
> in lignis si flamma latet funusque cinisque
> ex alienigenis consistant ligna necesse est,
> ex alienigenis, quae lignis exoriuntur.

The two blocks of three lines[4] are not only parallel in structure, but Lucretius fulfils quite literally his promise in 870 to 'use the same

---

[3] Cf. Asmis (1984), 321–30, with further literature.

[4] There is a textual problem here: the manuscripts give us between 872 and 874 the line *praeterea tellus quae corpora cumque alit auget*, which is clearly out of place. Diels transposed the line after 874 to begin a new section, lost in a lacuna, and this has now been confirmed by the Herculaneum papyrus of Lucretius published by Kleve (1989). Although the readings are very uncertain, fr. H seems to contain in successive lines the letters IGEN, LUSQ, and XVIR: that is, 874, 873, and a new line containing something like the phrase *ex viribus*, which will be second line of the new paragraph lost in the manuscript tradition. There are problems with this reconstruction—it is a little surprising that the end of the lacuna now coincides with the end of a complete sense-unit (since 875 begins a new paragraph)—but the papyrus does seem to confirm Diels's view that 871, 872, and 874 should be read together as a block.

number of words'. If we count *quaecumque*, however analysed, as two
words and include *que* as a separate word, then each section contains
twenty words.

Normally, however, the effects of the Lucretian block-structure
(which is of course by no means uniform throughout) are more diffuse.
The articulation of the argument into blocks is only one aspect of a
general stress throughout the work on segmentation, seen at all levels
of the poem. The division into books is strongly marked by separate
prologues, and a variety of less obvious but equally marked closural
features at their ends: each book has a central theme or cluster of
themes. Above the level of the book, the work articulates itself with
two parallel but overlapping structures: as three pairs of books, with
an expanding movement from the basics of Epicurean physics and
phenomena below the level of the compound (One and Two) through
man (Three and Four) to the world-system (Five and Six), and as two
groups of three books, with a movement from microscopic to macro-
scopic events, the opening of the second section being marked by the
prologue to Book Four, which, if genuine, functions as a 'proem in the
middle'.[5] Below the level of the book, the larger sections are carefully
delineated in introductory 'syllabuses', sometimes with retrospective
summaries of previous sections: the longest example is 5. 55–90 at the
opening of the final pair of books. Within each section, logical articulation through locutions like *nunc age, primum, deinde, praeterea*, etc. is
one of the most familiar markers of the didactic style. Below this comes
the block structure of the verse; below this, the formulaic phrases that
are at once poetic and philosophical, from *semina rerum* to *magnum per
inane*; below this the words themselves; below this the syllables into
which we are constantly invited to dissolve them; and at the most
elemental level of all, the letters and sounds that make up the poem, as
their analogues the atoms make up the world:

> Quin etiam passim nostris in versibus ipsis
> multa elementa vides multis communia verbis,
> cum tamen inter se versus ac verba necesse est
> confiteare et re et sonitu distare sonanti.
> tantum elementa queunt permutato ordine solo.   (1. 823–7)

This kind of articulation is of course a necessary feature of any work
of exposition or argument, from a technical manual to didactic poetry,
particularly where, as often, the instruction is emplotted as a progress

[5] Cf. Conte (1992).

from ignorance to enlightenment for the addressee. The *ars* is carefully divided into units that the tiro can master, each one a step on the path to mastery of the subject. This general didactic pattern is one of Ovid's targets at the opening of the *Ars Amatoria* (1. 35–40):

> Principio quod amare velis, reperire labora,
> qui nova nunc primum miles in arma venis.
> proximus huic labor est placitam exorare puellam:
> tertius, ut longo tempore duret amor.
> hic modus, haec nostro signabitur area curru:
> haec erit admissa meta premenda rota.

Principio and *proximus* are generically normal, but *tertius* is parodically hyperdidactic: such precise numeration is usually avoided even where the articulation of the subject is most explicit. The three topics are covered in Books One and Two, but if, as seems likely, the notion that Book Three was added later is a fiction and the *Ars* was always published in three books, the reader is misdirected to think that the three topics will occupy each one book, which would again be hyperdidactic.[6]

But although the segmentation of the text that we find at all levels of the *De Rerum Natura* is thus typical of didactic literature in general, it has fuller meaning within the context of an Epicurean poem about the universe. Friedländer coined the term 'atomology' to describe the way in which the *De Rerum Natura* played with the segmentation and resegmentation of words through etymology:[7] the wider appreciation of etymological play in ancient literature has led scholars to discount any particularly Epicurean element here[8] but the phenomenon is at the very least recontextualized. Epicurean semantics did contain a strong element of logical atomism, the resolution of complex concepts into more primary constituents. The *prolepsis* or 'first image' associated with each word,[9] as primarily a visual image, could easily be analysed in this way: a unicorn is a horse plus a horn. Lucretius' etymologizing dissolution of the constituent morphemes of words can thus be seen as an attempt to recover the original component parts of

---

[6] In the background are the topoi of the 'three steps to heaven' and the 'four bases', that is of the stages of courtship figured as a progression through which lovers pass in sequence: cf. Porph. (and Nisbet–Hubbard) on Hor. *C.* 1. 13. 15 ff., Donatus on Ter. *Eun.* 640, Lucian, *Amat.* 53, and e.g. Petron. *Sat.* 85–6.

[7] Friedländer (1941): cf. Deutsch (1939), Snyder (1980), Dionigi (1988).

[8] Cf. West (1982).

[9] All this is controversial: for the *proton ennoema*, see Epicurus, *Ep. Hdt.* 38, with Asmis (1984), 19–80, Fowler (1986), 228–9.

the compound concepts behind the words. But the careful segmentation of the Lucretian text bears a more important Epicurean message.
Epicureanism promises the truth about the universe, to *give an
account* of how things are. The Epicurean universe is not a place of
mystery and anomaly, but possesses a *ratio* which it is the task of the
philosophy to set forth. The *ratio* of Lucretius' account maps onto the
systematic *ratio* of the universe. It is not simply one story among
many, but segments the world according to its *natural* divisions, the
natural kinds which have their basis in the finite set of shapes amongst
the atoms, as Lucretius explains in 2. 478–521. The ordered divisions
of the text of the *De Rerum Natura* reflect the ordered divisions of the
world. To segment is to comprehend.

Moreover, this omnipresent stress on rational division can be
further contextualized within a general Epicurean emphasis on boundaries and limits. The message that Epicurus brings back from the
infinite in 1. 75–7 is one of a set limit to variation:

> unde refert nobis victor quid possit oriri
> quid nequeat, finita potestas denique cuique
> quanam sit ratione atque alte terminus haerens.

Against the infinite insecurity of God and the plenum, Epicureanism
offers the articulated certainty of what can and what cannot happen:
against the vain yearning for immortality, the *ultima linea* of death.[10]
This in turn merits being seen in the context of the textuality of the *De
Rerum Natura*. The link between letters and atoms goes back to the
first atomists:[11] as the National Socialist philologist Richard Harder
observed, 'die Wirklichkeit auf wenige letzte Einheiten zuruckführen
und aus ihnen wieder zusammensetzen, das ist ein echtes Alphabet-
Verfahren, ein richtiges Buchstabieren der Welt'.[12] But the articulation
of the book roll and the *capsa* is manifested on many levels above that
of the individual letters of Lucretius' words. Spoken language is often
imaged as 'ein ununterbrochene Strom',[13] without a clear beginning or

---

[10] *mors ultima linea rerum est* is the last line of Hor. *Epistles* 1. 16: its combination of
imagery, from surveying (cf. the opening of the letter) to the race of life (cf. *DRN* 6. 92)
is perfectly Epicurean.

[11] Cf. Pease on Cic. *ND* 2. 93.

[12] Harder (1942), 100. For the influence here of Harder's politics, see e.g. the closing
pages on the 'new orality' of Nazi Germany, with its stress on communal, 'volkisch'
values: the people gathered together at a communal festival form a mass with one mind
(one country, one leader, . . .: cf. the Nazi concept of the *Gleichschaltung* or synchroniza-
tion of all social groupings under the leadership of the party).

[13] Harder (1942), 100.

ending to delineate it from the surrounding continuum of discourse: by contrast, in a written work all is down in black and white, before the reader begins her own journey through the text. In 6. 92 Lucretius calls for help to Calliope as he approaches *supremae praescripta ad candida calcis*, but alongside the fiction of the reader and author proceeding together through the text is the recognition that before day broke on the first day of Spring in the opening of Book One, these words were already *praescripta*. And this again in turn reflects back onto the natural basis of Epicureanism. The *De Rerum Natura* does not advertise itself as a free composition, offering one way amongst many of looking at the world, but as the truth, the way things are; if as a poet Lucretius forges over untrodden ground (1. 926–7 = 4. 1–2 *avia Pieridum peragro loca nullius ante trita solo*), as a thinker he follows in the footsteps of his master (3. 3–4 *te sequor, O Graiae gentis decus, inque tuis nunc | ficta*[14] *pedum pono pressis vestigia signis*). Because the *ratio* of the account aspires to mirror the *ratio* of the world, the poem is in a sense already written: its order is something discovered, not composed. Epicurus is a saviour of mankind because he gave men certainty, and that certainty comes from knowing that this is the right way to see things, the only true way to divide the world:

> veridicis igitur purgavit pectora dictis
> et finem statuit cuppedinis atque timoris
> exposuitque bonum summum quo tendimus omnes
> quid foret, atque viam monstravit, tramite parvo
> qua possemus ad id recto contendere cursu.   (6. 24–8)

It is significant that these words come at the opening of the final book, and are followed a little later by Lucretius' prayer to Calliope at the end of his own race to the line. Epicureanism offers not just a certain solution to the ills of life, it offers a complete one: once the basic principles are grasped, the whole tempest of life is dissolved.[15] All you need to save your life is contained in these six books. This is the necessary corollary to the stress on the rationality of the world, because unless one's account is complete, there is always the possibility of doubt and fear (cf. 5. 82–90).

There is one further aspect of the relationship between the articulation of the text of the *De Rerum Natura* and Epicurean atomism that

---

[14] We are told that *ficta* is an archaic form for *fixa* from *figo*, but no reader could fail to think of *fingo* also: this is not, however, free invention, but the patterning and shaping of the feet to fit in the traces of Epicurus.

[15] Epicurus, *Ep. Men.* 128.

needs to be noticed, though it concerns not word and world but word and society: that is, the relation of this segmentation to Epicurean politics. The ways in which societies segment reality, and in particular the models that they use to express the relationship between segments, are clearly a central part of the ideologies of those societies. The dominant models at Rome tended naturally to be highly hierarchical, as in the account of the republic (or is it principate?) of the heavens with which Manilius closes his Stoic reply to the *De Rerum Natura* (5. 734–45):

> utque per ingentis populus discribitur urbes,
> principiumque patres retinent et proximum equester
> ordo locum, populumque equiti populoque subire
> vulgus iners videas et iam sine nomine turbam,
> sic etiam magno quaedam res publica mundo est
> quam natura facit, quae caelo condidit urbem.
> sunt stellae procerum similes, sunt proxima primis
> sidera, suntque gradus atque omnia iusta priorum:
> maximus est populus summo qui culmine fertur;
> cui si pro numero vires natura dedisset,
> ipse suas aether flammas sufferre nequiret,
> totus et accenso mundus flagraret Olympo.[16]

In contrast to this, the Epicurean world was often seen as peculiarly democratic,[17] in particular because of the absence of a controlling god to order the activities of the atoms:

> quae bene cognita si teneas, Natura videtur
> libera continuo dominis privata superbis
> ipsa sua per se sponte omnia dis agere expers. (2. 1090–2)

Now the Epicurean division of reality has its own hierarchies: just as the world of the atoms is in one sense more basic than the phenomena it explains,[18] so some propositions are more important than

---

[16] The ending has been much discussed: against the present ending, see Housman (1930), xlvi; Rech (1973), 157; and from a slightly different point of view Romano (1979), 72: more sympathetic are Lühr (1969), 68 and Salemme (1983), 65. It is worth observing the intensely closural gesture that the total destruction of the universe embodies. The *De Rerum Natura*, like the *Iliad* and many other works, had ended with the dark light of a funeral pyre: Manilius concludes with the funeral rites of the universe, and if it is counterfactual on this occasion—a technique borrowed from the end of the first book of Lucretius—then as a good Stoic again Manilius must be aware that such ecpyrosis will undoubtedly one day come.   [17] Cf. Fowler (1989), 146–7.
[18] Another controversial point: the degree to which Epicureanism is reductionist is much discussed (cf. Sedley (1989), Laursen (1988), Sharples (1993)). But to deny *some* priority to atomic explanation over other types would deprive Epicureanism of its distinctive approach.

others, and the arrangement of Lucretius' account respects that hierarchy. Nevertheless, it is important that the atoms as the basic elements of Epicurean explanation constitute an infinite plurality, interacting independently without external control. In the end, the world of atomism is democratic: one atom counts as much as another. Epicurean politics were not so simply democratic,[19] because democracy was associated with involvement in the political pursuit of empty glory: and the internal organization of the Garden and other Epicurean communities centred on the authority of the master and other *sapientes*. A better characterization would be liberal individualism, since the salvation of the individual was paramount, and the values conferred by society were at best the negative ones of freedom from attack. There were no stronger social ties, no greater sense of a communal continuum. This social atomism is more loosely consonant with the segmented text of the *De Rerum Natura*, but the parallel is there. To divide up the world and thereby make it intelligible, to stress boundaries and distinctions, to dissolve society into individual units pursuing their own ends: Epicureanism was the philosophy above all of segmentation, and thus too of the divided text.

The picture of Epicureanism that I have just offered is not an unfamiliar one. It associates Epicureanism especially with scientific rationalism, and with the liberal capitalism which has been its concomitant in the West. In the place of a mystic web of myths and obscure social ties, it offers the simple truth of plain words that map onto intelligible reality, and the free exchange of the market. It is hard to think of a philosophy less attractive to the postmodern mind. The old dream of finding the *ratio* of the universe and setting it forth in an ordered account has been abandoned even by many physical scientists, and the heroic rationalism which punctured the empty myths of religion and superstition has had to admit that it needs myths of its own to sustain itself. In place of a rhetoric which aims to uncover the truth and analyse the world into its proper parts, we have a rhetoric which constructs new worlds with ever more complex interrelations, where every construction is a partial and provisional one open to later redescription and supplementation.

The central ancient text for this view of the world is not the *De Rerum Natura* but Ovid's *Metamorphoses*, with its stress on change and the ability of the text to live through rereading and reuse.[20] The

---

[19] Cf. Fowler (1989).
[20] But Virgil's *Georgics* represent the first move away from the optimistic scientism of the *De Rerum Natura*: see esp. Schiesaro (forthcoming).

contrast between the two poems, however, is not as simple as it first appears, and a brief look at Ovid may enable us to return to Lucretian segmentation with more sympathy. The *Metamorphoses* is a *carmen perpetuum* (1. 4): we move from story to story by transitions like those in Buñuel's *Phantoms of Liberty*, in which minor characters of the preceding story come to take on a life of their own in the succeeding one, and the book divisions, far from being strongly marked with proems and conclusions as in the *De Rerum Natura*, scarcely relate at all in any obvious way to the divisions of fabula and story. Moreover, this seamless labyrinthine flow of the text is central to the ideology of the work, which takes its stand against all rigidity and hierarchy: *nihil est toto quod perstet in orbe.* | *cuncta fluunt* (15. 177–8) is fighting talk in a Rome predicated on eternally valid distinctions and divisions. But the stance of the *Metamorphoses* is more complicated than this overview suggests. The work famously begins with a description of the creation of the world from chaos which mirrors Ovid's creation of his new world in the poem. The god—or *melior natura*—who embarks on an Epicurus-like revolt against this *rudis indigestaque moles* (1. 7) and gives it shape and order is an obvious surrogate for Ovid himself: and just as before the division of chaos by *limitibus . . . certis* (1. 69) the stars could not shine, so *form* is essential to the *Metamorphoses*.[21] When the earth in 87–8 is clothed with new men, it becomes another instance of the poem's theme: *induit ignotas hominum conversa figuras*. Similarly, anyone who looks more closely at the book divisions of the poem quickly sees that far from being insignificant they are playing sophisticated games with the readers. It is one thing, for instance, to know that the book roll marks a strong break: it is another to discover that in between putting back Book Six and getting out Book Seven, the most famous of all epic road-adventures, the *Argonautica*, is already almost half over.[22]

This opposition between segmentation and the continuum in Ovid need not be left as an irresoluble dialectic. Chaos was not simply formless, but constantly changing: and the phrase used in 1. 17, *nulli sua forma manebat* will find an echo later in Pythagoras' sermon, 15. 252, *nec species sua cuique manet*. The beneficent action of god in

---

[21] Cf. e.g. Lämmli (1962), 133.

[22] At the end of Book Six, we have been told that Calais and Zetes went with the Argonauts and sought the Golden Fleece over an unknown sea in the first ship: at the opening of Book Seven the Argonauts are *already* well under way, *iamque fretum Minyae Pagasaea puppe secabant . . .* That epic *iamque* compresses more or less the whole of the outward journey into the gap between the books.

separating the elements in the creation is later parodied in the age of iron when centuriation is introduced: *communemque prius ceu lumina solis et auras | cautus humum longo signavit limite mensor*, 'the careful surveyor marked out with a long line the soil that had before been as common to all as the light of the sun and the breezes' (1. 135–6). The order that we see in heaven in 1. 170–6, with the separation of high and low gods, each in their proper places, an order that is explicitly equated with that of Rome, reflects this post-lapsarian division as well as the creative ordering from chaos with which the poem began:

> hac iter est superis ad magni tecta Tonantis
> regalemque domum: dextra laevaque deorum
> atria nobilium valvis celebrantur apertis.
> plebs habitat diversa locis: hac parte potentes
> caelicolae clarique suos posuere penates;
> hic locus est, quem, si verbis audacia detur,
> haud timeam magni dixisse Palatia caeli.

(By this way the gods fare to the halls and royal dwelling of the mighty Thunderer. On either side the palaces of the gods of higher rank are thronged with guests through folding-doors flung wide. The lesser gods dwell apart from these. Fronting on this way, the powerful and illustrious heavenly gods have placed their homes. This is the place which, if I may make bold to say it, I would not fear to call the Palatia of high heaven.)

The whole *Metamorphoses* is built around precisely the crossing of boundaries like this, between god and demi-god, divine and human: but it presupposes that those boundaries are there to be crossed, just as Steven Hinds argued that the crucial boundary between epic and elegy was always already transgressed but always already present.[23] The Ovidian viewpoint on segmentation is that it is inevitable and necessary, but always provisional: it is not wrong to divide up the world or the text, but it is wrong to think that one's divisions are eternal, that there is one right way to segment phenomena. Hence the constant thematization within the *Metamorphoses* of issues of identity and distinction: not in the name of a formless chaos, but to stress that form and beauty are all the greater if perceived precisely as not unchanging, not timeless, not eternal. So in the *Fasti*, when we again meet chaos at the beginning of the work in the person of Janus, he bears still the *confusae quondam nota parva figurae* (1. 113), the traces of his former chaotic state embodied in that double aspect of his that Philip Hardie and Alessandro Barchiesi have made central to our readings of the

[23] Hinds (1987).

Fasti.[24] Christopher Martin saw in the *Fasti* an opposition between the formlessness of human activity, mirrored in what he saw as its self-reflexive 'narrative chaos', and the eternal order of the stars: 'as all around us may change, including the names of the gods we worship and the reasons for which we worship them as we do, the stars remain as eternal guides, reminders of the one unambiguous form of order'.[25] But few will be so certain that that is the Ovidian way to read the opposition that Martin acutely detects. Change, however dizzying in its rapidity and totality, need not be formlessness, and we need not look to eternal verities for our guides.

From this glance at Ovid, we can see that what is problematic for the postmodern reader in the *De Rerum Natura* is not its thematization of segmentation but its belief in truth, in the discovery of correct ways to divide up the world rather than of simply persuasive or attractive ones. The *De Rerum Natura* itself, however, can be made to present more than one face. Like Ovid, Lucretius stresses that in the phenomenal world, all is change. If space and time at the atomic level are divided up into discrete units, and all events are bounded by these quanta, at the phenomenal level everything flows just as it had for Heraclitus:

> sic rerum summa novatur
> semper, et inter se mortales mutua vivunt,
> augescunt aliae gentes, aliae minuuntur,
> inque brevi spatio mutantur saecla animantum
> et quasi cursores vitai lampada tradunt.   (2. 75–9)

Although the atoms set limits to this change, enormous stress is nevertheless laid on the variety of the phenomenal world:

> postremo quodvis frumentum non tamen omne
> quidque suo genere inter se simile esse videbis
> quin intercurrat quaedam distantia formis.
> concharumque genus parili ratione videmus
> pingere telluris gremium, qua mollibus undis
> litoris incurvi bibulam pavit aequor harenam.
> quare etiam atque etiam simili ratione necessest
> natura quoniam constant neque facta manu sunt
> unius ad certam formam primordia rerum,
> dissimili inter se quaedam volitare figura.   (2. 371–80)

---

[24] Hardie (1991); Barchiesi (1991), esp. 14–17.
[25] Cf. Martin (1985), 274, cf. 263 on Janus' twin aspect as 'both a guardian of divine boundaries and a symbol of arbitrary, chaotic form', and 267–8, 272 on 'narrative chaos'.

Moreover, if Epicureanism delineates and sets apart, it is also the philosophy of the *omne immensum*, the infinite universe whose bound-aries are nowhere. Beneath our feet, there is no lower world, but atoms and void proceeding into infinity: however far one travels, one's spear-cast can never cross the boundary of what is into a new world of what is not.[26] If the message that Epicurus brings back from the infinite is one of the *alte terminus haerens* of our world, there is an infinite number of other worlds in which all the possibilities allowed by the theory of 'multiple explanations' can be actualized.

These tendencies to stress variety and the continuum rather than division and the truth can also be detected in the textuality of the *De Rerum Natura*. Although Epicureans resolutely set their faces against the providential unity of Stoic *sympatheia*, the individual *rationes* of phenomena are interconnected, and while Lucretius' exposition has to plot a course through the variety of the world, to arrange these *rationes* in order, he also has to suggest that they are interrelated. In particular, the twin targets of the fear of death and the fear of the gods are mutually implicated in a complicated syndrome that was well explored by David Konstan in his study of Epicurean psychology.[27] If the Epicurean stress on the intelligibility and rationality of the universe leads to an emphasis on an exposition mapping onto that systematic order—the twin senses of *ratio*, inner workings and reasoned account of them—then there are times when Lucretius chooses rather to stress the seamless complexity not only of the world but of his exposition. The poem as microcosm of the universe is segmented, but these segments are overlapping, and the connections between divisions complex: the *De Rerum Natura* in modern readings is a text whose parts are interconnected by an exceptionally rich web of correspondences. And as we proceed down the scale of segmenta-tion, we find a similar sense of complexity. One of the factors which have led some scholars to wish to play down the Epicurean context of the etymologizing in the *De Rerum Natura* is that Lucretius will often suggest more than one possible etymology for a word: *religio* for instance can be connected not only with *religare* (1. 931–2, 70–1) but also with *caeli regio* (1. 64) and *legio* (2. 40, 44). The words of the poem are as subject to dissemination and deferral as any others.

It was of course features like these which led many earlier scholars to posit an alternative voice in the *De Rerum Natura*, the *anti-Lucrèce*

---

[26] *DRN* 1. 967–83.
[27] Konstan (1973); cf. Fowler (1989), 137.

chez Lucrèce whose joy and enthusiasm for the myriad phenomena of the world worked against the dry reductionism of Epicureanism. These readings did scant justice to the complexity of Epicureanism's response to the world, and the dominant tendency of modern Lucretian criticism has been to stress rather how poetry and philosophy can be made to work together in the poem: a line of approach brilliantly summed up in Monica Gale's recent study *Myth and Poetry in Lucretius*.[28] Moreover, there are grounds for locating some of these tensions within Epicureanism itself, in particular in its anti-providentialism. The world is comprehensible and ordered, but it is not the perfect creation of a god. The articulation of Lucretius' poem is in fact in striking contrast to the accusations often made against Epicureans and to the form of the earlier Epicurean writers in Latin: if we may trust Cicero in the proem to the *Academica*, Amafinius and Rabirius avoided *partitio* and logical ordering.[29] But there is an Epicurean point to this. Epicurus elevated *physiologia* over dialectic in part because of the providentialist implications of an axiomatically ordered account of the world. The world is an ordered place, but it is also empirically complex and messy, and you cannot derive its complexity from a few simple axioms. The vision Epicureanism offers of an ordered but yet flawed world can be seen as a productive product of these tensions, rather than simply a philosophy of perfect rationality. Nevertheless, I am inclined to think that those who located a 'further voice' in the poem itself may yet be right. This is not simply a question of anti-Epicureanism, but the basic simplicity of the Master's saving truth is undoubtedly at odds with the complexity of the world many people prefer to inhabit. The message is essentially a negative one: if one can only free oneself of false myths and desires, and understand how little one really needs to be happy, then happiness is achieved. But when the jungle is cleared, what is left may be not a garden but just bare earth. The *De Rerum Natura*, 'simply' by virtue of its own complex textuality, engenders its own myths,[30] like Epicurus' revolt against *religio* or the activities of the feminine trio of Venus, Nature, and Mother Earth,[31] but while we may be happy to see those myths put at the

---

[28] Gale (1994).

[29] Cic. *Acad. Post.* 5 'vides autem ... non posse nos Amafini aut Rabiri similis esse, qui nulla arte adhibita de rebus ante oculos positis volgari sermone disputant, nihil definiunt, nihil partiuntur, nihil apta interrogatione concludunt, nullam denique artem esse nec dicendi nec disserendi putant' (cf. Reid ad loc., esp. *Fin.* 1. 22, 29, 2. 30, 3. 40).

[30] Cf. Gale (1994), esp. 99–128.

[31] Cf. Fowler (forthcoming).

service of the philosophy, it is still difficult to accommodate within Epicureanism any reason why we should need myth, why the plain and simple truth is not enough. The very images of truth and freedom which so attract us are themselves ways of seeing that are incompatible with the idea that there is just one way to look at the world—the way things are. A tension remains in the *De Rerum Natura* between the strong aspiration of Epicureanism as a scientific philosophy to the one true story and the intractable variety of stories that the work as a poem suggests, between the thinness and clarity of the message and the richness and confusion of the medium.

A Festschrift is one of the few traditional forms of publication where the 'personal' mode is allowed, and I would like to end this piece with some personal remarks. I read philosophy and literature for Greats at Oxford in the heady days of truth-functional semantics, and began graduate work with a strong commitment to realism (a commitment whose psychological roots I am happy to acknowledge). I was an Epicurean and a structuralist: somewhere beyond the confusion and variety of experience was the truth, about literature and about life. As with many people who begin with such a strong realism, when conversion came I swung to the other extreme, and I would now describe myself as a Rortyite relativist: use has replaced meaning, and I find that I can live without the foundations which used to be so important to me. If I am still attached to Epicureanism, it is as a myth and a way of seeing, not as the truth. I was supervised for my graduate work first by Robin Nisbet, and then by Donald Russell: if I attempt to blame our honorand for where I have ended up, he may well think it a poor repayment for all the effort that he put into supervising me. But I am afraid that there is some 'truth' in this view: it was through the sense of complexity of things which Donald managed to instil that I eventually lost my faith and ended up with a better one. For this, as well as for more mundane kindnesses, much thanks.[32]

[32] A version of some of the more general ideas in this chapter was offered to a Princeton conference on 'The Text Divided: The Poetics and Politics of Segmentation' in Spring Break 1994. I am grateful for comments to the participants; and to Peta Fowler, Monica Gale, Debra Hershkowitz, and the editors.

2

Authorial Rhetoric in Virgil's *Georgics*

RICHARD RUTHERFORD

As an undergraduate I learned from Donald Russell's wide-ranging lectures on ancient criticism; in my years as a graduate student his profound knowledge of Greek philosophy and rhetoric proved a constant aid while I puzzled over the writings of Marcus Aurelius. His expertise in these fields is familiar to all classical scholars; those outside Oxford may not know that for years he lectured on Virgil, and his renderings of passages from that poet's most perfect work, the *Georgics*, are well remembered. He has been known to say that too much is written about Virgil: but his well-known magnanimity will, I hope, forgive this writer's *insanabile scribendi cacoethes*, and his pupils all know that they can rely on him as a *candidus iudex*.

I

The relation between the didactic poet and his addressee was an ambiguous one from the start. Already in Hesiod, the situation of Perses seems to shift according to the poet's tone and purpose.[1] Much that Lucretius says in his great poem seems more fittingly addressed to everyman, or at any rate a more ordinary man, than to the philistine consular Memmius. Even in shorter poetry with a didactic tendency (Horace's *Epistles* come to mind), it may be hard to define the exact point at which the writer moves from personal address to an individual patron or friend, to a more broadly didactic stance, where he seems to be speaking to all mankind. The distinction is related to the contrast between poet as individual and poet as *vates* or prophetic bard.

In the *Georgics* the situation is rather more complex, for an obvious reason. The poem is formally dedicated to Maecenas, who is named at the opening of each book, but it is also in a sense addressed to Caesar,

---

[1] M. L. West (1978), 33–40; Bowie (1993), 23.

the future Augustus, who is more prominent in the proem, and is referred to or invoked, often in the most grandiose terms, at important points thereafter. The bulk of the poem, however, is conceived as instructions to farmers, who are defined as the chosen audience in the proem and addressed at various stages later (1. 101 'agricolae', 210, 2. 35–6, 3. 288 'coloni', 420 'pastor'). There is no need to waste space on the misconceived enquiry as to whether farmers would really read a poem like the *Georgics*, or whether Virgil really hoped to convince Caesar of the need for (say) a more traditional agricultural strategy: most scholars would answer both questions with an unhesitating negative. What concerns us here is the rhetorical and poetic consequences which follow from this split of addressees. Recent work on poetic 'voices' seems not to have considered this topic systematically. A simple model of the process by which a poem is communicated to its public postulates a direct relationship between poet and audience: the poet, as it were, reads aloud, speaking directly to that audience, as Virgil is said to have read the *Georgics* to Maecenas and Octavian until his voice gave out. In reality things are of course more complex: in poetry, as in oratory, we often find a number of addressees who may respond to or appreciate different aspects of the performance.[2] A subtler model might distinguish the actual author from the poet as seen or implied in the poem, and identify an implied addressee also distinguishable from 'real people' in contemporary society.[3] In what follows I offer some observations on a number of aspects of this relationship between 'poet' and 'addressee', which I hope will unite rhetorical analysis and interpretation.

The first general point is that, given this situation, Virgil's role as poet is inevitably an ambiguous one. On the one hand, he is a learned poet, writing for a sophisticated, wealthy, and highly literate audience; on the other, he is posing as an experienced countryman, practical and thorough, sometimes naïve or superstitious, giving advice to men of the soil, probably not men of great substance, advice which to Maecenas or Caesar would often seem trivial or sordid (brought out esp. at 1. 79–81, 176–7; cf. 3. 289f., 4. 3).[4] This is not to deny that

---

[2] Thus in Cicero's *Pro Caelio*, to take a simple case, the orator at various points addresses the prosecutors Atratinus and Herennius, and of course Clodia: he also plays the parts of Appius Claudius and Clodius in prosopopoiia; all of this is, in one way or another, intended to have an effect on the jury. A further aspect is opened up by the publication of speeches: once the case is over, the reader may be allowed to enjoy what the jurors missed (cf. Quint. 2. 17. 21 on the *Pro Cluentio*).

[3] Cf. de Jong (1987), etc.   [4] Cf. Perkell (1989), 40.

Virgil is himself (at least in upbringing) a countryman, nor that distinguished figures might take pleasure in the activities of the country and even the down-to-earth practicalities of harvest-time or grape-picking.[5] But the contrast between Alexandrian-neoteric ingenuity and didactic detail and prosiness is a real one, and there is ample evidence in the poem to suggest that Virgil was aware of it, and indeed that he exploited it to achieve particular effects, for instance by humorous transitions from the grand to the low, from the sublime to the commonplace.

The poet's formal statements of his subject provide an illuminating starting-point. The opening lines summarize the topics of the four books: crops and seasons, vines, cattle and sheep, bees; they do not, however, give any indication of the moral, philosophic, and religious themes which give depth and breadth to these expositions. After the apocalyptic vision of war and despair at the end of Book 1, the poet opens Book 2 with a deliberately down-to-earth, even prosaic résumé: 'hactenus arvorum cultus et sidera caeli'. The line sums up the first book once more in terms suited to the simple farming manual rather than the poem which has expanded its scope to include contemporary politics and the reflection of these events in cosmic terms. The concluding sphragis to Book 4 plays the same game: 'haec super arvorum cultu pecorumque canebam | et super arboribus' (559–60)—no hint of Aristaeus and Orpheus, or even of the bees, only a minimal statement of the poem's subject-matter. Comparable are the many passages where the countryman yields place to the bard and vice versa, often involving a humorous anticlimax as we return to more down-to-earth advice or seemingly prosaic material (e.g. 2. 288, 345, 3. 286, 384).[6]

The poet also presents himself as sharing in, observing, or affected by the country life which he praises and describes. This has obvious advantages for the exposition: rather than receiving impersonal admonitions, the reader is offered (so it appears) the fruits of experience. The poet's own recollection of pleasures and disappointments, his hopes and misgivings, raise the emotional temperature and vary

---

[5] Cf. Cic. *Cato Maior* 51–60; rather differently, *De Or.* 2. 22, echoed by Hor. *Serm.* 2. 1. 71–4. Later, note also Marcus Aurelius to Fronto, p. 62 van den Hout (i. 180–2 Haines).

[6] See further 1. 284 (incongruous juxtapositions in the 'Days' passage); 2. 177 (from *laudes Italiae* to differing types of soil); 4. 228 (after the sublimity of the bees' relation to the divine mind, back to the precise but earthbound detail of unsealing the hive—though even here 'augustam' and 'thesauris' preserve a certain grandeur). Cf. Wilkinson (1969), 71 ff.

the more obvious but potentially tedious sequences of imperatives. It is common sense (and sound rhetorical technique) for a speaker to emphasize what he has learned from the past.[7] Sometimes the authorial involvement goes further, as Virgil visualizes himself as part of a rural community: 'ergo rite suum Baccho *dicemus* honorem | carminibus patriis lancesque et liba *feremus* . . .' (2. 393 f.; cf. 192 ff.). Or he may celebrate a near-ecstatic self-surrender to the delights of country life (2. 486 f., part of a larger context to which we shall return). Rapturous pleasure in his subject-matter is also important in the transitional passage half-way through Book 3, where the poet reminds himself that time is fleeting by, 'singula dum capti circumvectamur amore' (285). There is word-play here: on the one hand he means love of his subject, on the other 'by love'—which has been the subject, for the last 80 lines.[8] Realistic detail is mingled with mild self-mockery as he exclaims apotropaically at the dangers of sea-travel (1. 456 'non illa quisquam me nocte per altum | ire . . .'),[9] or dreads the attack of a snake while he basks in the sun (3. 435 'ne mihi tum mollis sub divo carpere somnos | neu dorso nemoris libeat iacuisse per herbas').[10] Elsewhere he adopts a didactic role in a more explicit way, issuing edicts and organizing herdsmen or beekeepers (3. 295 'edico', 300 'iubeo', 329 'iubebo', 4. 264 'suadebo'). Yet this device can easily glide into more 'literary' poses: thus the superficially similar opening at 3. 440 'morborum quoque te causas et signa docebo' carries more than a hint of the learned didacticism of Nicander (cf. *Ther.* 528).

More serious is an interesting series of claims to 'autopsy' running through Book 1: for the didactic writer, as for the historian, to have observed something personally adds to one's credibility and authority.[11] At 1. 193 and 197 ('semina vidi . . . vidi lecta diu . . .'), an account of the tendency of grain to turn bad passes into memorable generalizations about natural decline: the prudent countryman becomes the

---

[7] e.g. Hom. *Il.* 1. 259 ff.; Thuc. 3. 37. 1; Arist. *Rhet.* 1393ª23–ᵇ4, 1394ª5–8.

[8] Rather similarly, perhaps, in *Ecl.* 6. 10–11: 'si quis tamen haec quoque, si quis | captus amore leget . . .'. The passage in the *Georgics* is an example of a metaphorical usage common in classical literature, whereby the writer speaks of himself as doing, or as otherwise involved in, the actions he describes: cf. C. W. Macleod (1983), 205; Nisbet–Hubbard on Hor. *Odes* 2. 1. 18; Lieberg (1982, 1985); and e.g. 'Longinus' 9. 11, 14 (if πλάνος is right), 15. 4. In the *Georgics* cf. also 3. 340: is 'prosequar' there a pun on the poet pursuing the travelling nomads?

[9] The misgivings are traditional in the genre: cf. Hes. *WD* 618–94; Aratus, *Phaenomena* 110 f.

[10] Compare further 2. 252 f., 3. 513, and perhaps 1. 448 'heu'.

[11] Cf. Nisbet–Hubbard on Hor. *Odes* 1. 2. 13 (where Horace is imitating Virgil); also Macleod (1983), 92 n. 14. For the historiographical background see Schepens (1980).

sombre voice of wisdom. In 318 the scene that the poet claims to have witnessed is grander and wilder, as he describes violent winds clashing in combat, with the world in flood and the king of the gods hurling thunderbolts. At the climax of the book, the same technique is employed with a difference: the verb is in the plural, as the poet speaks for his generation: 'quotiens Cyclopum effervere in agros l *vidimus* undantem ruptis fornacibus Aetnam' (471–2, cf. 502 'luimus', 503 'nobis'). Here the scenes witnessed are of chaos and unnatural disorder on a cosmic scale. The concerns of both poet and poem are extended in a way quite unexpected as we read the earlier parts of the book.

The author's use of the first person does not exist in isolation: as suggested above, it must be discussed along with the relation of the author to his addressee. I exclude here the special case of apostrophe addressed to inanimate objects or places (e.g. the high-flown compliments paid to wines at 2. 95–6, 102, rivers at 2. 159–60, etc.).[12] Simple general address to 'agricolae' and the like has already been mentioned. For variation, instruction can be conveyed not only in the second person singular or plural imperatives, but also by first plural indicatives (e.g. 1. 257), or by jussive subjunctives, whether first person plural or third person singular (1. 343) or plural. Most of these devices create a more vivid or dramatized scene; often, too, they stress the sympathetic collaboration of the poet, as in 2. 393 f., already quoted. Similarly in Book 4, it is '*our* misfortunes' (251, 'casus ... nostros') which are shared by the bees, also vulnerable to disease and death; and it is 'for us', including the poet, that some god has devised a remedy (315).

Variety of tone and pace can also be achieved by questions, which add a sense of urgency and challenge (1. 56, 2. 433, 3. 103, 250 'nonne vides ...?'), or by interjections (1. 63 'ergo age', 3. 515 'ecce'). In one passage alarm and urgent calls for action are vividly dramatized as the poet affects to spy a threatening snake: 'cape saxa manu, cape robora, pastor, l tollentemque minas et sibila colla tumentem l deice!' (3. 420 ff.) Sometimes the poet attributes a particular reaction or emotion to the addressee: wonder (4. 197), misgiving (1. 335 'hoc metuens', 459, 4. 239), and even fear (3. 408 'horrebis'). He himself shares in their experiences and, despite his position of authority, admits his own dismay at alarming signs, and waxes eloquent on the transience of

---

[12] In his commentary on 1. 215 Thomas remarks that Virgil's apostrophes and personifications become more frequent in Books 2 and 3: he does not develop the observation, which might repay further study.

human success (3. 66–8): in this last passage, 'miseris mortalibus' (not, for instance, 'agrestibus') reminds us that the poem is concerned with more than just the farming community.

II

The poet's self-presentation involves further complexities which affect our interpretation of the poem's generic status, and perhaps also its meaning.

In the above discussion invocations were not considered, but since these bear on the overall tone of the work, they require some comment here. The elaborate proem to Book 1 juxtaposes the twelve gods of the countryside with the living yet near-divine Caesar, placing the rural and poetic alongside the political, however fantastically conceived. The end of the book obviously echoes this beginning, but in a darker mood, with more Roman concerns reflected in the sonorous invocation of 'di patrii Indigetes ...'—no Alexandrian cleverness here, but native tradition and patriotic anxiety, even national guilt (501–2). The fantasy of Caesar being translated among the constellations, which in the proem seemed extravagant and fanciful, in the manner of Callimachus' *Lock of Berenice*, is echoed in more sombre terms at lines 503 ff., in which the poet fears that Caesar, the potential saviour, may be taken from them before he has done his vital work. The invoking of Bacchus in Book 2 (2. 388) and Pales in Book 3 (1. 294) require no discussion: they are the appropriate deities for the subjects under discussion. In Book 4 the only figure directly addressed in the proem is Maecenas, but Apollo's blessing is hoped for. At 4. 315 the new invocation to the Muses indicates a change to a more epic register, in preparation for the new phase of narrated mythology, the epyllion of Aristaeus. The Muses have not been involved in the composition of the *Georgics* so far, as 2. 475 and 3. 11 involve anticipation of future work. We are led to expect something grander in store, and our expectations are fulfilled by the imitations of Homeric epic, the introduction of speeches, the divine cast of characters, and the supernatural settings, beneath the sea and in the underworld. If the appeal to the Muses does indeed mark a shift in poetic style and ambition, it is perhaps appropriate that the narrative in the second half of the book should include as a central figure one of the great poets of myth.

Different issues arise with passages in which the poet's own role or status is defined or explored at greater length: esp. 1. 1–5, 2. 475–94, 3. 1–48, 284–94, and 4. 559–66.[13] In these passages we can find different conceptions of what a poet is or should be, what the worth and value of poet to community may be—questions which we know to have been aired in late Republican and Augustan Rome.[14] The main proem implies a view of the poet as a teacher, helping the ignorant countrymen with the support of a far greater helper, Caesar himself (1. 41 'ignarosque viae mecum miseratus agrestis'). Elsewhere this alignment of poet with ruler takes other forms. In the second book, at the climax of the *laudes Italiae*, Caesar and Virgil are both benefactors of Italy, the one defending her against foreign dangers, the other drawing upon fresh sources abroad to enrich her poetry (2. 170–6).[15]

These concerns come together in a different way in the last part of Book 2 and the proem to Book 3.[16] Both passages set Virgil apart from the rural life he describes. In Book 2 this is because he shows himself to be aware of the real meaning and value of that life, which the ordinary countryman is not (458 f.), and because he aspires to the higher themes of natural philosophy,[17] while accepting that he is unlikely to reach these austere heights of wisdom (475–86). In Book 3 a more positive note is struck, but again one which tends to separate the poet from his present subject-matter. Here Virgil seems eager to move on to a quite different, but again more ambitious project, a poem that will glorify Caesar, his victories and his ancestors. Here there is no hesitation or self-doubt, but exhilaration and ambition: in this, the most magniloquent of Virgil's self-characterizations, he himself is both encomiast of Caesar and triumphant victor in his own right.[18] It is almost with reluctance that he slackens his pace and returns to his present addressee (41) and his current project: the immediacy and anticipation of the encomiastic poem return in the last three lines of the proem (46 ff. esp. 'mox . . . accingar').

[13] On 4. 116–48 see Thomas (1982), 56–60.

[14] Cf. Williams (1968), 31–7, esp. on Cic. *Pro Archia* and Hor. *Ep.* 2. 1; Newman (1967), ch. 4; Brink (1963), e.g. 199–209.

[15] Space forbids discussion of recent interpretations which detect negative and disturbing elements in the *laudes Italiae* (see Thomas (1982), 36–51; the briefer account in his commentary seems to me much less satisfactory, esp. in his repeated use of the term 'lying'). While sympathetic to some of the points made, I feel that it is important not to underestimate the positive elements.

[16] The two passages are considered and compared from different points of view by Buchheit (1972), 45 ff., and Hardie (1986), 33–51.

[17] Innes (1979); Hardie (1986), chs. 1–2, a book from which I have learned much.

[18] See further Buchheit (1972).

Again, the interpreter of poetry of this refined complexity must guard against too literal a reading. The two passages should not be read naïvely as the outpourings of an emotional poet prone to self-contradiction; nor should we assume that different dates of composition sufficiently explain the different attitudes presented in them.[19] The motives will include a desire to pay tribute to Lucretius, Virgil's greatest Latin model, and a wish to celebrate the successes of the victorious Caesar and (perhaps more important) what they meant for Italy. But within the poetic world of the *Georgics* we may also see that these passages perform other functions. Both enlarge the scope of the poem's concerns. The first makes explicit the concern with nature and with the need to understand her ways, of which we have so far had only hints;[20] a stronger note of moralistic approval for the country life also enters. The other passage, the proem to Book 3, recalls the military language used in the first book and horrifically deployed in its finale; developed in the praise of Italy, where Caesar was seen as defending the frontiers of the empire (2. 170–2), this language is now used in a celebratory spirit, with wars won abroad and civil conflict forgotten. The *Georgics* is a poem much concerned with Italy, its fertility and beauty, its great potential for peace and prosperity.[21] In these passages, first the strength of Italy is described as resting on rural values associated with a primitive past, remote from and yet intertwined with intestinal violence; then, in Book 3, patriotic pride supersedes learned mythology, now dismissed as a hackneyed tune (3. 3–9). Whereas Virgil had faltered at the thought of tackling philosophy, he now warms to the project of panegyrical epic; yet the lofty strains of the proem do not entirely purge the reader's memories of the quietism

[19] Even a psychological reading as subtle as that of Hardie (1986), 44, 46f., seems to me unsatisfactory unless complemented by an account of the function of these passages within the poem as it stands.

[20] Notably at 1. 410–23 (the passage on the birds' premonitions), esp. 415 'haud equidem credo'; rather differently, 2. 325 f., on the origins of the world and the union of Earth and Sky (Aether suggests a philosophic tone, cf. Eur. *Chrysipp.* fr. 898 N., Lucr. 1. 250 ff., and other passages cited by Mynors ad loc.). Much more ambitious claims for Virgil's philosophic content are advanced by Ross (1987).

[21] Doreen Innes suggests that the audience of the poem may be seen particularly as inhabitants of Italian townships, an area between city and country: thus Hesiodic song is being translated to Roman *oppida* (2. 176), and Mantua is prominent in 3. 12 ff. (reversing the sadder allusion at 2. 198?). The ambiguities of Virgil's attitude to the country–city opposition may thus be related to the ambiguities of addressee; yet also, as a matter of historical fact, these townships would include persons of culture and devotion to the land, apt readers for such a poem (cf. Cic. *De Or.* 3. 43, 'nostri [sc. Romans] minus student litteris quam Latini').

and uneasy detachment from the political and military world which characterized the finale of Book 2. There are connections between the passages (both, for example, emphasize the poet's debt to Greece and Greek poetry), but the transition is startling, the means of reconciliation elusive.

By contrast, the conclusion of Book 4 opposes Caesar and Virgil, contrasting their careers and concerns. Caesar now seems remote and scarcely human, while Virgil's own efforts, summarized in banal terms (559–60), are seen as trivial, the product of inglorious ease in luxurious Naples. The passage, which associates his present work with the 'play' of the *Eclogues* (565), seems to represent a retreat, however ironic, from serious claims for his poetry.

III

As in the bucolic poems of his earlier years, Virgil repeatedly extends the scope of his formal subject and genre, both in his digressions and in the passages (such as the opening of Book 3) in which he points beyond what he has achieved to what could come later, or what he might achieve were his poetic gifts sufficient, or his powers fully mature. The literal or biographical sense of these passages (was he really engaged on a Trojan epic? would he really have turned to philosophy in his old age?) is less important than their effect in the overall context of the *Georgics*.[22] Self-praise needs to be balanced by self-protection:[23] through such gestures Virgil draws attention, without excessive display of pride, to what he has in fact achieved (as in the passage which pays tribute to Lucretius in Book 2). While hugely extending the poem's range beyond its ostensible subject-matter, he regularly stresses that he must be selective (2. 42, 3. 284, 4. 147), and also shows his awareness of the limited nature of his actual achievement; perhaps, in fact, his work is in the end play . . . but the reader will have to judge. The ambiguity of the poet's role, as teacher or entertainer, Lucretian instructor in cosmic truths or deft craftsman of Alexandrian artifice, committed supporter of Caesarian Italy or leisured versifier, reflects the complexity of poetry's relation to society in general. The story of

[22] On such passages as a literary device see Ogilvie–Richmond on Tac. *Agric.* 3. 3; Woodman (1975), 287f.; and e.g. Dion. Hal. *Dem.* 58 fin.

[23] Cf. Plut. *On Inoffensive Self-Praise* (esp. 539b–d, 541e, 542ab, passages which concern literary figures). For the ethical background see Betz (1978), 373–7, and also Russell (1993*b*).

Orpheus explores on a different, mythical plane the question of what poetry can and cannot achieve.[24]

The haunting inset story about Orpheus, which has called forth so many different readings, can only be treated selectively here.[25] It is natural, however, to associate Virgil with his fellow-poet (as ancient critics already saw Homer behind the bard Demodocus in *Odyssey* 8).[26] That identification need not be unqualified, and we may suspect, as with the song of Silenus in *Eclogue* 6, that the more plangent and self-indulgent aspects of his song represent only part of Virgil's own poetic range.[27] If, however, we see Aristaeus and Orpheus as opposed personalities, one passage in the most moving part of the epyllion leaps to our attention: the lines in which the singer is compared with a nightingale whose young have been stolen away by an *arator*:

> qualis populea maerens philomela sub umbra
> amissos queritur fetus, quos durus arator
> observans nido implumis detraxit; at illa
> flet noctem, ramoque sedens miserabile carmen
> integrat, et maestis late loca questibus implet.   (4. 511–15)

Here 'durus', formerly a term suggesting virtuous toughness and manliness, comes closer to 'callous, cruel', and the passage goes further than its model, Catullus 11, in that the farmer's act here is premeditated (unlike the random action of the plough in the lyric poem). Further, although we have seen the poet advocating ruthlessness and harsh action by the farmer in earlier passages (e.g. 3. 95–6, 468–9, 4. 106–7), those acts were normally justified by efficiency or the greater good; here, the cruelty of the *arator* seems unmotivated.[28] In short, the reader senses a gap opening up between farmer and poet, Aristaeus and Virgil; the poet of the *Georgics* appeals to a broader range of sympathies than those of farmers and realists.[29] Although it is over-schematic to assume equivalences between Aristaeus and Caesar, Orpheus and Virgil, it is perhaps not surprising that the subsequent

[24] Cf. Rutherford (1989*b*), a paper in which I tried to argue that the *Eclogues* similarly show a preoccupation with different paths of poetry and what they might offer a poet disturbed by the political turmoil of his time.

[25] For a brief satirical survey of recent views see Griffin (1985), 163–4.

[26] e.g. Σ EV on *Od.* 8. 63; cf. further Hardie (1986), 54–6.

[27] Somewhat similarly Griffin (1985), 173–6; cf. Rutherford (1989*b*), 45, 47.

[28] We should of course note that Proteus is actually speaking the lines in question; but we are given no particular reason to suppose that his words are to be viewed with any scepticism.

[29] For further comments on this passage see Perkell (1989), 48–9, 184, and elsewhere.

sphragis sets the two Roman figures in contrast with one another: *bello* contrasts with *oti*, *Euphraten* with *Parthenope*, *dat iura* with *carmina lusi*. In a sense poetry is dependent on politics: Caesar needs to be victorious for Virgil to be able to enjoy his literary pursuits. Yet at the same time Caesar's conquests, like Aristaeus' miraculous recovery of his bees, are not the whole story.

These comments, which range from small-scale stylistic observations to overall lines of interpretation, are both sketchy and selective: they cannot hope to do justice to the richness of a long and highly sophisticated poem, still less serve as a substitute for a rereading. This essay can perhaps illuminate certain patterns and ideas in the poem, without obscuring or doing justice to the far larger and subtler design of the artist. That criticism has a place, but one which must remain subordinate to the work of art, is one of the simple but vital truths which, with characteristic modesty and firmness, Donald Russell has regularly affirmed.[30]

[30] e.g. Russell (1973), 116; (1981*a*), 171–2.

3

Friendship and its Problems in Greek and Roman Thought

JONATHAN POWELL

It is easy to get the impression that the ancient Greeks and Romans in general were more worried about friendship than we are. I am not sure how one would prove or disprove the truth of this idea, but it is not hard to see where it comes from. The responsibility for it lies mostly with two authors: admittedly great and influential ones, but for all that only individuals whose representative status cannot automatically be taken for granted without further investigation. They are Aristotle and Cicero. Readers of the *Nicomachean Ethics* are usually surprised at the amount of space devoted to discussion of φιλία in a work on moral philosophy—a field in which, in modern times, discussion of friendship has hardly figured to any great extent. Readers of Cicero, in the same way, may be surprised that he should have seen fit to devote a philosophical dialogue to the topic of *amicitia*. Those who investigate the subject further will read Plato's *Lysis* (not normally one of his more popular dialogues) and Plutarch's treatises on 'How to distinguish the friend from the flatterer' and 'On having many friends'; they will collect the evidence for lost philosophical treatises on friendship—no less than seven of them, by Simmias of Thebes, Speusippus, Xenocrates, Theophrastus, Clearchus, Cleanthes, and Chrysippus; they will find letters of Seneca and a discourse of Epictetus on the subject; they will look at the examples of friendship in Valerius Maximus and Lucian's *Toxaris*; and they will comb the rest of ancient literature for observations on friendship, ranging from Hesiod, Theognis, and the

This chapter expands on some ideas adumbrated in my edition of Cicero's *Laelius de Amicitia* (Powell (1990a)), to which the reader is referred for more detailed information and bibliography; I have here restricted annotation to the bare minimum. A version of this chapter was read at the Institute of Classical Studies, University of London, in February 1993, at the invitation of Prof. R. R. K. Sorabji, to whom I am grateful for comments.

Seven Sages, through Xenophon's *Memorabilia*, to other works of Cicero and Seneca. The subject remained popular in late antiquity; others may speak with more authority than I can on the works of Maximus of Tyre, Themistius, and Libanius concerned with this subject. Altogether there appears to be quite a substantial volume of writing and thought about friendship in the ancient world, and this fact invites explanation.

The explanation often put forward or implied is that there was something about ancient society which made friendship more important, or more of a problem, than it is in modern society. It will be noticed, in the first place, that while Aristotle, Cicero, and the rest devote a substantial amount of space to the problems of friendship, they usually say rather less about those of marriage and the family (which figure so largely and anxiously in much of modern Western thought). We shall be told, almost as a matter of course, that this is because ancient marriage was purely utilitarian, devoted to the raising of legitimate children and the economic running of a household; hence (the standard argument runs) it was no more of a problem for the philosophers than other parts of the topic of Household Management (as discussed most notably in Xenophon's *Oeconomicus*). That affectionate companionship which we moderns are supposed at least to look for, and sometimes to find, in marriage, is consequently thought to have been impossible for the ancients, who therefore found it elsewhere: in homosexual relationships between an older and a younger man, in the case of Athenians of the classical period (and some other Greeks), or in friendships between equals, such as those discussed by Aristotle and Cicero. (In fact, there is evidence for an idealized conception of marriage in the ancient world, very similar to the modern one, from Homer through the Stoics to some of the more enlightened Roman writers.[1] It would, however, be possible to argue that this represented a minority view.)

Then something will doubtless be said about the nature of ancient political life, which depended on a network of personal alliances rather than any organized party structure. It might be thought that one-to-one political friendships were most important in the aristocratic states of Archaic Greece; their function in democratic Athens, for example, does not seem to receive so much emphasis or attention. However, Roman historians (with certain honourable exceptions) have notori-

---

[1] *Odyssey* 6. 182–4, admittedly in a speech of Odysseus; for the Stoics, Seneca, *Ep.* 104, Musonius Rufus, Περὶ γάμου; see further Treggiari (1991).

ously made a great deal of what they call the 'Roman concept of *amicitia*'. This is carried to the extent of virtually always leaving the Latin word *amicitia* untranslated; the word is usually glossed as meaning something like a political alliance between persons of approximately equal standing, although its use is sometimes extended, as for instance by Gelzer,[2] to include relationships of political patronage between superiors and inferiors (I am talking about its modern scholarly use, not its actual use in ancient authors). Once it is accepted that this is actually the meaning of the word *amicitia*, it follows that the use of the English word 'friendship' to translate it would be quite misleading. Perhaps, therefore, when the ancient philosophers treat friendship as an ethical problem, they are not really talking about friendship in our sense at all, but rather about *amicitia*. The importance of *amicitia* in ancient public life is thus held to be reflected in the prominence given to it in the ethical writings of the philosophers; and since our own public life is supposed not to be based on *amicitia*, and in any case what we mean by friendship is something different, the relative unimportance of this topic in modern ethical writing becomes apparently less surprising.

There may be some truth in such sociological explanations of the prominence of friendship in ancient philosophical literature, even when presented in an over-simplified form (or, some might say, a caricature) such as the above. However, there is another type of explanation available, not necessarily incompatible with the sociological type, but perhaps more appropriate given that what we are largely dealing with is the literature of ancient philosophy. As an alternative to looking in the philosophical writers for immediate reflections of their contemporary society, we might instead look at the internal coherence of what they have to say. Is there anything about the philosophical positions of Aristotle, or Cicero, or ancient philosophers in general, that makes it likely that friendship (or φιλία or *amicitia*) would be a problem for them? It seems to me that, once one has stated the question in this way, the answer is rather obvious. If it can be said that there was one central issue in Greek ethical thought since Socrates, it was surely the issue of whether and how an individual human being was capable of achieving such a level of 'wisdom' or 'excellence' as would enable him to take control of his own life and achieve a state of self-sufficient well-being, as far as possible independently of any factors outside himself. If you believe in this possibility, it follows logically that

[2] Gelzer (1975), 101–10.

you cannot allow a superior and successful man to be dependent on his friends for even the smallest portion of his εὐδαιμονία. If he is truly self-sufficient he clearly will not need friends. At the same time, natural human instincts are in favour of friendship and incline one to think that it is a good thing; and it was the common opinion of unphilosophical Greeks (as of many other people) that the number of your friends, or in other words your popularity, was an index of your success in life. Even if one insists, as the philosophers sometimes did,[3] that it is the quality and not the volume of your friendships that counts, one is still left with the problem of what, in strict logic, friends can contribute to the well-being of a person who is already perfectly happy. Wherein lies the good of friendship if not to increase one's own personal good?

This problem is central to the discussion in Plato's *Lysis*. The starting-point of the *Lysis* (not unexpectedly) is one of the innumerable romantic homosexual love-affairs that figure in the background of Plato's dialogues. Socrates shows that the behaviour of such lovers is very unlike that of friends or φίλοι. As examples of friends in the normal sense we see first of all the two boys Lysis and Menexenus, who cannot agree which of them is the elder or better; Socrates' cross-examination of Menexenus on this point is nipped in the bud when the latter is called away by the wrestling coach. Then Socrates gives an example of how to talk to a boy in an educative and therefore (according to Socrates) truly useful and friendly way, arguing that at his tender age Lysis knows nothing at all and will never have any friends until he has something to offer in the way of wisdom. This creates an expectation that Socrates will argue for a conception of friendship based on the usefulness of a wise person to one who is less wise: that is, a basically one-sided version of friendship.

At this point Menexenus reappears, and Socrates formally raises the topic of friendship and, in particular, of its origin: how one person becomes the friend of another. The first part of the argument largely turns on an ambiguity in the words φίλος and φιλεῖν, and doubtless the main purpose of this passage is to bring that problem into the light of day. The basic meaning of φίλος is the passive one, 'dear'; but when two people are φίλοι they are usually dear to each other, and to say that someone is your φίλος implies that he is friendly towards you as well as dear to you. The verb φιλεῖν presumably meant originally 'to treat somebody as one's φίλος', and in Homer it is often applied to

---

[3] Cf. Plutarch, Περὶ πολυφιλίας.

concrete hospitality. Later, as is well known, it simply means 'to love' or 'to like', and its passive, 'to be loved'. On the one hand, it seems to make sense to say that the relationship with a person who is φίλος is generally a reciprocal one. On the other hand, if you love wine or music it is not at all clear that wine or music loves you in return; and the same goes for unrequited affection between human beings. Socrates concludes that φιλία can be defined neither as a reciprocal nor as a non-reciprocal relationship, and leaves the argument in the air.

Socrates then makes a new start by referring to the proverbial notion that likeness draws people together and makes them friends. He immediately converts this into moral terms, concluding that the good are friends to the good because they are like each other in respect of their goodness. He rejects the idea that the bad can be friends to the bad, because the bad are always doing each other harm. In any case, the bad are unstable characters and are not even like themselves, so how can they be truly like anyone else? So we end up with the idea that only the good can be friends. This is found also in Xenophon's *Memorabilia* and has a chance of being genuinely Socratic; it recurs in Aristotle, in the Stoics, and figures very prominently in Cicero.[4]

But, continues the Socrates of the *Lysis*, the good are self-sufficient; so how can they need each other, value each other, or miss each other when separated? How, in other words, can they be friends? On the other hand, it cannot be true that the unlike are friends to the unlike; because what is unlike a friend is an enemy, and an enemy clearly cannot be a friend; and the good and the just cannot be friends to the bad and the unjust. In the rest of the dialogue, various strategies, some of them extremely complicated, are put forward for solving this difficulty. For the present purpose, these need not be pursued in detail. On the whole, they are idiosyncratically Platonic, to such an extent that they seem to have had relatively little influence on later thought. However, I shall revert to the end of the *Lysis* at the very end of this chapter.

Among the post-Platonic schools there were different attitudes to the concept of the self-sufficiency of the good and the wise. The Stoics notoriously embraced the doctrine without qualification. Aristotle and the Peripatetics held it in a qualified form, allowing some importance to external factors in determining εὐδαιμονία. For Epicureans self-sufficiency meant not complete independence of anything outside

---

[4] Xen. *Mem.* 2. 6. 16–20; Arist. *EE* 7. 1235ᵃ; Diogenes Laertius 7. 124; Sen. *Ep.* 81. 12; Cicero, *Lael.* 18–21.

oneself, but simply limiting one's desires to those that are easily and naturally satisfied; thus the problem did not arise for them in quite the same way as for others.

On the whole, few philosophers seem to have held so fast to the doctrine of self-sufficiency that they rejected friendship entirely; but there is evidence that a position of this sort was at least canvassed. Seneca, in his ninth letter, attributes to Stilbo (or Stilpo) the Megarian the idea that the wise man did not need friends, and that friendship can be a source of worry and hence inimical to tranquillity of mind. It appears that some of the Cyrenaic school also took such a view.[5] Theodorus of Cyrene put it in the form of a dilemma: the wise do not need friendship, while the non-wise are incapable of it. Such ideas are not confined to philosophical contexts; the Nurse in Euripides' *Hippolytus*[6] puts forward the view that excessively close friendships should be avoided because they are so troublesome, and quotes the proverb 'Nothing in excess' to support her statement; this passage is picked up by Cicero as a convenient object of refutation.

It might have been expected that the Stoics would adopt this sort of position, but in fact they do not seem to have done so. Their view of the self-sufficiency of the wise was tempered by another equally important Stoic doctrine, that of οἰκείωσις. The evidence is sketchy, but it suggests that Stoics held a positive view of friendship; part of their doctrine was that the wise were all naturally friends to each other, whether acquainted or not.[7] It is a plausible guess that the idealized view of friendship presented by Cicero in the *Laelius* (and elsewhere) is based, at least to some extent, on Stoic doctrine, although the evidence is certainly not sufficient to tie it down to a particular Stoic philosopher.

There may have been little difference in essentials between the Stoic ideal of friendship and that of Aristotle, which we know much more about, although presumably the Stoics cannot have regarded friendship (depending as it does on something outside the individual) as an integral constituent of the good life. Aristotle, however, clearly did: 'Without friends,' he says, 'nobody would choose to live, even if he possessed all other good things.'[8] But friendship according to Aristotle is not just an ἀγαθόν, from which a person benefits if he has it; it is also a kind of ἀρετή or at least accompanied by ἀρετή;[9] in other words, it is part of what it means to be a good-quality human being.

---

[5] See Powell (1990*a*), 103.   [6] *Hipp.* 253 ff.   [7] Cicero, *ND* 1. 121.
[8] *NE* 8. 1. 1155ᵃ. On Aristotle's view of friendship, see Price (1989).   [9] *NE* ibid.

This may at first seem puzzling. In ordinary Greek it does not seem that φιλία is the name of an ἀρετή any more than 'friendship' is the name of a quality of character in English. Both are names of *relationships*. But Aristotle may be thinking that there is a particular ἀρετή that goes with friendship, the quality of being a good friend to one's friends. (I am sure that he is *not* thinking of mere friendliness in the modern English sense, nor of a cynical competence in the management of friendships. It is possible that German *Freundlichkeit* preserves more of the appropriate meaning than does 'friendliness', which is no more than a generalized affability.) In any case, this form of ἀρετή is in the long run inseparable from the more general ἀρετή that makes one a good sort of person. Thus, so far from rendering one so self-sufficient that one does not need friends, the possession of ἀρετή in fact disposes one to be a better friend.

Then Aristotle produces his well-known classification of friendships into those based on ἀρετή, on utility, and on pleasure. His exact account of the logical relationship between these three types of friendship varies somewhat between the version in the *Nicomachean Ethics* and that in the *Eudemian*; but it seems fairly clear that the first type is held to be the only one in which the word 'friendship' has its full and proper sense. Hence friendship, in the full sense, is based on the possession of goodness or ἀρετή by both parties.

In Cicero, we find a twofold division of friendship, into a perfect or ideal kind and an inferior or ordinary kind.[10] The ideal type corresponds closely to Aristotle's concept of friendship based on goodness and presumably to the Stoic idea of friendship among the wise. Cicero takes pains to clarify that he does not mean to restrict it to those who are wise by Stoic standards. It is not clear whether the Stoics explicitly made such a classification, although it is clear enough that in practice they recognized the existence of ordinary imperfect friendships in the real world. Seneca tells us not to seek only wise men as our friends, because there are so few of them, and he stresses the opportunities that friendship gives to display one's own virtue rather than to benefit from association with others.[11] Advice on how to break friendships was, it seems, given by Chrysippus[12] much as it was by Aristotle and Cicero: such precepts cannot, of course, be taken to refer to the ideal friendship of the wise, and must imply a category similar to Cicero's *vulgares amicitiae*. The Stoics would obviously not take a high view of the

---

[10] *Lael.* 22, 76, 77, 100.   [11] *Ep.* 9; *Tranq.* 7. 4.
[12] In his second book Περὶ φιλίας, according to Plutarch, *Stoic. Rep.* 1039b.

ordinary, non-wise man's capacity for real friendship, any more than Socrates did, and this idea is developed later by Epictetus.[13]

As for the Epicurean view of friendship,[14] we actually know rather less about it than one might think. The majority of our evidence for it comes from the testimony of Cicero, which is respectfully hostile but still hostile; it is clear that he has an interest in magnifying any inconsistency in their position. Though friendship is the subject of a number of surviving Epicurean maxims, Epicureans did not, as far as we know, write whole treatises devoted specifically to the topic; and the maxims themselves tend to praise friendship in a general way, rather than offer any philosophical analysis of it. It may be that, although they clearly valued friendship very highly and regarded it as one of the greatest sources of good in life, they did not see it as so much of a problem as it potentially was for the other schools. Their account of the origin of friendship, which we know directly from a brief passage in Lucretius[15] and indirectly from Cicero's criticisms of it, is on all fours with the rest of their social theory, and treats friendship as originally a sort of contract for mutual benefit, even though according to Cicero, Epicurus recognized that real affection could develop out of such beginnings. The Epicurean seeks friendship because it is an easy and natural source of pleasure; Epicurus himself criticized those who suggested that friendship was incompatible with tranquillity of mind.[16] There was no obvious reason for an Epicurean to worry about the notion that the wise man had no need of friends; doubtless an Epicurean wise man could be happy without them if need be (since the pleasures of friendship were not placed in the category of ἀναγκαῖαι ἡδοναί), but that did not stop them from being a thing to be desired whenever they were available.

The evidence does not indicate whether this distinction between necessity and desirability was made fully clear by the Epicureans themselves, but it was certainly obscured by Cicero in his attacks on them.[17] To seek something because it is desirable does not necessarily imply, as Cicero suggests, that one cannot do without it or that there is some weakness in oneself; nor that in seeking it one is necessarily being coldly calculating. Yet Cicero is right to the extent that the Epicurean opinion of the origin of friendship does seem to reduce friendship to a

---

[13] *Diss.* 2. 22.
[14] Cf. Bollack (1969), 221–36; Rist (1972), ch. 7; id. (1980).; Mitsis (1987).
[15] Lucr. 5. 1019–20; cf. Cic. *Fin.* 1. 66 ff.
[16] Referred to in Seneca, *Ep.* 9.   [17] *Lael.* 26 ff.

mutual exchange of favours, and that it fails to account plausibly for the genuine affection and compatibility of personalities which is the basis of friendship according to the Stoic or Peripatetic view. It is to be noted that Aristotle recognizes utility as the basis of an inferior form of friendship, and this may have accentuated the differences between Peripatetic and Epicurean views: what the Epicureans say is the real thing is relegated by Aristotle to the status of a poor imitation.

The issue between Epicureans and the rest on the question of the origin of friendship (which is simply an aspect of the debate on the origin of any human association) clearly became something of a commonplace. Not only does Cicero make a great deal of it in the *Laelius* and refer to it in several of his other philosophical works; he had clearly long been familiar with it as a rhetorical topic. It is mentioned both by Cicero himself in the *De Inventione*, and by the unknown author of the *Ad Herennium*.[18] It also figures in Horace's list of proper subjects for after-dinner philosophizing in *Satires* 2. 6. 75.

This, in very broad outline, was the state of play in the philosophical schools on the general question of the nature of friendship. Two main themes run through it: the problem of reconciling friendship with self-sufficiency, and the question of the origin of friendship or the causes that make one person become the friend of another. Both of these questions receive their first major treatment in Plato's *Lysis*: here as elsewhere, Plato provides the germ of almost all later Greek speculation. Neither of these themes, perhaps, is likely to strike much of a chord in the average modern European mind; moral self-sufficiency is not a modern Western ideal, and speculations on the origins of friendship have been replaced by (supposedly) empirical psychological and sociological studies of what is called 'bonding'.[19]

The residue of ancient writing on friendship consists largely of practical precepts and advice on how to choose one's friends, how to gain the friendship of the persons chosen, how to behave towards them when you have made friends with them, and how to get rid of them if they prove to be less good friends than one expected. Particular writers may colour their discussion of these questions according to their more general philosophical position, but in general this type of thing moves mostly on the level of common sense and popular wisdom. Exhortations

---

[18] Cic. *Inv.* 2. 167; cf. *Ad Her.* 3. 4, 3. 10, 3. 14.

[19] For a recent example see Argyle (1992), 49 ff., 205–7. At this point the oral version of this chapter contained a more substantial section comparing ancient and modern attitudes and attempting to elucidate further the differences between them; for the present publication, this has had to be omitted.

to caution in the choice of friends and in the early stages of a friendship are found throughout. See, for example, Solon: 'Do not be hasty in
acquiring friends; and whatever friends you do acquire, do not be
hasty in finding them wanting.' Bias, or perhaps Chilon: 'Love in the
thought that you may some day hate; hate in the thought that you may
some day love.' Theognis: 'You will never know the mind of a man or a
woman until you have tried it out, like a team of horses.' Socrates (in
Xenophon): 'Most people take care over anything rather than the
acquisition of friends ... They know the exact number of their other
possessions, even when they have a great number, but they cannot tell
the number of their friends, few though these are.' Theophrastus:
'Judge before loving; do not love before judging.'[20] All this implies, not
that the ancients were more conscious than we are of the process of
making friends, but that apart from a few self-appointed wise men,
they were on the whole about equally unaware of it. These sayings are
often neatly and memorably formulated, but they offer us little
specific evidence for ancient society.

More particular advice is sometimes given on distinguishing true
friends from false ones. The false ones are usually characterized as
flatterers, κόλακες in Greek, *adulatores* or *assentatores* in Latin.
Again, those who are on the look-out for generalized differences
between ancient and modern society may well jump into the ring at
this point: the κόλαξ or flatterer will be said to be a more constant and
prominent part of ancient society than of modern, as is shown by his
frequent portrayal in comedy in the specialized form of the Parasite. It
is true that certain features of ancient society did encourage the flatterer. The rich in ancient times were expected to distribute largess as a
point of honour, and it was only to be expected that some unscrupulous characters would play on this. But this is a feature of aristocratic
societies in general, not of Greece and Rome in particular; one need go
no further than the English eighteenth century to see what were then
called 'toadies' in full cry. The twentieth-century tendency for the rich
to shut themselves away from the rest of society and dispense charity,
if at all, through impersonal and bureaucratic organizations, is a
peculiar aberration from the common pattern of human behaviour,
which the ancients would have found very difficult to comprehend.

[20] Solon, Diels–Kranz i⁶. 63; Bias or Chilon, see Powell (1990*a*) on *Lael.* 59;
Theognis 1. 125–6 Bergk; Xen. *Mem.* 2. 4. 4; Theophrastus ap. Plut. Περὶ φιλαδελφίας
8. 482b. All these sayings are adapted by Cicero in the *Laelius*, the second half of which
is a compendium of popular wisdom of this type.

But it is surely the case that we have our own twentieth-century Anglo-American versions of the κόλαξ; they just operate in slightly different ways. The other thing we must remember is that most of the ancient writing on this topic is directed at members of the aristocratic class, who would be likely to suffer from the attentions of flatterers; most of us modern classical scholars who read these writings are simply not important enough to attract flattery to any great extent. Satire and comedy always present flattery as absurdly obvious, and portray the objects of flattery as so stupid and vain that they cannot see what is happening. This exaggeration is necessary in order to have the desired effect on the audience, and should not be taken as a true reflection of ancient society in general. Cicero[21] points out that the problem in real life comes not from overt flattery, but from the more subtle varieties of insinuation. What distinguishes the flatterer from the true friend is not necessarily his manner of behaviour, but the level of insincerity behind it. We British tend to distrust anyone who is excessively demonstrative in friendly behaviour, but among the ancients (as in some other parts of the world today) much more display of affection was acceptable and, indeed, expected between friends. It appears, in addition, that there was some difference in convention between Greeks and Romans; it is standard in Roman literature to accuse Greeks of being expert flatterers, slippery and unreliable, always telling the listener what will please him rather than the truth.[22] This is reminiscent of English attitudes to Orientals or even to Irishmen, and is possibly symptomatic of a failure of understanding of the relevant social conventions: a Greek could probably tell when another Greek was putting on the blarney, but a Roman could not necessarily do so.

One particular topic in the ancient practical treatment of friendship deserves a little more consideration: the relationship between friendship and politics. What happens when the demands of friendship conflict with those of public responsibility? Aulus Gellius (1. 3) tells us the story of Chilon of Sparta, who was judging the case of a friend of his with two other judges, and was convinced that the man was guilty, but wished to help him; so he himself voted for condemnation, but persuaded the other judges to acquit. This is to our way of thinking a strange sort of compromise, yet it had the effect of helping the friend

---

[21] *Lael.* 99.
[22] The most obvious example is Juvenal 3. 86–93, 100–8. These two passages nicely illustrate the distinction between *adulatio* (flattery in the true sense, i.e. insincere praise) in the former passage, and *assentatio* (insincere agreement) in the latter.

without apparently infringing Chilon's duty to judge the case according to the law; the most a modern judge could do would be to refuse to
act, and in ancient Greece this would probably have been taken as a
tacit acknowledgement that the defendant was guilty. Cicero discusses
the same question in general terms in the *De Officiis* (3. 43–4), and
takes a line more in tune with modern ideas: one cannot be a friend and
a judge at the same time, and if one is a judge one must do one's duty
regardless of friendship. Yet Cicero does add that a good man 'will
concede so much to friendship, that he will hope for his friend's case to
be just, and that he will grant as much time for him to plead his case as
is allowed by law'. Is Cicero perhaps trying to have it both ways? Does
he really mean to say that litigants who are not friends of the judge
should have less time to plead their cases? Be that as it may, Cicero has
another strategy to which he alludes here and which he develops at
greater length in the *Laelius*: this is to say that friendship properly so
called can only really exist between perfectly wise and good men, who
would never have got into such a situation in the first place.

In the latter work,[23] he employs this argument in connection with
the conflict of friendship with politics. The discussion must be seen
above all in the context of the civil war, in which personal loyalties
were all-important in determining which side one was to fight for. In
an earlier historical context, that of the Catilinarian conspiracy,
Cicero had already enunciated (for good rhetorical purposes, in *Pro
Sulla* 6) the principle that one should not stand by a friend who com-
mits treason; there are some crimes of such magnitude that they
cannot be defended. Here, Cicero similarly says that one must not act
against the interests of one's country on behalf of a friend, and
produces examples such as Coriolanus and the Gracchi. But the
trouble in the case of the civil war of course lay in the definition of
'acting against the interests of one's country'; the legitimacy claimed
by the Pompeians was enough to tilt the balance for Cicero (though
even he took some time to declare himself), but for others the issues
may not have been so clear. Some of the arguments that could be
deployed are to be seen in the correspondence between Cicero and
Matius, which belongs to the same period as the *Laelius*, soon after
Caesar's death in 44 BC.[24]

Cicero's discussion is perhaps most notable for the fact that it preserves a clear statement of the contrary view, attributed to Blossius of

---

[23] *Lael.* 36ff.
[24] *Fam.* 11. 27–8; for bibliography see Powell (1990*a*), 6; see also Brunt (1988), ch. 7.

Cumae when defending himself before the tribunal of inquiry after the death of Tiberius Gracchus. According to Cicero, he said that he valued Tiberius Gracchus' friendship so much that he would do whatever Gracchus told him, even to the extent of setting fire to the Capitol. This comes near to the well-known saying of E. M. Forster: 'If I had to choose between betraying my country and betraying my friend, I hope I should have the guts to betray my country.'

If matters of patriotic allegiance are left aside, Cicero's remaining comments on the conflict of friendship and duty are rather unsatisfactorily vague, as Aulus Gellius points out, referring us to an allegedly superior discussion in Theophrastus' treatise on friendship.[25] I have attempted to explain the vagueness in my commentary on the passage; it seems most likely that Cicero is not, in fact, trying to justify himself for having compromised his own principles in public life, but rather to qualify the extreme position he has previously stated, and to display indulgence towards those surviving supporters of Caesar whom he could not afford to alienate entirely at that juncture in 44 BC. But whatever the reason for it, the discussion is anything but helpful to anyone who might get into such a position. Cicero's instincts in the end seem to come down to the feeling that good men are always on the right side in politics anyway. What Gellius quotes of Theophrastus' discussion is hardly more encouraging. Theophrastus simply advises us to weigh up the merits of each situation. A small advantage to a friend is not worth a great loss of one's own reputation; a small loss of reputation is worthwhile for the sake of a great advantage to one's friend.

One thing is clear from all this, and that is that friendship is not seen by Cicero or any other ancient author in exclusively political terms. If it were really true (and universally recognized in antiquity) that, as Sir Ronald Syme put it, '*amicitia* was a weapon of politics, not a sentiment based on congeniality',[26] then there would have been far less of a problem. The loyalty of a man to his friend was indeed based on personal sentiment as well as on political advantage; hence the possibility of a conflict of personal and political loyalty. It is quite possible that a political connection might develop into a genuine friendship, or vice versa; it also seems that, at least in the period documented by Cicero's letters, strong protestations of personal friendship and affection were in order in any profession of political support. The feelings so expressed might be sincere or they might not; but the language

---

[25] *Noct. Att.* 1. 3 = Theophrastus F 534 Fortenbaugh; *Lael.* 61.
[26] Syme (1939), 12.

of friendship would not have served as it did to induce help and support, if it had been seen in the purely cynical way encouraged by some modern historians. The *Laelius* begins with an allusion to Publius Sulpicius, the tribune of 88 BC, who became involved in bitter conflict with Q. Pompeius, the consul of the year. What shocked the public in this instance was not simply the fact that two politicians had fallen out with each other, but the fact that they did so despite having previously been on terms of close personal friendship. I have argued[27] that Sulpicius may have hoped that his friendship with Pompeius might ensure co-operation on the part of the latter, though Pompeius was not his natural political ally. When this failed, Sulpicius was driven into an attitude of hostility to his former friend. As Brunt[28] has pointed out, there is a constant interaction of motives in political life, and personal friendship can be as important as any other. This simple fact is still often obscured in modern discussions of Roman history; but one only has to read the *Laelius* with a reasonably open mind to see that Cicero knew perfectly well the meaning of personal friendship. Indeed, one of Cicero's truest remarks, which would be reduced to gibberish by the common persuasion of the meaning of *amicitia*, is that political life in Rome made it extremely difficult to maintain *amicitiae* (i.e. friendships!), since there were so many occasions when a conflict of interests might arise. Even so, he manages to point to some pairs of friends in which both members were in the thick of political competition, but no conflict arose.

Amicitia, then, is personal friendship. The real difficulty that a modern reader may have with the ancient philosophical accounts is not that they are based on a different concept of friendship from ours, but that they are too generalized to do real justice to experience. In practice, doubtless, the ancient writers did recognize such a thing as the compatibility of individual personalities (one need look no further than Aristophanes in Plato's *Symposium* to see that such ideas existed). This idea was to find its full expression in the memorable dictum of Montaigne: 'Parce que c'estoit luy; parce que c'estoit moy.' But it is not an idea that lends itself easily to philosophical analysis in ancient terms. An ancient philosopher, searching as always for causes and explanations, would probably have asked Montaigne: 'Yes, but what was it *about* you and De la Boétie that made friendship possible between you? Was it not some excellent quality of character in him that made you like him?' The ancient philosopher felt obliged to

----

[27] Powell (1990*b*), 446–60.   [28] Brunt (1988).

generalize and objectify even in such a personal matter as friendship; affection had to be rationalized as admiration. In the same way, love was presented as a response to an objectively existent beauty in the beloved. It is tempting to link this with specifically Platonic views of the world; but the tendency may not in fact be peculiar to Platonists or even to philosophers, since it is well known that the Greek graffito corresponding to our 'I love X' was ὁ δεῖνα καλός. More interestingly, perhaps, it is in Plato himself that we find what may be a genuine philosophical attempt to escape from this way of thinking. At the end of the *Lysis*, after rejecting numerous schematic accounts of the nature of friendship, Plato suggests that friendship may be based on what is οἰκεῖον, conventionally translated 'akin'. Now 'akin-ness' is not a quality that an individual can possess in the abstract, but a relation which subsists between two or more individuals. I can appear to talk, from my own point of view, of a person being φίλος or οἰκεῖος in the abstract, but what I mean when I do so is that such a person is φίλος or οἰκεῖος to me. Looked at objectively, what is meant is that there is a relationship of friendship or 'akin-ness' between the other person and myself. Being οἰκεῖος to another person does not depend on the possession of any qualities in particular, but is precisely a matter of what we call compatibility.

To a casual modern reader, the *Lysis* may seem to be an idiosyncratic piece of sophistry; but more careful consideration shows that most of the rest of ancient philosophical thought on friendship gets little further than Plato did, and often not as far. Aristotle's account is distinguished for its analytical approach and its practical common sense; Cicero combines the practical (derived from popular wisdom and, apart from that, largely from Aristotle and the Peripatetic tradition) and the ideal (which is probably more Stoic) in what is altogether less an analytical discussion than a heartfelt encomium of true friendship. Though the details of ancient discussions of friendship are conditioned to some extent by the nature of ancient society, by the position within it of the writers concerned and their expected audiences, and by certain of the peculiar preoccupations of ancient philosophical ethics, the concept of friendship as defined in these works contains nothing essentially unfamiliar to a modern reader; and I am inclined to think, though this is terribly unfashionable in our relativistic age, that the reason for this is that friendship in its essence is much the same for human beings in all societies. In fact, I am not really sure what it would mean to assert otherwise.

4

Poetry, Philosophy, and Letter-Writing in Horace, *Epistles* 1

STEPHEN HARRISON

Two long-running issues in the criticism of Horace's first book of *Epistles* now appear to be in a steady state: that of whether these twenty hexameter poems are in any sense 'real' letters, and that of whether Horace's professions of philosophical eclecticism in the programmatic *Epistles* 1. 1 (13–19) are borne out by the collection. On the first issue, most would now agree with a recent monograph that 'while the possibility remains that some of the *Epistles* were actually sent as letters, they are best judged as fictional discourse' and that these poems aim at 'a lively illusion of reality'.[1] On the second issue, Horace's lack of dogmatism seems to be re-established after attempts to make him more philosophically systematic, and he is now seen as an independent purveyor of familiar ethical generalizations.[2] These issues form the background to the questions addressed here. First, what kind of techniques does Horace use to present philosophical material (whatever it is) within the context of a collection of hexameter poetry? And second, how does Horace's fictionalized use of the letter-form (assuming that it is fictionalized) relate to ancient practice and prescription in the field of letter-writing? These issues will be dealt with separately in what follows, but as will emerge, they are crucially interrelated: letters were well known as a means of presenting philosophy in the ancient world (note the extant epistles ascribed to Plato and Epicurus, and the

A version of part of this chapter was read at the Annual Conference of the Classical Association at Durham in April 1992. It is a real pleasure to dedicate its final form to Donald Russell, *qui more Horati doctrinam summam cum summa humanitate semper coniunxit.*

[1] Kilpatrick (1986), xvii. The battle between Fraenkel (1957), 308–63, and Williams (1968), 1–30, on this question is now a distant Titanomachy.
[2] So Rudd (1993), Mayer (1986), Moles (1985). Kilpatrick (1986) sees Horace as an Academic, McGann (1969) sees him as an eclectic Stoic, but both these positions seem too dogmatic.

lost epistles of Aristotle), and some of the techniques used in the presentation of philosophy in the *Epistles* have clear links with the prescriptions of ancient epistolographical theory.

I. POETRY AND PHILOSOPHY

The idea of putting philosophy into hexameter poetry was not of course original to Horace. Its history stretches back to Parmenides and Empedocles, and the *De Rerum Natura* of Lucretius had come out in the 50s BC. There is clear evidence that Horace knew and used the work of Lucretius in the *Satires* and *Odes* as well as the *Epistles*,[3] but there are some important differences between the two poets. Horace deals not with the relatively recondite subject of Epicurean physics but with the central matters of ethics and personal conduct, common topics of educated conversation at Rome and closely applicable to everyday life; here, as has long been recognized, he is indebted to the *De Officiis* of Cicero, another publication of the previous generation, which tries similarly to apply the precepts of Greek ethics to the practice of Roman public and private life.[4] There is also the question of dogmatism, intensity, and grandeur: the doctrinaire missionary fervour and epic sublimity of Lucretius, though tempered at times by reflection and humour, is far from the mellow and humble protreptic persona adopted by Horace in the first book of *Epistles*.

Horace's presentation of philosophy in the first book of *Epistles* may be considered under two general headings: that of the poet's own self-representation as writer of the poems, and that of how the resources of hexameter poetry in particular are used in the exposition of ethics.

(i) *Self-Presentation*

The first and programmatic poem of *Epistles* I gives the reader vital indications of the kind of philosopher Horace will be (*Ep.* I. I. I–12):

> Prima dicte mihi, summa dicende Camena,
> spectatum satis et donatum iam rude quaeris,
> Maecenas, iterum antiquo me includere ludo.
> non eadem est aetas, non mens. Veianius armis

---

[3] Cf. e.g. *Ep.* I. II. 10, I. 16. 35; *Odes* I. 34; *Sat.* I. I. 25–6; cf. Rehmann (1969).
[4] Cf. McGann (1969), 10–14.

Herculis ad postem fixis latet abditus agro,
ne populum extrema totiens exoret harena.
est mihi purgatam crebro qui personet aurem:
'solve senescentem mature sanus equum, ne
peccet ad extremum ridendus et ilia ducat'.
nunc itaque et versus et cetera ludicra pono;
quid verum atque decens, curo et rogo et omnis in hoc sum.
condo et compono quae mox depromere possim.

Horace here describes his turning to philosophy as the retirement of a
gladiator, who does not wish to enter again the *ludus*, playing on the
double sense of that word, which means both 'gladiatorial school' and
'frivolous play';[5] the metaphorical message to Maecenas is clearly that
Horace will not write another book of erotic *Odes* after the recent
publication of *Odes* 1–3, and that he is keen to put such frivolities
behind him in his new ethical project. *Ludus* can refer specifically to
love as well as to erotic poetry, as it does in a similar context at *Epistles*
1. 14. 36, *non lusisse pudet, sed non incidere ludum*;[6] Horace is presenting himself as too old both for love and for its poetry, as at *Odes*
3. 26. 1–2: *vixi puellis nuper idoneus,* | *et militavi non sine gloria.*[7] The
image used there was of course the elegiac one of the *militia amoris*;
here in the *Epistles* the same idea is presented through the image of the
retired gladiator, a decidedly down-market and sordid version of the
same metaphor (Veianius is not an elevated character—as a gladiator
he was probably a slave).[8] The rural retirement of the gladiator (*latet
abditus agro*) reinforces the parallel with Horace the poet on his own
Sabine *ager* (*Ep.* 1. 16. 4): Horace's pensive withdrawal to the country
and its opportunities for philosophical reflection will be a major theme
in *Epistles* 1.[9] This lower tone is confirmed by the image of lines 8–9,
where Horace's poetry is compared to a clapped-out nag, clearly a
comic and low-life version of the chariot of poetry;[10] Horace will have to
slow down to a walk, suitable to the *Musa pedestris* of *sermo* (*Sat.*
2. 6. 17). Explicit allusion to philosophy comes at lines 10–12, where all
poetry is renounced in favour of moral philosophy. The protestation

[5] Cf. D. A. West (1967), 23–4.
[6] Cf. *TLL* 7. 1789. 32 ff.
[7] Cf. also *Odes* 1. 5. 13–16.
[8] On the status of gladiators cf. Hopkins (1983), 23–5.
[9] Cf. *Ep.* 1. 7, 1. 10, 1. 14, 1. 16.
[10] For the chariot of poetry cf. (e.g.) Pindar, *Ol.* 6. 23, *P.* 10. 65, *Isth.* 8. 68; Callimachus, *Aetia* fr. 1. 25–8; Virgil, *G.* 2. 542, 3. 18. It is particularly common in Greek
lyric poetry (cf. Hollis on Ovid, *Ars* 1. 39), and Horace may be exploiting this here in
making a renunciation of lyric.

is solemn, but tinged with not a little humour: Horace is after all renouncing poetry in the context of introducing a book of poems, a type of ironic fiction found elsewhere in his hexameter poetry.[11] As in the opening image of the *ludus*, ambiguous language indicates this irony: *condo* and *compono* are technical terms for the storage or laying down of wine in a cellar, but both verbs can also refer elsewhere in Horace to the composition of poetry.[12]

So the first book of *Epistles* begins with a self-representation which is far from sublime, and with a renunciation of poetry in favour of morality which is strongly stated but cannot be literally true; the erotic and symposiastic themes of the *Odes* do largely disappear, but the collection is indubitably poetic. The apparent conversion to philosophy is at least partly a fiction for literary purposes, since philosophical concerns are far from absent from Horace's earlier writings.[13] The poet is not a 'born again' fundamentalist missionary in the Lucretian mould, but is able to joke about his new career as a poetic purveyor of philosophy to his friends. This combination of self-depreciating humour and enthusiasm in conveying his philosophical interests is a hallmark of Horace's self-presentation in the first book of *Epistles*. This is confirmed by further examples. In *Epistles* 1. 4 Horace writes to Tibullus,[14] advising his fellow-poet to enjoy the material benefits of his comfortable life while he may, despite the emotional traumas he writes about in his love-elegies (12–16):

> inter spem curamque, timores inter et iras,
> omnem crede diem tibi diluxisse supremum.
> grata superveniet quae non sperabitur hora.
> me pinguem et nitidum bene curata cute vises
> cum ridere voles Epicuri de grege porcum.

Once again this famous self-characterization by Horace is clearly not an elevated one, and here again, as in the opening epistle, it is conjoined with earnest philosophical exhortations, here of an Epicurean kind no doubt suited to a hedonistic elegist.[15] Horace the philosophical teacher uses self-depreciation as a *captatio benevolentiae*.

[11] Cf. *Sat.* 1. 4. 41–2; *AP* 306.

[12] *Condo* = 'lay down' (wine) at *Odes* 1. 20. 3, 'compose' (poetry) at *Sat.* 2. 1. 82; *compono* = 'store' (wood) at *Odes* 3. 17. 14, 'compose' (poetry) at *Ep.* 2. 1. 76.

[13] Here I agree with Mayer (1986) and Rudd (1993) against C. W. Macleod (1979), who takes the theme of conversion too seriously and literally.

[14] The 'Albius' of this epistle and of *Odes* 1. 33 must be Tibullus; see Nisbet and Hubbard (1970), 368.

[15] As will be seen in (ii) below, line 13 is a translation of an Epicurean precept.

Horace commonly presents himself in *Epistles* 1 not as the great teacher and moral paragon but as a fallible fellow-pupil, while still urging a particular moral line. At the end of *Epistles* 1. 6, Horace refers to his advice as no better than anyone else's, but encourages Numicius to take it if he knows nothing else better (67–8), while at the beginning of *Epistles* 1. 17, in an equally prominent position, Scaeva is given instruction on the art of friendship, a philosophical subject in antiquity,[16] but by a Horace who is still learning and who is like a blind man leading the way (3–4). Twice Horace, advocating the consistent moral life, alludes prominently to his own inconsistency (*Ep.* 1. 8, 1. 15. 42–6), and the final poem of the book, although it is not concerned with philosophy as such, continues this modest self-presentation, in a direct contrast with the great closing claims for the poet made in *Odes* 2. 20 and 3. 30.[17] The rationale behind this modesty both as poet and as teacher of philosophy is clear enough: Horace is evidently going to get further in interesting his friends in ethical topics by not posing as an omniscient sage. The humorous and fallible self-image of the poet as philosopher in *Epistles* 1 helps to convey its protreptic message in the most effective and acceptable way.

(ii) *Poetic Packaging*

I now turn to the advantages of poetry in general and of the hexameter in particular in Horace's presentation and packaging of philosophical material in *Epistles* 1. Two techniques will suffice here. One is the use of single-line *sententiae*, 'one-liners', through which the poet can encapsulate a thought in a single syntactical unit in one easily memorable hexameter. There are many examples, of which the following list is merely a convenient selection.

1. *Ep.* 1. 1. 19   et mihi res, non me rebus subiungere conor
2. *Ep.* 1. 1. 52   vilius argentum est auro, virtutibus aurum
3. *Ep.* 1. 2. 46   quod satis est cui contingit nihil amplius optet
4. *Ep.* 1. 4. 13   omnem crede diem tibi diluxisse supremum
5. *Ep.* 1. 6. 23   hic tibi sit potius quam tu memorabilis illi
6. *Ep.* 1. 7. 98   metiri se quemque suo modulo ac pede verum est
7. *Ep.* 1. 11. 27   caelum non animum mutant qui trans mare currunt

---

[16] See conveniently Powell (1990*a*), 2–5, with further bibliography, and Powell in the preceding chapter of this volume.   [17] Cf. S. J. Harrison (1988).

8. *Ep.* 1. 14. 11   cui placet alterius, sua nimirum est odio sors
9. *Ep.* 1. 14. 44   quam scit uterque libens censebo exerceat
　　　　　　　　　　 artem
10. *Ep.* 1. 16. 17   tu recte vivis, si curas esse quod audis
11. *Ep.* 1. 17. 10   nec vixit male qui natus moriensque fefellit
12. *Ep.* 1. 17. 36   non cuivis homini contingit adire Corinthum
13. *Ep.* 1. 18. 9   virtus est medium vitiorum et utrimque reduc-
　　　　　　　　　　 tum

These thirteen one-line *sententiae* divide into two types: those which
express a very general philosophical or proverbial idea, and those
which translate or adapt known moral precepts of Greek philosophers.
Of the first type, 3 encapsulates the ideal of self-sufficiency (αὐτάρ-
κεια) desiderated by most ancient philosophies, 6 the general idea that
each man has his own individual measure, 7 refers to the common idea
that travel does not ease the mind, 8 to the commonplace that each
man dislikes his own lot and wants another (μεμψιμοιρία), while 6, 9,
and 12 are versions of known proverbs;[18] here it is worth recalling that
ancient proverbs were often expressed in metrical units.[19] For each of
the second type, we can trace a particular Greek prose source cast by
Horace into verse, as follows.[20]

1. cf. Aristippus in Diogenes Laertius 2. 75: ἔχω, ἀλλ᾽ οὐκ ἔχομαι
2. cf. Plato, *Laws* 5. 728a: χρυσὸς ἀρετῆς οὐκ ἀντάξιος
4. cf. Epicurus fr. 490 Us.: ὁ τῆς αὔριον ἥκιστα δεόμενος ἥδιστα
　　　πρόσεισι πρὸς τὴν αὔριον
5. cf. Plutarch, *De Tranq.* 10: ζηλωτὸν μᾶλλον εἶναι ἢ ζηλοῦν
　　　ἑτέρους
10. cf. Socrates in Xenophon, *Mem.* 2. 6. 39: ὅτι ἂν βούλῃ δοκεῖν
　　　ἀγαθὸς εἶναι, τοῦτο καὶ γενέσθαι ἀγαθὸν πειρᾶσθαι
11. cf. Epicurus fr. 551 Us.: λάθε βιώσας
13. cf. Aristotle, *NE* 2. 6 1107ᵃ: ἔστιν ἄρα ἡ ἀρετή . . . μεσότης . . .
　　　δύο κακιῶν, τῆς μὲν καθ᾽ ὑπερβολήν, τῆς δὲ κατ᾽ ἔλλειψιν

Thus it is clear that Horace is aware in the *Epistles* that hexameter
verse adds an extra dimension to the presentation of philosophical
precepts, enabling the poet to communicate philosophical views,
whether general or particular, with epigrammatic point and neatness

---

[18] Cf. Otto (1890), 221, 151, and 92 respectively for 6, 9, and 12.
[19] For the metrical patterns of Greek and Latin proverbs cf. K. Rupprecht in
RE 18. 1713. 17 ff.; Otto (1890), pp. xxxiii–xxxiv.
[20] These parallels are all collected by Kiessling–Heinze (1915).

in a single regular and memorable unit not available to writers of prose.

A second resource offered by the poetic medium is that of imagery. Of course, prose texts and prose expositions of philosophy need not be poor in imagery (Plato's dialogues and Seneca's letters are good counter-examples),[21] but the *Epistles* show that poetry, especially hexameter poetry with its long and rich tradition, offers greater opportunity for such ornament, and Lucretius had provided an important precedent for the extensive use of imagery in the poetic exposition of philosophy.[22] One particular technique which the *Epistles* share with Lucretius here is the use of analogy with the familiar and visual in giving expositions of non-visual philosophical ideas. A few examples. In the first poem Horace compares disorder of appearance and of soul (*Ep.* 1. 1. 94–100):

> si curatus inaequali tonsore capillos
> occurri, rides; si forte subucula pexae
> trita subest tunicae vel si toga dissidet impar,
> rides: quid mea cum pugnat sententia secum,
> quod petiit spernit, repetit quod nuper omisit,
> aestuat et vitae disconvenit ordine toto,
> diruit, aedificat, mutat quadrata rotundis?

Here Horace comically implies that the elegant Maecenas is more interested in minor aberrations in Horace's dress and appearance than in major aberrations in his moral and internal state. The minute and everyday details of dress and haircut give the thought a strong visual element, and suggest that moral confusion is just as common a state as untidiness of dress, a significant disadvantage in polite Roman society, so forcing it on the reader's attention. Very similar is the briefer image at 1. 10. 42–3:

> cui non conveniet sua res, ut calceus olim,
> si pede maior erit, subvertet, si minor, uret.

There discontent with one's material lot is aptly compared to an ill-fitting shoe, which will be uncomfortable if it is either too small or too big; again the sartorial detail brings the moral point home to the reader. Another instance is 1. 18. 84–5:

> nam tua res agitur, paries cum proximus ardet,
> et neglecta solent incendia sumere viris.

---

[21] For the rich imagery of these cf. conveniently Pöschl, Gärtner, and Heyke (1964), 303–16, 347–52.   [22] Cf. D. A. West (1969).

Here Horace advises Lollius to stick by friends who are attacked by others—he may be next, and will need their support in turn. This is reinforced by the vivid image of the burning house; in the close confines of a heavily inflammable Rome, conflagrations were all too common, and a neighbour's property in flames meant disaster for one's own.[23] All this is very similar to the technique by which Lucretius presents such invisible and arcane scientific matter as atomic motion through comparison in similes with things and events common in the visual life of late Republican Rome, most memorably public festivals or events in the theatre.[24]

The same can be said for the deployment of another image in the *Epistles*, the idea that philosophy is a cure for the soul just as medicine is a cure for the body. Again this is an image which begins in prose texts such as Democritus and Plato,[25] but in *Epistles* 1 Horace uses it a number of times, taking advantage of the capacity of a poetry-book to continue and develop an image.[26] This medical analogy appears prominently in the first and programmatic poem (1. 28–37):

> non possis oculo quantum contendere Lynceus,
> non tamen idcirco contemnas lippus inungi;
> nec quia desperes invicti membra Glyconis,
> nodosa corpus nolis prohibere cheragra.
> est quadam prodire tenus, si non datur ultra.
> fervet avaritia miseroque cupidine pectus:
> sunt verba et voces quibus hunc lenire dolorem
> possis et magnam morbi deponere partem.
> laudis amore tumes: sunt certa piacula quae te
> ter pure lecto poterunt recreare libello.

Here the poet encourages Maecenas and the reader in general to make as much effort to cure their moral ills as they would to heal physical complaints. The illnesses named as analogies in lines 29–31 are familiar and everyday ones, inflamed eyes and gout; the poet then goes on to treat moral ills in terms of bodily metaphor, with some careful and elegant ambiguity—*fervet* can refer to simple feverish heat as well as spiritual warmth, *lenire dolorem* is as appropriate to the relief of physical pain as to mental soothing, while *tumes* can suggest malignant

---

[23] Cf. (e.g.) J. E. B. Mayor on Juvenal 3. 7.

[24] Cf. D. A. West (1969), 49–63.

[25] Cf. Democritus B 31 D/K; Plato, *Gorg.* 480 b2; Summers on Seneca, *Ep.* 7. 1; Bramble (1974), 35 nn. 2 and 3.

[26] Collected by Bramble (1974), 35 n. 3. The most notable passages not discussed here are 1. 2. 37–9, 47–9, and 1. 6. 28–30.

physical swelling as well as the metaphorical swelling of ambition.[27] *Ter pure* suggests a formula of magical or medicinal relief of a physical kind,[28] an idea continued in *recreare,*[29] but *lecto . . . libello* points the surprise and the intentional ambiguity—the illness is one of the spirit, and its cure is a book, a text of philosophy, perhaps the very book which the poet is writing. The reader is being encouraged to read on in hope of a cure.

After this prominent introduction, the theme appears again in the next poem (2. 51–3):

> qui cupit aut metuit, iuvat illum sic domus et res
> ut lippum pictae tabulae, fomenta podagrum,
> auriculas citharae collecta sorde dolentis.

Once again the poet picks on everyday complaints, adding to the watery eyes and gout of the first epistle the pain of ears blocked with wax, arguing that they prevent the enjoyment of normal pleasures, and the point illustrated is similarly a trite one; the impossibility of pleasure for the rich man beset by cares is a favourite notion for Roman moralists.[30] Again, the point about moral health is effectively made through physical comparison and analogy. Equally effective is the image at 1. 3. 31–2, where the poet enquires of Florus whether the rift between Celsus and Munatius has been properly patched up, or whether it is still in operation:

> an male sarta
> gratia nequiquam coit ac rescinditur . . .?

Here the sundered friendship is clearly compared to an open wound where the stitches may or may not come together and heal; *sarta, coit,* and *rescinditur* are technical terms of medicine.[31] The point is clearly an ethical one: the moral harm of quarrelling is like the physical harm of injury, and the reconciled friendship is like the whole and healed body.

---

[27] For *fervere* of fever cf. *TLL* 6. 591. 75 ff., of mental warmth ibid. 6. 591. 81 ff.; for *lenire* of physical relief cf. *TLL* 7. 1142. 14 ff., of mental soothing ibid. 7. 1140. 68 ff.; for *tumere* of noxious swelling *OLD* s.v. 1(b), of ambition ibid. 3(a).

[28] For the number three in ritual/magic actions cf. Tibullus 1. 2. 54 *ter cane, ter dictis spue carminibus,* R. Mehrlein in *RAC* 4. 269–310; for ritual purity cf. Tibullus 1. 3. 25 *pureque lavari, OLD* s.v. *pure* 2(a).

[29] Cf. *OLD* s.v. 2(a).

[30] Cf. e.g. *Odes* 2. 16. 9–24, 3. 1. 17–24, 3. 16. 17–28, 3. 24. 1–8; Seneca, *Ep.* 84. 11, 115. 16; *Brev. Vit.* 2. 4.

[31] For *sarcio* of surgery cf. Celsus 7. 8. 4 and Scribonius Largus 206; for *coeo* of wounds healing cf. *TLL* 3. 1419. 11 ff.; and for *rescindo* of opening up wounds cf. *OLD* s.v. 2(b).

This link in imagery between physical and moral distemper is extended through another feature of the first book of *Epistles* already identified, the poet's detailed self-representation. Horace's own actual or potential ill-health is mentioned a number of times in the collection, and is linked from time to time with the unsatisfactory state of his mind. In 1. 8, in a letter to Celsus, on campaign with Tiberius in the East, the analogy is fully explored (3–12):

> si quaeret quid agam, dic multa et pulchra minantem
> vivere nec recte nec suaviter; haud quia grando
> contuderit vitis oleamque momorderit aestus,
> nec quia longinquis armentum aegrotet in agris;
> sed quia mente minus validus quam corpore toto
> nil audire velim, nil discere, quod levet aegrum;
> fidis offendar medicis, irascar amicis,
> cur me funesto properent arcere veterno;
> quae nocuere sequar, fugiam quae profore credam;
> Romae Tibur amem ventosus, Tibure Romam.

Again, as elsewhere, the terms used are neatly ambiguous: *audire*, *discere*, and *quod levet aegrum* refer equally well to listening to medically or spiritually curative advice, matching the balance in line 9 between *medicis* and *amicis* which suggests that friends try to do for the mind what doctors try to do for the body,[32] *veterno* in line 10 can refer to physical conditions such as dropsy as well as mental lethargy,[33] and the pithy one-liner of line 11 presents a moral dilemma akin to Aristotelian ἀκρασία as well as a problem with daily diet and habits.[34]

In 1. 7, Horace's Sabine estate is used as a starting-point for more general analogies between bodily and spiritual health. There Horace claims health as a reason for staying on his estate rather than coming to Maecenas in Rome; the opening, with its talk of the insalubrious summer conditions in the city, stresses that physical risk is a main factor in Horace's absence (1–13). But the rest of the poem, with its *exempla* of the Calabrian host, the vixen in the corn-bin, and the story of Philippus and Mena, makes it clear that the Sabine estate and Horace's capacity to remain there represent more than physical

---

[32] For friends as doctors of the soul, cf. similarly Propertius 1. 1. 25–8 with Fedeli's note on 1. 1. 25.

[33] For *veternosus* in the sense of *hydropicus*, 'dropsical', cf. Paul. exc. Fest., p. 507. 4 Lindsay (citing Cato).

[34] For Aristotle's account of ἀκρασία, where someone knows the right course of action but fails to do it through weakness, cf. *NE* 7. 1148ᵃ15 ff.; Horace's *sequar* and *fugiam* resemble Aristotle's use of διώκω and φεύγω in that same discussion (1148ᵃ17).

health. The estate and its gift through Maecenas' friendship allow Horace to remain healthy in spirit, that is to pursue an appropriate life-style of rural philosophical *otium* in dignified but grateful in-dependence, and the poem ends with a generalizing and proverbial 'one-liner' which stresses the ethical dimension (98 *metiri se quemque suo modulo ac pede verum est*).[35]

The extension and variation of a type of imagery illustrating a philosophical idea to provide a link with a central theme of the whole collection is typical of the resources available for the exposition of ideas in a poetry-book. In fact, we have seen that discussion of the analogy between mental and physical health has also mentioned and included the two other aspects of the first book of *Epistles* which have been classified above as poetic techniques—the elaborate self-presen-tation of the writer and the use of 'one-liners', showing that the poet is in full command of a range of poetical strategies, and uses them in an integrated way towards the objective of his collection, the entertaining and informative presentation of ethical issues both to his immediate correspondents and to a larger readership.

II. LETTER-WRITING AND *EPISTLES* I

Here we turn to our second issue, that of whether the first book of *Epistles* is written with some consciousness of formal works on letter-writing; we shall see in due course that this links closely with our first issue of the poetic presentation of philosophy. Some influence on Horace from the epistolographical tradition is not improbable; some case has been made for its use by Cicero in his correspondence,[36] and it would only be natural for Horace to employ it in recasting *sermo* into epistolary mode in the first book of *Epistles*. The Greek works devoted to letter-writing collected in Hercher's *Epistolographi Graeci* are jejune and concerned almost entirely with epistolary typology, and insignificant here;[37] most important are the pages devoted to letter-writing in Demetrius, *On Style*, variously dated between the late

[35] For the origin of this thought see the discussion of this 'one-liner' above.
[36] Cf. Keyes (1935).
[37] Hercher (1871), 1–13. On the theory and practice of Greek and Roman letter-writing cf. Thraede (1970) and Cugusi (1983). There is only one extant formal discussion of letter-writing in Latin, a few pages in the 4th-cent. *Ars Rhetorica* of C. Iulius Victor (text in Halm (1863), 447–8), which uses Greek precepts but Roman examples (from Cicero).

Hellenistic period and the early Imperial period.[38] Similarities between Demetrius' precepts and Horace's practice in the *Epistles* could suggest knowledge on Horace's part of epistolographical theory, even if Demetrius' work were written much later, since ancient handbooks of this kind are notoriously tralatician, and even those who wish to assign a late date to Demetrius recognize that his treatise contains elements of much earlier doctrine. It is possible, of course, that Demetrius' precepts merely reflected literary practice in letter-writing, and that any links with Horace could be owed to Horace's knowledge of actual letters rather than of theory, but the striking nature of some of the resemblances suggests a more direct connection.

Demetrius begins his section on letter-writing (*On Style* 223–35) by asserting that the style of letters requires plainness (ἰσχνότης), though this should also be combined with the more elevated quality of charm (χάρις, 235). In support of this, he cites Artemon, editor of Aristotle's letters and certainly a pre-Horatian writer, to the effect that 'a letter may be regarded as one of the two sides in a dialogue'. This, like plainness of style, is one of the conventional recommendations of ancient epistolography.[39] Here Horace fits the prescription, since most of the epistles in the first book are in effect his side of an exchange with the addressee, commonly an intimate with whom the poet might have regular contact and converse. More importantly, Artemon's view implies a colloquial stylistic level for letters, a view endorsed elsewhere in the epistolographical tradition;[40] of course, this is the natural register of Horatian hexameter *sermo*, making it a natural vehicle for letter-writing. Demetrius also stresses the small scale of the letter (228); in addition to mirroring the practicalities of ancient correspondence, brevity itself is another stylistic τόπος in epistolographical writing.[41] Here we can see an interesting contrast between the *Satires* and the first book of *Epistles*: the two books of *Satires* show an average poem-length of 119 lines (103 lines for Book 1, 135 for Book 2), the first book of *Epistles* one of 50 lines, dramatically different. The second book of *Epistles* and the *Ars Poetica* are of course rather longer, but there the epistolographical fiction is less immediately important; in *Epistles* 1 Horace is conforming more closely and consciously to the practice and prescriptions of letter-writing.

---

[38] For the earlier date cf. Grube (1961), 39–56, for the later Schenkeveld (1964), 135–48. I cite throughout the translation of Demetrius by D. C. Innes in Russell and Winterbottom (1972).

[39] Cf. Cugusi (1983), 32–3. [40] Cf. Cugusi (1983), 33, Thraede (1970), 27–61.

[41] Cf. Cugusi (1983), 34–6.

Further points made by Demetrius concern the content rather than the style of letters (227): 'A letter should be very largely an expression of character, just like the dialogue. Perhaps everyone reflects his own soul in writing a letter. It is possible to discern a writer's character in every other form of literature, but in none so fully as in the letter.' This aspect of self-revelation again fits Horatian *sermo* as a whole; Horace characterizes his *Satires* as self-revelatory, following the tradition of Lucilius (*Sat.* 2. 1. 30–4), and we indeed hear much there about Horace's earlier and present life. It is even more a feature of the first book of *Epistles*; as Gordon Williams has noted, 'a most marked feature of the *Epistles* is the way in which the form invites, indeed compels, statements apparently autobiographical'.[42] Horace continually presents the topics of his own life—his turning to philosophy (1. 1), his literary studies (1. 2), his social life (1. 5), his friendship with Maecenas (1. 7), the publication and reception of his poems (1. 13, 1. 19, 1. 20), his life in the country (1. 10, 1. 14, 1. 16), his health (1. 7, 1. 15), and of course the concluding self-description in the final poem (1. 20. 20–8). This relentless self-presentation recalls the intimate detail of actual correspondence such as Cicero's letters to Atticus; Horace relies here on the convention and practice of letter-writing as well as on the autobiographical element in Lucilian *sermo*. Here we can see a link with our earlier discussion of poetic self-presentation; the prominence of the writer himself in the first book of *Epistles* is both an effective protreptic tactic and an epistolary feature.

Most interesting of all in Demetrius' prescriptions for our purposes are those on the content of letters (230–2): 'We should also recognize that it is not only a certain style but certain topics which suit letters. Let me quote Aristotle, who is admitted to be an especially felicitous writer of letters: "I do not write to you on this; it does not suit a letter". If anyone writes on logic or science in a letter, he is writing something but certainly not a letter. A letter aims to be a brief token of friendship and handles simple topics in simple language. Its charm lies in the warmth of friendship it conveys and in its numerous proverbs. This is the only kind of wisdom a letter should have; for proverbs give popular sayings in everyday use. The man who is sententious and sermonizes seems to have lost the letter's air of a talk and mounted the pulpit.' All these aspects apply closely to the first book of Horace's *Epistles*, and link up neatly with the poetical tactics discussed in I above.

First, the non-technical and simple nature of letters. This might

[42] Williams (1968), 29. Cf similarly Heinze (1960), 298–304.

appear to be paradoxical for a book of poems which includes a fair amount of philosophical doctrine, but in fact, as outlined at the beginning, Horace's exposition of philosophy in *Epistles* 1 is generalizing, undogmatic, and fundamentally concerned with ethics, the most popular part of philosophy which was of universal interest in his own day, and not with the grittier topics of logic or physics; it is interesting to note that the quotation from Aristotle in Demetrius specifically refers to science and logic being excluded as inappropriate to letters. Second, the link of letters and friendship. In one sense, this is simply an obvious comment on the means of intimate communication in a pre-telephonic age, but it is again worth noting that almost all the poems in the first book of *Epistles* are addressed to known friends of Horace, a difference from the *Odes* and even the *Satires*, that they contain particularly warm expressions of personal affection (e.g. 1. 1. 105, 1. 10. 1–5), and that friendship and its rightful conduct is a major topic in the collection (e.g. 1. 7, 1. 17, 1. 18).

Third and perhaps most importantly, Demetrius' stress on the non-dogmatic and non-preaching role of the letter-writer, and his use of homely proverbs rather than technicalities and high-flown moral prescription, fits remarkably well with Horace's self-presentation in *Epistles* 1 as already discussed. Horace's humorous and self-depreciating role as author of moral protreptic in *Epistles* 1 is obvious from I(i) above, but here we can see how it fits neatly into the conventions of letter-writing. The use of proverbs, too, can be plausibly connected with the 'one-liner' technique identified in I(ii) above; not only does this technique resemble that of proverbial discourse with its pithy and memorable results (discussed, incidentally in ch. 9 of Demetrius, *On Style*), but several of the 'one-liners' identified in *Epistles* 1 are, as already noted, themselves known proverbs. The homely and generalizing wisdom of proverbs may also be appropriately compared with the overall strategy of *Epistles* 1 in proclaiming undogmatic and general ethical principles to which few would take exception.

III. CONCLUSION

In sum, I hope to have pointed to two features of the first book of Horace's *Epistles*, features which are crucially interrelated. First, I have indicated some of the strategies used by Horace to present his ethical material in hexameter poetry. Second, I have argued that some of the central features of Horace's treatment of his material are shared with ancient strictures on letter-writing, suggesting perhaps some knowledge on his part of epistolographical precept in his epistolary practice.

5

Ovid and the Failure of Rhetoric

RICHARD TARRANT

The Elder Seneca does not on the whole cut an imposing figure in the annals of literary criticism, but his effect on the interpretation of Ovid's poetry has been lasting and profound. The information Seneca transmits about Ovid's youthful study of declamation is a staple in any account of the poet's life; it has also provided a factual basis for the constantly repeated characterization of Ovid's writing as 'rhetorical'.[1] Exactly what is meant by this description is often hard to make out,[2] but at one level the aptness of the term can hardly be disputed: Ovid's poetry displays the techniques of formal rhetoric, and in particular the use of formally structured arguments as an instrument of persuasion, more often and more openly than that of any other Latin poet.[3] Only an austere critic indeed would deny the relevance of what Seneca tells us about Ovid's declamatory studies to this conspicuous feature of his writing. There is a danger, however, that having these biographical facts so conveniently available will inhibit or even replace criticism: knowing that Ovid attended the performances of the noted declaimers Arellius Fuscus and Porcius Latro, that he himself was thought to display considerable talent as a speaker, that he showed a marked preference for *suasoriae* over *controversiae* and rarely declaimed the latter unless they turned on questions of character—faced with this precious and uncommonly explicit testimony, even a critic wary of biographical fallacies may be tempted to view the rhetorical component of Ovid's

[1] The relevant passages are discussed by Higham (1958).

[2] 'That Ovid's style is "rhetorical" his critics all agree; not all trouble to define adequately what they mean by the term' (Kenney (1973), 131). In a similar vein Fränkel (1945), 167–9, anatomized the often conflicting senses in which the term 'rhetorical' had been applied to Ovid and mordantly concluded 'it may indeed be wise to let the question of Ovid's rhetoric rest until more urgent tasks are completed' (169), a sentiment that appears to have been taken to heart by most subsequent critics.

[3] His nearest rival in this regard is Juvenal, who programmatically points to his own training in declamation as a qualification to write poetry (1. 15–17 'et nos I consilium dedimus Sullae, privatus ut altum I dormiret').

writing as a mere reflex of his school training, to be deplored or excused according to taste but not calling for further investigation.

In this essay I should like to try a different approach to the place of rhetorical argument in Ovid; rather than seeing it as simply an ingrained or habitual mode of expression, I shall suggest that Ovid makes use of the procedures of formal argument to produce carefully directed effects, and that his relation to those procedures is fundamentally ironic.[4] My focus will be on the rhetoric of persuasion, the context in which Ovid or the various speakers in his poetry most often employ formal techniques of argument;[5] the aspect of these attempts at persuasion that I want especially to examine is their striking lack of success. From the first poem of the *Amores* to the final books of the *Tristia* and the *Epistulae ex Ponto*, ingenious and finely crafted arguments fail to move the persons to whom they are addressed; this type of failure is so frequent and so conspicuous that it deserves to be recognized as a leading theme of Ovid's writing. In a short discussion I can only hope to sketch the outlines of the argument, but I hope there may be some advantage in tracing the motif through all phases of Ovid's career; the *Amores* receive somewhat fuller treatment than the other works, since the motif of failed persuasion appears there in an especially well-marked form.

In the opening scene of the *Amores*, Ovid portrays himself as embarking on an epic account of kings and battles when Cupid deflects his efforts to elegy by stealing the last foot of his second line (1–4). The

---

[4] In some of its consequences my argument parallels that of Kenney (1969) regarding Ovid's use of legal terminology; Kenney's study shows that in passages with a strongly marked legal flavour Ovid usually exploits the potential for incongruity latent in any application of legal terms to a non-legal setting.

[5] As long ago as 1918, Kirby Flower Smith noted the prominence of *suasoria*-type argument in nearly all of Ovid's works: 'some of the most notable pieces in the *Amores* are really *suasoriae*, ... the *Heroides* are nothing more or less than so many *suasoriae* in epistolary form, ... the *Ars Amatoria* is one long lesson in the art of suasion. I may add 'that in the *Metamorphoses* many of the finest passages are suasorial, and that all those passages painting the conflict of warring impulses in the human breast ... are really so many adaptations of the *controversia ethica*. I need not mention the *Tristia* and the *Epistulae ex Ponto*. They are all *suasoriae*' (Smith (1918), in reprint (1920) 72; I was led to Smith's essay by references to it in Higham (1934)). Although reductively stated, Smith's observation is both acute and suggestive; he did not take it further, however, since for him the prominence of suasorial argument in Ovid was adequately explained by Ovid's documented fondness for this form of rhetorical exercise. A similar biographical approach is taken by McKeown (1987), 69–71, in discussing the role of *suasoria*-type argument in the *Amores*.

poet remonstrates with the god in a vigorously argued speech that fills the centre of the poem (5–20); he accuses Cupid of acting outside his proper sphere by meddling in poetry and protests that he cannot write elegy since he is not in love and so lacks the proper *materia*. Cupid speaks less than a full line in reply (24 'quod . . . canas, vates, accipe . . . opus'), but accompanies his words with an arrow to Ovid's heart that overcomes all resistance. The poem ends with Ovid's resigned acceptance of his changed project. In the 'plot' of the poem Ovid's failed effort at dissuasion is the element given the fullest treatment; the gross disparity of scale between Ovid's speech and Cupid's response places still more stress on the former.[6] We are surely meant to notice how assertive and articulate Ovid is in a situation where gods usually issue directions and poets acquiesce in silence,[7] but the poem's outcome also exposes Ovid's fluency as vain and suggests a correlation between extended or elaborate argument and ultimate powerlessness.

Amores 1. 1 is both an introduction to a collection of poems and a microcosm of that collection's qualities; the prominence in the poem of formal persuasive argument, and its futility, are thus by implication programmatic for the *Amores* as a whole. Again and again the lover-poet attempts to overcome an obstacle or to direct a situation with carefully argued speech; in most cases his efforts signally fail to achieve their intended effect, whether the recipient of the persuasion is a door-keeper (1. 6), the rising sun (1. 13), or a disobliging river (3. 6). These failed efforts at persuasion assume a variety of forms. In the most straightforward type (represented by *Amores* 1. 1 and found several times in the first book of the revised edition), the failure is dramatized as the endpoint of the poem's action, as in 1. 4, 1. 6, 1. 13, and 3. 6. Several sets of paired poems (1. 11–12, 2. 7–8, 2. 2–3, 2. 9A and B, 3. 11A and B) offer a variant in which the persuasive effect aimed at by the first half is undone by the second; in 1. 11–12 and 2. 2–3 an appeal is rejected by the person approached, in 2. 7–8 (the Cypassis poems) the lover reveals his earlier self-defence to have been

---

[6] In *Met.* 1. 454 ff. Ovid describes a quarrel between Apollo and Cupid that closely parallels the confrontation of *Amores* 1. 1. Although the poetic subtext of both scenes is similar (subordination of traditional epic to erotic subjects), the economy of the scene in the *Metamorphoses* gives roughly equal speaking roles to Apollo and Cupid; I infer that the markedly unequal distribution of speech in *Amores* 1. 1 is meant to characterize at the outset the persona Ovid will adopt in the *Amores*. Comparison with Propertius 1. 1 (in which the lover's conquest by Amor is complete before the poem begins) makes it still clearer that fluent speech in the service of persuasion is a feature of Ovid's distinctive identity as elegiac lover-poet.

[7] As noted by McKeown (1987), 8, introductory note to 1. 1.

a sham, and in the remaining two pairs his arguments against continuing in love fail to overcome his own inner resistance.[8] In yet another
variation the lover himself deflates his argument by retracting it at the
end of the poem (2. 14) or by shifting his ground in a way that makes
nonsense of his carefully constructed case (1. 10). A more subtle form
of this move can be seen in Ovid's version of the *propemptikon* (2. 11),
where the lover foresees the likelihood that his arguments will not
dissuade Corinna from a proposed sea-voyage and so changes tactics
to wish her well and imagine her safe return.[9] Finally, in a sizeable
group of poems the lover's arguments are left unanswered at the end
and their lack of success is more or less clearly implied rather than
being made apparent: 1. 3, 2. 3,[10] 2. 17, 2. 19, 3. 4, 3. 10, 3. 14. (The
ironic treatment of persuasion in 1. 3 is unusually complex in that the
lover's assurances of *fides* are apparently meant to seem convincing to
his intended mistress but are undermined in the eyes of the reader.)[11]

Against this background even the lover's apparent rhetorical successes in the *Amores* take on an ironic tint. In the first 82 lines of 3. 2 he
tirelessly strives to win the attention of the woman seated next to him
in the Circus; his exertions are finally rewarded by a smile and an
unspoken promise ('risit et argutis quiddam promisit ocellis' 83) and
the poem ends with his eager invitation to adjourn to another venue
('hoc satis hic; alio cetera redde loco' 84). As in 1. 1, the contrast
between the lover's extended speech and his addressee's brief but
decisive reply deflates the lover's rhetorical pretentions; in this case
there may also be a suggestion that persuasion of such length was
hardly necessary to produce the desired response. Under the heading
of ostensibly successful arguments one might also consider 1. 9 'Militat omnis amans', since it ends with a triumphant assertion of QED
('qui nolet fieri desidiosus, amet' 46). At best, however, the poem

---

[8] For the paired status of these poems see Damon (1990).

[9] The movement of thought in the poem may be conventional (cf. Cairns (1972),
120–1), but it is perhaps significant that Ovid reckons with the possibility of failure to
persuade Corinna while Propertius in 1. 8 portrays himself as successfully preventing
Cynthia from leaving for Illyria. (I owe this point to Cynthia Damon.)

[10] *Amores* 2. 3 serves an atypical dual function: as the second half of a pair with 2. 2
(cf. Damon (1990), 280–5), it reveals the failure of the appeal in the previous poem; but
it also contains a renewed attempt to win over Bagoas, the outcome of which can be
presumed to be equally unsuccessful. In other sets of paired poems the situation is firmly
closed at the end of the second poem; the Bagoas poems thus represent a further
variation on diptych structure.

[11] With many critics (e.g. Barsby (1973), 53, 55) I take it that the stress on deception
in the poem's mythological *exempla* (22 *lusit adulter*, 23 *simulato . . . iuvenco*) gives the
lie to the lover's protestations of lasting fidelity.

represents a form of pseudo-persuasion: its formal addressee, Atticus, has no real function as the recipient of the argument, and in any event the absurdity of what is 'proven' is as essential to the poem's humour as is the appearance of logic with which the case is argued.

In nearly half the poems making up the *Amores* Ovid combines attempts to persuade through argument with absence of actual persuasion, ironically suggesting a perverse causal connection between them. The impression of such a link is strengthened by a striking contrast: the exceptional scene of erotic success described in 1. 5 unfolds without a single word being spoken on either side.[12]

For an elegiac lover-poet to fail to get his way is of course nothing new; indeed, an inability to control events is a set feature of the love-elegist's persona. Ovid's innovation in the *Amores* was to couple the lover's typical lack of success with irrepressible verbal fluency in such a way as to make the lover's powers of speech emblematic of his lack of other forms of control. This ironic portrayal of the lover as rhetor assumes a fundamental incompatibility between its two constituent terms. 'Quis, nisi mentis inops, tenerae declamat amicae?' asks the *praeceptor* of the *Ars Amatoria* (1. 465); the implications of the question are also relevant to the lover of the *Amores*.

Extended argument with persuasion as its object is central to the *Heroides* as to no other work of Ovid; perhaps not coincidentally, the futility of those arguments is also nowhere else as obvious. Unlike the *Amores*, in which the outcome of a poem's 'plot' cannot be fully predicted on a first reading, the *Heroides* deal with some of the most familiar stories of antiquity. Every reader knew that Hippolytus did not give in to Phaedra's advances, that Theseus never returned to Naxos, and that Aeneas persisted in leaving Carthage for Italy; the corresponding letters are therefore suffused from the start by the inevitability of their failure. Indeed some of the women writers seem themselves aware of the tragic end of their stories, most conspicuously Dido, who concludes her letter with directions to her sister Anna for her funeral and her epitaph (7. 191–6).[13] Furthermore, while formally

---

[12] The absence of speech lends the scene a dream-like quality, although I am not persuaded by the view of Nicoll (1977) that the poem describes a dream rather than a 'real' event.

[13] It is noteworthy that Penelope, who is unusual in that her story is destined to turn out happily, ends her letter on a despairing note: 'certe ego, quae fueram te discedente puella, | protinus ut venias, facta videbor anus' (115 f.). (As regards the efficacy of her persuasion Penelope is of course no more successful than the other heroines, since it was not her letter that brought Ulysses home to Ithaca.)

the single letters[14] resemble those *Amores* in which the lover's efforts to persuade receive no response within the poem, the absence of any reply from the male addressees in itself strongly suggests that the appeals directed to them are being made in vain. The women of the *Heroides* speak into a void, sometimes with no confidence that their words will even reach or be read by the absent beloved;[15] the lack of a response helps account for two features of the *Heroides* often regarded as faults, the length of the letters (there is no one to interrupt) and the strained ingenuity of many of the arguments (often a sign of growing desperation).[16] In this context the *Heroides* may be seen as a female counterpart to the male-centred *Amores*, more varied in tone but showing the same interest in the failure of speech to persuade.

The longer poems of Ovid's middle years, starting with the *Ars Amatoria*, continue to present persuasive rhetoric in ironic terms, but they do so in increasingly complex ways. (The notable exception is the *Fasti*, in which efforts to persuade play a very limited role and which I shall therefore pass over in this discussion.) It might seem paradoxical to speak of a failure of persuasive rhetoric in the *Ars*, since Ovid's persona in that poem boasts loudly and often of his success in inculcating the precepts of his craft;[17] but, as with the virtuoso performance in 'Militat omnis amans', one may doubt whether anyone other than the *praeceptor* himself is actually convinced by his arguments. What seems beyond question is that despite an apparent equation of the *praeceptor*

---

[14] The double letters, if Ovidian, form a distinct group composed at a later date. The case against Ovid's authorship of the double letters has been placed on a new footing by the Toronto dissertation of Hansen (1992); by means of a variety of computer-assisted tests, Hansen has shown significant differences between the double letters and Ovid's other works in a large number of metrical and lexical details. I continue to harbour doubts regarding Ovid's authorship of several of the single letters, but the point does not impinge directly on the present argument.

[15] Cf. *Her.* 1.61f. (Penelope), 5.1 (Oenone), 13.1f. (Laodamia). Conversely, Ariadne's expectation that her letter to Theseus will actually be read (10.3f.) seems unfounded.

[16] But in some places probably the result of textual disturbance: I find it hard to believe, for example, that the end of Penelope's letter (from line 97 onward) was meant to be as inanely repetitive as the manuscript tradition makes it appear (unless Ovid wished to show Penelope unravelling under the stress of her situation). The argumentative fullness which for good poetic reasons marks these letters made them particularly open to the sort of expanding or embellishing interpolation by readers that I have elsewhere called 'collaborative', cf. Tarrant (1989).

[17] e.g. 1.19–24, 263–4, 2.3–4, 509–12, 535–42, 733–42. Even contradictory advice is presented as part of the grand scheme, cf. 2.427f. 'qui modo celabas monitu tua crimina nostro,|flecte iter et monitu detege furta meo.'

with the poet, Ovid has created an identity for his speaker that invites readers to view him with amused detachment and the claims he makes for his *ars* with a large degree of scepticism. This effect is produced at a general level by the *praeceptor*'s air of self-importance and the portentous attitude he takes toward his subject,[18] and at the level of detail by a number of instances in which the speaker seems blithely to ignore the implications of his own statements. At the start of the second book, for example, the *praeceptor* compares the elation of a young Roman who has gained a mistress by following his instructions to the triumphant feelings of Paris as he carried Helen off from Sparta or of Pelops when he had won Hippodamia by his chariot victory (2. 5–8). The doom-laden associations of these myths do not appear to trouble the *praeceptor*, nor does he find anything amiss in enumerating a long series of epic and tragic stories in which men are destroyed by passionate women (Agamemnon and Clytemnestra, Jason and Medea, etc.) and then drawing the inference 'ergo age, ne dubita cunctas sperare puellas:|vix erit e multis, quae neget, una, tibi' (1. 343f.).[19] The *praeceptor*'s blindness to the import of the myths he so freely draws upon parallels his failure to recognize the futility of his entire enterprise. In his self-aggrandizing way the *praeceptor* proudly asserts that his task is difficult (2. 537 'ardua molimur, sed nulla, nisi ardua, virtus'), but Ovid's reader remains fully aware that it is in fact impossible.[20]

The *Metamorphoses* poses special problems for my discussion, since the use of formally organized speech for persuasive ends is only one of

[18] Smith (1918), 63, nicely spoke of Ovid capturing the serious, almost reverential feeling of an expert for his subject and uniting it 'with the dogmatic certainty of the university professor'. For the sake of my argument I am here singling out the ironic dimension in Ovid's portrayal of the *praeceptor*, but the poem would not be as effective a satire as it is if the speaker were merely a figure of fun. Ovid's treatment of the *praeceptor* is in this respect similar to his portrayal of another 'professorial' character, Pythagoras in *Metamorphoses* 15. Pythagoras' numbingly thorough lecture style is gently mocked and his advocacy of vegetarianism is made to sound like sentimental claptrap, but he is also used to articulate ideas of universal change central to the poem.

[19] To be fair to the *praeceptor*, the conclusion in 343f. rounds off the section beginning at 269f. ('prima tuae menti veniat fiducia, cunctas|posse capi'), within which the discussion of violent female lust serves as a supporting argument, introduced at 281f. and concluded at 341f.; the optimism of 343f. is therefore not grossly contradicted by the preceding mythical examples, but it shows no awareness of their ironic potential. On this topic see P. Watson (1983), Ahern (1989).

[20] At two crucial stages in the pupil's progress the *praeceptor*'s instruction consists of doing what comes naturally: 1. 609f. ('fac tantum cupias, sponte disertus eris'), 2. 705f. ('sponte sua sine te celeberrima verba loquentur,|nec manus in lecto laeva iacebit iners').

many narrative elements in the poem and even within any given episode is not normally the exclusive focus of attention; isolating instances of the motif for analysis therefore involves an even greater risk of over-simplification here than elsewhere in this essay. It can at least be shown, however, both that the theme appears often enough in the poem to be significant and that the ironic perspective seen in Ovid's earlier works operates here as well.[21] Certainly in erotic contexts, where continuity with Ovid's elegiac poetry is strongest, formal attempts at persuasion are consistently unsuccessful, from Apollo's speech of self-commendation delivered on the run to Daphne (1. 504–24) to Byblis' *Heroides*-style letter of seduction to her brother Caunus (9. 530–63) to the elaborate effort of Vertumnus in disguise to move the obdurately virginal Pomona (14. 663–764, including the inset story of Iphis and Anaxarete).[22] Some examples of failed amatory persuasion are set off by unique circumstances: Narcissus is understandably unable to impress the youth whose face he sees in the surface of a clear pool (3. 442–62), and Polyphemus' notions of persuasive argument are too brutish to have much chance of swaying Galatea (13. 789–869, especially the threat to dismember his rival Acis (860–6)),[23] while the unsuccessful approaches of Salmacis to Hermaphroditus (4. 320–8) and Circe to Glaucus (14. 28–36) are perhaps doomed

[21] Every general statement about the *Metamorphoses* (apart possibly from this one) has to admit of exceptions. Ceres' impassioned plea to Jupiter for Proserpina's release from the underworld (5. 514–22) is as successful as the fates will allow and is not narrated in an ironic way. (It is noteworthy, however, that this scene forms part of Calliope's prize-song (5. 341–661), which pointedly shows the gods in a favourable light by stressing their power and their respect for one another's prerogatives; the positive view of Ceres' speech therefore reflects the partisan outlook of the singer.) Jupiter also carries conviction when he enlists support for his decisions from the other gods (1. 182–98 and 209–43, 9. 243–58, 428–38), but in his case persuasive argument is backed by the possibility of force (cf. 2. 397 'precibus . . . minas regaliter addit').

[22] In the first and last of these episodes the suitor is ultimately successful (at least to a degree), but through other means: Apollo wins assent from the transformed Daphne when he renounces hopes of marriage and offers her a position as his special tree (1. 557–67), and Vertumnus overcomes Pomona's resistance by putting off the guise of an old woman and showing himself in his true form (14. 765–71). The case of Apollo is of particular interest in that both his failed and his successful approaches to Daphne are expressed in formal speech. The faults of his earlier attempt are analysed in rhetorical terms by Gross (1985), 62–5, but what most distinguishes the two speeches is the shift from self-praise to tribute and the substitution of honour for marriage as the object sought. (A question of generic propriety may also be involved, since both speeches use clear elements of hymnic style: there is perhaps something indecorous in Apollo's pronouncing in effect a hymn to himself, whereas a hymn addressed to Daphne has at least some chance of eliciting a gracious response.)

[23] The story of Polyphemus is told by Galatea to Scylla, who is similarly cool to the entreaties of Glaucus in the succeeding episode (his appeal occupies 13. 917–65).

by their unbecoming forwardness. Whatever the particular reasons, it remains true that nowhere in the *Metamorphoses* is love successfully initiated by formal speech; by contrast, when Ovid describes the beginning of mutual love he presents it as a gradual and unspoken process (4. 59f., of Pyramis and Thisbe, 'notitiam primosque gradus vicinia fecit;ltempore crevit amor'; similarly 9. 718–21, of Iphis and Ianthe).[24]

The middle books of the *Metamorphoses* contain several prominent examples of rhetorical speech in the form of soliloquies by female characters caught in a violent conflict of emotions. These monologues cannot be simply grouped together with more clear-cut efforts at persuasion;[25] they are relevant, however, in showing off another facet of Ovid's ironic and sceptical view of formal rhetoric, since in none of the six episodes concerned does recourse to formal speech bring about a positive resolution of the crisis. Medea's monologue (7. 11–71) ends with an abrupt swerve in the direction of virtue (69–71), but her resolve melts at the sight of Jason a few lines later (79). For Scylla the daughter of Nisus (8. 44–80) and Byblis (9. 474–516) speech offers the means by which desire outwits *pietas*, with fatal consequences. Althaea (8. 480–511) comes to realize that her dilemma permits no proper solution; the decision to avenge her brothers by sacrificing her son Meleager is not the product of her reasoning, but an abandonment of reason (cf. 509 'male vincetis, sed vincite, fratres'). Myrrha (10. 320–55) retains a precarious hold over her incestuous passion, but her attempted suicide is thwarted by her nurse's well-meant but disastrous intervention. The episode of Iphis, a girl passed off as a boy by her mother to save her from exposure and now awkwardly betrothed to and in love with another girl, gives the futility of speech a further twist. Unlike her bolder counterparts, Iphis makes no attempt to justify or pursue her love for Ianthe, and her monologue (9. 726–63) despondingly elaborates the hopelessness of her case; yet Iphis is the only one of these soliloquists whose story ends well, thanks to just the sort of divine assistance her argument rules out (753f. 'nec, ut omnia fiant,l esse potes felix, ut dique hominesque laborent').[26]

---

[24] Even true lovers fail to move each other with set speeches: cf. 11. 421–43 (Alcyone's attempt to dissuade her husband Ceyx from a sea-voyage).

[25] Smith (1918), 72, invoked the rubric of *controversia ethica* to relate the *Metamorphoses* monologues to Ovid's declamatory pursuits.

[26] The type of speech that does save Iphis, an appeal to Isis for help by her mother Telethusa (9. 773–81), is effective in several other episodes as well: cf. e.g. 1. 544ff. (Daphne to Peneus [text disputed]), 5. 618–20 (Arethusa to Diana), 10. 274–6 (Pygmalion to Venus), 10. 483–7 (Myrrha to the gods generally). In fact such appeals for help

The *Metamorphoses* does, of course, have its rhetorical success stories, the most conspicuous being Orpheus' plea to the underworld gods for the life of Eurydice (10. 17–39) and the victorious speech of Ulysses in the *Armorum Iudicium* (13. 128–381), but these specimens are not such as to rehabilitate the unappealing image of rhetorical argument projected by the poem. Orpheus' speech has often been denounced for its emotional shallowness and its faults attributed to Ovid's own debased taste in rhetoric,[27] but Ovid is surely being mischievous in claiming that this glib performance unlocked the hearts of Pluto and his bride and caused the Furies to weep. On its merits Orpheus' speech ought to fail, but the story requires that Eurydice be released, and so Ovid can make ironic play with Orpheus' success. Ulysses' speech to the assembled Greeks is a far more impressive display of skill, but its speciousness is evident from start to finish (which is what makes it such a joy to read). The episode does indeed illustrate the power of rhetoric to move its listeners, but the import of Ulysses' success is thoroughly negative, showing how dishonest rhetoric can extort an unjust victory from an audience wanting in discernment.[28] Furthermore, although Ovid presents the outcome of the *Armorum Iudicium* as a triumph of eloquence over valor ('fortis ... viri tulit arma disertus' 13. 383), he gives Ajax a speech that is hardly less clever than its rival; beside producing the droll picture of an *Aiax declamans*, the effect is to award victory to the speaker more adept (or unscrupulous) in using the tricks of the rhetor's trade.

Exile[29] presented Ovid with an unexpected literary challenge, which he met by producing a body of elegiac poetry without direct precedent in

or mercy are usually mentioned only if they are successful. (An appeal of a similar sort is contained in *Amores* 2. 13, a prayer to Isis on Corinna's behalf, and the only straightforwardly successful appeal in the *Amores*.)

[27] A selection of critical views is given in Bömer's note on 10. 17; note in particular Frécaut (1972), 245 'le long discours d'Orphée à Pluton et à Proserpine renferme une habile argumentation digne d'une suasoire'—not, apparently, a compliment.

[28] Ovid's earlier description of the Greek chieftains at leisure (12. 155 ff.) makes it clear that they lack appreciation for the finer things: 'non illos citharae, non illos carmina vocum I longave multifori delectat tibia buxi ... pugnam referunt hostisque suamque, I inque vices adita atque exhausta pericula saepe I commemorare iuvat. quid enim loqueretur Achilles, I aut quid apud magnum potius loquerentur Achillem?' This audience then listens with apparent delight to Nestor's gruesome and interminable account of the fight between the Lapiths and Centaurs.

[29] Unlike Fitton Brown (1985), I believe that Ovid was actually banished to Tomis on Augustus' orders; my comments, however, mainly concern the exile-poetry as poetry rather than as the product of Ovid's experience in exile.

Greek or Latin literature. While the epistolary character of the *Tristia* and *Ex Ponto* links them with Horace's *Epistles* and Ovid's own *Heroides*, in other respects the exile poetry marks a return to the form of the *Amores*, relatively short poems in which the poet is the ostensible speaker and which deal with a consistent theme and set of circumstances. Attempts to persuade through rhetorically elaborated speech dominate the later poetry even more than the *Amores*, with even more conspicuous lack of success. In this respect Ovid's first and last collections of poetry are curiously alike: since both the elegiac lover and the exile repeatedly strive to undo a condition that is essential to their existence in those capacities, their efforts must always fail if the poetry is to continue. To create an identity as a poet of exile, Ovid required an ultimate addressee who would be as immune to persuasion as the traditional elegiac mistress; unfortunately for him, that was a role the *princeps* and his successor were only too willing to play.[30]

The interest in depicting repeated failure in persuasion that characterizes the extremes of Ovid's career[31] may have come naturally to a poet trained in scholastic rhetoric. Donald Russell has aptly described declamation as 'a toy model of oratory'.[32] One respect that distinguishes it from the real thing is its resistance to time and change. The mythological and historical situations used as the basis for Roman *suasoriae* appear to have remained fairly constant from the late Republic to the time of Juvenal; even in Ovid's youth it must already have seemed that in the schools of rhetoric Agamemnon would forever deliberate whether to sacrifice his daughter, that Alexander would constantly be about to set sail across the Ocean but would never actually do so. For this type of declamation practised on a fixed set of themes to remain possible, each successive specimen of the art must

---

[30] Ovid's rhetorical position in the exile-poetry is also compromised by the limits placed on what he could say about his situation. Unable to disclose the nature of the *error* that had so angered Augustus, he cannot credibly argue that his punishment was out of proportion to the offence; bound to endorse the image of the *princeps* as clement, he cannot adequately express his conviction that Augustus has treated him cruelly; dependent on his addressees for any link with the civilized world of Rome, he must praise them for their attentions even as he implies that they have abandoned him. The poetry of exile presents itself as a series of *cris de cœur*, but its most pathetic aspect is the sense it conveys of never openly saying what it feels.

[31] The *Heroides* as a collection also presents itself as a series of failed attempts to persuade.

[32] Russell (1983), 87.

fail, or more precisely it must constitute an effort at persuasion which is never seen to succeed.

Ovid's early training may have inclined him toward an ironic view of persuasive technique, but the importance of this outlook in his poetry calls for an explanation in its own terms (even if the one I shall give is phrased in a way that Ovid might have found embarrassing). Most of the instances of failed persuasion in Ovid are attempts to arouse or renew love, with efforts to deflect anger assuming an analogous role in the poetry of exile; whatever their individual circumstances, these approaches ultimately fail because they apply rational argument to an irrational emotion, they try to control the uncontrollable.[33] Ovid's fascination with figures who engage repeatedly in this doomed effort may imply a wish that passion were more amenable to reason, even as his consistently ironic portrayal of their failure attests to his realistic awareness that it is not.[34] However that may be, Ovid's studies in failed rhetorical persuasion deserve to be appreciated for their artistry and not dismissed as the excesses of a poet who did not know when to leave well enough alone.[35]

[33] While in many instances the particular arguments employed are flawed in rhetorical terms, technical defects are not the most significant factor in the failure of these efforts: a more accomplished speech from Apollo would not have halted Daphne's flight, nor would Cupid have allowed Ovid to continue his epic unmolested if he had been presented with an airtight argument for doing so.

[34] Another reason why the poetry of exile, despite its admitted lack of finish, carries so powerful an emotional impact: Ovid knew that his pleas would be unavailing, and at a certain point the continued writing of poetry became for him the bare assertion of the will to live.

[35] 'Nam et Ovidius nescit quod bene cessit relinquere'—another well-worn judgement for which the Elder Seneca is to blame (*Contr.* 9. 5. 17).

6

Ut ornatius et uberius dici posset: Morals into Epigram in the Elder Seneca

GRAHAM ANDERSON

Donald Russell has epitomized the peculiarities of Greek declamation in a characteristically terse treatment.[1] His title *Greek Declamation* might invite the assumption that Roman declamation was somehow 'different', if often parallel in its aims, methods, and manner. Roman declaimers[2] might have been expected to claim superiority to the Greeks in sense of responsibility, moral conviction, *gravitas*, and operation within a single and highly regarded legal system; but such distinctions are difficult to press when the overall body of Roman declamatory material is examined. Declaimers' silliness, ethical perversity, and legal fantasy were familiar criticisms in antiquity itself.[3] Moreover, in some cases at least writers who used the medium were only too well aware of its moral dubiety. When Petronius presents declamatory performance in the school-scene of a novel it is quite clearly being undercut. When his anti-hero Encolpius declaims against the morality of declamation itself,[4] we have in effect a new exploration of the relationship between morality and declamation—or rather two: in the first place we are told that declamation is immoral (in a declamation); we are then further informed that this declamation-against-declamation is itself immoral: it is only a ploy to impress the professor according to Ascyltos—himself hardly a one to talk.[5] Yet there is still a morality of a kind in the Roman declaimers, but the manner of their preservation and the peculiar nature of declamation itself make it an

---

[1] Russell (1983). I am grateful to the editors for several useful references, and for help in clarifying the argument at a number of points.

[2] See still in particular Bonner (1949). For a more theoretical approach, G. A. Kennedy (1972).

[3] For ancient attacks on declamation, see G. A. Kennedy (1972), 330–7 (among much); for the larger context of contemporary perceptions of 'cultural decline', Williams (1978), 6–51.

[4] *Sat.* 1. 1.

[5] *Sat.* 10. 2.

often elusive business to disentangle from the texture of school rhetoric. I choose to illustrate chiefly from the Elder Seneca:[6] in spite of his presentation of mere reminiscences, this assiduous listener and memorizer offers by far the richest texture of materials; and he also offers a not uncritical understanding of the medium he describes.

It is of course possible to find insistence that the declaimer would have had access to the methods and contents of philosophy. The ideal of what Quintilian was to style the *vir bonus dicendi peritus* was at least as old as Isocrates. In the youthful and derivative *de Inventione* Cicero could claim *si quis omissis rectissimis atque honestissimis studiis rationis et offici consumit omnem operam in exercitatione dicendi, is inutilis sibi, perniciosus patriae civis alitur* ('if anyone ignores the pursuit of reason and duty, the most upright and honourable pursuits, and expends all his energies in the practice of speaking, he is being brought up to do no good for himself and to be a danger to the state'). In the more mature oratorical works Cicero continues to insist on philosophical training for an orator, though admittedly he may not have been typical in this reaction against the technical narrowness of Hellenistic theory.[7] Cicero cites Aristotle as having resorted to the exercise of the generalized *thesis* to encourage richness of expression on either side of the question: *ad copiam rhetorum, in utramque partem ut ornatius et uberius dici posset* 'to afford speakers plenty to say, so that there should be greater elegance and richness of expression on either side'.[8] Already we can foresee the blending of ethics with the infinite and potentially mechanical divisions of the rhetorical exercise; and this blending will bring with it the apparent endorsement of moral non-alignment.

In the specialized world of declamation we shall look for a good deal less 'philosophy' as the dogmatic schools would have understood it:[9] the declaimers' audiences are for the most part already assumed to know the difference between right and wrong, and the names of Aristotle or Chrysippus need not be invoked to persuade them. The one mention of Plato in Seneca's declaimers is significantly in his familiar role as an honorary rhetor: *eloquentissimi viri Platonis oratio, quae pro Socrate scripta est, nec patrono nec reo digna est* ('the speech of the most eloquent Plato, written on behalf of Socrates, is unworthy of

---

[6] Citations are from Winterbottom (1974). For the nature of Seneca's presentations in general, Sussman (1978); Fairweather (1981).

[7] e.g. *Orator* 4. 16; 5. 17; 14. 45.

[8] *Orator* 14. 45.

[9] For superficial and typical criticisms against philosophy in the context of declamation, cf. (Ps.-)Quintilian, *Decl.* 268. 4–15.

both defender and defendant');[10] while Socrates himself, a favourite standby in historical anecdote, has no mention outside the same passage. Seneca does interestingly describe one declaimer (Papirius) Fabianus,[11] who appears subsequently to have turned to philosophy. No contrast is drawn between his use of ethical and of declamatory material: Seneca's observations are merely on matters of style and presentation. Predictably Fabianus dissociates himself from the *luxuria* associated with the style of his teacher Arellius Fuscus; otherwise it is asserted that his philosophical temperament fits him more to ekphrasis of places and character than to portrayals of such emotions as anger and grief.[12] Philosophy in use is being viewed as a stylistic commodity.

This relative detachment of declamation from philosophy might be felt to bear out the general suspicion of amorality attached to the rhetorical schools: even before any consideration of content or teaching is involved, we have to reckon with a deep-seated popular unease with 'education' as such, and with the supposed superiority it confers: anything that makes people 'better' than their parents will often be felt to confer a questionable sort of betterness. That is one of the moral strands already discernible in Aristophanes' *Clouds*; it is hardly absent from the climate when Roman schools of moral debate were being established: the Elder Cato reacted unfavourably to the performance of Carneades in very similar terms.[13] The closure of Latin schools by the censors Crassus and Domitius Ahenobarbus in 92 BC would naturally have reinforced prejudice and suspicion: two-sided moral argument is something that has to be left to the shifty Greeks: and whatever the real reasons for the measure, political or cultural, *ludus impudentiae* ('school of shame') was the unenviable term of abuse brought into play.[14]

Moreover, to some extent the actual *suasoriae* and *controversiae* invite associations of immorality through their very subject-matter.

---

[10] *Contr.* 3 praef. 8. Its alleged unworthiness prompted rewritings by rhetors and sophists till the end of antiquity: Libanius' massive version represents a culmination (*Decl.* 1, vol. 5, pp. 13–121 Foerster).

[11] Useful summary in Bornecque (1902), 185f., who notes two passages on the instability of fortune, and four on the condemnation of riches; but both themes are in any case grist to the declaimers' mill.

[12] *Contr.* 2 praef. 1ff. We might of course have had a rather different account had Fabianus moved from philosophy to rhetoric.

[13] Pliny, *NH* 7. 30. 112f.; cf. Cicero, *Resp.* 3. 6. 9, Quintilian 12. 1. 35.

[14] Tacitus, *Dialogus* 35. 1, with Gudemann ad loc. For discussion and rejection of political motivation for the closure, Bonner (1977), 71f.

The perennials of pirate chiefs and prostitute priestesses, separately or in combination, and tyrants' outrages, explicit or implied, give some idea of what schoolboys or adolescent young men were expected to be talking and thinking about. And one moral imputation which recurs often enough in the Elder Seneca is the notion that Greek declamation was less morally austere than Latin: in the treatment of the prostitute priestess Aemilius Scaurus had accused the Greeks *qui nihil non et permiserint sibi et inpetraverint* ('who took every licence and got off with it'),[15] and Seneca's illustrations bear him out.

Yet most of the subjects of the declamation schools did deal, however inadequately, with recognizably moral issues, however these might be distorted by the artificialities of the schools. It might be argued that one of the principal purposes of a training in public speaking was to be able to arouse the emotions of one's audience;[16] themes with a potential for moral indignation clearly served such a purpose: one should aim at the audience's sense of fairness (*aequitas*). It is not fair that a son should lose his inheritance because of some heroic act, or that a young girl should be debarred from office for acting in self-defence to protect her honour.[17] But the means of implying as much vary widely and are in some respects subtly subliminal.

I. THE MEDIA OF MORALITY

Moral values could be introduced or implied at a number of levels in the declamations as Seneca reports them. Simple statements may carry moral implications. In a situation where a mother has implicated her daughter in a poisoning, Triarius asks: *Quid ergo? Mater mentita est? Tolle matris nomen: post damnationem noverca est* ('Well then, was it a mother who told a lie? Strike out the name "mother": after her own condemnation she is now a stepmother').[18] The emotional registers of *mater* and *noverca* require no further elaboration: mothers are good and stepmothers are bad; one who acts like the other (by implicating her own daughter in a charge of poisoning) must be worst of all.

But what in moral terms is simply a proposition may be already well

---

[15] *Contr.* 1. 2. 22. For further examples, see the index of Winterbottom (1974), s.v. Greeks.

[16] The characterization of *ethos* was also important both as an end and as a means; cf. Russell (1983), 87–105; and note the treatment of the abandoned son and the lovelorn girl which I discuss below.

[17] e.g. *Contr.* 1. 8; 1. 2.   [18] *Contr.* 9. 6. 17.

on the way to becoming little more than a *sententia*. And with too much convolution the moral point is easily lost, obscured, or simply sacrificed to rhetorical effect, as in a case a few sections later:[19] the anguished father whose wife is accused of poisoning proclaims that he would have been tempted to take revenge on any sons of the accused—but not on the daughter, more in danger from her mother for having been named under torture as an accomplice. This idea is finally subsumed into the sententia *Sed propter hoc a me tuta erat quod a matre non erat* ('But for this reason she was safe from me, that she was not safe from her mother'). The original moral conflict has been stifled, and this *sententia* is there for its own sake.

In addition, certain topics are capable of carrying standard moralizing material: it takes no more than a contrast between rich and poor in a declamation subject[20] to trigger off a host of purple passages on the theme of Rome's degeneracy. Latro offers *Quietiora tempora pauperes habuimus, bella civilia aurato Capitolio gessimus* ('When we were poor we had more peaceful times; once the Capitol was gilded we waged civil wars').[21] But Arellius Fuscus can twist the same theme to opposite effect:[22] *Colit etiamnunc in Capitolio casam victor omnium gentium populus* ('Even to this day on the Capitol the nation that has conquered the world pays homage to a hut'). It is not too far to that other standard adjunct of the themes of rich and poor, the mutability of fortune:

fragilis et caduca felicitas est, et omnis blandientis fortunae speciosus cum periculo nitor: et sine causa saepe fovit et sine ratione destituit. Vidi ego magni exercitus ducem sine comite fugientem; vidi ⟨ab⟩ ambitiosa turba clientium limina deserta sub domino sectore venalia.

(Happiness can be dashed to ruin, and every false glitter of good luck comes with danger; often it has embraced a man for no good reason, often deserted him without explanation. I have seen the general of a great army fleeing without a single companion; or doorsteps deserted by their crew of social climbers put up for sale with the owner himself as auctioneer.)[23]

But as is clear from the relatively few longer extracts, a propensity for moral indignation and pathos is also clearly implied in extended narrative. A father has acknowledged his grandson by the prostitute who has looked after his ailing son, the child's father; the other son accuses

---

[19] *Contr.* 9. 6. 20.   [20] *Contr.* 2. 1.
[21] *Contr.* 2. 1. 1.   [22] *Contr.* 2. 1. 5.
[23] *Contr.* 2. 1. 1.

him of madness. But it is not by argument alone that the father is able
to make his point:[24]

Beside him sat a sad-looking woman, sad-faced, ill, herself for all the world like
the patient, with downcast eyes ... He consigned to my bosom son and soul
together. I brought him home. (My other son) calls me mad to adopt the baby.
But what else was I to do? Was I to deny anything to my own son when he
begged me on behalf of *his* son? I forgive you (my other son and accuser) for
being so hard-hearted. For you did not see your brother (lying there) sick.
There he lay, one moment the heir to a huge estate, now dying on the miserable
bed he had been forced to beg for. He had no crowd of slaves or friends standing round his bedside; lying between the baby and a weak woman he held on till
I arrived. As I came in, he raised his already closing eyes at the mention of my
name, and held back a life ebbing away. 'Father,' he said, 'it is not out of dis-
respect that up till now I have not asked your forgiveness: I had given over that
duty to my brother.'

Such a passage might belong as easily to a Dickens novel as to a Latin
controversia: the speaker has gone to town on the emotive qualities of
death-bed melodrama and heart-rending family relationships, as well
as the motif of the 'prostitute with the heart of gold', familiar from
New Comedy. And underneath the convolutions the declamation-
theme itself is only just recognizable as a variant of 'the Prodigal Son',
the debauchee who finds forgiveness for riotous living from his father,
but only indignation from his sanctimonious brother.[25]

   Moral values can also be skilfully implied in the character-por-
trayal[26] necessary in declamation-subjects: as when Publius Asprenas
presents the disinherited war hero as addicted to courage in the same
way as others are addicted to vice:[27]

The emotion that first entered our hearts is the one that exercises control over
us. We cannot unlearn luxury, avarice, idleness, envy, or fear—and every single
day all these faults are either criticized or punished, so fast do we cling even to
our vices. Believe me, father, I am unable to control myself when the familiar
noise of battle has broken out. I feel the urge to attack the foe, to scatter with
the sword the enemy formations. It is this aggression, this vigour that has
adorned your house with enemy spoils three times over.

In the unreal world of declamation even the *miles gloriosus* can become
a moralist.

---

[24]   *Contr.* 2. 4. 3.
[25]   For development still further (the prodigal youth who looks after *abdicati*!), cf.
(Ps.-)Quintilian, *Decl. Min.* 260, esp. 7 f. I owe this reference to Doreen Innes.
[26]   For the Greek counterpart, Russell (1983), 87–105.   [27]   *Contr.* 1. 8. 5.

We can see a cross-section of these means at work in relation to a single subject. The case of Cimon, ungrateful to Callias,[28] is worth attention for a skilful balance of inherent and unambiguous moral positions: Cimon himself undergoes imprisonment to release for burial the body of his father Miltiades, imprisoned on an embezzlement charge. Callias marries his daughter to the noble youth, having first ransomed him; Cimon catches his wife in adultery and opts for the death of both parties in defiance of her father, his benefactor. He is accused of ingratitude. In practice it is difficult for Cimon not to secure the moral high ground: he can benefit from his father's prestige, yet his own virtue is founded on a noble act in favour of the former when disgraced; and he can be presented as austerely virtuous in dealing with adultery. It is difficult for the other side to overturn the fact that Cimon would not have asked to be released from prison, and could presumably be presented as not having been forward in wooing Callias' subsequently dubious daughter either. Votienus Montanus (9. 1. 3) sums up the two issues neatly in a brace of epigrams: *Ego adulteros dimittam? quid aliud facerem si alligatas haberem manus?* 'Am I to let adulterers go? What else would I do if I were still a prisoner?', i.e. 'now that you have freed me I have the moral compulsion to dispose even of your, my liberator's, own daughter'.[29] Persuasion depends, as so often, on the resonance of the words themselves: everyone can be relied upon to abhor adultery, and its punishment entails a ruthless logic.[30] The moral authority of Miltiades also carries weight, in highly evocative pleas such as the *eidolopoiia: videbatur mihi omnis maiorum meorum circa me turba fremere dicentium: ubi sunt illae manus quae solvere Miltiadem?* 'I sensed the whole crowd of my ancestors raging round me: Where are those hands that freed Miltiades?' (and have not yet been raised against adulterers, as they ought to have been);[31] the epigram of Gargonius condemned by Seneca for bad taste is in effect only a vivid projection of the same 'historical indignation': *istud publicum adulterium est, sub Miltiadis trophaeis concumbere* ('That contemptible action amounts to committing adultery in public, to have intercourse under the trophies of Miltiades').[32] The speakers undoubtedly succeeded in conveying the moral imperatives that arise

[28] *Contr.* 9. 1.
[29] *Contr.* 9. 1. 3.
[30] Not so in real life: cf. Petronius' clever treatment of the case of Glyco's steward, who will provoke indignation against Glyco when thrown *ad bestias*, *Sat.* 45. 7 ff.
[31] *Contr.* 9. 1. 4.
[32] *Contr.* 9. 1. 15.

naturally from the case; but the characteristic tendency to drift into epigram for its own sake is still in evidence.

Some Awkward Cases

Ideally for a *controversia* to work there ought to be balancing principles on either side, and declamatory practice disliked subjects with no contest,[33] though obviously there was corresponding glory for those who took an evidently unsustainable side and won.[34] Two laws or two contrary moral principles should be at odds, or a law at odds with justice in a particular instance. *Controversia* 5. 5 has all the appearances of being a technical legal matter: a rich man burns down a poor man's tree (since he has refused compensation for its removal); he offers fourfold compensation for the burning of the tree, but only actual compensation for the accidental burning down of the poor man's house consequent upon it. But the balance of the whole case is entirely changed by the strong moral presumption in favour of the poor man who faces the arrogance of his rich neighbour. Purple passages are quoted at length on the disproportionate extravagances of the rich:

'It was blocking the view.' Well, don't crowds of slaves block *our* way when we're walking the streets? Don't walls raised to a huge height block the light? Don't boulevards stretching over great distances and houses sprawling as far as cities almost shut us off from public places?

Against this Juvenal-before-his-time there can be little to balance on the other side—except the claim that the roots of the tree were in fact undermining the rich man's wall, a morally neutral technical matter if proven.[35]

In some cases the moral balance of the declamation is likely to seem different to us from the way it would have appeared to the original audience. This is particularly true of *Controversia* 7. 6 (*demens qui servo filiam iunxit*). The slave abstained from raping his master's

---

[33] Hermogenes lists the one-sided case (μονομερές) as the first of his categories of ἀσύστατα (p. 32 Rabe); cf. also the case of Parrhasius and Prometheus which I discuss more fully below, Sen. *Contr.* 10. 5. 12: *nihil est autem turpius quam aut eam controversiam declamare in qua nihil ab altera parte responderi possit, aut non refellere si responderi potest.*

[34] All the more so in real cases: note Cicero's praise of Antonius' success in the defence of Norbanus, *De Oratore* 2. 197–204. The speciality of making the ἥττων λόγος appear the greater already characterizes the new-fangled teaching in Aristophanes' *Clouds.*   [35] For the authentic legal background, see now A. Rodger (1972).

daughter when a tyrant had allowed it. When the tyrant is overthrown the master gave his daughter in marriage to the freed slave. He is accused by his son of insanity. It is difficult to empathize with the son's indignation in a society so much less hierarchical than the slave-owning societies of antiquity. One's instinct is to see the nobility and continence of the slave as deserving of the highest reward, not least in the eyes of the daughter herself; it seems correspondingly pedantic and pusillanimous, as some treatments of the themes did, to insist that the slave merely did his duty and has been disproportionately rewarded. One suspects that in a New Comic or novel scenario the slave would have turned out an aristocrat after all, and all would have been well; but we still have Euripides' version of the story of Electra in which the free-born farmer is not rewarded with the heroine at the end—nor can he be, since he is still socially incompatible. In the present case the clanking machinery of the epigrams once again tends to take over the case: there are over six pages of conceits recollected against the marriage, and only one in favour of the slave, a balance not wholly retrieved in the *divisio* (e.g. 7. 6. 7: *Ex servo gener, ex domina uxor, ex domino socer factus est. quis has nuptias non tyranni putet?*: 'from a slave he is now a son-in-law; from a mistress she is now a wife; from a master [her father is now the slave's] father-in-law. Who would not consider this a marriage imposed by a tyrant?'). On the other side it is suggested *inter alia* that great men had married freedwomen (Marcus Cato is the example adduced); that 'slave' and 'free' are arbitrary titles;[36] or that the daughter herself approved of the slave.[37] Seneca says almost in passing that the following epigram was *valde excepta* ('highly acclaimed', Winterbottom): *eum non contempsi generum qui tyrannum contempserat* ('I did not disdain as a son-in-law a man who had disdained a tyrant'). But it clearly represented a minority view.

Another instance, *Controversia* 9. 5, has the flavour of a contemporary custody and child-abuse case: only the police and social services are absent. Two children in a house have died, after the (maternal) grandfather had been refused admission; the cause of death could be either indigestion or poisoning, of which a stepmother is suspected; the grandfather has removed a third child, and is accused *de vi*. Although poisoning and stepmothers are involved here, we are in a more realistic world, far removed from that of tyrants and pirate chiefs. Since it is not actually clear that any foul play has taken place, the grandfather may indeed be technically 'in the wrong', but it is

---

[36] *Contr.* 7. 6. 17–18.   [37] *Contr.* 7. 6. 18.

difficult for anyone to blame him even in the hysterical world of the declaimers: though the opposition can manage the construction that the grandfather's motive was really to slander the stepmother as a poisoner (9. 5. 8); or that the grandfather had become unreasonable when demanding entry (9. 5. 11). But Latro's point is difficult to get round: the grandfather acts as he does *pro nepote adfectu ablatus* ('carried away with emotion on behalf of his grandson') (9. 5. 8).

A number of themes, whether ordinary or extraordinary, reveal moral ambiguities of one sort or another. One notes particularly 'A man caught in adultery with a tyrant's wife snatched the sword from the tyrant and killed him. He claims the reward; an objection is raised.'[38] The theme itself contrives two favourites of the world of the schools: slaying someone taken in adultery; and tyrant-slaying, usually with some complication. One thinks of Lucian's *Tyrannicida*, where the tyrannicide claims his reward after 'killing' the tyrant only by a bizarre kind of proxy (by accidentally leaving the murder weapon already used on the tyrant's son, which the tyrant then uses to commit suicide). Here one might say that the real result of the exercise as practised was simply the production of epigrams succinct even by the standards of the *controversia* itself: (*novo inauditoque more pugnabant, tyrannicida pro adulterio, tyrannus pro pudicitia*; 'it was a new and unheard of kind of fight they fought, the tyrant-killer in defence of adultery, the tyrant in defence of chastity'). But that such a theme could arise at all betrays a revealing complex of attitudes, glimpsed from time to time in the epigrams: 'I want the tyrant to fall at the hands of the state; let it be an outraged citizen who kills him, let him intersperse the wounds he inflicts with curses—the sort a husband is accustomed to hurl at an adulterer, not an adulterer at a husband'; or again 'it should be the tyrant who draws the tyrant-slayer to the acropolis, not his wife; he should be led on by hatred, not by love. When he prepares to make the climb, let him bring indignation, and a sword; let him go to the quarter where he should find the tyrant' (and not the boudoir). The assumption is clear enough: in the morally black-and-white world of the tyrannicide, no one is 'qualified' to obtain such glory unless he is himself of unimpeachable moral character. Of course an attempt is made to distinguish intention and motive: this man, so it is argued, had no intention of killing the tyrant, only of debauching his wife (a contention difficult to prove). And a moral *exemplum* is adduced to the effect that even the best end may not justify the means

[38] *Contr.* 4. 7.

(the Roman people did not wish their enemy to be defeated by poison or treachery, as when the senate would not have Pyrrhus poisoned, or the Faliscans defeated by treachery).

One might have expected one subject to be self-evidently revolting and by nature one-sided: the case of Parrhasius and Prometheus (*Contr.* 10. 5). The most probably fictitious terms have the painter purchasing an old man from the Olynthian captives sold by Philip of Macedon—to model the sufferings of Prometheus by being subjected to tortures which prove fatal. But it is not the rights or wrongs of the matter that are the real subject of the case: it is rather the question of whether Parrhasius is guilty of injuring the state (of Athens) by putting the picture in the temple (of Athena). Seneca concedes that the Greek declaimers consider it *nefas* to speak on Parrhasius' behalf. The implication is that on a combination of moral and aesthetic grounds such a product could only be seen as an abomination and an affront to human dignity: no Greek would have wished to defend Athens for committing worse atrocities against Olynthus than Philip himself had done. But we do not find Seneca quoting their indignation as such, which he himself seems to imply is misplaced, as it results in the kind of one-sidedness already referred to. As often, it is a flourish of epigrams that breaks out, exploiting the paradox that a man is killed to mimic the creator of mankind himself. Indeed Seneca seems more concerned about the tendency to plagiarism than about the 'human rights' issue that appears so self-evident to us.

One declamation-subject received unique treatment in antiquity itself. In *Suasoria* 6 the Elder Seneca sets himself the task of comparing the (often miserable) declamation performances on the last agonizing decisions in the life of Cicero with the accounts in Livy and others of what actually happened. The object is quite explicitly to discredit declamation practice (which Seneca has by this time tired of recollecting): *sed fortasse efficiam ut his sententiis lectis solidis et verum habentibus ⟨robur a scholasticis⟩ recedatis*: 'But I may perhaps cause you to dissociate yourselves from the schoolmen when you've read these solid and genuinely vigorous sentiments' (6. 16). In this case the subject itself was unusual: it could be felt as fairly recent history and Roman, as opposed to the much-derided kind of historical subjects that might generally occupy the scholastici and form the major part of Seneca's own *suasoriae*. Here at any rate was a 'realistic' modern instance—as 'modern' as say Adam von Trott against Hitler, where again a plain and unequivocal moral principle was at stake; and here we have the citizen

ranged against the tyrant without the complications of sword, ravished
daughter, disinheritance, and rewards for tyrannicide.

In fact some efforts on such a topic do achieve some kind of genuine
moral indignation and dignity which rescues them above the accumu-
lations of mere *sententiae*:[39]

> It is no humble mound that will hide you, [Cicero], nor does your virtue end at
> the same time as your life. Memory, the immortal guardian of men's deeds,
> through which the great achieve everlasting life, will pass you on sacrosanct to
> all ages. Nothing will perish except the body, a thing of fleeting frailty, victim
> to disease, exposed to chance, vulnerable to proscription; but the soul, which is
> drawn from truly divine origins, and is subject neither to old age nor death, will
> be freed from the chains of its burdensome body and rush back to its own
> home, and the stars to which it belongs ... [*and as much again*].

At their most dignified, even the Senecan declamations could begin to
sound like the funeral speech in Thucydides 2 with some added
Platonic touches. But the moments when such dignity and balance are
attained are rare.

II. MORALITY IN THE SENECAN *SUASORIAE*

The *Suasoriae* in Seneca's discussions are sharply distinguished from
the *Controversiae* by their exclusively historical setting (but not of
course historical authenticity); the fact that one was only expected to
argue on one side did not prevent individual speakers from taking 'the
other side' in these exercises, though as in the *controversiae* themselves
the two sides are not always morally balanced.

In the case of *Suasoriae* 2 and 5, declaimers Greek and Latin alike
were in their element and could go wild over situations connected with
Xerxes and the Persian wars. It is worth noting that speakers did
actually speak to advise the Spartans against holding their ground at
Thermopylae; and with more dubious arguments on behalf of taking
down trophies to avoid the threat of a further invasion by Xerxes. The
favourite case, that of Alexander the Great,[40] does not revolve exclusively on an ethical point; if he is to go beyond (the Ocean?) there will be
all manner of new dangers, but of course anything of that nature could
be presented as an obvious challenge to so courageous a figure. It is
rather on the grounds of tempting providence, or outraging the

<hr/>

[39] *Suas.* 6. 5 f.   [40] *Suas.* 1.

natural order, that the moral objection depends: (1. 4 'It was as something sacred that nature poured Ocean round the world'; 1. 1 'Let it be enough for Alexander to have conquered as far as it is enough for the world to have light ...'). Note also that the counselling of expediency plays a part in these exercises, and with good reason:[41] despots like Alexander were liable to retaliate against unpalatable advice. Hence the line taken by Cestius, who 'used to say that in Alexander's hearing a speaker's opinion must be expressed in such a way that his feelings should be soothed by plenty of flattery, but that some sense of proportion had to be preserved so that he should appear to show deference rather than flattery' (*Suas.* 1. 6). Advisers to disinherited sons take few risks; advisers to Alexander have to invest themselves with the risks of courtiers.

III. DECLAMATION IN LITERATURE

If morality in the declamation schools was not always the foremost consideration, the influence of the schools certainly saw to its appearance elsewhere. The role of declamation in Ovid's early career is vividly documented by Seneca himself.[42] We can see the results at work in two contrasting declamations (for such they are) in *Metamorphoses* 8. In both cases the poet sets out to provide a test case for love versus family loyalty. Will Scylla prefer loyalty to her father, king of Megara, to her infatuation with his besieger Minos?[43] The reader is scarcely left in any doubt from the very outset that love is going to triumph over reason: the sight of Minos in equestrian garb is enough to send the naïve young princess into a world of adolescent fantasy and special pleading. One might describe the speaker's monologue as a *suasoria* addressed to herself,[44] whose argument could be paraphrased as follows:

I could be a hostage and settle the war;
I could ask him what would be the dowry—anything but my father's city;
and yet conquest can be advantageous, at the hands of a just conqueror;

---

[41] Over and above the conventional handbook juxtapositions of συμφέρον and δίκαιον.

[42] *Contr.* 2. 2. 8–12. He had been a pupil of Arellius Fuscus, ibid. 8.

[43] Ovid. *Met.* 8. 47–77.   [44] Cf. Tarrant in this volume: above, 63 ff.

and indeed we will be conquered;

better through my betrayal which will save time and avoid injury to
   Minos;

Would to the gods I had no father—and yet everyone is their own
   god;

If I don't betray the city, some other girl will;

I will be courageous ...

Of course Scylla's moral position is constantly shifting; it is difficult to
identify precise turning-points, but the first major leap is to convince
herself that conquest is inevitable, and that she is acting in the best
interests of her fellow-citizens; the second is the rather Euripidean
sententia in which she accords divine status to self-help, brushing aside
loyalty to her father (*di facerent sine patre forem!—sibi quisque profecto |
est deus* 72 f.); and the last the unbearable notion that some rival will
beat her to it. A *suasoria* has become a psychological study of self-
deception, and an illustration of irrational moral shift. Well might
Seneca complain that Ovid did not find the contrary arguments of the
controversia to his taste (*Contr.* 2. 2. 12). He is able to put a ludicrous
inadequate substitute for it to good use—to characterize a legendary
schoolgirl crush. If there is any doubt as to the humorous implications
of the argument, Ovid has already set Scylla up with the traditional
topoi of the infatuated lover: Minos looks good in anything, but she is
really carried away at the sight of his riding bare-headed (24–36).[45]

In the second case Meleager's mother Althaea debates whether to
save her son's life in spite of his murder of her brothers.[46] Here for the
purposes of the debate the moral argument is a good deal less clear-
cut, though again modern Western views of kinship would call into
question whether there was any real issue involved. Here there is no
gradual transition from one moral position to its opposite: Althaea
simply vacillates back and forth through a series of *sententiae* on the
theme of son versus uncles: *fratres, ignoscite matri . . . pereat sceleratus
et ille . . . mens ubi materna est?* . . . ('brothers, pardon the mother in
me ... and yet may even (my own son) perish for his crime ... Where is
my maternal instinct? ...'). Any moral imputations are only brought
home in the carefully deferred pathos of Ovid's description of
Meleager's end, simultaneous with that of the log his mother has
burned: *simul est exstinctus uterque, | inque leves abiit paulatim spiritus*

---

[45] *Met.* 8. 24–36. For the general context of humour in Ovid, Frécaut (1972).

[46] *Met.* 8. 460–511, *passim*. Much of the debate is not expressed in speech (*pugnat
materque sororque*, 463).

auras | *paulatim cana prunam velante favilla* ('both went out together, and little by little his breath left for the insubstantial air, as little by little a white ash covered the embers', 523 ff.). All Ovid has needed to do is state the inevitable consequence of Althaea's sympathetic magic. But he does not need to say that her choice was morally mistaken.

We have already seen that Petronius was able to manipulate the conventions of moral discourse for their ironic effect. Perhaps still more striking is the theatrical monologue declaimed by Encolpius over the corpse of a shipwrecked sailor. J. P. Sullivan[47] has demonstrated in detail the texture of this speech as a mosaic of commonplaces, this time paralleled by moralizing epigrams in Seneca the Younger; these are duly reversed, giving in effect the 'other side' of a *controversia*, when Encolpius turns the body over and finds that it belongs to none other than his tyrannical and corrupt old enemy Lichas, whereupon he is able to pour forth epigrams to gloat over the misfortunes of a rival; the declamation is an instrument of *Schadenfreude*, and its mutations mirror those of the volatile and evidently unprincipled Encolpius himself. And hostility to Lichas gives way to (quasi-)philosophical reflection: *tamquam intersit, periturum corpus quae ratio consumat, ignis an fluctus an mora* ('as if it would matter what way a corpse that has to die should be consumed, whether by fire or wave or the passage of time').[48] For the declaimer anger is acted out in a perpetual academy.

But not all such outbursts are cynically conceived. For a final instance we might return to Alexander the Great, as familiar to Silver poetry as to the world of the Latin declaimers. Lucan has Julius Caesar visit Egypt to visit the tomb of Alexander the Great, and the declamatory *topos* of Alexander at the world's end is here once more (10. 36–45):

> Oceano classes inferre parabat
> exteriore mari. Non illi flamma nec undae
> nec sterilis Libye nec Syrticus obstitit Hammon.
> Isset in occasus mundi devexa secutus
> ambissetque polos Nilumque a fonte bibisset:
> occurrit suprema dies, naturaque solum
> hunc potuit finem vaesano ponere regi;

---

[47] In Sullivan (1968), 196–204, on *Sat.* 115. 8 ff., 12–19. This is not to take sides on Sullivan's principal contention, that it is specifically Seneca that Petronius has set out to parody at this point; but there seems certainly no doubt that it is moral platitudes that are the target.

[48] *Sat.* 115. 17.

qui secum invidia, quo totum ceperat orbem,
abstulit imperium, nulloque herede relicto
totius fati lacerandas praebuit urbes.

(He was making ready to sail his fleet on the outer Ocean. Neither flame nor
sea, neither barren Libya nor Syrtic Ammon stood in his way. He would have
followed over the Western edge of the world, gone round the poles and drunk
from the source of the Nile: but his last day came upon him, and only nature
could impose this end on the mad ruler, who jealously snatched away the rule
he had imposed on the whole earth, and leaving no heir to all his fortune left
the cities to tear one another apart.)

But here there is no need for 'Alexander debates . . .'; with hindsight
Fate can be made to catch up on all tyrants, a message perhaps not lost
on Nero's own regime. And such nuances might well have been the
boldest recourse against a Hellenophile emperor with activities on the
Eastern frontier. The material of the declaimers can be made to bear
serious political indignation: the Pisonian conspiracy was to show that
not all could have been mere posturing.

IV. CONCLUSION

The relationship between morality and declamation, then, is a complex one. The standard view that sees declamation as a kind of reverse
of moral discourse is not wholly justified: here we have a flexible
medium in which moral principles could be straightforwardly presented, or silently implied, or subtly manipulated. Epigrams themselves could be the end of declamatory rhetoric; but they could equally
well be invested with moral conviction and effectiveness. Declamation
could break out of the schoolroom and threaten to take over literature;
but it could also be focused upon by literature moral or amoral alike.

We can perhaps best see that vehicle in action in a unique scenario
where the declaimer—a doctor—can belittle the usefulness of his
brothers, a philosopher and a rhetor respectively: *Quid civitati prosunt?*
Amputant vitia? Nimirum nemo luxuriosus est, nemo pecuniae cupidus?
('What use are [philosophers] to the state? Do they cut out vices? Of
course none of them enjoys a luxurious life-style, none of them is
greedy for money, is he?') (268. 15) And again: *Nonne Demosthenem*
illum oppressum veneno suo scimus, nonne Ciceronem in illis in quibus
totiens placuerat rostris poena sua expositum? ('Don't we know the
famous case of Demosthenes overcome by his own poison? Don't we

know that Cicero was exposed on that very rostrum where he had so often won favour in order to pay the penalty imposed on him?' (268. 20) The last two *sententiae* are particularly suspect, amounting as they do to 'Demosthenes died by his own poison, Cicero by his own punishment'. The political contexts of both deaths have disappeared in the artistic compression. Well might both rhetor and philosopher be found wanting by the eloquent doctor: both combined to provide him with the medium for spurious morality.

7

Seneca, Stoicism, and the Problem of Moral Evil

HARRY HINE

I. SENECA ON THE ORIGINS OF MORAL GOODNESS

'There are many good reasons for valuing the Letters [of Seneca]: for their realism of scene and language, for their psychological revelations, for their brilliant technique. But we shall not read them right if we do not also take the main theme seriously.' Thus Donald Russell advises us near the end of his characteristically sympathetic and illuminating guide to reading Seneca's *Letters*. My own study, which is concerned with a point of Stoic doctrine, starts, as it happens, from the passage with which Donald's essay ends, the conclusion of *Letter* 90. Another of his comments is worth repeating before we begin: he frankly acknowledges that 'In much of this letter, Seneca, as elsewhere, appears diffuse, unsubtle, incoherent in his moral vehemence.'[1] One may add that, with the rhetorical training that set a high premium on finding an unfamiliar twist to a familiar topic, he was well capable of devising a new angle on an ethical problem, which makes it sometimes hard to decide whether in a given passage a sketchily presented idea is a novel improvisation of his own or an adumbration of established Stoic doctrine. One must proceed by probing the coherence of the ideas in a given passage with what is found elsewhere in Seneca and other Stoic sources. That is what I shall seek to do with some of the ideas at the end of *Letter* 90.

That letter is about the role of the philosopher in human technological progress, and throughout the letter Seneca takes issue with Posidonius. Posidonius attributed to philosophers the early inventions and technological discoveries on which progress depended. Seneca rejects this attribution, or says that even if philosophers made these

---

[1] Russell (1974); both quotations are from p. 93.

discoveries, it was not in their capacity as philosophers that they did so. For him, technological advance is always ambivalent, it can be turned to beneficial and morally good purposes, but it can also be used for morally bad ends, to further luxury; therefore, Seneca argues, no philosopher could have sought it.

However, right at the end of the letter Seneca's argument takes a new direction: up to now he has implicitly accepted that there were philosophers around when the first steps were being taken in technological progress (though at § 16 he says more guardedly *illi sapientes fuerunt aut certe sapientibus similes*, 'they were philosophers, or at any rate resembled philosophers', cf. § 36), but now he denies that there were any philosophers in the earliest stages of human development (§§ 35–46). For in the Golden Age men were innocent, and acted instinctively; but they were not philosophers, and their behaviour was not truly virtuous. 'Philosophy alone gives happiness; it does more than reproduce the bliss of the Golden Age, because it offers not innocent ignorance but virtue born of struggle.'[2]

Let us explore this passage (§§ 35–46) more closely. The distinction between the behaviour of these primitive men and true philosophy or wisdom is initially described in sections 35–6 and then more fully explored in sections 44–6. The intervening sections 37–43 contrast the behaviour and happiness of early men with that of later and contemporary men, so for our purposes we may regard it as a digression. I give the surrounding sections:

(35) Hanc philosophiam fuisse illo rudi saeculo quo adhuc artificia deerant et ipso usu discebantur utilia non credo. (36) †Sicut aut† fortunata tempora, cum in medio iacerent beneficia naturae promiscue utenda, antequam avaritia atque luxuria dissociavere mortales et ad rapinam ex consortio ⟨docuere⟩ discurrere: non erant illi sapientes viri, etiam si faciebant facienda sapientibus.... (44) Sed quamvis egregia illis vita fuerit et carens fraude, non fuere sapientes, quando hoc iam in opere maximo nomen est. non tamen negaverim fuisse alti spiritus viros et, ut ita dicam, a dis recentes; neque enim dubium est quin meliora mundus nondum effetus ediderit. quemadmodum autem omnibus indoles fortior fuit et ad labores paratior, ita non erant ingenia omnibus consummata. non enim dat natura virtutem: ars est bonum fieri. (45) illi quidem non aurum nec argentum nec perlucidos ⟨lapides in⟩ ima terrarum faece quaerebant parcebantque adhuc etiam mutis animalibus: tantum aberat ut homo hominem non iratus, non timens, tantum spectaturus occideret. nondum vestis illis erat picta, nondum texebatur aurum, adhuc nec eruebatur. (46) quid

[2] Russell (1974), 93.

ergo ⟨est⟩? ignorantia rerum innocentes erant; multum autem interest utrum peccare aliquis nolit an nesciat. deerat illis iustitia, deerat prudentia, deerat temperantia ac fortitudo. omnibus his virtutibus habebat similia quaedam rudis vita: virtus non contingit animo nisi instituto et edocto et ad summum adsidua exercitatione perducto. ad hoc quidem, sed sine hoc nascimur, et in optimis quoque, antequam erudias, virtutis materia, non virtus est. vale.

((35) I do not believe that this philosophy existed in that primitive epoch when there were still no arts and crafts, and useful discoveries were still being made through experience. (36) ** the fortunate age when nature's benefits were readily available for all to use, before greed and luxury set men at odds with one another and taught them to abandon partnership for robbery: those were not wise men, even if they acted as wise men should ... (44) But however exceptional and free from wrongdoing their life was, they were not wise men, since this name is reserved for the very highest achievement. I would not deny that they were men of elevated spirit, and, so to speak, fresh from the gods; for there is no doubt that the world produced better things before it became worn out. But although they all had stronger natures, readier for hard work, still their characters were not perfect in every respect. For virtue is not a gift from nature: becoming good is an art. (45) They did not search deep in the dregs of the earth for gold or silver or transparent gems, and as yet they spared even dumb animals: there was a long way to go before human beings killed each other not from anger, not from fear, but just to watch. As yet they had no brightly coloured clothing, as yet they did not embroider with gold, as yet they did not even dig for it. (46) What then? Their ignorance made them innocent: there is a big difference between not wanting, and not knowing how, to do wrong. They lacked justice, they lacked prudence, they lacked self-control and bravery. Primitive life had qualities resembling all these virtues; but a mind does not attain virtue unless it is trained and instructed and brought to perfection by constant practice. At our birth we have this as a goal, not as a possession, and even in the best people, before you educate them, there is the raw material of virtue, not virtue itself.)

Here, as so often, Seneca does not spell out his ideas systematically, but the main point is clear. Primitive men, says Seneca, were not philosophers, even if they behaved as philosophers should (§ 36), nor were they really virtuous, for they lacked the four cardinal virtues, though their behaviour resembled virtuous behaviour (§ 46). Why were they not really wise or virtuous? One reason is stated very clearly, that they lacked knowledge: this is stated in general terms at § 44, *non erant ingenia omnibus consummata. non enim dat natura virtutem: ars est bonum fieri*, 'still their characters were not perfect in every respect. For virtue is not a gift from nature: becoming good is an art'; then more precisely at § 46, *ignorantia rerum innocentes erant; multum autem inter-est utrum peccare aliquis nolit an nesciat*, 'Their ignorance made them innocent: there is a big difference between not wanting, and not know-ing how, to do wrong'. This ignorance is to be understood, first, in the light of § 45: primitive men did not dig for gold, silver, transparent stones, or wear gold-embroidered clothes, nor did they hunt animals. In other words, they did not know about precious metals and stones, and so they were not tempted to greed, envy, and other wrongs. Then later in § 46 Seneca presents another aspect of the requirement of knowledge and training, the need for philosophical instruction and practice: *virtus non contingit animo nisi instituto et edocto et ad summum adsidua exercitatione perducto*, 'but a mind does not attain virtue unless it is trained and instructed and brought to perfection by constant prac-tice'. So primitive men lacked two sorts of knowledge: knowledge of precious metals and stones that might have tempted them to go astray; and the philosophical knowledge and training that is necessary for the wise man.

But what exactly is 'not knowing how to do wrong' (*peccare nescire*, cf. § 46). One might accept that innocent, unreflective good behaviour is different from the conscious, informed goodness that is morally self-aware, and yet at the same time try to argue that it would be possible to develop an understanding of what vice would be like even if there were not actually any vice in the world. But Seneca does not think on these lines: for the stress on the need for regular *exercitatio*, 'practice' (§ 46) suggests not just mental exercise but active moral resistance to vice; and earlier, in § 36, despite textual problems at the start, he clearly seems to state that wise men did not appear before avarice and luxury had appeared. As Blundell[3] correctly infers from the passage, '[Seneca] even implies that evil has to come into the world before virtue can exist, and to that extent evil must be seen as a necessity.'

Is Seneca here giving his own response to Posidonius' ideas, when he says that virtue only arose out of moral struggle with vice, or is there a basis in earlier Stoic theory? One might suspect that Seneca's own personality coloured or even inspired his argument here. Certainly he had an ascetic streak, with his youthful attachment to vegetarianism (*Ep.* 108. 17–23) and his lifelong fondness for cold baths (*Ep.* 53. 3, 67. 1, 83. 5) and hard mattresses (*Ep.* 108. 23). In *Letter* 66. 49 ff. he expresses a personal preference for virtue exercised in overcoming hardship, rather than the softer virtues: 'Permitte mihi, Lucili virorum

[3] Blundell (1986), 218.

optime, aliquid audacius dicere: si ulla bona maiora esse aliis possent, haec ego quae tristia videntur mollibus illis et delicatis praetulissem, haec maiora dixissem. maius est enim difficilia perfringere quam laeta moderari', ('My excellent Lucilius, allow me to speak more daringly: if some good things could be superior to others, I should have preferred these that are seen as disagreeable to those soft and enticing ones, I should have called these superior. For forging a way through difficult circumstances is superior to keeping a check on pleasant ones'). He has greater praise for Mucius Scaevola's hand, burnt in the fire, than for the unscathed arm of the bravest man (§ 51); compare how at *Letter* 67. 5 ff. he argues that such virtues as facing torture bravely are just as desirable as pleasanter virtues. In these passages the struggle is not with moral evil, but with physical pain, a moral indifferent as far as Stoics are concerned, but the rather masochistic admiration for virtues that require intense struggle might in itself have been enough to persuade Seneca that the innocence of the Golden Age was not real virtue.

Furthermore, the insistence that the earliest men had to learn to be virtuous and philosophers mirrors what Seneca says at the beginning of *Letter* 90, that individual contemporary men are not born with philosophy or virtue, but have to acquire them; they are not gifts of fortune, but can be acquired by all (*Ep.* 90. 1–2, cf. 76. 6, 123. 16, *Dial.* 4. 10. 6; *SVF* 3. 215, 224–5). Indeed, according to Seneca, we all come to virtue via vice (*Ep.* 50. 7 *ad neminem ante bona mens venit quam mala; omnes praeoccupati sumus; virtutes discere vitia dediscere* ⟨*est*⟩, 'nobody acquires a good mind before a bad one; the bad has made a pre-emptive strike on all of us; to learn virtue is to unlearn vice'). It was for a Stoic a matter of simple observation that we all start off wicked—wise men were notoriously thin on the ground in any case—and Seneca could have inferred from empirical observation of the contemporary state of affairs that a similar progression must have occurred in the earliest stages of human existence.

However, one can point to possible sources for his ideas in earlier writers. There are certainly precedents for Seneca's questioning of the philosophical status of these early men. As Theiler shows,[4] there is a similarity to Dicaearchus' denial that the Seven Sages were really philosophers: he said they were really clever men and lawgivers, not philosophers (Diog. Laert. 1. 40 = Dicaearchus fr. 30 Wehrli, cf. fr. 31), probably on the grounds that they did not devote themselves full time

---

[4] Theiler (1982), ii. 384–90 (comm. on F 448).

to philosophical activity as Plato or Aristotle did. Dicaearchus' point is echoed by Cicero, *Laelius* 7: *nam qui Septem* (sc. *sapientes*) *appellantur, eos qui ista subtilius quaerunt in numero sapientium non habent* ('for the Seven (wise men) are not reckoned as wise by the more fastidious investigators of such matters'); and at *De Officiis* 3. 16 Cicero makes a similar point about certain early Romans as well, this time with a clear Stoic underpinning: 'nemo enim horum sic sapiens, ut sapientem volumus intelligi, nec ii, qui sapientes habiti et nominati, M. Cato et C. Laelius, sapientes fuerunt, ne illi quidem septem, sed ex mediorum officiorum frequentia similtudinem quandam gerebant speciemque sapientium' ('For none of these is wise in the sense in which we wish to use the word, nor were those men wise who were reckoned and sur-named wise, Marcus Cato and Gaius Laelius, nor even were the Seven, but by the frequency of their outwardly virtuous actions they re-sembled and looked like wise men').

Such passages are about later stages of human history, but they could easily have persuaded Seneca to deny, *a fortiori*, that the earliest men were sages. But they do not account for the particular argument that moral evil is a pre-condition of moral goodness. Next we should look to the Stoic doctrine of the necessary coexistence of good and evil for the possible roots of Seneca's thinking.

II. THE NECESSARY COEXISTENCE OF GOOD AND EVIL IN STOICISM

Our sources for Stoicism are particularly sketchy on the problem of evil: Seneca and other extant Stoic writers understandably devote much attention to the practical problem of helping people to cope with suffering, but less to the theoretical problem of how the existence of evil can be reconciled with other Stoic doctrines. Furthermore, the problem was a complex one, with two aspects. (1) On the one hand, the Stoics had to explain the existence of moral evil—that is of evil men—in what was supposed to be a beneficently organized universe. (2) On the other hand, they had to explain the existence of pain, death, bereavement, famine, earthquake, and all such sufferings and disas-ters. According to Stoic doctrine, from the sufferer's point of view these were not true evils at all, that is they were not moral evils, but moral indifferents; but the Stoics still, by courtesy, as it were, referred to them as evils; for even if they are not evils from the sufferer's viewpoint, nevertheless to inflict such things on somebody else is prima facie a moral evil, so the problem of explaining their existence in the Stoic universe was a very real one.[5]

Our sources chiefly concentrate on the second aspect of the problem of evil, where the Stoics deployed a variety of arguments: that suffering was a source of moral training, that it provided exemplary punishment of evildoers, that it was an inevitable by-product of other, good goals, or that it was caused by evil spirits, and so on.[6] This emphasis is readily intelligible in psychological terms, for pain and suffering are more immediate in everybody's experience than the question why there should be any morally evil people.[7] However, both aspects of the problem of evil are addressed by the Stoics' argument that good could not exist unless evil did too. The fullest statement is in Gellius 7. 1. 1–6 (*SVF* 2. 1169, Long and Sedley 54Q):

Quibus non videtur mundus dei et hominum causa institutus neque res humanae providentia gubernari, gravi se argumento uti putant, cum ita dicunt: 'si esset providentia, nulla essent mala.' nihil enim minus aiunt providentiae congruere, quam in eo mundo, quem propter homines fecisse dicatur, tantam vim esse aerumnarum et malorum. (2) adversus ea Chrysippus cum in libro περὶ προνοίας quarto dissereret: 'nihil est prorsus istis' inquit 'insubidius, qui opinantur bona esse potuisse, si non essent ibidem mala. (3) nam cum bona malis contraria sint, utraque necessum est opposita inter sese et quasi mutuo adverso quaeque fulta nisu consistere; nullum adeo contrarium est sine contrario altero. (4) quo enim pacto iustitiae sensus esse posset, nisi essent iniuriae? aut quid aliud iustitia est quam iniustitiae privatio? quid item fortitudo intellegi posset nisi ex ignaviae adpositione? quid continentia nisi ex intemperantiae? quo item modo prudentia esset, nisi foret contra inprudentia? (5) proinde' inquit 'homines stulti cur non hoc etiam desiderant, ut veritas sit et non sit mendacium? namque itidem sunt bona et mala, felicitas et infortunitas, dolor et voluptas. (6) alterum enim ex altero, sicuti Plato (cf. *Phaedo* 60b) ait, verticibus inter se contrariis deligatum est; si tuleris unum, abstuleris utrumque.'[8]

---

[5] Long (1968); Kerferd (1978); Long and Sedley (1987), i. 323–33, esp. 332–3. I am supplementing, not disagreeing with, what they say (Long (1968), 331 does not think the assertion of the necessary conjunction of contraries is relevant, but Long and Sedley (1987), i. 332 take a different view).

[6] See Long and Sedley (1987), i. 332 for a brief review.

[7] Obviously evil men can be a threat and a source of suffering, so later Stoics do discuss how to treat them: e.g. Epictetus argues that other evil men are just externals as far as I am concerned, and I should not be angry with them (1. 15. 1–5, 1. 18); cf. n. 8 below.

[8] In §§7–13 Gellius goes on to give a different argument not so relevant to our purpose, that certain undesirable things are necessary concomitants of desirable things.

(Those who do not believe that the world is constructed for the sake of god and men, or that human affairs are governed by providence, think they have a weighty argument when they say, 'If providence existed, there would be no evils.' For they say that nothing is more incompatible with providence than the existence of such a quantity of sufferings and evils in the world that is said to have been made for the benefit of men. (2) When Chrysippus argued against this view in *On Providence* Book 4, he said: 'There is really nothing more silly than those who think there could have been good things if there had not been bad things at the same time. (3) For since good things are the contraries of bad things, it is necessary for both to be established opposite each other and, as it were, resting on each other in mutual opposition and dependence; for no contrary exists without its contrary. (4) For how could there be the idea of justice unless there were injustices? Or what is justice but the removal of injustice? Again, how could courage be understood except when set beside cowardice? or self-control except when set beside lack of self-control? Again, how could there be prudence if there were not imprudence on the other side? (5) So why do foolish men not also demand this, that there should be truth but not falsehood? For the same applies to good and bad, happiness and misfortune, pain and pleasure. (6) For, as Plato says (*Phaedo* 60b), the one is bound to the other, facing in opposite directions; if you take one, you have taken away both.')

The passage switches, apparently, between a psychological argument (that we could not have any *perception* or *understanding* of justice without injustice or of bravery without cowardice (§ 4)), and an ontological one (that justice *is* nothing except the absence of injustice, and there *could be* no self-control or prudence without their opposites (§ 4)). In other authors there are briefer statements specifically about the coexistence of moral good and evil, but they do not add any detail: Chrysippus ap. Plutarch, *On Stoic Self-Contradictions* 35, 1050e–f, cf. *On Common Conceptions* 13, 1065a–b (*SVF* 2. 1181): ἐπιτείνει δὲ τὴν ὑπεναντίωσιν ἐν τῷ δευτέρῳ περὶ Φύσεως γράφων τάδε· "ἡ δὲ κακία πρὸς τὰ δεινὰ συμπτώματα ἴδιόν τιν᾽ ἔχει ὅρον·[9] γίγνεται μὲν γὰρ καὶ αὐτή πως κατὰ τὸν τῆς φύσεως λόγον καί, ἵνα οὕτως εἴπω, οὐκ ἀχρήστως γίγνεται πρὸς τὰ ὅλα· οὐδὲ γὰρ ἂν τἀγαθὸν ἦν" ('He increases the contradiction when he writes as follows in *On Nature* Book 2: "A particular distinction can be made between vice and terrible misfortunes: for even vice itself occurs according to the principles of nature and, so to speak, occurs for the benefit of the universe: for otherwise good would not have existed either"'); cf. Posidonius F29 Edelstein–Kidd = F403 Theiler εἶναι δὲ καὶ τὴν κακίαν ὑπαρκτὴν διὰ τὸ ἀντικεῖσθαι τῇ ἀρετῇ ('Vice too is real because it is opposite to virtue').

---

[9] ὅρον Rasmus ex CN loc. cit.: λόγον SR codd.

These passages certainly seem to maintain that no contrary can exist without the other contrary. However, this fallacy had had the ground swept from under it in a passing comment of Aristotle's in *Categories* 11, 14ᵃ6 ff.: ἔτι τῶν ἐναντίων οὐκ ἀναγκαῖον, ἐὰν θάτερον ᾖ, καὶ τὸ λοιπὸν εἶναι· ὑγιαινόντων γὰρ ἁπάντων ὑγίεια μὲν ἔσται, νόσος δὲ οὔ ('And with contraries it is not necessary that, if one exists, the other should exist too; for if everybody is healthy, health will exist, but not disease'); and more examples follow. It is hard to see what the Stoics might have thought they could say in response to this, and if that was their argument, it is another case of their apparently being unaware of a passage of Aristotle that was relevant to their own philosophical ideas.[10] But is it possible that, at least with regard to virtue and vice, some Stoics modified the argument about the coexistence of contraries to the form that we have seen adumbrated in Seneca? That is to say, they did not just base their argument for the necessity of vice on a general assertion about the necessary coexistence of all contraries, but argued specifically that proper virtue cannot develop except in a climate where there is vice.

Other passages in Seneca and elsewhere suggest that the Stoics used another argument for the necessary dependence of virtue on vice. It was a common theme of Stoic writers that misfortunes or evil men provide material on which the wise man or the person aspiring to virtue can train and exercise.[11] But a few passages seem to go further

---

[10] See Sandbach (1985) on the question of the Stoics' knowledge of Aristotle's treatises. This passage of *Cat.* should perhaps be added to his list of passages of which the Stoics show no knowledge.

[11] See Rutherford (1989a), 232–3 on the Stoic image of suffering as a training ground; on Seneca, Motto and Clark (1985). Cf. Sen. *Dial.* 1. 2. 4 *marcet sine adversario virtus: tunc apparet quanta sit quantumque polleat, cum quid possit patientia ostendit* ('Without an opponent virtue goes soft: its scale and power are apparent when suffering reveals what it is capable of'), though this could refer to adverse circumstances rather than an evil human adversary; cf. *HF* 433 *Imperia dura tolle: quid virtus erit?* ('Take away harsh commands—what will be left of virtue?'). Epictetus 1. 6. 32–6 argues that Heracles could never have displayed his virtue if there had not been any monsters and evil men in the world, but he also says that it would have been folly for Heracles to introduce the monsters into his native land in order to display his virtue; however, since they did exist there, they gave him the chance to display his virtue. Marcus Aurelius 9. 42. 1 reflects that evil men must exist in the world, and he urges himself to ask: τίνα ἔδωκεν ἡ φύσις τῷ ἀνθρώπῳ ἀρετὴν πρὸς τοῦτο τὸ ἁμάρτημα; ('What virtue has nature given man to counter this misdeed?'), and he speaks of gentleness being an antidote against the unfeeling man, and so on. Thus he assumes that for every vice there is a virtue by means of which others can counter it; but he does not argue or imply that the vices must exist in order for the virtues to be exercised. Compare Epictetus 3. 20. 9–15 on the good I can derive from dealings with wicked men, as well as from disease and other sufferings; again there is no suggestion that wicked men must exist for the sake of the resulting good.

and argue that the sufferings or the evil men are essential in order for the wise man to be able to exercise his virtue at all. At *Dialogues* 9. 7. 5 Seneca is talking about the paucity of good men in human history; but the ages of Socrates and of Cato are more promising than other ages:

vix tibi esset facultas dilectus felicioris, si inter Platonas et Xenophontas et illum Socratici fetus proventum bonos quaereres, aut si tibi potestas Catonianae fieret aetatis, quae plerosque dignos tulit qui Catonis saeculo nascerentur (sicut multos peiores quam umquam alias maximorumque molitores scelerum; utraque enim turba opus erat ut Cato posset intellegi: habere debuit et bonos quibus se adprobaret et malos in quibus vim suam experiretur): nunc vero in tanta bonorum egestate minus fastidiosa fiat electio

(You would scarcely have an opportunity to make a happier choice if you looked for good men in the company of Plato and Xenophon and the offspring who issued from Socrates, or if you had access to the age of Cato, which produced a number of men who deserved to be born in Cato's lifetime (just as it produced many men worse than ever before, perpetrators of the most terrible crimes; for both groups were necessary for a Cato to be recognized: he needed both good men to whom he could prove himself and evil men on whom he could test his strength): but today when good men are so scarce you must be less choosy).

Here the significant phrase is *habere debuit . . . malos in quibus vim suam experiretur*: 'he needed evil men on whom he could test his strength'; without them he could not have been a Cato.

Rather as in *Letter* 90, Seneca here is brief, and this could be a passing thought that has no wider basis in Stoic doctrine. But the passage finds an echo in one of Plutarch, which claims that virtuous men cannot be virtuous except in relation to vicious men (Plut. *CN* 13, 1065b–c, *SVF* 2. 1181): . . . ἀρετὴ δ᾽ ἄνευ κακίας οὐκ ἔχει γένεσιν, ἀλλὰ ὥσπερ ἐνίαις τῶν ἰατρικῶν δυνάμεων ἰὸς ὄφεως καὶ χολὴ ὑαίνης ἀναγκαῖόν ἐστιν οὕτως ἐπιτηδειότης ἑτέρα τῇ Μελήτου μοχθηρίᾳ πρὸς τὴν Σωκράτους δικαιοσύνην καὶ τῇ Κλέωνος ἀναγωγίᾳ πρὸς τὴν Περικλέους καλοκἀγαθίαν. πῶς δ᾽ ἂν εὗρεν ὁ Ζεὺς τὸν Ἡρακλέα φῦσαι καὶ τὸν Λυκοῦργον εἰ μὴ καὶ Σαρδανάπαλον ἡμῖν ἔφυσε καὶ Φάλαριν ('. . . but virtue cannot come into being without vice, but as snake's venom or hyena's bile is needed for some medical prescriptions, so the wickedness of Meletus matches the justice of Socrates, and Cleon's vulgarity matches the nobility of Pericles. How could Zeus have managed to produce Heracles and Lycurgus if he had not also produced Sardanapalus and Phalaris for us?'); Plutarch proceeds to ridicule this argument: ὥρα λέγειν αὐτοῖς ὅτι καὶ φθίσις γέγονεν

ἀνθρώπῳ πρὸς εὐεξίαν καὶ ποδάγρα πρὸς ὠκύτητα, καὶ οὐκ ἂν ἦν
Ἀχιλλεὺς κομήτης εἰ μὴ φαλακρὸς Θερσίτης ('It is time for them to
say that mankind has received consumption for the sake of good
health, and gout for the sake of swift-footedness, and that Achilles
would not have been long-haired if Thersites had not been bald').
However, these objections are not fair, if the Stoics were not talking
about the coexistence of all contraries, but were arguing that specific
virtues cannot be exercised except in reaction or relation to particular
vicious men: there is a necessary correlation between the wickedness of
Meletus and the justice of Socrates, and so on.[12]

We may generalize from these passages and suggest that the Stoics
may have argued that there are some forms of virtue that by definition
require evil men before they can be exercised. For example, bravery in
the face of undeserved punishment, refusal to act unjustly in the face
of unjust behaviour, seem implicit in these examples. One could think
of other instances: retributive justice can only exist where there are
wrong deeds meriting retribution, and the virtue of self-control presupposes impulses to do wrong (these cases are implicit at Plutarch,
On Common Conceptions 13, 1065c ... οἱ λέγοντες μὴ ἀχρήστως
γεγονέναι πρὸς τὴν ἐγκράτειαν τὴν ἀκολασίαν καὶ πρὸς τὴν δικαιοσύνην τὴν ἀδικίαν, '... those who say the creation of licentiousness has
not been without use for self-control, and that of injustice not without
use for justice').

But, one might say, even if it is conceded that adversity of some kind

---

[12] Another passage of Plutarch may reflect similar Stoic arguments, although the
context in Plutarch is slightly different: he is scorning the Stoic argument that suffering
is a sort of accidental waste product of the universe, like the chaff from flour production
(Plut. *SR* 37, 1051c–d, *SVF* 2. 1178): τὸ μὲν οὖν τὰ τοιαῦτα συμπτώματα τῶν καλῶν
κἀγαθῶν ἀνδρῶν, οἷον ἡ Σωκράτους καταδίκη καὶ ὁ Πυθαγόρου ζῶντος ἐμπρησμὸς ὑπὸ
τῶν Κυλωνείων καὶ Ζήνωνος ὑπὸ Δημύλου τοῦ τυράννου καὶ Ἀντιφῶντος ὑπὸ Διονυσίου
στρεβλουμένων ἀναιρέσεις, πιτύροις παραπίπτουσιν ἀπεικάζειν ὅσης ἐστὶν εὐχερείας ἐῶ
('I say nothing of the irresponsibility of comparing to chaff that gets lost this sort of
accident that happens to good and upright men, such as the condemnation of Socrates
and the burning alive of Pythagoras by the Cyloneans and the torturing to death of Zeno
by the tyrant Demylus and of Antiphon by Dionysius'). The passage gives a series of
philosophers and a poet who died violent but presumably courageous deaths; it seems
unlikely that the Stoics themselves used the sufferings of these people as examples of
minor side-effects, and part of the original point may have been that such display of
bravery is possible only in a world where evil men exist and inflict undeserved suffering
on others. This point is perhaps implicit in Seneca *Ep.* 13. 14: *cicuta magnum Socratem
fecit. Catoni gladium adsertorem libertatis extorque: magnam partem detraxeris gloriae*
('The hemlock made Socrates great. Wrench from Cato the sword that claimed his freedom, and you have removed the greater part of his glory'); if hemlock and sword were
necessary, presumably the evil people who brought about the death of Socrates and the
suicide of Cato were necessary too.

is needed for the exercise of virtue, are there not other forms of virtue that do not depend on the existence of evil men, virtues such as distributive justice, or courage in the face of illness and accident that are not the fault of other human beings? Would it not have been sufficient for such virtues to be exercised? Do we have any further need of the virtues that do depend on evil men and evil impulses? Maybe the Stoics never addressed this problem; they were after all confronting a world in which evil men manifestly do exist and consequently certain virtues are required to deal with them. But this does not explain why such virtues must exist in the first place. Maybe the Stoics were persuaded that all conceivable virtues must exist by the doctrine of the completeness of virtue: compare, for example, Plutarch, *On Stoic Self-Contradiction* 27, 1046e–f (= *SVF* 3. 299) τὰς ἀρετάς φασιν ἀντακολουθεῖν ἀλλήλαις, οὐ μόνον τῷ τὸν μίαν ἔχοντα πάσας ἔχειν ἀλλὰ καὶ τῷ τὸν κατὰ μίαν ὁτιοῦν ἐνεργοῦντα κατὰ πάσας ἐνεργεῖν· οὔτε γὰρ ἄνδρα φασὶ τέλειον εἶναι τὸν μὴ πάσας ἔχοντα τὰς ἀρετὰς οὔτε πρᾶξιν τελείαν ἥτις οὐ κατὰ πάσας πράττεται τὰς ἀρετάς ('They say that the virtues imply one another not only in that the person who possesses one possesses them all, but also in that the person who is doing anything in accordance with one is doing it in accordance with all; for they say both that a man is not perfect if he does not possess all the virtues, and that an action is not perfect if it is not performed in accordance with all the virtues'); Seneca, *Letter* 71. 16 (*virtus*) *habet numeros suos, plena est* ('virtue has all its components, it is complete').

To summarize so far, we may postulate a Stoic argument that some vices are necessary in order for certain virtues to exist; and, possibly, a supplementary argument that these virtues must exist in order for the wise man's virtue to be complete. These arguments are different from the one we started from, in Seneca's ninetieth letter, that vice must exist in order for genuine moral choices to be made, and that without such choices there cannot be any virtue. But although these are two different arguments, they share a common purpose, to demonstrate the necessity of the existence of moral evil. Furthermore, they can both be seen as attempts to develop, with particular reference to virtue and vice, the general assertion of the necessary coexistence of contraries, and to develop it in such a way as to avoid the objection raised by Aristotle in *Categories* 11; though it is best left an open question whether or not the Stoics knew this passage and were consciously responding to it.

III. DIVINE AND HUMAN GOODNESS

However, there is an important objection to these arguments: what about divine virtue? If, as the Stoics maintained, divine virtue is no different from human virtue (*SVF* 1. 564, 3. 149, 245–54, 526), do the arguments not prove either that vice must coexist with virtue in god, or else that, if there is no vice in god, god has no virtue either? Plutarch makes the point at *On Common Conceptions* 13, 1065b (just after the quotation from Chrysippus given above on p. 100): οὐκοῦν ἐν θεοῖς ἀγαθὸν οὐδέν ἐστιν, ἐπεὶ μηδὲ κακόν ('So there is nothing good among the gods, since there is nothing evil either'). He then continues with a related objection, based on the Stoic doctrine that, immediately after an ecpyrosis, no evil is present in the universe: οὐδέ, ὅταν ὁ Ζεὺς εἰς ἑαυτὸν ἀναλύσας τὴν ὕλην ἅπασαν εἰς γένηται καὶ τὰς ἄλλας ἀνέλῃ διαφοράς, οὐδὲν ἔστιν ἀγαθὸν τηνικαῦτα, μηδενός γε κακοῦ παρόντος ('and whenever Zeus dissolves all matter into himself and becomes one and removes all other distinctions, nothing good exists then, since there is nothing evil').

Did the Stoics have any answer to this challenge? We need to treat separately the two different arguments for the dependence of goodness on evil. The second argument examined above, that certain virtues can only be exercised in relation to vicious men, causes no problem, for god too can presumably exercise those virtues in relation to vicious men, or indeed perhaps in relation to evil demons (referred to in *SVF* 2. 1104, 1178). But the first argument, that virtue can only exist where vice is a genuine alternative, is more troublesome. Here, however, we find a possible answer in Seneca.[13] As we have seen, he insists that human beings are not born with virtue but have to acquire it; but he also asserts, in contrast, that the gods *are* born with virtue: *Letter* 95. 36 *nam ut dii immortales nullam didicere virtutem cum omni editi et pars naturae eorum est bonos esse . . .* ('for, as the immortal gods have not learnt any virtue, having been brought into being with every virtue, and it is part of their nature to be good', so, he goes on, a few exceptionally talented men make moral progress swiftly and effortlessly).[14] Later in *Letter* 95 he says that the gods are incapable of doing

---

[13] On this topic see Lausberg (1970), 176–8, on fr. 122. Below I follow her punctuation of the fragment.

[14] Cf. *Ep.* 124. 14 'quattuor hae naturae sunt, arboris, animalis, hominis, dei: haec duo, quae rationalia sunt, eandem naturam habent, illo diversa sunt quod alterum inmortale, alterum mortale est. ex his ergo unius bonum natura perficit, dei scilicet,

wrong: § 49 *quae causa est dis bene faciendi? natura. errat si quis illos putat nocere nolle: non possunt* ('What makes the gods act benevolently? Nature. It is erroneous to suppose that they do not want to do harm: they are incapable of it'). Indeed, Seneca maintains that the wise man is superior to god in that he owes his virtue (courage, in this passage) to himself, not to nature: *Letter* 53. 11 *est aliquid quo sapiens antecedat deum: ille naturae beneficio non timet, suo sapiens* ('There is one respect in which the wise man surpasses god: god is unafraid thanks to nature, the wise man thanks to himself'). However, we may well suspect that Seneca is being carried away by his own rhetoric in this last passage, for in a fragment quoted by Lactantius he points out that god is identical with nature, so he really receives his virtue from himself: fr. 122 Haase (ap. Lactant. *Inst.* 2. 8. 23) 'melius igitur Seneca omnium Stoicorum acutissimus, qui vidit nihil aliud esse naturam quam deum. "'ergo'" inquit "'deum non laudabimus, cui naturalis est uirtus? nec enim illam didicit ex ullo.' immo laudabimus. quamuis enim naturalis illi sit, sibi illam dedit, quoniam deus ipse natura est"' ('Seneca, most acute of all the Stoics, is better: he saw that nature is nothing other than god. "'So'", he says, "'shall we refrain from praising god, for whom virtue is natural? For he did not learn it from anybody.' No, indeed we shall praise him. For although it is natural for him, he bestowed it on himself, since god himself is nature."'). But even if the superiority of the wise man to god is Senecan embellishment, the basic point, that god is virtuous by nature whereas men are not, and that god cannot do wrong whereas men can,[15] could well be authentically Stoic; after all, god is eternal (e.g. Diog. Laert. 7. 134), so he cannot acquire his virtue in the same way as men do. If this is granted, then divine virtue is significantly different, and Plutarch's objections do not hold: for it is only human virtue that must be acquired after moral struggle in a climate where vice exists.

alterius cura, hominis' ('there are these four natures—plant, animal, human, divine; the last two, which are rational, have the same nature, but are different in that one is immortal, the other mortal. So nature makes perfect the good of one of them, that is of god, and effort makes perfect the nature of the other, that is man').

[15] It cannot be objected that this makes god innocent, not good, according to Seneca's distinction in *Ep.* 90. 46; for god is not ignorant of anything in the way that innocent men are: he knows everything about the universe and about his own nature.

8

Rhetoric as a Protreptic Force in Seneca's Prose Works

DESMOND COSTA

(1) Quantum inter philosophiam interest, Lucili virorum optime, et ceteras artes, tantum interesse existimo in ipsa philosophia inter illam partem quae ad homines et hanc quae ad deos pertinet. Altior est haec et animosior; multum permisit sibi; non fuit oculis contenta; maius esse quiddam suspicata est ac pulchrius quod extra conspectum natura posuisset. (2) Denique inter duas interest quantum inter deum et hominem. Altera docet quid in terris agendum sit, altera quid agatur in caelo. Altera errores nostros discutit et lumen admovet quo discernantur ambigua vitae; altera multum supra hanc in qua volutamur caliginem excedit et e tenebris ereptos perducit illo unde lucet.

(3) Equidem tunc rerum naturae gratias ago cum illam non ab hac parte video qua publica est, sed cum secretiora eius intravi, cum disco quae universi materia sit, quis auctor aut custos, quid sit deus . . . (4) Nisi ad haec admitterer, non tanti fuerat nasci. Quid enim erat cur in numero viventium me positum esse gauderem? An ut cibos et potiones percolarem? ut hoc corpus causarium ac fluidum, periturumque nisi subinde impletur, farcirem et viverem aegri minister? ut mortem timerem, cui uni nascimur? Detrahe hoc inaestimabile bonum, non est vita tanti ut sudem, ut aestuem. (5) O quam contempta res est homo, nisi supra humana surrexerit! Quamdiu cum affectibus colluctamur, quid magnifici facimus? Etiamsi superiores sumus, portenta vincimus. Quid est cur suspiciamus nosmet ipsi quia dissimiles deterrimus sumus? Non video quare sibi placeat qui robustior est in valetudinario. (6) Multum interest inter vires et bonam valetudinem.

Effugisti vitia animi; non est tibi frons ficta, nec in alienam voluntatem sermo compositus, nec cor involutum, nec avaritia quae, quicquid omnibus abstulit, sibi ipsi neget, nec luxuria pecuniam turpiter perdens quam turpius reparet, nec ambitio quae te ad dignitatem nisi per indigna non ducet: nihil adhuc consecutus es; multa effugisti, te nondum.

Virtus enim ista quam affectamus magnifica est, non quia per se beatum est malo caruisse, sed quia animum laxat et praeparat ad cognitionem caelestium dignumque efficit qui in consortium deo veniat.

(7) Tunc consummatum habet plenumque bonum sortis humanae cum

calcato omni malo petit altum et in interiorem naturae sinum venit. Tunc iuvat inter ipsa sidera vagantem divitum pavimenta ridere et totam cum auro suo terram, non illo tantum dico quod egessit et signandum monetae dedit, sed et illo quod in occulto servat posterorum avaritiae. (8) Non potest ante contemnere porticus et lacunaria ebore fulgentia et tonsiles silvas et derivata in domos flumina quam totum circumit mundum et, terrarum orbem superne despiciens angustum et magna ex parte opertum mari, etiam ea quae extat late squalidum et aut ustum aut rigentem, sibi ipse dixit: 'hoc est illud punctum quod inter tot gentes ferro et igne dividitur? (9) O quam ridiculi sunt mortalium termini! ... (10) Si quis formicis det intellectum hominis, nonne et illae unam aream in multas provincias divident? Cum te in illa vere magna sustuleris, quotiens videbis exercitus subrectis ire vexillis et, quasi magnum aliquid agatur, equitem modo ulteriora explorantem, modo a lateribus affusum, libebit dicere:

it nigrum campis agmen.

Formicarum iste discursus est in angusto laborantium. Quid illis et nobis interest nisi exigui mensura corpusculi?' (*NQ* 1, praef. 1–10)

In an essay devoted to Seneca's art of persuasion it is fitting to let him have the first word. Here he is introducing Book 1 of his *Natural Questions*, one of the works that came from the last and astonishingly productive three years or so of his life. It is thus a work written in his maturity at the height of his powers—he never outlived his creative powers—and this extract is a moving protreptic, an exhortation to study philosophy, which incidentally reveals several of Seneca's favourite tricks of rhetorical persuasion. There is no need nowadays to labour his supremacy as a rhetorical technician: his father's interests and influence on him from childhood, coupled with his own remarkable natural talent, made him the greatest prose artist of his generation. His contemporary fame, Quintilian's later strictures on him, and his adoption as a role-model for prose style from the seventeenth century onwards, all testify in different ways to his unassailable position in Latin literature.

But even the most dedicated Senecans should and do admit his stylistic failings (the failings in his life are not relevant here). There are many passages in which Seneca's love of his own technique gets the better of him, and he indulges himself to what seems to modern readers boring extremes. So all too often we are treated to an interminable series of *exempla*, far exceeding the need to prove the necessary point, or a stretch of rhetorical questions filling half a page of text and pushing at an open door in the reader's mind: Seneca, in a word, is being too clever or learned, and does not have that quality of the supreme artist, knowing when to stop. With that admission, however, it remains true that when Seneca is at his most earnest in urging the claims of philosophy as the supreme pursuit of the human mind, he is also at his most persuasive, at least in part because he is more controlled and delicate in deploying his rhetorical armoury. We are not simply dazzled by linguistic fireworks, with the attendant danger that we are apt to forget what the display is in aid of anyway, and Seneca's restraint here may rise from the very seriousness of what he is trying to say. This passage from the opening of the *Natural Questions* may illustrate his more controlled evangelism.

The opening at once engages the interest of the addressee, Lucilius, in the importance of exploring philosophy, before Seneca goes on to reveal his own interest and his credentials for stating philosophy's claims (3. 'equidem . . . naturae gratias ago'). This I/you relationship is characteristic of much of Seneca's work, as C. J. Herington[1] has shown: not just in the *Letters*, where a close relationship with an addressee is to be expected, but throughout the treatises, where the rapport is sustained by second-person verbs even when the notional addressee has faded from view. In this way, as our passage shows, Seneca maintains the teacher/taught roles, the more advanced *proficiens* talking to the relative novice and through him to a wider readership.

But before we pick up Lucilius again in section 6 we meet philosophy, and Seneca loses no time in clarifying the important divisions of the subject into what roughly speaking we would call ethics and metaphysics or theology. Both are important but the second much more so, as the succession of comparatives stress—*altior, animosior, maius, pulchrius*. The rest of the paragraph (2) illustrates one of Seneca's styles, the directly didactic, with short punchy clauses, lack of connecting words, hammer-blow repetition and balance (*altera . . . altera . . . altera . . . altera*), verbal play (*agendum . . . agatur*). This is the controlled Seneca, without an otiose word and showing little of the *abundantia* for which he is rightly criticized elsewhere.

Seneca then, as a good teacher, shows that he knows what he is talking about and has travelled at least some way along the road he is pointing out to Lucilius—the same stance he adopts to the same addressee in the *Letters*. There is no suggestion that he has arrived at the goal of *sapientia* himself—there are several disclaimers against this

---

[1] Herington (1982), 515: he points out the comparative rarity of third-person verbs throughout the prose corpus.

in the *Letters*—but he knows something, and he certainly knows the value of the exercise. Again rhetorical devices are deployed (4–5): the argumentative question ('quid enim . . .? . . . quamdiu . . .? . . . quid est . . .?'), the repeated rejected answers ('an ut . . . ut . . . ut . . .?'), the exclamation ('O quam . . .!'), piquant word- and thought-play ('homo/ humana'), the snappy summarizing statement that rounds off the paragraph ('multum interest . . .'), which itself is teasingly elliptical, because we have to work out what *is* the difference between *vires* and *bona valetudo*. We note in passing the characteristic Stoic duty to struggle against our passions (*affectibus*), and the equally characteristic Senecan twist given to a topos: even if we are victorious we have not won through entirely, and we must not be complacent in simply comparing ourselves with morally worse people.

Back to Lucilius in the next paragraph (6) and the second-person singular, and Seneca is showing another quality of a good teacher: encouragement for his pupil. Lucilius has indeed much to his credit in the absence of certain bad qualities of character; but these are not positive achievements ('nihil adhuc consecutus es'), and the important advances have yet to be made which bring an awareness of heavenly things and association with god. This is a good point to remind ourselves that Seneca's approach to instructing Lucilius (and the other recipients of his philosophical works) was essentially heuristic: he was showing them how to find things out for themselves. They must use their minds to attain *virtus* and *sapientia* (the terms are often virtually synonymous) through studying philosophy; and the role of philosophy is largely concerned with the fundamental truths of nature and the gods. The two important *Letters* 88 and 90 discuss the function of philosophy, and stress that it is different in kind from other educational pursuits and from men's inventive faculties, and it is the apex of our mental achievement through which we finally arrive at *sapientia*. This little section focusing on Lucilius has its own unity signposted by *multa effugisti* at the end picking up the opening words *effugisti vitia*. This is a minor example of ring-composition, a device which Seneca occasionally uses to unify larger structures: for example, the treatises *De Brevitate Vitae* and *Consolatio ad Helviam*.

The next task for Lucilius is through philosophy to free his mind from earthly preoccupations, and by exploring the secrets of nature to acquire a true sense of values which will enable it to despise human greed. The *avaritia* (7) here picks up the earlier *avaritia* and *luxuria* (6), and it is one of Seneca's favourite objects of attack. He is not alone in this, of course, and shares this stance with most moralizing writers, but this vice and the associated greed of gluttony are particular targets throughout the treatises. The dominant image of this last section of our extract is of the mind soaring up to the heights of the cosmos, where it can absorb the profound secrets of the world and learn to despise the trivial frippery which preoccupies mortals. Only in this way will it realize the fullest potential of its human existence. This is another familiar Senecan picture, and it reflects at least partly the Stoic theory that the soul or mind (*animus* can be translated by either English word according to context) of each human being derives from the cosmic *pneuma*, which informs the universe, and seeks instinctively to return to it. The contrast between the soaring mind and the petty money-grubbers below is further pointed by the comparison of its inter-stellar ambit with the unappealing earth, mostly covered by sea and otherwise squalid, parched, or frozen (8). The apostrophe given to the mind is another frequent dramatic device of the treatises, and here too Seneca quotes from one of his favourite authors, Virgil, to deflate pretentious human armies to the scurrying of a colony of ants (10).

Another rhetorical feature which our passage illustrates is rhythm. From the fifth century BC Greek rhetorical writers recognized prose rhythm as a tool of their trade, and this technique became highly sophisticated as used, for example, by the Greek orators and Plato, individual writers developing their own favourite rhythmical units. It is important to keep reminding ourselves that the poets did not have a monopoly of metrical or rhythmic effects, and the reason is of course that oratorical prose, and much other, was heard rather than read no less than poetry itself. Roman writers and theorists took over Greek ideas, and their greatest practitioner, Cicero, stated that the period-ending, *clausula*, was the rhythmically most important part of the sentence (*De Or.* 3. 192). By Seneca's time rhetoric as a practical activity had declined for political reasons, but rhetorical theory had become even more self-conscious and refined, and Seneca himself showed a total mastery of the repertoire, including a very obvious devotion to rhythm. There is some statistical evidence of a greater attention to rhythmic effects in his later prose works, and it may well be that the interest and expertise he acquired in metre while writing the tragedies (which unfortunately cannot be firmly dated) can be seen, for example, in the rhythms of the *Natural Questions* and the *Letters* which he wrote towards the end of his life.[2] However that may

[2] Soubiran (1991), 376–7.

be, we surely have in Seneca an almost unique example of a writer highly adept in the skills of both prose and verse composition, and a neat link between the two fields can be seen in his preoccupation with prose rhythm. This is most obvious in his *clausulae*, where he shows a particular fondness for certain metrical cadences. Two of his favourites are $-\cup--\times$ and $-\cup--\cup\times$ allowing resolution of two shorts for a long, and several examples of both can be found even in the short passage we are looking at. It is probably pointless to probe further into any writer's motives for using a particular rhythm (e.g. by trying to link rhythm with sense) beyond assuming that it pleased his ear or was used by another writer he admired. But clearly this practice was regarded as an important formal element in the structure of *Kunstprosa*, and Seneca has his place in the company of the most distinguished practitioners.

Mention of the effect of rhythmic prose on the ear leads us to a more general point that can be made about Seneca's prose. A very great deal of it is hortatory: in particular, he is urging the study of nature and the world through philosophical inquiry. It is likely that most people respond more readily to encouragement from the living voice than from the written word, and this coupled with the fact that a large amount of Greek and Latin literature was read aloud rather than silently suggests that Seneca was consciously composing in a style intended to be heard and not just seen as words on a page. He would probably have vigorously disclaimed any resemblance between himself and fifth-century sophists or Hellenistic Cynic preachers, but in a sense he stands in a line of succession from them in the urgency of his moral convictions and even in the similarity (to the Cynics) of some of his lessons (e.g. simplicity, the value of independence). The difference is that, so far as we know, he preached exclusively by the written word—but one clearly in a sense to be heard. The traditional label *dialogi* for the Ambrosian treatises, misleading as it is in some respects, reflects this aspect of the works, and the *Letters*, like any letters, are spoken words put on paper and sent to a friend. Seneca's voice, like Cicero's and Lord Chesterfield's in their letters, can be heard without much effort of the imagination talking to Lucilius. Of course, in suggesting there is a spoken style to be heard in the prose works there must be qualifications. There is the formal studied art of the written style obvious on every page, and presumably not even Seneca's everyday conversation was a string of *sententiae* and carefully balanced antitheses; but many of the treatises as well as the letters have a shapelessness and a spontaneity which show the teacher talking in a familiar unstructured way to his pupil or his friend. So we are, as it were, listening to two registers: we are hearing (not just reading) the rhetorical sound effects of the artful stylist, and also the spontaneous directness of the speaking voice. This should be remembered when we quite justly accused Seneca of being too diffuse, of simply not knowing when enough is enough, when he piles antithesis on antithesis and *exemplum* on *exemplum*, far beyond the need to convince us. He does run on to excess, but just as reading aloud gives a fuller value to the more restrained rhetoric of much of his prose, so by varying the tone it can diversify and relieve the monotony of the catalogues; and there is, after all, something to be said for varying the approach when guiding people in their conduct and their studies.

No survey, however cursory, of Seneca's rhetorical repertoire should ignore the fine descriptive passages which occur from time to time in the treatises and *Letters*. Various kinds of *descriptio* were recognized exercises in declamation, and it is clear that Seneca's inclination and his virtuosity enjoyed picturing the natural world, terrestrial and celestial, in passages of lavish and memorable prose. The link with his protreptic intent is that they tend to occur in contexts where he is encouraging a philosophical attitude by widening our view in comparing the majesty of nature with trivial human existence. In other places he seems just to be indulging himself in a piece of virtuoso pictorial writing, a sort of ekphrasis, which arises from and decorates his current theme. An example of the latter type of passage is the tremendous description of the cataracts of the Nile, from which this extract comes.

Excipiunt eum [the Nile] Cataractae, nobilis insigni spectaculo locus; ibi per arduas excisasque pluribus locis rupes Nilus insurgit et vires suas concitat. Frangitur enim occurrentibus saxis et per angusta luctatus, ubicumque vincit aut vincitur, fluctuat et, illic excitatis primum aquis quas sine tumultu leni alveo duxerat, violentus et torrens per malignos transitus prosilit dissimilis sibi (quippe ad id lutosus et turbidus fluit); at, ubi scopulos et acuta cautium verberavit, spumat et illi non ex natura sua sed ex iniuria loci color est, tandemque eluctatus obstantia in vastam altitudinem subito destitutus cadit cum ingenti circumiacentium regionum strepitu. (*NQ* 4A. 2. 4–5)

The vigour and the *sound* of this description hardly need detailed exposition, and it is a good illustration of the earlier point that much of Seneca's prose needs to be read aloud to achieve its full effect. How else can we hear, for example, the welter of *s*'s Seneca uses to describe the Nile boiling and seething as it struggles through its rocky channel?

In contrast with the violent surge of that description are two passages which both portray the peace and serenity of the heavens. They are also different in being both closely linked to a protreptic theme. In *Letter* 90 Seneca pictures the glorious sight of the heavens as viewed in wonderment by primitive men.

Non inpendebant caelata laquearia, sed in aperto iacentis sidera superlabebantur et, insigne spectaculum noctium, mundus in praeceps agebatur, silentio tantum opus ducens. Tam interdiu illis quam nocte patebant prospectus huius pulcherrimae domus; libebat intueri signa ex media caeli parte vergentia, rursus ex occulto alia surgentia. (*Ep.* 90. 42)

In one of his most carefully written works Seneca consoles his mother on his own exile, and a clinching argument is that there are two supremely important things no exile can be deprived of: universal nature and his own virtue. No matter where we are sent on earth we can still look up to the heavens, marvel at celestial phenomena, and thus associate with the divine.

Undecumque ex aequo ad caelum erigitur acies, paribus intervallis omnia divina ab omnibus humanis distant. Proinde, dum oculi mei ab illo spectaculo cuius insatiabiles sunt non abducantur, dum mihi solem lunamque intueri liceat, dum ceteris inhaerere sideribus, dum ortus eorum occasusque et intervalla et causas investigare vel ocius meandi vel tardius, dum spectare tot per noctem stellas micantis et alias immobiles, alias non in magnum spatium exeuntis sed intra suum se circumagentis vestigium, quasdam subito erumpentis, quasdam igne fuso praestringentis aciem, quasi decidant, vel longo tractu cum luce multa praetervolantis, dum cum his sim et caelestibus, qua homini fas est, inmiscear, dum animum ad cognatarum rerum conspectum tendentem in sublimi semper habeam, quantum refert mea quid calcem? (*Helv.* 8. 5–6)

We do not know whether Seneca's words soothed Helvia's grief, but this and the previous passage show that he could deploy with great skill other styles than his more familiar effects of staccato epigram, antithesis, and hammer-blow repetition.

Other similar passages that could be quoted to illustrate the expansive or descriptive style are *Ad Marciam* 17. 2–4, a description of Syracuse which, like the last piece, also fits thematically into a *consolatio*; and *De Beneficiis* 4. 5–6, on god's gifts to man. Again, both are linked with the lesson Seneca is putting over, and as with the previous passages we have looked at, something in the sequence of ideas triggers off a development of the argument which is expressed in a virtuoso section which Seneca obviously enjoyed writing as much as we should enjoy reading it.

It is commonplace to criticize Seneca's faults, and Macaulay's famous jibe[3] that reading him is like dining on nothing but anchovy sauce, though exaggerated, has enough truth to be taken seriously. Usually, recommending Seneca as an enjoyable writer is a case of preaching either to the converted or to the unconvertible, as readers react in extreme ways to him; but at least we should recognize the range of his art. We now know more about that because we know more about ancient rhetoric in general, and for this we owe a deep debt of gratitude to the work of the great scholar to whom this volume is dedicated.

[3] In a letter to Ellis of 30 May 1836: see G. O. Trevelyan's *Life and Letters of Lord Macaulay* (World's Classics edn.; Oxford, 1932), i. 414.

9

Burning the Brambles: Rhetoric and Ideology in Pliny, *Natural History* 18 (1–24)

MARY BEAGON

There has been a tendency for literary critics of the Elder Pliny to denigrate the frequent rhetorical flourishes in the *Natural History*: Pliny was trying, inexpertly, to brighten up his work in accordance with the increasingly rhetorical literary tendencies of his age; he was in effect haphazardly ransacking his own *Studiosus*, the training handbook for aspiring orators which Gellius tells us included a selection of clever sayings to use in speeches; the addition of rhetorical baubles to a shambolic collection of facts only exacerbated the work's undisciplined nature.[1]

More recent assessments have been more positive. Pliny can be seen to have grafted factual material on to a coherent ideological structure based on his concept of Nature. The rhetorical material, far from being irrelevant, is integral to this strong thematic structure, articulating the ideals of a crusading and committed individual. I have argued at length elsewhere for this view of the *Natural History* and in the present chapter will therefore take it for granted.[2]

It is perhaps necessary to make a distinction between the mechanics of Pliny's literary style and the ideas contained in the rhetorical passages. There is no way of avoiding the conclusion that Pliny's Latin is very often clumsy, convoluted, and almost impossible to translate. Thus far, his critics are correct to condemn him. Yet this need not mean that the thoughts expressed therein are worthless, even if the language in which they are couched makes them difficult to unravel.[3]

---

[1] Norden (1909), 314; Duff (1966), 307–9; Rose (1966), 347. *Studiosus*, Pliny, *Ep.* 3. 5. 5; Gellius 9. 16. 4 ff.

[2] Rhetoric: Wallace-Hadrill (1990), 80–1; Nature: Schilling (1978), 272–83; Sallmann (1986), 251–66; Beagon (1992).

[3] Note, however, the rather reluctant concession of D. J. Campbell (1936), 34: 'his best efforts have an almost Tacitean ring'.

If the thoughts themselves appear commonplace, the *Natural History*'s thematic coherence should persuade us to look again. For however 'commonplace' a particular sentiment, it will have a bearing on a specifically Plinian ideal. In short, Pliny's rhetoric is not an irrelevant indulgence but the positive choice of a rational mind committed to a clear basic scheme.

That scheme, as has been mentioned, is Nature; more precisely, it is a view coloured by the influence of Stoicism and of Roman moral ideology. Man is central to his view of nature: man's life in Nature, his relationship to the natural world, and his use and abuse of Nature and her products are the main strands of his thought.[4] Nature is divine (2. 27), and in celebrating her greatness Pliny perhaps sees himself as a lone figure repaying the debt owed to her by his ungrateful fellow men: 'I alone of Roman citizens have praised you in all your manifestations' (37. 205). More obviously, he sees his composition as a great benefit to mankind (pref. 15–16); a didactic work on a grand scale with no less a purpose than to indicate to man how to live in accordance with Nature. If the subject-matter and aims are of unparalleled scope, so too is the consequent literary achievement: no other writer has tackled the whole subject (pref. 14).

Rhetorical passages continually emphasize the size and importance of Pliny's undertaking. They enlarge upon his main ideas and explain the significance of his factual material, illustrating, for example, the *maiestas*, *varietas*, and *potestas* of *Natura* and her generosity to an ungrateful human race.[5] They are positioned at structurally significant points, frequently the beginnings and endings of individual books. Therefore, just as assigning Pliny's factual material to putative 'sources' is no longer the sole aim of Plinian studies, so too his rhetoric deserves more than purely linguistic or stylistic attention. It is now necessary to ask not merely what Pliny said and how, but also why he bothered. With these criteria in mind, then, I propose to examine one example of Pliny's rhetoric with stress not on its form alone, but primarily on the significance of that form. The text in question is the beginning of Book 18, the longest of the thirty-seven books of the *Natural History* and one which marks the middle point of the work (Book 1 being devoted to a lengthy index).

First, a text and translation of the passage in question. The text is

[4] Beagon (1992), 55–9.
[5] e.g. 2. 14–27, 154–7, 7. 7, 11. 1–4, 18. 1–5, 251–3, 266–7, 20. 1, 21. 1, 22. 1, 25. 1–3, 27. 1–9.

that of the Budé edition (Le Bonniec, 1972), except in two places where the Teubner edition of 1892 (Mayhoff) is used.

(1) Sequitur natura frugum hortorumque ac florum quaeque alia praeter arbores aut frutices benigna tellure proveniunt, vel per se tantum herbarum inmensa contemplatione, si quis aestimet varietatem, numerum, flores, odores coloresque et sucos ac vires earum, quas salutis aut voluptatis hominum gratia gignit. Qua in parte primum omnium patrocinari terrae et adesse cunctorum parenti iuvat, quamquam inter initia operis defensae. (2) Quoniam tamen ipsa materia accedit intus ad reputationem eiusdem parientis et noxia, nostris eam criminibus urguemus nostramque culpam illi inputamus. Genuit venena, sed quis invenit illa praeter hominem? Cavere ac refugere alitibus ferisque satis est. Atque cum arbore exacuant limentque cornua elephanti et uri, saxo rhinocerotes, utroque apri dentium sicas, sciantque ad nocendum praeparare se animalia, quod tamen eorum excepto homine tela sua venenis tinguit? (3) Nos et sagittas unguimus ac ferro ipsi nocentius aliquid damus, nos et flumina inficimus et rerum naturae elementa, ipsum quoque quo vivitur in perniciem vertimus. Neque est ut putemus ignorari ea ab animalibus; quae praepararent contra serpentium dimicationes, quae post proelium ad medendum excogitarent, indicavimus. Nec ab ullo praeter hominem veneno pugnatur alieno. (4) Fateamur ergo culpam ne iis quidem quae nascuntur contenti; etenim quanto plura eorum genera humana manu fiunt! Quid? non et homines[a] quidem ut venena nascuntur? Atra ceu serpentium lingua vibrat tabesque animi contacta adurit culpantium omnia ac dirarum alitum modo tenebris quoque suis et ipsarum noctium quieti invidentium gemitu, quae sola vox eorum est, ut inauspicatarum animantium vice obvii quoque vetent agere aut prodesse vitae. Nec ullum aliud abominati spiritus praemium novere quam odisse omnia. (5) Verum et in hoc eadem naturae maiestas: quanto plures bonos genuit ut fruges! quanto fertilior in his quae iuvant aluntque! Quorum aestimatione et gaudio nos quoque, relictis exustioni suae istis hominum rubis, pergemus excolere vitam, eoque constantius quo operae nobis maior quam famae gratia expetitur. Quippe sermo circa rura est agrestisque usus, sed quibus vita constet[b] honosque apud priscos maximus fuerit.

[a] hominis *codd.*: -nes *vett. edd.*, *Mayhoff*.
[b] stet *Le Bonniec*: vita constet *Codex Toletanus, edd.*

(My next topic is the nature of cereals, of gardens and flowers and the other products of beneficent earth, with the exception of trees and shrubs [*described in the previous five books, 12–1* 7]; herbaceous plants alone offering a limitless field of study if one considers their variety, number, flowers, scents, colours, and the juices and properties of those plants which earth produces for the well-being or pleasure of mankind. And in this section, it is my pleasure first of all to plead earth's cause and to give aid to the mother of all creation, although I have already defended her at the beginning of my work. Since, however, our subject itself brings us to consider her also as the producer of poisons, they are our own crimes with which we charge her and our own faults which we impute to her. She has produced poisons, but who discovered them other than man? It is enough for the birds and beasts merely to avoid and shun them. And although the elephant and wild ox sharpen and whet their horns on a tree, the rhinoceros on a stone, and the boar files the tips of his tusks on tree and stone alike, and even animals know how to prepare themselves to wound; yet which of them besides man also dips its weapons in poison? But we men even poison our arrows, and we make destructive iron yet more destructive; we dye even the rivers and the elements of nature, and turn the very breath of life into a pestilence. Nor is there reason to think that animals do not know about these things. I have previously described the preparations that they make to guard themselves in fights with snakes and the medicines they have devised for healing after the battle. Nor does any animal other than man fight with borrowed poison. Therefore let us confess our guilt, who are not content even with natural poisons; so much more numerous are the varieties made by human hands! Why, are not even men themselves sometimes born poisonous? Their tongue flickers, black like the serpent's, and the corruption of their mind scorches what it touches; they malign all things and, like birds of evil omen, curse even the darkness that is their own element and the quiet of the night itself with their moaning, the only sound they utter; so that, like animals of ill omen, when they so much as cross our path they forbid us any activity useful to life. And they know no other reward for their hateful vitality than to hate all things. Yet in this instance also Nature's greatness remains the same as ever; how many more good men has she produced as her harvest! How much more fertile is she in products which aid and nourish! I too, then, will continue to enrich life with the value I place on these things and the joy I derive from them, abandoning those human brambles to their bonfire; and I will continue all the more resolutely because I derive greater reward from industry than I do from renown. My subject is indeed the countryside and rural practices, but it is on these things that life is based and the greatest honour was bestowed by our ancestors.)

Paragraphs 6–24 then describe in detail how agriculture underpinned all aspects of life and was consequently an occupation of the greatest distinction in earlier days.

The length of this introduction is remarkable. The other individual books of the *Natural History* have on average 7–10 introductory paragraphs. One obvious reason for the discrepancy is the length of Book 18. At 365 paragraphs, it is twice as long as most of the other books. More significant, however, is the importance of its position in the work as a whole. Book 18 is the half-way point of the *Natural History*, a suitable place for a reiteration of intent. Pliny specifically refers back to the first book proper of the *Natural History*, Book 2, when he remarks that he is going to undertake again the task of defending Earth which he had already performed *inter initia operis* (2. 154–7). Earth plays a vital part in Pliny's 'man in nature' theme as she is the one area of Nature which is always *benigna*, *mitis*, *indulgens* towards the human race (2. 155).

A key element of Pliny's main theme thus receives a timely reworking. So too does Pliny's mission in writing up that theme. In para. 5, he insists, as he had in the main preface to the *Natural History* (pref. 16), that his work, although rustic (and therefore in some opinions lowly, cf. 9. 59), is in fact of greatest value to 'life', the intrinsic value of his labours being a reward in itself. Critics are mentioned, as they were in pref. 28, but as a tiny minority among the products of Nature—poisons or brambles. They may be confidently swept aside by an author describing the benefits of Nature, the vast majority of her products, and thus 'cultivating' (*excolere*) rather than corrupting life (5).

The actual subject-matter of Book 18 itself also gives its introduction a particular importance. Agriculture is an area of man's 'life in nature' where his interaction with Nature is at its most intimate. Thus it is a crucial element in Pliny's thematic structure. Its importance is given an extra dimension by the Roman ideology of the soil[6] which affects Pliny and indeed all Roman writers who touch on this topic. There is all the more reason for Pliny to eulogize Earth and reiterate his intention of aiding this most profitable of relationships between man and Nature. Moreover, after the initial five paragraphs on general themes, a further nineteen follow, devoted to an introductory essay specifically on agriculture.

Another reason for such a substantial introduction may have been that Pliny felt particularly self-conscious as a writer in the context of agriculture. The existence of a practical handbook on this subject by his contemporary Columella may have generated a certain amount of competition. Comments in the *Natural History* suggest attempts to improve on or outdo the latter author.[7]

It was suggested above that the subject, holding as it did a central place in moral ideology, was a highly charged one for any Roman writer. Comments a little further on in the *Natural History* suggest

[6] Farming an honourable occupation, ensuring sturdy, virtuous, responsible fighters and citizens: Cic. *Off.* 1. 42. 150–1; Cato, *De Agri.* pref.; Varro, *RR*, esp. 2 pref. 3; Virgil, *G.* 2. 458–74; 513–42; Colum. *RR*, esp. 1 pref. 12–17. cf. Beagon (1992), 161–4.

[7] Beagon (1992), 173–5.

that Pliny felt particularly conscious of his role in a revered literary tradition. In 18. 22–4 he claims that the honourable nature of agriculture is shown by its distinguished literary tradition, kings and generals having written on the subject. He also takes particular care to make a general acknowledgement of his sources in 18. 23, but singles out Varro for special mention. A number of sayings which he has borrowed from Cato (18. 26) are also specifically attributed to their author. Acknowledgement of indebtedness to specified authors occurs sporadically if at all in ancient writings. Pliny himself is not unusual in having a rather thin scattering of such references in the main part of the *Natural History*. More common, particularly in the prefaces of prose works, was a tendency to name or enumerate a quantity of writers to show off the author's erudition.[8] Varro (*RR* 1 pref. 8–11) has a formidable list of names and Pliny himself boasts of the 20,000 facts he has gleaned from 2,000 volumes (pref. 17). Some authors, it is true, voice a respect for and debt to their predecessors, as does Cicero for example in *De Orat.* 1. 22. Yet, when the subject of indebtedness is enlarged upon at any length, as in Vitruvius 7 pref. 1–15, there is an air of rather self-conscious virtue, as if the writer was being rather more scrupulous than was normally thought necessary. We may compare Pliny's similarly pious tone when pointing out with evident pride his index of sources (pref. 20–3).

Finally, Book 18's topic, agriculture, offers particular opportunities for rhetorical fireworks. A device by which the writer of a practical treatise might capture the reader's sympathy was to set his subject's lack of literary polish against its actual worth. We find Vitruvius suggesting that an elaborate style would not be suitable in a technical manual for practical use (5 pref. 1–3), Pomponius Mela that his subject would not lend itself to the grand treatment.[9] It is agriculture, being quite literally down to earth, yet holding such an elevated place in moral ideology, which offers the greatest scope for rhetorical play on this theme. Pliny has already done this specifically in his main preface. There, Nature and the rustic, uncouth language often needed to describe her are set in contrast to those subjects such as history, war, and politics which are elevated and dignified according to the conventions of literary criticism (pref. 12–14, cf. 20). Further on, Titus is asked to accept this humble literary offering as if it were a rustic sacrifice of milk and salted meal (pref. 11). In fact, the apparently

---

[8] Janson (1964), 97. cf. also Vitruvius 7 pref. 11–7.
[9] Janson (1964), 99–100.

humble offering was one of Rome's most ancient religious rites and sprang from her agricultural roots—as Pliny relates in 18. 7. The same paradox underlies the literary apologia in 18. 1–5, though it is only specifically brought out in the concluding lines; 'quippe sermo circa rura est ... sed quibus vita constet, honos apud priscos maximus fuerit.' That sentence, as we have seen, acts as spring-board to a detailed defence of agriculture's importance. The agricultural subject-matter of Book 18, then, makes it a particularly appropriate context for a literary defence of Pliny's mission as a whole.

It is also worth pointing to the frequent use of words drawn from agriculture in the context of literary production and criticism. Some are predictable. We take for granted, for instance, the idea of a writer's 'flourishing' talent and the finished product as the 'fruit' of his labours. Thus, Vitruvius describes the writers whom he admires for their usefulness: 'praecepta ... cotidiana perpetuis industriis *culta* ... recentes et *floridos* edunt *fructus*' (9 pref. 2). They live on in their works, 'sententiae ... vetustate florentes' (9 pref. 17). *Florens* and *floridus* frequently appear in critiques of orators and their styles.[10] Horace's depreciation of his poetry to Augustus as 'sermones repentis per humum' (*Ep.* 2. 250–1) derives from conventional descriptions of a 'plain style' as being down to earth rather than lofty.[11] But when the subject of the literary work actually is the soil and the fruits of the soil a new dimension is added and even greater scope is offered for play with transferred vocabulary. Pliny rises enthusiastically to the challenge at the beginning of Book 18. Critics are snakes and brambles opposing his mission 'to cultivate life'. These and others will be discussed in due course.

The unusual length of Book 18's introduction invites consideration not only of its placement within the *Natural History* but also of its form. At twenty-four paragraphs long, it is, perhaps, closer in scale to Pliny's main preface (33 paras.) than to the introductory remarks of the other individual books. It is more consciously and systematically related to the overall aims and ideas of the *Natural History*, especially in the first five paragraphs, than are the introductions to the other books. The latter have general remarks on Nature but these are more narrowly related to the topic about to be discussed. A similar pattern, of less elaborate and lengthy introductions to the subsequent books, is

---

[10] Cic. *Brut.* 285; Quint. *Inst.* 2. 5. 18.
[11] See Brink (1982), 254. Being down to earth stylistically is also safe, cf. Brink (1971), 112; security is a prime feature of Pliny's *Terra* (2. 155).

the norm for the other extant agricultural handbooks in more than one volume.[12] In one sense, the beginning of Book 18 might be seen as consisting of two prefaces. Paragraphs 6–24 are more akin to the 'specific' introductions of the other books, introducing the actual topic of the book. This passage is, of course, linked to the first five paragraphs as an elaboration of the latter's concluding assertion of the importance of apparently lowly subject-matter. Those first five paragraphs, on the other hand, form a brief reiteration of the *Natural History*'s overall theme, touching on many of the ideas in the main preface and on key passages elsewhere.

In the latter part of this paper I propose to examine the structure and content of this general mini-preface, 18. 1–5, in more detail. We shall see how Pliny, adopting a conscious artistry, draws together important ideas scattered throughout the *Natural History* and presents them as a coherent case for his work to the reader.

There were, as we saw, two main features of these paragraphs: the reiteration of Pliny's main theme, Nature; and of his intention that, by writing the *Natural History*, he should 'be of benefit to life', that is, aid his fellow men to live in accordance with Nature. The passage is wrought so as to make the second idea emerge ingeniously from the first. The initial stress on the beneficence of Earth mirrors the tone of the earlier defence of *Terra* in Book 2. It stresses the quality which exonerates her from malice in the production of poisons, a point which Pliny was also anxious to make in Book 2. There he suggests Nature had intended poisons as a gift to man to ensure a peaceful suicide if necessary (156). Earth was depicted as the ultimately selfless parent, giving herself uncomplainingly to her greedy, thoughtless offspring. In Book 18. 1 Pliny's defence is once more of Earth as *cunctorum parens*. The stress in the same passage on her *varietas* picks up a point frequently made in the *Natural History* to extol the greatness of nature.[13] Here, it also helps to explain why poisons crop up at all. The use of *herba* in particular as an example of this *varietas* is important. Their medicinal function occupies no less than six books (22–7) of the *Natural History* exclusively, and several more partially. They are, for

---

[12] Columella, *RR* 19, is an exception: the author attempts to complement the *Georgics* by writing on gardening in verse and therefore provides a more self-consciously elaborate preface. Of the other technical writers, Celsus' prefaces to subsequent books are confined to statements of the topic to follow, rarely exceeding a paragraph in length. Vitruvius, however, who has only a short main prefatory letter to Augustus, does provide rather longer and more varied subsequent prefaces.

[13] *Varietas*: e.g. 9. 102; 11. 123; 21. 1.

Pliny, Nature's ultimate 'aid' to the human race[14] and he reflects this here when he says that Earth produces them '*salutis* aut voluptatis hominum gratia'. However, they also provide more potential poisons than any other part of the natural world and so their mention paves the way for the 'defence' idea.

The very fact that Pliny decides to renew his defence of Nature at this point is significant. It is, after all, uncalled for by the immediate subject-matter of Book 18: no poisons are mentioned there and none in fact for several more books after 18. It would therefore seem to have two purposes. There is the structural one already described, with important ideas from earlier in the work, such as the description of Earth, being revived. It is also, as we shall see, an ingenious way of ultimately working in a defence of his own mission which was outlined in the main preface. By the end of the passage, the defence of Earth has become a defence of the author and his work.

The defence device is to be found particularly in Roman dramatic prefaces and those of Terence can be seen to use much forensic language.[15] The passage in pref. 28, where Pliny talks directly of the critics of his earlier literary output, has normally been cited as a rough parallel in prose to the playwrights' practice. A closer look at both pref. 28 and 18. 1–5, however, suggests a more neatly personalized use of the device in a manner appropriate to the *Natural History*'s subject. In 18. 1 Earth is, as it were, on trial in a human lawcourt; 'patrocinari terrae et adesse cunctorum parenti iuvat, quamquam inter initia operis defensae'. However, it is her accusers who are found to be guilty: 'nostris eam criminibus urguemus nostramque culpam illi inputamus' and 'fateamur ergo culpam' (2). In contrast, the critics of Pliny's work in both passages are described not in human legal vocabulary but in terms drawn from the natural world. In pref. 28 this is done humorously. The publication of the critics' works is a longer process even than the gestation period of the elephant; so long that in fact they must have been having a series of miscarriages. In 18. 3–5 Pliny treats potential critics of his present work more seriously, as noxious natural products: poisons, with corrupted and corrupting minds and serpent tongues, and birds of evil omen whose appearances are intended to halt beneficial activities such as Pliny's writing.

Returning to the defence of Earth: Pliny proceeds to put the blame on man; it is his use of poisons, not nature's production of them, which

---

[14] 22. 1, 23. 1–2, 24. 1 and 4, 25. 25, 26. 10, 27. 3, 28. 2.
[15] Janson (1964), 97; Goldberg (1986), 31–60.

is at fault. In this misuse, man is unique. Animals know how to sharpen the horns and other weapons Nature has given them *ad nocendum*. Man alone adds poison to his weapons, just as he pollutes all other natural elements and can never resist 'improving' nature's gifts. Animals use their knowledge of poisons only in so far as they prepare antidotes and cures for wounds received when fighting poisonous animals such as snakes. This passage is structurally important. It takes Pliny from Earth's defence to his own via the suggestion that some men, whom the ensuing description suggests are critics of his work, do not just misuse poisons but are actually poisonous in themselves. The transition is helped by the mention of snakes. Pliny uses his own earlier description of these creatures' flickering black tongues (*HN* 11. 171) to enliven the portrait of such men.

Further important links are provided by reflections of Pliny's ideas on the relative strengths and weaknesses of men and animals. Animals have better natural defences than man, who is born naked and helpless (7. 2–5). However, man is uniquely endowed with the power of speech (11. 271) and with the power of rational thought.[16] It is his power of *ratio* which gives him the ability to pervert as well as to live in accordance with Nature. These ideas underlie Pliny's remarks in 18. 3 on animal weaponry and man's misguided attempts to improve both the weapons he makes for himself and other perfectly sufficient natural products. They also provide extra links in the train of thought from this passage to the description of the 'human' poisons. There is emphasis on these creatures' tongues and minds, the vehicles of man's unique speech and rationality. Here, however, both faculties have been poisoned. Thus, the weapons of the critics, tongues and minds, recall the poisoned arrowheads of man in 18. 3, and contrast with the uncorrupted weapons of the animals. Critics can, of course, be depicted as fighting with sharp teeth and nails. Horace fears the nails of a critic (*Ep.* 1. 19. 46) and is attacked by *invidia*'s tooth (*Sat.* 2. 1. 77). *Dens* indeed often operates figuratively, denoting envious carping.[17] To have their weapons poisoned

---

[16] Rational thought: Beagon (1992), 44–7, 60–8, 133–7, 156–7.

[17] Cic. *Balb.* 57, cf. Ovid, *Met.* 15. 235; Sen. *Con.* 10 pref. 8 (the 'teeth' of the notorious orator Labienus, see below, p. 130 and n. 25). In the case of the satirist, weapons are used by the writer as well as his critics. Worth comparing with Pliny on animal weaponry is Horace, *Sat.* 2. 1. 39, where the author's pen-dagger is likened to the purely defensive fangs and horns given respectively to the wolf and the bull by nature. With Pliny's black-tongued venomous snakes compare Horace's striking metaphor from nature to describe 'true' malice: *nigrae sucus lolliginis* (*Sat.* 1. 4. 100).

is a distinctively Plinian improvement in keeping with his general themes.

The human poisons are next compared to birds of evil omen (*dirarum alitum*, picked up by *inauspicatarum animantium* further on). Their groaning, the only sound they make, pollutes even the darkness which is their own element and the quiet of the night. The description has obvious echoes of Pliny's description of the ill-omened screech-owl in 10. 34–5, a bird of the night whose cry is not a song but a groan. The screech-owl is an evil omen when it leaves its natural darkness and wilderness and appears in daylight, in inhabited places. Pliny's human omens, however, pollute even their own natural environment, making them in a sense even more unnatural than their avian counterpart.

The impression that Pliny is referring to human critics of his own work emerges gradually as the passage unfolds. The fact that these creatures 'forbid activity or being of service to life' (*vetent agere aut prodesse vitae*) seems to be a clear reference to Pliny's own intentions in writing the *Natural History*.[18] This is confirmed in the next few lines where Pliny reasserts his belief in nature's overall goodness and pledges to continue his mission: '*pergemus excolere vitam*'.

As critics of Pliny's work, the negative behaviour of these ill-omened men is of obvious significance. Their *invidia* contrasts with the normal beneficence of Nature, epitomized in the tireless generosity of Earth. While it is a quality not entirely absent from the natural world (*HN* 6. 1; 8. 115), it is, in Pliny's optimistic scheme, rather anomalous; as are manifestations of ill-omened animals. *Invidia* is also, of course, familiar from the descriptions of critics in other authors.[19] Pliny's development of an analogy drawn from his own subject-matter, the natural world, once again has the stamp of individuality and relevance to his particular case. Their only cry is a moan which pollutes their own element. Pliny thus describes vividly the destructive sound of their literary 'voice' and the negative effect it has within the otherwise creative literary sphere. Their behaviour is a direct negation of his own; he renders service to 'life'; they try to prevent any such activity. For Pliny, this active service is its own reward ('*operae nobis maior quam famae gratia expetitur*'); his critics, however, get a kick only out of hating everything ('*nec ullum aliud*

---

[18] Importance of helping man: pref. 16, 2. 18. See Citroni Marchetti (1977), 124–48, and now her book (1992).

[19] e.g. Hor. *Sat.* 2. 1. 77, Cic. *ND* 1. 5 and φθόνος in Call. *H.* 2. 105–11. With Pliny's poisonous, nocturnal critics, compare Ovid's venom-drooling, sleepless *Invidia*, *Met.* 2. 760ff. cf. also refs. in n. 17.

abominati spiritus praemium novere quam odisse omnia').[20] The phrase *abominati spiritus* renders neatly the paradox of calling their negative behaviour 'activity', or indeed of calling their existence 'life'. Nothing could be further from the air of frenetic energy which Pliny so often imparts to his writings and their aim ('vita vigilia est', pref. 19, etc.).

Finally, Pliny reasserts the domination of the positive side of Nature; bad men, like other bad products, are an insignificant part of creation. The vast majority of her fruits aid and nurture (*iuvant . . . alunt*). The value and delight which he derives from them (quorum *aestimatione et gaudio* nos . . . pergemus excolere vitam . . .') in turn encourage Pliny to continue his own life-enriching project. His *aestimatio* of Nature's gifts is suggested both here (*quae iuvant*) and on frequent occasions elsewhere in the *Natural History* by reference to their *utilitas vitae*.[21] Agricultural products are, of course, Pliny's next topic and the final remarks of paragraph 5 enlarge upon their *aestimatio* in terms of their practical importance and the honour in which they have been held. They are also the gifts which most obviously fill the twin criteria mentioned here of aiding *and* nurturing.

The *gaudium* instilled by nature's gifts is also particularly suited to this context. In one sense, the delight these give is a reminder that there is a pleasurable as well as a purely useful side to Earth's bounty: compare paragraph 1 'flores . . . quas salutis aut *voluptatis* hominum gratia gignit [natura]'. While Pliny disapproved of many manifestations of luxury, he did not take this to the extremes of approving a strictly ascetic life-style. In another sense, *gaudium* has connotations of productivity and exuberant fertility.[22] This meaning, too, was no

---

[20] Who were these critics? Pliny pref. 28 suggests they were more than a conventional topos, by elaborating. Specific philosophical schools are named: Stoics, Peripatetics, and Epicureans, as well as the expected *grammatici*. See Holtz (1987) for the respective linguistic pretensions of the different schools. Citroni Marchetti (1992), 17–21 and 46–9, postulates friction with aloof intellectuals such as the so-called Stoic Opposition, who would look down on Pliny's utilitarian ideal and its links with the Flavian ethos. She links *odisse omnia* of the critics in 18. 5 with Pliny's disapproval of the *apatheia* affected by philosophers. This, he says, could lead to harsh inflexibility and even to Timon's 'hatred of the human race' (7. 79). Similarities with the doubts expressed by the 'more philosophical' Cicero (*Tusc.* 3. 31, 4. 25–7) and Seneca (*Tranq. An.* 15. 1; *De Ira* 2. 7–10) seem more striking than the differences Citroni Marchetti notes. She is surely right, however, to suggest an intended contrast in 18. 1–5 between the egotistical meanness of the critics and the selfless giving of mother Earth.

[21] *Utilitas*: see 11. 5 on the multitude of uses for trees, *sine quis vita degi non possit.* 37. 201 lists natural products—crops, wine, olive oil, flax, cloth, young cattle— *quo carere vita non debeat*; cf. also the plant refs. in n. 14.

[22] Virgil, *G.* 4. 120; Colum. *RR* 10. 257; Pliny, *HN* 3. 40, 19. 56; cf. Beagon (1992), 90. *Laetari*: *G.* 1. 1; Cato, *De Agri.* 6. 1. 2.

doubt intended by Pliny. He has just mentioned Nature's *fruges* and her great fertility in their production (*quanto fertilior . . .*). It is thus appropriate to his overall theme. It is also an apt expression in the immediate context of Book 18, for the abundant fertility of Nature is most obviously manifest for man in the life-sustaining crops of agriculture.

In reasserting Nature's overwhelming goodness, Pliny sweeps to one side his critics, who are referred to in another memorable and original analogy as 'brambles of the human race'. Once again, he draws on his subject, Nature, for material with which to stigmatize her opponents. Appropriately, the material is reject material, to be consigned to Nature's dustbin. The successive abortions of pref. 28 are nature's mistakes, the poisonous or ill-omened animals of 18. 3–4 natural anomalies. The brambles of the present comparison are typical of the weeds which must be cleared from the earth and burned before she can produce crops (cf. 18. 300).

The aptness of the brambles analogy cannot be overstressed. There are various points of reference between it and the text, but above all, it goes to the heart of Pliny's thinking on man's relationship to Nature. He admits to problems caused by man's misuse of Nature and by Nature's own dangerous side as exhibited in phenomena ranging from earthquakes to poisons. Yet the overall picture is of a positive and largely harmonious partnership. The fruits of the Earth keep man healthy and nourished. Man aids the relationship when he grafts new fruit trees (17. 58), tills the fields—and keeps earth clear of the brambles which would otherwise threaten to envelop her (17. 96).[23] It is no accident that Pliny picks upon the bramble as a paradigm of his enemies. As such, they are also the enemies of the philosophical ideal of man in nature; their negativism is set against the positivism which dominates Pliny's thought on the subject.

It should go without saying that the opposition between the bramble and the cultivation of Earth is also of specific significance for the immediate context of Book 18 with its agricultural subject-matter. It is, however, worth highlighting the striking use Pliny makes in this

---

[23] Man's misuse: e.g. 9. 139, 19. 54, 33. 1–4, 34. 138; cf. 2. 147. Savage nature: e.g. 2. 236, 4. 88, 6. 1. Harmonious relations prevail: 32. 41, 17. 58, 17. 96, 32. 1. Man's co-operation as a civilizer of nature (cf. 17. 96) is a Stoic concept most famously expressed by Cic. *ND* 2. 99, cf. Beagon (1992), 131. See Beagon, 'Nature and Views of her Landscapes in Pliny the Elder' (forthcoming) on the contrast between Pliny's optimistic interpretation of the man/nature relationship with regard to brambles and Lucretius' pessimism (a battle between *vis naturae* and *vis humana*, 5. 206–7).

passage and again a little later in Book 18 of *colere*. In the context of the bramble analogy, Pliny talks of abandoning the human brambles to their bonfire while he gets on with his task: 'nos ... excolere vitam'. Thus, he brings out a literal as well as a figurative sense of the contrast: his writings on man in nature are a 'cultivation of life' itself. Further on in Book 18 he puns on the meaning of *colo*—'to cultivate' but also 'to worship' the earth (18. 21). This, too, is relevant to the portrayal of Pliny's mission as *excolere vitam*. Nature in the *Natural History* is portrayed as divine and part of Pliny's task is to praise the greatness of her works. His postscript to the *Natural History* takes the form of an invocation to Nature as a deity (37. 205). As 'Nature is life' (pref. 13), there is doubtless a religious significance to *excolere* in the present passage.

Lastly, the aptness of the bramble as an analogy for a literary critic is clear. Their sharp thorns are an alternative portrayal of their destructive laceration of others' literary efforts, just as Horace gave them teeth and claws and Pliny poisonous bites. References in Pliny and other authors show them to be an invasive and tenacious weed which is continually threatening to take a stranglehold on cultivable ground.[24] Similarly, the critic can suffocate the shoots of another's literary creativity. Even the bonfire to which they, like other weeds, must be consigned if they are not to spring up again, has a literary parallel in the practice of burning writings which had fallen out of favour. This was, of course, more often than not for political reasons in the early Empire. According to Dio (56. 27), however, writings of a more generally derogatory and slanderous nature also suffered this fate under Augustus.[25] Burning also features in Vitruvius' anecdote about the Hellenistic critic Zoilus who attacked the work of Homer and was executed for parricide. One version of his fate had him thrown on a burning funeral pyre; fit punishment, so the context implies, for literary as well as filial savagery (Vitr. 7 pref. 7–8).

[24] Brambles: besides Lucretius (n. 23), cf. Virgil, *G.* 2. 411 and Colum. 11. 2. 19. As the epitome of intractable nature, they feature in another literary comparison. Quintilian 9. 4. 5, arguing for 'artistic' as opposed to 'natural' structure in rhetoric, suggests that art is not born fully grown but must be cultivated. Hence the vine is trained but the equally natural bramble is discarded.

[25] Political burning: most notoriously, the histories of Cremutius Cordus (Tac. *Ann.* 4. 34; cf. Tac. *Agr.* 2. 1, *Ann.* 6. 29, Sen. *Contr.* 10 pref. 3, Suet. *Tib.* 61. 3). Slander: Cassius Severus, Tac. *Ann.* 1. 72, 4. 21, Suet. *Calig.* 16; Labienus, Sen. *Contr.* 10 pref. 4 ff. These two latter may also have caused political discomfort: Labienus wrote history as well as speeches. Conversely, the sharpness of Cordus' tongue had gained him the personal enmity of Sejanus.

Pliny refers to the bonfire as *exustioni suae*. The possessive pronoun has parallels with the phrases used in paragraph 4 to describe the critics' violation by their utterances of their own element of night. They are negative to the point of being self-destructive: they are consumed by *invidia* (18. 4) and *odium* (18. 4), and so, perhaps, by a fire which is of 'their own' making. Against such self-destructiveness, we can once again set Pliny's description of his own selfless efforts, *excolere vitam*, which could, by analogy with the phrase *colere vitam*, 'live', mean 'live life to the full'.[26] Indeed, in the main preface of the *Natural History* Pliny says that, because he writes mainly at night, his work in effect adds hours to his life: 'pluribus horis vivimus' (pref. 18–19).

The selflessness of Pliny's mission is stressed at the conclusion of the brambles analogy. He will press on with his work, despite his critics, 'eoque constantius quo operae nobis maior quam famae gratia expetitur'. This is a sentiment closely parallel to that expressed in the main preface (16), where he takes Livy to task for composing his history *animi causa*, whereas in fact it would have been more praiseworthy to have composed *operis amore*. A special place belongs in learning to those 'qui difficultatibus victis utilitatem iuvandi praetulerunt gratiae placendi' (pref. 16).[27]

Paragraph 5 ends with a justification of subject-matter similar to that in the main preface. This time, however, he looks forward to a particular part of his work, the specifically 'rustic' material of Book 18 itself, rather than nature generally. Its apparent inelegance as a literary topic is outweighed by its importance as the very basis of life and by the honour traditionally assigned to it. The first thought, 'essential to life', of course, applies to Nature as a whole as well as to farming in particular as the field of the closest interaction between man and Nature. The second thought, however, *bonos apud priscos*, refers more specifically to farming and to that Roman ideology of the soil mentioned in the earlier part of this chapter. The thought thus leads naturally into the agricultural preface for Book 18 (paras. 6 ff.).

Detailed examination of 18. 1–5 should, I hope, have laid to rest the notion that Pliny's rhetorical prose is inept or disorganized. Modern critics, like their ancient counterparts, have been unfairly maligning him. The passage has been carefully crafted with reference

---

[26] *Colere vitam*: cf. *OLD* 'to live one's life (in a specified way)', e.g. Virgil, *G.* 2. 532, Cic. *Fam.* 3. 13. 2, *Rhet. Her.* 4. 20.

[27] Usefulness of work: Frontinus, *De Aqu.* 1. 1–2, Largus 1 pref. 1–4, Vitr. 9 pref. 1–18; Janson 98.

to arguments elsewhere in the *Natural History* and to the intentions outlined in the main preface. The result is an impassioned plea for the task he has in hand. In this respect, comparing it to the main preface is misleading. In the main preface, the burden of the work was still before the reader. There was a good deal of the sort of preliminary depreca-tion found in most literary prefaces. The epistolary form encouraged a light and modest touch. The reference to his literary critics was more humorous than barbed. Even there, however, the conventional apolo-gia was given a consciously individual touch. As has been rightly observed,[28] Pliny delights in the deliberate irony of the phrase *sterilis materia, rerum natura, hoc est vita* (pref. 13). Nothing could be less sterile than his picture of *fertilitas naturae*.

In the context of Book 18, however, the need for subtlety has passed. The reader is deeply involved in the work itself, having covered no less than seventeen books and with another seventeen to go. Polite pleasantries to an imperial dedicatee are no longer appropriate. Pliny now appeals directly to the reader. Critics are directly attacked without restraint. The tone is confident, even defiant. There is plenty of evidence for Nature's greatness in the *Natural History* to date; recalling this, the reader should approach Book 18, the heart of the work, and the whole of the second half, with confidence. The begin-ning of Book 18 is not so much an introduction as a strategically placed rallying cry.

[28] *Sterilis materia* irony: Howe (1985), 574; Wallace-Hadrill (1990), 82.

10

On the Sacking of Carthage and Corinth

NICHOLAS PURCELL

1. DESTROYING CITIES

One of the most potent ways of labelling enemies in the ancient rhetoric of war was identifying them by their city. Cities were among the most highly developed symbols of state identity, and Roman leaders, like the kings whom they came increasingly to imitate, had to form their plans and policies around cities and their various claims to status or power.

Founding, refounding, and major embellishment were normal ingredients in rulers' city-policy. Destruction was just as effective, directly proportional in its impact to the fame or beauty of what was destroyed. The ruination of cities is a statement in the same symbolic language as founding or beautifying them: a Dresden or a Dubrovnik attracts both the tourist and the Baedeker raid. In antiquity, the city embodied much more than art or cultural heritage. Attacking famous ancient cities in the manner of Alexander or Demetrius Poliorcetes was important to a conqueror's image. The style of the attack, the fate of the people, and the extent of the damage all had their resonances. Sacks were normal: wholesale destruction evoked Nineveh, Miletus, King Xerxes at Athens, and, above all, Troy.

At Carthage and Corinth in 146 BC the Romans made a carefully considered statement in the old symbolic language, one which went far beyond any recent experience of city war. Only the existence of that language can explain the extraordinary fact of Rome's formally extinguishing the independent civil existence and physical identity of two of the largest and most ancient cities of the Mediterranean world within a few months.

They were both very special cities. Their physical features, and relation to the geography of land and sea, continent and island (a principal defining characteristic of an ancient city) were highly distinctive. The art of fortification had improved on nature in both cases. At Carthage, the great third-century brick walls across the isthmus between the coastal lagoons, where the city was accessible from the mainland, were triple, and designed to house and display the machinery of war, being linked with barracks for 20,000 infantry, stables for 4,000 horses, and quarters for 300 elephants.[1] Corinth's fortifications (including Long Walls extending to the harbour of Lechaeum) combined with its location on the highly symbolic Isthmus to make it one of the 'fetters of Greece'.[2] The citadels—the impregnable Acrocorinth, or Byrsa at Carthage—symbolized the city's strength and independence (like the Capitolium at Rome). The harbours of both Corinth and Carthage were also proverbially fine. Size was another notable feature. Exaggeration made the circuit of Carthage an alleged 365 stades, a literally astronomical figure, also claimed for the walls of highly symbolic Babylon.[3] The size of Corinth made Mummius fear that it would, if spared, inevitably act as a focus for other cities, as if it was naturally high in the urban hierarchy, federal by predestination.[4] The manpower of Carthage, visible in its repeated recovery from military disaster, had been as marvellous as other aspects of the size of the metropolis.

Hi duos illos oculos orae maritimae effodierunt. The victims of the Romans of 146 formed a pair, and their nature was maritime.[5] In 149 Censorinus' ultimatum demanded that Carthage should be removed ten miles from the sea—precisely the minimum that Plato had recommended if a city was to avoid the contagion of sea-borne communications.[6] The Romans wished to render the city unmaritime, reversing the process which Herodotus identified for Athens in the fifth century, by which its people 'became *thalassioi*'.[7] Appian's Censorinus rejects the plea of the Carthaginian ambassadors for mercy in 149 with an eloquent statement of the ancient themes of the close tie between naval empire and water-borne trade, and of the instability of the sea's *tachyergia*, contrasting the Athenians' insecurity while they maintained their thalassocracy with their long subsequent peaceful exist-

---

[1] Pol. 38. 7. 3; Appian, *Lib.* 95; Lawrence (1979), 299–301; Lancel (1989).

[2] Lawrence (1979), 157.

[3] Strabo 17. 3. 14 (832), about double the correct figure. Carthage 'in circuitum viginti tria milia patens', had to be 'per partes capta', Livy, *Per.* 51. Appian, *Iber.* 15. 98, the size of Carthage and its empire, combined with its *eukairia* by land and sea, made the sack inevitable; cf. 95, the set-piece on Carthage's remarkable site.

[4] Dio fr. 72 = Zonaras 9. 31.

[5] Cic. *ND* 3. 91.

[6] Appian 73; Hoffmann (1960).

[7] Hdt. 7. 139.

ence; the great land-empires of the Assyrians or Persians were truly stable, and Rome itself is twelve miles from the sea.[8]

Censorinus' disingenuousness is extraordinary. Rome had been a contender for thalassocracy since the late fourth century, and the power that it had sought had been economic as well as purely naval. His own arguments show that the two were inseparable. The language in which the issues of economics were discussed was that of morals, and the constant preoccupation with the nature and spread of *tryphe* and the ethical problems connected with it reveals a truth that is not explicit in the annals of political decision-making: Roman leaders were acutely aware of the economic geography of the Mediterranean in the second century BC. In claiming that Carthaginian sea-power was politically corrupting, they made plain its economic worth.

Roman policy had once before involved prohibiting the sea-coast to a defeated foe—the Capuans in 210 BC.[9] That coast was speedily adapted to Roman ends, with the establishment of *coloniae maritimae*, and before long, the economic exploitation that was to make the coasts of Italy famous. Fiscal innovation and new forms of exploitation of local resources characterized the Roman management of their newly won Spanish interests. The same period and places saw new fiscal practices on the part of those who managed the revenues of the *populus Romanus*. The new structures of revenue established at Carthage by their enemy Hannibal and the highly productive agriculture of Africa provided models.[10] These were also imitated by their ally Massinissa, whose opportunistic transformation of his domain had brought him to war with Carthage over such resources as the region Emporia.[11] And so, after 146 both city territories became *ager publicus*, 'insignia et infulae imperii' for Cicero (the symbolic ploughing of the site of Carthage was later explained as symbolizing the alienation of the city's *usus fructus*).[12] It was noted that commercial exchange between Italy and Africa, which had not been possible before, now commenced.[13] The agrarian lore of Mago was translated into Latin.[14]

[8] Appian, *Pun.* 86–9.

[9] Livy 26. 34. 9 'ne quis eorum propius mare quindecim milibus passuum agrum aedificiumve haberet'.

[10] Diod. 20. 8. 3–4; Pol. 1. 71. 1; Appian, *Pun.* 69. On Carthaginian prosperity, Wolff (1986).   [11] Rossetti (1960).

[12] *Lex agraria* of 111 BC, 81 and 89 (Carthage); 96 (Corinth). Strabo 8. 6. 23 (381); Cic. *Leg. Agr.* 1. 5–6; Pausanias 2. 2. 2; Zonaras 9. 31. 8. For the ploughing, Modestinus, *Dig.* 7. 4. 21.

[13] Fenestella fr. 9, 'nullo commercio inter Italos et Afros nisi post deletam Carthaginem coepto'.

[14] Rome's debt to Carthage: Kolendo (1970); Mago, Pliny, *HN* 18. 22, etc.

Censorinus' ultimatum also reflects a Thucydidean view of the *nautikos ochlos* that accompanied economic and naval power. Malign *otium*, bringing *luxuria, cupiditas, dissipatio*, destroyed Corinth and Carthage: 'they abandoned the practices of agriculture and arms out of desire for trade and sailing'.[15] Livy made Hannibal advise the Carthaginians on the choice that they had between softness and *otium* on the one hand, and military strength on the other.[16] Polybius gave parallel portraits of Hasdrubal and Critolaus as weak men but effective demagogues.[17] In both cities the populace was politically powerful, numerous, and hostile to Rome. It was the *banausoi* and *ergasteriakoi* that brought the last meeting of the Achaeans to disaster.[18] A similar view is found in second-century documents. A letter of Q. Fabius Maximus to Dyme, in particular, defined the disaster of Achaea as being a *synchysis* which has involved the planning of the most disastrous disturbance and damage for all the Greeks, with the raw materials of *asynallaxia* and *chreocopia*, and things alien to the freedom given to the commonalty of the Greeks and to Our Will.[19] 'Democratic' social unrest was incompatible with the terms on which Greece was to be privileged under Roman rule. This was presumably the spirit in which Mummius reformed the constitutions of the cities of the league.[20] Imitating fifth-century claims to restore Greek freedom, Flamininus had set himself up as the Liberator: now Romans could claim that the tyranny of certain sorts of mob was inimical to the kind of self-determination that would be guaranteed by subordination to Rome.

The prominence given to the desperation of the enemies of Rome wins our sympathy and attracts our allegiance against the Roman aggressor, but in antiquity such scenes of popular frenzy are more likely to have served to justify the mission of Rome in propagating stability in the face of social violence. And it was a nice exculpation to argue that Rome was only the agent in a historical process which had doomed these cities anyway. In general, in this period, the ethnicity of Rome's opponents mattered less than their social position. There is

[15] *RP* 2. 4. 7.　　　　[16] 33. 45. 7.　　　　[17] Pol. 38. 8. 7–15.

[18] Pol. 38. 12. 4–5, cf. Diod. 32. 26. 2–3. Strabo 8. 6. 23 (381–2); Crinagoras, *Anth. Pal.* 9. 284, disapproval of the social standing of Caesar's colonists. Mummius' care not to enslave non-Corinthians, Dio fr. 72 = Zonaras 9. 31. Justin 34. 2. 6 'urbs ipsa Corinthus diruitur: populus omnis sub hasta venditur ut hoc exemplo ceteris civitatibus omnibus metus novarum rerum incuteretur'.

[19] Sherk, *Roman Documents from the Greek East*, 43 = Sherk tr. 50; *ABSA* 40 (1939–40), 60–70; *Insc. Cret.* III. 4. 9.

[20] Paus. 7. 16. 9; cf. Pol. 39. 5 on the grant of *politeia* and *nomoi*.

more ideology and less bluff pragmatism in these actions than it has been usual to claim.[21]

The calculation of city-status also played an important part in the sieges and the destructions, and their aftermath. The hostilities at Carthage were dramatically connected with the marvellous harbours: the blocking of the culvert by the Romans to prevent supplies arriving and the digging, against all likelihood, of a new port. In the siege and its narratives the painful process by which the Romans displayed their mastery of even these fortifications was set out in detail: the emphasis on how strong and unique the city had been before magnified the Roman achievement. Wall countered wall, harbour works were built to render harbours useless, the Roman camp stood like a rival city before its opponent, bearing its own name and that of the family that had humbled Carthage before, Castra Cornelia.[22] The epic siege was matched by a specially horrible sack. The thaumatology of siege warfare is parasitical on the rhetoric of praising cities. Through their conquest of famous places the Romans displayed their mastery of the order of nature. The lesson of Harpagus, Alexander, and Demetrius learned by Scipio at Carthage was developed further by him at Numantia and reached its highest expression under Caesar.

Almost as if to point up the material damage, the inhabitants were not massacred, and their leaders treated with some consideration.[23] At Corinth the punishment of enslavement was restricted—remarkably, given Roman claims about the collective guilt of the Achaeans—to the inhabitants of the city itself. The triumph of Mummius was made singular, as is too rarely recognized, by the fact that the artistic loot of Corinth *replaced* the normal display of humiliated opponents. This was a victory over things. Aemilianus and Mummius carried out a peculiarly emphatic destruction, which focused particularly on the removal of the perimeter walls.[24] The systematic abolition of a great urban nucleus in the ancient world was not the work of a few hours of frenzy, but a difficult, slow, and labour-intensive activity.[25] The motive for

[21] Rostovtseff (1941), 739 subordinates the political changes to the need for pacification, order, and obedience to Rome. Briscoe (1967) also takes the pragmatic view, while Gruen (1976) advocates the still more extreme view that the Romans had no social policy whatsoever. [22] Appian 134.

[23] Hasdrubal was led in Scipio's triumph, but he and Bithias and other top Carthaginians lived out their lives in honoured custody in Italian cities: Eutrop. 4. 14. 2; Zonaras 9. 30, cf. Pol. 38. 8. 4. Mercy for nephew of Massinissa: Val. Max. 5. 1. 7.

[24] Orosius, *Adv. Pag.* 4. 23. 1–7 at 6 on reducing the *muralis lapis* to dust at Carthage, cf. ibid. 5. 2–7, for Corinth.

[25] Thus Ridley (1986), 143 n. 9.

embarking deliberately on two such expensive operations is to be sought in the rhetoric of war rather than in any practical considerations; the destructions have the closest of ties with the grandeur of the urban claims of the defeated cities. That was explicit in many of the gestures used by the Roman commanders, of which the Carthaginian curse is the most famous.

II. THE SYMMETRIES OF HISTORY

The cities were also distinguished by their age and their history. The richness of the symbolism of cities derived from the density of the written and oral tradition about their past and its glories as well as from their fabric. History itself had to be city-history.

Scipio Aemilianus was moved by the catastrophe of Carthage to quote Homer to Polybius, comparing the scene to the destruction of Troy.[26] For Polybius' Scipio history was a sequence of empires (we shall return to that point) and even Rome's future doubtful: but the precedents were perhaps more important. Carthage suffered the fate of Troy: the sack of Corinth fitted a sequence of earlier disasters, including the burning of Athens by Xerxes.[27] Was Mummius at all conscious of the theme, clearly attested for the first time in the *Aeneid*, that the sack of Corinth was the Roman revenge for the sack of Troy?[28]

Mythical and historical precedent magnified the greatness of the wars and of the generals. Scipio had during the war of Massinissa and Carthage a grandstand view of a fight between 110,000 men—such as, he would say in awed but immodest tones, only Zeus and Poseidon had had before, as they watched the Iliadic battles from Ida and Samothrace.[29] In weeping over his enemy he could be represented as following the example of Antigonus Gonatas over Pyrrhus.[30] But he was also imitating Achilles. His famous vision of the transcience of power is a clear bid to put Rome on the map of historical culture.

Chronology could also be used to magnify the significance of cities: this was the 666th year of the history of Carthage, and the 952nd of

[26] Polybius almost certainly recorded the event in his own history. Walbank, *Comm.* 722–5 is important on this famous question; also Scullard (1960), 59–74.

[27] Pol. 38. 1. Appian 132, Assyria, Media, Persia, and Macedon all cited as precedent.

[28] The theme also mentioned by the unfortunately undatable epigrammatist Polystratus, *Anth. Pal.* 7. 297.

[29] Appian 71, cf. Astin (1967), 248–9.   [30] Hornblower (1981), 104–6.

Corinth's.[31] Caesar seems to have been aware of the neat fact that it was precisely one century after the sacks that he refounded the two cities.[32] Livy also reckoned in *saecula*: its last year of existence had been the seven-hundredth year of the existence of Carthage, a point which Rome had comfortably passed, as Augustus' *ludi saeculares* in 17 BC had made clear.[33] Scipio's reflection on the fate of Rome's metropolis was appropriate in a year when the foundation of Rome was celebrated by the performance of *ludi saeculares* that had been postponed from 149. Myth was deployed to emphasize the great age of the two cities: the stories of the self-immolation of Hasdrubal's wife make Carthage's history end as it had begun, with a noble woman's pyre.[34] The antiquity of Carthage and the comparison with Rome can hardly have escaped even those of her enemies who were not familiar with the Punic literary tradition.[35]

The battles of Himera and Salamis, in which the Greeks fought off the alien threat from west and east respectively, had happened at precisely the same moment, according to Herodotus. The Greek conceptual division of the Mediterranean into two domains shaped the theme of the two options for world conquest, that of Dionysus or that of Heracles, as it appeared in the historiography of Alexander or of *condottieri* like Rome's enemy Pyrrhus. The Romans inherited a perspective of this kind, notably in their sensitivity about the union of foes in east and west, like the pact between Hannibal and Philip V.[36] Our pair of sacks must be seen in a similar context; the effect achieved by Scipio in one sphere could be seen as being reciprocated by Mummius in the other. The three triumphs over Carthage, Andriscus, and Corinth were seen at the time as being in a sense parallel. The parallelism of East and West in Caesar's refoundation of both cities is explicitly asserted by Plutarch.[37]

---

[31] Velleius 1. 12. 5–6.

[32] e.g. Diod. 32. 37.

[33] *Per.* 51 'Urbem expugnavit septingentesimo anno quam erat condita'. Appian 51: Hasdrubal Eriphus made the same point in 202.

[34] Pol. 38. 19. 7–10 has the opening of this scene, with her reproaches of Hasdrubal, but breaks off before the suicide, recounted at Appian 131. Cf. the dramatic fate of Diaeus the Achaean leader, who after Leucopetra returned home, set fire to it, killed his wife and threw her into the flames, and took poison: *Vir. ill.* 60. 2.

[35] Censorinus 17. 11: 'de quartorum ludorum saecularium anno triplex opinio est. Antias enim et Varro et Livius relatos esse prodiderunt [in 149]. at Piso Censorius et Cn. Gellius sed et Cassius Hemina qui illo tempore vivebat post annum factos tertium adfirmant'. *Periti Punicae* at Rome: Pliny, *HN* 18. 23.

[36] Appian 111, Carthaginian embassy to Andriscus; Athenaeus 5. 213e, Carthaginian survivors join Mithridates.

[37] Plut. *Caes.* 57, cf. Strabo 17. 3. 15 (833). Refoundation: Shaw (1981); Cristofori (1989).

The Romans themselves used their own religious procedures to signal the symbolic importance of the sacks, their mutual connection, and the permanence of their effects. The famous and controversial 'curse' with which they afflicted Carthage has become almost proverbial, attracting—interestingly enough—contamination from other cultures' ritual practice in sacking cities.[38] Macrobius quotes the invocation, and states that it was used at both Corinth and Carthage.[39] His text is closely related to the old Roman ritual of *evocatio*, in which the desired effect is that the gods of the community should have nothing more to do with it.[40] Here the curse seems to have been specially concerned with habitation, particularly in the two most important sections of the old city, Byrsa and Megara. The special desolation of Carthage became a backdrop for the hopelessness of the exile, of which the stock scene was the sojourn of Marius in a hut among the ruins.[41] The emptiness was also stressed by Cicero, for whom *religio* was one of the concerns of Aemilianus in leaving the site vacant, and Appian, who was interested in the impact on the subsequent history of Carthage, the attempt to refound the city by Gaius Gracchus, and the eventual successful plans of Caesar and Augustus, who succeeded in obliterating the sinister legacy of the grim past in refounding Carthage where Gaius Gracchus had failed, and represented themselves as rejecting the grotesquerie of the curse.[42]

Using a symbolic ploughing, the ritual of 146 reversed the founder's act, and converted city to countryside, making the place *meloboton*, as the Thebans had intended for Athens in 404.[43] The buildings were seen to be destroyed, and the removal of *moenia* and *tecta* through *religio*

---

[38] Ridley (1986) shows that the salt-sowing derives from the fate of Shechem (Judges 9: 45); Piccaluga (1988) (I owe this reference to the kindness of Nicholas Horsfall) blames Gregorovius.

[39] Macrobius, *Sat.* 3. 9. 10–1, from the *vetustissimus liber* of one Furius. Florus (1. 33. 5 'civitas . . . tuba praecinente deleta est') suggests a ritual element to the destruction at Corinth, in saying that it took place to the sound of the trumpet.

[40] On *evocatio*, Bassanoff (1947). For the view that Scipio, equating Capitoline Juno with Carthage's Tanit/Juno, had brought the cult to Rome, Serv. *Aen.* 12. 841 'constat bello Punico secundo exoratam Iunonem, tertio vere bello a Scipione sacris quibusdam etiam Romam translatam'. Cf. C. Gracchus' choice of the name Iunonia.

[41] Cf. the elegiac gloom of Romans about the ruins of Corinth, esp. Cic. *Fam.* 4. 5. 4. Diodorus 32. 36–7 finds the horror of Corinth worse than that of Carthage because there were some Greeks left to look at the ruins. See also Antipater of Sidon, *Anth. Pal.* 9. 151.

[42] Cic. *Leg. Agr.* 1. 2. 5; cf. 2. 51. Appian, *Pun.* 135–6. The vanquished enemy was restored, in a display of *clementia*; both cities were relabelled 'Concordia Iulia'; Weinstock (1971); Vittinghoff (1951), 82.

[43] Modestinus, *Dig.* 7. 4. 21; Pliny, *HN* 26. 19; Piccaluga (1988), 156–7.

had for Cicero the implication that the site would be left vacant for all time.[44] The people were removed, in this case through mass-enslavements, in a demonstration of power which the Romans had made their own in the course of the conquest of Italy, and that went back to the Persians and beyond.

The curses and the sacks must, therefore, be considered simultaneously: the thoroughgoing destruction carried with it some of the same symbolic force as the rituals involved in the consecration. The two are inseparable. Other cities reduced in war, though terribly damaged, might rise again; but in 146 it was considered essential that there should never again be a Corinth or a Carthage. So solemn a religious decision is incompatible with the view that the chronological juxtaposition of the two events was coincidental.

In all this the obliteration of the city was linked extremely closely to the understanding of what the city had previously been, to its urban identity. The Romans in 146 made similar statements through their disposition of the movable items, the spoils of their war. Both Scipio and Mummius, of course, embellished Rome: indeed both, significantly, spent their spoils on the Capitolium itself.[45] But the spoils policy was a good deal more complex and revealing than that.

Other spoils went to beautify the cities of Rome's dominion and commemorate the victory as widely as possible.[46] Scipio also arranged the return of many statues and offerings from Carthage to the communities from which they had originally been plundered.[47] The 'artworks' that a conquerer removed from subject cities were often also divine representations and therefore dangerous: removing them was a kind of *evocatio*, and their restoration made a powerful historical point about the dissolution of the dominion of Carthage.

The communities of Sicily were involved formally in the recognition and restitution of their property, which included cult-statues central to their religious identity, like the Artemis of Segesta, the Hermes of

[44] Cic. *Leg. Agr.* 1. 5, cf. 2. 51, 'de consilii sententia consecravit', suggesting that the decision was taken on the spot after discussion; with Appian 134, the *decemviri* decreed the destruction of anything that remained standing after the sack.

[45] Pliny, *HN* 33. 57.

[46] Scipio's generosity was commemorated at Marruvium, which had perhaps suffered depredations in the second Punic war; *ILLRP* 326 = *CIL* i². 625. The Hadrianic text is likely to be a restoration of the original. Libraries of Carthage given to the *reguli Africae* by the Senate, Pliny, *HN* 18. 22.

[47] Eutrop. *Brev.* 4. 12. 2 'spolia ibi inventa quae variarum civitatum excidiis Carthago collegerat et ornamenta urbium civitatibus Siciliae Italiae Africae reddidit quae sua recognoscebant'.

Tyndaris, and the Apollo of Acragas.[48] Rome's sack of Carthage reversed the damage done to Acragas by Himilco's sack in 406/5 BC: the spoils returned included the infamous bull of the tyrant Phalaris; for Cicero, Phalaris' *domestica crudelitas* was now outshone by the demonstration of Roman *mansuetudo*.[49] Cicero's allusion to the joyful rituals with which the statues had been welcomed home shows the historical sensibilities at work *at the time*. The cruel regime of Carthage was contrasted with the generous dominion of Rome: the rededication of the Apollo of Myron at Acragas was a *testimonium societatis*, and the divine spoils of this *evocatio* benefit not the capital but a wider commonalty—the *socii* of Rome. The statues became Scipio's *monumenta*.[50] Besides his invincibility, they commemorated his *aequitas* and *humanitas*—no bad thing for the sacker of the third city of the Mediterranean.[51]

Mummius likewise 'despoiled Corinth of statues and paintings, and filled the cities of Italy with them—taking nothing at all, however, for his own home'.[52] Inscriptions confirm these donations to towns in Italy, and even to the new provincial community of Italica in far-off Spain.[53] He can hardly not have been imitating Aemilianus.[54] Just as the redistribution of Carthaginian loot cemented *societas* in the West, moreover, so the Attalids who had provided signal help to Rome in the Achaean war took a share of the art of Corinth to adorn their newly embellished capital Pergamum.[55] Mummius also knew that it was his business to understand what the statues represented. The removal or reinstatement of monuments provided a good way of settling old scores, as we hear in the context of a statue of Philopoemen, whose fate was discussed formally in an interesting historical perspective by Mummius and the Commissioners.[56]

---

[48] Sicily, Livy, *Per.*; Cic. *2 Verr.* 2. 86–7; 5. 72–102, cf. Val. Max. 5. 1. 6. Plutarch also emphasizes recognition, *Mor.* 200b = *Reg. et Imp. Apophth., Scipio Aem.* 6.

[49] Diod. 13. 90; cf. 32. 25. Cic. *2 Verr.* 4.

[50] Cic. *2 Verr.* 4. 74, the base of the Artemis of Segesta displayed his generosity *grandibus litteris*.

[51] Cic. *2 Verr.* 2. 86–7.

[52] 'Corinthum signis tabulisque spoliavit, quibus cum totam replesset Italiam, in domum suam nihil contulit', *Vir. ill.* 60. 3.

[53] The Apollo of Placentia is a possible instance of his generosity; *CIL* ii. 1119 = *ILLRP* 331, the dedication at Italica; cf. *ILLRP* 327 (Trebula Mutuesca); 328 (Cures); 329 (Nursia); 330 (Parma).

[54] His victory *monumentum*, like Aemilianus', was a temple of Hercules: Festus 282L, Plut. *Mor.* 816c. On Mummius' temple of Hercules, *CIL* vi. 331 = *ILLRP* 122.

[55] Paus. 7. 16; 1 and 8.

[56] Pol. 39. 3; cf. Plut. *Philopoemen* 21.

Mummius acquired a reputation for philistinism. But there was more method in his behaviour. A name for *abstinentia* was no bad thing, but there was a more important point to be made too. Romans notoriously faced the problem of deciding how their own claims about themselves and their power in the world related to the cultural achievements of their predecessors. They also had to cope with not unreasonable accusations of greed. The anecdotal tradition about Mummius and his followers addressed both problems: it marked out a moral and cultural gradient. 'Playing the most abstinent of men'[57] Mummius, who took nothing at all for his own house, was *megalophron* rather than *philotechnos*.[58] 'Mummius the philistine' was another reassuring tradition. In the cities of Sicily, Aemilianus posed as a benevolent outside overlord, vouching for their rights and civic identity. Mummius was remembered as the first Roman, whether senator or private citizen, to make a formal dedication in a Greek sanctuary. His offerings from the spoils of Achaea were seen at Olympia by Pausanias.[59] For all his ignorance of the visual arts, he became a patron of the religious and cultural life of Greece: even the sacker of Corinth could present himself as an insider, a benefactor vindicating the true freedom of Greece.

Rome's actions in 146 were intended to make history, in the literal and deliberate sense, to insert Rome among the great powers of Mediterranean history.[60] To make this possible, Carthage had to be represented as an *aemula imperii*. This, drawing on the sense of the long hostilities, the vision of three struggles with Carthage, became the normal Roman view.[61] Cato's calls for the destruction of Carthage argued, to judge by Nasica's reply, that power can be won through the discomfiture of rivals. Nasica's own argument, 'the "rival keeps us in order" view', equally entails the recognition, implausible after 202, of Carthage as an equal.[62]

---

[57] Livy, *Per.* 52 'L. Mummius abstinentissimum virum egit'.

[58] Livy, *Per.* 52; Strabo 8. 23; Dio fr. 76; cf. *rudis Mummius*, Velleius 1. 13. 4. Libraries of Carthage, n. 46. Magnanimous Mummius shared his takings even with his aristocratic competitors, Strabo 8. 6. 23 (381).

[59] Paus. 5. 24. 4; cf. Guarducci (1938). Dedications at Olympia, Delphi, and the Isthmus, Walbank, *Comm.* 736. *Artes theatrales* first on show in Rome at his triumph, Tac. *Ann.* 14. 21; Pietilä-Castrén (1991).

[60] Appian 57–65, Carthage's was the second or third *hegemonia* on earth.

[61] Sall. *Cat.* 10. 1; Strabo 17. 3. 5 (832); Velleius 1. 12. 5 on *invidia imperii*, cf. 6 'hunc finem habuit Romani imperii Carthago aemula'. Appian 51, Carthage had once been Rome's *ampheriston* but was no longer.

[62] Diod. 35. 33, perhaps from Posidonius: Gelzer (1931). Already in Cato, *Rhod.* Appian 65: *ORF* 62–7. Calboli (1978), 137–41 argues that Rhodes was a less well-matched rival for Rome.

Representing the wars as a struggle for survival suggested that the eventual victory was justifiable as a working out of fate. Hasdrubal put extravagant trust in divine help; Scipio knew better and could afford to feel contempt for Hasdrubal's confidence.[63] It was obviously in Rome's interest to present the destructions as events in the millennial working out of Providence, and Roman decisions as interlocking with a matrix of divine retribution for wrongdoing or for simply having the bad luck to be exposed to corruption because of your maritime position. The images of the two cities in the sources have been created to make this argument more plausible.

The theme of rivals for empire is thus central to the decision-making of 150–146. Cicero in 63 BC, speaking of the prudent abolition of the civic identity of Capua after the Hannibalic war, made the point with great clarity:

Our ancestors decided that there were only three cities in all the lands that could sustain the burden and the reputation of a world-empire: Carthage, Corinth, and Capua.[64]

This profoundly historical view of the relations of Rome with its predecessors, and its sense of a sequence of world-rulers, also brings us back to the maritime nature of Carthage and Corinth. The sea was essential to the urban identity of both: integrally linked with the economic prosperity and manpower resources of the cities, it defined their place in the layout of the world and the geography of Empire that was so closely connected with it.

III. WHO SHAPED THE RHETORIC OF WAR?

These events were epoch-making for Greeks and Romans not by accident, but because they were intended to be.[65] The sophisticated choice of the targets and of their fates made statements about thalassocracy, political morality, and precedent which served to pattern Rome's dominion for a century. Who selected the complex set of bellicose images involved in the obliteration of Carthage and Corinth—the decision to act, the implementation, the aftermath, the representations?

---

[63] Pol. 38. 7. 9 and 11; 8. 1 for Scipio's contempt.

[64] *Leg. Agr.* 2. 87: Capua had been spared because it was close by and could be supervised. Cf. Appian on Carthage's *eukairia* (n. 3 above).

[65] Historical myths and outgrowths from the earlier sources on the subject, Dubuisson (1989) and Krings (1989).

Imperatores, imitating kings, staged pivotal moments of high drama and rhetoric in which their characters and virtues might be seen and their gestures or *obiter dicta* recorded as they determined the fates of peoples on behalf of Rome. It is the contribution that they thereby made to contemporary rhetoric that demands our attention rather than the attempt to reconstruct the unrecoverable temperaments beneath the outward show or to apportion the decision-making between them and the Senate. The same ideas, arguments, and associations were present in the rhetoric used by all, and that is clear from the tradition that attributes the decision in both cases to the Senate, even though ancient historians interested in individuals might have been expected to attribute these sacks to the commanders; and to do so would have helped exculpate the Roman state from responsibility for actions that were not regarded subsequently as wholly admirable.[66] The famous stand-off between Scipio Nasica Corculum and the aged Cato on the survival of Carthage actually served to stress the role of debate, persuasion, and collective responsibility.[67]

Historians lament that 'it is precisely the thinking of leading senators which is as usual the most elusive part of the whole history'.[68] In fact, the material usually dismissed as rhetorical embellishment actually offers a route towards some understanding of the way in which monstrous decisions were conceived and explained. The public pronouncements constituted 'a nice demonstration of the Will of Rome', a set of statements about the nature of their policy to the world at large.[69] Roman ratiocination was exhibited, and the sanctity of treaties and the honour of ambassadors were stressed to elevate the standing of all Rome's diplomatic dealings, and make Rome the arbiter of international behaviour, and the avenger of wrongdoing.[70] The rules of imperialism were being propounded. Rome was setting out a repertoire of instances of how they dealt with other people, and once the Carthaginians had come to instantiate treachery or the Corinthians insubordination, their punishment was inevitable.

Considerable blame attached to Rome as a result of these acts.[71] The tradition is noteworthy for the commonplaces of apology. These frequently sound half-hearted. An extreme case is Cicero's atrocious

---

[66] Contrast Scipio's later sack of Numantia, decreed without reference to higher authority: Appian, *Iber.* 15. 98, with Astin (1967), 153.

[67] Appian 69.   [68] Harris (1979), 240.

[69] Pol. 39. 5. 1; Fabius' letter to Dyme (n. 19) uses the same term.

[70] 'Corinthon ex s.c. diruit quod ibi legati Romani violati erant', cf. Pol. 39. 6.

[71] Appian 76, explicit on Rome's duplicity in 150–149.

nonchalance 'nollem Corinthum'.[72] But we should not be surprised. This is not the advancing of weak excuses *faute de mieux*. Logic and law are being reshaped to suit Rome. Rome is claiming the preposterous superiority of being allowed to advance systemic reasons for obliterating cities, and not needing to bother with convincing pragmatic rationales. The topoi of half-hearted shame bolster complacency. Posing as the arbiter of international behaviour entailed wrongdoing. The shocked recognition of the duplicity of Rome was part of the desired effect. Convincing reasons for the wars and the destructions would have given them a totally different rhetorical effect, and not the one that was wanted at the time. What was produced was no uneasy apologetic, but a radical and unprincipled propagandizing.

The escalation of deliberate violence in the second century reflected two new circumstances: the Romans began to build in a style worthy of their power, and to equip themselves with literature in their own tongue, and a historical tradition. Rome was now ready for comparison with rivals in the usual terms of city-rhetoric as outlined above. All it needed were exegetes to put the messages about. Those were found in the world of international exchanges of ideas, above all in embassy-oratory, philosophy, and historiography.

Polybius, with his well-known statement of the concern felt at Rome for Greek opinion, was one such publicist. Philosophers could also rationalize the suffering. The complicity of men like Clitomachus (a Carthaginian who moved to the Academy in Athens and comforted his former fellow citizens with the argument of Carneades that the Wise Man should not be upset by the capture of his city) with the Roman rhetorical project constitutes a more interesting and more repellent ethical problem for the historian than the swagger of Scipio, Censorinus, or Cato.[73]

In conclusion, I wish to draw attention to one instance in which this problem appears with particular clarity. In 155 BC the Athenians sent an embassy to Rome to ask for remission of a fine for damage done to the territory of their neighbour Oropus.[74] The envoys succeeded in this

---

[72] *Off.* 1. 35. Cf. also Pol. 38. 1. 5.

[73] See also Cic. *Tusc.* 3. 53–4, commenting on the extent to which the mass-enslaved of Rome's 2nd-cent. wars became resigned to their lot.

[74] Paus. 7. 11. 2–3, the principal source, excuses the Athenians on the grounds of financial desperation, omitting the wholesale expulsion of the Oropians (*Syll.* 675). The (enormous) fine was supposed to be proportional to the damage. Polybius (32. 11. 5) found the case *idion kai paralogon*, but his account does not survive: Walbank, *Comm.* ad loc. for what we know.

political aim, and in so doing impressed the Romans deeply with the efficacy of philosophy and rhetoric. The enthusiastic Hellenist A. Postumius Albinus, then *praetor urbanus*, joked dangerously with the visitors: he had learned that he was quite unqualified, on the Stoic view, compared with a genuine Sage, to govern even that non-city, Rome.[75] Carneades, one of the ambassadors, nervously passed the buck: that was actually the personal opinion of his colleague Diogenes of Babylon, the fifth Scholarch of the Stoa.

Now this is certainly true. We have a considerable fragment of Diogenes, including this passage:

[The statesman] is not only a good dialectician and grammarian and poet and orator, but also ... shares in the government of cities, and not only with those inhabiting Athens or Lacedaimon. For among the foolish there exists neither any city nor any law: but in the confederacy made up of gods and sages he is even correctly titled commander by land and by sea, quaestor and tax-collector.[76]

The latest interpreters of this text rightly see that the Romans were not hostile to this view, or to the philosophers who expressed it. But they are inclined to take reactions like Postumius' as academic, good-humoured, casual.[77] Diogenes probably did indeed hold a strong and subtle doctrine of the nature and rareness of true sages. He probably really did consider Rome and all its notables to be *aphrones* of the regular kind. It is just possible that the doctrine was not alluded to at all in the speech which he delivered justifying the Athenian brutality at Oropus. But it is hard to believe that Postumius was so stupid as to fail to link the new doctrine, however he heard it, with the Athenians' exculpation of their action: it would have been curiously embarrassing otherwise to involve the fifth Scholarch in excusing the *aphrosyne* of one set of fools to another.[78] But whatever the case that was made

[75] Gellius 6. 14. 8–10 = Pol. 33. 2; Cic. *Acad.* 2. 137 '"ego tibi, Carneade, praetor esse non videor, quia sapiens non sum, nec haec urbs, nec in ea civitas". tum ille "huic Stoico non videris".'

[76] *P. Hercul.* 1506, col. 8, translation by Obbink and Vander Waerdt (1991), modified.

[77] Obbink and Vander Waerdt (1991), 395 'the story generously portrays the Roman praetor, in his official capacity, as engaging in urbane philosophical banter (if not completely on top of the argument) in a foreign tongue with distinguished visiting intellectuals'. The story actually portrays the cynical glee with which a ruthless and highly intelligent imperial politician accepts complicity with a crawling subordinate community that has, unprovoked, done hundreds of talents of damage to a defenceless neighbour, recognizing that the argument lends unlimited philosophical and cultural cachet to the replication of the criminal behaviour on a universal scale.

[78] The explicit reference to Athens and Sparta as types of the non-foolish city strengthens this view.

about Oropus, and whatever purity of principle and consistency of philosophical mind characterized the inner Diogenes, to write those words in the years after Pydna was—at best—colossal folly.

Imagine our reaction to a contemporary philosopher who said to a Dictator 'good men are very rare, but when one is found, he may function as Führer, embodying the will of Party and People'. Even if he was certain that his interlocutor could never qualify as that good man, his failure to see that he was certain to be misunderstood would be criminal. No Roman could have read or heard Diogenes' words without at least the passing thought that it might be his to be Wise. Certainly similar claims became omnipresent in Roman thought over the next decades. Maybe Postumius misunderstood: it seems to me more likely that he fully appreciated the potency of the doctrines that the Athenian delegation and others like it rashly evoked for their own ends in front of the receptive Roman audience. What did Diogenes and the fortunate Athenians who escaped penalty for the fate of Oropus think when they heard what the generals by land and sea, their *tamiai* and *praktores*, had done to those cities of fools, Carthage and Corinth?

This chapter has presented a small selection of the ways in which people in antiquity drew on a set of ideas about cities, in talking about the destruction of Carthage and Corinth. Most of these ideas are in various ways 'rhetorical', and historians have therefore usually preferred to pass most of them by. Narratives derived only from the least 'rhetorical' material form a curious sterile, bleached picture of meaningless brutality, like the aggressions of chimpanzees. Philosophers and literary scholars take the tropes and themes to have been officially manumitted by their rhetorical nature from the slavery of historical analysis, and produce a bland, undemanding cultural portraiture, with the urgency and sense of controversy of features in an in-flight magazine.

The material should be divided, not into categories of more or less rhetorical, but according to the context of place or time in which it was used. The statements that were made about these events were rich and complex, and inseparable from the events and the agents of their effects. That does not free those who made them from the charges of cynicism or self-interest, but it presents the literary scholar, the philosopher, and the historian with raw material that demands their integrated attention: of the sort that Donald Russell has always given, and which we are all more than ever bound to give too.

II

Reflections on Ekphrasis in Ausonius and Prudentius

ANNA WILSON

Thybris ea fluvium, quam longa est, nocte tumentem
leniit, et tacita refluens ita substitit unda,
mitis ut in morem stagni placidaeque paludis
sterneret aequor aquis, remo ut luctamen abesset.
ergo iter inceptum celerant. rumore secundo   90
labitur uncta vadis abies, mirantur et undae,
miratur nemus insuetum fulgentia longe
scuta virum fluvio pictasque innare carinas.
olli remigio noctemque diemque fatigant
et longos superant flexus, variisque teguntur   95
arboribus, viridisque secant placido aequore silvas.
                              Virgil, *Aeneid* 8. 86–96

Tiber soothed its rising night-long flow,
Turned back, halting in its silent swell,
Gentle—as marsh or quiet swamp—
To level its water and to ease the oar.
And so they hasten on the journey now begun. Propitious sounds: 90
The well-pitched bark slips through the shallows; waves marvel—
And the grove—at the strangeness as the flash of shields
And the painted hulks glide on the river.
These men day and night at the oar strain, overcome
The twisting lengths; roofed over by ever-changing   95
Trees, cut through luxuriant woods on quiet water.

The controversy over Aeneas' Tiber journey is old. Was Virgil or was
he not, in the closing phrase, *viridisque secant placido aequore silvas*,[1]
describing a ship cutting through the reflections of trees on Tiber's

This piece is dedicated with affectionate gratitude to a kind and learned friend, in
memory of a seminar that we gave to undergraduates at St John's many years ago. I
would also like to thank the editors for their prompt and helpful comments.

[1] *Aen.* 8. 96.

water? Nineteenth- and twentieth-century commentators have tended to take the negative view, maintaining correctly that the words need mean only that the ship passes up the river between the woods.[2] That was not at all the late antique view: Servius declares in favour of reflected trees[3] and, as we shall see, it is likely that this would have been the response to the line of two fourth-century Latin poets. Certainly the words themselves are not decisive. However the description as a whole invites the image of reflection. The Tiber has calmed its waters; their surface is level;[4] river and grove wonder at the water's strange freight of glittering shields and coloured ships. Reflection might seem a very natural expression of that wonder. The conditions for reflection then, are all there implicitly. Whether or not Virgil intends us to take the final line overtly in that sense, there can be little doubt that such a scene as he describes would in practice have been mirrored in the water.

That poets and critics of the fourth century might well respond more imaginatively to these lines than recent scholars has a great deal to do with their understanding of the nature of ekphrasis as well as with their distinctive poetic style. The Greek progymnastic tradition on ekphrasis is far more extensive than that surviving from Latin rhetorical writers,[5] yet both alike base their prescription on the necessity for such clarity and vividness in the description that the subject-matter is virtually seen by the listener's or reader's eye, with ἐνάργεια (Latin *evidentia*) as the fundamental requirement.[6] It is exhaustive description that marks off ekphrasis from διήγημα or *narratio*, and this involves the precise and logical enumeration of individual aspects of the event or subject-matter, to build up rather than merely suggest a

---

[2] e.g. Heyne (Leipzig and London, 1830–41): 'nimis acute Servius et alii secant imagines nemorum quae in pelucida fluvii superficie apparebant', Henry, *Aeneidea* (London and Dublin, 1873–92), Page (London, 1951), Gransden (Cambridge, 1976), Fordyce (Oxford, 1977). Conington (London, 1875) is broadly sympathetic to the Servian view, but wonders if it may be too modern a concept.

[3] Serv. ad. loc: 'ostendit adeo perspicuam fuisse naturam fluminis, ut in eo apparerent imagines nemorum quas Troianae naves secabant.'

[4] 8. 87, 89.

[5] See, however, Fontaine's argument (1959), i. 326–8, that the Greek *progymnasmata* are reliable witnesses of Latin practice. This is accepted by M. Roberts (1989), 39 n. 6 who further argues (38–55) that the rhetorical theory of ekphrasis was crucial to late antique poetics. On the role of the Greek *progymnasmata* for ekphrasis in the Byzantine world, R. Webb (1992).

[6] For ἐνάργεια, Theon 11 (Spengel, ii. 119. 26 with σαφήνεια), Hermogenes 10 (Rabe, 22. 47), Aphthonius 12 (Spengel, ii. 46. 15–16); for *evidentia*, *Rhet. ad Her.* 4. 55. 68, Quint. 8. 3. 61–71, 9. 2. 40–4.

complete picture.[7] Michael Roberts, in presenting the methods of
ekphrasis as a stylistic key to much fourth-century poetry, has argued
well that this enumerative technique or *leptologia* relates to the frag-
mentation or miniaturization of the elements found in that poetry, and
that the metaphorical terminology of rhetorical theory, particularly
such strongly visual words as *flos*, *lumen*, *color*, is closely allied to the
brilliance and jewel-like patterning that he identifies as characteristic
of the descriptive writing of the period.[8]

In line with this, effects of light and colour appeal strongly to these
poets, and in this respect the description of light or images reflected in
water offers irresistible opportunities. The hymn of Prudentius on the
two churches of St Peter on the Vatican and of St Paul on the Via
Ostiensis[9] contains a description of the baptistery of St Peter, which
gradually narrows its focus from the river Tiber that separates the two
martyria to the water in the font within the baptistery, and in so doing
provides a good example of the type of organization of detail prescribed for ekphrasis:

> Dividit ossa duum Tybris sacer ex utraque ripa,
>   inter sacrata dum fluit sepulcra.
> Dextra Petrum regio tectis tenet aureis receptum
>   canens oliva, murmurans fluento;
> namque supercilio saxi liquor ortus excitavit   5
>   fontem perennem chrismatis feracem.
> Nunc pretiosa ruit per marmora lubricatque clivum,
>   donec virenti fluctuet colymbo.
> Interior tumuli pars est ubi lapsibus sonoris
>   stagnum nivali volvitur profundo.   10
> Omnicolor vitreas pictura superne tinguit undas,
>   musci relucent et virescit aurum
> cyaneusque latex umbram trahit inminentis ostri;
>   credas moveri fluctibus lacunar.
> Pastor oves alit ipse illic gelidi rigore fontis,   15
>   videt sitire quas fluenta Christi.
>   *Peristefanon* 12, *Passio Apostolorum* 29–44

(Holy Tiber parts their bones to either bank
   as it flows between their consecrated tombs.
The right ward holds Peter housed beneath golden roofs,

---

[7] Roberts (1989), 40–7.

[8] Roberts (1989), *passim*, but particularly with reference to *varietas* at a verbal level
in the Latin theorists, 45–65.

[9] On the cult of these two martyrs at Rome, Chadwick (1957), 31–52.

is white with olive, murmurs with the flow:
Water, risen from the rock's heights, has roused   5
   an everlasting healing spring.
It runs through precious marble now and smooths the slope
   to lap and eddy in the green font.
Inside the tomb there, ringing, falling,
   a pool swirls in icy depths.   10
Bright mosaic overhead stains crystal waters,
   moss reflects light and gold glows green,
Blue moisture lures the arching purple's shade:
   almost, the ceiling ripples with the tide.
The Shepherd nourishes with that freezing spring   15
   Sheep he sees thirsting for the streams of Christ.)

By contrast with Virgil, here the Tiber itself divides, instead of being
divided. Juxtapositions of colour contrasts are prominent throughout
and images of water are constantly interwoven with them: the gold of
the *martyrion*'s roof, the whitish grey of the olive grove, and the mur-
muring of the miraculous stream (3–6), the precious marble, white
perhaps, through which the water runs and the green mossy basin in
which it ends its journey down the hillside (7–8). The icy or snowy
(*nivali*) depths of the water inside the tomb (10) carry one last hint of
white before an explosion of colour and light as the water's surface
and the mosaics overhead respond to one another, merging and
exchanging their individual characteristics. The vivid change is for-
cibly signalled in line 11 by the two heavily contrasted adjectives,
omnicolor of the mosaic picture[10] and *vitreas* of the waters, and by the
verb *tinguit*, as the colour passes from the jewel-like mosaic to stain
the colourless but highly reflective water. Two powerful contrasts
follow, expressing a reciprocal exchange between the two environ-
ments. The green moss catches the light from the gold background of
the mosaic overhead, and the mosaic itself picks up the greenish tinge
of the moss (12). The imperial purple tones of the figures in the mosaic
are sucked down into the dark blue-black of the water's surface and in
response it is the water's nature rather than its colour that has its com-
plementary effect above as the mosaic seems to echo the shifting
surface beneath (13–14). This play of light between water and ceiling
may owe much to Virgil's simile of the motes of sun or moonlight
reflected dancing on a ceiling from the water in a pail.[11] If so Virgil's

[10] Roberts (1989), 66–121 draws interesting parallels between 4th-cent. mosaic work
and the encrusted, 'jewelled style' that he finds in the poetry.

[11] *Aen.* 8. 22–5.

light airiness has been replaced here by a sombre and ornate richness characteristic of Prudentius' age. In the final baptismal imagery of the shepherd watering the flock from the icy stream (15–16), the relationship between the water and the building that houses it has become so closely integrated that the two seem inseparable. Indeed the possibility that the mirrored mosaic did in fact depict Christ as shepherd surrounded by twelve apostolic sheep should be considered.

If Prudentius handles the effects of light reflected from water briefly yet with very rich colouring, Ausonius, in a long passage from his extended ekphrasis of the Moselle, focuses largely on a single colour, the green of the hillsides lining the river's banks and seen within its waters, and is chiefly interested in the deceptive nature of reflection, in appearances taken for reality. As elsewhere in the work, scene following upon scene matches the poetry's gradual passage down the Moselle. Since the river's beauty is his chief theme, Ausonius keeps his language and tone bright, and in this he accords with the requirement of the Greek rhetorical writers that in ekphrasis the *lexis* and exposition should match the nature of the subject-matter.[12] Yet if the bright tone is consistent, variety of mood is sought between successive scenes and sometimes within them. Thus at the end of an imaginary portrayal of Naiads, Satyrs, and Pans frolicking energetically in the river, Ausonius half-humorously invokes religious silence about their amorous behaviour[13] and turns to a tranquil theme that may be enjoyed without reserve:

> Illa fruenda palam species, cum glaucus opaco
> respondet colli fluvius, frondere videntur   190
> fluminei latices et palmite consitus amnis.
> quis color ille vadis, seras cum propulit umbras
> Hesperus et viridi perfundit monte Mosellam!
> tota natant crispis iuga motibus et tremit absens
> pampinus et vitreis vindemia turget in undis   195
> adnumerat virides derisus navita vites,
> navita caudiceo fluitans super aequora lembo

---

[12] Theon 11 (Spengel, ii. 119. 29–120. 2): τὸ δὲ ὅλον συνεξομοιοῦσθαι χρὴ τοῖς ὑποκειμένοις τὴν ἀπαγγελίαν, ὥστε εἰ μὲν εὐανθές τι εἴη τὸ δηλούμενον, εὐανθῆ καὶ τὴν φράσιν εἶναι· εἰ δὲ αὐχμηρὸν ἢ φοβερὸν ἢ ὁποῖον δή ποτε, μηδὲ τὰ τῆς ἑρμηνείας ἀπᾴδειν τῆς φύσεως αὐτῶν. Hermogenes 10 (Rabe, 23. 49–50): ἔτι μέντοι συνεξομοιοῦσθαι τὰ τῆς φράσεως ὀφείλει τοῖς πράγμασιν· ἂν ἀνθηρὸν τὸ πρᾶγμα, ἔστω καὶ ἡ λέξις τοιαύτη, ἂν αὐχμηρὸν τὸ πρᾶγμα, ἔστω καὶ ἡ λέξις παραπλησία.

[13] *Mos.* 169–88.

> per medium, qua sese amni confundit imago
> collis et umbrarum confinia conserit amnis.
>
> *Mos.* 189–99

> That sight's for outright pleasure: the bright river
> Answers the shady hill, the leaves unfold   190
> In running water; the stream looks set with vines.
> What colour in the shallows, when Hesperus has spread
> Slow shadows out, drowned the river in green heights!
> Hillsides float whole on the eddies, and—not truly there—
> A tendril quivers, grapes swell in waves of glass.   195
> A muddled boatman tallies his green vines
> And rocks on the waters in his bark-built boat
> Midstream, where the hills' image merges in the flow
> And the river knits close the shadows' boundaries.

Here stillness is all, and the undisturbed surface of the water, by contrast with the earlier splashings of the Naiads. The reflection of the
mountain in the river is expressed as one half of a dialogue (*respondet*).
The appearance (*videntur*, 190) of the water growing leaves and
planted with vines is more vivid than the real vines, as is the slowly
lengthening green shadow of the mountain that the evening star pours
onto the reflective surface. The verb *perfundit*, like the following
natant (194) turns the images of the solid realities almost as fluid as
the water where they float. Only in the adjective *absens* (195) of the
tendril and *derisus* (196) of the comically depicted boatman counting
his vines[14] does Ausonius admit to the fiction. For the rest, it is in the
mirroring water that the grapes swell and the vines are counted as the
stillness gives way to slight motion, and a single human being is quietly
admitted to the scene.

Line 200 shatters this quiet as the boys' skiffs come racing and
looping[15] to and fro across the water:

[14] The phraseology of 196, 'adnumerat virides derisus navita vites', is very close to
Pliny's description of ash and poplars reflected in the river Clitumnus in the ekphrasis of
Epp. 8. 8. 4: 'Ripae fraxino multa, multa populo vestiuntur, quas perspicuus amnis velut
mersas viridi imagine adnumerat', except that there it is the river itself that counts the
trees. There seems some probability that Ausonius may have been acquainted with this
letter. See also next note.

[15] Ausonius offers *et varios ineunt flexus* as the small boats twist to and fro at 202. He
may intend a light-hearted contrast with the determined effort of *Aen.* 8. 95: 'et longos
superant flexus'. Pliny also plays on the delights of boating on the Clitumnus for
pleasure, contrasting the effort of rowing upstream with the ease of floating downstream
when the river does all the work, and remarks 'Iucundum utrumque per iocum
ludumque fluitantibus, ut flexerint cursum, laborem otio otium labore variare' (*Epp.*
8. 8. 4).

Haec quoque quam dulces celebrant spectacula pompas,   200
remipedes medio certant cum flumine lembi
et varios *ineunt* flexus viridesque per oras
stringunt attonsis pubentia germina pratis!
puppibus et proris alacres gestire magistros
impubemque manum super amnica terga vagantem   205
dum spectat ⟨*viridis qua surgit ripa colonus,*
non sentit⟩[16] transire diem, sua seria ludo
posthabet; excludit veteres nova gratia curas.   (200–8)

The view offers lively games as well,   200
As the oared skiffs, mid-river, fight it out,
Cross and recross their circles; on green banks
Clip the young shoots of grass cropped short.
Excited masters leap on stern and prow,
And young crews range the river's back,   205
⟨*The farmer*⟩ views them ⟨*from the green bank's rise,*
Forgets⟩ day's passing, rates his business
Less than their game: new pleasure sets old cares aside.

The exuberance of the earlier description of the country deities
returns but this time in a picture of more innocent fun. The river had
linked the reflected shadows from the banks at line 199; now it is the
passage of the boys across its surface that connects them. Contrasting
with the innocence, slightly more serious ideas are introduced to mock
epic effect. The boys are the *magistri* of their tiny boats (204).[17] Their
games can turn the mind of the onlooker from his own *seria* (207).[18]
The game on the water is also a contest (*certant,* 201), which recalls
more grandiose mock sea battles, particularly the *naumachia* given by
Augustus after Actium,[19] and these in their turn recall real sea battles
that are far from harmless.

This idea is handled in a panel of three highly epic similes (208–
18)[20] dealing with such *naumachiae*, on an exaggerated scale to gently

[16] Böcking's supplement, exempli gratia.

[17] Important for the similes that follow is the fact that *lembi*, the word used for the
boy's boats at 201, can also be applied to the lighter and swifter types of warships. See
Green's commentary (Oxford, 1991), ad loc.

[18] The similarity of 207–8 to Virgil, *Eclogue* 7. 17, 'posthabui ... mea seria ludo' has
been remarked.

[19] Doreen Innes reminds me that at *Ep.* 1. 18. 61–4 Horace describes a mock *Actia
pugna*, in which the unfortunate Lollius and his brother may find themselves in leading
roles with *pueri* (here slaves rather than children) serving as crews, as one of the trials to
be expected in pleasing his patron.

[20] The picture of Liber striding across Vesuvius to watch these Cumaean games
(208–10) draws on Virgil's comparison of Aeneas to Apollo on Cynthus watching the
dancing choruses before his altar, *Aen.* 4. 143–9.

comic effect. Within these, *seria* are catered for by references to
Actium and to the engagements against Sextus Pompeius (211, 214–
15), but are undercut and largely forgotten in that the *ludi*, the celebratory mock battles, are the real point of the comparison. Venus
stages the Actian *naumachia* with cupids for sailors, and collisions do
no harm (211, 217). Given the space Ausonius allots both to the boys'
contest and to the similes of the *naumachia*, with its forceful associations with actual naval warfare, it should be recalled that battle
scenes are one of the prime subjects for ekphrasis in all the rhetorical
handbooks, and that both Hermogenes and Aphthonius include sea as
well as land battles in their lists.[21] Playfully Ausonius includes within
his larger ekphrasis of the river an elaborately contrived mock version
of one of the main school topics for ekphrasis, hence the elaborate
comparisons. Descriptions of great rivers as well as of battles both
belong among the themes of grandeur.[22] Ausonius subverts both by his
delicate and light-hearted treatment.

In the last of the three similes Ausonius brings back the theme of
reflection in order to apply it at much greater length to the boys on the
river:

> innocuos ratium pulsus pugnasque iocantes
> naumachiae Siculo quales spectante Peloro
> caeruleus viridi reparat sub imagine pontus:
> non aliam speciem petulantibus addit ephebis   220
> pubertasque amnis et picti rostra phaseli.
> hos Hyperionio cum sol perfuderit aestu,
> reddit nautales vitreo sub gurgite formas
> et redigit pandas inversi corporis umbras.
> utque agiles motus dextra laevaque frequentant   225
> et commutatis alternant pondera remis,
> unda refert alios simulacra umentia nautas.
> ipsa suo gaudet simulamine nautica pubes,
> fallaces fluvio mirata redire figuras.   (217–29)

> Or like the harmless shunts, the *naumachia*'s mock
> Warfare, with Sicily's Pelorus looking on,
> That the dark sea reshapes in green reflection,
> Such is the air that youth, the river,   220
> The painted boat-prows lend these frisking boys.
> The sun drenches them with Hyperion's scorching,
> Mirrors their boating shapes in glasslike swirl,

---

[21] Hermog. 10 (Rabe, 22. 47); Aphthon. 12, (Spengel, ii. 47. 1).
[22] Innes (1979), 167, 169.

Refracts skewed images turned upside down.
As right and left they whip their darting strokes,   225
And lay alternate weight, shifting the oars,
The wave paints wet portraits, doubles the seamen back.
The boys on the water laugh at their look-alikes,
Gawp at the lies the river offers them.

Where earlier the peaceful picture of the vineyards had been set in
the calm of evening,[23] these reflections are those of the sun in the
middle of the day (*Hyperionio . . . aestu*, 222), and the contrast is
emphasized by the use of the same verb *perfundere*. Other colours join
the green, *caeruleus* of the sea in the opening simile, and brilliant
colours are implicit in the phrase describing the skiffs on the river: *picti
rostra phaseli*.[24] Yet it is the nature of the reflections that interests the
poet. By contrast with the stress on the reality, however unreal, of the
reflected vines and mountains in the previous passage dealing with still
water,[25] the handling here is very different. This water moves, and
Ausonius pays far more attention here to the real boys and to their
swift boats (220–2, 225–6, 228).

The verbs are carefully matched. Five times the same prepositional
prefix is found, and the sense always involves some kind of repetition
or return: *reparat* (219), *reddit* (224), *redigit* (225), *refert* (227), *redire*
(229).[26] Such consistency helps to point up the increasingly ambiguous
nature of the reflected images, at once both true and false likenesses.
From the relatively straightforward *imagine* and *nautales . . . formas*
(219, 223), Ausonius moves to ideas of distortion in *pandas inversi
corporis umbras* (224). *Simulacra* (227) is ambiguous, in that it can be
used equally well of 'phantoms' as of 'likenesses', and is set here in
apposition to *alio nautas*, a phrase conveying difference as well as
similarity. The rare *simulamine* (228)[27] carries the notion of dis-
sembling still more obviously in its etymology and deception is made
explicit in *fallaces . . . figuras* (229). Similarity, the passage argues, is

[23] 192–3: *seras . . . Hesperus*.

[24] 221, perhaps one of several bows in the direction of Virgil's passage, in this case to
'pictasque innare carinas' (*Aen.* 8. 93). The boys' wonder at their reflections (229
mirata) may also vary 'mirantur et undae, | miratur nemus' (*Aen.* 8. 91–2) as do the
flexus cut by their boats those of the Tiber itself in Virgil (8. 95). Likewise lines 225–6
describing the energetic strokes of the boys as they row may owe some of its inspiration
to the *Aeneid*'s *remigio . . . fatigant* (8. 94), most notably the decision to place *fre-
quentant* at the end of line 225.

[25] 189–90, 194–6.

[26] Contrast the very different effect of *respondet* at 190.

[27] Elsewhere only at Ovid, *Met.* 10. 727.

also difference, illusion, deception, and the point is fully articulated in the couplet that closes the entire episode:

> talis ad umbrarum *ludibria* nautica pubes
> *ambiguis* fruitur *veri falsique figuris*.

Firs, however, Ausonius balances his earlier sequence of epic 'battle' comparisons with a single fully developed simile.

> sic, ubi compositos ostentatura capillos   230
> (candentem late speculi explorantis honorem
> cum primum carae nutrix admovit alumnae)
> laeta ignorato fruitur virguncula ludo
> germanaeque putat formam spectare puellae:
> oscula fulgenti dat non referenda metallo   235
> aut fixas praetemptat acus aut frontis ad oram
> vibratos captat digitis extendere crines:
> talis ad umbrarum ludibria nautica pubes
> ambiguis fruitur veri falsique figuris.   (230–9)

> As, ready to show off her hair once combed   230
> (When the nurse first hands to a beloved charge
> The searching mirror's glint and grace),
> A young girl thrills, delights in a strange game,
> Thinks that she looks on her twin-sister's face:
> Kisses bright metal, answerless,   235
> Tests the firm pins, or at the forehead catches
> With finger-tip to smooth stray shining strands—
> So, as reflections mock, the boys afloat
> Play with deceptive images of true and false.

The quiet domestic scene[28] stands out against the earlier similes of *naumachia* and the flashing movement of the boys' boats. A static enclosed interior replaces the movement on the open river. The multiple points of contact between the simile and the surrounding text extend beyond the reflective nature of mirror and water, both of which are represented as having an active role in this exchange of images (*redire* (229), *explorantis* (231)). Initially the girl's delight in the game (*laeta . . . fruitur . . . ludo* (233)) echoes that of the boys (*gaudet* 228), yet the vocabulary of the final couplet about them (*ludibria, fruitur,* 238–9)) is also anticipated. In the second half of the simile the deception involved in the image is uppermost and this too is picked up in the

---

[28] See Green (Oxford, 1991), ad loc, as well as for the literary background to the simile, which he dismisses out of hand as trite. He is surely correct in suggesting a link with artistic representations of such scenes.

closing phrases (*ad umbrarum ludibria, ambiguis ... veri falsique figuris*, 238–9). The introduction of the nurse as a second character both recalls and contrasts with the onlooker of lines 206–8. Yet the boys' delight in the pretence of their own reflection (*suo simulamine* (228)) whilst the girl believes that the image belongs to another, albeit to an identical twin (*germanaeque ... puellae* (234)), one who is the same and yet other.[29] Naïveté is implied of both, but to different effect. The boys are not really deceived at all. Their fun lies in indulging the shifting shapes on the waters as part of their game. The young girl is portrayed at a moment of genuine and very intimate confusion, and the poet dwells playfully yet sympathetically on her response as she tries in vain to kiss what seems a second self, lovingly to secure and rearrange the stray curls that catch at the light. The distinction between the two images is highlighted as well as their similarities. As throughout the whole passage the deceptiveness in the mirrored reflection is what appeals to the poet's imagination. It may be worth asking ourselves yet again whether the far subtler and more restrained poet of the Augustan age was entirely immune to such an appeal.

[29] Cf. the *alios ... nautas* of line 227.

B
LATER GREEK LITERATURE

12

Sense of Place in the Orations of Dio Chrysostom

MICHAEL TRAPP

I

Sense of place is a quality the ancient epideictic orator was frequently called upon to display. Both the call and his response could take a number of different forms. He was, characteristically, a traveller who spoke to many different gatherings and in many communities other than his own. It was often highly important for him to convey a lively sense of his own appreciation of where he was and to whom he was speaking: an assurance to his audience that they had before them someone whose rich sense of their identity and worth qualified him to address their concerns, and to receive their close attention. This is most obviously true of civic encomia, in which community and place are directly addressed and praised.

At the same time, again in virtue of his role as traveller—the mask of Odysseus was constantly available for epideictic appropriation[1]—he could bring to his place of performance a knowledge and experience of other places and peoples, to be deployed both for the entertainment of his present audience, and for telling comparisons and contrasts with their own experience and self-image. There could also be a historical dimension: some of those other places available to him belonged to the honoured past, and were known to him in virtue not of his physical travels, but of his exploration of the classics of literature. In both cases, the orator had the opportunity to underline his own superior experience and authority even as he informed and entertained his audience.

Sensitivity to considerations such as these can, I believe, enrich our

I should like to offer my thanks to the editors, particularly Doreen Innes, for helpful comments on my first draft.

[1] See below, n. 7.

reading of a wide range of ancient texts, among them the orations of
Dio Chrysostom, to which one of Donald Russell's most recent works
is devoted.[2] Two of the three speeches in his edition lend themselves
particularly well to this kind of attention, as examples of the skilful use
of other places.

II

Oration 7, the *Euboicus*, is a sermon on the moral indifference of
wealth, delivered to an unspecified audience (or audiences) in the
eastern provinces.[3] It is introduced and given persuasive force by a
lengthy evocation of a contrasting other place: the shore and de-
populated interior of Euboea, 'near the very heart of Hellas' (§ 1),
where Dio claims once to have experienced virtuous poverty at first
hand. The persuasive strategy is simple: the more attractive the
portrayal of the poor rustic setting—both physically and in terms of its
cultural associations—the more acceptable the message about poverty
will be. What rewards closer attention is the care and the subtlety with
which the evocation of this privileged location is effected. The reader is
conducted through a carefully contrived series of stages from the
purely (and vividly) physical (Dio shipwrecked and left alone on a
beach with the roaring surf and the wave-beaten body of a stag, the
baying of hounds just audible from the cliff-tops above him—§§ 2–3)
to the heavily moralized scene of rustic hospitality with which the
Euboean section of the oration ends (§§ 65–80). In between, an
impression of both the physical appearance of the area and the values
it preserved in the face of great hardship is built up through Dio's
report of his conversation with his rescuer: first, a general account of
the huntsman's family fortunes and present resources, as the two
make their way through the landscape under discussion (§§ 10–20);
then the story of the huntsman's visit to town (§§ 21–63). The latter
begins by intensifying the atmosphere of rustic simplicity, presenting
familiar urban features (towers, harbours, a theatre) through the eyes
of an uncomprehending countryman (§§ 22–3);[4] then, in the reported
debate that follows (a fictitious court-case within a reported speech
within an epideictic oration), further physical details of the landscape

[2] Russell (1992).
[3] Russell (1992), 8–13; Jones (1978), 56–61; Desideri (1978), 225–8.
[4] Cf. Russell (1992), ad loc.

and of the huntsman's own homestead and resources supplement what
had already emerged at the beginning of the conversation. It is only
after all this that we are finally presented with the homestead itself,
and the welcome Dio received within it. This in turn leads on to direct
discussion of the moral status of the rustic poor, and that to the
question of suitable occupations for the urban poor.

Complexity of a different kind, but still related to the evocation of
place, can be seen in *Oration* 36, the *Borystheniticus*.[5] Here, speaking
to an audience in his home town of Prusa, Dio regales them with an
account of a visit and a speech to another audience, in Borysthenes on
the far side of the Black Sea. That Borysthenite audience in its turn, he
records, was introduced by him to an Eastern myth, borrowed from
the Magi of Persia. Thus, just as the Borysthenites within the speech
were invited to contrast their own outlook with that of another, distant
place, so the Prusan audience (and any subsequent audience and
readers) are invited to compare themselves with both Magi and
Borysthenites.

The main topic of the speech as a whole is the nature of a true city,
seen as an image of the larger order of the cosmos. Intertwined with
this, though, and hardly subordinated, is a sustained reflection on the
nature of educated culture (παιδεία): specifically, on the competing
claims of poetry and philosophy within Hellenic culture, and on the
claims of Hellenic culture itself to be a bearer of truth.[6] Central to both
themes is Dio's presentation of Borysthenes and its inhabitants. The
polis the Borysthenites inhabit stands at the very margins of the Greek
world. Physically, it is a mere shadow of its former self, and bears the
all too visible scars of its past misfortunes; it was only comparatively
recently refounded to suit the needs of the barbarian tribes that
surround it (§§ 4–6). The inhabitants themselves are presented as at
best half-Hellenes. On the credit side, they retain some traces of their
Milesian origins in their sexual habits (§ 8), they share a proud
devotion to the poetry of Homer (§ 9), and that allegiance is matched
by a splendidly Homeric—and pointedly anti-Roman—hairstyle (§ 17).
Yet at the same time, their knowledge of Hellenic παιδεία is virtually
restricted to Homeric epic (they know nothing of gnomic poetry, and
next to nothing of Plato and philosophy: §§ 9–10, 27), their style of

---

[5] Russell (1992), 19–23; Jones (1978), 61–3; Desideri (1978), 318–27; Schofield
(1991), ch. 3.

[6] See esp. §§ 31–8 for the comparison of poetry and philosophy, and §§ 39–42 for the
characterization of the myth of the Magi as fundamentally un-Hellenic in ethos, yet at
the same time validated by transcendent authority.

dress is heavily influenced by Scythian fashions (§ 7), and they themselves are painfully aware of being out of regular contact with all but the shabbiest and most disreputable representatives of Hellenism (§ 25). This is a place and a people described in a way that deliberately emphasizes their marginal status, because that marginal status, compared one way with the Magi and their exotic cosmic myth (originally revealed to Zoroaster in a wild mountain landscape: § 40), and the other way with the settled civility of Prusa, provides a telling medium for reflection on the themes of the oration.

Description of the city and its people, furthermore, is prefaced with a vividly conceived account of the geographical setting (§§ 1–3). As in the parallel case of the opening of the *Euboicus*, this serves at the very least the standard proemial function of securing an audience's interest and attention: the travelled orator, like his prototype Odysseus, so carefully evoked at the beginning of both speeches, sets out to unfold the results of those travels.[7] In the *Borystheniticus*, however, Dio seems to have been aiming at something more. In the first place, his geographical account of the city's surroundings echoes Herodotus as loudly as Homer,[8] giving a double reference to classic precedent, and a double claim to the personal authority due to the reflective and knowledgeable traveller. Secondly, and more importantly to the present theme, the physical details highlighted have been deliberately chosen for their thematic appropriateness. The city stands near the junction of two rivers, the Hypanis and the Borysthenes. On the landward side, these rivers enclose a sharp prow (or ram—ἔμβολον) of hard ground, but between their point of juncture and the sea there extends an expanse of marshland, in which their currents are all but lost, and where clumps of trees give unwary arrivals by sea the illusion of masts and anchored ships. Thus at the outset, the reader is confronted by a place of confluence, where boundaries—between earth and water, freshwater and salt, and nature and human artefact—become blurred. This prepares for the presentation of city and its inhabitants, as a place and a people on the uncertain boundaries of civilization.

Examples of the skill with which Dio constructs and positions his descriptions of other places, and of their thematic importance, could easily be multiplied. For the main part of this chapter, however,

---

[7] 7. 1 ff. with Russell (1992), 8 and 110; 36. 1. Cf. Moles (1978), 97 and Jones (1978), 46–51.

[8] Hdt. 4. 53.

I should like to turn in another direction, to consider an example of the controlled and pointed evocation not of the elsewhere, but of the here and now of performance. In this case too we shall find signs of a skill that goes beyond the standard conventions and expectations of every-day epideictic.

III

The implicit brief of the thirty-second, Alexandrian, oration is easily reconstructed. At the time of Dio's intervention rowdy behaviour in and after musical performances in the theatre and races in the hippo-drome has long been known as a distinguishing characteristic of the Alexandrians. The rioting and bloodshed that have ensued have caused problems in the past, above all in bringing the local population into conflict with the resident Roman garrison. Now again the same behaviour, perhaps combined with some inept civic diplomacy, threatens to attract the unfavourable attention not only of the Prefect, but also of the Emperor; not only local comfort, but the very status of the city of Alexandria in the Empire, may be in jeopardy. The Alexandrians must be encouraged to mend their collective ways, or face the consequences.[9]

The speech can thus fairly be categorized as an exercise in practical protreptic: exhortation to a revision of values and behaviour, in the context of a particular place and a particular set of circumstances (as opposed to more generalized exhortations to philosophy or liberal culture).[10] The tone of the whole is one that must have presented itself to the original audience as gently and insistently philosophical; it is throughout the values of reason and order that Dio seeks to recommend and reinstate.[11] The philosophical emphasis begins to become clear already in § 3, with a reference to the peculiarly Hellenic pursuits of παιδεία and λόγος, neglected once by the Athenians as

[9] For discussion of the dating and structure of the *Alexandrian*, see above all Jones (1978), ch. 5; also Desideri (1978), ch. 2.

[10] e.g. Themistius, *Or.* 24; Maximus of Tyre, *Dial.* 1; Galen, *Protrepticus* (*Scr. Min.* 1. 103–29 Marquardt).

[11] On the philosophical colour of the *Alexandrian*, see von Arnim (1898), 435–6; Moles (1978), 88; and Jones (1978), 44. Jones' overall verdict, no doubt influenced by his desire to establish an early (Vespasianic) date, is somewhat misleading: 'Beneath the sophistic trappings, the outlines of the mature philosopher begin [*sic*] to be visible.' Philosophical values, and Dio's own status as a philosophical emissary, are more prominently on view than that.

they are now by the Alexandrians; further allusions to the salutary effects of Homeric poetry and philosophical λόγοι follow in §§ 5 and 7, and in §§ 8–19 the audience is confronted with a set-piece disquisition on the nature and the value of true, therapeutic philosophical discourse—of the kind that the so-called 'philosophers' of contemporary Alexandria fail to deliver, but is now (implicitly) to be forthcoming from Dio himself. By the end of the proem, in § 28, Dio has run through a large number of the familiar topoi of philosophical protreptic.[12] Thereafter, the protreptic colouring becomes more diffuse, but returns in strength in § 75, where Dio conjures up a divinity to harangue the Alexandrians in the words of Homer's Telemachus—a clear echo of the Socrates of the *Clitophon*, addressing erring mankind 'like a god on the tragic μηχανή'.[13]

What I wish to explore now is how Dio turns reference to place to these protreptic ends. He does so first and foremost by the deliberate manipulation of the topics of civic encomium, but other forms of reference play an important supporting role in his response to the brief he has set himself.

When an epideictic orator addresses an audience as the representatives of their city, the standard expectation is that he will praise them: for the physical magnificence and importance of their city, for its well-favoured geographical position, for the excellence of its constitution and laws, for the virtues, achievements, and characteristic activities of the people themselves in the past and the present. The rules and proprieties of such praise are conveniently set out in the treatises ascribed to Menander Rhetor: above all, in Treatise I, Book iii, 344. 15 ff. (Spengel).[14] Dio's tactic in the *Alexandrian* is to take up each of these standard and expected topics, but to give it a critical spin.[15] The critical spin—which is after all the ultimate *raison d'être* of the performance—is thus, by being so rooted in an obvious awareness of the city's conventional image, recommended to the audience in a way that a more detached and abstract approach could not achieve.

That Dio is seeking to place his own oration against the familiar background of encomium begins—like the protreptic orientation—to

[12] Cf. e.g. the presentation in Maximus, *Dial.* 1; for an (almost) exhaustive discussion of lost and surviving προτρεπτικοί, see Hartlich (1889).

[13] *Clit.* 407ab, with Slings (1981), ad loc.

[14] Russell and Wilson (1981). Doreen Innes draws my attention to Hendriks, Parsons, and Worp (1981), for an account of city encomium with special reference to Alexandria.

[15] A tactic clearly also facilitated (as Doreen Innes has pointed out to me) by Dio's—and his audience's—awareness of encomium's counter-tradition, ψόγος.

emerge in its very first paragraphs: both the verb ἐπαινεῖν and the noun ἔπαινος occur twice in the first two. Just how that background is being put to work for present purposes, however, becomes most starkly clear in §§ 35–8. Here, for a minute or so, Dio gives the impression of falling into something more like the standard, comforting mode. Alexandria, he acknowledges, is the second city of the civilized world, vastly superior to all but one in size and situation; its great river, the Nile, beggars description both for its extraordinary behaviour and for its practical usefulness; situated 'at the crossroads of the world', it outstrips all in the volume of its trade and in the magnificence of its buildings. These are all the familiar heads of praise for Alexandria in the category of θέσις (position).[16] Then comes the sting. This has been a mere passing glance in the direction of encomium, firmly between inverted commas, there only to serve as a foil to the real message:

Perhaps you enjoy hearing this, and think that you are being praised when I say it, as you are by others who from time to time set about flattering you. But my praise was for water and earth and harbours and places—for everything sooner than for *you*. At what point did I say *you* were prudent and temperate and just?   (§ 37)

For it is of course the moral qualities of a city's inhabitants that really count. You would think—Dio adds sarcastically—that the Alexandrians themselves flowed from Ethiopia, to see how smug they are when their river is praised for its marvellous source!

§§ 35–8 encapsulate a manœuvre basic to the oration as a whole.[17] The more carefully one reads it, the more manifest it becomes with what skill and with what consistency Dio weaves his critical message in and through references to precisely those local features—of position, origins, pursuits, and achievements (θέσις, γένος, ἐπιτηδεύσεις, πράξεις)—that would standardly feature in an encomium of the city of Alexandria. Not every reference is in itself critical—indeed it would seem important to the persuasive venture that some at least should not be; but the overall effect is sobering in the very thoroughness with which it takes on and dismantles the main topics of Alexandrian pride.

The Nile, singled out in § 38 as a spectacular irrelevance, has already entered the discussion in a more neutral fashion in § 15, as the basis for an illuminating image. Wishing to insist that all good things

---

[16] Cf. e.g. Strabo 17. 1. 7–10.

[17] Cf. Jones (1978), 40 with nn. 48–55, for a brief analysis and comparison with examples of the same manœuvre in other speeches.

(including, implicitly, his own discourse) come from the gods, while evil is a result of human vice,[18] Dio compares the flow of water from the river's divine source, and its pollution by the filth from man-made drainage channels. More pointedly, the image of the city as the world's crossroads, also highlighted in § 36, is picked up again and turned around in §§ 40–3. Here, to insist that good behaviour is of particular importance in Alexandria, Dio reminds his audience that their position puts them on view not only to visitors from Greece and Italy, but also to Syrians, Libyans, Cilicians, Ethiopians, Arabs, Bactrians, Scythians, Persians, and Indians; and he invites them to consider—projecting his own criticisms—what these various visitors might report back on their return home. This line of thought is to recur, with even greater weight, in § 96, where Dio invites the Alexandrians to reflect on what is being reported to a still more significant potential visitor—the Emperor.

Encomiastic convention calls also for attention to the city's past—above all to the circumstances of its foundation. In the case of Alexandria, the natural expectation would be for flattering reference to the great Alexander, and to the city's proudly Hellenic origins. Dio once again acknowledges but subverts these expectations. Alexander is named twice, but in neither case is Dio straightforwardly compliment-ary; a story of origins is duly told, but it is not a story that flatters. The second reference to Alexander, in § 95, where he is compared to Heracles in claiming to be the son of Zeus, is flanked by a pointed reference to Heracles' madness, and the suggestion that a Centaur or a Cyclops would be a better comparison for the Alexandrians than Heracles. The first reference to Alexander, which is in itself still more cursory, comes in the story of origins, in §§ 63–6. According to this tale, which is given the form of an Aesopic fable, the Alexandrians are the descendants of a particular tribe of Macedonians who were them-selves originally the animals charmed and domesticated by the singing of Orpheus. This in turn explains why it is that, unlike other sturdier and more warlike Macedonians, the Alexandrians are so wildly susceptible to the music of the lyre, and why their own citharodes are such shamelessly degenerate artists. The Alexandrian audience are the descendants of the sheep and the birds in Orpheus' original audience, the citharodes (who are to music what Cynics are to philosophy, §§ 62, 66) the descendants of the dogs. Here once more, what might have been a gesture towards ethnic pride becomes instead a gesture of

---

[18] A good Stoic message: cf. Cleanthes, *Hymn to Zeus*, 15 ff.; but see also Maximus, *Dial.* 41 for a similar message from a non-Stoic vantage-point.

censure. The Alexandrians are indeed Macedonians, but Macedonians of a kind who need to watch themselves more than others; they are indeed devotees of the arts, but in an inappropriately excessive way.

The fable also touches on the topic of the Alexandrians' characteristic pursuits (ἐπιτηδεύσεις)—the third heading under which they might expect in other circumstances to be praised. Two of their pursuits—concert-going and the races—are of course the direct targets of Dio's criticism, and between them divide the main body of the speech (concerts, §§ 47–74; races, §§ 75–95; both together, §§ 41–6). But Alexandria was known also for its higher culture, and this too comes under fire: in particular, the Museum, the special relationship to the poetry of Homer, and philosophy.

The Museum, as the single most powerful token of the city's claim to cultural eminence, is held back for the peroration, in § 100. Devotion to the degenerate music of the 'Cynic' citharodes, and to frivolity in public entertainments in general, warns Dio, threatens to reduce this famous institution to an empty name and a shadow without substance. But this final reference only sets the seal on a sustained critique of Alexandrian culture that has run through the whole oration, since the opening claim (in § 3, cf. § 16) that true παιδεία has lost its place.

Homeric quotation, and the use of Homeric episodes as material for moral argument, is of course a standard device.[19] There is, however, a specially rich and persistent use here, which it is highly tempting to see as yet another backhanded acknowledgement of a local distinction—Alexandrian philology. The first 'quotation', in § 4, in a disparaging description of the Alexandrians' favoured kind of performer, is a playful cento, compounded from three separate passages, which simultaneously insults its audience by its content, while flattering them on their ability to appreciate how cleverly it has been stitched together. Thereafter, a series of allusions and quotations runs through the oration (16, 21, 23, 28, 30, 34, 38, 47), culminating in two carefully contrived set-pieces. In the first, building on an allusion to the chariot race of *Iliad* 23 in §§ 74–80, Dio mocks the Alexandrians' behaviour in the hippodrome in a 36-line pastiche, in which not only the race itself but also such scenes as the quarrel of Achilles and Agamemnon are pressed into service to describe the yelling and squabbling of the crowd. He also observes, cuttingly, that the only hero to have been overtly excited by the Iliadic race was Ajax—whose subsequent career makes him anything but a useful role-model. Then, hard on the heels

[19] See Kindstrand (1973).

of this sarcastic *tour de force*, in §§ 88–90, Dio develops the conceit that the moral destruction of Alexandria by real horses is a reprise of the physical destruction of Homer's Troy by a wooden one; the Alexandrians need to appreciate that they are 'captives' in as serious a sense as the Trojans. Finally, in a parting shot in § 99, the Alexandrians' self-image as wits and jokers is dismissed as the kind of boast more appropriate to a Thersites than to a great and noble city. It seems reasonable to see a special sting for the Alexandrians in all this. They do indeed have a special claim on Homer, and Homer's poetry is indeed a special element in their civic glory, but their current behaviour distorts and degrades that claim; until they mend their ways, it is more appropriate to address them in cento and parody than in genuine Homeric verse, and to compare them with the losers and the low-grade of the *Iliad*, rather than with its heroes and victors.

Alexandrian philosophy, finally, is both acknowledged and criticized.[20] It is a central conceit of the oration that Dio, like Hermes sent from Zeus (§ 21), or Odysseus showing the way past the Sirens (§ 47), is bringing the saving message of philosophical values to the sick community of Alexandria (§§ 12–19). However, he goes out of his way to insist that this mission is only necessary because of a failure on the part of those among the local population who might have done the job for him: the so-called philosophers who divide between those who never venture outside their lecture-rooms into the real world (§§ 8, 20), those who do, but whose discourse has been fatally infected by corrupt local tastes (§§ 10, 68), and the low, buffoonish Cynics, who only inflame the maladies they ought to be curing (§§ 8–9, 17–20).[21] Here too, a standard source of local pride is acknowledged even as it is demolished.

The fourth and final heading for encomium is achievements (πράξεις), subdivided by Menander Rhetor into justice (which includes piety), self-control, prudence, and courage.[22] As with the previous category (pursuits), Dio combines direct attack and more oblique disparagement. Under direct attack is the Alexandrians' claim to self-control and prudence: the former in the whole account of their uproarious conduct during and after concerts and races (see especially §§ 41–6, 51–9); the latter in Dio's solemn warnings of the risks that

[20] Cf. Strabo 14. 5. 13.

[21] All familiar complaints: for the first, cf. (e.g.) Callicles in Plato, *Gorgias* 484cff. and Maximus, *Dial.* 1. 8; for the second, Epictetus 3. 21 and 3. 23; for the third, Epictetus 3. 22, Lucian, *Peregrinus* 3 ff., Julian, *Or.* 6.

[22] 361. 13–28 Sp.

their conduct has exposed them to in the past (§§ 69–72), and may expose them to in the future (93–6). Slightly more oblique is the light cast on their claims to piety and divine favour (Menander's φιλο-θεότης and θεοφιλότης), and to courage.

The question of courage is touched on twice: first, in the Aesopic fable, which implicitly contrasts the flighty Alexandrians, descendants of Orpheus' sheep and birds, with the other, sterner Macedonian tribes, and the lions who did not stay to listen to his playing (§§ 63–5); secondly, in the minatory references to recent Alexandrian history—the return of Ptolemy Auletes and the repression of a riot by a Roman general—which underscore the self-destructive yet ultimately ineffectual nature of native bellicosity (§§ 69–72). References to divine favour and religious observance are more diffuse and evenly distributed. The very first, to Sarapis, the Alexandrian divinity *par excellence*,[23] in §§ 12–13, is relatively neutral, in keeping with the moderately conciliatory tone with which the oration begins. As devotees of the god, Dio observes, the Alexandrians should be particularly receptive to the notion that good advice (like his own) can be sent from the gods, since they are themselves so used to receiving messages from Sarapis in dreams and oracles. This sop to local pride is swiftly reinforced by a disparaging allusion to a nearby rival, the oracle of Apis at Memphis: while the Memphiots must make do with the piecemeal utterances of mere boys, Sarapis has seen to it that the Alexandrians are now to be presented with a full-scale disquisition from a grown man.[24] Here already local pride is turned to self-advertisement, in a way that also suggests that the Alexandrians do not properly understand their own θεοφιλότης, and need an outsider to explain it to them. Subsequent allusions to Alexandrian cult and allegiances are still less flattering. The final reference to the Museum in § 99, already mentioned in connection with Alexandrian claims to παιδεία, is again relevant: for betrayal of the Museum is also, as Dio presents it, betrayal of the cult of the Muses and the Graces.[25] And in between, in §§ 56–8, betrayal of the Muses (and Apollo) is linked to distortion of the cult of Dionysus too.[26]

Manipulation of the conventional image of the place of performance, as codified above all in civic encomium, is thus a highly

---

[23] Fraser (1972), 246–76.
[24] For the implied image of philosophical discourse as oracular utterance, and the philosopher as ὑποφήτης of divinity, see e.g. Maximus, *Dial.* 11. 6.
[25] Fraser (1972), 312–19.   [26] Fraser (1972), 201–6.

important element in Dio's strategy in the *Alexandrian*. It remains, however, to demonstrate briefly that the other form of sense of place, distinguished at the outset, is in play as well.

In §§ 40–3 Dio invites the Alexandrians to reflect on what their status as the 'crossroads of the world' really means, and to do so in terms of the reports carried back by visitors to other, supposedly less favoured locations. This invitation to his audience to see themselves in relation to other places is followed up by a reminder of the clear moral vision that outsiders can bring to the Greek world, as exemplified above all by the Scythian sage Anacharsis (§§ 44–5).[27] The appeal to local pride is clear, but it is not only pride that is in question. It is also a matter of practical political prudence. Through a whole series of veiled allusions to 'your superiors' or 'rulers' (§§ 29, 51, 52(?), 59, 69), which lead up to open and detailed mention of both Roman governors (§ 72) and the emperor himself (§§ 95 ff.), Dio reminds the Alexandrians that there is one 'other place' of overriding importance to their continued prosperity, relations with which they disregard at their peril. The Empire's second city is bidden to reflect on its place in the larger structure of the world, by cultivating a more vivid sense of those who observe it from outside. Both the one city more powerful than itself and its many inferiors[28] can be equally vital to its own flourishing.

Besides cities of the present, comparisons are also drawn from the great places of the past and of Hellenic tradition, in ways that seek to flatter the Alexandrians' cultural grasp even as they are challenged to re-examine their conduct and outlook. So it is that Athens and Sparta take their place in Dio's discourse, alongside Rhodes and Rome. In his conciliatory opening (§§ 3–4), Athens offers the Alexandrians a companion in error—for even that great city once temporarily lost its grasp on the centrality of παιδεία and λόγος. But the note of challenge and criticism soon begins to sound: most immediately in § 6, where the Athenian habit of allowing comedy the freedom to preach and criticize is an example of a good the Alexandrians foolishly deny themselves (a point which is underlined by the subsequent use of comic quotation in §§ 16 and 23). In §§ 60 and 69 it is the turn of Sparta, as offering a better model of musical taste—and particularly of the correct evaluation of citharodes—than that represented by the Alexandrians' current

[27] For whom see Kindstrand (1981).

[28] Among which Rhodes (§ 52) seems to have special force as a comparison, presumably because of its earlier status in the days of the Ptolemies, and its more recent fortunes in dealings with Rome.

blind devotion. In §§ 77–8 Athenian and Cretan myths of bestial affections are used to pour scorn on the local passion for horses. And in §§ 92–3 Athens and Sparta join forces with Corinth and Megara to exemplify the renown that communal pursuits can bring—whether for good (as in their cases) or for bad, as now threatens Alexandria.

IV

Dio's exploitation of place in the *Alexandrian* thus encompasses evocation of both the here and now of performance and of the other places of geography, history, and myth. What I hope to have shown is that it is throughout as carefully tuned to the overall purpose of the oration as were the descriptions of Euboea and Borysthenes in *Orations* 7 and 36. Dio has a fine line to tread between conciliation and criticism, and reference to place is one of the stabilizers that enables him to combine reproof with a mollifying acknowledgement of his audience's underlying cultivation and self-image. The *Alexandrian* is by no means unique in this respect—similar cases can be argued, for example, for the *Rhodian* and the *First Tarsic* (31, 33)—but it is probably the most accomplished example in Dio's surviving *œuvre*. More generally, I hope to have shown how attention to the ways in which references to place are constructed and deployed might enrich reading not only of Dio, but of other oratorical texts too.[29]

---

[29] For the handling of references to place in Cicero, see now Vasaly (1993).

13

Dio Chrysostom, Greece, and Rome

JOHN MOLES

Donald Russell's commentary on Dio happily unites the best Greek orator and the greatest connoisseur of Greek prose of their respective ages. No scholar has argued more persuasively for the literary, philosophical, and indeed moral excellence of *Euboicus*, *Olympicus*, and *Borystheniticus*.[1] I here offer a sketch of their attitudes to Rome.[2] While my interpretations differ from Donald's, they owe his scholarship an incalculable debt.

I

The extant *Euboicus* (*Or.* 7) is a patchwork of different versions but one version seems to have been delivered in Rome[3] (which Dio visited after his exile, the context of his Euboean adventure). Allusions to aqueducts (106), parks, suburban villas, and groves (145) indicate a large city; the sentiment 'we are criticizing the things most important among the Greeks' (122) and some apparent harmless accommodation of Roman prejudices suggest a Roman audience,[4] as does a powerful counter-element: the final tirade against sexual exploitation and prostitution, which suggestively links the ideas of capture in war, literal enslavement, enslavement in the provision of degrading sex, enslavement of the human spirit, and depravity at the highest levels of

---

[1] Russell (1992), with Moles (1993).

[2] I thank Malcolm Schofield, Simon Swain, Tony Woodman, and the editors for valuable comment.

[3] Russell (1992), 1, 13, 156, cf. 139–40, 146.

[4] Brunt (1973), 17. For 'we' cf. *Or.* 79. 4–5 (p. 180). Roman delivery of one version does not exclude, indeed it entails, delivery also elsewhere (some passages suggest a Prusan perspective, e.g. 83–90 on Odysseus' continued tribulations on his return home likely bear on Dio's troubles in Prusa (for Odysseus/Dio see p. 179)).

society (133–4).[5] Thus the speech has both general significance for great (Greek) cities and particular reference to Rome.[6]

Dio's message is plain: the rural Euboean hunters show that the poor can live a natural, self-sufficient, and virtuous life (81, 103), city life is potentially corrupting and frequently corrupt in practice (24–48), but even the urban poor can find occupations consistent with virtuous living (104–52).

Several areas, however, require sharper definition: (1) the balances between idealization and realism and between fictionality and fact in the narrative; (2) Dio's own role; (3) the relationship to imperial policy; (4) Dio's attitude to Roman social mores.

(1) On the one hand, the narrative is set idyllically 'practically in the middle of Greece' (1), exploits pastoral topics and novelistic, New Comedy and Odyssean plot-structures;[7] the description of the grazing (14–15) has Golden Age and *locus amoenus* resonances; the debate in the theatre (24–63) recalls famous literary debates;[8] the hunter's hospitality (65) is coloured by reminiscences of Plato's *Republic*; his naïveté provokes amusement (as he himself realizes (21–2, 24–5, 43–4, 47–8, 59, 62)).

On the other hand, the narrative is 'authenticated' both by Dio's eyewitness testimony and personal experience (1) and by the parallels between the hunter's treatment of 'Sotades' (55–8) and his treatment of Dio (2–10, 64–80); the hunters suffer hardship when their master is killed by a Roman emperor (12); there are realistic allusions to transhumance (13), to an 'exchange economy' (69), to the Euboean city's economic decay (34, 38–9), and to *emphyteusis* arrangements (37) popular under Nerva and Trajan;[9] the terms of the honorific decree (60–1) are officially correct;[10] the hunter is several times allowed the last laugh (47–8, 50, 59, 63–4): his naïveté reflects a higher truth.

Thus the hunters' ideal life is presented with knowing irony and fictionality, but also seriously propounded and anchored in reality: hence Dio can reasonably propose that the principle of self-sufficiency be transferred into city life (103).

---

[5] Note the ambiguous and defensive discussion of this passage in Jones (1978), 129. The reference to 'barbarian bodies or those of Greeks who previously were not at all slaves but now live in abundant and considerable slavery' makes these sex-slaves into a particularly degrading example of that moral and political slavery to which in Dio's view all non-Romans are subject under the empire (cf. *Orr.* 31. 125; 34. 39, 51; 12. 85 (p. 183)). Of course the attack upon Roman sexual depravity is *also* an attack upon *any one*'s sexual depravity.

[6] *Pace* Swain (1994).   [7] Russell (1992), 8–9.   [8] Russell (1992), 9.
[9] Russell (1992), 120–1.   [10] Russell (1992), 126.

In the second half of the speech, while Dio's recommendations for the urban poor are practicable enough, parallels and disclaimed parallels with Platonic programmes (107, 110, 113, 118–22, 125, 130) create a rather similar balance between ideal and actuality.

Within the whole speech, therefore, the balances between ideal and reality, between seriousness and entertainment and between moral absolutism and accommodation of audience prejudice are finely judged for exposition of a message at once general and specific.

(2) Dio's philosophical persona compounds the Cynic (1, 9, 66, 75, 103), Socratic (81, 100), and Platonic (1, 102–3, 124–6),[11] with a corresponding progression from individual moral philosophy to Platonic social and political philosophy. As a Cynic and/or Odyssean figure (1, 3),[12] Dio himself exemplifies wandering, suffering, and poverty. He also suggests an analogy between his 'wandering' life and 'wandering' (philosophical) speech (1, 127): his own biography is interwoven into the discourse. There are also implicit parallels between Dio's life and experience and the hunter's (4, 9–10, 32). Consequently, Dio's comment at 81 acquires a double meaning: 'I have not *gone through* this whole account pointlessly, nor, as I might perhaps seem to some, because I wished to talk idly, but because I was setting out an example of *the life I undertook*[13] from the beginning and of *the way of life* of the poor, an example I *knew myself . . .*'.[14] The example consists of Dio's life as well as the hunters'.

Further, 81 echoes 1: 'I shall now *relate at length* something which I saw *for myself* and did not hear from others. For wordiness and difficulty in rejecting any of the topics that *come one's way* are perhaps not only characteristic of an old man: they may possibly be just as characteristic of the wanderer as of the old man. The reason is possibly that both have had many *experiences* that they recall with some pleasure. So *I shall tell* of the sort of people I encountered virtually in the middle of Greece and *the sort of life* they lived.' These echoes suggest that the work's beginning is not lost[15] and unify 1–81 into a strong moral statement centring on the role of Dio himself as both observer and exponent of poverty.

[11] Hardly the Stoic, despite the Cleanthes allusion (102) and general Stoic influence (Brunt (1973)).

[12] Russell (1992), 8.

[13] ὑπεθέμην = (i) 'propounded', (ii) 'undertook' (cf. e.g. Andoc. 6. 19).

[14] For the double sense, 'know of' and 'know through experience', cf. 65–6.

[15] Discussion in Russell (1992), 109, 132; I think the Euripidean quotation has simply fallen out at 82, like the Sophoclean at 102.

(3) Date, location, echoes of Trajanic agrarian schemes, and Dio's friendship with Trajan might seem to make *Euboicus* a manifesto for Trajanic 'back-to-the-land' policy.[16] But this interpretation fails against Dio's fierce attacks on Roman corruption and his brusque, Cynic-style, dismissal of imperial wealth by comparison with the hunters' poverty (66): 'and yet I knew the homes and tables of rich men, not only private individuals but also satraps and kings, who seemed to me at that time the most wretched of all, and though they seemed so before, they seemed still more so when I saw those men's poverty and freedom and saw that they lacked nothing of the pleasure of eating and drinking, but rather even in those respects effectively had the greater riches'. The Roman setting and Dio's past and present intimacy with Roman emperors give this sentiment enormous force. Dio can pronounce authoritatively on the relative value of poverty and riches, on the ideal of rural life, on contemporary rural and urban decline in Greece, and on the corruptions of Roman city-life because he has direct personal experience of all these different states.

(4) Granted the double focus of the attack on urban corruption (both general and Roman), Dio's condemnation of Roman luxury remains uncompromising. Poverty is simply superior to wealth; sexual exploitation is disgusting; there is no praise of the magnificence of Rome as a city, nor acknowledgement of the benefits of the Roman peace (note the casual 'just now there is peace' (49)); and the miserable economic conditions of the Euboean city are implicitly linked, in part, to Roman misrule (12).

In this unsatisfactorily preserved but excellently conceived speech Dio projects himself as a moral authority who attacks contemporary urban decline and corruption and Roman corruption in particular, and offers practical solutions. The speech coheres with his claim in *Oration* 13, delivered in Athens, that he had told the Romans that true happiness came from the practice of virtue, not from the acquisition of ever greater luxuries from the whole world, and that the poorer and more self-sufficient the Romans became, the happier they and their subjects would be (31–7). Similarly, *Oration* 79, a radical attack on urban luxury, seems both to envisage, and to have been delivered in, Rome and refers to 'us in Rome'.[17]

---

[16] Desideri (1978), 257 n. 28 with bibliography.
[17] Moles (1983).

II

In the long *prolalia* to *Olympicus* (1–16), the sophists resemble the peacock in being beautiful, vain, and empty-headed, whereas Dio resembles the owl in being apparently no wiser than anybody else yet besieged by crowds, without eloquence and a mere complainer, scorned for his dowdiness but admired, a divine messenger and purveyor of wisdom, a warner whose warnings are spurned until too late, the embodiment of philosophy and ancient wisdom. The multiple ironies are transparent: in this triumphant come-back speech[18] delivered, just after his exile had ended, at the cultural and religious centre of Greece, the moral and philosophical claims that Dio makes for himself could not be greater.

Dio's analogy between his wanderings and wandering speech (16) introduces his recent visit to the Roman army as it prepared for war against the Dacians (16–20). Is Dio here 'wandering' from his subject?

The allusion to the Dacians' ancient and modern names (16) suggests their antiquity, in implicit contrast with the Romans. Dio himself appears in Cynic guise—'wanderer', 'alone', 'unarmed' and peaceable amongst armed men, yet 'fearless' and 'safe' from physical assault, an 'observer' of military 'sights' (16–20, cf. *Or.* 6. 60–2).

Dio desired 'to see men contending for empire and power and the others for freedom and fatherland' (20). Within a Cynic perspective 'empire and power' are false values and 'freedom' a good. Other details reinforce this reading: the tart allusion to congratulatory embassies 'which join in prayers with the tongue only', a remarkable sentiment from Dio, intimate of emperors (17); the Roman army's lack of leisure (19) to listen to speeches (granted the formal moral ambiguity of 'leisure', Dio's present audience do have the leisure to listen, and rightly so, and a pupil of Musonius would surely have required even an army to make the leisure);[19] the statements that Olympia and the 'history' of Zeus are divine things better and more profitable, older and greater, than the Dacian war and Dacian history, however great these may be on the human plain (20–1). Finally, we recall that in Aesop's fables the ancient owl's wisdom consisted of warnings about devices to entrap and kill birds (7–8): if the Greeks are birds, what are the Romans?

[18] I believe the date to be 97, *pace* Russell (1992), 16, 171, but cannot argue it here.
[19] Cf. Tac. *Hist.* 3. 81; Moles (1990), 373 n. 130.

In the introduction to Dio's grand main theme of the providential organization of the universe (23–4), these ideas are sustained. Hesiod, poet of peace, is preferred to Homer, poet of war, and after 16–20 listeners might hear in Hesiod's hymn to Zeus' omnipotence (*WD* 5–7: 'easily he makes strong, and easily he brings the strong man low', etc.) the possibility of Rome's humbling (cf. *Or.* 13. 34: 'Rome's greatness is not very secure').

Dio also constructs a hierarchy of 'sights': having dismissed the 'sight' of the Roman army, he now depreciates the 'sights' of the games by comparison with the 'sight' of Phidias' great statue (25). The conception of Zeus as ruler of the universe and of the entire human race, Greeks and barbarians alike (27), so far from providing a heavenly paradigm for the Roman world-empire,[20] evokes a higher reality, which demotes that empire. And Dio locates true human wisdom in the ancients, the first men, who were closest to God and responded most freshly to heavenly 'sights' (27–8). Their current earthly representative is Dio himself, 'ancient' philosopher, not military man.[21] Further, Dio's comparison of the Epicureans' 'banishing' of the gods from the world to unfortunates banished to deserted islands (37) recalls the Roman emperor's merciless power, and the introduction of Phidias' 'contest' or trial (49–50) confirms the relative triviality of the 'contest' between Rome and Dacia. Phidias justifies his claim that this is the greatest 'contest' ever by the fact that it is *not* about empire or military resources but about Zeus' governorship of the universe and his own likeness of him (53). He insists that his god, unlike Homer's, is one of peace (74). Thus the Dacian episode is no 'wandering' from the true discourse but sets up a mirror which both by itself and through refraction with the rest of the discourse reflects negatively on Roman militarism.

Now *Olympicus*, like *Euboicus* and *Borystheniticus*, contains elements which in isolation might appear complimentary to Rome. Thus, as in *Euboicus*, allusion is made to peace in Greece (formally fifth-century Greece during the truce covering the games): 'our god is peaceful and altogether gentle, as befits the overseer of a faction-free and concordant Greece' (74).[22] But the 'mirror' deflects contemporary compliment of an aggressive imperialist power. Here, as at the end, the

[20] Desideri (1978), 331; Russell (1992), 14.

[21] Russell (1992) 18 and 194 rightly stresses the sudden and undeveloped intervention of 'the philosopher' as the fourth and greatest interpreter of the divine (47–8): the point, I believe, is that he is making the speech.

[22] Russell (1992), 206.

Greeks are behaving rightly, not the Romans. Similarly, while the enumeration and exegesis of Zeus' titles (74–7) *can* be employed to promote links between Zeus and the emperor, as by Dio himself before Trajan (*Or.* 1. 37–41), this analogy is excluded here, both by the 'mirror' of the section on Dacia and by the immediate context: Phidias again rejects Zeus' warlike aspects (78–9).

The speech ends (85) with a theatrical *coup*, testimony to the mimetic powers alike of Phidias the sculptor and of Dio the orator and philosophical and religious exegete: the statue of Zeus seems to look upon the Eleans and all Greece in goodwill and concern and to address them. Greece herself becomes the final 'sight' of the speech. After congratulating the Greeks for offering sacrifices as magnificent as their means allow, for maintaining as from their beginning the Olympic games, and for preserving inherited festivals and mysteries, Zeus expresses his anxiety for Greece by quoting the words of Odysseus to his father Laertes (*Od.* 24. 249–50). Having congratulated Laertes on his care for his garden, Odysseus says: 'you yourself enjoy no good care, but you bear grievous old age, you are badly unkempt and unfittingly clothed'. What does this abrupt and pessimistic conclusion mean?

Clearly, Laertes represents old Greece and, as a lament for its present wretchedness, this conclusion fulfils Dio's description of the owl's song as 'mournful' (1). No doubt there is also an allusion to Dio himself,[23] old and unkempt like both Laertes and Greece and the embodiment of Greek philosophical and religious values. Such allegorizing has been anticipated by Dio's remarks about Phidias' covert representations of himself and Pericles on Athene's shield (6). But there is another, barbed, point.[24] Odysseus next says that it is not because Laertes is lazy that his master has no care for him but because he is a slave (24. 257). Greece therefore is suffering not through her own fault but because her master, Rome, treats her as a slave. The integralness of the Dacian section is again manifest: Greece is unfree under Roman rule. Allusion to Dio himself also yields criticism of Rome, his exile (cf. 37) having been inflicted by the merciless Domitian.

To describe *Olympicus* as an attack upon Roman imperialism would diminish a rich and profound speech. Nevertheless, criticism of Rome

---

[23] Reiske (1784), i. 418 n. 34; Geel (1840), 122–3. It is also Δίων who makes Δία speak; for the significant association of names cf. *Or.* 4. 27; such (con)fusion of roles is unproblematic: Moles (1990), 328.

[24] Argued, independently, in Simon Swain's forthcoming book, *From Plutarch to Philostratus*.

must be integrated into any overall interpretation. Dio is telling the
Greeks that Greek culture and religion are more important than the
Roman empire, that the eternal divine governance of the universe is a
far greater reality than that transient empire, and that Greece's
decline is largely Rome's fault. He also proffers the divine governance
as a source of deep spiritual comfort and joy to all men, Greeks and
barbarians (who must logically include Romans). It remains true that it
is Greek poets, artists, and philosophers (naturally, on this occasion,
Dio himself) who have most perfectly represented the divine, and that
contemporary Greece is suffering from Roman misrule.

III

Donald Russell's and Malcolm Schofield's fine readings[25] have demonstrated *Borystheniticus'* complexity and subtlety, clarified difficulties,
and proposed convincing solutions; but there is more to say.

As in *Olympicus*, a central concern is Greekness, focused here with
peculiar sharpness by the city's marginal, perilous, and ruinous state.
As in *Euboicus* and *Olympicus*, the narrative provides a mirror for the
audience, here the Prusans. As in *Euboicus*, there is a mixture of the
realistic and the literary, the serious and the humorous. While much of
Dio's topography seems historically acurate, it has been influenced by
literary accounts, especially Herodotus',[26] and, while the information
about Dio's behaviour at Borysthenes seems circumstantial, details of
both narrative and topography recall Plato's *Phaedrus*.[27] Moreover,
Dio has greatly exaggerated the Borysthenites' poor Greek, ignorance
of Greek culture and philosophy, and lack of contact with Romans.[28]
One effect must be to amuse the sophisticated Prusans (cf. *Euboicus*).

After the initial description of place we learn that barbarians, Borysthenites, and Scythians buy salt from the same mines (3), and although
Borysthenes is under continual barbarian attack (no Roman peace
here),[29] after its most disastrous capture it was refounded with
Scythian help in order to maintain trade between Greeks and barbarians. This contrasts with most of the Pontic cities, whose fate illustrates 'the dispersal of the Greek world into many places' (5). The

---

[25] Schofield (1991), 57–92.   [26] Russell (1992), 22, 212.
[27] Trapp (1990).   [28] Jones (1978), 63.
[29] Whether Olbia was garrisoned in Dio's time is unclear (Russell (1992), 220): *if* it
was, Dio's silence is eloquent.

old city has been physically fragmented 'so that you would not surmise that the surviving towers once belonged to a single city', and not a single statue remains undamaged among the holy places (6).

The first of the two Borysthenite characters is well mannered but, like the Borysthenites generally, wears barbarian clothing. As his name Callistratus indicates, he is an excellent warrior. But he is also interested in oratory and philosophy and wants to sail away with Dio as his pupil. His military prowess and handsome 'Ionian' appearance attract many lovers. In their homosexuality at least the Borysthenites maintain ancestral tradition and are likely to win barbarian converts, leading to barbarian debasement of the practice (7–8). Notwithstanding Dio's general hostility to homosexuality, the allusion here is not overtly hostile (otherwise the practice could not be debased) but strengthens the dialogue's Platonic texture. Callistratus is a lover of Homer,[30] as are the Borysthenites generally because of their warlike nature and devotion to Achilles. Although, surrounded by barbarians, they no longer speak Greek clearly, almost all know the *Iliad* by heart (9). These details link warfare, homosexuality, love of Homer, and Achilles to create an image of Greekness rather like that espoused by Alexander the Great, but they also suggest a tension between that image and love of wisdom.[31]

Dio's challenging attempt to interest Callistratus in the gnomic poet Phocylides instead of Homer (10) has several implications: Dio himself will perform a provocative Socratic role; as Platonic *eromenos* and would-be pupil of Dio, Callistratus has good philosophical potential; like Achilles, Homer is an excessively warlike model (causing philosophical 'blindness'); Phocylides better inculcates civic virtue; Dio will eventually broach a philosophical mode analogous to Phocylides' severe poetic mode (i.e. a Stoic mode). The relative depreciation of Homer, Hellenic icon, illustrates how for Dio, custodian of Hellenism, the constituents of Hellenic παιδεία are negotiable according to particular moral and practical needs.[32]

Dio's analogy between sampling Phocylides' poetry and sampling a merchant's wares (11) suggests that virtue is not necessarily the exclusive preserve of Greeks (he himself had planned to observe the Getae (1)). Phocylides' poem shows that even a small city perilously

---

[30] Also, presumably, 'thigh-lover': for such plays cf. Ach. Tat. 8. 9. 3; *Anth. Pal.* 11. 218 (Crates).

[31] *Or.* 2 offers interesting parallels: Moles (1990), 339.

[32] Similarly in *Orr.* 2 (cf. Moles (1990), 339) and 18 (the reading-list for an unnamed Greek statesman).

located (like Borysthenes) can be more truly a city than a great city foolishly and lawlessly governed ((13) cf. both *Euboicus* and *Or.* 13). Dio
soothes Callistratus over Homer and with a great crowd of Borysthenites they go, symbolically, within the city, in contrast to the fleeing
Scythians of the previous day (evidently not true 'city' people (14–16)).

The Borysthenites' philosophical potential is emphasized by their
Hellenic manner and enthusiasm to hear Dio, even though they are
still under arms. The meeting takes place, again symbolically, within
the temple of Zeus. The seating arrangements reflect respect for age,
and the sight of so many long-haired and long-bearded Greeks of the
ancient type would have delighted a philosopher (Dio teasingly suggests that he is not himself such). Greekness and philosophy are closely
associated. Only one man was clean-shaven, through desire to flatter
the Romans and advertise his friendship with them: he is rightly
derided and hated (17).

The smug Prusan audience now has *its* preconceptions challenged.
For Prusa had far closer dealings with Rome than had Borysthenes
and Dio often mentioned his own friendship with Romans, including
the emperors (e.g. *Orr.* 40. 5, 13–15; 43. 11; 44. 6, 12; 45. 2). The point
must be that while such associations may be necessary, it is essential
not to compromise one's cultural Greekness, as Dio himself visibly did
not, or one's moral integrity, as Dio claimed not to have done. This
passage, like the Dacian episode and the end of *Olympicus*, shows that
there are occasions when Dio registers direct hostility to the encroach-
ments of Roman imperialism and culture. The passage also reveals
another function of his exaggeration of Borysthenite simplicity and
lack of culture: to define the *essence* of Greekness. Despite their faults,
the Borysthenites are here the Prusans' moral superiors.

After stressing the city's ancient and Greek character, Dio goes into
Socratic mode, insisting on the importance of correct definitions.
Those without this ability are like barbarians (18–19): true Greekness
entails philosophical competence. By the Stoic definition of a city as a
group of men dwelling in the same place under law (where 'man' = 'a
mortal man endowed with reason'), there never has been, and never
will be, a city on earth: only the community of gods merits the name.
Nevertheless, it is worth distinguishing between fairly good examples
(ruled by good persons) and utterly corrupt ones (20–1). This section
need not disturb interpreters who detect complimentary allusions to
the Roman empire or to the reigns of Nerva or Trajan:[33] while Dio

[33] Desideri (1978), 318, 321–2; Russell (1992), 23.

cannot commend the empire whole-heartedly, he might still commend it reservedly. Yet the allusion to the solitary shaven Borysthenite discourages such interpretations.

Dio's desire to discuss the fairly good communities (23–4), that is, to philosophize in the tradition of Plato's *Republic*, is now diverted by Hieroson's intervention into the long final exposition about the divine city or government. Is Hieroson abandoning hard political thought for cloudy abstractions?[34]

On the contrary, his old age, respected status, courtesy and frankness, awareness of the question of Greekness (which, like Dio, he partly defines in moral terms), consciousness of Dio's divine role, love of Plato (an advance upon the general love of Homer), metaphorical desire, though he is all but blind, to look upon the sun itself, name ('preserver of holy things'), and the 'erotic' excitement which he and his companions feel at the prospect of hearing about the divine government (24–6): all these factors validate his intervention. We have progressed from Callistratus, 'fine warrior', to Hieroson, 'preserver of holy things', from war to peace and to concern for the city and for the preservation of holy things currently neglected (6). *Olympicus* exhibits the same progression and fundamental concerns.

Hieroson now requests Dio to discuss the divine city, not the mortal (27); the restated distinction seems to exclude any allusion to the Roman empire. Dio's exposition will mix Stoicism (his own creed, but difficult) with Platonism (as more appropriate to the Borysthenites, because a few read him and he has some affinity with Homer), and will be marked by Platonic elevation (28–9). While this mixture of both doctrine and mode reflects the respective tastes of Dio and his internal audience, it must also appeal to Dio's Prusan audience and any other audiences. A Stoic exposition will persuade only those who are themselves Stoics or susceptible to Stoic arguments, whereas harmonization of Stoic and Platonic positions, however forced,[35] must have larger appeal, especially given the greater attractiveness of Platonic modes of exposition.

Dio's initial assertions that the Stoics do not literally define the universe as a city but liken the present arrangement of the universe to a city and that this doctrine aims to harmonize the human race with the divine (29–31) may seem again to open the possibility of integration of the Roman empire within the universe, especially as he states that the term city can be applied only to a kingdom in the proper sense,

---

[34] Schofield (1991), 63.   [35] Schofield (1991), 88 on 31–2.

as exemplified by the kingship of Zeus.[36] After arguing that poets offer partial insight into religious thought, Dio restates the 'account of the philosophers', whereby there exists a fellowship of gods and men which apportions citizenship to those possessed of reason (32–8).

He next, however, embarks on an 'amazing myth sung in secret rites by the Magi' (39), who learned it from Zoroaster. This myth concerns the physical organization of the universe and its periodic conflagration and rebirth. The Magi, he says (42), stubbornly assert the truth of their myth, whereas Greek poets try to persuade their audience. At a critical point in the development Dio elaborately apologizes (43): 'what follows concerning the horses and their driving I am ashamed to tell in the manner in which they say it in their exposition, not caring in the least whether their image is in all respects a good likeness. For I might perhaps seem absurd [lit. 'out-of-place'] singing a barbarian song to follow songs that were elegant and Greek [i.e. the 'city-of-the-universe' section], but nevertheless I must dare to do so.' His final words to his Prusan audience excuse his imaginative flights as due to Borysthenite insistence (61).

Questions of Greekness and barbarian-ness again obtrude. Clearly, Dio aims to make both his audiences *think*. But to what effect?

There are two basic interpretative principles. (*a*) While the myth has a Mithraic veneer, its substance is solidly Stoic, with some of the imagery (the chariot and horses) derived from Plato's *Phaedrus* and some from Stoic contexts.[37] (*b*) One would expect Dio to approve that substance: his general philosophical position is Stoic, as he notes in *Borystheniticus* (29), and he says similar things in *Or.* 40. 35–41. The length, power, and eloquence of Dio's treatment here suggest some sort of assent and he finally refers not to a 'myth' but to an 'account' (60–1), thereby blurring the distinction of 38–9.

Why, then, Dio's stress on the myth's 'barbarian', 'out-of-place' quality and on the Magi's 'stubbornness' in asserting their myth, despite their apparently inaccurate imagery, a stress which entails elaborate apologies? Is Dio seriously suggesting that truly Greek 'songs' are not only charming but sober and rational (43), thereby conveying a salutary warning against the Borysthenites' irrational barbarian tendencies?[38] This interpretation fails to account for the implicit approval of Hieroson's desire to learn about the divine city, the disingenuousness of describing as 'Mithraic' material that is essen-

---

[36] Desideri (1978), 322; Russell (1992), 228.
[37] Russell (1992), 22.   [38] Russell (1992), 23.

tially Stoic and Platonic and the fact that Dio himself would naturally approve such material.

To some extent the stress on the myth's bizarreness reflects Dio's stance towards the entire 'divine-city' material, which is one simultaneously of ironical disavowal and ironical assertion of his powers to scale such Platonic and Homeric heights (29). To some extent also, within the 'divine-city' material, the stress distinguishes, conventionally, between the rationalism of an 'account' (38) and the cloudiness of 'myth' (39). This again reflects Dio's double agenda: appeal both to Stoic and to Platonic material; the 'account' belongs to the 'more accurate philosophy' of Stoicism (26), the 'myth' deploys 'Plato's liberty of style' (27), its details necessarily less 'accurate' than Stoicism's. Appeal to Magian authority is also Platonic (*Alcib.* 122a; [*Axioch.*] 371a). These factors, however, do not fully explain why Dio describes as Mithraic what is not Mithraic but just as Stoic as the formally contrasting 'account'-material of 29–38, nor why he stresses its bizarreness so heavily.

One factor concerns the Borysthenites' status as would-be Greeks surrounded by barbarians. They are given both a Stoic account of the divine city and a basically Stoic myth which is proclaimed as 'Mithraic', 'barbarian', and 'out-of-place' and which disputes Greek traditions (40–2, 48–9). This myth could not be more serious in its concerns—the organization of the universe and its successive destructions and rebirths—nor more universal in its application—to all men, irrespective of race, at all times. Dio seems to say that virtue and true understanding of the gods and the universe can be found in unexpected 'places': as in *Olympicus*, Greek thought is especially honoured, but other human beings may contribute to the understanding of the highest truths of the universe—even the Iranians, represented by the Sauromatians (Sarmatians) with whom the Borysthenites are constantly at war (3, 8).

It is particularly pointed that Dio relates the 'Magian' myth in response to Hieroson. For the latter's observation (25) that, in contrast to Dio, visitors to Borysthenes are only nominally Greeks and are actually more barbarous than the Borysthenites themselves, with whom they exchange poor-quality goods, echoes Dio's earlier merchandise simile (11, cf. 5). But whereas Dio allowed the possibility of good-quality merchandise from any source, Hieroson assumes the impossibility of good-quality barbarian merchandise. Furthermore, he apologizes for his request for a Platonic exposition on the ground that 'it may be "out-of-place" for a barbarous speaker to delight in the most Hellenic of writers' (26).[39]

Dio's 'apology' for 'out-of-place' Magian material interacts with Hieroson's preconceptions in contradictory ways. *Qua* apology, it acknowledges Hieroson's request for impeccably Hellenic material. But Dio provides Hieroson with formally non-Hellenic material. Yet this formally non-Hellenic material is actually not non-Hellenic. Yet in turn, the rhetorical effect of providing formally non-Hellenic material is not erased, especially for the Borysthenites, who cannot penetrate the philosophical disguise. For them it remains both disconcerting and educative to receive the highest truths about the universe wrapped up in the teachings of their Iranian enemies. We may also recall Dio's own projected visit to the Getae, who here, as in *Olympicus*, are not necessarily despicable: they too may represent that 'alien wisdom' which may benefit even Greeks trying very hard to be Greeks. For Greekness is not just language and culture: it includes virtue.

Other factors concern Dio's external audience or audiences. As in *Euboicus* and *Olympicus*, one effect is to boost Dio's own claims as philosopher and embodiment of Greekness. There is also the question of philosophical doctrine. Not only non-Stoics but by Dio's day even some Stoics rejected the doctrine of the universe's cyclical destruction and rebirth.[40] Hence elaborately distancing irony might seem an appropriate rhetorical mode for exposition of such material.

How should the Prusans take the 'Magian' material? Just as the Borysthenites are racially challenged by Dio's giving them an 'Iranian' myth, the Prusans are also racially challenged (although differently): they, presumably, expect exotic tales from Dio the returning traveller, but the exotic material which Dio so flamboyantly produces turns out to be Greek.[41] The effect is disconcerting but also, apparently, ingratiating. Greek values seem to be affirmed and the Prusans can feel superior to the gullible Borysthenites as Dio passes off standard Greek philosophical material for Eastern wisdom. But the material's unexpected presentation and the earlier jolt to Prusan self-esteem must unsettle their self-satisfaction. Even for them, the rhetorical effect of the myth's 'barbarian' presentation remains. Its hybrid nature seems to suggest the ultimate harmony of Greek and barbarian peoples within the universe. Here again, the Borysthenites provide an ambiguous paradigm for the Prusans and other Greeks: in some ways

---

[39] On this sentence see Russell (1992), 224–5.

[40] Rist (1969), 175–6, 202.   [41] Russell (1992), 232.

their barbarism prevents their fulfilment as true Greeks, in other ways it adumbrates the ultimate fusion of Greek and barbarian within the universal city ruled by God the king.[42]

What of the Romans? As in *Olympicus*, allusion to the Romans brings them within the interpretative framework. But nothing indicates that the cosmic city offers a paradigm for the Roman empire. While an analogy between Zeus, king of all, and the emperor is always a theoretical possibility, exploited, as we have seen, by Dio himself in addressing Trajan, it is here deliberately short-circuited by the sharp criticism of the single shaven man, which performs an 'exclusion' function analogous to that of the Dacian section in *Olympicus*. The attempt to interpret the 'regeneration' of the universe as a metaphor for the rebirth of the Roman empire under Nerva and Trajan[43] also founders on Dio's insistence that the newly created universe is 'far more resplendent than it appears today' (58). Rather, this periodic regeneration is an essential manifestation of divine providence. Moreover, before his regeneration and expansion of the universe the 'erect' divine Fire 'occupied as great a "place" as possible' (53): the 'place' that ultimately matters is not Borysthenes or Prusa, the Greek world (5), barbary, or the Roman empire: it is the 'place' of the universe. Dio's lengthy and remarkably sexy description of the act of regeneration (55–7) is also integral to the whole speech. For the Borysthenites' homosexuality and 'sexual arousal' in anticipation of Dio's discourse (26) represent a striving, however imperfect, towards the true, divine, love that is at the heart of the universe. (The Platonic 'ladder of love' is also relevant here.)

As in *Olympicus*, Dio offers his audiences these great Stoic reflections on the workings of the universe not in order to reconcile them to the Roman empire but to give them a higher vision. Both in space and in time this vision dwarfs and transcends that empire, but it can provide a context and a standard for the expression of true Greekness, because it is Greek thinkers who have come closest to an understanding of the divine. Greekness, however, cannot be an exclusive thing, for Greeks may benefit from barbarian wisdom and we are all children of God (cf. *Euboicus* 138). This vision is at once what ought to be and what, ultimately, is, and the right way to handle problems of racial identity and conflict lies in emulation of the cosmic harmony. The

---

[42] Within Dio's interpretation of Stoic theology 'God' is a wholly appropriate term: Russell (1992), 14–15.

[43] Russell (1992), 23, 233.

requisite adjustments of attitude and behaviour will naturally vary according to circumstances: the Prusans, beset by Romans, must desist from flattering them, the Borysthenites, beset by barbarians, should preserve, deepen, and in some ways redefine their Greekness, but should also become more receptive to barbarian religious thought. As in *Olympicus*, Dio is not 'anti-Roman' as such; he cannot be: the Romans are necessarily (potential) fellow-citizens of the Greeks (and of everybody else) in the cosmic state. What he pointedly resists is the universalizing claim of the Roman empire, whether it proclaims itself the earthly instantiation of that state or encroaches upon the Greek way of life (17). Dio's warm and humane interpretation of Stoic cosmopolitanism encompasses concern for Greek cultural integrity, openness to barbarian wisdom, and a profound sense of kinship between all human beings and between humans and the divine. This is a fine and noble speech, as well as being an extraordinarily subtle one. Donald Russell is right to discern in both *Olympicus* and *Borystheniticus* that 'sublimity' whose 'cosmic dearth' was lamented by Dio's great contemporary, 'Longinus'.[44]

IV

Dio, we agree, adjusts his message to his audience. He can criticize the Roman empire before Greeks (*Olympicus*, *Borystheniticus*); to the Romans (*Euboicus*) and to Trajan (*Orr.* 1–4)[45] he is the insider who delivers honest advice and warnings. This is a matter of practical moralism, not of inconsistency. Now in some respects Dio was, I still believe, a dreadful fraud,[46] hence his self-projection as a moral and philosophical paradigm was a double-edged ploy, which often encountered, and indeed created, resistance among his contemporaries (even though it is generally tempered by irony and wit). Yet, in Donald Russell's humane words, Dio is also, sometimes even at the same time, 'a moralist of convincing earnestness and charm'.[47] The greatness of these three speeches derives from their combination of literary excellence, profound moral seriousness, and intense engagement with the problems of being Greek in the Roman empire.

[44] Russell (1992), 2–3.   [45] I here rely upon Moles (1990).
[46] Moles (1978).   [47] Russell and Winterbottom (1972), 504.

14

The Poetics of the *Paraphthegma*: Aelius Aristides and the *Decorum* of Self-Praise

IAN RUTHERFORD

The subject of this chapter is one of the most boastful works of prose to survive from antiquity, Aelius Aristides' *Concerning a Remark in Passing*, which he wrote to justify an incidental comment in praise of himself dropped while delivering a prose-hymn in honour of Athena.[1] This may seem an inappropriate choice for a volume of essays honouring Donald Russell, whose modesty is famous. But the issues covered in the paper are ones that have engaged him throughout his professional life. And, though he has never written on this particular work, I suspect that he has been touched by its charms.

During his incubation in the temple at Pergamum (probably in AD 145–7) Aristides delivered a prose-hymn in honour of Athena (apparently not the extant 37K, which is shown to be later by the subscription).[2] In the middle of this performance, or perhaps at the end,[3] he discussed the nature of his *Prooimia* (105), and this discussion included praise of his own abilities, and of the idea of divine inspiration. This remark-in-passing or παράφθεγμα, as Aristides called it, was made in consequence of a dream (21). He received criticism from a member of his audience for making it, and took up the challenge posed by the critic in *Concerning a Remark in Passing*.

What was the παράφθεγμα? Aristides seems to have in mind some or all of the following factors. First, a παράφθεγμα is an interruption or incidental remark judged against the speech as a whole (cf.

---

[1] I thank the editors for helpful criticism.

[2] On the dating, see Behr (1968), 53. It might, however, be the one mentioned in *Hieros Logos* 4 (50. 25).

[3] In the middle suggested by μεταξύ in 2; at the end suggested by 21, where the παράφθεγμα seems to come after the completion of the speech. In the latter case, there would be a parallel with the *Cheirons* of Cratinus (92).

πάρεργον versus ἔργον);[4] second, because it was a passing comment, it was not premeditated, and it was not part of the prepared or written text of the hymn.[5] (Thus, even if the written text of the hymn survived, the παράφθεγμα would presumably not be part of it, unlike the discussion of the technique of the prose-hymn in the first part of the *Hymn to Sarapis*.) Third, the word also implies that the remark was to some extent a mistake, and this implication is confirmed by the fact that Aristides glosses it with the verb παραληρέω.[6]

The level of self-assertion in the παράφθεγμα was presumably very high. Since *Concerning a Remark in Passing* dates from the period of the incubation, and since in that work he reproduces the text of a dream which is placed in context in the *Hieroi Logoi* (116, discussed below), a good guess might be that the παράφθεγμα included reference to one or more of Aristides' dreams. Candidates would be the dream in which Rhosander appeared and told him he surpassed Demosthenes in dignity (*Hieros Logos* 4 (50). 19), or the one in which Aristides found a common tomb for himself and Alexander the Great ('I rejoiced and conjectured that we both had reached the top of our professions, he in military and I in oratorical power': ibid. 48–9), or perhaps the one in which Plato was writing in his bedroom (ibid. 57), or that in which Sophocles and Aeschylus were living in his house (ibid. 60). It is easy to see that the claims of divinely favoured status implied by dreams like this could have produced uproar from the audience.[7]

An extra twist to the concept of the παράφθεγμα is added by the fact that at one point, Aristides seems to compare it to the παράβασις in drama (both comic and tragic) (97).[8]

---

[4] For this sense, see LSJ sense 2.

[5] That seems to be the implication of 96, for example.

[6] This is sense 4 in LSJ. For παραληρέω, see cc. 9, 137.

[7] There are similarities between παράφθεγμα and dream. Both are non-deliberate, involuntary. Both are self-aggrandizing. Both come from god, and represent the gods', and in particular Asclepius', validation of the speaker. Both are also insubstantial: dreams are in some sense non-real, and the παράφθεγμα too was unreal, not having been included in the text of the speech. It is almost as if the παράφθεγμα was a dream-like section within the *logos*.

[8] See Behr (1981), ii. 386 n. 143. As elsewhere, I follow the translation of Behr, with occasional modifications. Tragic παράβασις is also attested in Pollux, *Onomastikon* 4. 111 (1. 234 Bethe), where it is attributed to Euripides' *Danae* and Sophocles' *Hipponous*; see de Martino (1982), 16; Bain (1975), 14ff. Approval by Aristides of the παράβασις in Old Comedy is clear also in *Or*. 29 (*Concerning the Prohibition of Comedy*), where he praises it for its 'admonition' and 'education' (28). Cf. Behr (1968), 95–6. Also, in *Against Capito* (11 ff.) he applies the term παράβασις to a short section in *To Plato: In Defence of Oratory* (295 ff.) in which he concedes that Plato's motives in journeying to Sicily may have been good.

καὶ κωμῳδοῖς μὲν καὶ τραγῳδοῖς καὶ τοῖς ἀναγκαίοις τούτοις ἀγωνισταῖς ἴδοι
τις ἂν καὶ τοὺς ἀγωνοθέτας καὶ τοὺς θεατὰς ἐπιχωροῦντας μικρόν τι περὶ
αὑτῶν παραβῆναι, καὶ πολλάκις ἀφελόντας τὸ προσωπεῖον μεταξὺ τῆς
Μούσης ἣν ὑποκρίνονται δημηγοροῦσι σεμνῶς· σὺ δ’ ἡμῖν οὐδὲ τοσοῦτον
μετέδωκας ἀναπνεῦσαι, καὶ ταῦτα ὢν οὐδείς, ἀλλ’ ἀγαπᾶν σοι προσῆκον, εἰ
καὶ ἐν οἰκέτου τάξει παρῆσθα τοῖς γιγνομένοις.

(And one would see that the directors of contests and the spectators permit the
comic and tragic poets and the relatives of these contestants (?) to step aside
and talk about themselves a little. And often removing their masks in the
middle of the Muse whom they are impersonating, they solemnly make public
speeches. But you have not even allowed us to share in this much respite,
although you are a nobody and ought to be satisfied even if you were present at
the events as a slave.)

The παράφθεγμα and the παράβασις are similar in so far as both are
marked off from the rest of the speech and in so far as both involve
self-description. The fact that both words begin with the same preposition may have influenced Aristides in making this comparison
(although the force of the preposition is different); he uses a similar
play on words when he calls the self-advertising inscriptions placed on
dedications by their dedicatees παραγράμματα (i.e. a cross between
ἐπιγράμματα and παραφθέγματα) (88).[9] Perhaps Aristides changed
his position during the παράφθεγμα, and came closer to the audience,
or moved to the side.[10]

Concerning a Remark in Passing purports to be a defence against the
critic's charge of arrogance. An utterance which is beside the point
(πάρεργον) thus becomes the main subject of a speech, a paradox
whose spiritual father is perhaps the paradoxical sophistic encomium
on subjects inherently unworthy of praise, such as Polycrates' eulogy
of salt.[11] The work has a tripartite structure. The first section, after the
introduction, is a catalogue of instances of pride in Greek literature
(11 ff.), included to demonstrate that self-assertion is allowable if the

[9] So Behr (1981). The *paronomasia* is found one more time when Aristides says:
παρελήρησα (137).
[10] The same comparison may underlie the use of the word *paraskenion*, contrasted to
skene in the following section (136): καὶ σὺ τὴν σκήνην θαυμάζων τὰ παρασκήνια ᾐτιάσω
καὶ τοὺς λόγους ἀφεὶς ἐτήρεις τὰ παραφθέγματα. ('And although you expressed admiration for the stage, you criticized the scenery at the sides; and neglecting my speech, you
carefully observed my remarks in passing.') Here the *paraskenion* is the scenery at the
sides of the main stage. Did Aristides perhaps change his position between speech and
παράφθεγμα, like a chorus coming forward?
[11] Pease (1926).

speaker is a good man. It draws on almost all the major genres of classical literature, with the exception of tragedy and New Comedy; he includes nothing after Demosthenes. He begins with a series of examples from Homer (Thersites versus Achilles; Nestor; Odysseus among the Phaeacians (25–43); Zeus (45–50). Most of this section concerns Homer's portrayal of heroes, though he mentions the passage about the 'blind old man of Chios' at the end of the *Homeric Hymn to Delian Apollo*, which he naturally takes as a self-description by Homer.[12] Then he passes to lyric poetry: Sappho, Alcman (51–4), Pindar, Simonides, epigrams (55–67); surprisingly, he is not specially interested in hymns (he does, however, cite the opening of Pindar, *Paean* 6). After poetry, he turns to history (68–74), oratory (75–9) (particularly Demosthenes, *De Corona*), and philosophy, taking the example of Socrates (80–3), criticizing the arrogance he displays in Plato's *Apology* which belies his reputation for self-deprecation.[13] After that he moves to the oratory of the generals Iphicrates of Athens and Epaminondas of Thebes (84–8); then to painters (88–90); back to literature and comic poets (91–4); and then Isocrates, *Panegyricus* (96–7). He ends with the observation on the dramatic *parabasis* cited earlier.

The aim of this section is complex. The ostensible purpose is to show that pride is a traditional Greek characteristic, but he is particularly interested in examples that are more audacious than his own remarks, so that he can argue *a fortiori* that his παράφθεγμα was comparatively trivial. Alcman's implicit comparison of himself to a Muse or a Siren is more arrogant than Aristides' statements (52); Pindar includes self-praise right at the beginning of *Paean* 6 (58); Demosthenes' arrogance in *De Corona* is premeditated, whereas the παράφθεγμα was extempore (75); Isocrates was allowed to praise himself in the *Panegyricus*, and Aristides not allowed to say this even outside his speech (96); Cyrus in Xenophon's *Hellenika* rages *before* battle, whereas Aristides raged *during* it (104–5).[14] The two aims are in a certain tension, as Aristides admits when he expresses a concern that he is criticizing examples of excessive praise so much that he might end up proving that self-praise is bad (59).

[12] The implications of Aristides' treatment of the *Homeric Hymn* have been explored by de Martino (1982), 26 ff.

[13] Thus far Aristides follows the structure of the reading-list: poetry, history, oratory, philosophy. This is the same as the order in Quintilian, *IO* 10. 1, and in Dio of Prusa, *Or.* 18 (*Peri Logon Askeseos*). The order in Dionysius, *On Imitation* 2 is slighly different: poetry, history, philosophy, oratory.

[14] So in the secondary catalogue (137) Solon wrote a poem about his achievements, whereas Aristides merely made a passing comment.

After the catalogue follows the second major section: a discussion of Aristides' oratorical technique and the sources of his genius (98 ff.). The inspiration of the orator can be represented as fire (110: a borrowing from Heraclitus?)[15] and even the flooding of the river Nile. Above all, the force of possession is irresistible (112): if the speaker's words are not uttered, they are unbearable (114). In an amazing mixed metaphor, he says that the heat of divine inspiration guides his speech like a ship (115).[16] In the middle of all of this, he describes the divine sanction of a dream sent by Asclepius (corresponding verbatim to a dream reported in *Hieros Logos* 4 (50. 52) (dated to AD 147)) (116–18):

ἀνάγκη τὸν νοῦν ... κινηθῆναι τὴν πρώτην ἀπὸ τοῦ συνηθοῦς καὶ κοινοῦ, κινηθέντα δὲ καὶ ὑπερφρονήσαντα θεῷ συγγενέσθαι καὶ ὑπερέχειν. καὶ οὐδέτερόν γε ... θαυμαστόν. ὑπεριδὼν τε γὰρ τῶν πολλῶν ὁμιλεῖ θεῷ θεῷ τε ὁμιλήσας ὑπερέχει

(It is necessary ... for your mind to be removed first from the common and ordinary, but when it has been moved and become scornful, for it to associate with god and to be superior. And neither ... is remarkable. For he who has scorned the general populace converses with god, and he who has conversed with god is superior.)

Because Aristides' mind and rhetorical technique are divinely inspired, he goes on, it is necessary for him to comment on his speeches to the audience; otherwise there is a risk that his techniques will go unnoticed, because when he makes full and rapid use of all the elements of language, the effect is to bewilder and browbeat the audience (119) (a passage that made an impression on contemporary rhetoricians).[17] This is followed by more reflections on inspiration: the orator is said to contain a divine 'footprint' in himself, and his is the task of ensuring that divine 'seed' (of oratory) be disseminated to his audience (122). The orator must be shown to respect and show deference because it is the law of nature that the weak obey the strong (123). The effect of inspiration on the orator is so overwhelming that he perceives the

[15] Heraclitus, *DK* 22B64 (= Hippolytus, 9. 10): τὰ δὲ πάντα οἰακίζει Κεραυνός ('Thunder is at the helm of the whole universe'), where Hippolytus interprets Κεραυνός as 'fire'. Cf. Dio Chrysostomus, 36. 34. There are also parallels for it in hermetic doctrine. The possible Persian background to the Heraclitean doctrine about fire is investigated by West (1971), 170 ff. See also Russell (1992) on Dio 36. 39–61.

[16] Aristides compares himself to a ship at sea during his illness at *Hieros Logos* 3. 17.

[17] Two passages from *Concerning a Remark in Passing* are cited in *On Political Language*, formerly attributed to Aristides. These are 119 ff. at 54. 16 ff.; and 145 at 55. 15 ff. (references are to Schmid (ed.), *Ps. Aristides*). On these borrowings, see Boulanger (1968), 242–3.

speech as the words of someone else (127).[18] And yet for all their brilliance, Aristides' performances are not extravagant like those of a sophist (a theme which has a parallel in Aristides' other invective, *Against Those Who Betray the Mysteries of Rhetoric*).

Toward the end of this section he develops the unusual idea that possession is like illness or the effect of being bitten by a snake (132). Hence Aristides is like Philoctetes, a comparison which throws the critic into the role of the shifty Odysseus.[19] The comparison with Philoctetes also implies, I think, that the rhetorician, like Philoctetes, provides an indispensable service to his community. The idea that Asclepius encourages rhetoric as well as physical healing (i.e. healing = rhetoric) is found in the *Hieroi Logoi*, where he plays with the idea that the illness had the beneficial effect of improving his oratory.[20] But the idea that inspiration, the pre-condition for excellent oratory, is itself like an illness is not found there.[21]

After the section on inspiration, Aristides moves on to the third, shorter section, which is a supplementary catalogue (135–6). He faults the critic for not being lawful in criticizing trivial aspects of Aristides' speech (137), and the theme of law provides a transition to the lawgiver Solon (137 ff.), whose poetry contains calculated self-assertions that are much stronger than those of Aristides.[22] After that he turns to Plato's *Phaedrus* (143 ff.) and Plato's role as a lawgiver in the *Laws* (146 ff.). He finishes off the supplementary catalogue with the examples of the generals Epaminondas and Chabrias. Finally, there is a short conclusion to the work as a whole, rounding it off with the provocative thought that even the critic probably desires that his children be like Aristides (154).

---

[18] τῶν ἐμαυτοῦ λόγων ἠκροώμην ὡς ἀλλοτρίων.

[19] Aristides himself usually puts himself in the role of Odysseus: see Schröder (1987).

[20] Cf. *Hieros Logos* 4 (50). 27: Pardalas said that he thought that the reason for the illness was that Aristides should get better at oratory. *Concerning Concord* (23). 16 (composed in AD 167): Aristides regarded the disease as profitable. *An Address Concerning Asclepius* 42. 15 (end) (composed in AD 177): Asclepius watches over the oratory of Asclepius.

[21] Note that just as the inspiration is like 'fire', so Aristides sometimes describes his diseases as 'fiery'. I note in particular *Hieros Logos* 1 (47). 56, where the doctor Theodotus says that fasting is a bastard outlet for the inflammation which goes out through the chest (ἡ ἀσιτία δὲ . . . νόθος τις ἔξοδός ἐστι τοῦ πυρὸς διὰ τοῦ στήθους διεξιοῦσα). Another attack of πῦρ at *Hieros Logos* 2 (48). 39. Frost and fire at *Hieros Logos* 2 (48). 46. More fevers at *Hieros Logos* 3 (49). 1 (referring to AD 146) and *Hieros Logos* 3 (49). 16 (referring to AD 148). Aristides dreams of a statue being enveloped by fire at *Hieros Logos* 4 (50). 50 (referring to AD 147).

[22] Law in fact was a theme already in 123, 125: you invert the law of nature. Cf. also much earlier at 18.

The basic structure is a central section on inspiration surrounded by catalogues of instances of pride in Greek literature. The surrounding sections justify the παράφθεγμα on the grounds of precedent and general attitude, and on the grounds that other writers praise themselves in their λόγος whereas Aristides only did so in the παράφθεγμα. The central section justifies it on the grounds that Aristides was inspired, that his technique is so complex that it needed to be explained, and also that Aristides' unique status as a divinely inspired and sanctioned orator actually gives him a greater right to praise himself than other writers have, so that it is all to his credit that he does it less than them.

The overall impression the work makes is one of tedious megalomania. One might single out his use of Homer's description of Zeus boasting (45) as a paradigm for his own boasting; the merciless assault on the poor critic, who apparently approved of the prose-hymn as a whole (3, 9); the statement in the proem (10) that the original prose-hymn was worth more than the Nomes of Egypt and the land of Babylon combined; and the concluding reflection that the critic secretly wishes his children to be like Aristides.

The premiss that self-praise is basically offensive (ἐπαχθές) and has to be justified is not new. The earliest trace comes in Aristotle's discussion of the ἀλαζών in *Nicomachean Ethics* 4. 7 (1126^b–27^a). The issue for Aristotle is the truth of what one says: the boaster, by exaggerating his own merits, is guilty of falsehood, whereas in the rhetorical tradition the issue is avoiding offensiveness; only in passing (4. 7. 9) does Aristotle suggest that the 'sincere' man will tend to understate rather than to overstate his excellences, since this is 'in better taste' (ἐμμελέστερον).[23] Later on, a rich rhetorical tradition developed dealing with περιαυτολογία, as the rhetoricians called it, mostly dating from the first to third centuries AD. The same theme occurs in literary texts also: a few decades before Aristides, Plutarch wrote *On Praising Oneself Without Giving Offence*, which suggests ways of doing just that; the influence of the rhetorical tradition is clear. About the same time, Tacitus lamented in the preface to the *Agricola* the fact that self-praise by distinguished men in the form of autobiographical notes used

[23] Radermacher (1897); Pohlenz (1913); 358ff.; see the introduction to the Loeb 5. 110ff. (de Lacy and Einarson); some Roman material is collected by Rudd (1966), 46–7. The technique is mentioned by Alexander Noumeniou at *Peri Rhetorikon Aphormon* Spengel 3. 9ff., citing the proud words of Achilles at Homer, *Iliad* 21. 108; also by Quintilian, *IO* 11. 1.

to be acceptable, whereas now it meets with suspicion, and only slander passes unchallenged.

Most of what the rhetoricians, and Plutarch, say on the subject falls under three headings: (*a*) use it only where it is clear you are forced to; and (*b*) mitigate it; or (more rarely) (*c*) disguise it. Let us look at them in detail.

(*a*) Use it only when you are forced to. Quintilian in his discussion of *decorum* (*IO* 11. 1. 16) says that Cicero's self-assertiveness is always justified by his situation because he is threatened. The same point is made in Ps.-Hermogenes, *On the Method of Power* (442. 6 ff.) and in Ps.-Aristides, *On Political Language* (62. 7). Plutarch, whose account is the fullest, says that περιαυτολογία is inoffensive when you are defending yourself (c. 4), when you are unfortunate (c. 5) or wronged (c. 6), or reproached for your triumphs, like Demosthenes in *De Corona* (c. 7). Plutarch also adds the new point that it is permissible when it serves a useful purpose (cc. 15–17).

(*b*) Mitigate it. Ps.-Hermogenes mentions a technique called 'change of person' (442. 10 ff.), which means that when Demosthenes wants to say something mildly praiseworthy about himself, he addresses the Athenians, but when he wants to say something excessively praiseworthy about himself he addresses Aischines. Ps.-Aristides, *On Political Language* says that self-praise is justified if someone narrates some of his virtues, but rejects others (62. 9 ff.), if before he praises himself he apologizes to the jury (62. 10 ff.), or if he shows that his opponents do exactly the same thing (62. 15 ff.). Similarly, Plutarch says that self-praise can be mitigated by mixing praise of oneself with praise of the audience, as Demosthenes does (c. 9), or one can attribute one's successes to the gods (c. 11), or qualify the praise, pointing out that one's true excellences are not the ones suggested (e.g. great achievements) but others (e.g. personal qualities) (c. 12), or introducing minor shortcomings to temper the praise (c. 13), or imply that one's merits imply shortcomings (c. 14).

(*c*) Disguise it. Ps.-Hermogenes, *On the Method of Power* (441. 15 ff.), Ps.-Aristides (62. 12), and Plutarch (c. 10) all recommend speaking in generalities, so that the audience can infer that the speaker is a good man ('disguise'), and Ps.-Aristides may say the same thing (62. 12).[24] The idea of disguise is also found in Ps.-Dionysius in *On*

---

[24] Radermacher (1897), 421 ff., referring to Gregory of Corinth, Walz 7, p. 1299; also Ps.-Dionysius, B, 96. 14 ff. Usener.

Figured Speeches 1. 8 (53. 14ff.), where the Apology of Socrates is analysed as a covert encomium of Socrates, in which the offensiveness of
the theme is thrown into shadow by the necessity of the defence.

The comparatively high incidence of this theme in the literature of
the first to third centuries AD was noticed by the Russian critic Mikhael
Bakhtin, who suggested that it indicates a change in attitudes to the
relation between the individual and society. As the individual became
more alienated from society, he argued, and the 'classical wholeness of
the individual broke down', the social codes that govern self-presentation in society were obscured, and a crisis developed about what
degree of self-assertion was allowable.[25] Elegant as it is, this hypothesis
is unnecessary. Most of the περιαυτολογία tradition in rhetoric is the
working out of a problem in *decorum* created by a conflict between the
social pressure to assert oneself in public and the social criticism of
excessive assertiveness. This problem would have been particularly
urgent because it has to be faced on every page of the rhetoricians'
favourite model, Demosthenes' *De Corona*, which is a masterpiece of
successful self-praise.

What does Aristides draw from Plutarch and from the tradition of
περιαυτολογία-theory in general? Some of the passages they cite to
illustrate self-praise from classical literature are the same, which
suggests a common source.[26] There are also a few similar arguments:
mitigation enters Aristides' theory of self-praise in so far as παράφθεγμα is mitigated by the fact that it was just that—a παράφθεγμα—
and not direct speech. And at one point he says that the critic also
engages in παράφθεγμα and free speech (147) (although he does not
say that the critic praises himself), which is reminiscent of one of the
arguments in Ps.-Aristides.

He is sympathetic to the idea that self-praise is justified if in a good
cause (one of Plutarch's points). This comes up in the case of Odysseus, who praised himself in front of the Phaeacians in order to
admonish a young Phaeacian (41; *Od.* 8. 408), and also in the case of

---

[25] Bakhtin (1981), 133; Morson and Emerson (1990), 394.
[26] They both quote Achilles at *Iliad* 9. 328: 'twelve cities I destroyed': Plutarch 541d
and Aristides 16. They both mention the defence of Epaminondas: Plutarch 540e;
Aristides 88, 148. They both mention Pericles' speech at Thucydides 2. 60: Plutarch
540c; Aristides 71. Cyrus in Xenophon, *Cyropaidia* 7: Aristides 104; Plutarch 545b.
Nestor in Homer: Aristides 30–36; Plutarch 544e; Demosthenes: Plutarch 541e; Aristides 75–9.

Solon (141).[27] And this fits the fact that both the original παράφθεγμα and *Concerning a Remark in Passing* itself were intended to educate imbeciles like the critic (e.g. 122). However, this idea is remarkably absent in his discussion of the speeches of Nestor: one of Plutarch's prize examples of self-praise for the exhortation of others is the speeches of Nestor in the *Iliad* (c. 15), but, although Aristides dwells on the speeches of Nestor (30–7), he does not mention the possibility that they were intended to encourage.

Despite these similarities, the thrust of Aristides' position is the diametrical opposite of those of Plutarch and the rhetoricians. Aristides believes that any virtuous person ought to be allowed to praise himself, and Aristides more than most, since he is a genius. Hence, one would not expect Aristides to be interested in the idea of disguising self-praise, and in fact he is not. And he does not try to justify self-praise on the grounds that he is threatened. In fact, this argument is conspicuous by its absence. In his discussion of the speeches delivered by Iphicrates, the Athenian general (which Aristides regards as possibly Lysianic), he remarks that he shows great pride in the early one about the bribe (85–6), but maintained this attitude even when his life was placed in danger by the prosecution of Aristophon (86). Plutarch would have said that in the second case the self-praise was more excusable, but Aristides makes no such observation.

Aristides shares with the theory the basic belief that self-praise has to be used only when it is necessary; it is just that his view of what constitutes such necessity is very different. (Paradoxically, a strong point of contact between Aristides and περιαυτολογία-theory is thus also a strong point of contrast.) For Aristides, pride is a necessary possession of Greeks (150). For Aristides, inspiration imposes necessity (112, 115).[28] For Aristides, it is necessary that the orator draw attention to techniques that would go unnoticed (105, 119).[29] Above all, Aristides

---

[27] ἡγεῖτο γὰρ, οἶμαι, τὰ εἰς αὑτὸν αὐτῷ ταῦτα ἐγκώμια πεποιημένα λυσιτελεῖν τοῖς ἄλλοις γίγνεσθαι παραδείγματα. ('He believed, I think, that this laudation which he wrote for himself was of use to other men as an example.') Observed by de Lacy and Einarson in their edition of Plutarch, 149 n.

[28] 112: οὕτω κἂν τοῖς ἀγῶσι τοῖς περὶ τοὺς λόγους τοὺς περὶ τῶν θεῶν πολλὰ τοιαῦτα αὐτῶν τῶν λόγων ἰδίᾳ κινουμένων ὥσπερ ἔκφορα γίγνεται, καί τινα ἠχὴν παρέχεται τότε ὁ λόγος ἀναγκαίαν καὶ ἀκόλουθον τῇ ῥύμῃ καθάπερ βέλος τι σὺν ῥοίζῳ φερόμενον. ('So too in contests involving speeches inspired by the gods, many such parts of speeches, which have a rhythm of their own, are as it were carried off course, and then the speech sounds in a way which is *inevitable* and consistent with its rapid course, like a missile carried along with a whizzing noise.')

[29] 105: ταῦτα παρεφθεγξάμην ἐπιστροφῆς ἕνεκα καὶ κοινῆς ὠφελείας τῶν ἀκουόντων, ὃ καὶ τῶν προοιμίων ἐπαινοῦμεν καὶ προσδεῖν αὐτοῖς φαμέν. ('I made these

represents Asclepius as announcing in the dream that it is necessary for the mind to be raised to a higher level (116). Thus, Aristides justifies self-praise on the grounds that he has no choice: his superiority, his inspiration, his pride, and his calling attention to his rhetorical skills are all irresistible.

There is also a further point. Hitherto, I have considered only Aristides' defence of his παράφθεγμα, but it is also possible to look at *Concerning a Remark in Passing* as a whole, since the work is itself a vehicle for self-encomium (much more, I imagine, than the comparatively brief παράφθεγμα). The chief point to make here is that, whereas Aristides does not avail himself of the traditional justification of self-praise on the grounds that the speaker is threatened, this justification may underlie *Concerning a Remark in Passing* as a whole, which is written in the σχῆμα of a defence. In fact it adds a twist to the conventional justification, since the explosion of self-praise in *Concerning a Remark in Passing* is justified not merely by a threat to Aristides' reputation or position, but precisely by a threat to his right to praise himself.

To sum up: to justify παράφθεγμα, Aristides appeals to the irresistible force of divine inspiration, but also to the conventions of Greek poetry, which require that epic heroes assert their superiority in the face of their adversaries, and which allow a lyric poet to pose as a divinely inspired genius. His ostensible target is the contemptible critic, but I would suggest that the real and implied target is likely to be the conventional rhetorical theory of self-praise, which would have outlawed the παράφθεγμα. Aristides draws a few insights and details from rhetorical theory, but the differences of emphasis are much more striking than the similarities. What he offered the world is a whole new theory of self-praise in which less stress is placed on social *decorum* and more on the brilliance of the subject. It is a *tour de force*, and, rebarbative as Aristides' boasting is, the direct honesty of his approach is refreshing compared with the evasive hypocrisy of

remarks in passing as an admonition and as a means of assisting the whole audience as to what we approve in our *Prooimia* and where our deficiencies lie'); 119: φημὶ γὰρ αὐτῶν ἕνεκα τῶν λόγων συμβαίνειν ἀνάγκην πολλάκις παραφθέγξασθαι τόν γε καθαρῶς ἁπλοῦν καὶ φιλάνθρωπον. εἰ δὲ μή, τοὺς πολλοὺς ἐκφεύγειν ἐστὶν ἃ τῶν κρειττόνων μὴ λαθεῖν. ('I claim that it often becomes necessary for the completely ingenuous and generous man to make remarks in passing on account of the speech itself, but that if he does not, it is necessary that certain features which are too good to go unrecognized escape the notice of the people.')

the traditional theory. What ultimately subverts it, and makes it ridiculous, is that Aristides' surviving writings are nowhere near impressive enough to earn their author this sort of panegyric. But that is another story.

15

The Moralism of Plutarch's *Lives*

CHRISTOPHER PELLING

For there is always a risk that civil life will damage the reputation of those who owe their greatness to warfare, and are ill-suited to democratic equality. They expect to enjoy the same supremacy in this new sphere, whereas their opponents, worsted by them on campaign, find it intolerable if they cannot overtake them even here. Thus they delight in taking a man with a glorious record of campaigning and triumphs, and when they have him in the forum they take care to subdue him and put him down; whereas they behave differently to a man who lays aside and yields the honour and power he enjoyed on campaign, and they preserve his authority unimpaired.

(*Pomp.* 23. 5–6)

When Antony had taken his fill of the sight he ordered the head and hands of Cicero to be impaled over the rostra, as if this were a matter of outraging the corpse; in fact he was making an exhibition of his own outrageous behaviour at fortune's expense, and of the dishonour which he brought on his office.

(*Ant.* 20. 4, cf. *Cic.* 49. 2)

Nothing brought more delight to the Romans as a whole, and nothing won them over more firmly to Otho's side, than the fate of Tigellinus. No one had realized it, but the fear of punishment, which the city demanded as its public due, had already been one sort of punishment in itself; a second sort had been the incurable diseases which racked his body; but the wisest judges put particular weight on those impious and unspeakable cavortings with prostitutes, a style of life to which his depraved taste clung even as it came near to gasping its last. This, thought those wise persons, was the worst punishment of all, outweighing a multitude of deaths.

(*Otho* 2. 1–2)

I. PRELIMINARY

Plutarch, it is agreed, is a 'moralist', a writer who employs his persuasive rhetoric to explore ethics and point ethical truths; but moralism can take different forms. Take the three passages printed above. The first essays a generalization about human experience; the second adopts a particular ethical voice for describing behaviour, commending one mode—not a particularly controversial mode—of viewing an action; the third is similar, but this time the voice is more individual, intimating a view which Plutarch might hold but his audience might find more paradoxical.

It is good to see Plutarch so admired once again, but there is one way in which our generation is out of step. Most ages who have admired Plutarch have been appreciative of his moral content, and have found no difficulty in extracting morals from the *Lives* for their own day. Sometimes, indeed, this has been unnerving, as in the eighteenth century, when Rousseau and others found Plutarch's treatment of liberty so inspiring: Macaulay, not specially tongue in cheek, even held Plutarch responsible for some 'atrocious proceedings' of the French Revolution.[1] But the late twentieth century has no taste for moralism. 'Moralizing' tends to have an adjective before it—'mere', or 'shallow', or 'hackneyed'. Plutarch's rehabilitation as a biographer has largely sprung from an increased alertness to his artistry, but fewer critics of the *Lives* have dwelt on the ethical thought. Prime among them has been Donald Russell, whose work has contributed so much to the revival of Plutarch's fortunes.

Most of us lack the instinctive understanding of moralism which previous generations enjoyed. We accept that it concerns values and conduct; it is a natural next step to assume that a moralist will be telling readers to live their own lives differently—to put it in grammatical terms, that a moral should be an imperative, 'act like this', 'avoid that'. And so, of course, it sometimes is. This is the way in which Plutarch sometimes describes it himself: at *Demetrius* 1. 6 he compares himself with Ismenias the flute-player, who would use bad examples as well as good: this is how you should play, this is how you should not. Yet this is where the modern discomfort begins, particularly when we approach those *Lives* which most invite ethical appraisal. Is the moral of *Antony* the encouragement to public figures to control their sexuality, for

[1] Macaulay (1898; 1st pub. 1828), 185–92; cf. Hirzel (1912), 160–6.

ladies like Cleopatra might be catastrophically distracting? Is *Coriolanus* or *Marius* a simple lesson in the need for education and flexibility?
Are we to assume an audience which really needed telling these things,
all agog for any Cleopatra which came along, all arrogantly proud of
their lack of education or their class-bound inflexibility? These, surely,
were morals which everyone already knew all too well. We may feel
tempted to take a step which is often rewarding in treating tragedy,
and to make these moral views features of the audience rather than the
writer, assumptions which the audience would *already* have and which
the writer could therefore exploit for his own purposes. In Plutarch's
case, these purposes might then be viewed as an extension of the self-
characterization which Stadter has so illuminatingly stressed,[2] Plutarch's presentation of himself as a man of sage, humane, sympathetic
understanding, bonded with the audience in moral harmony. That can
work simply, with Plutarch describing events in a voice which his
readers would welcome as their own: thus, perhaps, the example from
Antony with which we began. Or it can be subtler, as with the *Otho*
case: not all of Plutarch's audience would think in quite the terms he
adopts, but this stronger and more mannered self-projection is still
engaging rather than alienating.

There is something in this approach, but we should also be aware
how similar this Plutarchan phenomenon is to one visible in other
genres, where self-projection is a less profitable approach. If we feel
impatient at the simpler formulations of a Plutarchan moral, then it is
similar to the impatience we feel at those who reduce Sophocles'
Antigone to a sermon on its closing lines, 'respect the gods'—a formulation which the audience would indeed have found unsurprising,
and one which does not match up to the moral intensity of the play
itself. And *Antigone* may be a thought-provoking example in other
ways. In tragedy, as in epic, we have grown more used to thinking
about moralism. We have learnt that works can be ethically reflective
and exploratory, without always producing conclusions which can be
reduced to a simple expository imperative 'do that', 'avoid this'. The
Iliad can explore war and heroism without being simply pro-glory or
anti-war; tragedy can explore paradoxes of polis-life without always
crudely reinforcing or crudely subverting polis-ideology.

This distinction between 'expository' and 'exploratory' moralism is
one to which we will return, though it may by then appear a little
rough. The same is true of a further distinction, that between

[2] Stadter (1988), 292.

'protreptic' and 'descriptive' moralism, with 'protreptic' seeking to guide conduct, 'descriptive' being more concerned to point truths about human behaviour and shared human experience.[3] Such 'descriptive' moralism is suggested by such formulations as *Cimon* 2. 5, where Plutarch includes bad qualities 'as if in shame at human nature, if it produces no character who is purely good or of unqualified virtue'. That may not give Plutarch's audience any firm guidance on how to behave, but it still points a moral truth of the human condition, just as it may be a human truth that men as great as Alexander or Pompey or Antony may be fragile in different ways. The *Pompey* passage with which this chapter began is a good small-scale example of this. It is immediately clear that descriptive moralism often involves a protreptic aspect as well: don't go around killing people like Cleitus or drinking yourself into oblivion; if you are a military man, find out about politics too; avoid Cleopatras. But this may at least remind us that the moralism may have a range and depth which goes beyond the simpler protreptic reductions, just as *Oedipus Tyrannus* is better seen as a study of a great man's fragility than as a warning against intemperate behaviour, or for that matter against intense curiosity.

II. CONTEMPORARY FLAVOURING, OR TIMELESSNESS?

This chapter will explore these distinctions through a more precise question, one which centres on more narrowly political moralizing. What sort of political guidance do the *Lives* offer, and how close is their relevance to Plutarch's own day? If we think of other ancient biographers, some of the most interesting recent work has centred on their moral categories, and the way in which these reflect the contemporary interests of the writer's milieu. Wallace-Hadrill (1983) has brought out how Suetonius' distinctive categories reflect his Hadrianic setting—the stress on *civilitas* and clemency, the preoccupation with *spectacula* and *ludi*, the lack of interest in military courage, and so on. Dionisotti (1988) has emphasized that Nepos' *Lives* recurrently focus on the clash of freedom and tyranny, the desirability of public men's obedience to the state, the dangers of unrestrained self-seeking, all themes which resonate with the experience of the Second Triumvirate. The famous passage of the *Eumenes* is a particularly explicit example:

---

[3] For this distinction cf. Pelling (1988), 15–16.

That phalanx of Alexander the Great had crossed Asia and vanquished Persia; glory, and also licence, had become ingrained; now they presumed to issue commands to their leaders rather than obey them, just as our veterans do today. Thus there is a danger that history will repeat itself, and that they too will destroy everything through their licence and lack of moderation, their victims including those who once stood on their side along with their former enemies. If one reads the history of those veterans, he will see the parallels and will judge that the differences are only those of period. (Nepos, *Eumenes* 8. 2–3)

The most thoughtful attempt to relate Plutarch to his political milieu, that of Jones, was sceptical of such precise contemporary allusions in the *Lives*. He found hints of contemporary concerns with harmony and concord, but he also emphasized, for instance, that Plutarch could criticize the self-deification of Hellenistic kings without feeling that this need reflect on Roman emperor worship.[4] And it is clear that Plutarch responds much less well than Suetonius or Nepos to the search for contemporary flavouring. Let us consider the qualities which most regularly excite Plutarch's interests. If we consult Wardman's catalogue, we find an emphasis on steering a middle path between demagogy and tyranny; on disarming the envy of opponents; on winning military victories but not abusing success; on giving a lead in battle but not exposing oneself to unnecessary personal risk; on an appropriate degree of ambition.[5] If we consult Bucher-Isler, we find the thickest lists of examples for bravery, energy, prudence, justice, cowardice, arrogance, lack of self-control, and awkwardness in personal encounters.[6] Of course, these virtues and vices have some relation to his own time; they have some for any time, including our own; but do they really have more relevance for Plutarch's own day than for any other?

Take that emphasis on military qualities, bravery, keeping a cool head when successful, not exposing oneself to unnecessary danger; or, if we turn to a more 'descriptive' type of moralism, that type variously illustrated by Pompey and Marius and Coriolanus, the brilliant general lost in the tricks of politics. In the *Praecepta rei publicae gerundae* Plutarch emphasizes that, in matters of war and peace, the world has changed:

Consider the greatest goods which cities can enjoy, peace, freedom, prosperity, a thriving population, and concord. As for peace, the peoples have no need of politicians at the present time; every war, Greek and barbarian, has disappeared. (824c)

[4] Jones (1971), esp. 108–9, 123–4. [5] Wardman (1974), 49–132.
[6] Bucher-Isler (1972).

No wonder that Plutarch's contemporary Suetonius has relatively little to say about warfare; yet the *Parallel Lives* are preoccupied with soldierly virtues and are full of wars, often with disproportionate space and emphasis—the Parthian wars in the *Antony* or the *Crassus*, for instance.

Some might seize on this same example in a different way. Wars may have vanished from the world of small-town Greece, but Plutarch knew of the wider world of Rome. Trajan was probably planning a Parthian war at the precise time when Plutarch was preparing *Antony* and *Crassus*. Was this in Plutarch's mind?[7] We should doubt it. The same line of reasoning, applied to *Marius*, would convince us that Trajan was planning to attack Germans and Cimbri; to *Caesar*, that he was turning to Gaul. If we search for references to Dacia in the *Lives*, they are conspicuously scarce: Caesar's Dacian aspirations are given a couple of lines (*Caes.* 58. 6–7).[8] And at this same time Trajan was also emphasizing a connection with Hercules, pointing to the traditional Stoic associations of toil and beneficence to humanity.[9] Plutarch's Antony plays the Hercules as well, but in a very different way—a swaggering bluffness, with more than a breath of the comic *miles gloriosus* (*Ant.* 4). If any contemporary association had been caught, it would have been extraordinarily gauche, and Trajan surely never crossed Plutarch's mind. Plutarch has other reasons for emphasizing Parthia, where so many of Antony's frailties and virtues showed themselves so plainly; a few chapters later the Actium campaign reprises many of the same points, but this time events are even more catastrophic. Parthia can point many truths about an Antony, impetuous, valiant, irrepressible, lovable, and deeply flawed; but those are traits which might recur with other people at other times. They are points about a timeless human nature, not about AD 110–15. Similarly the German fighting reveals many of the best features of Marius, which will show themselves in so distorted a form when he returns to politics; and Caesar's fighting in Gaul marks the successful version of the energy and φιλοτιμία which will guide Caesar's rise as well as sealing his end.

This 'timelessness' deserves further stress. The *Lives* are narratives of particular past events, but Plutarch, like so many Greek writers

---

[7] Different answers to this question are given by Scuderi (1984) on *Ant.* 34. 9 and 37. 1 and by Pelling (1988) on *Ant.* 34. 9 and intr., 4.

[8] Here the same goes for Suetonius, *Divus Iulius* 44. 3.

[9] Jones (1978), 116–19; cf. Pelling (1988) on *Ant.* 4. 2.

about the past, had a gift for extracting points of general, timeless significance from such details of narrative: often he makes such generalizations explicit, as in our initial example from *Pompey*. Often too the timelessness is less explicit, and becomes more a question of the categories of interpretation which he tacitly prefers. One aspect is his liking for formulating political controversy in fairly standard terms, exploiting categories which cut across different cultures and periods, such as the antithesis of *demos* and *oligoi*.[10] These categories do not always sit comfortably on the periods which he is describing, but they do not fit his own day any more closely, and he is not imposing distinctively contemporary preoccupations. In particular, he frequently remoulds his material to present powerful demagogic leaders anxious to lead the *demos* in rebellion, and rise on the people's shoulders to establish personal tyrannies. It is hard to imagine a political atmosphere more remote from Trajanic Rome; and it is more remote still from the Greek world of the *Praecepta rei publicae gerundae*. That is not a world of fierce *demos–oligoi* confrontation and tyrannical aspiration. True, the *demos* has to be handled tactfully: leaders may have to put on a spurious show of disagreement over trivialities, for instance, but only in order to carry the really important matters with less bother (813a–c); and 'overthrows of tyrants' are explicitly one of the spheres of glorious activity which the world no longer admits (805a).

Critics sometimes comment on this 'timelessness' as a weakness of Plutarch's historical vision. We say that he assumes every generation to be more or less the same, so that he applies the same moral categories to each period in turn; that he fails to weigh his judgements of characters against the moral norms and expectations of the societies in which they lived.[11] Perhaps we have overstated this. He is certainly capable of generalizing about different societies and bringing out what was morally distinctive about each. Thus he identifies the bellicosity of Rome. '"Did not Rome make her great advances through warfare?" That is a question requiring a lengthy answer for men who define "advance" in terms of wealth, luxury, and empire rather than safety, restraint, and an honest independence' (*Numa* 26(4). 12–13). And several times Plutarch dwells on the destructive moral decline of

---

[10] Pelling (1986*a*) and de Blois (1992).

[11] Thus Bucher-Isler (1972), 73–4; Wallace-Hadrill (1983), 108; Pelling (1986*a*), e.g. 177, 187. As so often, the most perceptive judgement is that of Donald Russell, in this case Russell (1966*a*), 141–3.

Rome, the greed, the selfishness, the luxury, the provincial ransacking and extortion.[12] He also adduces circumstances of time or background to explain quirks of a particular character: the Spartan educational system helps to explain a Lysander or an Agesilaus (*Lys.* 2. 2–4, *Ages.* 1. 5); the perpetual warfare of the time can explain why Marcellus' taste for Greek culture took such an uncomfortable form (*Marc.* 1. 3–5).

It is notable too how rarely Plutarch's moral judgements are wholly anachronistic. Sometimes they are, as when he criticizes the Gracchi for their φιλοτιμία (*Ag.–Cl.* 2); but he does not attack Caesar for his intense version of the same trait. That is a *Life* where explicit moralism is scarce: such criticism would have been insensitive to the ambitious norms of Roman political life. He is more interested in tracing how Caesar's φιλοτιμία operated, how it built him and then destroyed him, as the pressures of success forced him to measures which fed the resentment against him. That is a more descriptive style of moralism, 'how φιλοτιμία works' rather than 'avoid excessive φιλοτιμία'; and one which is both timeless in its application and a reasonable extrapolation even from the peculiar norms of Roman politics. Nor does he criticize Flamininus when he is prepared to make peace with Philip rather than allow a successor to take over the war and win the glory (*Flam.* 7. 1–2). Plutarch is very clear in bringing out what Flamininus was doing, clearer than his source Polybius.[13] Yet he does not inveigh against him, even in a *Life* so concerned with φιλοτιμία and the ways in which it could be corrupted. He knows that Roman politics were like that, that this is how Roman generals thought.[14] He limits his criticisms of Flamininus' φιλοτιμία to the vindictiveness in the hunting down of Hannibal (*Flam.* 20–1), and that is surely a fairer point; just as he is not anachronistic in criticizing Pompey so strongly for yielding to the pressure of his lieutenants, or Lucullus for the extremity of his hedonistic retirement (*Pomp.* 67. 7–10, *Lucull.* 40–1). These are points which contemporaries too could have made, and in some of the cases clearly did make.

Plutarch's approach, then, was not 'timeless' in the sense that he was insensitive to historical change; it is simply that points particularly apposite to one period or one milieu were less interesting to him. Immediately one says, 'one can only understand Pompey by relating

---

[12] *Pomp.* 70, *Sulla* 1. 5, 12. 8–14, *Phoc.* 3. 3 (on Cato), *Aem.* 11. 3–4, *C. Mai.* 4. 2, 16. 8, 28(1). 2–3.

[13] Polybius 18. 10. 11–12.

[14] Pelling (1986*a*), 177.

him to the social circumstances of Picenum in the first twenty years of his life', one is making points less likely to be relevant to an audience of different circumstances. It was the more general, more widely applicable points which engrossed Plutarch more, and that is the sense in which he had a taste for the timeless.

III. PHILOPOEMEN AND FLAMININUS

Philopoemen and Flamininus provides an interesting test case for these questions of timelessness and contemporary relevance. In this pair he is treating the first important intrusion of Rome into Greece. The 'freedom of the Greeks' is a recurrent theme, one which is highlighted by the mirroring great central panels of each *Life*. After Philopoemen has killed the Spartan 'tyrant' Machanidas he is fêted by the Greeks at the Nemean games of 205. The whole theatre turned to him as the lyre-player recited the line of Timotheus, 'he wrought Greece her freedom, her grand and glorious crown' (*Phil.* 11. 3–4). Freedom recurs throughout that *Life*: Philopoemen's last years are spent in trying to assert the dignity of Greece against the Roman intruders, 'endeavouring to draw the most powerful speakers and statesmen in the direction of liberty' (*Phil.* 17. 3). Yet, paradoxically, it was one of these Roman intruders who finally gave Greece that liberty: Flamininus, at that proclamation of the Isthmian games of 196, a second theatrical festival which provides the equivalent central panel of his *Life* (*Flam.* 10–11). Plutarch there makes the paradox explicit: after all those great national struggles for liberty, it was now the Roman outsiders who brought them that freedom.

They thought about Greece and all the wars she had fought for freedom; and now it had come almost without blood and without grief, championed by another people, this finest and most enviable of prizes . . . Men like Agesilaus, Lysander, Nicias, and Alcibiades had been great warriors, but had not known how to use their victories to noble and glorious ends; if one discounted Marathon, Salamis, Plataea, and Thermopylae, and Cimon's victories at the Eurymedon and in Cyprus, all Greece's wars had been fought internally for slavery, every trophy had been also a disaster and reproach for Greece, which had generally been overthrown by its leaders' evil ways and contentiousness . . . (*Flam.* 11. 3–7)

It was the Greeks' own φιλονικίαι which had been so self-destructive. In the context of the pair that is a most suggestive theme, for φιλονικία is Philopoemen's word (*Phil.* 3. 1, 17. 7): the contentiousness that led him to take on other Greeks, eventually even destroying the ancestral constitution of Sparta. Flamininus is φιλότιμος, Philopoemen is φιλόνικος (*Flam.* 22(1). 4), and the two men's qualities have come to embody something of their two countries as well. Philopoemen was indeed the 'last of the Greeks', and in several senses.

These emphases of the pair—freedom, Greek contentiousness, Roman intervention—would certainly have a resonance for Plutarch's own generation. The 'freedom of the Greeks', that delicate possession which Philopoemen upheld and Flamininus bestowed, remained delicate in his own day. In AD 67 Nero had come to Corinth and proclaimed the freedom of Greece: Plutarch himself compares that announcement with the great proclamation of Flamininus (*Flam.* 12). Yet that freedom had turned sour. Nowadays, as the *Praecepta rei publicae gerundae* stress, the constant threat of Roman intervention lay over Greek public life. 'As you enter on any office, you should not merely remind yourself, as Pericles did whenever he took up the general's cloak, "Be careful, Pericles; you rule over free men, over Greeks, over Athenian citizens"; but you must also say to yourself, "You rule as a subject: the city is subject to proconsuls, the procurators of Caesar"' (813d–e). An important theme in the *Praecepta* is the need for Greek local politicians to act with responsibility, but also with dignity: they should develop the art of controlling their cities without constant recourse to Rome, and without allowing the sort of disorder or affray which would force Rome to intervene (814c–816a). The Greek cities had as much freedom as their masters chose to give them; that had to be accepted (824c); and that freedom was too valuable to be abused. And one of the greatest dangers was, precisely, φιλονικία, 'contentiousness': that produced the disorder which forced Rome to intervene even more actively than she might have wished (814e–815b). Nearly three centuries earlier, Philopoemen's differences with Aristaenus centred on the degree of deference which Greeks owed to Rome, and the ways of minimizing Roman intervention (*Phil.* 17. 2–5), Aristaenus arguing 'that they should do nothing to oppose or offend the Romans', Philopoemen preferring a more active independence though making some concessions; yet Philopoemen himself embodied that contentiousness which endangered the freedom he championed.

These issues clearly had their counterparts for Plutarch's audience. The need to steer a path between dignified self-respect and provocative self-assertion was still problematic; contentiousness and greed could easily prove Greece's worst enemies. Of course *Philopoemen* grazes those questions, and the issues would strike Plutarch's audience as absorbingly familiar. But how sharp a political moral did Plutarch intend that audience to draw, and how specific were the lessons for their own political life?

The *Praecepta rei publicae gerundae* again give some guidance, and illustrate the facility which Plutarch has, and which he expects in his audience, in extracting morals from past events and applying them to new contexts. The work is full of *exempla* from the distant past, and its addressee, Menemachus of Sardis, is expected to draw conclusions from the worlds of Themistocles and Pericles, Nicias and Archidamus, Pompey and Cato and use them to guide his conduct in his own very different world. At the same time Plutarch expects discretion as well as facility in applying those morals.

We laugh at small children when they try to pull on their fathers' boots and wear their crowns; but what of the leaders in the cities, when they stupidly stir up the ordinary people and encourage them to imitate their ancestors' achievements and spirit and exploits, even though those are all quite out of keeping with present circumstances? Their behaviour may be laughable, but the consequences they suffer are no laughing matter. There are many other deeds of the Greeks of old which one may recount to mould the characters of the people of today and give them wisdom. At Athens, for instance, one might remind them not of their deeds of war, but of the nature of the amnesty decree under the Thirty; or of the way they fined Phrynichus for his tragedy about the fall of Miletus; or of how they wore crowns when Cassander refounded Thebes, but when they heard of the clubbing at Argos, with the Argives killing 1,500 of their fellow-citizens, they gave orders for a procession of purification around the whole assembly; or of the episode during the Harpalus affair, when they were searching the houses but passed by the one of the newly wedded bridegroom. Even now one can imitate these things, and make oneself like one's ancestors; as for Marathon and Eurymedon and Plataea, and all those examples which make the ordinary people swell up and fill them with shallow ostentation—we should leave them in the schools of the sophists. (814a–c)

Plutarch clearly hopes his audience will be too sensible to assume too close a correlation between the glorious deeds of the past and anything that might be practicable in present circumstances.

The *Praecepta* passage is mainly concerned with more distant and heroic events, Marathon, Eurymedon, and Plataea. *Philopoemen* and *Flamininus* relate to a period when circumstances were more similar to those of Plutarch's own day. But even here the moral implications of the story remain at a very general level. A self-respecting, dignified stance for independence is good, though one might have to make some (unspecified) concessions; contentiousness, on the other hand, is bad: simple morals like that come out clearly enough, and would have struck Plutarch's audience as utterly unsurprising: everyone knew such things. But they are not enough to make this *Life* into a manual for contemporary statesmen, and anyone seeking more specific political advice would search in vain. Plutarch gives little idea of how the balance should be struck, of what counted as a wisely gauged line of action or what was perilous. Plutarch's striking vagueness at 17. 2–7 about those 'concessions' which Philopoemen made, or the way in which he tried to 'draw the most powerful speakers and statesmen in the direction of liberty', is here significant.[15]

Nor does Plutarch strain to illustrate another theme he preached in the *Praecepta*, that contentiousness can itself be self-destructive, forcing Rome into more direct intervention. He might have done: there were instances where Philopoemen acted in provocative ways which nearly inspired Roman intervention; there were several Greek appeals to Rome and her representatives to interfere with Philopoemen's Spartan settlement in the 180s. Yet Plutarch tells us nothing of all this, though he knew his Polybius well. Sometimes Plutarch visibly shies away from making a moral too contemporary and too sharp. *Philopoemen* stresses Greek contentiousness and it stresses the Roman presence, but it does not bring the two themes together: one can even trace some sleight-of-hand in separating the two themes. The climax of contentiousness is Philopoemen's destruction of the Spartan constitution (*Phil.* 16. 4–9), but Plutarch removes this from its chronological context in order to treat it at a moment when the Romans are far from our thoughts.[16] When Plutarch turns to the increasing Roman

[15] Contrast Polybius 24. 12–14, which has clearly influenced Plutarch's presentation of Philopoemen and Aristaenus, but phrases the disagreement in more detail: Philopoemen's legalism was more thoroughgoing than Aristaenus', but he would co-operate with requests within the terms of the alliance; and so on. Polybius' own readers could extract from that passage much harder and more illuminating guidance for *their* own day.

[16] Thus *Phil.* 16. 4–9 describes this destruction of the Spartan constitution (189 BC) with clear disapproval (ἔργον ὠμότατον . . . καὶ παρανομώτατον, 'a most savage and unprecedented deed'); then *Phil.* 17 turns to the Roman question, reverting to events of 192/1. The Roman question builds to a climax as Philopoemen shows his independence and contentiousness by restoring some Spartan exiles (17. 6). These are in fact the same exiles as he restored in the context of the constitutional dismantling, and Plutarch has referred to them already at 16. 4; but no one would have inferred this from his narrative. He has now come back to the same context, and could, if he had chosen, have delayed

intrusion, he prefers to explain it in a different way, associating it not with contentiousness but with the sycophancy of 'the demagogues' instead (17. 2), a phrase of great vagueness, and one of less contemporary relevance to Plutarch's audience. That intrusion even seems to come at a time when Greek contentiousness, τὸ φιλόνικον, is fading:

Rather as diseases become less acute as the body loses its strength, so the Greek cities were becoming less contentious as they grew feebler.   (18. 2)

That is no way to preach the continuing dangers of contentiousness to a contemporary audience, in a world which was immeasurably feebler still. If a moral is to be drawn, it illuminates not the Greek present, but the Greek past, just as those spectators at the Isthmian games of 196 were thinking of the Greek past when they reflected on Flamininus' gift of freedom. Contentiousness had typified Greece for many generations, but was fading by the beginning of the second century BC: that is the moral we would draw from *Philopoemen* and *Flamininus*, and it is only the *Praecepta* which remind us that contentiousness was a problem still, three hundred years later.

The contemporary resonance of freedom and contentiousness still matters; but it is just that, a resonance. The themes would seem particularly alive and engrossing to the audience, who would find the atmosphere disturbingly familiar; but those readers would be hard put to it to extract any specific guidance for their own political lives. We have already seen that Plutarch prefers the more timeless to the more particular, that he favours modes of historical explanation which transcend the particular period which he is describing; he likes points which transcend the particular circumstances of his own day as well. We might be reminded of the ways in which contemporary affairs impinge on tragedy. It matters that certain plays were performed during the Peloponnesian war, in a context of great human suffering, often generated by Athens herself; but to move from that to specific contemporary allusions is a more delicate matter. Such material touched a nerve, and it might enrich the way spectators pondered their own political and moral problems, but it rarely told them what to conclude or how to act.

the constitution item till here. As it is, the dismantling of the constitution and the Roman question are left in separate trains of thought.

IV. CONCLUSIONS

It is time to return to those more general questions about moralism with which we started. Perhaps three conclusions can be drawn. First, it has continued to prove profitable to relate this 'contemporary reson-ance' to Plutarch's reception, and to think first of the audience rather than the author. The audience already know that contentiousness is dangerous and freedom is a delicate possession, and bring these assumptions to their reading: Philopoemen's and Flamininus' stories chime in with these pre-existent assumptions. We should not only think of the historical interpretation subserving the moralism: the moral assumptions of the audience also predispose them to accept the interpretation. There is evidently a two-way process here, with audience ready for the text, and the text affecting the audience.

Secondly, let us concentrate on the second of the two ways, the moral impact of the text on this receptive audience. It may still look as though Plutarch was telling the audience things that they knew already, and doing so in an expository rather than exploratory way, even if these expository morals are uncontroversial ones, and general rather than specific. Yet it is surely more complicated than that. By the end of the *Life* the audience will have found various shafts of light falling on those initial presumptions, and they will have seen them in various new perspectives; they will have seen that the taste for liberty and the contentiousness coexisted even in a great national hero; they may have sensed wider points about the Greek past; they will under-stand more sharply what range of actions φιλοτιμία can inspire, in Flamininus' case as well as in Philopoemen's. None of this will lead them to doubt their initial presumptions. Freedom is still precious and inspiring, contentiousness still a peril. But their grasp of these morals will not merely be reinforced, it will also be more nuanced. In Plutarch's case the new perspectives are not specially challenging ones; they are piquant rather than shocking, just as it may be piquant to discover that Antony or Cleopatra can be moving in their fall, or that Aristides and Themistocles were mutually incompatible; we may never doubt that the choices made by Antony and Cleopatra were reprehensible, or that Aristides and Themistocles were both great national heroes, but the new insights are again piquant. Perhaps, too, that exploratory/expository distinction is coming to seem inadequate. These new piquancies may not lead in any particular direction; they provoke thoughts rather than command a single unambiguous conclusion, and in that sense they are exploratory rather than expository. But the initial assumptions survive, indeed are reinforced, and no doubts are felt about them: that is more clearly an 'expository' aspect.

Once again, it is interesting to compare tragedy. There too the audience bring their own moral assumptions, and these assumptions are deepened by new insights. True, those new, exploratory insights are more challenging ones. Beliefs in the superiority of Greeks to barbarians, in the ideology of the Athenian polis, in the justice of the gods—all are put to a much sterner test than Plutarch ever essays. In tragedy the new perspectives are more than piquant, they are disturbing and shocking. But there too the initial assumptions generally survive, and are deepened rather than reversed by these new insights and perspectives. Reader-response theorists tend to speak as if the 'negation' of an audience's social or moral ideology is the distinctive contribution of challenging literature; as if, indeed, negation is vital to literature's socially formative role.[17] That seems crude. We might rather recall recent work on Augustan literary and artistic propaganda, which has again shifted the focus more to the audience. Propaganda only works with an audience ready to receive it, when it deepens rather than replaces assumptions;[18] straightforward negation is a poor way of influencing opinion, and it is more effective to add to ideas rather than counter them; more effective still, if one thinks of great Augustan poetry rather than the more basic Augustan propaganda, to see ideology put to a stern test, and nevertheless, arguably, survive. That parallel also suggests that the moralism is still authentic in a more traditional sense, in Plutarch as in tragedy: that it does seek to affect and impress an audience, and to encourage particular moral views—even if these views were identical, or closely related, to those which the audience already held. Augustus was too accomplished a propagandist to waste time on telling his audience what they already knew unless there was some further advantage to this. Propaganda reinforces, it crystallizes, it strengthens the will. Plutarch's interpretations

[17] Cf. e.g. Iser (1974), pp. xii–xiii; (1978), 73, 85; the train of thought is especially clear in Jauss (1983), 25–8, 39–45. Fish (1972), 1–2 prefers to talk of dialectically 'decertainising' moral assumptions, rather as the Russian formalists talked of 'defamiliarization'. These formulations may be more fruitful for tragedy, but even these overstate the case for Plutarch. His audience remain quite certain of their original assumptions, and the persisting familiarity of these assumptions is crucial to the audience's receptiveness to the historical analysis.

[18] D. F. Kennedy (1984) has been very influential. Cf. esp. Zanker (1988) for artistic aspects.

too provide clear and crystallized examples of moral truths, both descriptive and protreptic, which enhance those pre-existent moral insights. Once again we have that two-way process between writer and audience.

'Both descriptive and protreptic': this, thirdly, brings us back to that further initial distinction. The notion of 'descriptive' moralism may still be a useful one: at least, it is useful to see how some *Lives*, like *Caesar*, veer to the descriptive end of the spectrum, while others, like *Aristides* or *Brutus* or *Aemilius Paullus*, tend to the protreptic. But it is also now clearer that there is indeed a spectrum, that the distinction between protreptic and descriptive moralism is a blurred one, and the two forms go closely together: just as, in the *exempla* of the *Praecepta*, descriptions of past human experience can inspire us as we face current problems. *Philopoemen* gives little specific guidance for contemporary politics, but that does not mean that it has no protreptic force. The description of Philopoemen's fighting for liberty can elucidate the dangers, it can point to certain truths of Greek historical experience, and it can also inspire: it can sensitize an audience to the issues; readers have their own moral decisions to make, and they will confront them with greater insight once they grasp how similar behaviour has worked in the past. The protreptic may consist in an invitation to recognize the importance of the issues and to explore them in a particular way, rather than to draw specific practical conclusions; but that is still protreptic. Descriptive and protreptic moralism feed off one another, and that is central to Plutarch's moral programme.

16

'Subject to the Erotic': Male Sexual Behaviour in Plutarch

PHILIP STADTER

Early in the *Life* of Pompey, Plutarch reports that the great general, when a young man, was madly in love with the courtesan Flora, so much so, in fact, that in later years she boasted that he never left her without a bite. Soon Pompey's friend Geminus also became infatuated with Flora, but she rebuffed him, reminding him of her tie to Pompey. However, after Geminus spoke to Pompey, Pompey surrendered Flora to him and never tried to see her again, much to Flora's dismay.[1]

The anecdote is puzzling for several reasons. Though at first it seems to demonstrate Pompey's attractiveness (*erasmion*), which has just been mentioned, the elements of dignity and majesty associated with it are lacking, even denied by the reference to love-bites.[2] The theme of self-control recurs in the following anecdote regarding the beautiful wife of the freedman Demetrius, in which Pompey's awareness of his susceptibility to her beauty leads him to abandon his characteristic courtesy. Nevertheless, he will be accused by his enemies of abandoning the public good to please his wives. The nexus of themes is complex. What does Plutarch think of Pompey's liaison with Flora, and its abrupt rupture? Does he mean the anecdote to be complimentary or critical? What does it imply about Pompey's character? Finally, a question which will help us answer these three, what does it reveal about Plutarch's own attitudes toward sexual behaviour? Plutarch's judgements and sensibilities shape every paragraph of his *Parallel Lives*, in which he holds up models for himself and for his

---

[1] Plut. *Pomp.* 2. 2–3. This topic seems especially appropriate in a collection dedicated to D. A. Russell, who has done so much for Plutarch studies, and recently has translated some of Plutarch's most important works on sexual matters: *Eroticus*, *Advice on Marriage*, *Virtues in Women*, and *Gryllus*, Russell (1993*a*). The title comes from *Ages.* 20. 9, ἔνοχον ὄντα τοῖς ἐρωτικοῖς, cf. *Cim.* 4. 9.

[2] Love-bites are uncommon in the *Lives*: I note only Lamia's at *Demetr.* 27. 8.

readers of qualities to be imitated and avoided in their lives.[3] His eye for the revealing incident and his comprehensive view of human nature make his observations valuable windows into upper-class attitudes at the beginning of the second century.

Most of Plutarch's *Lives* are silent on sexual conduct, apart from mentioning the existence of a wife or children. Unlike Suetonius, Plutarch had no category of vices, including lust, which formed a staple part of his biographical pattern.[4] Sources would have been a problem: when he did not have access to scurrilous attacks, such as those found in Old Comedy or politically motivated slander, he was less likely to find sexual material. In addition, he did not share the modern belief that sexual acts and fantasies are fundamental components of personality, and must be sought out or invented as necessary keys to a life history. Nevertheless, in about a quarter of the *Lives* he does report such behaviour either in his protagonists or others, enough to reveal some of his attitudes and judgements.

Michel Foucault, in his *History of Sexuality*, found in Plutarch's *Advice on Marriage* and *Dialogue on Love* evidence for a 'domestication' of *eros* through the valorization of the marital bond and a shift in the concept of self-control, which no longer expressed male domination but human frailty and the male need for careful defence against troubles.[5] In this view, *eros* is not only a passion, but a unifier and cause of affection, and male limitation of pleasure is seen as desirable. Much more attention therefore is given to the arts of self-control, involving constant examination, self-checking, and self-renunciation. Foucault's approach has been faulted for its preoccupation with the theorizing of philosophers rather than with actual practice.[6] More important is that he misses both the essential conservatism of Plutarch's approach and the personalist and pragmatic slant which he brings to the question, especially in the *Advice on Marriage*.[7] Plato, where he actually addresses sexual morality, is surprisingly close to

[3] *Aem.* I. 5.

[4] Cf. Wallace-Hadrill (1983), 157–8.

[5] Foucault (1990), Pt. 5, ch. 2, 'The Pleasures of Marriage', pp. 176–85, and Pt. 6, ch. 1, 'Plutarch', 193–210.

[6] Cf. e.g. G. E. R. Lloyd in *New York Review of Books*, 33/4 (1986), 24–8, Averil Cameron, *JRS* 76 (1986), 266–71, M. Lefkowitz, *Partisan Review*, 2/4 (1985), 460–6.

[7] Cf. Patterson (1992), Russell (1972), 90–3, Goessler (1962), 44–69. Cf. also Babut (1969), 354–5, noting Plutarch's aversion to the rigidity of Stoic ethics and recognition of the actual needs and limitations of human nature. Plutarch's sensitivity to human needs is consistent with his *philanthropia*, on which see H. Martin (1961), de Romilly (1979).

Plutarch.[8] Plutarch continues to think that the mature, self-restrained male is the dominant figure in a sexual relationship.[9] In these two works, his distinct preference for heterosexual married love over homosexual boy-love is noteworthy, but must be coupled with his insistence on the male's sensitivity and respect for his younger and less educated wife. The *Advice on Marriage* is directed to a young couple of his acquaintance; the *Dialogue on Love* presents a sophisticated and passionate reinterpretation and rebuttal of two of Plato's most famous dialogues, the *Symposium* and the *Phaedrus*.[10] The *Parallel Lives*, treating concrete actions of individuals, permit us to refine and possibly correct our reading of his understanding of sexual behaviour.

Plutarch rarely examines the details or morality of specific sexual actions: thus he does not criticize Pompey's association with the courtesan. However, he often expresses a concern, or explicitly or implicitly makes a judgement, on kinds of male sexual behaviour. An examination of the anecdotes and observations on male sexual behaviour in the *Lives* establishes three types of problematic sexual behaviour: irrational excess, unseasonable lust, and violence; and three positive features: rational self-control, a harmonious relationship, and stimulus to virtue. After surveying these, it will be possible to suggest how these examples of sexual behaviour are used by Plutarch to reveal the character of his protagonists. I consider first the negative cases, then the positive.[11]

Self-control was the common ground of most ancient ethical theories, and Plutarch is no exception. While lack of control, *akolasia*, or licentiousness, *aselgeia*, is always a weakness, it becomes a major concern for him when sexual excess interferes with a man's duties or noble projects. Plutarch ignores physical weakness caused by excessive sexual indulgence[12] but condemns the obsession with sexual or amatory pleasure which distracts the mind from responsible government, especially from war.

The great and tragic example is Antony, whose passion for Cleopatra overrode all considerations of right action. Antony is shown as

[8] Cf. A. W. Price (1989), 223–35, utilizing especially the *Laws*. The rather different view of Lucas (1990) is based on the *Republic*.

[9] Cf. Patterson (1992), Le Corsu (1981), 274.

[10] Cf. Trapp (1990), 157–61.

[11] I omit from consideration the legal sections of *Lycurgus* and *Solon*, interesting as they are, since they do not present men in action. Many instances of sexual behaviour are treated from a different point of view by Le Corsu (1981).

[12] Elsewhere he discusses it: cf. *Advice on Health*, esp. 130a, though in general he seems more preoccupied with overeating and drinking in this work.

weak and unable to resist Cleopatra's charms from the very beginning
(*Ant.* 25. 1). He constantly sets other obligations second to Cleopatra's
demands, until at the battle of Actium he abandoned his men and his
cause to follow her, 'the woman who had already destroyed herself and
would destroy him as well' (*Ant.* 66. 8). *Antony* and *Demetrius* form
the only pair in the *Parallel Lives* explicitly stated to be negative examples. It is significant that the principal weakness of both is a notable
lack of self-restraint in sexual matters, which has a profound effect on
their overall behaviour and success.[13] But whereas Plutarch can say
that Demetrius never let his debauchery interfere with his military
campaigns,[14] Antony was ruined by his tie to Cleopatra.

Not only is an excess of passion reprehensible and even dangerous,
but also the kind of subservience to a woman which such passion
encourages, since, as has been noted, Plutarch believed that even in
the best relationship, the man should be dominant. Antony, because of
his infatuation with Cleopatra, cannot resist her will in any way.
Plutarch is explicit: before Actium, he is 'an appendage to the woman'.
When he follows her ship away from the battle, he is 'dragged by the
woman'.[15] In another case, Plutarch criticizes Ptolemy IV, who was so
given to licentiousness, drinking, and women's ways that the most
important decisions were made by his mistress Agathoclea and her
procuress mother Oinanthe.[16] Ptolemy's domination by his mistress is
demeaning and reprehensible, both personally and politically (*Ag. Cl.*
58. 12).

Two types of sexual behaviour are not only excessive but unnatural.
Incest Plutarch finds repulsive, and he considers Stesimbrotus vicious
for suggesting that Pericles had relations with his own daughter-in-
law.[17] The Persian king Artaxerxes' love for his daughter Atossa is

---

[13] Note also that in the other notably negative pair (though not explicitly identified as
such), *Coriolanus–Alcibiades*, Alcibiades' sexual desirability and flaunting of his power
over his lovers form a significant motif and contrast markedly with Plutarch's silence on
Coriolanus' sexual behaviour. In this case the outstanding feature is Alcibiades' shame-
lessness, whether fleeing as a youth to a lover's house, arrogantly taking Anytus' silver,
forcing his wife to put up with prostitutes in the house, or seducing the wife of Agis of
Sparta. In these cases *eros* is a weapon of power, not of union. Cf. *Alc.* 3. 1, 4. 5–6, 8. 4–
5, 23. 7. On this *Life* see esp. Russell (1966*b*) and (1972), 117–29.

[14] *Comp. Demetr.–Ant.* 3. 2. The sentiment is not entirely borne out by the narrative
of the *Life*: cf. Pelling (1988), 22.

[15] *Ant.* 62. 1: προσθήκη τῆς γυναικός; 66. 8, ἑλκόμενος ὑπὸ τῆς γυναικός.

[16] *Ag. Cl.* 54. 1–2. 'The king himself was so morally ruined (διέφθαρτο τὴν ψυχήν) by
women and drink that when he was most sober and serious, he would celebrate mysteries
and go about in the palace, with a drum, raising money.' Cf. also *Amat.* 753d.

[17] Cf. *Per.* 13. 16. The charge is δεινὸν ἀσέβημα καὶ μυσῶδες.

named an ἔρωτα δεινόν, a frightening or strange love, which he first tried to conceal and restrain. But then, shamelessly encouraged by his mother, he formally married his daughter, ignoring the opinions and customs of the Greeks.[18] Artaxerxes' inability to control his passion, demonstrated by his incest, soon led to vicious intrigues in the royal family. When his son Darius asked that he be given Aspasia, the Phocian concubine who had previously belonged to Artaxerxes' brother Cyrus, the king was extremely displeased. Artaxerxes allowed his son to take her, then within a few months appointed her priestess of Diana in Ecbatana, a post which required that she remain chaste (27. 1–5). This affront drove Darius to plot against his father, encouraged by Tiribazus, who had been twice promised the hand of one of the king's daughters, only to find that in each case the king kept them to be his own wives, first Amestris and then Atossa (27. 6–10). Finally, the younger son Ochus, with the help of his stepmother and lover Atossa, killed off the other heirs and succeeded on his father's death (30, cf. 26. 3). In this case, incest and uncontrolled passion destroy the family and civil society.

However, such is not always the case. Cimon, who was accused of incest with Elpinice (*Cim.* 4. 6–9), nevertheless receives a generally positive portrait, perhaps because he was very loving toward his legitimate wife Isodice and some reported that the marriage to Elpinice was also legitimate, since she was too poor to have a proper dowry. Certainly Cimon's willingness to give her in marriage to Callias when the opportunity arose was accepted by Plutarch as proof that he was not given to unnatural lust. Plutarch's awareness of serious faults in Cimon's character, especially in his youth, tempers but does not negate his admiration for a Hellenic hero. His apology for human weakness in the proem of the life (*Cim.* 2. 3–5) prepares the reader for moral failings which nevertheless do not vitiate his hero's achievements.[19]

Though not so disgusting, Plutarch finds equally unnatural the marriage of an elderly man to a young woman. Cato the Elder, after his first wife died, 'continued in excellent health, to the extent that he as an old man had relations with a younger woman, and made an unseasonable marriage'. It seems that he first made use of a young woman, who secretly came to visit him. However, since it was a small

---

[18] *Artax.* 23. 3–7. Cf. 27. 2: the marriage was παρὰ τὸν νόμον. The story appears to be from Ctesias. Heraclides said that he married another daughter too: cf. 23. 6, 27. 8–9.

[19] In *Lucullus*, instead, the great leader falls into luxury and sloth at the end of his life.

house and his son and his wife lived with him, the affair became known, and distressed the young bride and angered her husband. When he perceived the problem, Cato resolved the matter on the same day by marrying at once the young daughter of a client, one of his under-clerks, much to the surprise of the son (*Cat. Maj.* 24. 1–7). Later Plutarch criticizes the marriage as tarnishing Cato's otherwise excellent reputation for *sophrosyne* (*Comp.* 6. 2–3). First, bringing in a wife of much lower social and economic status, when he already had a grown son, himself with a wife, was inappropriate and demeaning to his own dignity and that of his son.[20] Second, if he really were interested in eugenic breeding for his household and for the state,[21] he would choose a wife from the noblest possible family. Cato's behaviour, which to some might seem refreshingly direct and practical, a convenient answer to a physical or emotional need, to Plutarch indicates personal weakness, petulance, and not a little hypocrisy. The old man's sexual behaviour reveals for Plutarch that Cato's famous *sophrosyne* was not flawless. The Aeschylean contrast between seeming and being had been mentioned at the beginning of the *Aristides*: Cato seemed self-controlled to his admirers, but Aristides truly was such.

Other men criticized for marrying late to a young woman include Sulla and Cicero.[22] Instructive for Plutarch's sympathies is the case of the Spartan politician Cleonymus, who in old age married a young woman of royal blood, Chilonis. However, Chilonis was in love with Acrotatus, a young man in his prime and the son of king Areus, and despised Cleonymus (*Pyr.* 26. 17–18).[23] Both Cleonymus' marriage and his policies turned the people against him, so he called in Pyrrhus to help him at Sparta. As Acrotatus heroically led the Spartans' successful defence against Pyrrhus, all the women envied Chilonis'

[20] Plutarch stresses the social class of Cato's client/father-in-law: he was an underling and a public wage-earner. The woman, like her father, was a client of Cato's (*pelatis*, *Cat. Maj.* 24. 5, cf. *Rom.* 13. 7, *De Fort. Rom.* 323b). A grown son (a point also noted in the parallel story of Peisistratus, *Cat. Maj.* 24. 8) would also see a young wife and possible children as a threat to his expectations of property. According to Roman law, a father could by testament favour one child over another.

[21] A philosophically acceptable if impractical notion: cf. *Cat. Min.* 24. 4–5. The secret use of the prostitute, especially when there is also a new bride in the house, indicates a lack of self-control and a propensity to sexual indulgence unsuitable in an old man.

[22] Cf. *Sull.* 35. 5, *Cic.* 41. 4–6.

[23] The word used of Chilonis, ἐπιμανεῖσα, implicitly criticizes her adulterous desires: the word appears in *Il.* 6. 160 of Anteia's love for Bellerophon, and in Plut. *Brut.* 5. 2 of Servilia's passion for Caesar, and *Brut. Anim.* 991a of women's passion to copulate with male animals.

love for him and the old men cried out, 'Go, Acrotatus, and lay Chilonis. Just make brave sons for Sparta!'[24] Plutarch's disapproval of Cleonymus' late marriage combines with his philo-Laconism to justify even the adultery of Chilonis and Acrotatus. As in the case of Cato, he also implies that sexual relations in marriage are tied to child-rearing, and not to sexual satisfaction alone. The love of Chilonis and Acrotatus joins two young, noble people in a relation which through their children should prove beneficial to the community; Cleonymus' marriage, like his politics, is focused on his own selfish ends, and therefore wrong.[25]

Sexual violence, a particular aspect of excess, is a third area of concern for Plutarch. He particularly associates it with tyrants, continuing a tradition found as early as Herodotus. Thus the Spartan Pausanias, when in Byzantium, was doubly vicious: first he forced Cleonice, unmarried and a child of noble parents, to come to his room, and then, when she tripped in the dark and surprised him, he drew his knife and killed her. For this her ghost haunted him at night, speaking of the justice which follows upon hubris, and the Ionians supported Cimon in expelling him from Byzantium (*Cim.* 6. 4–5). Sexual licence not only characterized Pausanias' tyranny, but was directly responsible for his fall. Similarly, Plutarch shows that Archias, one of those tyrannizing Thebes, was destroyed by his own vices. Those plotting to free Thebes enticed him to a party with promises of married women to debauch, distracting him from all precautions. When the long-expected women finally came, they were in fact conspirators in disguise, and Archias and his party were quickly killed.[26] In the same *Life*, Alexander of Pherae's cruelty, violence, and lust directly led to his death.[27]

Plutarch twice associates homosexual passion with vicious, arrogant assault. He paints in graphic detail Demetrius Poliorcetes' pursuit of the beautiful Athenian youth Democles, just one example of the violence he used against free women and youths of the city (*Demetr.* 24. 3–5). Democles' extraordinary courage and modesty create a

---

[24] *Pyr.* 28. 6: οἶχε Ἀκρότατε καὶ οἶφε τὰν Χιλωνίδα· μόνον παῖδας ἀγαθοὺς τᾷ Σπάρτᾳ ποίει.

[25] For another late marriage, cf. Antiochus' to a woman of Chalchis, οὐ καθ᾽ ὥραν οὐδὲ κατὰ καιρόν (*Flam.* 16. 1–2, cf. *Phil.* 17. 1). Note however, that Antiochus won goodwill from the Chalchidians by marrying a local woman.

[26] *Pelop.* 9. 4–11. 4, cf. *De Gen. Soc.* 577c; 596f.

[27] *Pelop.* 28. 5–10, 35. 5–12. Cf. also the cases of Nicocrates of Cyrene, killed by Aretaphila; Learchus of Cyrene, killed by Eryxo; and Aristodemus of Cumae, killed by Xenocrite, *Mul. Virt.* 255e–257e, 260d–261d, 261d–262d.

stunning contrast with Demetrius' lust. The king followed Democles to a bathhouse:

When Democles realized that the place was deserted and what he must do, the boy removed the cover of the bronze cauldron and leapt into the boiling water, killing himself. He suffered what he didn't deserve, yet his attitude was worthy indeed of his country and of his own beauty.

The relentless, thoughtless pursuit of Demetrius, the efforts of Democles to avoid contact with him, and the final heroic act to escape his attacker become in Plutarch's words a moral *exemplum* of noble innocence violated by a crude and domineering rapist.[28] Similar emotions are expressed in the unusual story which opens the *Cimon* (1. 2–4). A Roman officer presses himself upon a young man of Chaeronea, Damon, who finally kills him in the market-place,[29] and great risk to the town follows. In this case, the violent lust of the Roman has brought death to himself, to his beloved, and to many others. The story presents a horrible example of excess which lessens the negative impact of Cimon's erotic but non-violent tendencies.[30]

For Plutarch as for many writers it was easier to give examples of vicious than of virtuous behaviour. But the areas of unsuitable sexual behaviour which have been discussed so far have their counterparts in behaviour of which Plutarch clearly approves.

The opposites to the wantonness and violence which Plutarch finds so reprehensible are restraint, sensitivity, and faithfulness. Plutarch accepts restraint or *sophrosyne* as the norm, the basic behaviour of the educated man, so rarely makes it a special feature of the character of one of his heroes.

Alexander furnishes perhaps the clearest example. In contrast to his father Philip, Alexander already showed his self-restraint as a child (*Alex.* 4. 8). In his treatment of the captured Persian queen and noblewomen, he matched their beauty with 'his own beauty of restraint and

---

[28] Cf. *Comp. Demetr.–Ant.* 4. 4–5: Demetrius forced οἰκτρῶς ἀποθανεῖν τὸν κάλλιστον καὶ σωφρονέστατον Ἀθηναίων, φεύγοντα τὸ καθυβρισθῆναι.

[29] Apart from other reasons Damon might have had, he had just outgrown the age for such affairs: Ἄρτι τὴν παιδικὴν ἡλικίαν ἀπηλλαχότος. Cf. the similar expression of Alcibiades, *Alc.* 7. 1 (τὴν δὲ παιδικὴν ἡλικίαν παραλλάσσων).

[30] Cf. also the story of L. Flamininus, who had a prisoner killed at a banquet to please his favourite, who had never seen a man die, *Flam.* 18. 4–10, *Cato Maj.* 17. 1–4. The story was a famous case of debauchery: Plutarch cites Valerias Antias, Livy (39. 42, citing a speech of Cato), and Cicero *De Senectute* (12. 42). *Amat.* 768f mentions several young men who killed abusive lovers.

temperance'.[31] Like Xenophon's Cyrus, he does not wish even to see their beauty.[32] He falls in love with Roxane, but again is most *sophron*, waiting until he has married her to touch her (47. 7–8). However, for Plutarch, Alexander's model *sophrosyne* does not mean complete chastity, such as practised by Cato the Younger, but rather restraint and fidelity to one person. Alexander before marrying Roxane had had a child by Barsine (21. 7–9). Plutarch is careful to point out Barsine's nobility and that it was a court decision, taken on Parmenio's advice.[33] His second marriage, with Stateira, was also political (70. 3). Alexander's homosexual behaviour is mentioned only once, in a rather light context, when the Macedonians in the theatre urged Alexander to kiss his beloved, Bagoas (67. 8). Plutarch offers no comment on the story. However, neither in the *Life* nor in his other works does he mention the supposed love relationship of Hephaestion with Alexander.[34] On the contrary, two of the anecdotes on Alexander's continence have him rejecting as shameful suggestions to purchase young boys for his use (22. 1–3). Alexander's *sophrosyne* consists in not taking personal advantage of his power as conqueror. This treatment of Alexander's sexual self-restraint forms part of the larger picture of his character, which sees his basic challenge as the need to conquer himself. The conqueror of Asia can only be a true king if he has control of himself, sexually and otherwise.

Sexual behaviour, for Plutarch, has a positive value beyond the mere exercise of self-control, when it creates a bond of unity between a man and woman in marriage and acts as a force for harmony in the larger community. The Romans' seizure of the Sabine women furnishes an example. Plutarch stresses two factors in the story. First, the capture was not a wanton act of violence, but was absolutely necessary to the survival of Rome, which desperately needed women (*Rom.* 14. 7). The Sabine women were taken not for sexual pleasure but for bearing children. In fact, by the time the Sabines organize to retaliate, these children are already born, and being carried in the arms of their mothers. Second, the women became a bond between the two groups, on the one hand their fathers, brothers, and relatives, on the other

---

[31] *Alex.* 21. 11, τὸ τῆς ἰδίας ἐγκρατείας καὶ σωφροσύνης κάλλος. He also insisted on restraint by his soldiers: cf. *Alex.* 12 (with *Mul. Virt.* 259d–260d) and 22. 4.

[32] *Alex.* 22. 5, cf. Xen. *Cyr.* 5. 1. 8, 16. Later, Darius marvels at his *sophrosyne* (30).

[33] The source of the information, Aristobulus (*F. Gr. Hist.* 139 F 11), regularly tries to whitewash Alexander's faults, so is not in fact a reliable witness here.

[34] Contrast the implicit meaning of Arrian, *Anab.* 1. 12. 1 and 7. 14. 4, with Herodian 4. 8. 4–5.

their husbands and the fathers of their children, a bond which required reconciliation and harmony rather than a battle which would harm one side or the other, and thus the women themselves (19). Plutarch insists, moreover, that violent as the initial act was, the Roman men immediately after the seizure respected their wives and made them mistresses of their homes (19. 8–9, cf. 15. 5). The result was that the Sabines joined with the Romans in harmony to build a stronger city. Plutarch thus redefines the attack on the women from an act of sexual aggression to a necessary and politic action to build up the city, in which the initial violence is only a prelude to domestic harmony and union.[35]

This view of the sexual act as ideally leading to harmony is confirmed by the negative evaluation Plutarch gives of Theseus' many sexual exploits. In the course of *Theseus*, Plutarch recalls in detail Theseus' involvement with Ariadne and with Antiope, then lists other stories of 'marriages' which were 'neither honorable in their occasions nor fortunate in their outcomes' (*Thes.* 19–20, 26–8, 29. 1–2). In the *Life* itself, there is a certain tendency to gloss over these events,[36] but in the comparison the criticism is explicit. 'The wrongs committed in the rapes of the women admit of no fair excuse', first because they were so many, and second because they were not for begetting children, but rather appeared to be 'from hubris and for pleasure', with an explicit comparison to Romulus' action (*Comp.* 6. 1–2). Theseus' sexual activity spawned wars, whereas Romulus' Sabine rape brought peace and friendship to Rome.

Agis presents on a personal level a similar story of reconciliation. Chilonis, the daughter of Leonidas, was married to Cleombrotus. When the two men were at odds, Chilonis offered sympathy and support first to her father when he was being wronged, then to her husband when circumstances changed. By an impassioned appeal, given at length by Plutarch, she was able to save Cleombrotus' life, and went with him into exile (*Ag. Cl.* 17. 2–18. 4). Again, although Plutarch is discreetly silent on sex, the wife serves as an agent of gentleness and harmony between hostile men. He is more explicit in describing Cleomenes' bond with Agiatis, which blossomed from a forced marriage into a loving one. Cleomenes adopts her way of thinking about her former husband Agis'

---

[35] Cf. the stories in the *Virtues in Women* of Pieria and Polycrite, who brought harmony to their cities through love (*Mul. Virt.* 253f–255f).

[36] Note e.g. the emphasis on Paeon's version of the Ariadne story, favourable to Theseus (20. 3–7).

revolution, and grieves deeply when she dies—some eighteen years later (*Ag. Cl.* 22. 1–3; 43. 1–3).[37]

Proper sexual behaviour builds harmony between men and women, and between cities. It also reinforces other virtues, especially courage. Although he provides a number of examples for both men and women in the *Amatorius*, in the *Lives* Plutarch says little about how heterosexual love makes men more brave, and gives only a few anecdotes of women: Porcia's willingness to die (*Brut.* 53),[38] Cleopatra's resolution at the end of the *Antony*, and the extraordinary courage of the wife of Panteus (*Ag. Cl.* 59–60).[39]

Instead, this concept of love-inspired courage justifies the civilly sanctioned homosexual relationships of Thebes and Sparta. In *Pelopidas* 18–19 Plutarch speaks admiringly of the Sacred Band at Thebes, the body of 300 men specially supported by the city, begun by Gorgidas and continued under Epaminondas and Pelopidas. Cautiously he refers to a tradition that the band was composed of pairs of lover and beloved, and quotes the correction of Homer's Nestor uttered by the Theban general Pammenes, that a phalanx is better arranged by lovers than by phratries.[40] In the Sacred Band, as with Heracles and Iolaos, the soldiers' love for their partners gave them enormous courage in the face of danger. Plutarch argues that these love relationships were encouraged by the Theban magistrates to better regulate the spirited temper of youth, and associates the practice with the goddess Harmonia, daughter of Ares and Aphrodite.[41] The lover–beloved relationships in the Sacred Band belong to a context of martial and moral education, leading 'to the most harmonious and orderly way of government'.

[37] Note that when he dies in Egypt, Cleomenes has with him his former beloved Panteus, now himself married. Panteus saw that all were dead, and killed himself over Cleomenes' corpse. Much of the sensibility and the pathetic treatment of love in this pair derives from Plutarch's source, Phylarchus, yet Plutarch himself clearly finds it edifying. Cf. also his praise of Solon for encouraging the sexual bond between man and wife, *Sol.* 20. 5.

[38] Cf. Goessler (1962), 130–42.

[39] Cf. also the stories in *Virtues in Women* of Aretaphila, Camma (also in the *Amatorius*), Chiomara, and Eryxo (*Mul. Virt.* 255e–258c, 258e–f, 260d–261d).

[40] Pammenes' *bon mot* recurs at *Amat.* 761b and *Qu. Conv.* 618d. This Pammenes was a famous Theban general in whose house the young Philip of Macedon stayed when a hostage in Thebes (*Pel.* 26. 7). According to others, though not Plutarch, he was Philip's lover (Libanius, *Prog.* 9. 3, *Suda* s.v. Karanos, cf. also Arist. *Eud. Eth.* 1243b21). Although Pelopidas led the Sacred Band in 371 (*Pel.* 20. 3) Plutarch does not mention his boy-loves, although he does refer to his marriage and children (*Pel.* 3. 7).

[41] He expressly denies that the institution is connected with the more violent story of Laius and his beloved Chrysippus. For these stories, see *Amat.* 761c–d, and Dover (1978), 199–200.

Agesilaus provides the fullest treatment in Plutarch of how Spartan homosexual relations worked in practice.[42] Agesilaus, like his partner king Agesipolis, was 'subject to love affairs'. Plutarch finds it necessary to explain that 'these Laconian loves had nothing shameful about them, rather a great sense of respect, of honour, and of zeal for excellence' (*Ages.* 20. 9, cf. *Lyc.* 17. 1, 18. 8–9). Agesilaus revealed his self-restraint when taking his leave from Spithridates and his son, for whom he had an attachment.[43] He resolved not to kiss the boy, and exalted when he could keep his resolution. As Plutarch notes, he may not have refused a second time (11. 6–10).[44] Here the king acted well, but Plutarch later criticizes him for acting to spare Sphodrias, who deserved to be punished, because he was the father of his son's beloved (25. 1–26. 1, cf. *Comp.* 1. 6).[45] In both 11. 6 and 20. 9, Plutarch speaks as if no physical contact were involved in the Spartan practice.[46]

Outside of these two cases, Plutarch has little to say about male homosexuality. As has often been noted, especially in discussions of the *Amatorius*,[47] Plutarch's attitude on the subject is somewhat ambiguous. He appears to accept what he considers a traditional Greek custom of boy-love, but considers it fundamentally unnatural and under no circumstances wishes it to drive out heterosexual love or to diminish the respect due to women or the importance of their role. In the *Lives* he tends to suppress notices of homosexual activity or treat it as problematic (in Sparta and Thebes), except for classical Athens. In *Themistocles* he can dismiss as typical of young men (*meirakiodes*) the fact that the rivalry between Aristides and Themistocles originated when they were young men and both in love with the boy Stesilaus. In *Aristides*, however, he suggests that the rivalry should have broken off when the boy grew up, and uses it as a springboard for a fuller treatment of political rivalry.[48] Boy-love should not continue beyond a certain point, nor disturb the harmony of the state. If Solon loved

---

[42] On the topic, cf. Cartledge (1981).

[43] Literally, '*eros* for the boy had dripped into him (ἐνεσταγμένος)' a poetic expression (cf. Homer, *Od.* 2. 271). The story, like much of the *Agesilaus*, comes from Xenophon's *Agesilaus* (5. 4–5), where it is cited as an example of sexual self-control (ἀφροδισίων ἐγκράτεια), but has been rewritten by Plutarch.

[44] Cf. also his kindnesses to the son of Pharnabazus, whom he found attractive, *Ag. Cl.* 13. 1–4.

[45] According to *Lys.* 22. 6 Agesilaus was beloved of Lysander, but this is not mentioned in *Agesilaus*.

[46] Nor is it suggested in *Pelopidas*. In *Amat.* 768e–f he firmly rejects physical homosexual relations as disgraceful to both parties.

[47] Cf. esp. Foucault (1990), 193–210.   [48] *Them.* 3. 2, *Arist.* 2. 3–4.

Peisistratus, as some say, the memory in later years, when they disagreed, kept them from vicious actions.[49]

To sum up this brief survey, then, Plutarch's concerns in commenting on male sexual behaviour in the *Lives* focus on a few broad categories: rational self-control, defined most often by its opposite, self-indulgent excess; a relationship creating peace and concord, with its opposite extremes of incest, violence, unseasonable lust, and female domination; and incitement to virtue.

In the cases of Antony and Demetrius, Theseus and Romulus, Cato the Elder and others the survey has shown how Plutarch uses sexual behaviour to illumine and evaluate character. However, Pompey's treatment of Flora with which this paper began, as well as other instances, does not seem to fit neatly into any of the above categories. No excess of passion can be ascribed to one who surrenders his love so readily, yet this seems a strange example of self-restraint. The anecdote, by its placement early in the *Life* and its vivid presentation, clearly was meant to influence the reader's interpretation of Pompey's character. To what end? Plutarch's details are significant. The lovebites, Flora's sense of loss, and her fond memory in later years, point to a loving relationship, confirmed by Plutarch's words, 'although he seemed in fact to love her'. The anecdote creates a strange sense of loss, as well as wonder at such generosity toward a friend. A tension is apparent. One senses that Pompey has made a mistake, though his action appears rather admirable. The problem lies not so much in his callous attitude toward Flora as in his unwillingness to respect his own feelings. Plutarch sees sexual love as creating a bond, which Pompey here does not recognize. The anecdote prepares the reader to discover as the *Life* unfolds that Pompey at major points in his life abandons his own best interests and those of the state to serve his friends, and to be betrayed by them.[50] His lack of good judgement in a sexual relationship becomes a paradigm of his lack of judgement in the political arena.[51] This anecdote and that of the wife of Demetrius point to a lack of a true equilibrium, apparent, as Plutarch hints at 2. 10, also in his marriages, especially with Julia. Flora he abandons too readily, Julia he

---

[49] *Sol.* 1. 4–7, where Plutarch notes Solon's susceptibility to young men and his protection of aristocratic affairs in his legislation. Alcibiades' loves alternate between licence (an indication of his future unreliability) and the steadying influence of Socrates.

[50] Cf. *Pomp.* 46. 2–4 and *Comp. Ages.–Pomp.* 1. 5, 7; 2. 3, 4. 9 and note esp. the alliance with Caesar, and the self-serving advice of Scipio.

[51] Agesilaus' self-restraint in refraining from a kiss seems wiser than Pompey's generosity in abandoning his love Flora.

loves to distraction—forgetting his obligations to the Republic and serving Caesar's goals.[52] When she dies, he errs in the other direction, rushing toward a useless and destructive war (*Pomp.* 70. 2–3). Pompey's marriages though full of affection do not promote civic peace; his acquiescence in the demands of his fathers-in-law Caesar and Metellus Scipio, like his surrender of Flora to Geminus, annuls the nobler aspects of *eros*. In sexual relations as in politics he is unable to achieve the harmonious balance and noble self-assurance which his excellent qualities promised.

Sexual anecdotes, like other stories in Plutarch, explore and explain elements of character. They do not point, in the Freudian mode, to underlying features of the subconscious, but provide telling indications of character traits. *Cato Minor* offers confirmation: the unfeelingness and artificiality of Cato the Younger's stoicism is shown in his dealings with women. Plutarch remarks with amazement that Cato had never been with a woman prior to his marriage (*Cat. Min.* 7. 1). He does not make a judgement here, but later he describes the total misfortune Cato met with regard to women,[53] misfortune alluded to already in 7. 3, in the comparison with Laelius.[54] His two sisters and his wife were promiscuous (24. 3–6), but his relation with his second wife Marcia was particularly unusual, and to Plutarch, problematic.[55] Hortensius had asked Cato to give him his daughter in marriage, although she was at the time married to Bibulus and had given him two sons. Hortensius wanted also to have a well-born 'land' (*choran*) to plant children in. When Cato demurred, Hortensius asked for his wife Marcia, and Cato agreed, stipulating only that her father should be consulted. Plutarch notes that Hortensius' request according to human opinion was strange, but according to nature it was fine and good for the state. Nevertheless, he found it puzzling: like Pompey, Cato does not have good sense. He does not understand the nature of the sexual bond, which should bring harmonious union. His insensitive lack of common human feeling is the other side of his philosophic rigidity. It isolates him from other political figures and ultimately leads to the defeat of his cause.[56]

---

[52] Cf. *Pomp.* 47. 9; 48. 8; 53. 1, 5.

[53] *Cat. Min.* 24. 4: φαίνεται δ᾽ ὅλως ἀτύχημα γενέσθαι τοῦ Κάτωνος ἡ γυναικωνῖτις.

[54] *Cat. Min.* 7. 3: Laelius was 'more fortunate, since in his long life he knew only the one woman he married at the beginning'.

[55] *Cat. Min.* 25. 1: προβληματῶδες γέγονε καὶ ἄπορον.

[56] Note that Cato forced Pompey's alliance with Caesar by refusing to accept a marriage alliance with Pompey, lest he be won over via the women's chambers (*Cat. Min.* 30. 10). *Advice on Marriage* emphasizes a husband's need for sensitivity: cf. Patterson (1992).

Sexual anecdotes interpret character, as these two examples attest. In addition, Plutarch often uses such anecdotes to indicate a progression from the first to the second *Life* of a pair. As in other matters, so also with sexual behaviour, the second *Life* is often more exaggerated or complex than the first.[57] In *Phocion–Cato Minor*, for example, Phocion is a leader who rises above the level of ordinary politicians. Like Cato, his integrity is without question. Sex is almost totally absent from the *Life*, but two points are noteworthy: first, Phocion had two wives, of whom the first was not spoken of at all, and the second was as distinguished for modesty and simplicity as was Phocion for integrity (19. 1, cf. 18. 3); second, his son, though otherwise not good, bought the freedom of a young woman from a procurer. Phocion, that is, combined integrity with a sound family life, and was able to teach his son something about the nature of a loving relationship.[58] Cato, while trying to lead a philosophic life, including complete control of sexual desires, is seen to be out of touch with reality, so that he becomes a self-righteous prude among lascivious women.

On the other hand, the *Lysander–Sulla* uses Sulla's undisciplined sexual behaviour to indicate his greater viciousness. Lysander, despite his other weaknesses, is seen as self-controlled toward every kind of pleasure (*Lys.* 2. 2, cf. *Comp.* 5. 6); the only aspect of his sexual life mentioned is his love for Agesilaus (22. 6). Sulla, however, shows every kind of sexual failing: 'His licentiousness in love affairs and urge towards pleasure was a kind of disease, which did not cease as he grew older' (*Sul.* 2. 6). The final scene, of Sulla in a wild debauch with his young wife Valeria and his old lover Metrobates, leaves an impression of a dissolute and self-serving tyrant.[59] More sophisticated is the case of *Demetrius–Antony*, in which both leaders are given to sexual indulgence. Plutarch castigates Demetrius for his licentiousness and violence, but finds a redeeming feature in his ability to put aside pleasure when military duties called.[60] Antony shows the same tendency toward sexual indulgence, but after encountering Cleopatra, no

[57] Cf. Pelling (1986*b*), Stadter (1992).

[58] The story of the son sounds like a New Comedy plot, but Plutarch seems to approve, citing the argument that if buying the freedom of a male friend is good, then it should be good for a female friend also. Cato's son instead apparently seduced the wife of his host in Cappadocia (*Cat. Min.* 73. 3–4). In the very first chapter Phocion's own simple life is contrasted with Demades' licentiousness (*Phoc.* 1. 1).

[59] *Sull.* 36. 1–2, cf. Stadter (1992), 45.

[60] Plutarch even finds a creditable factor in Demetrius' multiple marriages: these followed Macedonian practice, whereas Antony's treatment of Octavia violated Roman custom (*Comp.* 4. 1–2).

longer can abandon his passion when other obligations arise. Nevertheless, his final relationship with Cleopatra is much more than physical indulgence, and their love goes far beyond the ménage of Demetrius with Lamia. The final scenes show Antony and Cleopatra bonded together in love, lending significance to Plutarch's comment, early in the *Life*, that Antony's eroticism was 'not without Aphrodite'.[61]

Plutarch sees sexual behaviour as a manifestation of a man's character. For the tyrant or the violent man, sex is an arena for power and the domination of others. Theseus, Demetrius, Sulla, and subsidiary figures like Alexander of Pherae or Pausanias express and reveal their viciousness through sexual violence. The ideal statesman instead shows his self-control in the same arena, creating harmony in his household and in his city. General considerations may be stated: excess appears in a promiscuous obsession with sex, but also in the unnatural passion of incest, or self-deluding senile lust. Harmony is built on self-control, fidelity, and heterosexual marriage and childbearing. However, Plutarch's treatment of sexual behaviour is more subtle than such principles might suggest. He does not directly moralize about sex, but looks at the whole behaviour of his subject. Although sex's ideal sphere is in relation to a wife, for childbearing and mutual support, Plutarch recognizes and accepts heterosexual activity outside marriage.[62] Homosexual boy-love, despite his strictures in the *Amatorius*, can have a positive role under very controlled circumstances, in the civic structures of Thebes and Sparta, although it should not involve physical contact. Overall, men should be strong and sensitive, dominating and restrained, but often are not. Conduct which may be acceptable in one man, given his circumstances and traits, may prove disastrous in another. Sexual behaviour reveals character flaws and strengths which surface in other areas as well, and so contributes to a full and complex portrait. Pompey's uxoriousness is not that of Antony, nor Cato's austerity that of Brutus. Using Pelling's term, Plutarchan protagonists possess 'integrated' characters, in which the different traits and tendencies blend together into a whole. Self-control and excess, violence and nobility are revealed in sex life as in political life, by a person's actions.

---

[61] *Ant.* 4. 5. Cf. Pelling (1988), 18–26.

[62] e.g. with Pompey, or with Pericles' liaison with Aspasia (*Per.* 24). But even there he insists upon both the affection of the couple and the non-sexual aspects of the relationship.

17

Lucian's Choice: *Somnium* 6–16

DEBORAH LEVINE GERA

The *Somnium*, Lucian's allegedly autobiographical account of the circumstances which led to his choice of career, is a delightful, but enigmatic work. The rhetor from Samosata begins by telling of a family conference held when he came of age in order to determine his future. His father decides that young Lucian should be apprenticed as a sculptor to his maternal uncle.[1] Lucian, who has often been punished in the past for moulding figures of wax scraped from his writing tablets at school, is, he tells us, delighted at the prospect. On the very first day of his apprenticeship, he manages to ruin a slab of marble. His uncle beats him and the tearful Lucian runs home. That night he has a dream in which two women—work-stained, poorly dressed Techne and refined, comely Paideia—fight over him and his future. Each of the two women addresses him directly, trying to convince him to adopt her way of life. Dirty, mannish Techne offers a life of labour and pains-taking craftsmanship as a sculptor, while the ladylike Paideia promises Lucian admiration and honour, if he should become educated and learn how to speak. Lucian does not even need to hear out Paideia to the end of her speech: hers is the path he chooses. Paideia immediately rewards the young Lucian for his decision by taking him for a ride in her chariot across the heavens. The young man scatters seeds of some kind to the admiring people below and then returns home, newly garbed, where Paideia proudly presents him to his father. His choice, Lucian states at the conclusion of the *Somnium*, can serve as an inspiration to other young men of little means.

What are we to make of this elusive little work?[2] How many authentic autobiographical details lie behind this entertaining account? Did

[1] For the exact profession of Lucian's uncle—stonemason, sculptor, or herm carver—see Jones (1986), 8 n. 12 and Romm (1990), 96 n. 59.

[2] Nesselrath (1990), 115 n. 9 maintains convincingly that the *Somnium* is not a true *prolalia*, but 'a special-occasion piece'. See too M. D. Macleod (1991), 249 and cf. Anderson (1977), 314 n. 5; Stock (1911), 25–7.

Lucian come, in fact, from a family of moderate means, and was there ever such a family conference about his future profession? Is it simply a coincidence that Lucian's family were sculptors, conveniently reminding us of that most famous stonemason of all, Socrates?[3] (Later in the *Somnium* (12), Lucian will make this implicit link with the philosopher explicit and have Paideia mention Socrates as one who chose her path and rejected Techne.)[4] Finally, how are we to understand Lucian's dream? Did the satirical sophist really have such a dream or is it a literary invention, pure and simple? Dreams, in particular dreams which led to an important decision in life, are well attested in the second century AD and it has been noted that a dream of Galen's father, which led to the choice of a medical career for his son, is a particularly close parallel to our situation.[5] Thus Lucian's dream conforms to the practices of his time, but perhaps he invents the dream precisely because his contemporaries report theirs so seriously: he may be parodying or making use of the fashion.[6] In any event, it is clear that Lucian is influenced here (whether consciously or otherwise) by earlier, literary dreams. One such dream is Xenophon's first dream in the *Anabasis*, which Lucian himself mentions.[7] Socrates, whose presence in the *Somnium* has already been noted, also dreams a dream at a crucial moment in his life and his dream, like that of Lucian, is both clear (ἐναργής) and involves an elegant, impressive woman who has a message for him (*Crito* 44a–b).[8]

[3] Hall (1981), 16–17, 446–7 n. 26, 460 n. 57 argues for accepting the details Lucian gives us as authentic; see too Baldwin (1961), 206 and Jones (1986), 9. Bompaire (1958), 528–32 and Anderson (1976*a*), 80–1 are much more sceptical.

[4] This technique of first hinting at a famous personage and then later actually referring to him by name appears several times in the *Somnium*. Thus Lucian first paraphrases Demosthenes and then mentions the orator by name (9, 12). The parody of Xenophon's account of Prodicus' tale of Heracles at the crossroads is followed both by a mention of Xenophon and the playful use of the oath 'by Heracles' (17). (Cebes' *Tabula* is another version of the Prodicus myth where Heracles is conspicuously absent, but the phrase ὦ Ἡράκλεις appears several times—see 4. 1, 12. 1, 19. 1 and Fitzgerald and White (1983), 38 n. 67.) Cf. Bompaire (1958), 259–60 n. 5 on 'l'art de la citation camouflée' in Lucian.

[5] Galen 10. 609, 16. 223, and 19. 59 (Kühn); the parallel is noted by Jones (1986), 10. Bowersock (1969), 73–4 discusses the dreams of other 2nd-cent. figures.

[6] See Anderson (1976*a*), 25 on false dreams as 'a constant source of fun' in Lucian; cf. Baldwin (1973), 14.

[7] *Anab.* 3. 1. 11–13; cf. *Somn.* 17. Although commentators think that Lucian may actually have Xenophon's other dream in the *Anab.* (4. 3. 8) in mind (cf. e.g. M. D. Macleod (1991), 251), this first dream seems relevant because the young and agitated Xenophon is dreaming a dream which will affect his entire future and turn him into a leader.

[8] Note how both writers quote Homer: in Lucian, Homer is used to announce the fact

The striking literary influence on Lucian's reverie, whether actual or invented, is, of course, Prodicus' tale of Heracles at the crossroads, as found in Xenophon (*Mem.* 2. 1. 21–34). In adapting this allegory by Prodicus for his own purposes, Lucian is far from unique. Time and again, writers make use of Prodicus' scheme of having two women who are very dissimilar in looks and manner represent, discuss, or serve as guides to, two different ways of life.[9] Many authors—Philo, Silius, Justin, Clement, Philostratus, Basil—make use of the general outlines of Prodicus' story, telling of Virtue and Vice (or at times Pleasure), but recast the tale in their own fashion. Others—Ovid, Dio Chrysostom, Maximus, Themistius—experiment more freely with the story mould and have the two women represent different contrasting qualities, such as Kingship and Tyranny or Friendship and Hypocrisy. Here, Lucian plays the part of young Heracles, while Paideia and Techne, the two women doing battle over his professional future (rather than his soul), are clearly modelled upon Arete and Kakia. At first sight, there are no difficulties or ambiguities in the *Somnium*: the way of life offered by Techne is rejected outright, while Paideia and her path are embraced wholeheartedly by the sophist.[10] Lucian, it seems, proudly announces to his readers, that he, like Heracles before him, has chosen the better of the two women, the woman whose way of life is obviously to be preferred. Or has he? A closer look at this section of the *Somnium* (6–16) will show that Lucian's choice is not as simple or straightforward as it seems.

The two women of Lucian's dream appear on the scene with a flourish: each of the two seizes the poor young man and tries to pull

of a dream (*Somn.* 5), while in Plato the message to Socrates is conveyed in Homeric verse (*Crito* 44b2). Jones (1986), 10 with n. 19 also compares the dreams of Xerxes in Herodotus (7. 12–19) and of Atossa in Aes. *Persae* 179–99 to the *Somnium*. Cf. Dodds (1951), 107–8 for a more general discussion of 'godsent' dreams which contain prophecy, advice, or warning.

[9] The most notable passages are: Ovid, *Am.* 3. 1. 1 ff.; Philo, *De Sacr. Ca. et Ab.* 20ff.; Cebes, *Tabula*; Silius Italicus, *Pun.* 15. 18–128; Dio Chr. 1. 66–83; Justin Martyr, *Apol.* 2. 11; Maximus 14. 1; Clement, *Paed.* 2. 10. 110; Philostratus, *VA* 6. 10; Themistius, *Or.* 22. 280a–282c; Basil, *De Leg. Gr. Lib.* 5. 55–77. For additional parallels cf. I. Alpers (1912), *passim*, Waites (1912), 12–19, Fitzgerald and White (1983), 37 n. 62, and Trapp (1990), 143 n. 2. In what follows I shall range freely over these parallel texts, generally ignoring strict chronology and citing writings which are both earlier and later than the *Somnium*. My interest is in examining the wide range of variations inspired by the Xenophon–Prodicus tale, rather than tracing direct influences.

[10] Waites (1912), 12 points out that in these Prodicus-based tales there is a 'law of precedence by which the party to be defeated regularly begins the argument' and then notes that Techne 'dooms herself to defeat by beginning' (16; cf. 45).

him over to her side, so that he is, he tells us, nearly torn apart. The women argue with one another vociferously even before they address him and each tries to establish her claim over young Lucian (*Somn.* 6). Paideia and Techne are, of course, competitors (cf. πρὸς ἀλλήλας φιλοτιμούμεναι 6), as are all the women in these Producus-based tales, whose theme is precisely the choice or contrast between their two different ways of life. Hence when these pairs of contrasting women address the young man they are trying to influence, they often debate passionately with one another (as in Xenophon, Ovid, Philo, Silius, and Justin), but actual physical aggression is rare. Perhaps the closest parallel to the *Somnium* scene is one found, according to Philostratus (*VA* 6. 10) in picture books (ἐν ζωγραφίας λόγοις) where Kakia and Arete are depicted as seizing Heracles in the middle and trying to draw him towards them. Often, however, the two competing women in these tales arrive quietly on the scene together and patiently wait their turn to speak.[11] In Xenophon, Arete and Kakia appear together, but as they come nearer to Heracles, Arete continues to walk at the same pace, while Kakia, anxious to be first, runs ahead (*Mem.* 2. 1. 23).

This difference between the two women is frequently found in later versions: physical aggression or quick motion of any kind is typically associated with the negative women or Vice. Basil, for instance, tells us that Vice tries to draw Heracles to herself after speaking to him (*De Leg. Gr. Lib.* 5. 70–1). Elsewhere the bad women do not actually use force, but they are invariably more restless, more active than their positive counterparts. In Cebes' *Tabula* (6) the Opinions, Desires, and Pleasures (all of whom are less than positive figures) jump up, embrace, and then lead away the masses who enter.[12] Tyranny, Dio's negative figure, is unable to sit still: she frequently looks around and jumps up from her throne. This restlessness extends to her facial expression and her face changes colour in accordance with her rapidly changing emotions (1. 80–1). Other versions of Vice move too seductively, smile too freely, or cast alluring glances, as in Philo, Silius

---

[11] Ovid, *Am.* 3. 1. 31–5; Philo, *De Sacr. Ca. et Ab.* 26; Silius Italicus, *Pun.* 15. 68–9; Justin Martyr, *Apol.* 2. 11; Themistius, *Or.* 22. 280a.

[12] Fitzgerald and White (1983), 141 n. 21 note that these actions of jumping up and embracing (ἀναπηδῶσι . . . καὶ πλέκονται) are 'characteristic of personified vices'. There is one instance in the *Tabula* where mobility is attributed to positive figures: Enkrateia and Karteria stretch out their hands and help the traveller climb the difficult path leading to Paideia (16; see too 18. 3 vs. 7. 3 and compare Eudaimonia seated on a throne at 21).

Italicus, and Justin Martyr.[13] Clement assigns to his Kakia movement
and posture which are intended to please (*Paed.* 2. 10. 110. 1) while
Themistius' Hypocrisy bows and scrapes to encourage those who
come to her (*Or.* 22. 282a). Even Ovid's Tragedy has somewhat
violent movements (*Am.* 3. 1. 11, 31–2). Sometimes the bare mention
of rapidly darting or rolling eyes suffices to indicate that the woman
described is negative or too licentious in her ways (Xenophon, *Mem.*
2. 1. 22; cf. Ovid's Elegia at *Am.* 3. 1. 33). If many of these negative
women are too free in their movements and expressions, their rivals,
the various versions of Arete, move quietly and sedately and are often
said to have immobile or steadfast expressions. Cebes' Paideia has a
calm face (18. 1), while in Dio Chrysostom, Basileia is composed,
steadfast, and with an unwavering expression (1. 71).[14] Themistius,
writing in Dio's wake, gives Philia a simple, noble gaze and a steady,
unmoving smile (22. 281b). Philo's Virtue has a firm, unhurried tread
(*De Sacr. Ca. et Ab.* 26), while that of Silius Italicus has a steady
expression (*Pun.* 15. 29). Basil assigns Arete an intense glance (*De Leg.
Gr. Lib.* 5. 72).

In short, repose is a positive quality, almost always associated with
the good member of these Prodicus pairs, while motion of almost any
kind is seen as disreputable. Lucian's brawling, shouting figures are, of
course, meant to be comic, but no other pair of women is quite as
undignified as Lucian's two and actually come to blows. By having
both women push and pull Lucian seems to indicate that there is no
real difference, in demeanour at least, between the two: both Paideia
and Techne are assigned a quality—(forceful) motion—which is
almost always allotted to the undesirable half of a Prodicus pair.[15]

If Paideia and Techne are very alike in their initial behaviour, they
are altogether dissimilar in physical appearance. When he assigns the
two women contrasting appearances, Lucian is following in the wake
of many others, for in all these Prodicus-based tales the physical differences between the two women are used to illustrate or symbolize the
different ways of life they represent.[16] Techne, the stonemason, is at

---

[13] Philo: *De Sacr. Ca. et Ab.* 21; Silius Italicus, *Pun.* 15. 26–7; Justin Martyr, *Apol.*
2. 11. Maximus' Κόλαξ is much more active than his Φιλία (14. 1h).

[14] Even the old priestess who is Dio's source for his tale of Basileia and Tyranny is
quiet and controlled. She does not, we are told, gasp for breath or whirl around while
prophesying, as is commonly done (1. 56).

[15] Later (*Somn.* 14), Techne will be turned to stone, the ultimate in repose.

[16] Cf. Basil's perceptive comment on Prodicus' presentation of Arete and Kakia:
εὐθὺς μὲν οὖν καὶ σιωπώσας ἐμφαίνειν ἀπὸ τοῦ σχήματος τὸ διάφορον (*De Leg. Gr. Lib.*
5. 65–7).

first sight a totally unattractive figure. She is a masculine-looking labourer with filthy hair. Her hands are calloused, her clothes are tucked up, and she is covered with dust. Above all Techne is rough and masculine (*Somn.* 6). Paideia, on the other hand, has a lovely face and figure and is neatly dressed μάλα εὐπρόσωπος καὶ τὸ σχῆμα εὐπρεπὴς καὶ κόσμιος τὴν ἀναβολήν (6) and there is little doubt that she is the more attractive of the two.[17]

While a marked contrast between the two women is a standard feature of these tales, it is rare for one of the women to be quite so unattractive as Lucian's Techne.[18] Here too the tone or pattern is set by Prodicus, as paraphrased by Xenophon. Virtue in Xenophon is comely, yet modest, while Vice is attractive in an artificial, blatant way (*Mem.* 2. 1. 22). Many later authors take up this distinction between the good, naturally beautiful woman and the bad, artificially attractive one, but generally both women have a pleasing physical appearance. Thus Philo has a detailed description of the elaborately dressed, courtesan-like Pleasure and a briefer account of Arete, who is modest and unaffected in appearance (*De Sacr. Ca. et Ab.* 21, 26). In Cebes' *Tabula* there are a whole series of positive women—Paideia, Virtues, Knowledge, and Eudaimonia—and all are described in similar fashion: they are attractive, simply dressed, and they do not use artificial adornments (18, 20, 21). Interestingly, Pseudopaideia also *seems* to be altogether pure and neat, according to the author of the *Tabula* (12),[19] while less surprisingly a series of negative figures, such as Covetousness and Flattery, look like courtesans (9). Dio Chrysostom's Basileia is beautiful, radiant, and dignified (1. 70–2), while Tyranny, who tries to imitate Basileia, is much more embellished, restless, and colourful (1. 78–81). Themistius describes his good woman, Philia, as being in the first bloom of youth, while her rival, Hypocrisy, tries to imitate her, but resorts to cosmetics (*Or.* 22. 281a–b, 282a). Maximus' Virtue is graceful, gentle, and modestly clothed, while Pleasure is bold, uses cosmetics, and is elaborately dressed (14. 1b–c). Clement of Alexandria describes Arete as pure, dressed in white, and decorated only with modesty, while Kakia is overdressed and painted (*Paed.* 2. 10.

---

[17] Bompaire (1958), 349–50, recognizes Prodicus' influence on the description of Paideia here, but compares similar 'clichés descriptifs' found elsewhere in Lucian (*Pisc.* 13; *Merc. cond.* 42; *Rhet. Prae.* 6); see too Anderson (1976a), 67.

[18] See I. Alpers (1912), 51–2 and 54–5 for a survey of the various descriptions of Virtue and Vice respectively.

[19] Cf. I. Alpers (1912), 55.

110. 1).[20] Thus most authors of these tales contrast an artless, attractive good woman with an artificial, but alluring, bad one. Other writers heighten the contrast between the two women so that Virtue's beauty is solely that of the spirit. Physically, Virtue seems to glory in her lack of artifice and indifferent looks, and she may be, at times, ugly. In Silius Italicus (*Pun.* 15. 23–31), for example, Voluptas smells of perfume, has flowing tresses carefully set off with a pin, and is clad in shining purple and gold, but Virtus lets her hair grow free and unstyled; in face and gait, we are told, she is more like a man (*et ore | incessuque viro propior* 29–30). Justin Martyr claims to be following Xenophon's account, and his Kakia is dressed seductively, but Arete cares nothing for superficial ornaments and is squalid in face and dress ἐν αὐχμηρῷ . . . προσώπῳ καὶ . . . περιβολῇ (*Apol.* 2. 11). Philostratus tells of representations of Heracles at the crossroads in which Arete is worn out with toil and has a rough look. She goes about barefoot, in a plain dress, with squalor as her ornament (τὸν δὲ αὐχμὸν πεποιημένη κόσμημα *VA* 6. 10). Kakia, on the other hand, is dressed in purple and adorned with gold; her hair is plaited and her face painted. Basil (*De Leg. Gr. Lib.* 5. 65–72) describes Virtue as emaciated and squalid (κατεσκληκέναι καὶ αὐχμεῖν), while Vice is elaborately dressed. In all the instances we have looked at thus far, Virtue may be beautiful, plain, or even occasionally unattractive, but Vice (or her negative counterpart) is never ugly.

In fact, in all the many variations on Prodicus' tale there seems to be only one instance where Vice is altogether unappealing—an anonymous rhetor terms Kakia filthy and squalid (ῥυπώσης καὶ αὐχμηρᾶς), as opposed to blooming, fresh Arete.[21] One can well understand why other authors do not choose to describe the two women in such simplistic, black-and-white terms of Beautiful Virtue versus Ugly Vice. If the tale of a choice put to young Heracles (or his counterparts) is to be morally instructive and interesting, it must comprise a genuine choice and involve a real dilemma of some kind. And the way to create such a quandary is to present a pair of two genuine alternatives, where the bad or misguided option is at least superficially compelling, while the good alternative is less obviously attractive. Portraying Virtue as altogether beautiful and Vice as entirely ugly involves no choice

---

[20] See too Ovid's lovely, dainty Elegy who is quite different from vigorous, impressive Tragedy (*Am.* 3. 1. 7–14). I. Alpers (1912), 37 quotes two further passages from rhetors—an anonymous rhetor and Troilus—where Arete is described as naturally beautiful in contrast to artificially enhanced Kakia.

[21] Rhetor II ignotus (*Rhet. Graec.* v. 606), as quoted by I. Alpers (1912), 38.

whatsoever: such a tale is too simplistic and unilluminating, for all but the most moralizing or didactic of authors. None the less, Lucian (who normally is not what one would term a moralizing, didactic author)[22] seems to favour here precisely such a black-and-white presentation, for his dirty, mannish, hard-working Techne is altogether unappealing. We should bear in mind, perhaps, that Lucian is describing a dream that he had as a young and not overly subtle boy, but if we look more carefully at Techne's qualities we shall find that in other contexts—in Lucian's own writings and in other variations on Prodicus' tale—her characteristics are more positive than they seem here.

Techne is squalid (αὐχμηρά), austere (σκληρά), and masculine (ἀνδρική, ἀνδρώδης *Somn.* 6) and all three of these qualities are associated with various versions of Virtue (or her equivalent) in other writers. We have already seen that Justin, Philostratus, and Basil all describe Arete as squalid (above, p. 243), and in Justin, Arete's way of life is also linked with austerity, the pursuit of τὰ . . . νομιζόμενα σκληρά (*Apol.* 2. 11).[23] Masculinity is, as we have noted, a feature of Silius Italicus' Virtue (*Pun.* 15. 29–30), and the companions surrounding Dio's Basileia, Dike, Eunomia, and Eirene, are admired by Heracles for their manliness (ὡς εὐσχήμονες καὶ μεγαλοπρεπεῖς καὶ ἀρρενωποί 1. 73). In Lucian's own *Piscator* (16), Arete is depicted as a woman who is ἀνδρώδης. But, for our purposes, the most interesting figure described by Lucian in one of his works is the old-fashioned teacher of rhetoric found in the *Rhetorum Praeceptor*. The *Rhetorum Praeceptor* is a highly ironic account of the two ways to become a rhetor: an old-fashioned teacher serves as a guide on the hard road, which involves long and careful study, while on the easy way, an effete, foppish teacher can produce a rhetor almost instantaneously. The work is addressed to an aspiring young student of rhetoric who must choose between the two; the similarity with Lucian's own situation in the *Somnium* is apparent.[24] In the *Rhetorum Praeceptor* the unfashionable teacher of rhetoric clearly represents

---

[22] Surely Stock (1911), 27 is right to make light of Lucian's claim at the end of the *Somnium* that he wrote the work in order to encourage other poor young men to pursue their education.

[23] It is interesting to see how closely Plato's description of Eros (as son of Penia) matches that of Techne: Eros is not as most people think ἁπαλός τε καὶ καλός . . . ἀλλὰ σκληρὸς καὶ αὐχμηρὸς καὶ ἀνυπόδητος καὶ ἄοικος (*Symp.* 203c–d).

[24] Jones (1986), 106 notes this resemblance but finds 'no significance in the similarity'; see, however, Anderson (1976a), 138–9, 165 and cf. Romm (1990), 97–8.

the better alternative of the two,[25] and he bears more than a passing resemblance to Techne. He too is quite lacking in surface charms: Lucian describes him as a hairy, sunburnt man who sweats and pants while toiling along the rough road to rhetoric. Like Techne, he is hard and manly, even overly masculine (καρτερός τις ἀνήρ, ὑπόσκληρος, ἀνδρώδης τὸ βάδισμα . . . ἀρρενωπὸς τὸ βλέμμα *Rhet. Prae.* 9; πέρα τοῦ μετρίου ἀνδρικῷ 10; cf. ἡ σκληρὰ ἐκείνη καὶ ἀνδρώδης *Somn.* 6). The path he recommends—serious and prolonged study of ancient models such as Plato and Demosthenes—is long and arduous. Techne's way of life is similarly laborious, as Paideia is careful to point out (*Somn.* 9, 13). Finally, it is interesting to note that the narrator of the *Rhetorum Praeceptor* compares the models for study prescribed by the old-fashioned teacher to the works of ancient sculptors (9)—the very province of Techne![26]

If the similarities between Techne and the unfashionable teacher are noteworthy, the reverse side of the coin, the resemblance between Paideia and the foppish, modern teacher, Lucian's target in the *Rhetorum Praeceptor*,[27] is perhaps even more interesting. The modish teacher and Paideia are, of course, both teachers of rhetoric and both promise their prospective pupils that they will become rhetors fairly quickly. Paideia speaks vaguely of a short period of time (cf. οὐκ εἰς μακράν σε διδάξομαι *Somn.* 10; μετ᾽ ὀλίγον . . . ζηλωτὸς . . . ἔσῃ 11) and seems to transform Lucian into an orator during the course of their chariot ride, while the modern teacher of *Rhetorum Praeceptor* promises to turn his pupil into a rhetor before sunset (πρὶν ἥλιον δῦναι 15; cf. αὐτίκα μάλα 11, οὐκ εἰς μακράν 24). This is in sharp contrast to his rival, the old-fashioned teacher, who requires neither days nor months, but Olympiads for the road he sets his pupils (9). (Techne does not specify how long Lucian's apprenticeship to her craft need last.) The modern teacher's way is as simple as it is brief: all the potential

---

[25] See Atkins (1934), 338–42; Hall (1981), 307–9 (with n. 80 on 555–6). Bompaire (1958), 135, and Romm (1990), 94–5, see the old-fashioned teacher as a more ambiguous figure.

[26] Cf. Romm (1990), 94–8. Themistius has a noteworthy description of his virtuous woman, Philia. She is not attractive, but possesses a true, old-fashioned beauty like that of the statues of old, which need time and sharp eyes in order to be appreciated: εὐειδὴς μὲν οὔ, ὡραία δέ, ἀληθινοῦ καὶ ἀρχαίου γέμουσα κάλλους, ὁποῖα τὰ ἀγάλματα τῆς παλαιᾶς τέχνης ἃ χρόνου δεῖται εἰς τὸ θαυμάσαι καὶ ὀφθαλμῶν ἀκριβεστέρων (*Or.* 22. 281a). If Lucian's Techne can be said to possess any sort of beauty, it is precisely of this kind.

[27] For the real-life identity of Lucian's victim in the *Rhet. Prae.*, often thought to be Pollux, see e.g. Baldwin (1973), 34–6, 70–4 and Jones (1986), 105–8.

rhetor need do is concentrate on a few superficial rules, such as wearing fancy dress and sprinkling his speech with Atticisms and neo-
logisms (*Rhet. Prae.* 14–17). The young pupil of the *Rhetorum
Praeceptor* is, then, faced with the classic choice between a long and
arduous path and a short and easy one, and the narrator's warm
commendation of the latter road is patently false: we are meant to
understand that the difficult way is actually far superior. In the *Somnium* young Lucian is offered an equally clear-cut choice, for Paideia
seems to require of him nothing more than his willingness to submit to
her tutelage, while Techne's way involves great exertion. But in the
Somnium it seems that the easier of the two options is also the better
one. Once again we are confronted in the *Somnium* with a simplistic,
black-and-white scheme, which involves no quandaries or dilemmas:
not only is Paideia far more attractive than the manly, work-stained
Techne, but her path is easier and much more agreeable. No wonder
then that young Lucian does not even wait to hear her out and elects to
choose her way on the spot.

Lucian is not the only author to present such an unequal pair of
alternatives. In Dio Chrysostom, the road leading to the good woman
(Basileia) is smooth, while that leading to the bad one (Tyranny) is
rough, and this is true of Dio's imitator, Themistius, as well. None the
less, just as we have seen that most writers who make use of Prodicus'
scheme prefer to offer a more interesting choice than that between
Beautiful Virtue and Ugly Vice, so too many writers, when using the
allegory of two roads to represent two ways of life, favour a more
complex alternative than the *Somnium*'s Easy, Good Road versus a
Hard, Bad one. In several authors, when there is a long, arduous road
and a short, easy one it is the longer and more difficult road which
leads to virtue (or some other positive quality) and should be chosen,
as in the *Rhetorum Praeceptor*.[28] Other writers try to soften this stark
contrast and present these opposite roads in such a way that the way-
farer will be confronted with two genuine alternatives and yet be able
to see the advantages of the better way. In these authors, the steep,
difficult road to virtue may turn smooth at some stage; analogously,
the easy road leading to vice clearly becomes undesirable at some
point. Thus Hesiod, who was the first to make use of this allegory of
two roads (*Op.* 287–92), has the steep road to virtue turn easy once

---

[28] See Philo, *De Sacr. Ca. et Ab.* 35–42; Silius Italicus, *Pun.* 15. 46ff., 107–10;
Maximus 14. 1k; Basil, *De Leg. Gr. Lib.* 5. 63–4; Rhetor I ignotus and Troilus, as quoted
by I. Alpers (1912), 37.

the top is reached. In Cebes' *Tabula* there is a similar reversal of the rough and smooth roads after one has reached the summit of virtue (15. 2–16. 5; 18. 3; 27. 3).[29] In Ps.-Diogenes, *Letter* 30, there is a different set of alternatives: the road to virtue is *short* and steep while the other, inferior way is long and smooth. In sum, Lucian's easy choice in the *Somnium* is too easy or simplistic for most of the writers who make use of the 'two roads' motif.

Let us return to Paideia and the modern teacher of rhetoric found in the *Rhetorum Praeceptor*. Another feature they share in common is the emphasis they place on external appearances, both in relation to themselves and their pupils. Paideia proudly points to her own splendid apparel, promising Lucian that if he chooses her he too will be dressed in the same way. Indeed, during their chariot ride, she outfits him in elegant new clothes, and subsequently exhibits his finery to his father (*Somn.* 11, 13, 16). It seems that clothes make the man: a mere glance at his son's new garb suffices to indicate to Lucian's father that his son has become a rhetor, a person of consequence. The modern teacher of rhetoric is a dainty creature with mincing steps, who smiles delicately and speaks gently, since manliness is uncouth and not in keeping with a delicate and charming rhetor (*Rhet. Prae.* 12). This veritable Sardanapallus or Agathon is balding, but has curls and smells of perfume (11–12). He gives his pupil specific instructions on the kind of clothes he is to wear, stressing the importance of purple (11, 15, 16; cf. 20). This emphasis on external finery seems superficial, to say the least. We have already seen that in Prodicus pairs it is normally Vice or Pleasure who is elaborately costumed, painted, and decorated, while Arete (or the better of the two women) is dressed unpretentiously, often in white, with purity or simplicity as her chief ornament. In Justin's version of Prodicus' tale, for example, a delicately and seductively dressed Kakia promises Heracles that if he follows her he will spend his life decked out in similar fashion, just as Paideia promises Lucian in the *Somnium*; it is Justin's unkempt Arete who holds out the promise of less transient adornments (*Apol.* 2. 11).

One further point Paideia and the modern teacher have in common is their appreciation of fame. Paideia promises young Lucian that he will be admired and envied, honoured and praised; she will even grant him immortality. I will make you so well known, she adds, that

---

[29] See Fitzgerald and White (1983), 38 n. 67; 41 n. 88. They note (p. 14) that in Xenophon, too, there is a similar kind of reversal for Vice's pleasures ultimately lead to hardship, while Virtue brings happiness (*Mem.* 2. 1. 31–2).

everyone will point to you saying 'here he is' ὥστε ... ἕκαστος ... δείξει σε τῷ δακτύλῳ, οὗτος ἐκεῖνος λέγων (*Somn.* 11–12). The foppish modern teacher is proud of being notorious and pointed at as well: καὶ τὸ δείκνυσθαι τῷ δακτύλῳ τοῦτον ἐκεῖνον (*Rhet. Prae.* 25; cf. 6, 12, 17, 20–1, 26).[30] Both Lucian, Paideia's pupil, and the modern teacher's prospective student have a chariot ride offered to them. In the *Rhetorum Praeceptor* the prospective pupil is told (albeit somewhat ironically) that he, rather than Zeus, should be driving Plato's winged chariot (πτηνὸν ἅρμα ἐλαύνοντα φέρεσθαι 26),[31] while Lucian of the *Somnium* is actually taken by Paideia for a ride across the heavens on a chariot drawn by winged horses, as a reward for choosing her.[32] Surely it is significant that what Lucian remembers from this ride is the praise of those who saw him from below, while he forgets the kind of seeds he has sown to them. Lucian's 'view from above' does not lead to any deep, philosophical perspective; instead Paideia's pupil portrays himself as a 'travelling performer ... who recollects an endless succession of upturned admiring faces more clearly than the message he has tried to convey'.[33]

Despite the many points of contact between Paideia and the modern teacher of rhetoric, it would be wrong to tar the two with the same brush. While the new-fangled teacher is an absolute contrast to his old-fashioned rival, and is clearly an altogether negative figure, Paideia has several positive aspects and in many ways her ambitions for Lucian are identical to those of her rival, Techne. Both women hold out the promise of fame for Lucian, his family, and his native city (Techne states: κλεινὸς αὐτὸς ... ζηλωτὸν ... τὸν πατέρα ἀποδείξεις ... περίβλεπτον ... τὴν πατρίδα *Somn.* 8; cf. Paideia's words: ζηλωτὸς καὶ ἐπίφθονος ἔσῃ ... τιμώμενος καὶ ἐπαινούμενος καὶ ... εὐδοκιμῶν καὶ ... ἀποβλεπόμενος 11) and both mention the prospect of immortality, an eternal reputation (8, 12). Paideia also pledges to tend to Lucian's soul in addition to his body, embellishing it with 'self-

---

[30] This is no mere coincidence: we find the identical motif of pointing at a figure and saying "οὗτος ἐκεῖνος" used in conjunction with a third figure, Herodotus, who, Lucian claims, became a celebrity overnight with little effort (*Herodotus* 1–2). Such fame seems of equivocal value at best.

[31] Cf. Pl. *Phaedrus* 246e and see Trapp (1990), 153 on Lucian's 'particular taste' for this allusion.

[32] I. Alpers (1912), 44–5 compares Virtue's promise to Scipio in Silius Italicus ... *mox celsus ab alto | infra te cernes hominum genus* (8. 106–7). In Themistius (*Or.* 22. 280a–b), Arete rewards Heracles for choosing her by granting him a *closer* look at the two peaks at the end of the road.

[33] Duncan (1979), 16. On the 'view from above' see also Rutherford (1989a), 155–61.

control, justice, piety, gentleness, decency, intelligence, fortitude, love of beauty and an impulse towards the sublime' (*Somn.* 10; M. D. Macleod 1991 trans.). This list of qualities is reminiscent of the series of companions or personified virtues who often accompany the good figure in other variations on Prodicus' tale.[34] As such the list is impressive, perhaps a little too impressive. Paideia rattles all these virtues off in one breath and seems to be paying lip-service to these ideals. It is worth quoting here a scholiast's grudging view on how false these promises have proved in Lucian's case: ἀλλὰ μὴν ψευδεῖς αἱ τῆς διδασκαλίας ὑποσχέσεις ἀπεφάνησαν· οὐ γὰρ τοιαύταις σου τὴν ψυχὴν ἀρεταῖς κατεκόσμησεν ἀλλὰ ταῖς ἐναντίαις, ὡς αὐτὸς σὺ ταῦτα ἐξ ὧν γράφεις ἀποδεικνύεις. One further good quality assigned to Paideia is her appreciation of Demosthenes: she boasts of having made him great (*Somn.* 12). The Attic orator seems to have been a great favourite of Lucian[35] and in the *Rhetorum Praeceptor* it is the old-fashioned teacher of rhetoric who believes in close study of Demosthenes (9, 10); his more modern rival ridicules Demosthenes' writings (17; cf. 21).

Paideia of the *Somnium* is then a complex or ambivalent figure, perhaps closest in kind to another allegorical woman in Lucian, Rhetoric of *Bis Accusatus*. In this composition, which is again seemingly an autobiographical work, Rhetoric describes her first encounter with the young Syrian (i.e. Lucian). The situation is very similar to that of Lucian's dream: 'When the defendant was a mere boy still talking with a foreign accent and almost wearing a turban in Syrian style, I found him wandering about in Ionia, not knowing what to make of himself, so I took him in hand and gave him an education.'[36] Rhetoric marries the Syrian, has him enrolled as a citizen and faithfully follows him in his travels abroad, where he is a great success thanks to her embellishments and teachings. Thus Rhetoric seems to have fulfilled all the promises Paideia has made to Lucian. None the less the Syrian deserts her and he explains why: Rhetoric has changed. She was modest and respectable when ὁ Παιανιεὺς ἐκεῖνος, Demosthenes, carried her off, but she now uses make-up and dresses (and behaves) like a courtesan (*Bis Acc.* 31). The Syrian also admits that he has tired

---

[34] We find such companions in the versions of Philo, Cebes, Silius, Dio Chrysostom, and Themistius; cf. I. Alpers (1912), 48–51.

[35] See Baldwin (1973), 69; cf. Anderson (1976*b*), 64–5.

[36] *Bis Acc.* 27; transl. M. D. Macleod (1991), 1–2. The young Syrian boy with his foreign speech and inappropriate dress is not unlike the poorly dressed Techne who also does not speak perfect Greek—cf. βαρβαρίζουσα πάμπολλα (*Somn.* 8).

of Rhetoric: at 40 he is too old to argue in the lawcourts and hold forth on hackneyed themes. Rhetoric, who is in many ways the counterpart of Paideia, has proved a disappointment: at some stage she has been transformed from Arete to Kakia, from Virtue to Vice, and has become more like the modern teacher of rhetoric in the *Rhetorum Praeceptor* than the old-fashioned one. Hence the Syrian has taken up with a new figure, Dialogue, the son of Philosophy, who is now Rhetoric's rival for his affections. Unfortunately, Dialogue is not an altogether compatible mate either: he is too serious, a dour, skeletal figure who arouses respect, but is neither pleasant nor attractive. The Syrian is forced to wash the dirt off him, make him smile, and couple him with Comedy (*Bis Acc.* 34). Grave, unattractive Dialogue is, then, reminiscent of Techne of the *Somnium* and Lucian cannot accept him, just as he cannot choose the female stonemason: he finds it necessary to modify him, turn him into a lighter, more carefree figure. By the time he wrote the *Bis Accusatus* Lucian had reached the satisfactory solution of writing comic dialogues, but in the slightly earlier *Somnium*[37] one can, perhaps, sense underneath the surface the disillusion or disappointment Lucian feels with the path he has chosen. As a boy still trembling from his uncle's blows, Lucian tells us, he made the obvious choice, preferring attractive Paideia to hard-working Techne. As an adult, when writing the *Somnium*, the sophist from Samosata indicates by means of his ambiguous presentation of the two women that he cannot celebrate this choice whole-heartedly. At the very end of the *Somnium* (18), Lucian states in mock-modesty that he is no less distinguished than any sculptor: are we meant to think that he is more distinguished?[38]

[37] The *Bis Acc.* is generally dated to AD 165 on the basis of internal references, while the *Somn.* is thought to be a few years earlier. See Hall (1981), 13–16, 20 and M. D. Macleod (1991), 3–4, 249; cf. Jones (1986), 8 n. 10.

[38] I would like to thank David Satran for his comments on an earlier version of this paper. It is a privilege to contribute to a volume in honour of a man who, like Lucian's teacher of old, has spent Olympiads on the close, careful study of ancient texts. His scholarship is an inspiring illustration of the fruits to be found at the very summit of the long and arduous road.

18

Apollonius in Wonderland

SIMON SWAIN

One of the most important figures in the history of later Greek literature is the sophist and biographer Flavius Philostratus. He is known principally for two works. The *Lives of the Sophists* is his account of the rhetorical stars of the high Empire, whose theory and practice Donald Russell has done so much to illuminate. The eight-book *In Honour of Apollonius of Tyana*, which was allegedly written for the cultured empress Julia Domna, is a biography of a different sort, but is nevertheless from the same sophistic school that has been central to Russell's interests. The following observations on some of its later readers will, I trust, entertain and instruct.

In the person of Apollonius Philostratus celebrates the famous mystical philosopher of the first century AD.[1] By emphasizing Apollonius' Hellenism and his closeness to god, he prefigures the concerns of many other Greek pagans in later antiquity, when Apollonius became an object of veneration and worship as a true Hellene. Philostratus did not invent Apollonius' Hellenism. It is to the fore in some of the *Letters* which are rightly or wrongly attributed to him. But he clearly built it up to suit his own interests. Hellenism comes out most strongly in Apollonius' final confrontation with the tyrant-emperor Domitian in Books Seven and Eight of the life. One of the ways readers are prepared for this show-down is by the earlier description of the treatment Apollonius receives from the model king of India, Phraotes. Phraotes' philosophical utopia is founded upon the wise teaching of the Brahmins under their leader Iarchas. Greek and the Greek character command their highest respect (2. 26 ff., 31; 3. 12, 16, 36). It seems, indeed, that Apollonius is sent to the Indians not only to discover the proper relation between culture and power, but also to

This note could not have been written without the generous help of Alexis Sanderson.

[1] On Apollonius and Philostratus see esp. Bowie (1978).

have his own wisdom confirmed by them. We may compare Dio of Prusa's musings on the Indians' respect for Homer and on their translation of his poems (*Or.* 53. 6–7).[2] Much of what Philostratus says about Apollonius has been disbelieved (for reasons obvious to any reader). The Indian excursion is especially suspect owing to the Brahmins' role in ancient literature as a species of wise man *par excellence*. But reference to a record of Apollonius' trip in Sanskrit literature has recently been brought forward—with due caution—and if the record were genuine, students of Philostratus would clearly have to review some of their baser suspicions.[3]

The evidence for Apollonius in India is mentioned by an Indian Sanskritist, V. Bhattacharya.[4] He refers to two texts. First is the *Gururatnamālā* by Sadāśivabrahmendra. This is a hagiographical work celebrating the pontiffs of the Kāmakoṭi monastery in the south Indian city of Conjeevaram. It was written in the second half of the sixteenth century, since Sadāśivabrahmendra was a pupil of the fifty-fifth pontiff who held office from 1534 to 1586. Second is a commentary on this work by Ātmabodhendra which was produced in the first half of the eighteenth century under the fifty-ninth pontiff (1704–46).[5] The verse in Sadāśivabrahmendra which mentions Apollonius runs as follows: 'I take refuge in Gauḍapāda, the first scholar to expound the Bhāṣya of Phaṇīśa [i.e. Patañjali, the author of the yoga system], whose feet were reverenced by Ayārcya his [former] opponent, who was the leader of Apolonya and the other Niṣāka (?) holy men.' It was first drawn to the attention of historians by M. Hiriyanna, who noted its important implications, if authentic, for the chronology of Gauḍapāda. He was the earliest exponent of the non-dualist Vedānta (the Hindu philosophy of the oneness of God, soul, and universe), which is the theology of the Kāmakoṭi pontiffs, and is usually thought to have lived in the sixth or seventh century AD.[6] The commentator Ātmabodhendra glosses the verse by saying that when Gauḍapāda was seeking the truth of the self under the guidance of Śuka on a peak of the Himalayas, he influenced Ayārcya and his followers, including the Yogins Apalūnya and Damīśa from the western border and the chief of Taxila, Prāvṛti, to abandon their erroneous Buddhistic theology for his

[2] Cf. Aelian, *Varia Historia* 12. 48.
[3] Bowersock (1989), 97 n. 1. Cf. Anderson (1986), 173 n. 106.
[4] Bhattacharya (1943), pp. lxxii–lxxiv.
[5] These works are published together in *Vedāntapañcaprakaraṇī* (Kumbhakonam, 1895). The following translation is Sanderson's.
[6] Hiriyanna (1926).

own. He reports two sources for his extra information, the *Gauḍapā-dollāsa* of Harimiśra and the *Patañjalivijaya* of Rāmabhadra Dīkṣita. This is where the matter becomes interesting, for of the first no manu-script is known, while the second, which was written by a man of the same school as Ātmabodhendra living around 1700, contains no refer-ence to Greeks but only to Gauḍapāda as the disciple of Śuka.[7]

There is more. For if it does not seem fantastic enough that Apollo-nius' presence in India should have been remembered for fifteen hundred years to then appear in an obscure sectarian tract, it can in fact be proved that the Sanskrit references to him are bogus. They are due neither to memory nor to familiarity with Philostratus, but depend upon a work on Apollonius written in *modern English*. This is obvious from the rendering of 'Iarchas' as 'Ayārcya'. For the Sanskrit 'c' here is pro-nounced like English 'ch' and therefore does not represent the value of Greek χ (or its Latin equivalent 'ch'), but that of the English digraph which was mistakenly read and pronounced in 'Iarchas'. *We are, then, dealing with a forgery*. Philostratus' disbelievers may rest easy after all.

To complete the removal of this bogus evidence it remains to inquire who the forger was and what his aims were. Various considera-tions make the interpolation in the hagiographical work and its com-mentary a late one. Neither Sadāśivabrahmendra nor Ātmabodhendra had any motive to allude to foreign scholars (an entirely untraditional approach) and anyway lived in a world untouched by English or Euro-pean culture. The motivation is rather the neo-Hinduistic thinking which became widespread at the end of the last century when men like Bal Gagandhar Tilak, Surendranath Banergea, and Bipin Chandra Pal were busy harnessing traditional Hindu religion and literature in opposition to British rule. Appropriation of all wisdom for India was a natural part of this. But there may also be a particular connection with Greece. For though the precise identity of the forger is unknown, it might be recalled that the revered Bengali holy man, nationalist, and exponent of the Vedānta, Swami Vivekananda, took an interest in the wisdom of the ancient Greeks and its affinities with Indian philosophy (Indians and Greeks being of the same stock), and suggested that the mingling of Greek and Indian qualities following Alexander's con-quests had had a profound effect on world history.[8] The application

---

[7] The work is published under the title *Patañjalicarita* (Kāvyamālā, 51; Bombay, 1895); the reference is at 7. 31.

[8] See Raychaudhuri (1988), 270–3. I have not discovered a reference to Apollonius in Vivekananda's own works.

here of Apollonius' visit to the Brahmins is clear, and we may guess that the idea of citing him and inventing his conversion came about under the influence of thinking of this sort. The use Apollonius made of his wisdom in resisting tyranny may also have appealed to our forger. At any rate the later nineteenth-century nationalists were keen on rehearsing the stories of men like Mazzini who stood up to foreign despots.

A reasonable guess can also be made as to the English source which caused the forger's confusion. It is likely enough that this was the article published in 1860 by O. de Beauvoir Priaulx.[9] If this is so, we may say that the verse and commentary and the other information were inserted some time between this date and 1895 when the texts they appear in were published.

In sum, the Hellenic Apollonius has come full circle. Philostratus sent him to India to be told how important true Greek culture was. Many centuries later he returns there to show the supposed heirs of the Greeks that his wisdom was Indian all along.

[9] More or less a summary of the *Apollonius*, though not totally credulous; cf. Charpentier (1934), 16 (whose own work combines similar leisureliness with lunatic etymologies).

19

Female Characterization in Greek Declamation

RICHARD HAWLEY

During the past twenty years or so, classical scholarship has seen a phenomenal growth in two areas which have seldom overlapped: the examination of gender in antiquity and the study of so-called 'later' Greek literature. This paper is a contribution to both spheres. Classical scholars are now constantly reminded of how ancient texts constructed social ideals of masculinity and femininity. But most literary critics have clung to the safe and traditional classical period, from archaic times to the second century AD. The second current of criticism which has inspired this paper is one for which Donald Russell has provided much impetus. He has so often and eloquently performed an encomium of later Greek literature that the generations of scholars who have flourished under his inspiration are now reassessing these intriguing texts. The central texts of this brief paper will be the declamations and *progymnasmata* (preparatory exercises) of the fourth-century AD rhetor Libanius, but many of the observations can be applied to others among the *rhetores Graeci*.

As we know from Russell's masterly *Greek Declamation* (1983), that curious species of littérateur which flourished during the first centuries of the Roman empire, the declaimer, underwent a detailed and systematic education in the art of rhetoric. Central to this education were the *progymnasmata*, where the trainee orator progressed from the basic narration of a story, through exercises on expansion and refutation, comparison and contrast, to the complex exercise of ἠθοποιΐα, characterization. The orator had to be able to develop versatility into a seemingly casual art. He had to know how to address any kind of audience appropriately, and how to adopt any number of stereotypical personae.[1] One group of those personae was women: but not just one type, rather a range, from the ideal wife to the ex-prostitute.

[1] See esp. Russell (1990).

The world of Greek declamation is peopled by characters from myth, literature, and the classical past.[2] This is as true for its female as for its male characters. There were historical women upon whom rhetors might draw as examples. The most famous collection of such stories is Plutarch's *Virtues of Women*. But the rhetors preferred to use mythical or anonymous generic women (the chaste prostitute, the talkative woman).[3] This avoidance of historical women can be easily explained when we recall the function of the declamations and preparatory exercises, as textbook examples of principles applicable anywhere, any time. The choice of historical examples might prove too specific. For instance, Theon cites the historical women Artemisia, Tomyris, Sparethra, and Semiramis as examples one may use for a σύγκρισις (comparison) between men and women who were brave (2. 114. 17–115. 10 Spengel). These women are only famous for their bravery and may not be appropriate in other settings. We may also observe that many declamations concerned themselves with points of law. When declaimers set their scenarios in the world of the fifth or fourth century BC (especially Athens), it is not hard to explain the absence of women speakers by referring to the convention that then men alone spoke in court or the assembly, with women only speaking in minor roles as witnesses or swearers of oaths. The first point, therefore, that we should notice is that the declaimers' favourite sources for women were archaic epic and drama of the fifth and fourth centuries BC. The women of the *Iliad* are especially popular, presumably because they also feature heavily in tragedy.[4]

Secondly, unlike much modern literary criticism, women were not thought of in rhetorical texts as a special or separable group. Nor were they singled out as victims of any literary 'oppression' or 'textual harassment'; they were not considered as alien or inferior subjects.[5] Our best proof of this important point is the way in which the technical treatises on *progymnasmata* cite women as examples of various rhetorical tricks.

In Hermogenes, for instance, examples of linguistic devices can just

[2] Russell (1983), 106–8.

[3] Cf. Peisistratus' semi-mythical Athena look-alike, Phye: Maximus Planudes 5. 378. 9–13 Walz; Hermogenes, *Peri. Heur.* 104. 16–20 Rabe.

[4] Cf. the ἠθοποιΐα of Laodameia in Nicolaus, *Prog.* 9 (1. 392. 22–394. 18 Walz), a famous figure from e.g. Euripides' *Protesilaos*.

[5] This lack of anti-feminine bias is common in ancient literary criticism. In the character lists of e.g. Horace, *Ars Poetica* 114ff., 120ff., or Ovid, *Am.* 1. 15. 17–18, women are included on equal terms with men.

as much concern themselves with women as with men. In *Progymnasmata* 2. 17–18 (4. 21–6. 2 Rabe), περὶ διηγήματος, Hermogenes chooses the story of Medea to illustrate five types of σχήματα. The first is the ὀρθὸν ἀποφαντικόν, used, he says, for ἱστορίαι because it is clearest: 'Medea was the daughter of Aetes; she betrayed the golden fleece'. Here we have the nominative case. The second σχῆμα is the ἀποφαντικὸν ἐγκεκλιμένον: 'the story says that Medea, the daughter of Aetes, was enamoured of Jason'. An exercise in using oblique cases. Thirdly, the ἐλεγκτικόν, with its use of questions: 'what terrible thing did Medea not do? was she not enamoured of Jason, and betrayed the golden fleece, and killed her brother Apsyrtos?' Fourthly, the ἀσύν-δετον: 'Medea the daughter of Aetes was enamoured of Jason. She betrayed the golden fleece. She slaughtered her brother Apsyrtos.' Fifthly and finally, the συγκριτικόν: 'Medea the daughter of Aetes instead of showing sexual restraint (σωφρονεῖν) fell in love, and instead of protecting the golden fleece betrayed it, and instead of saving her brother Apsyrtos slaughtered him.'

It is clear that there is no specially 'feminine' reason for choosing Medea as the example. Medea's story just happens to contain the elements desired for the exercise. She is cited as an example of an ἀπίθανον by Sardianus, Theon, and the Anonymous Scholia to Aphthonius.[6] It is unlikely that a mother such as Medea would harm her children. Similarly it is the unlikeliness of the story that explains other references to Medea dyeing old men's white hair black, cutting up old men, cooking them in a pot and rejuvenating them.[7] Again, stories which concern famous mythical women may be popular exercises for ἀνασκευή or κατασκευή, but the characterization of the women is limited and stereotypical.[8] Women's participation in such events is not especially exploited for the issue of gender.[9]

But gender does begin to play a part in questions of ἦθος, character, and πάθος, emotion. Unlike men, women as a gender seem more

[6] Sardianus 71 *app. crit.*, 75. 10–12 cf. 85. 3 Rabe; Theon, *Prog.* 6, 2. 94. 17–32 Spengel; Anon. Schol. in Aphth. 2. 28. 26–29. 22 Walz.

[7] Sardianus 78. 6–9 Rabe; Theon 2. 96. 11–13 Spengel.

[8] e.g. Daphne in Aphth. 10. 20–13. 18, 14. 8–16. 6 Rabe; Medea in Nicolaus, *Prog.* 6. 5, 1. 301. 8–304. 24; 6. 9, 312. 7–314. 7 Walz; Niobe in Nicolaus 1. 304. 25–307. 9, 310. 11–312. 6 Walz. Of Nicolaus' eleven topics for the ἀνα-/κατασκευή, seven centre on women (Penthesileia, Danae, Pasiphae, Niobe, Medea, Alcestis, Amazons).

[9] Cf. Helen in Theon, *Prog.* 8. 40 (2. 110. 26 Spengel). She is a negative character whom one may redeem with praise; that she is female is irrelevant. Gender is similarly unimportant when Theon (*Prog.* 13, 2. 129. 19–22 Spengel) cites a legal issue for debate concerning a maid and her jewellery.

chosen for their stereotypical associations with πάθος. Theon indeed
remarks (*Prog.* 6, 94. 31–2 Spengel) μαλακώτεραί πως αἱ γυναῖκες
πρὸς τὰ πάθη. Aphthonius includes in his section on ἠθοποιΐα a type
which he calls 'mixed', where ἦθος and πάθος are combined (35. 2, 6–
7 Rabe). Sardianus cites among the examples of such speeches 'what
Medea would say as she is about to kill her children' (207. 15–16
Rabe). We are lucky that just such a speech has been preserved among
the *progymnasmata* of Libanius (8. 372–6 Foerster). The piece offers
Medea's reasoned motivation (λογίσωμαι 3), offered through a linear
chronological narration of her past history. The style is clear, almost
staccato, full of asyndeton and repetition of emphatic words. The first
sentence stresses that though she is wronged (ἀδικουμένη 1), she will
not be passive but act in revenge. Medea dwells on how her secrecy will
prevent her being suspected (2). Her narration of Jason's arrival in
Colchis is structured to show the obstacles which stand in his way,
before Medea appears to remove them (4–6). She trusted Jason's oaths
and left with him (6). So far the elements could have come straight
from Euripides' *Medea* and its many classical imitations. But then
Medea speaks (with what seems less of a classical colouring) of the
reasons for Jason's desire to marry the Corinthian princess as a desire
for power (7), a desire called a passion (τὸν ἔρωτα τῆς δυναστείας).[10]
Medea then rouses herself to action with a self-address (cf. Eur. *Med.*
1056) and imperatives. Euripides' famous monologue for Medea
(1021–80) is then cleverly recalled when Libanius' Medea lists all the
things which will *not* prevent her proceeding with her revenge: nature
(Medea as a mother), memory of birth-pangs, the children's voices or
appearance (8).[11] The children are then called to come to her, in a vivid
penultimate section (10). She sees their shape and forms as recalling
those of Jason (10) but, she says, that only makes her more determined
to kill them. The final section sums up her future, as in Euripides,
culminating in her journey to Athens, where, she says, τὴν λύπην
ἀποθήσομαι. This phrase may exploit the double meaning of λύπη:
Medea will indeed lay aside *grief*, but not stop causing others *pain*.

Libanius presents the feminine here along quite stereotypical lines.
But this suits the requirements of a brief introductory exercise,
designed for universal application. Euripides' monologue for Medea is
one of the most striking of women's speeches in classical Greek

---

[10] Cf. *Ad Her.* 2. 3: 'num honorem, num pecuniam, num dominationem, num aliquam cupiditatem'.

[11] Birth-pangs: cf. Eur. *Med.* 1030–1; appearance: 1071–7, esp. 1072.

literature. Another is that of Andromache to Hector in *Iliad* 6. This too provides grist for the rhetor's mill. Under ἠθοποιΐα (9), Hermogenes speaks of it as a μίμησις ἤθους, and gives as his example 'Andromache's words to Hector' (20. 8–9 Rabe). The same speech is cited later when he subdivides ἠθοποιΐα into three groups: ἠθικαί, where ἦθος is dominant; παθητικαί, where πάθος dominates; and a mixed type (21. 10–18 Rabe). Predictably, Andromache is chosen to exemplify the pathetic type (p. 21. 13–14 Rabe). Luckily for us, Libanius gives as an example of ἠθοποιΐα 'what words would Andromache say over Hector?' (8. 376–8 Foerster).[12]

This speech is set after Hector's death, but does not use the lamentations of the Trojan women in *Iliad* 24 as its source for ideas, but rather the striking encounter between Hector and Andromache in *Iliad* 6. Libanius takes what are Andromache's fears for the future in Homer and realizes them in his dramatic 'present'. Thus the time at which the speech takes place is carefully chosen to exaggerate the πάθος. The fall of Troy is a favourite setting for rhetorical πάθος: Aphthonius offers a παθητικὴ ἠθοποιΐα of Hecuba (*Prog.* 9, 35. 4 Rabe); Choricius twice develops the scene at length (131–50, 152–74 Foerster–Richtsteig). The speech of Libanius' Andromache is typical: short on ἦθος, long on πάθος. Andromache stresses the πάθος of Hector's premature death: it will now cause (in a measured emotional crescendo) the death of Priam, his brothers, Hecuba, the baby, Andromache herself, and the whole city (2). Libanius adds an extra touch of πάθος by using the deictic pronoun of the baby, τουτὶ τὸ παιδίον. We envisage her, child in arms, as she was in *Iliad* 6. She develops the commonplace contrast between former happiness and present misery (2–3), blaming Achilles and, in a non-Homeric touch, Thetis, because she bore Achilles (4). Further πάθος is added by her vocative address to the dead Hector (5). Andromache says that she can 'see' the Trojans being massacred, the wives being molested, the young girls being humiliated, the children being dragged along, the iron, the fire (5). The list of all the pathetic groups of the city, coupled with the emotive repetition ὁρᾶν τὸν σίδηρον, ὁρᾶν τὴν φλόγα, completes this section. Finally and emotively, she addresses her baby (ὦ παιδίον), visualizes her own death, and concludes with the humiliation which she would think ultimate: to be forced to have sex with Hector's killer (6). Again we have a string of literary reminiscences, skilfully manipulated, and commonplaces: dramatic switches of fortune, images of the stormed city. But these

---

[12] Cf. Nicolaus, *Prog.* 11, 3. 489. 17 Spengel.

pieces, even when explicitly supposed to reveal ἦθος according to Hermogenes, illustrate the limitations of ancient conceptions of character.[13] The women are more interesting for the rhetorical devices which they employ and for the emotions which these may arouse, than as what we might think of today as 'individuals'. Both Medea and Andromache simply illustrate two traditionally female associations: the family and emotion.

Within the *progymnasmata* of Libanius, we find several other treatments of mythical women, especially those made famous by Attic drama, and of topics which concern women. Other ἠθοποιΐαι feature Niobe (8 and 9),[14] Polyxena (16), Medea again, this time addressing Jason about his new marriage (17), a prostitute who has become chaste (18 and see below), and a sculptor who has fallen in love with a statue of a girl (27). Among the ἐκφράσεις (detailed descriptions), we find Hera (16), an anonymous Trojan woman (17), Polyxena (18),[15] Medea (20),[16] Pallas (22), and beauty (30). The ἔκφρασις of Medea explicitly says that the description is of her as she was in Corinth where she committed the murders (20. 2), an act of πάθος (20. 3). Medea seems once again to be a particular favourite, especially in the ἔκφρασις tradition.[17] The remaining exercises also include a θέσις on whether one should marry (13. 1)[18] and the defence of a law about intrafamilial marriage.

More detailed treatments of women may be found among the declamations proper. Here the debt to Attic drama remains strong, especially to Middle and New Comedy. Libanius' *Declamation* 6 presents Orestes' defence, heavily influenced by traditional images of the tragic Clytemnestra. The world of comedy provides the inspiration for the talkative wife of *Declamation* 26.[19] Legal difficulties concerning sexual misconduct (μοιχεία) give three declamations (38, 39, and 40).[20] *Declamation* 43 offers the defence of a woman who kills her

---

[13] See in general Pelling (1990).

[14] Cf. Aphth. *Prog.* 9, 35. 15–36. 20 Rabe, with Sardianus' analysis 212. 7–214. 22 Rabe.

[15] Attributed by Walz to Nicolaus, *Prog.* 12. 1 (1. 394. 19–396. 16).

[16] Attributed by Walz to Nicolaus, *Prog.* 12. 3 (1. 400. 1–401. 8).

[17] Cf. Philostratus the Younger, *Imag.* 7 (Medea among the Colchians) and 11. 1–2 (on the Argo); Callistratus, *Imag.* 13 (on the statue of Medea) cf. *Anth. Pal.* 16. 135–41.

[18] Cf. Hermogenes, *Prog.* 11, 24. 8 Rabe; Theon, *Prog.* 12, 2. 120. 15 Spengel; Nicolaus, *Prog.* 13. 3. 494. 5 Spengel; *Prolegomena* to Hermogenes, *Peri Staseon* in *Proleg. Syll.* 253. 28–254. 10 Rabe; Aphthonius, *Prog.* 13, 41. 17, 42. 11–46. 18 Rabe with Sardianus 234. 23, 235. 23, 241. 23–5 Rabe; Quintilian 2. 4. 25, 3. 5. 8.

[19] Discussed in Russell (1983), 91–6.

[20] 38: a rich man sleeps with a poor man's wife; 39: a father sleeps with his son's wife; 40: a father kills his daughter and her husband after a dowry swindle.

tyrant husband and then asks for her children's lives as a reward, when the law demands their death. The traditional portrait of the money-grubbing prostitute supplies the background for *Declamation* 32, where an avaricious man begs the authorities for poison in order to avoid having to pay his prostitute lover. But in all except *Declamations* 6 and 26, the woman's role and subsequent characterization are only, at best, of secondary interest. The emphasis is on points of law, patriotism, and general morality. Even in Orestes' defence, Clytemnestra is the passive object of accusations. One interesting touch, however, comes near the end (57) and is thus given dramatic emphasis. Orestes imagines for the jury the kind of thoughts which might have run through Clytemnestra's mind as she prepared to murder her husband. Only she did not reason like this (58), rather ἐτόλμα καὶ διεπράξατο (she dared and did the deed).

The same lack of individuality characterizes the talkative wife of *Declamation* 26. As Russell's discussion and Foerster's notes show, all the wife's traits are stereotypical and can be paralleled from comedy. She is given an accumulation of 'non-feminine' interests: politics and law (26. 15), military affairs (26. 16), the economy (26. 18), literary history (26. 22). She is impervious to the famous line from Sophocles (*Ajax* 293) that silence brings a woman κόσμος (26. 40). Her poor husband does not even want her present when he takes poison, for fear that she may make speeches instead of the usual feminine lamentations (26. 51).

In order to show how Libanius uses traditional feminine stereotypes I shall look in more detail at *Declamation* 25, *That Lais should not be recalled from exile*. Corinth has exiled an *hetaera* (prostitute), Lais, after she had corrupted a large number of the city's young men. During her absence many men were convicted of sexual misconduct and condemned to death. In order to stem the tide of these deaths, someone proposes her recall. Libanius' speaker opposes this proposition. Because this appears to be a rare example of a declamation which centres on a historical rather than mythical woman, one might hope to see greater subtlety in feminine characterization. However, the name Lais was common among prostitutes and she developed a semi-mythical persona.[21] In this way her historical specificity and individuality are minimized: she simply represents another character type, and

---

[21] Athenaeus mentions and sometimes confuses two. The elder was associated with Corinth (e.g. 4. 137d, 13. 582c; Pausanias 2. 2. 5); the younger probably the daughter of Timandra/Damasandra of Hyccara (13. 574e).

the rhetor is free to develop more general themes. The introductory προθεωρία neatly encapsulates many of the themes which the μελέτη (exercise) will develop. First among these is the bad reputation (ἀδοξία) among other Greeks which the city of Corinth will gain if she readmits Lais. Her recall thus affects both morality and politics.

The moral tone starts the speech, as the speaker swears by the personified Sophrosyne (sexual moderation) that he is ashamed (αἰσχύνομαι) at the city's wantonness (ἀκολασία). But the political implications soon emerge, as the speaker compares and contrasts public and private, offering a paradoxical statement (ἄλογον 2) that now immorality is openly paraded while decency is despised. The word for decency, εὐκοσμία, neatly covers the meanings of proper behaviour on both a private moral and a public political level. In this way the declamation may centre on Lais and her recall, but offers the potential for amplification on public morality and the dangers of fickle political decisions.

The first nine sections of the speech concentrate on how immorality infects the city. It has led to an inversion of proper standards, which the speaker illustrates by contrasting past and present. Once Corinth was respected for its decent men (3), now the common good is despised and private lives are dishonoured. Once men respected their own wives and were thus rewarded by the gods with noble children (4). Libanius underlines this former idealized state of happiness by his repetition of words with the prefix εὐ-: εὐδοκιμεῖν, εὐδαιμονία, εὔνοια, εὐπραγία, εὐγένεια, εὐημερία. But then some δαίμων . . . σκαιός (5) brought Lais to the city. The speaker has emphasized the former good fortune of Corinth, now he dwells upon the corruption imported through Lais. His description of Lais' activities and character (5) is completely reliant upon the negative stereotype of the *hetaera* which we find in Attic comedy, especially Middle and New Comedy.

Lais is one who hunts out youth (θηρᾶσαι), an activity which the speaker later says in a generalization is true of all πόρναι. She is clever, but evil; educated, but in the ἐργασία (work) which is prostitution; deceitful; fickle. She causes fights among her jealous lovers. But the speaker emphasizes that she also robs the city of its wealth, which, along with the weakening of young men, pollutes the city (λυμαίνεσθαι). Lais thus harms the city at large through its vulnerable young and wealthy men. But Lais' evil influence also corrupts their wives. The speaker develops a long section on the ways in which Lais' activity makes the formerly respectable wives jealous (7–9). Using generalizations, he follows the classical stereotype most often held by men, that women are strongly motivated by sexual jealousy: this, for example, is held by Jason to be Medea's true reason for anger in Euripides' *Medea* (esp. 569–73). The wives try to stress their σωφρο-σύνη (sexual moderation) to impress their husbands, condemning ἀκρασία (wantonness 7). But when this fails, and the men avoid their wives, they feel that they have to compete with Lais on her own terms and 'sell their youth', as the speaker politely puts it (8). A similar situation is envisaged by Apollodorus in his speech *Against Neaira*: if Neaira is acquitted, she will 'confuse the status of respectable women with that of prostitutes' (113). The contrast between the wives and the πόρναι also attributes typical characteristics to πόρναι: they encourage the men to be deceitful, for the men may praise their wives at home, while in the agora they are bewitched (ἐγοητεύοντο) and ensnared by clever words (λόγοις ποικίλοις 8). Prostitutes in Middle and New Comedy are often compared to witches, such as Circe, and to dangerous animals; they are also said to use wheedling words of erotic persuasion.[22]

Corinth was, of course, renowned in antiquity for its prostitutes, who derived benefit from Corinth's position as a port. This too is developed as part of the fictional construction of the speech by Libanius. When Lais lived in Corinth, the Greeks used to laugh at the city, as if it were an anchorage for wantonness (τῆς ἀκολασίας ... ὁρμητήριον 12). But then the gods encouraged the honourable and moderate men to find the single solution (μίαν λύσιν 13) to their problem by exiling Lais. The speaker makes the decree concern chastity itself, and swears by Athena (13): an appropriately asexual deity. The motives for the decree were to prevent the wives from being insulted and the young men from being corrupted (13). But all has gone wrong. Instead a proposal has been made to recall Lais. Here the speaker quotes *oratio recta*, sarcastically referring to Lais' supporters and their words as χρηστοί (good): instead of one Lais, they say, there are now many. The only way to save the women is to drain the young men's desire for pleasure by recalling Lais.

---

[22] Enchantresses: Men. *Dis Exapaton* 19–30; Anaxilas, *Kirke* 12–13 K–A; Aristophanes, *Ploutos* 302–3 (of Lais as Circe); Ephippus, *Kirke* 11 K–A; Plautus, *Epidicus* 604. Dangerous: Theophilus, *Philaulos* 11 K–A; Timocles, *Ikarioi Saturoi* 16 K–A, *Orestautokleides* 27 K–A; Xenarchus, *Pentathlos* 4 K–A. Animals: Amphis, *Gynaikomania* 9 K–A; Anaxilas, *Neottis* 22 K–A; Eubulus, *Kekropes* 53 K–A; Timocles, *Epistolai* 10 K–A. Wheedling words: e.g. Critias 88 B F1. 3 D–K (γυναικῶν ἠπεροπεύμα at the symposion).

The speaker strongly resists this proposal and recalls a famous line from Sophocles' *Ajax* (293 originally concerning a woman's silence) when he remarks that σωφροσύνη brings κόσμος (order/beauty) to those who practise it (15),[23] and that it strengthens cities and gives them the greatest fame and wealth. The speaker then returns to the wives, now corrupted. There are other ways in which they may be saved (17): we may educate them (παιδαγωγήσομεν) by the law (18), so that they are forced to be chaste, praise good behaviour and then attempt to persuade them. They are not beyond saving, for they were corrupted not by Lais' exile but by envy of her. The speaker here is clearly a man speaking to other men. The use of the verb παιδαγωγεῖν implies that the women are to be treated like children.[24]

The speaker also attacks the proposer of the recall decree, using second person addresses and quoting his *oratio recta* on several occasions. He tries to paint his opponent as one who will criticize those who voted originally for Lais' exile (22) and as one who encourages Lais' return to prevent the city running short of men (26). Once more Lais' effect upon respectable wives is used to advocate that the new proposal be defeated. How many women, he asks in a forceful rhetorical question, have watched their husbands with Lais and wept for their 'widowhood', how many have not even been able to find comfort in children, for Lais even prevented many of them from having children (27).

Lais is thus presented as a threat to the city's reputation among the Greeks, to the city's concept of law and order, to respectable wives, to the continuation of the city by preventing the birth of children, to the city's wealth, and to the youth of the day, who abandon thoughts of bravery in battle for luxury (27). She is, in short, a νόσημα (plague) for the city (29). She is even an inspiration for the abuse of language, for once well-bred young men are now called pimps (33); and the decree proposer twists the law to find authority for the recall in what the law omits to make clear (38–9). Lais is responsible for all this. But the speaker emotionally hesitates

[23] Cf. the use of the same quotation in *Decl.* 26. 40 (see above). The idea was a commonplace: e.g. Sophocles F 64. 4 Radt; Aeschylus, *Sept.* 230–2; Euripides, *Heracl.* 477–8; Aristophanes, *Lys.* 515–16; Plautus, *Rudens* 1114; Democritus F 274 D–K; Xenophon, *Oec.* 7. 5; Lycophron, *Alex.* 2–3; Heliodorus 1. 21.

[24] Although *paidagogoi* are usually of inferior status to their charges, the emphasis here is on the childlike nature of the women. For the husband as educator of the wife: cf. Plutarch, *Praec. Coniug.* 48 = *Mor.* 145b–c; Xen. *Oec. passim.*

to use her name (34), preferring to call her ἡ ἄνθρωπος (34), a term of abuse for women also found in classical authors.[25]

Famous Athenian prostitutes (Aspasia, Myrrhine, Theodote, Phryne)[26] are also wheeled on in a list of *exempla* to confirm that what happens in one city need not necessarily happen in all, for each city has its own laws. This is part of a build-up to the final attack on the proposer, which includes appeals to the gods (42) and lengthy and vivid *oratio recta* to reveal to the citizens the proposer's true thoughts.[27] These thoughts are predictably shameful. The proposer seeks to gain Lais' affections by manipulating the citizens, who he says are 'in the palm of his hand' (χειροηθεῖς 44), so that he, first and foremost, may win her favour as a way to assuage his own lust. He is also presented as so confident of success that his final thoughts are 'I think I can already see my dearest coming to visit'. This use of *oratio recta* is a splendid touch, carefully designed to appeal to the fictional audience. It is also an example of how one *progymnasma*, here an ἠθοποΐα, can be neatly embedded in a longer declamation. The final paragraph (45) returns to the themes of piety and the gods, the city's reputation throughout Greece, and closes with an ominous reminder that Lais, again an unnamed ἄνθρωπος, is one who offers her body to men for money. The contrast of lofty gods and filthy sex, couched in the form of a rhetorical question, makes a suitably striking conclusion.

This declamation offers us much insight into the way in which these literary stereotypes persisted and were exploited by rhetors such as Libanius. It is a great pity that Libanius had not made Lais give her own defence. There is, however, one πόρνη who does deliver a speech among Libanius' *progymnasmata*, in the ἠθοποΐα *What speech would a prostitute who has been chaste (πόρνη σωφρονήσασα) utter?* Here Libanius again engages with the old stereotypes, in a speech based upon one of the paradoxical situations so beloved of declaimers. The characteristics of the classical πόρνη are enumerated, only to be qualified by words such as οὐκέτι (no longer), or by the use of the past tense. The πόρνη now shuns Aphrodite and loves Athena's ἐπιείκεια (decency 3), so much that she will put up an inscription encouraging

---

[25] Also used of a prostitute in e.g. Lysias 4. 9, 4. 19. For use of ἄνθρωπος as a term of abuse: Dover (1974), 282–4.

[26] Aspasia: e.g. Athenaeus 13. 569f–70a, 589d–e; Myrrhine: e.g. 567f, 'the most expensive' 590c, Samian mistress of Demetrius 593a; Theodote of Athens: e.g. 574e, 588d; Phryne: e.g. 584c, 590d–91f.

[27] Cf. the use of similarly vivid *oratio recta* in *Decl.* 6. 57 for Clytemnestra's imagined motivation, which is then dismissed (see above).

other women, perhaps wives,[28] to avoid wantonness, which can make uncertain the identity of a child's father. The piece plays with past, present, and future through the interplay of verb tenses. It closes with her intentions of future noble actions, which will include the destruction of the brothel (ἐργαστήριον). This may recall the similar destruction of the φροντιστήριον at the end of Aristophanes' *Nephelai*. For, like Strepsiades and philosophy, this πόρνη has tried prostitution, only to turn against it with such vehemence that she wants to destroy its very physical manifestation.[29] A prostitute who becomes chaste might seem to offer a type of 'individuality'. But she is a paradoxical product of the rhetorical school, which draws once more upon classical models. The 'good *hetaera*' is just another stereotype from New Comedy. Much of the humour of Menander's *Samia*, for example, comes from male inability to appreciate that the prostitute Chrysis has now given up her profession to live as a wife with Demeas.

In this chapter I have tried to show some of the ways in which Greek declamation may treat women. The technical treatises present mechanical examples of rhetorical constructions and devices, where gender is not an issue. The practical exercises of Libanius reveal an almost equally mechanical construction for the ἠθοποιῖαι of Medea and Andromache, for example, and offer little insight into femininity. But the length of the exercise is not a determining factor, for the longer declamations also preserve the stereotypes in situations which allow the writer to display his detailed knowledge of classical literature and thus of traditional negative feminine stereotypes. Many of the mythical situations and characters are chosen simply to develop more general topics such as law and order, patriotism, πάθος, or morality. Greek declamation is thus not a mine of new images of femininity. But it is valuable as a medium through which literary images of women were transmitted from the classical world into the world of the empire and thus beyond. These images are already centuries old and relegated to the comfortably distant world of antiquarian ideals. But this does not mean that they lose all relevance for historians of these periods. We should recall that these images are enshrined in texts which are used to educate young men who will later hold positions of influence and power. Furthermore, as we know only too well today,

---

[28] The women may be wives since the context is that of children and legitimacy.

[29] For the belief that prostitutes who leave the profession are more sexually reliable than other women: Athenaeus 13. 577a 'when such women turn to sexual moderation (τὸ σῶφρον), they are better (βελτίους) than those who pride themselves upon it'.

it is extremely easy for society to cherish, revive and re-advocate ancient images of gender and sexuality, whenever the political need may arise.[30]

[30] A shortened version of this paper was delivered to the senior research seminar at Liverpool University on 10 December 1993. I am grateful to all those then present and to the editors of this volume for their helpful comments.

20

Names and a Gem: Aspects of Allusion in Heliodorus' *Aethiopica*

EWEN BOWIE

Names can evoke a vast range of associations. Dropped into the calm flow of a narrative they set up ripples which persist long after they have first splashed into the reader's awareness. Any classicists reading a novel with a character named Donald Russell would expect him to be learned, helpful, and companionable, with a nice sense of humour. A novelist who then constructed a quite different character would challenge readers by a constant play between his construction and their expectation. Inventing (or borrowing) names for characters is one trick open to novelists (and to Athenian comic poets, as Antiphanes reminded his audience)[1] that is largely denied to genres that work with traditional myths. Thus whereas writers (who are most often poets) drawing on a mythological tradition can exploit the ethical qualities which that tradition associates with certain characters (e.g. *sit Medea ferox*),[2] others with freely invented plots and dramatis personae can create expectations of character and behaviour by telling choice of names; though here too a tradition can establish expectations, as for the servile name Davus in New Comedy.[3] The first part of this discussion explores the way in which Heliodorus, a novelist who draws on a wide range of sophisticated literary tricks, exploits the potential of names to create expectations, partly simply to entertain the reader by offering a character or actions that defeat these expectations, partly to force the reader's attention on the all-important ethical qualities of his principal characters. The second part of my discussion considers a different rhetorical technique for using subordinate elements of a narrative to throw its main features into greater relief.

---

[1] *PCG*, vol. ii, Antiphanes fr. 189 = 191 Kock.
[2] Horace, *Ars Poetica*, 123.   [3] Cf. Horace, *Satires* 2. 7. 2.

I. ALLUSIVE NAMES

I wish to examine first the names chosen by Heliodorus for the important sub-plot that constitutes the story of Cnemon. Cnemon is introduced early in the main narrative, as a young Athenian captive
quartered with the loving couple Charicleia and Theagenes when they
too have been captured by the Egyptian bandit Thyamis (1. 7).
Cnemon is later to provide a naïve and enthusiastic audience for the
priest Calasiris' long narrative of the couple's story-so-far. But his
immediate function is to postpone the impatient reader's comprehen-
sion of the couple's identity and origins, offering instead an explanation of his own presence. As John Morgan has superbly shown, the
characters and actions of Cnemon's story act as a foil to the main narrative. After Cnemon has told his story it becomes increasingly clear
from Heliodorus' authorial narrative of the couple's adventures in
Egypt that they have very different ethical qualities from the characters in Cnemon's Athenian tale (as indeed has been hinted in their brief
appearances and utterances before it). I quote Morgan's summary of
his view:[4]

It provides a prolonged portrait of perverted, immoral, simply bad love, which,
by being placed programmatically at the start of the whole novel, will inform
and structure the reader's appreciation of the true love of the central characters, and at the same time provide points of reference for some of the hostile
elements that threaten their love, notably the Persian princess Arsake ...
Between them, the negative love of the *novella* and the positive love of the
novel form a framework of moral values, the expression and reinforcement of
which is the fundamental *raison d'être* of the *Aithiopika*.

Morgan goes on to illustrate this by a well-documented series of polar-
ities: Charicleia and Theagenes display a love that is mutual, altruistic,
faithful, lifelong, and spontaneous; the sexual relations of the Athenians in Cnemon's story are unreciprocated, egocentric, promiscuous,
ephemeral, and mercenary.

　　Why does Heliodorus set this story of Cnemon in Athens? Partly, no
doubt, because Attic literature of the classical period was, next to
Homer, the core of the educational syllabus, and re-creation of the
social, political, and architectural milieu of fifth- and fourth-century
Athens was a game enthusiastically played by many genres of imperial

---

[4] Morgan (1989), at 107.

Greek literature, not least those that betray the influence of rhetorical training. Heliodorus is doing his bit (not always accurately) to satisfy the Greeks' interest in the Athenian past when he presents a Panathenaic procession, public dining in the Prytaneion (both I. 10), an accusation before the *ecclesia*, enrolment in a *phratria* and in a *phyle* (I. 13), and Demaenete hurling herself to her death into a *bothros* in the Academy where the polemarchs sacrificed to the heroes (I. 17).[5] But this evocation of classical Athens cannot be the whole explanation. There are other classical sites that had become theme-parks by the imperial period which go quite unmentioned—Olympia and Sparta are the most obvious—and there are other cities, like Pergamum, Smyrna, or Ephesus, which would have made a plausible setting and had an interesting classical past to evoke.

The explanation, I suggest, is rather to be found in the plot and characters of Cnemon's story. They recall the less edifying side of New Comedy, a genre well-populated with pimps, *hetaerae*, merchants, slave-girls, and ingenuous young men who are too easily led astray, and a genre whose plays were chiefly written for the Attic theatre and typically set in Athens. New Comedy was also the first genre in Greek literature to exploit at length the story-pattern in which boy meets girl, they fall in love, and are eventually married—the pattern that had been developed by the addition of travels, trials, and temptations to become the stereotypical novel. That the Greek novel numbered New Comedy among its ancestors was certainly obvious to Heliodorus. It is clear, too, that the extreme attachment to chastity with which Heliodorus burdens his loving couple, and his story's religious and mystical colouring, take them and it still further from New Comedy than earlier novels went. Chariton's heroine Callirhoe, who is prepared to marry Dionysius of Miletus in order to secure the future of her unborn child by the hero Chaereas, would stand more easily on the comic stage than Charicleia; so too Achilles Tatius' Cleitophon, who succumbs to the advances of the Ephesian matron Melite. I would suggest, therefore, that Cnemon's story reminds us of certain aspects of the novel's inheritance from New Comedy in order that their condemnatory presentation may establish this novel's healthy distance from it. Heliodorus is suggesting that this was one sort of literature from which the novel developed and which some other novelists had incorporated

[5] It may be an aspect of Heliodorus' exclusive focus on heterosexual love that he does not reveal, as Pausanias does (I. 29. 15), that these heroes were the homosexual pair Harmodios and Aristogeiton.

(novelists like Lucian in his *Metamorphoses*): he himself gives it a subordinate role, only as a counter-plot against which the true love of Theagenes and Charicleia can be measured.

Heliodorus offers a pointer to this interpretation in the name of the story's chief character and narrator. Cnemon is not a common name. In literature it seems to appear only three times outside Heliodorus. Its début is in Menander's *Dyskolos* as the name of the cantankerous old man who gives the play its name. It is revived *circa* AD 160 by Lucian in his *Dialogues of the Dead* (18 MacLeod) as a suitable name for a deceased misanthrope (who had made his will before dying, so was presumably not young). It is exploited again by Aelian in two pairs of his *Letters of Farmers*, ἀγροικικαὶ ἐπιστολαί 13–16, written *circa* AD 220. Two of these are sent to a misanthropic Cnemon living near a shrine of Pan in the deme Phyle, the other two are his replies; his character is manifestly drawn from Menander's play, and indeed the reader of the *Letters* is meant to think of them as identical. On the evidence we have, then, the chief literary text that the name Cnemon would evoke is one from New Comedy.[6] Unlike many another name given to young men in New Comedy, Cnemon's absence from other literary texts means that Heliodorus can be sure of its associations for almost any reader. Furthermore the age and character of Cnemon in Menander's play offers Heliodorus the chance to set up an amusing conflict with readers' expectations—Cnemon is a malleable youth, easily interested in sex, rather than an aged misanthrope.

Once he has the name Cnemon, Heliodorus can build another sort of literary joke around it, making Calasiris bamboozle young Cnemon by a deliciously *ad hominem* quotation of Homer (whom he claims to

---

[6] I am grateful to Elaine Matthews for providing me with material from the database of the *Lexicon of Greek Personal Names* for the names Cnemon, Thisbe, Nausicles, Nausicleia, and Charicleia, and for the warning that for certain areas (including Syria and Egypt) it is incomplete. So far that database has no 'real-life' use of Cnemon. Apart from the instances cited in my text Cnemon appears (*a*) in Ammonius (*c.* AD 500), *In Aristotelis librum de interpretatione*, ed. A. Busse in *CAG* iv (part v) (Berlin, 1889), 114. 29–31 = 93ʳ οὐ γὰρ δὴ περὶ ὧν μηδεμίαν ἔχομεν ἢ ἐκ πείρας ἢ ἐκ μαρτυρίας γνῶσιν, εἰ μὴ τοῦ Κνήμονος καὶ τοῦ Τίμωνος εἴημεν μισανθρωπότεροι, τολμήσομεν ἀποφαίνεσθαι: Ammonius must know either Menander's *Dyskolos* or Aelian, probably the former; (*b*) in an ostracon of the 4th or 5th cent. which bears lists of names, almost all others of which are mythological and most are Homeric, Crum (1902), 83, No. 525, with the sequence ΘΑΛΗ-ΙΚΡΕΩΝ ΚΝΗΜΩΝ ΛΩ--Ι ΠΕΛΟΨ ΠΡΟΙΤΟΣΠΗΛΕ--. A similar list, but without Cnemon, is found in P. Bouriant, No. 1, most accessible in Ziebarth (1913), No. 46. The compiler of the list on the ostracon could be drawing either on Menander or Heliodorus.

have been Egyptian) as evidence for the possibility of identifying gods by the way they move their feet and shins:

for readily did they recognize the tracks of his feet and shins as he departed, for the gods are easily recognized.[7]

The reader is surely meant to be amused by the dexterity of Calasiris (i.e. Heliodorus) in dragging in (by the back heels!) the only line of Homer with the phonemes κνημάων. But this joke can hardly be the motive for giving the young man the name Cnemon. It helps, however, to remind the reader of Cnemon's Comic origins.

We are told Cnemon's name right at the beginning of his story (1. 8). Almost immediately we learn the name of his father, Aristippus. Although a much commoner name than Cnemon, its best known bearer was the pupil of Socrates from Cyrene who followed a very different philosophical path from Plato and made pleasure, ἡδονή, the τέλος. Aristippus is generally treated unsympathetically by Plato, Xenophon, and later philosophers in other schools. He was said to have had the famous *hetaera* Lais as his mistress, and, when offered the choice of three *hetaerae* by the tyrant Dionysius, walked off with all three. His works included one addressed to Lais; among his pupils was a man called Aithiops, a detail that might well have caught the eye of our writer of the *Aethiopica*.[8] In a novel with strong Neoplatonic colouring the reader of Cnemon's story is both amused and has her expectation of its contents directed by the discovery that one of the principal members of its pleasure-seeking Athenian circle—and the father of a young man who at this stage in the narrative may be expected to turn out as crabbed as his Menandrean eponym—bears the name Aristippus.

The two men's names, Cnemon and Aristippus, are set off against two women's names which take the reader away from Athens and evoke a complex of erotic associations. The more important of the two is borne by the slave girl whose collusion with Cnemon's stepmother was responsible for Cnemon's and his father's exile from Athens, and whose appearance in Egypt creates the opportunity for both readers and characters to believe that Charicleia has been murdered. The name of this girl—who, it turns out, was killed by mistake for Charicleia—is Thisbe. In classical Greece Thisbe is the name not of a

---

[7] ἴχνια γάρ μετόπισθε ποδῶν ἠδὲ κνημάων | ῥεῖ' ἔγνων ἀπιόντος, *Iliad* 13. 71–2, quoted at 3. 12. 2.

[8] These details in Diogenes Laertius 2. 67, 74, 84, 86.

person but of a place in Boeotia. By Ovid's time it is enjoying in the Latin-speaking West its most famous use in literature, as the name of one of a pair of ill-starred lovers, and his *Metamorphoses* offer the fullest version of the story that moderns know from *A Midsummer Night's Dream*.[9] It is set in Babylon. The couple, of outstanding beauty, live in adjacent houses and fall in love with the boy/girl next door. Parents impede, so they arrange a tryst under a mulberry tree by Ninus' tomb. Thisbe arrives too soon, sees a lion and flees into a cave, leaving a veil which is stained by the blood of the lion's prey. When Pyramus sees it he thinks she has been killed by the lion and he kills himself, his blood staining the mulberry so that henceforth it is red, not white. She returns and follows suit. Ovid elaborates both suicides with appropriate rhetoric.

Ovid is thought to be using a Hellenistic Greek original.[10] It is surely from this Hellenistic source that Heliodorus has also drawn his recherché name Thisbe. Like Cnemon, the name Thisbe is rare in the Greek world in both literary and documentary contexts. Other than Heliodorus only three extant Greek writers use it: the epigrammatist Metrodorus (early fourth century AD) has it as the name of a playful and attractive παρθένος along with commoner girls' names in one of his arithmetical puzzle-poems (*AP* 14. 116. 6). Later, in the second half of the fifth century, Nicolaus of Myra tells and Nonnus implies a version of the love of Pyramus for Thisbe in which the crisis arises from Thisbe's pregnancy and the lovers are metamorphosed into a river and a spring respectively.[11] That version is already implied by mosaics from Antioch of the early third century AD, where, as in Nonnus, Pyramus and Thisbe are juxtaposed with Alpheius and Arethusa.[12] A conflation of the two stories appears on a mosaic floor of the second half of the third century AD from the House of Dionysus at Nea Paphos: Pyramus is given the iconography of a river-god, but the scene has the big cat (looking more like a panther than a lion), garment, and blood of Ovid's narrative.[13] The love-unto-death of Pyramus and Thisbe is clearly the chief literary association of the

---

[9] 4. 55 ff.: see also Servius Auctus on Virgil, *Ecl.* 6. 22, Hyginus, *Fab.* 242f.

[10] H. Gärtner in *Kleine Pauly* s.v. Thisbe, Bömer on Ovid, *Met.* 4. 55 ff., pp. 33–6; but Ovid's version is argued to be his own by Holzberg (1988).

[11] Nicolaus of Myra, *Rh. Gr.* 1. 271. 21–8 Walz; Nonnus, *Dionysiaca* 6. 346–55.

[12] Levi (1947), vol. i, pp. 109–10; vol. ii, pl. xviiic: the mosaic, from the House of the Porticoes, portrays four heads to which the names are attached.

[13] Nikolaou (1963), 56 ff., esp. 64–5 and (1967), 100 ff. A good coloured illustration in Karageorghis (1981), 190, pl. 148 cf. now Kondoleon (1995), 148–156.

personal name Thisbe in the imperial Greek world, from the first-century poet of a Greek epigram from Ostia who compares the life-long love of a dead couple to that of Thisbe and P[yramus][14] to the late fifth century AD. The story was also well known in the Latin West, as is attested, for example, by a wall-painting at Pompeii.[15] In the West Thisbe is also widely used as a real name in the early imperial period, chiefly for slaves. At least one of these occurrences must be credited to knowledge of the Ovidian story, since we find a *libertus* named Pyramus and his wife, also a *liberta*, named Thisbenis(?): it may be assumed that the names were given to the slaves when purchased by or born in the household of a whimsical reader of Ovid.[16] In the Greek East, however, Thisbe does not establish itself as a common personal name: so far (cf. n. 6) I have found only one instance, where Thisbe is the name of a slave enfranchised at Delphi *circa* AD 47–66.[17] In Thisbe, then, Heliodorus has found another name which would for most Greeks have definite literary associations, associations likely to be untrammelled by encounters with its use in real life.

The first associations would be that of an oriental setting, clearly a favourite with novelists. Our earliest novelistic fragments, the Ninus romance, are set partly in Babylon and in one of them (fragment A)[18] it seems that marriage between Ninus and his beloved has for the moment been vetoed. It is also to Babylon that Chariton's Callirhoe was taken so that the Persian king could decide whether she belonged to the Milesian Greek Dionysius or the Persian satrap Mithridates (4. 6ff.), and where Callirhoe faces yet another suitor; and of course Babylon was the starting-point of Iamblichus' *Babyloniaca*.[19] The second set of associations is with the overpowering love that Thisbe and Pyramus feel for each other, love that leads each to suicide rather than live without the other.

The first of these themes is picked up in the main narrative when

[14] *IG* xiv. 930. 12.

[15] For the Pompeian painting and other attestations of the story see Kondoleon (1995), 148–156.

[16] *CIL* ix. 1830 (Beneventum): 'C. Herennius I C.l. Pyramus felcit sibi et I Herenniae Thisbe I ni coniugi suae et I Herenniae Faventinae I Lauro et Quintae suis'. For another clearly libertine case cf. *CIL* xi. 1434 = *ILS* 1667 (Pisa, early 2nd cent. AD): 'D.M. I M. Ulpio Aug. lib. I Vernae I ab epistulis I Latinis I Vibia Thisbe I uxor I infelicissima'. There are 6 more instances of Thisbe in *CIL* ix, and 16 from Rome in *CIL* vi.

[17] *Fouilles de Delphes*, iii. 6, No. 123, where the other women are called Alcippe and Nico.

[18] For a translation see Reardon (1989), 806–7; text and trans. in Stephens and Winkler (1995).

[19] Iamblichus' *Babyloniaca*, ed. E. Habrich, 2 ff., trans. Reardon (1989), 785.

Theagenes is to be dispatched to the Persian king as a present (5. 9). Of the second set of associations that of lifelong and overriding love is of course fundamental to the presentation of Charicleia and Theagenes. But there is also a constant threat that one of the lovers will commit suicide. It is already there at 1. 2, where Charicleia gazes at the blood-stained and almost dead Theagenes and promises she will kill herself with a sword if he dies—a scene that recalls, among other antecedents, the death of Pyramus. The appearance of the name Thisbe at 1. 11 thus reminds the reader of danger that the love of Theagenes and Charicleia, unlike that of *this* Thisbe, may lead them to suicide rather than to the 'right' ending of the story. When both Thisbe and Charicleia are concealed in a cave, so that we are invited to compare and contrast their qualities, we recall the cave of the Pyramus story. When Theagenes thinks that the body of Charicleia has been discovered in the cave he delivers rhetorical last words, like Pyramus, before seeking his sword to stab himself precisely as the tale of Thisbe has threatened that he might: just in the nick of time Cnemon stops him and tells him that Charicleia is in fact alive (2. 1).

The use of Thisbe's name, therefore, helps to underline some of the positive themes of Heliodorus' story and to remind us, time and again, of how the world from which Cnemon comes is different from that of Charicleia and Theagenes. Moreover, like the name Cnemon its function within the sub-plot retains an element of humorous incongruity—the inconstant Thisbe bears the name of a famous paradigm of the committed lover.

A supporting role in this reader manipulation may be played by Thisbe's friend and workmate, the *hetaera* Arsinoe. It may of course be that the Ptolemaic queens of that name extruded other associations from a reader's mind, especially in a novel where much of the action is played out in Egypt. If so, perhaps the name is chosen simply as a historical joke. But imperial Greek readers could also have known a story in Antoninus Liberalis (39) taken from the *Leontion* of Hermesianax: a Phoenician fell in love with Arsinoe, a princess of Salamis in Cyprus, but both she and her parents rejected him; he starved himself to death, and when she gloated over his unhappy end from a window she was turned to stone by Aphrodite. This might, then, be another carefully chosen name for an *hetaera* who helps Thisbe to dupe Demaenete—with consequences fatal for Demaenete and disastrous for Cnemon and his father—and who belongs to a set of characters with the wrong view of love. Again there is some entertaining incongruity in a name associated with real and fairy-tale princesses being borne by a *demi-mondaine* from Athens.

I now turn briefly from the story of Cnemon to the main narrative. I begin with a name chosen chiefly for its humorous effect, that of the bandit leader's henchman called Thermouthis (1. 30 etc.). When Cnemon attempts to lose him, by the comic technique of feigning diarrhoea, Thermouthis is in fact killed off by a snake-bite (2. 20. 2). Although his is indeed an Egyptian name, readers of Aelian will have recalled that *thermouthis* was also the name of an Egyptian snake.[20]

Heliodorus uses three other names that have a genuine Egyptian ring. Two of these, given to Calasiris' sons, Thyamis and Petosiris, seem to be chosen simply to impart Egyptian décor. But that of Calasiris himself has associations that are, like his character, more complex. The term καλάσιρις was known to readers of Herodotus as the name of an Egyptian warrior class and of a linen garment worn by Egyptian priests, not unsuitable for the vegetarian priest in Heliodorus.[21] But Calasiris may have further resonances. As a priest with a special channel of communication to the divine he may be seen as an Egyptian version of *Cal*chas, prominent of course in the opening scene of the *Iliad*, some lines of which (1. 46–7), describing Apollo's descent from Olympus, are echoed right at the beginning of the *Aethiopica* (1. 2. 5). The name may also recall the Indian naked sage *Cal*anus, who followed Alexander back from India and when he fell ill in Persia had himself burned alive on a huge pyre, refusing to say farewell to Alexander because he would greet him in Babylon (where Alexander in fact later died).[22] Allusion to a prophet and to a guru well established in Greek literary traditions enhances Calasiris' own claim to a similar status.

Alongside the names which are, I argue, evocative of other literature, there are many which are either unremarkable[23] or are chosen as straightforwardly appropriate to their bearer.[24] Among the latter the names Charicleia and Theagenes were presumably chosen with special care. The chief criterion was clearly the sense of the component Greek terms, as is brought out by the spontaneous oracle at 2. 35. That

---

[20] Aelian, *De Natura Animalium* 10. 31.

[21] Hdt. 2. 81, 164.   [22] Arrian, *Anabasis* 7. 2. 4, 3. 1, 18. 6.

[23] e.g. Anticles (2. 10), Charias, and Teledemos; Demaenete; Isias of Chemmis.

[24] e.g. the Ethiopian priest Sisimithres, anagram of Isis and Mithres. For Heliodorus' convincing choice of Persian names (Orondates, Arsace, Mitranes, Bagoas) and largely unambitious attempt at Ethiopian names (Sisimithres, Persinna, Hydaspes, Hermonias: only Meroebus carries Ethiopian colour) see Morgan (1982), 247.

spells out for the reader that the name Charicleia starts with grace, χάρις, and will end with κλέος, glory. Theagenes is descended from Thetis through Achilles, as Calasiris states (2. 34) and as the hymn to Thetis at 3. 2 emphasizes. There the significance of Theagenes' name may end.[25]

One might dismiss as a simple *redende Name* the name given to the merchant Nausicles, who lives by sea-borne trade. But here too there is a nice nuance. Nausicles' daughter can without surprise be called Nausicleia: but once she is given that name, this father and daughter invite reading as a contrast to the father and daughter who also share name-forms, Charicles and Charicleia, while the name Nausicleia also kindles recollections of the *Odyssey*'s Nausicaa. These recollections underline the lack of commitment and staying power in Cnemon, who jumps at the offer of Nausicleia's hand instead of honouring his undertaking to escort Charicleia until Theagenes is found (6. 7–8). How different was the behaviour of the traveller who did not allow marriage to Nausicaa to deflect him from his commitment to return to Penelope, and who is a prototype in different ways for both Theagenes and Charicleia! To achieve these effects Heliodorus has given his merchant a name widely used in real life: but Nausicleia, though plausible enough, is nowhere attested, and has clearly been invented by Heliodorus for his literary purpose.[26]

II. AN ALLUSIVE GEM

Nausicles offers a convenient transition to a rather different type of intertextual allusion. When Calasiris is at last reunited with Charicleia, now in the possession of the merchant Nausicles, who has claimed (with her connivance) that she is his lost chattel Thisbe, Nausicles hints that a ransom should be paid to him for her restoration. In one of his puzzling performances of apparently magical tricks[27] Calasiris pretends to conjure out of the fire a ring set with an amethyst—in fact

[25] But it is worth asking whether an author with some interest in the allegorical interpretation of Homer (cf. above with n. 7) might have chosen the name Theagenes to evoke the 6th-cent. BC Greek from Rhegium who was the first to interpret Homer allegorically and to investigate his life and works, cf. Pfeiffer (1968), 9–11.

[26] The *Lexicon of Greek Personal Names*, vol. ii (1994) records 13 instances of Nausicles for Athens, and its database none of Nausicleia (but cf. n. 6).

[27] Cf. his pretence to exercise magic arts when Theagenes and Charicleia suffer from lovesickness at Delphi, 3. 16–17, 4. 5, and for the problem that arises in interpreting his character, Sandy (1982).

it is one of the opulent tokens with which the infant Charicleia had been dispatched from Ethiopia. Heliodorus describes the jewel in detail and offers learned explanations of the sources of amethysts and of the meaning of the name (5. 13). The scene that is engraved on it is allowed half a page of virtuoso description (5. 14). It is described first as a μίμημα ζώων: its depiction (γραφή) is of a shepherd boy, playing on transverse *auloi* to his flock; his sheep graze to the music and their lambs gambol in circles round the rocks on which he stands, giving the effect of a pastoral theatre. Such ekphraseis have long been seen as a favourite constituent of the sophistic novels: characteristically, and above all in Heliodorus, they make an important contribution to the reader's interpretation, offering a μίμημα which not only displays the writer's rhetorical skill but invites the reader to relate the scene or object in some way to the main narrative.[28]

What is the jewel's contribution here? Set against the very different and exotic landscape around the village of Chemmis,[29] where crocodiles scuttle across the tracks, this miniature works partly to offer the sort of contrast with which Homeric pastoral similes point up Iliadic battle narrative. The apparently untroubled and relaxed shepherd boy himself contrasts with the anxious central characters. But the subject-matter is *so* alien to that of the *Aethiopica* that some deeper explanation is called for. It is not hard to see, even if (to my knowledge) modern scholars have not yet suggested it. Any reader of our corpus of ancient novels must surely be tempted to think that Heliodorus is alluding to that literary miniature, the ποιμενικὰ τὰ κατὰ Δάφνιν καὶ Χλόην,[30] usually simply referred to as *Daphnis and Chloe*. That work itself begins with an ekphrasis of a γραφή, its hero is a herding boy, and at least two of Heliodorus' phrases recall expressions in Longus. Heliodorus' ἀρνείων ἁπαλὰ σκιρτήματα (5. 14. 3) recalls Longus 1. 9. 1 σκιρτήματα ποιμνίων ἀρτιγεννήτων. His reference to the ποιμενικὸν θέατρον (ibid.) reminds us of the scene towards Longus' denouement where Lamon proclaims Daphnis' skill to Dionysophanes and Cleariste: Cleariste wants to test the claim that Daphnis has made

---

[28] Rommel (1923); Bartsch (1989), who mentions the jewel only briefly, noting the animation of the scene (123) and the jewel's contribution to the advancement of the plot (149). Dubel (1990) has a good discussion of the description of the jewel and its emphasis on craftsmanship, but draws no conclusions from its subject's difference from the rest of the novel.

[29] I shall discuss elsewhere the implications for the novel's interpretation of Heliodorus' choice of the name Chemmis for the village where so many strands of the first half of the story are drawn together.

[30] The text of **V**. That of **F** is ποιμενικὰ περὶ Δάφνιν καὶ Χλόην.

his goats μουσικάς, so Daphnis makes his human audience sit down like that in a theatre—καθίσας ὥσπερ θέατρον (4. 15. 2)—and plays to his goats on a syrinx; they respond to different tunes in different ways, cf. Heliodorus' sentence 'the sheep seemed to pasture obediently and contentedly to the tune's melody'.[31] Earlier (1. 13. 4) Daphnis' goats are said to lie down as if listening to his syrinx tunes.

The *theatron* image is of course one much exploited by Heliodorus, who often describes characters within his narrative either as themselves a *theatron* or as playing as if to a *theatron*.[32] If, as I am arguing, there *is* an allusion to Longus here, the theatrical analogy is an element which encourages us to recall the text in which the allusive description is set. We are invited to contrast the huge Aida-like stage across which Heliodorus has his characters process with the miniature and enclosed world of Longus. Such a comparison may cause us to reflect that, despite the virtuosity displayed by Longus in his *mimesis* of his confined pastoral universe, only the grand operatic stage created by Heliodorus really deserves comparison with the theatre. The narrative setting also allows us to see the gem as standing for a literary work. Calasiris, who often seems to play the role of the author in the first half of the work, here decides to exchange an item of great value for Charicleia (who has sometimes been seen by scholars as emblematic of the work *Charicleia* in which she has the leading role). A jewel evoking another novel is judged by Calasiris to be worth less than his Charicleia. Heliodorus has crafted an appropriate assertion of his own work's pre-eminence in the novelistic tradition and given it prominence in a pivotal scene near the mid-point of the novel.

---

[31] Morgan's translation of τὰ δὲ ἐπείθετο, ὡς ἐδόκει, καὶ ἠνείχετο πρὸς τὰ ἐνδόσιμα τῆς σύριγγος ποιμαινόμενα, 5. 14. 2. The ability of the skilled herd-person to control grazing animals by music alone appears also at Longus 1. 27; 2. 28. 3, 29. 3.

[32] See esp. the excellent discussion of Bartsch (1989), 129–41.

21

περιγίνεσθαι as a Medical Term and a Conjecture in the *Cyranides*

DAVID BAIN

Donald Russell is, among other things, that rare bird, a renowned expert in the field of Greek prose of the post-classical period. I offer this minor contribution to the study of later Greek vocabulary in the confident expectation that he will acknowledge with sympathy the difficulties that confront anyone seeking to investigate such a topic using the existing lexica of the Greek language.

LSJ give as their second meaning for περιγίγνομαι, 'live over', 'survive', 'escape' and cite examples from Herodotus, Thucydides, and Plato. As Nadia van Brock has observed,[1] they omit to mention[2] that it is also a medical term. In medical writings περιγίνεσθαι is frequently to be found, used of the recovery (complete or partial) of patients from serious illness, regularly in opposition to ἀπόλλυσθαι.[3] The many Hippocratic examples may now be seen clearly set out in the excellent and indispensable *Index Hippocraticus*.[4] The usage is, however, as van Brock points out, not confined to the Hippocratic medical works. There are several occurrences in other medical writers, Aretaeus for instance providing eighteen examples. Since Aretaeus was one of those later authors who chose to write in an artificial Ionic and is known to

---

[1] Van Brock (1961), 216ff.

[2] An omission incidentally which is not shared by Stephanus.

[3] See van Brock (1961), 216 for examples and, for the persistence of this opposition, compare the instances quoted in this chapter, the two passages from Galen mentioned below, in this paragraph, and the passage of Stephanus quoted at the end.

[4] See Kühn and Fleischer (1989): s.v. II. I. I have noticed two other instances—no doubt there are many others—where LSJ completely neglect the Hippocratic corpus. There are over 20 examples in Hippocrates of νέμεσθαι used metaphorically of diseases, inflammations of the skin, etc. spreading. LSJ s.v. νέμω B 2c note this usage, but do not cite any of these examples. The *Index Hippocraticus* gives 5 examples of ῥύπος meaning 'ear-wax'. LSJ merely cite Aristotle, *Problemata* 960ᵇ18, ὁ ἐν τοῖς ὡσὶ ῥύπος, and follow this with the note 'cf. Artem. I. 24, *P. Mag. Osl.* I. 332 [= *PGM* 36. 332]'.

have borrowed phraseology directly from the Hippocratic corpus,[5] it might be argued that this is simply slavish imitation of Hippocrates. It is useful, therefore, to be able to point to examples in the most important later Greek medical writer, Galen,[6] as evidence of the survival of this usage in living medical language. Most of the occurrences of the word used in this sense in his work are in fact direct quotations from the Hippocratic corpus, but Galen can be found using it independently when paraphrasing and commenting on Hippocratic writings.[7] For example, he twice uses it in his commentary on the Hippocratic treatise *Prognosticum*: οἱ δὲ νεώτεροί, φησι, πρὶν ἐκπυηθῆναι τὸ οὖς οἱ πολλοὶ ἀπόλλυνται. ἐπεὶ ἤν γε ῥυῆι τὸ πῦον ἐκ τοῦ ὠτός, ἐλπὶς περι-γενέσθαι (CMG 5. 9. 2, p. 323. 20); τὸ δὲ ἐκ τούτων ἤτοι περιγίνεσθαι τὸν ἄνθρωπον ἢ ἀπόλλυσθαι δηλωτικόν ἐστι τοῦ τὴν κρίσιν ὀνομάζειν αὐτὸν ἐπὶ πάσης τῆς ὀξυρρόπου μεταβολῆς, οὐ μόνης τῆς ἐπὶ σωτηρίαν (ibid., p. 331. 16). The first of these examples is particularly significant as the word περιγίνεσθαι is absent from the Hippocratic text Galen is elucidating: τῶν δὲ ἐμπύων τῶν ἐκ τῶν περιπνευμονικῶν νοσημάτων οἱ γεραίτεροι μᾶλλον ἀπόλλυνται· ἐκ δὲ τῶν ἄλλων ἐμπυημάτων ἀποθνήσκουσι (Hp. *Progn.* 18, p. 219. 3–5 Littré).

It is pleasing also to be able to point to an example of περιγίνεσθαι in veterinary medicine which provides further confirmation of its currency in late antiquity. My colleague, J. N. Adams, has drawn my attention to its occurrence in the sense 'recover, survive' in a passage in the veterinary writer Apsyrtus.[8] In part of a section dealing with the treatment of tetanus in mules the text of the Berlin *Hippiatrica* runs as follows, οἱ δὲ ταῖς καυτηρίαις χρώμενοι πρὸς τὰ τοιαῦτα, εἰς κόπον φέρουσιν· καὶ περιγενόμενος γὰρ ὁ τοιοῦτος ἐλάττων ἐστὶν εἰς τὴν ὑπηρεσίαν τὸν ἐπίλοιπον χρόνον[9] (*Hippiatr. Berol.* 34. 4 (*CHG* i. 180. 7–10)).

---

[5] See F. Kudlien in *CMG* 2²173 f., Deichgräber (1971), 18 f., and van Brock (1961), 16 n. 2, 103, 135 f., 201. Aretaeus' direct borrowings, however, appear to emanate from a restricted range of works in the corpus: see Schmidt (1980), 35.

[6] I am grateful to my colleague G. C. Neal for carrying out computerized word searches of the works of Galen on the C version of the CD-ROM of the Thesaurus Linguae Graecae.

[7] Cf., in addition to the passages cited in the text, 17. 1. 138. 10, 18. 1. 150. 10, 18. 2. 235. 15 Kühn.

[8] The date of Apsyrtus cannot be determined with certainty. See Doyen-Higuet (1984), 111 ff. Traditionally he has been placed around AD 300, but Björck (1944), 7–12 sought to place him as early as AD 150.

[9] Pelagonius translates these words as follows: 'multi cauteriis utuntur: etsi evaserit cauteritus, inutilis viribus erit' (Pelagonius 269. 4). *evado* in turn is a technical term of Latin medical writers: see Adams (1995), 612.

I would like now to propose that an example of this usage should be introduced by emendation into another late medical text (medical, at any rate, of a sort). I have in mind a section of the Hermetic medico-magical text, the *Cyranides*, a work first put together in the fourth century AD. The passage in question comes from the fourth book, which was added by a redactor to the original three-book *Cyranides*.[10] It contains descriptions of the medical properties of aquatic creatures (Books Two to Four of the *Cyranides* make up a bestiary).

In the chapter dealing with the curative powers of the water snake (περὶ ὕδρου), the writer, in a personal reminiscence,[11] describes the successful application of its stone[12] in curing a woman of dropsy: ἐγὼ οὖν ποτε ὑδεριώσηι γυναικὶ περιῆψα τὸν λίθον καὶ ἀλυπότατα περιεγενόμην τοῦ πάθους. παπύρωι γοῦν ἑκάστης ἡμέρας τὴν κοιλίαν αὐτῆς ἐμέτρουν καὶ παρὰ τέσσαρας δακτύλους ⟨μειούμενον⟩[13] ἀεὶ τὸ μέτρον ἑκάστης ἡμέρας εὕρισκον καὶ εἰς τὸν κατὰ φύσιν ὄγκον τῆς γαστρὸς τὴν γυναῖκα ἔστησα. εἶτα ἀφειλόμην τὸν λίθον (*Cyranides* 4. 65. 19 ff.).[14]

Ἀλυπότατα περιεγενόμην τοῦ πάθους, which is attested by eight of

---

[10] On the date, nature, and form of this work see K. Alpers (1984), 17 ff. and Bain (1990), 295–7.

[11] This is one of several personal reminiscences or observations to be found in the work: cf. 1. 1. 57, 1. 4. 18, 2. 5. 24, 2. 20. 25, and 2. 40. 24 ff. Such personal remarks are common in medical writers, less common, but still attested in magic works: cf. *PGM* 4. 790 f. and 6. 374.

[12] This is what is known as a bezoar: for the use of bezoars in magic see Marquès-Rivière (1938), 258 ff., von Lippmann (1931), 56, van Tassel (1973), and Waegeman (1987), 75.

[13] ⟨μειούμενον⟩ C.-E. Ruelle (ap. de Mély (1898)). A few lines above (15 ff.) the text runs: σημείωσον [τὸ ἄγγειον] οὖν καὶ εὑρήσεις τὸ ὕδωρ καθ᾽ ἑκάστην ἡμέραν μειούμενον κοτύλας δύο. In this sentence the participle μειούμενον is transmitted by only one of the manuscripts used by Kaimakis in this chapter, D (K has ἐλαττούμενον: M (see n. 16) has a different, but coherent text, καὶ σημείωσαι καὶ εὑρήσεις τὸ ὕδωρ εἰς τρεῖς ἡμέρας ἡμιμερές (this word is absent from LSJ: Sophocles and Lampe attest it from Anastasius of Sinai: 'ob. post 700')). Ruelle, the first editor of the *Cyranides*, who did not at the time of editing have available to him the manuscripts D and K, restored forms of μειοῦσθαι in both places, taking note of the Latin version (see n. 20) which reads 'signa et invenies quod quaque die decrescet aqua cotylas duas' (201. 1) in the first sentence and 'iunco itaque illius mensurabam et quotidie decrescebat ultra quattuor digitos donec ad locum suum venter rediit, et abstuli' (201. 3 f.) in the second. It is questionable whether μειούμενον is necessary in the second passage: see LSJ s.v. παρά, III. 5b. (Here the corresponding text in M differs considerably from that of the other manuscripts: ἐγὼ οὖν ποτὲ ὑδεριῶσι τὸν λίθον περίηψα καὶ ἀλυπότατα περιεγενόμην τοῦ πάθους. παπύρωι οὖν ἑκάστηι ἡμέραι τὴν κοιλίαν τοῦ ὑδεριῶντος ἐμέτρουν καὶ τέσσαρας δακτύλους ἀεὶ παρὰ [? = *cis*] τὸ μέτρον [? l. παρὰ τέσσαρας δακτύλους ἀεὶ τὸ μέτρον] εὕρισκον καὶ κατὰ φύσιν ἔστησα καὶ ἀφειλόμην.)

[14] Kaimakis (1976). On the deficiencies of this edition see K. Alpers (1984), 56 and Meschini (1983), 145 ff.

the twelve manuscripts[15] used by Kaimakis in this chapter and is also the reading of Marcianus Graecus 512 (678) (= M), a recently discovered and extremely important witness for the text,[16] is defensible if taken to mean 'I overcame the ailment quite painlessly'. De Mély (1902) renders by 'sans la faire souffrir, je suis devenu maître de sa maladie'. For περιγίνεσθαι used like this in a medical context compare the phrases περιγενέσθαι τῶν νοσημάτων and περιγενέσθαι τῆς ἐπιληψίας found in the section on epilepsy in the first book of Alexander of Tralles (vol. i, p. 573 Puschmann). In both cases the subject is the practitioner. An earlier example is perhaps to be found in Asclepiades[17] ap. Galen, 12. 694 ἐπὶ δὲ τῆς χρήσεως τὰ ἐριώδη τῆς πλατάνου ἐνθεὶς εἰς κάλαμον ἀφῃρημένα τὰ γόνατα ἔχοντα, ἀπογλυφὴν δ᾿ ἔχοντα καθ᾿ ὃ μέρος ἐπιτίθεται, τῶι μυκτῆρι ἐμφύσα, συντόμως περιγίνεται τῆς αἱμορραγίας. The subject of the verb would appear to be 'it' (the whole procedure).[18] It is difficult, however, in a context of healing to think of περιγίνομαι used in anything other than its technical sense 'recover'. I suggest, accordingly, that in the *Cyranides* passage we should consider the possibility of changing the person of the verb and emending περιεγενόμην to περιεγένετο. (The surrounding first person verbs will have led to assimilation of the ending.) Dropsy is a serious enough complaint for mention of survival to be made. For instances in the Hippocratic Corpus of περιγίνεσθαι used specifically of recovery from dropsy, note *Prorrh.* 2. 6 (Littré, 9. 22) ἄριστ᾿ μὲν οὕτω πάντα διακεῖσθαι τὸν ἄνθρωπον, καὶ ἀσφαλέστατα ἂν γένοιτο ὑγιής· εἰ δὲ μή, ὡς πλεῖστα τουτέων ἐχέτω, ἐν ἐλπίδι γὰρ ἔσται περιγενέσθαι and 7 (Littré, 9. 24) ὅστις μὲν γὰρ ταῦτα πάντα ἔχει, περιεστικώτατος γίνεται ... ἥκιστα περιγίνονται αἵ τε παρθένοι καὶ αἱ γυναῖκες ... (both cited by van Brock, 219).

---

[15] GHF have ἀπολυπότατα for ἀλυπότατα and L has ἐγενόμην for περιεγενόμην.

[16] For the discovery that the work entitled περὶ ἰατρικῆς in manuscript Marc. Gr. 512 (678) contains a version of Books 2–4 of the *Cyranides* written in the late 13th cent. see Meschini (1983), who provides an excellent edition of new material found in the manuscript. (Her edition is not absolutely complete. She passes over small sections in the chapters on the goat, puppy, and the dove, omitting thereby the splendidly cynical advice contained in the chapter on the puppy, καὶ τῶν νοσημάτων ἀκμαζόντων τοὺς μισθοὺς ἀπῄτει [sic]. μετὰ γὰρ τὴν τελείαν ὑγίειαν οἱ πολλοὶ ἀχάριστοι γίνονται (f247r).) The full collation promised by her has yet to appear. I have collated the part of the manuscript containing the *Cyranides* from photographs kindly supplied to me by the director of the Biblioteca Nazionale Marciana, Dr Marino Zorzi, and also examined it *in situ*. For a discussion of its value for the reconstitution of the text see Bain (1993).

[17] For Asclepiades (Pharmakion) see Fabricius (1972), 192 ff. and 246 ff.

[18] Even here it might be possible (against Kühn) to take περιγίνεται to mean 'recover' if one understood 'the patient' as the subject of the verb.

In addition I feel, perhaps subjectively,[19] that the adverb ἀλυπότατα is more easily referred to the sufferings of the patient than the activity of the doctor (cf. καθαρθήσεται ἀπόνως, 1. 6. 6). For the adverb accompanying περιγίνεσθαι when the subject is the patient, compare Hp. *Morbo Sacr.* 8. 7 Grensemann (of infants attacked by epilepsy) οἷσι δ' ἂν βόρειόν τε καὶ πάνυ ὀλίγον παραρρύηι καὶ ἐς τὰ δεξιά, ἀσήμως περιγίνονται and Hp. *Joints* 69 (pp. 222. 20–233. 1, Kühlewein), πήχεως δὲ κνήμης ἀποπεσούσης καὶ ἔτι εὐφορωτέρως περιγίνονται.

Possible support for my conjecture is to be found in the Latin version of the *Cyranides*.[20] Although it contains nothing to correspond with the adverb ἀλυπότατα, it does use a third person verb: 'ego enim quondam mulieri ydropicae circumcinxi lapidem et liberata est' (201. 3: one manuscript, G, has 'sanata est'). It may be, however, that this represents a Greek version which had the reading ἀπηλλάγη (cf. 2. 11. 13: καὶ τελείως τοῦ πάθους ἀπαλλαγήσεται (ἀπαλλάσσεται, M; ἀπαλλάξει, D; ἀπαλλάσσει, WKS):[21] the Latin version here, however, has 'et perfecte a passione sanabitur' 108. 3–4). The Latin version with the third person verb and the omission of the adverb does at least supply evidence that once there existed other versions of the text at this point.

It is a characteristic of the textual tradition of the *Cyranides* that different manuscripts or groups of manuscripts present roughly the same material by means of widely differing phraseology. This is only to be expected given the kind of text it is. It belongs to a category of text

[19] Obviously ἀλυπότατα could be applied equally well to the patient or the doctor since ἄλυπος means both 'causing no pain' and 'feeling no pain'. Others no doubt will prefer the adverb to be applied to the boastful doctor. There are no instances of ἀλύπως in the Hippocratic corpus, but all five instances of the adjective refer to conditions or things rather than to the feelings of patients. I am grateful to Professor H. M. Hine for drawing my addition to the Hippocratic usage. It does not seem to me an insuperable objection to my conjecture.

[20] The Latin translation, an important and early witness for the text (it dates from 1169), is cited by page and line number from Delatte (1942). This edition, contained in pp. 11–206 of Delatte's work, has been almost totally ignored by scholars working on the *Cyranides*. The translation is on the whole extremely faithful to the Greek, often retaining the original word order. Although it contains the occasional lapse (I hope to discuss this topic elsewhere), it is an indispensable aid to the editor of the *Cyranides*, on many occasions leading to the reconstruction of a text superior to that transmitted by the Greek manuscripts (cf. e.g. the discussion of 4. 65. 15 ff. in n. 13 and see also Meschini (1983), 146 and n. 7 and Bain (1990), 301 and n. 27). It is quite incredible that Kaimakis makes no use of it whatsoever.

[21] Any of these alternatives would be acceptable: for intransitive ἀπαλλάσσω see LSJ s.v. II and, for medical writers particularly, van Brock (1961), 226.

happily described by Robert Halleux as a 'texte vivant'.[22] (The discovery of M provides many further examples which I hope to discuss elsewhere. A particularly striking instance occurs at 3. 36. 46f. where the seven manuscripts used by Kaimakis (and the Latin translator) present a version in which various diseases are said to run away from the patient who has eaten boiled stork: ἐσθιόμενος δὲ πελαργὸς ἐφθὸς ἅπαξ τοῦ ἐνιαυτοῦ ἔαρος ἀρχομένου πρὶν αὐτὸν εἰς τὸν πόλεμον ἀποπτῆναι ἀβλαβῆ καὶ ἀνώδυνον διαφυλάττει ἕνεκεν νεύρων καὶ ἄρθρων τὸν ἐσθίοντα. φεύξεται γὰρ ποδάγρα, χειράγρα, γονάγρα, ἰσχιάδα (nominative), ἀρθρῖτις, ὀπισθότονος καὶ ὅσα νευρικὰ πάθη. In M, on the other hand, it is the patient that escapes the diseases: φεύξεται γὰρ ποδάγρας, γονάγρας, ἰσχιάδας, ἀρθρητάς (?: the reading is not certain), ὀπισθότονον καὶ ὅσα νευρικὰ πάθη καὶ ἀρθρητικά.)

Περιγίνεσθαι meaning 'survive' followed by a genitive denoting the circumstance survived is attested in LSJ s.v. ii. 1 (Herodotus 5. 46: περιεγένετο τούτου τοῦ πάθεος). A parallel in medical writings for the syntagm produced by my emendation is provided by the seventh-century Alexandrian commentator on Hippocrates' *Prognosticum*, Stephanus 'the philosopher': πλὴν δεῖ σε καὶ τοῦτο γινώσκειν, ὡς πολλάκις μεγάλη ἐστὶν ἡ φλεγμονή, ὥστε πνιγμὸν ποιῆσαι, καὶ τὸ τηνικαῦτα οὐ δεῖ ἐγχειρεῖν τῆι θεραπείαι, ἐπειδὴ οὐ περιγίνονται τοῦ πάθους, ἀλλὰ πνιγμωδῶς ἀπόλλυνται.[23] Compare also the description of a man in Byzantium cured as a result of obeying the instructions given to him by the Saints Cosmas and Damian who had appeared to him in a dream: οὕτως διὰ τῆς τοῦ θεοῦ εὐσπλαγχνίας καὶ τῆς τῶν ἁγίων ἐπισκέψεως περιεγένετο τοῦ πάθους, εἰς τέλος παραγγελίας εἰληφὼς παρὰ τῶν ἁγίων, μὴ ἀναχωρήσειν τῆς ἁγίας αὐτῶν αὐλῆς ἄχρις ἐνιαυτῶν ἕξ.[24]

[22] 'À la différence des textes littéraires ou philosophiques, les lapidaires, commes les herbiers, les bestiaires, les réceptaires et les antidotaires, sont des textes vivants, que le copiste se donne toute liberté de remanier par addition de matériel nouveau, suppression, fusion d'articles, bouleversement de l'ordre, etc.', Halleux in Halleux and Schamp (1985), 193. Under 'etc.' one might include 'variations of phraseology': cf. Bain (1990), 297.

[23] *CMG* xi. 1. 2, p. 260. 32 ff. On Stephanus see now Temkin (1991); 228 ff.

[24] The text is quoted from Deubner (1907), 176 (miracle 30, lines 68 ff.).

22

Julian and Marcus Aurelius

DAVID HUNT

For Donald Russell, teacher, colleague, and friend

In keeping with the fanfare of superlatives which heralds Julian's entry into the narrative of Ammianus' history, only the great and the good provided adequate precedents for the youthful new Caesar. Thus in the eyes of the historian Julian's virtues amounted to a comprehensive replay of all the qualities of the best of his predecessors—the wisdom of Titus, the military success of Trajan, the clemency of Pius, 'and in his striving after truth and perfection he was the equal of Marcus Aurelius, on whom he endeavoured to model his own actions and character'.[1] The mention of Marcus in this list of imperial *exempla* is accorded a special authority of its own; for whereas the others might be dismissed as figments of the historian's craft, it was Julian himself, it is claimed, who actually adopted the philosopher-emperor as his guiding example. Ammianus' statement mirrors a similar observation in the *Breviarium* of Eutropius: Julian was 'not unlike Marcus Antoninus, whom he even took pains to copy'.[2] Both writers could claim first-hand knowledge of the emperor—Ammianus was serving as an officer in Gaul when Julian first arrived there as Caesar at the end of 355, and later shared with Eutropius personal experience of the Persian campaign of 363 in the course of which Julian met his death[3]— and consequently their remarks have commanded the respect of the scholarly tradition. It has become axiomatic to link Julian's name specifically with that of Marcus Aurelius: one recent biographer of Julian, for example, has attributed to him an admiration of Marcus which 'went beyond all conventions'.[4]

---

[1] Amm. Marc. 16. 1. 4. For Ammianus' conception of Julian, and his place in the *History*, see Matthews (1989), 468–70.   [2] Eutr. 10. 16. 3.

[3] For Eutropius' participation in the campaign, see *Brev.* 10. 16. 1.

[4] Athanassiadi (1992), 200 n. 31.

Yet this is surely to underestimate precisely the influence of 'convention' in determining these contemporary accounts of Julian. Along with Trajan, Marcus stood highest in the canon of approved Roman rulers in late antiquity, according to which it was customary to measure the merits of present incumbents.[5] To look no further than the surviving books of Ammianus (we lack, of course, his account of the Antonine era itself), Marcus repeatedly sets the standard for the historian's assessment of contemporary emperors in his narrative. Thus Valentinian's elevation of his brother and son as fellow-*Augusti* had its precedent in Marcus' joint rule with Lucius Verus (27. 6. 16); while in the obituary-notice of the same emperor, Ammianus was not averse to comparing his best characteristics with 'Trajan and Marcus' (30. 9. 1). Constantius II, on the other hand, by his ruthless suppression of suspected opponents showed himself 'dissimilis' from the revered Marcus, who had preferred to destroy unopened the correspondence of the rebel Avidius Cassius rather than have to discover the identity of his accomplices (21. 16. 11).[6] The historian could also appeal to Marcus as the saviour of the empire in the face of potentially disastrous invasions, and uphold him as the model for current emperors in the task of restoring Roman fortunes.[7] It is then no surprise to find Ammianus' Julian, the prince who arrived in Gaul carrying the people's hopes for recovery (15. 8. 21), cast in the historical role of Marcus *redivivus*.

Ammianus also finds other uses for the Julian–Marcus motif. As the historian traces Julian's movements eastwards towards his disastrous Persian adventure the tone and subject-matter of the narrative become less uniformly eulogistic than the quasi-panegyrical account of the young Caesar's dashing exploits in Gaul.[8] Julian's flaws surface with increasing intensity, in the process of preparing the reader for a climax of heroic failure on the battlefield in Persia. In this more equivocal phase of the narrative, the 'Marcus parallel' is redeployed to

[5] Syme (1971), 89–94, principally for the Latin tradition; for Greek writers, Stertz (1977).

[6] Ammianus follows a tradition of Marcus' *clementia* towards the associates of Avidius already to be found in Dio, 71. 29. 1–2.

[7] Thus the youthful Gratian could ill afford to neglect the empire 'at a time when even Marcus Antoninus, had he been emperor, would hardly have been able to remedy the lamentable state of public affairs without colleagues like himself and a most prudent policy' (31. 10. 19). On Marcus' rescuing the empire from barbarian attacks, see 31. 5. 13–14.

[8] Ammianus' criticisms of his 'hero' were first discussed by Thompson (1947), 72–86; cf. Matthews (1989), 105–14.

contribute to the undermining of Julian's perfection. It is alluded to, for example, in the much-quoted passage where Ammianus diminishes Julian's lofty proclamation of religious freedom into a calculated ploy to encourage Christian factionalism ('experience had taught him that no wild beasts are such dangerous enemies to man as Christians are to one another').[9] The historian reinforces his critical tone at this point by accusing Julian of misinterpreting a dictum of Marcus Aurelius, in which the earlier emperor on his travels through the eastern provinces had remarked upon the disorderliness of the Jews as surpassing that of his erstwhile barbarian foes across the Danube.[10] By appending this (mis)use of the hallowed precedent of Marcus, Ammianus has only added to Julian's discredit over his treatment of dissident Christians: the saying attributed to his exemplar of right behaviour, so the historian avers, would not in fact bear the interpretation which Julian wanted to place upon it.[11] Marcus reappears in the context of criticism of imperial policy in Ammianus' obituary-notice of Julian, where among the emperor's *vitia* the historian resumes the accusation (found earlier in his narrative) of excessive indulgence in sacrificing—which threatened a dearth of cattle if Julian had returned triumphant from Persia.[12] Ammianus here introduces a Greek couplet addressed to Marcus, in which 'white oxen' lament their forthcoming fate at the altars of the victorious emperor. As earlier, the criticism has a sharper edge for being coupled to Julian's exemplary predecessor.

These instances of Marcus' appearance in the narrative to drive home criticism of Julian's failings only serve to confirm the linkage of the two emperors as a literary mechanism in the hands of the historian. We may still legitimately wonder what basis in actual fact, if any, supported the assertions of Ammianus and Eutropius, and of modern scholars, that Julian consciously set out to model himself on Marcus Aurelius. The obvious recourse is to Julian's own surviving works. Yet here the impact we might expect to be registered by a cherished exemplar is remarkably elusive. The *Meditations*, for instance, have left no clearly discernible trace in Julian's works (even though their

[9] 22. 5. 4. Julian himself laid claim to more philanthropic motives: *Ep.* 114 (Bidez), 435d–436b; 115, 424c.

[10] Ammianus' use of the statement attributed to Marcus is discussed by Sabbah (1978), 268–71, but missing the point of its tone critical of Julian. Marcus' words are not reported elsewhere: Birley (1987), 193.

[11] Ibid.: 'sed parum advertit hoc *ab eo nimium discrepare*'.

[12] 25. 4. 17; cf. 22. 12. 6, 14. 3.

existence was known to his contemporary Themistius).[13] There are indications that Julian may have been familiar with some correspondence of Marcus, if a puzzling passage in one of his letters, discussing his reading-matter in Gaul, is rightly interpreted as referring to correspondence between Marcus and his *ab epistulis Graecis*, Alexander of Seleucia.[14] It was Bidez who first postulated that Julian knew letters of Marcus, observing that, in writing to Libanius, Julian praised his oratory in terms which echo language used by Marcus when commending the eloquence of Fronto.[15]

Yet scattered hints that Julian had read some letters of his distinguished predecessor fall far short of confirmation that he looked back to Marcus with a special reverence. Only once in his works does Julian actually identify Marcus Aurelius as a potential exemplar,[16] but in a context in which he proceeds to discard as unattainable the goal of aspiring to Marcus' 'perfect virtue'. At the opening of his *Letter to Themistius* Julian professes that he had once thought to rival outstanding precursors like Marcus and Alexander, but his intimidation before the virtue of the one and the valour of the other had led him to opt out of public life in favour of intellectual retreat. Themistius in turn has sought to convince him by means of another list of divine and human *exempla*—Heracles, Dionysus, and the great lawgivers Solon, Pittacus, and Lycurgus—that it was possible to combine the contemplative and the practical life: it was open to Julian, Themistius had argued, to surpass these predecessors and prove himself both philosopher and king.[17] Marcus' appearance in this passage, as one possible model among others (Julian had looked to 'Alexander, Marcus and *anyone else* outstanding in virtue'), and amid traditional reflections on the compatibility (or otherwise) of wisdom and action, is hardly convincing proof of any direct and specific influence on Julian's behaviour. In any event Julian is unpersuaded. The rest of the *Letter* is a

[13] Bouffartigue (1992), 73–6, *contra* Lacombrade (1967). Farquharson (1944), p. xiv, could find in Julian 'no certain verbal reminiscence of Marcus' work'; cf. also Rutherford (1989a), 10.

[14] Jul. *Ep.* 11 (Bidez), 425c; cf. Bouffartigue (1992), 75–6.

[15] Jul. *Ep.* 97, 382d, with Bidez, n. 6, ad loc.

[16] I leave aside the disputed Fayum papyrus (Hunt–Edgar, *Select Papyri*, No. 216), an imperial pronouncement on the subject of *aurum coronarium* citing the precedent of Trajan and Marcus, which was first attributed to Severus Alexander, but which Dessau and others (including Bidez) have claimed for Julian. For rejection of Julianic authorship, see Pack (1986), 132–4, following Moreau (1964), 37–9.

[17] 253a–254a; cf. 262d, Julian should move 'from the shadow of philosophy to the open air'.

restatement of misgivings about the life of a ruler and an endorsement of philosophic withdrawal—not the lesson to be drawn from the career of Marcus.[18]

It is the work familiarly known as the *Caesars*, dating from the period of Julian's sojourn in Antioch during the winter of 362–3,[19] which seemingly offers the best prospect of confirming his particular commitment to the example of Marcus Aurelius.[20] Inspired by the example of Plato (306c), Julian offers an edifying fable, depicting a banquet of the gods gathered to celebrate the feast of Kronos (i.e. the Saturnalia). The host is Romulus, identified by his divine name Quirinus, who invites to the symposium not only his fellow-gods but also his descendants who were emperors of Rome. It is the occasion for the gods to have their fun at the expense of the mortal guests, and Silenus is on hand as the 'court jester' figure to poke jibes at the succession of earthly rulers arriving for the feast, in due chronological order from Julius Caesar to Constantine and his sons. There is an additional guest in the person of Alexander, who is included at the insistence of Heracles as being worthier than any of Romulus' Roman successors (316b). This advent of Alexander is the cue for a talent contest between him and the emperors, with the gods as judges of their respective merits. Julius Caesar, Augustus (or 'Octavian' as he is always called in the *Caesars*), and Trajan are 'shortlisted' to compete with Alexander as warriors, while to complete the comparison Marcus Aurelius gains inclusion as a philosopher (317b–c), and Constantine at the other extreme as a ruler 'enslaved to pleasure and enjoyment' (318a). Having each made his case for superiority, the five candidates in turn are cross-examined by Hermes as chief investigator, aided and abetted by interventions from Silenus. A secret ballot of the gods determines Marcus the victor (335c). Hermes concludes with an invitation to all the mortal contestants to join the company of the gods, each to choose for himself a suitable mentor: while Marcus attaches himself to the senior deities Zeus and Kronos, Constantine finds his 'archetype' not among the gods at all, but with the more enticing company of Τρυφή (Luxury), spotted lurking close by.

---

[18] On the interpretation of the *Letter to Themistius*, see Athanassiadi (1992), 90–6, and commentary by Prato and Fornara (1984); but for persuasive arguments for an earlier date for the work, Bradbury (1987). The distancing from Marcus may be implicit, but the coolness towards the Alexander model is clearly stated: 257a–b, 264d.

[19] On the title of the work, and time of composition, see Baldwin (1978), 450–3. For the complex literary background, Bouffartigue (1992), 397–400, and on Julian and Lucian, Nesselrath (1994).   [20] See e.g. Bowersock (1978), 15–16, 101–2.

Recent interest in Julian's *Caesars* has tended to focus on identifying the sources of its (sometimes unconventional) observations about his imperial predecessors,[21] and on the political context of its composition at Antioch in the winter of 362–3: the addition of Alexander to the cast list of emperors is given immediate relevance by the imminence of Julian's prestige military enterprise in Persia.[22] The role of Marcus, on the other hand, has attracted little comment. It has seemed a predictable and unremarkable consequence of Julian's assumed admiration of the philosopher-ruler that the one emperor who had no difficulty winning over his divine judges with the terse announcement that his aim in life had been to 'imitate the gods' (333c), and successfully countered the cross-examination, should naturally emerge winner of the contest.[23] Yet it is possible to challenge the assumption that the *Caesars* is a vehicle for Julian's devotion to the historical precedent of Marcus Aurelius. To take the work too seriously, for example, is perhaps to miss some of its point.[24] Despite disclaiming a talent for humour (306a) Julian recounts a fable to suit the merry-making of its Saturnalia setting. The serious content implied by the invocation of Plato and the promise of a tale which offers 'perhaps much that is worth hearing' (306b) is none the less articulated in a tone in keeping with the playfulness of the season. The interrogator Silenus offers a *mixture* of γελοῖα and σπουδαῖα, in the tradition of the Socratic symposium (314d).[25] The same mixture is illustrated by the juxtaposition of Hermes' mock-solemn proclamation of the opening of the contest (a parody of the herald's summons to the games) with humorous banter between Silenus and Poseidon alluding to Trajan's and Alexander's fondness for drink: even the contents of the gods' *clepsydra* would not be safe in their presence, should they mistakenly suppose it to contain nectar (318c).[26] Julian's readers, we might justifiably conclude, are being warned off over-zealous interpretations of his fable.

Marcus Aurelius' first appearance, in the procession of emperors

[21] So Alföldi (1968); Bowersock (1982); Baldwin (1978), 453 ff.; Bouffartigue (1992), 401–7.

[22] Athanassiadi (1992), 197–200; Matthews (1989), 137–8.

[23] e.g. Baldwin (1978), 466 'one is hardly surprised by the victory of Marcus Aurelius'; Matthews (1989), 137 'the winner is of course Julian's model, Marcus Aurelius'.

[24] I thus beg to differ from Bowersock (1982), 159 'we must not look for humour here'. For the *Caesars* as a subversively comic piece, see now Relihan (1993), 119–34.

[25] On the resemblance of Silenus to Socrates, cf. Plato, *Sympos.* 215a–b.

[26] Baldwin (1978), 461, misses this passage in claiming that 'the *Caesares* does not include the commonplace of Trajan's addiction to drink'. For the proclamation of the games, cf. Lucian, *Demonax* 65, with Bouffartigue (1992), 295.

arriving for the banquet, attracts no headlines.[27] He is introduced
under his private name 'Verus', and in the dubious company of his
adoptive brother (and fellow-emperor) Lucius (312a), who would be
familiar to fourth-century devotees of imperial biography in the guise
of a playboy prince whose bad habits contrasted with the virtuous
conduct of his senior partner.[28] This tradition offered plenty of opportunity for the jester Silenus to deploy his talents to Marcus' advantage.
Yet Julian explicitly rejects the possibility: 'there was nothing for
Silenus to scoff at'. Instead it is Marcus' own failings which are alluded
to, the twin ἁμαρτήματα of excessive affection for a wayward wife and
over-indulgence of a ruinous son—Marcus would have done better to
elevate his worthier son-in-law (the unnamed Ti. Claudius Pompeianus, Lucius' successor as husband to Lucilla).[29] Although it is true that
Marcus' great virtue does not go unnoticed (312b: τὸ μέγεθος . . . τῆς
ἀρετῆς), he still arrives before the gods a tarnished figure, his domestic
shortcomings only accentuated by the indignity of seeing Commodus
not even admitted to the presence of the gods, and falling back to earth
(312c). If Marcus Aurelius is to be the idol of the *Caesars*, his entry—it
must be said—marks an unpromising beginning.

If there is a hero in the queue of emperors approaching the gods'
threshold, then the strongest candidate is Claudius II ('Gothicus'),
whose 'greatness of soul' attracted the admiring gaze of *all* the
immortals (313d). Such unqualified divine approval was directed at
Claudius as the progenitor of the imperial dynasty of which Julian
himself was to be the last representative (Julian's full name was Fl.
Claudius Julianus).[30] Similar approbation greeted the show of unanim-
ity with which the quartet of Diocletian and his colleagues arrived
(including 'my grandfather Constantius'), to be granted precedence at
the banquet over 'most' of the other emperors (315a–b). In this final
family group places are also found for Constantine and his sons,
whereas Licinius and Magnentius fail to gain admission (despite the
appearance, in the latter case, of 'many fine deeds': 315d–316a).[31] The

---

[27] Baldwin (1978), 462 'Marcus Aurelius enters the dialogue on a subdued note'.

[28] The tradition reflected in SHA *Verus*, 4. 4–6. 6; cf. Barnes (1967), 69–70.

[29] On this leading associate of Marcus, see *PIR*² C 973. For the unfavourable biographical tradition surrounding Faustina and Commodus, Syme (1983), 34–40.

[30] Claudius' merits as the founder of the second Flavian dynasty had also featured in
Julian's first *Panegyric to Constantius*, 6d–7a. On the 'fraud' which linked Constantine's
family to Claudius, see Syme (1983), 63–79.

[31] As one who preceded Julian in challenging Constantius II, the usurper Magnentius
could not be entirely beyond redemption: cf. Zosim. 2. 54, for similar acknowledgement
of his apparent merits.

catalogue of emperors arriving for the banquet thus culminates on a theme of dynastic solidarity (whatever divisions may emerge later in the story), with those who had challenged the imperial monopoly of Julian's family excluded from the gods' table. Marcus' arrival, by comparison, had made no distinctive impact.

It is with the contest generated by the introduction of Alexander that Marcus' part in the *Caesars* seems destined to assume greater importance. Marcus finds himself added to the shortlist of warrior-emperors in competition with Alexander, as the representative of philosophy: it is the combination of the practical and intellectual life which will constitute the make-up of the perfect ruler. So Marcus makes a second entry on to the scene, noticeably more striking than the first: he is every inch the philosopher, the bearded ascetic whose appearance betrayed his devotion to study and carelessness of worldly matters of dress and food (317c–d). Neither Alexander nor his other Roman competitors (to whose ranks Constantine is also added) are accorded any description to match this glimpse of Marcus' solemnity. Whereas his first advent before the gods had been muted and over-shadowed, his body now 'gleamed like the purest light'.[32]

It is the more surprising, then, that Marcus plays little part in the competition which follows. The lion's share is devoted to the speeches of Caesar and Alexander—for the rival claims of these two generals, and their respective military achievements, evoked significant associations for Julian: his military spurs had been won following Caesar's footsteps in Gaul, and (as we have seen) he was now on the eve of an Alexander-style invasion of Persian territory. But neither of them offers any pretensions of being a philosopher: that is left for the next speakers, Augustus and Trajan, who in addition to their military boasts both avow that they were ardent students of philosophy (in Trajan's case, at least, a somewhat surprising admission).[33] It might have been expected that this would be the cue for Marcus, whose turn is next, to advertise his intellectual virtues—the philosopher-ruler *par excellence*. Yet he is accorded the briefest speech of all. Where the other contestants have bragged of their achievements, he has no need of words to tell the gods what they already know, 'for nothing at all is

---

[32] Farquharson (1944), p. xv, thought this passage the closest he could find to Marcus' own language, citing *Medit.* 10. 1, 11. 12; but Marcus there describes the bright light of the soul *obscured* by its bodily surroundings, not (as in Julian) the brightness of the body itself.

[33] Augustus, 326a–b ('I was never guilty of any offence against philosophy'); Trajan, 328b ('I revered your daughter, philosophy').

hidden from you' (328c). Despite seeming strangely laconic when set against the more fulsome eloquence and factual claims of the other speakers, his contribution is perceptive enough to win the gods' admiration for its wisdom.

Marcus' moment arrives during the cross-examination of the speakers. While Alexander is reduced to tears and the others have their bravado severely punctured under the interrogation of Hermes and Silenus, Marcus is able, 'like a skilful boxer' (334a), to counter the challenge of the prosecution. Silenus first indulges in some sophistry at the expense of Marcus' professed aim of 'imitating the gods': why, then, did he continue to take mortal nourishment rather than ambrosia and nectar? The emperor responded that he supposed that even the bodies of gods needed to be fed by the fumes rising from sacrifices (333d). Julian here places on the lips of Marcus what may be taken as a riposte to those among his own critics who complained, not least during the court's residence in Antioch, of his excessive devotion to the practice of sacrificing.[34] Silenus returns to the attack by repeating the accusations of over-indulgence towards his wife and son which had greeted Marcus' first arrival for the banquet; Marcus parries by appealing to Homeric precedents of family devotion among the immortals, as well as invoking the established custom of hereditary succession as something which 'all men pray for' (334d–335a). Significantly Julian has reintroduced the theme of dynasticism, which he had earlier endorsed in recounting the arrival of Claudius II and the Tetrarchs. As with the justification of sacrificing, Marcus' counterarguments in the face of his accusers become the channel for voicing sentiments which were of political importance to Julian himself, for it was the tradition of dynastic succession which legitimized Julian's own imperial role.[35] In this respect Marcus offered a conveniently doubleedged precedent: Julian might make the best of his own childlessness with the defence that he had no wish to bring harm to the empire by fathering an unworthy heir.[36] Certain features of Julian's own regime are thus based on an appeal to the *exemplum* of Marcus Aurelius as depicted here, and the arguments which he successfully deploys

[34] Amm. Marc. 22. 14. 3; Jul. *Misop.* 346c ('who will endure an emperor who frequents the temples so often?'). See J. Fontaine, *Ammien Marcellin: Histoire* (Budé), vol. 4/ii, n. 589; above, p. 289 and n. 12.

[35] Hence, for example, his ostentatious respect for his dead rival Constantius: Liban. *Or.* 18. 119–20; Mamert. *Grat. Act.* (= *Pan. Lat.* 3(11)). 27. 5 ('oblitus inimici meminit *heredis*').

[36] Liban. *Or.* 18. 181.

against Silenus' questioning: the Marcus of this section of the *Caesars*, turning the tables on his opponent, comes close to adopting the persona of Julian himself.

It is perhaps then surprising that it is only a majority vote of the gods which gives the palm to Marcus (335c): an unspectacular victory, and one clouded by the thought—which Julian does nothing to dispel—that some of the immortals preferred other candidates. Marcus is permitted only qualified dominance of the proceedings. The ballot is in any case rendered seemingly irrelevant by Hermes' proclamation that all the mortal competitors, winner and losers, are free to enter the company of the gods and seek out the mentor of their choice. Marcus of course, as their dutiful adherent, makes for the greatest of the gods, Zeus and Kronos; but his and the others' choice of divine guardian fades into insignificance by comparison with the emphasis placed at the conclusion of the *Caesars* on Constantine's eager consorting with Τρυφή ('Luxury') and her associate Ἀσωτία ('Profligacy').[37] Here at last the real import of the work is vividly, even savagely, revealed. For in this company Constantine also encounters Jesus, holding out the prospect of easy absolution for all conditions of earthly criminals through the waters of baptism: 'let any seducer, any murderer, any accursed and infamous character, approach without fear; for with this water I will wash him and straightway make him clean' (336a–b). It is fitting refuge for Constantine and his sons who, in Julian's eyes, bore the guilt for the domestic murders of his kinsmen in the summer of 337 (to say nothing of Constantine's involvement in the deaths of Crispus and Fausta in 326)[38] and were only spared the ultimate fate of parricides, it is here asserted, because of Zeus' regard for their (and Julian's own) ancestors Claudius and Constantius I. That same dynastic heritage, on which Julian has repeatedly insisted in the *Caesars*, is at last revealed to be a bloodstained and divided one, polluted by the family massacre for which he held Constantine and his sons responsible.

The underlying *tendenz* of Julian's humorous fable is thus graphically exposed in its final tableau. Ridicule of Constantine (and of his

---

[37] 336a, cf. 329a, where the infatuation is first recorded. Constantine's fondness for τρυφή and ἀσωτία was to become a regular motif of the hostile pagan tradition: cf. Zosim. 2. 32. 1, 38. 1 (deriving from Eunapius).

[38] For the pagan version of the bloodshed of 326, cf. Zosim. 2. 29 with discussion by Paschoud (Budé) ad loc. For Julian's accusations concerning the massacre of 337, see his *Letter to the Athenians*, 270c–d, and *Against the Cynic Heracleios*, 228b. For a summary of events, Barnes (1981), 261–2.

Christian revolution) and the blame for dismembering Julian's imperial dynasty are the dominant notes, and the idolization of an exemplary Marcus Aurelius—in any case, as we have seen, a restrained component—is subordinated to this theme. It is the clash of opposites reflected in Marcus and Constantine which reinforces the serious message: the winner of the imperial contest is everything which Constantine is not. Both are late entries to the competition, representing the two extremes of public deportment: one the studious ascetic, the other a pleasure-loving libertine. Where Marcus impresses by his wisdom and devotion to the gods, Constantine is an ignorant braggart proclaiming trivial achievements which are easily belittled, and not even having the wit to understand Silenus' scoffing at 'gardens of Adonis' (329c–d).[39] Marcus lives for the noble purpose of 'imitating the gods'—which he defines under questioning as 'having the fewest possible needs and doing good to the greatest possible number' (334a)—Constantine for blatant self-interest, amassing wealth for the gratification of himself and his friends (335b).[40] In the end Marcus assumes his rightful place alongside the leaders of the gods he reveres, while the ἀθεότης (336b) ('godlessness') of Constantine and his sons disdains the divine gathering in favour of more enticing company. In contrast to the sober and unadorned philosopher's habit of Marcus, Constantine is suitably arrayed for his new companions in gaudy multi-coloured garments (336a).

The Marcus seen in Julian's *Caesars* is thus not—beyond the conventional image of the philosopher-ruler—a depiction of the second-century emperor (alone of the competitors he is not, as already noted, given a speech to detail his historical achievements), but a contemporary creation, constructed as the antithesis of the godless wastrel who is the Christian Constantine. As in his arguments against Silenus' questioning, the role of Marcus in the *Caesars* is a projection of Julian's own self-identification, embodying the austere asceticism and practising piety which were the hallmarks of his own regimen, and of the religious crusade over which he sought to preside.[41] Even down to his long beard (317c) the Marcus of the *Caesars* is cast, not as his real self,

---

[39] Cf. Plato, *Phaedrus*, 276b. The notion became proverbial to denote ephemeral glories (*Suda* A517 Adler).

[40] Cf. Zosim. 2. 38. 1, with Amm. Marc. 16. 8. 12, 25. 4. 23; for refs. to Constantine in surviving books of Ammianus, see Matthews (1989), 447–50.

[41] For the *Caesars* as a companion-piece to the polemic of the *Contra Galilaeos* (also composed at Antioch in the winter of 362–3: Liban. *Or*. 18. 178), see Baldwin (1978), 451, Bowersock (1978), 102.

but in the image of Julian.[42] His part in the fable finds its ideal *exemplum* in Julian, and not the other way round.

Yet if in composing the myth of the *Caesars* Julian paused to reflect on the real Marcus Aurelius, he might indeed have found the historical precedent in some respects too close for comfort. For his predecessor in 175 the city of Antioch had turned into the seat of a rebel government, its citizens declaring their loyalty for Avidius Cassius; and Marcus' only visit there as emperor had occurred against the background of this failed *coup d'état*.[43] Julian's own imperial residence in the same city nearly two centuries later was also to be marred by an increasing spirit of disaffection, as he encountered the defiance of a population out of sympathy both with his personal austerity and with his zealous paganism. It was the recent legacy of Constantine, rather than the distant (and largely imaginary) virtues of Marcus Aurelius, which was to prove the more influential model for the majority of Julian's subjects.

[42] Julian's beard, long and trimmed in goatee fashion (Amm. Marc. 22. 14. 3, 25. 4. 22), was an object of ridicule in Antioch, and of course the starting-point for his *Misopogon*, 338b–339b. Representations of Marcus, as the famous equestrian statue in Rome, show him with shorter, stubby growth.

[43] On Avidius' following in Antioch, see SHA *Marcus*, 25. 8–11.

C

ANCIENT LITERARY CRITICISM

23

Criticism Ancient and Modern

DENIS FEENEY

mihi de antiquis eodem modo non licebit?

Cic. *Or.* 171

Classicists have long taken it for granted that an acquaintance with the literary criticism of the ancients is a useful skill for the student of their literature to master.[1] This rather general and often unarticulated assumption, part of a larger professional concern with unanachronistic historical fidelity, has recently been given a much sharper focus in the work of Francis Cairns and Malcolm Heath.[2] The latter scholar in particular has claimed, not merely that ancient literary criticism is a useful supplement to the critical apparatus of the modern scholar, but that ancient literary criticism is in effect the only apparatus which the modern scholar may use for the purpose of 'poetics', an activity defined as 'a historical enquiry into the workings of a particular system of conventions in a given historical and cultural context'.[3] In the case of fifth-century Attic tragedy, for example, despite the fact that we have no contemporary critical testimony to speak of outside Aristophanes, we are assured by Heath that 'even a fourth-century writer is a priori more likely to be a reliable guide to tragedy than the unreconstructed prejudices of the modern reader'.[4]

---

[1] I am putting as much stress on the 'and' in the title as Donald Russell did when I heard him introducing R. D. Williams's talk at Oxford on 'Virgil and Homer'. I first tried out some of these ideas on the Bristol English–Latin Seminar in November 1991; and an audience at Berkeley heard a (suitably disguised) version in April 1994. My thanks to those present for their comments. I must also thank several people who read a draft of the chapter: Stephen Hinds, Jacques Lezra, Laura McClure, Terry McKiernan, Georgia Nugent, Neil Whitehead, and Jeffrey Wills (who suggested my motto from Cicero). The editors had me think again on various points, and made me wish I had had the space to develop the case further.

[2] Cairns (1972); Heath (1987) and (1989).

[3] Heath (1987), 1 n. 1.

[4] Heath (1987), 3.

In order to set up the ἀγών which I wish to conduct in this essay, let me, to the accompaniment of litotes, bring on to the stage the scholar whom we honour with this volume, a man more versed than most in ancient literary criticism, and a man whom few would convict of possessing more than his share of 'unreconstructed prejudices'. A striking leitmotif of Donald Russell's synthetic judgements on ancient literary criticism is his apprehension that, however much 'we cannot help reasoning that the Greeks and Romans must after all know best, since the language and the culture were their own', nonetheless, 'this ancient rhetorical "criticism" . . . is fundamentally not equal to the task of appraising classical literature'.[5] This is true, by Russell's account, of the ancient critics' principles of style and allegory (6–7, 98, 131), of their study of *imitatio* (113), literary history (117, 168), and genre (149, 152).[6] Both in *Criticism and Antiquity* and in his valedictory lecture, when he stands back to sum up his impressions of pervasive antithetical currents in ancient literature—impressions which could have been formed only by the most broad and searching reading—he concedes that they do not correspond to anything formulated by an ancient critic (indeed, to anything that *could have been* formulated by an ancient critic).[7]

My own rhetoric will probably have indicated which of the agonists wins my vote, and I have already elsewhere indicated that I think the ancient critics are to be used 'as an aid, even a guide, but not as a prescription, or a straitjacket'.[8] But I would like to develop those earlier brief remarks and justify in detail my partiality for Donald Russell's position. Then I would like to suggest why all critics everywhere should expect to find themselves in his predicament. For the issues raised by my σύγκρισις rapidly multiply. An examination of the role of ancient criticism in the study of ancient texts soon spins into its corollary—currently very topical—of the examination of the role of modern criticism in the study of ancient texts;[9] and that issue in turn confronts us with the problem of what we take to be the explanatory

---

[5] Russell (1981a), 1, 6. Page references in the next sentence of the text are to this book.

[6] For his reservations about the penetration of ancient *imitatio*-studies, see also Russell (1979), esp. 9.

[7] Russell (1981a), 6–7, and (1989), 21. Cf. G. A. Kennedy (1989a), 493, on the fact that 'the ancient criticism we have seems oblivious of major historical features of the literatures'; and Williams (1968), 31, on ancient reflections on the nature of poetry: 'the answers of theorists lagged quite a lot behind the practice of poets'.

[8] Feeney (1991), 3.

[9] De Jong and Sullivan (1994).

power of criticism anyway. No doubt by the end of the essay I will have taken up positions which Donald Russell would not care to occupy with me, but at least we will have begun in the same camp, and he may be sure that my own forays could not have been undertaken except under his auspices, and with the well-supplied commissariat of his scholarship.

We must begin by delineating the difficulties involved in Heath's claim that ancient testimony is our sole legitimate interpretative key: 'when we are dealing with the evidence of witnesses who are contemporary or near contemporaries, there is at least a presumption of general reliability; certainly, they are more likely to prove reliable guides than the untutored intuition of a modern reader—which is, in practice, the only alternative, and a patently treacherous one'.[10] For all its polemical tone, such a statement captures a basic frame of mind shared by many classicists, and it takes an effort to shake oneself free of its allure.

For a start, we may observe how many ancient aesthetic objects are removed from our critical attention by the strict application of Heath's law. He has concentrated on topics where a good deal of ancient critical evidence is extant (Attic tragedy, the problem of unity), but, even rhetorically, it is worth asking how he would propose we discuss the ancient novel, which was 'drastically undertheorized', as J. R. Morgan puts it, 'even to the extent that there was no word for it in either Greek or Latin'.[11] If modern critics of ancient literature are to confine themselves to the critical horizon of the surviving ancient evidence, then scholars of the ancient novel might as well shut up shop. Or how are we to talk of ancient art according to Heath's model when, for example, there is in the extant corpus of classical literature precisely one reference to vase-painting?[12]

Heath is far more alert to the difficulties of periodization than his precursor Cairns, who, in order to justify his use of a third/fourth-century AD model for interpreting literature back to the archaic period, had to make his now notorious claim that 'in a very real sense antiquity was in comparison with the nineteenth and twentieth centuries a time-free zone'.[13] Still, despite Heath's acknowledgement of

[10] Heath (1987), 3.
[11] Morgan (1993), 176. I can only agree with Morgan: 'The obvious point is that there is a lot which is in excess of ancient theory, but that just means that theory had not caught up with practice' (224).
[12] Ar. *Eccl.* 996; my thanks to Barry Powell for this interesting information.
[13] Cairns (1972), 32.

the possible anachronism of using ancient critics who are not contemporary with their texts,[14] he remains on thin ice in describing Aristotle as a near contemporary witness to Attic drama. Euripides and Sophocles had been dead for anything between forty-five and eighty-five years by the time the *Poetics* were composed, and Aeschylus for anything between ninety-five and one hundred and thirty-five. By this kind of calculation Pope is a near contemporary witness of Shakespeare's aesthetic, and Tennyson a near contemporary witness of Pope's—and this is quite apart from the problem, to which I return shortly, of what *kind* of witness Aristotle is.

The difficulties in historical perspective glimpsed here open up larger problems with the historicist stance represented by Heath and Cairns. One of the main flaws in this kind of approach is that it cannot do justice to the very sense of history which it purports to champion, for critics such as Heath and Cairns exhibit a systematic refusal to come to terms with the fact that their own critical practice is historically sited.[15] The claim that only a given culture's modes of criticism can work for that culture has some kind of initial plausibility, perhaps, but we have to recognize that this claim itself comes from an identifiable modern philological tradition. Heath is always denouncing modern prejudice, but the idea that we can only read ancient literature in terms of ancient criticism is itself a modern prejudice.[16]

And it is one which it is theoretically impossible to control in the way Heath wishes to, for any modern selection of ancient critical techniques and approaches is inherently partial, in every sense of the word. Heath asserts quite rightly that 'we do not inspect "the poem itself" without presupposition, and our presuppositions dispose us to find plausible or implausible interpretations of one or another kind';[17] but precisely the same is true of our inspection of criticism. At the most basic level, there is simply so much ancient criticism, and it is so multifaceted, that the modern critic must pick and choose: as Andrew Ford

---

[14] Heath (1987), 2–4; (1989), 10–11, 122.

[15] Heath (1987), 79 recognizes that 'the preoccupations of literary criticism ... are historical and change in the course of history', but his argument proceeds as if he is exempt from the implications of his insight. My own emphasis on the historical sitedness of the critic is of course ultimately indebted to Gadamer (1960). For classicists' perspectives on the 'hermeneutics of reception', see Martindale (1993a) and Nauta (1994).

[16] Quite unrealizable, at that, as pointed out by D. F. Kennedy (1993), 8: 'If historicism achieved its aim of understanding a culture of the past "in its own terms", the result would be totally unintelligible except to that culture and moment ... Far from past being made "present", it would be rendered totally foreign and impenetrably alien.'

[17] Heath (1989), 122.

well says of the Homeric scholia, in the course of a sympathetic but dissenting review of Heath (1989), 'we are always taking from them what we find congenial and discarding the rest'.[18] Despite acknowledging the problematic nature of the critical material,[19] in his *modus operandi* Heath does not actually treat the corpus of ancient literary criticism as something that requires interpretation on a footing with the literature. But the corpus is itself, if you like, 'literary', not an inert tool. This is immediately obvious in the case of an Aristotle or a Horace, but it is also true of Servius and the largely anonymous company of the scholia. We are not dealing with a problematic body of material ('literature') which can be explained with the aid of a less problematic body of material ('criticism'): we are dealing with numerous, often contesting, strands of problematic material which interact with each other in innumerable categories of time and space.[20]

The critical terrain, in short, is riven and complex, and our modern image of it is an interpretative construct, every bit as open to anachronism and *parti pris* as our construction of the 'literature'. An example of this is to be found in Heath's use of Aristotle's *Poetics* as evidence in reconstructing the 'emotive hedonism' which he sees as the ruling aesthetic of the tragic drama of the previous century. In using Aristotle as *evidence* for poetic practice in this way, he first of all removes Aristotle from a philosophical context, for, as Halliwell says, in the *Poetics* 'the theory is *normative*, and its principles, while partly dependent on exemplification from existing works, are not simply deduced from them. The theorist's insight claims a validity which may well contradict much of the practice of playwrights hitherto.'[21] Further, Heath's reading of what Aristotle has to say about the emotions is very much at odds with other recent interpretations of the *Poetics*, notably that of Halliwell, by whose account Aristotle's concept of aesthetic pleasure is one 'in which cognition and emotion are integrated'; indeed, 'Aristotle's conception of the emotions, pity and fear, itself rests on a cognitive basis'.[22] This kind of approach to

[18] Ford (1991), 147; I must declare my debt here to this finely argued essay. Cf. Martindale (1993*b*), 123 on Heath's approach: 'we all ... in order to validate our readings, appropriate, *selectively*, pieces of past data. There are reasons for this selectivity, but those reasons are always and never good enough as it were.'

[19] Heath (1987), 2–3.

[20] Ford (1991), 146–7.

[21] Halliwell (1987), 83 (his italics); cf. 9–10, and Halliwell (1986), 3–4.

[22] Halliwell (1986), 76; see his whole discussion of pleasure, 62–81, and, for specific engagements with Heath, Halliwell (1989) and (1992), 255. Only after writing this chapter did I see the powerful article of Lada (1993); see esp. 114–18.

Aristotle has been behind some compelling recent studies of tragedy, especially those of Martha Nussbaum[23]—though her ethics-based approach is not without its own risks, especially that of making the play, as Terry McKiernan puts it, 'a piece of moral philosophy worn inside-out, with the example or parable on the outside and the argument that the example illustrates hidden within'.[24]

All this has serious implications for Heath, since it is an important part of his purpose to discredit 'intellectualizing' readings of Attic tragedy. If Heath has to read Aristotle in a reductive way in order to make this possible, he also has to disparage another strand of ancient criticism—just as venerable and authoritative, it may seem to other observers—that is, the didactic one, as exemplified in the only genuinely contemporary substantial evidence we have, Aristophanes' *Frogs*. Heath's distinctive intellectual honesty has him acknowledge the prominence of the didactic bent in the ancient tradition, but he dismisses it as a 'habit', not something interesting or important, and certainly not something which gives 'support for the intellectual interests of modern tragic interpretation'.[25] When an ancient critic makes a remark about a text's emotional impact, Heath will commend him, but not when he makes a remark about its didactic impact; it is difficult to see this preference as one that emerges naturally from the material under inspection. Although I have a good deal of sympathy with many of Heath's objections to the intellectualizing reading of Greek tragedy as it is actually practised, I do not see how he can write it down by elevating one strand of ancient criticism over another.

Heath represents a set of assumptions shared by many classicists, even if he pushes them to their extremest limit. There are doubtless many ways of accounting for the appeal of such an approach—a concern with professional rigour; a belief that only an historicizing approach is intellectually respectable; a desire to make criticism as 'objective' as philology, so that this movement in literary criticism in Classics becomes the counterpart of the anxieties of students of modern literatures over what exactly their τέχνη is (a dilemma that goes back to Socrates' interrogation of Ion). I suspect, however, that

---

[23] Nussbaum (1986), esp. 12–15, and (1990), esp. 378–91, on the theoretical issues.

[24] My thanks to him for letting me quote from an unpublished essay on ethics in tragedy. Similar reservations in B. Harrison (1991), 15–17.

[25] Heath (1987), 47. Heath's main ground for rejecting intellectualizing interpretations as part of 'poetics' is that the poets cannot have intended them (44–5); but, even if we conduct the debate on these terms, I do not see on what evidence he can claim that they did not.

the main reason why so many classicists attribute such authority to ancient literary criticism is that it relieves them of the distasteful task of attributing any authority to modern literary criticism. The historicist bent of classical training predisposes many of us to be hostile to the idea that the ancient world can be illuminated by modern schemes which may be quite at odds with the conceptual apparatus of the Romans and Greeks,[26] yet it is an issue which we continually confront, and Charles Segal is quite right to describe it as 'perhaps the central hermeneutic question of our field today'.[27]

It should be clear from my discussion so far that in my opinion we are all (including Malcolm Heath) doing modern literary criticism all the time, and that students of ancient literature have to learn to live with the hermeneutic gap: 'interpretation ... involves a constantly moving "fusion of horizons" between past and present'.[28] Just as in the case of ancient literary criticism, however, we are of course always engaged (consciously or not) in selecting which currents of modern criticism to value and which to disparage, and it becomes a decided problem to justify or even to isolate the criteria by which we perform this selection.[29] If we grant that there is a necessary gap of incommensurability between our criticism and the ancient text (a protasis which not all my readers will accept), does it follow that all modern modes of analysis are equally valid or rewarding?

Attempts have been made to suggest continuities, or at least deep similarities, between certain ancient and modern preoccupations, especially in semiotics and scepticism.[30] The value of such connections will reside in the use to which they are put in practice, and the 'naturalness' of the connections may of course always be challenged on the grounds that we are finding only what we are predisposed to look for: when Simon Goldhill says that the 'fifth century underwent "a linguistic turn"',[31] it is easy to remark that only the intellectual heir of the twentieth-century's 'linguistic turn' is in a position to talk in these

---

[26] Martindale (1993*a*), 5–6 on historicism in the Classics.

[27] Segal (1992), 153.

[28] Martindale (1993*a*), 7; cf. the points made by D. F. Kennedy (1993), quoted at n. 16 above. The most obvious example of Heath's use of the techniques of modern literary criticism is in his synoptic discussion of individual tragedies in the compass of a few pages; this is not a form of criticism practised in the ancient world, or in the modern world either until John Dryden's 'Examen of *The Silent Woman*' in his 1668 *Essay on Dramatic Poesy* (my thanks to Richard Knowles for this information).

[29] On this problem, see Goldhill (1994), 52.

[30] G. A. Kennedy (1989*a*) and (1989*b*), pp. xi–xii; Sullivan (1994), 14–21.

[31] Goldhill (1986), 2.

terms. Still, when we are dealing with semiotics and rhetoric we may feel more confidence in finding analogies between our interest in language and theirs if we reflect that analogy is itself, after all, one of *their* words. We have, I think, a different kind of problem—though not of course *per se* a disabling one—when there appear to be clear discrepancies between ancient and modern approaches.

Of the critical techniques currently in play, the most problematic from this point of view is probably psychoanalysis, because its scientistic apparatus lays open the issue of its truth-claims in a particularly overt form. These truth-claims have for some time been under attack on their own terms anyway, and it is clear that in psychiatric and psychological education and practice the psychoanalytic model of the mind has nothing like the authority that it had even twenty years ago.[32] Even if, for the sake of argument, we concede that the model has some kind of validity for late nineteenth-century and twentieth-century European culture, we still need to contend with the fact that anthropologists and historians are practically united in doubting the value of applying it to other cultures.[33] It is bad luck for exponents of psychoanalytic criticism in Classics—whether they acknowledge it as such or not—that they are entering a field dominated by the Foucauldian view of sexuality and the self as variably constructed cultural phenomena, in which the current agenda is to 'define and refine a new, and radical, historical sociology of psychology'.[34] Very few practitioners do in fact make the kind of claim for the transhistorical and transcultural applicability of Freudianism that is advanced by Caldwell, for example,[35] but

[32] Grünbaum (1984) and (1993); for an ancient historian's perspective, S. R. F. Price (1990), 360–70; a highly critical overview in Crews (1993), with reaction and discussion in Crews (1994). My thanks to Jude, and to my neighbour, Dr James Gustafson, for their conversations about contemporary psychology and psychoanalysis.

[33] S. R. F. Price (1990), 370: 'Freudian theory is thus at best extremely problematic, and its imposition on another culture singularly futile'; Dinnage (1993), 66: 'Anthropologists now tend to feel, understandably, that psychoanalytic studies of societies, particularly of non-Western societies, apply unproven theories and a Western bias to cultures with quite different assumptions.' As Neil Whitehead points out to me, such perspectives in anthropology only became possible once the Freudian model had lost a good deal of its authority in its own home culture.

[34] Halperin (1990), 40; cf. esp. 41–6 for the 'essentialist/constructionist' debate over 'homosexuality'. Of course our reconstruction of that ancient sexuality and self will always be in dialogue with our own deeply acculturated sense of sexuality and self, of which some kind of Freudianism—however diluted—is inevitably a part; cf. D. F. Kennedy (1993), 40–3.

[35] Caldwell (1990), 344; cf. Segal (1992), 153, justifying his use of psychological and anthropological models with the assertion that 'certain categories of human experience are universal'.

this only throws into relief the usual evasion of the issue. Repression, unconscious, desire, lack, other: with what stringency are these terms being used?

A major difficulty is brought into focus with a question asked by Segal: 'One of the big problems with applying any kind of psychological criticism is to try to decide what is the object of the analysis. Are you trying to analyze the author; or ... the relationship between the reader and the text ...; or ... a particular character?'[36] Increasingly the answer to this question is 'the text', or 'the narrative'.[37] Françoise Meltzer puts the case very economically (though remaining faithful to the idea that Freud does have something to teach us about the psyche), in discussing Freud's necessary use of the known in order to describe the unknown (*das Unbewusste*, the original of 'the unconscious'): 'Freud will be "condemned" to describe the unconscious rhetorically, through analogies, metaphors, similes, etymological play, and anecdotes. And the way that future critical theory will choose to read those rhetorical tropes employed by Freud will ultimately ... tell us as much about the "economy" of rhetorical structures and the inner workings of narration as it will about the psyche.'[38] The linguistic turn of Lacan in particular and of post-structuralism in general is presumably largely responsible for this shift of emphasis towards looking at psychoanalysis as a model of figural language; important, too, have been the mounting reservations about the feasibility of analysing literary constructs ('characters', 'authors') as if they were human beings in an interactive setting;[39] and there may be a part played also by a tacit loss of faith in the scheme as a model of the mind—particularly in trans-cultural studies. The use of psychoanalytical models by Brooks and Quint may be regarded by the acolytes, for whom Freud and Lacan remain clinicians, as a domestication.[40] Still, for most critics the use of

---

[36] Segal (1992), 171. I must declare my debt here to the highly interesting response of S. Georgia Nugent to the APA Panel on 'Roman poetry and recent developments in psychoanalytic criticism', 28 Dec. 1993.

[37] Brooks (1984) has been particularly influential; his work has stimulated fine work on the *Aeneid* in Quint (1993), 50–96. An interesting parallel to this move is to be found in the emergence of narrative therapy, on which see White and Epston (1990), a reference I owe to Dr James Gustafson.

[38] Meltzer (1990), 149.   [39] Bonime and Eckardt (1993).

[40] Meltzer (1990), 161: 'as with Freud, the unconscious for Lacan represents a clinical problem, a force underlying the behavior of real, living and breathing patients; it is not only an abstract concept to be imagined in differing ways. If the literary critic is ultimately faced with the text, the practicing analyst faces the patient ... "Unconscious" at the moment of such confrontations begins to mean and to matter in fundamentally separate ways.'

psychoanalysis in narratology is doubtless made more acceptable by
the fact that the figural nature of the model's claims is so much more
obvious than it is when the psyche is the object of analysis. But then
one is left wondering what the power of the model really is, and
whether any more is being said than that Freud was some kind of
narratologist *avant la lettre* (a description which need not be read dis-
missively, depending on how much value you accord narratology).

Whatever models we employ, we have to acknowledge that there is
no use pretending that we are not employing them, and we also have to
acknowledge that we will often be employing them unconsciously
(they will be 'employing' *us*). As students of long-vanished cultures, we
face continually the challenge of respecting our place in history as
observers and the place in history of the artefacts we are observing.[41]
There is—unfortunately, in the opinion of some—no universally valid
way of adjudicating this process, for the criteria by which we perform
it are always under negotiation.

These issues are intractable enough, but we need, in conclusion, to
uncover a larger presupposition which underpins the approach not
only of Heath but of most critics, classicists or not. This is the assumption that criticism somehow explains literature, is adequate to it in
some worthwhile sense. Let us begin with the comparatively mundane
observation that great works can or even must break the bounds of
interpretative possibility, redefining the critical practice needed to
read them, addressing an audience which is not (yet) there: in Wordsworth's formulation, 'every author, as far as he is great and at the
same time *original*, has had the task of *creating* the taste by which he is
to be enjoyed: so has it been, so will it continue to be'.[42] Margaret
Hubbard makes this point very cogently of Horace's *Odes*, for
example, adducing Cicero's philosophical works as an analogy.[43] From
this perspective, Heath's search for the most contemporary witnesses
presents us with the apparent paradox that it is precisely the contemporary generation who are often worst placed to respond to
original works in ways which later generations will find at all helpful
(this will of course be an unacceptable conclusion for those who
remain convinced that the goal of classical philology's interpretations
is no more than to reconstruct the ideal contemporary response).

[41] The oscillations involved in being self-conscious about this double commitment are
the subject of ch. 1 of D. F. Kennedy (1993).

[42] From *Essay Supplementary* to the *Preface* (1815); my thanks to David Hopkins for
this quotation.

[43] Hubbard (1973), 25.

Heath himself acknowledges the 'obvious danger ... in arguing from Greek literary theory and criticism to the underlying principles of Greek literary practice—that is, from secondary to primary poetics'; as he puts it, 'it is inevitably uncertain whether any given critic or theorist has correctly grasped the nature even of contemporary literary composition'.[44] We have to face the fact that a seance with an Augustan *grammaticus* on the subject of Horace's *Odes* would almost certainly yield us very little that we would value (except that his very incomprehension might jolt us into realizing just how shocking and novel these now tamely canonical poems were on first appearance).[45]

It is precisely his distance on the tradition which makes it possible for Donald Russell to make the synthetic critical judgements he does,[46] and acknowledging this fact helps put us in a position to appreciate the pitfalls of confusing the modes of explanation with the modes at work in the phenomenon being explained. The analogy with the use and study of language is perhaps instructive. Alcaeus and Stesichorus had an active knowledge of Greek incomparably superior to that of anyone now alive, yet they knew no formal Greek grammar, and the Regius Professor understands—in some meaningful sense of the word—the workings of the Greek language in ways that they could not, and in ways that for certain purposes we will value more highly than whatever intuitions about language may be gleaned from witnesses of the archaic period. Similarly, the anthropologists have been tussling for a long time with the problems involved in recognizing that the very act of analysis, by constructing a sense-making whole, creates an intelligibility of a kind that is not accessible to the members of the society being analysed.[47] The clearest discussion of this dilemma which I know

[44] Heath (1989), 10; cf. the points made by G. A. Kennedy (1991), 116.

[45] This paragraph is not meant to impugn the value of such contemporary critical evidence as we may have for any period; nor is it meant to deny the practical usefulness of reconstructing, as best we can, how a contemporary reader might have reacted to any particular work. The problem is that most critics are very good at getting into a position where they can claim that there is an uncanny overlap between the way they read a text and the way the ideal contemporary reader would have read it too. Further, scholars of this persuasion imply by their practice that something like the *Odes* or the *Aeneid* could somehow be apprehended in one take, 'exhausted', if you will, by their first readership. Finally, the search for the ideal contemporary reader's response makes it practically impossible to entertain the notion of a diverse, contentious initial audience.

[46] Above, n. 7; cf. Russell (1967), 141–3, where he 'stands back from the detail' of the rhetorical tradition in order to put the large picture within the frame of a modern critical theory, only then being in a position to advance his propositions about how to read Catullus and Propertius.

[47] Even if they would no longer adopt the patronizing perspective of Malinowski—as reported by Macintyre (1970), 113—'who insisted that the native Trobriander's account

of is provided by David Trotter, reviewing a book on the semiotics of gesture: 'the cognitive power which the idea of codification generates in the historian's own understanding of language has been projected onto the world he is studying, where it becomes a moral and social power universally available'.[48]

For our purposes, it is not a matter of saying that one of these modes of knowledge or experience is preferable to the other in each case. Rather, we must recognize that the incompatibility which many detect between modern criticism and ancient literature is not something *sui generis*, but an example of a gap which will be found between any critical act and its object of study.[49] There are diverse ways of dealing with the gap. For myself, I would follow the lead of Bernard Harrison, who constructs a theory designed to show 'why since Plato [literature] has been permanently at war with theory, and why its role is endlessly to exceed and transgress the insights and outlooks fostered by theory'.[50] Classicists, of all people, should have the historical perspective to see that any critical act is provisional: in this way we may resist not only the historicists' claim to objective recovery of contemporary response, but also the whiggish triumphalism of many of the modern schools. For the gap which Donald Russell rightly sees between the literature and theory of the ancients has always been there, and always will be.

---

of Trobriand society must be inadequate, that the sociologists' account of institutions is a construction not available to the untutored awareness of the native informant'. The language/grammar analogy is itself used in this connection, normally in a recuperative fashion, as if the interpretative scheme of the observer is genuinely valid for the participant, only 'unconsciously': Lawson and McCauley (1990), 77.

[48] Trotter (1992), 14.

[49] Indeed (as Jacques Lezra suggests to me), if literature is itself in some ways a form of literary criticism, then literature may be thought of as building this gap into what is constitutively literary.

[50] Harrison (1991), 17; cf. Felman (1982), 207, on 'literality [*sic*] as that which is essentially impermeable to analysis and to interpretation, that which necessarily remains unaccounted for, that which, with respect to what interpretation does account for, constitutes no less than *all the rest*: "All the rest is literature," writes Verlaine.' I had not realized, until Stephen Hinds pointed it out to me, that my historical perspective here gives way to a transhistorical essentializing definition of 'the literary'. Well, let it give way.

24

On Impulse

MICHAEL WINTERBOTTOM

'Iuba, Scipio, Labienus in legionarios impetum fecerunt' (*B. Afr.* 52. 1). But one might suffer *impetus* from something less rational than a general: from a wild beast, or a disease. One might be carried along by one's own *impetus* when making an attack on another: *fert impetus ipsum* (Virg. *A.* 12. 369). The *impetus* assailing one might come from within oneself, a mental impulse, a burst of passion. When the word came to be used in literary criticism, it brought with it more than a hint of lack of control and even violence.

All the same, the great orator could not do without *impetus*: 'Quid denique Demosthenes? non cunctos illos tenues et circumspectos vi sublimitate impetu cultu compositione superavit?' (12. 10. 23).[1] A speaker needed drive, the onward movement that would carry the audience with him; and, with it, force.[2] Hence the appropriateness of the common comparison with a river; for a river too has its *impetus*.[3] On this model, the slender and circumspect Lysias hardly measured up at all: 'puro tamen fonti quam magno flumini propior' (10. 1. 78).[4] The

Some of the same material was exploited in a short paper given at the conference on 'Understanding the passions in Roman literature and thought' at the University of Exeter in July 1992, and in a lecture at the University of Helsinki in September 1993. This final version is offered to Donald Russell in admiration and affection; like anything else one might have written for him, he would have done it better himself. I hope that he will at least find it appropriate, in the sense that its origin lies in my (unpublished) thesis on Quintilian Book Two, of which he was, with R. G. Austin, an examiner in 1962.

[1] All references, unless otherwise specified, are to Quintilian's *Institutio*.

[2] For the combination see also 6. 2. 10, 12. 2. 11 ('impetu quoque ac viribus ... est opus, ut vis amnium ...'), 12. 10. 64 (if my text is right); Cic. *Orat.* 229.

[3] *TLL* s.v. impetus 604. 56f.

[4] The Callimachean echo (perhaps not carried over from Dionysius) was not noticed by Peterson ad loc.: ἥτις καθαρή τε καὶ ἀχράαντος ἀνέρπει πίδακος ἐξ ἱερῆς ὀλίγη λιβὰς ἄκρον ἄωτον (*Hymn* 2. 111–12). The big river ('Ασσυρίου ποταμοῖο μέγας ῥόος, 108) comes just before. Other river passages in Quintilian include 5. 13. 13; 5. 14. 31 (eloquence, like big rivers rather than *ieiuni fontes*, should make a way for itself if it finds none available to it); 9. 4. 7; 9. 4. 61 (in a long period the ears 'ductae velut prono decurrentis orationis flumine tum magis iudicant cum ille impetus stetit').

middle style at least was a river, 'lenior ... amnis et lucidus quidem, sed virentibus utrimque ripis inumbratus' (12. 10. 60). But it was the grand style that had the real thrust: 'ille qui saxa devolvat et pontem indignetur et ripas sibi faciat multus et torrens,[5] iudicem vel nitentem contra feret, cogetque ire qua rapiet' (12. 10. 61). There might be, as in the case of Cicero, such a blending of styles as to disguise the force, 'ut ipsa illa quae extorquet impetrare eum credas, et cum transversum vi sua iudicem ferat, tamen ille non rapi videatur sed sequi' (10. 1. 110). The judge, in his helpless boat athwart the current, might have some illusion of being in control. In fact, *vis* was sweeping him away.[6]

But if the boat is out of control, how controlled is the river? The orator might make the audience go where he would, but might he not be carried away by his own *impetus*?[7] A safer analogy was that of the horseman. Sometimes, indeed, the orator had to ensure that the *impetus* of his own speech was not lost.[8] Too much attention to fitting words into pleasant mosaics could lead to a failure of heat[9] and drive, 'ut equorum cursum delicati minutis passibus frangunt' (9. 4. 113). On the other hand (though Quintilian is here talking about writing), when we find ourselves going too quickly, we should stop 'ut provideamus et ferentes[10] equos frenis quibusdam coerceamus, quod non tam moram faciet quam novos impetus dabit' (10.

---

[5] Tac. *Dial.* 24. 1 'quo torrente, quo impetu saeculum nostrum defendit!' (with Gudeman[2] ad loc.). Also 3. 8. 60 ('tumultuosius atque turbidius' follows) and 10. 7. 23 'id potius quam se inani verborum torrenti dare quasi tempestatibus quo volent auferendum'.

[6] No fun: 'non aliter quam qui adverso vix flumine lembum I remigiis subigit, si bracchia forte remisit, I atque illum in praeceps prono rapit alveus [9. 4. 7 suggests that Quintilian understood this as the river] amni' (*G.* 1. 201–3). Virgil pairs this passage with horses out of control (1. 512–14): see what follows.

[7] Sen. *Con.* 7. 1. 20 'quidam principia tantum habuerunt in sua potestate, deinde ablati sunt impetu'; Sen. *Ben.* 1. 10. 1 'sed longius nos impetus evehit provocante materia'. At 12 pr. 3 'suo iam impetu fertur' means 'carried *along* by', as in *Aen.* 12. 369 cited earlier.

[8] Cf. 3. 8. 60; 9. 4. 35 (worry about hiatus); 10. 7. 14 ('infelix verborum cavillatio'); 11. 2. 46 (weak memory); 11. 3. 134 (sitting down); 12. 9. 18 (over-preparation). Also Sen. *Ben.* 7. 8. 2 ('eloquentiae ... non concinnatae nec in verba sollicitae' contrasted with 'prout impetus tulit').

[9] Also associated with *impetus* at 10. 3. 6 and 17 (note also 10. 7. 13 'si calor ac spiritus tulit'). At 10. 3. 18 it is used in connection with emotions and contrasts with *diligentia*. See also n. 11 below, and *calescimus* in Ovid, *Fast.* 6. 5, cited below, p. 321; also Plin. *Ep.* 2. 19. 2 (lost in recitation) and 7. 9. 6 ('recalescere ex integro et resumere impetum fractum').

[10] *Si vera lectio*. It would, I think, be transitive ('carrying us away'). I am not sure the analogy works well; perhaps better that with long-jumping at 10. 3. 6 ('et velut repetito spatio sumit impetum').

3. 10).[11] The horse is an irrational beast, but he can be ruled by rational man, made to run in the right direction and at the right speed.

This is a comforting picture: the orator in control of his mettle-some medium. More comforting still if he is, like the charioteer in Plato's *Phaedrus* (253–4), in full charge of lower elements of the soul. He should certainly govern his own emotions: 'bonus altercator vitio iracundiae careat; nullus enim rationi [i.e. the speaker's own rational judgement] magis obstat adfectus, et fert extra causam plerumque, et deformia convicia facere et mereri cogit' (6. 4. 10). But it was all very difficult. Quintilian followed Cicero in believing that to move others one must be moved oneself, and he explains how such emotion should be induced: 'nos illi simus quos gravia indigna tristia passos queremur, nec agamus rem quasi alienam, sed adsumamus parumper illum dolorem' (6. 2. 34). He had been able to do the trick himself: 'frequenter motus sum ut me non lacrimae solum deprenderent, sed pallor et veri similis dolor' (6. 2. 36). *Like* the real thing: so perhaps it was only an act (compare the tragedians in 6. 2. 35), and the speaker's self-control was not prejudiced.[12] At least it was only for a little.

What, meanwhile, of the auditors? They are not even the horses of this analogy. We have, for them, to return to the raging river; and in the face of its fury, the judges, though rational, are under *force majeure* that makes them more helpless than a bridled horse. And they are thus dominated because the orator can play on their emotions and deprive them for a time of their reason. In the end their pity will weaken: 'fatigatur lacrimis auditor et requiescit et ab illo quem ceperat impetu ad rationem redit' (6. 1. 28). But in the meantime 'cum irasci favere odisse misereri coeperunt, agi iam rem suam existimant,[13] et, sicut amantes de forma iudicare non possunt quia sensum oculorum praecipit animus, ita omnem veritatis inquirendae rationem iudex omittit occupatus adfectibus: aestu fertur et

---

[11] Cf. also the slave employed by C. Gracchus to play the flute in order to regulate his *pronuntiatio*, 'quia ipsum calor atque impetus actionis attentum huiusce temperamenti aestimatorem esse non patiebatur' (V. Max. 8. 10. 1). Something similar is related of Haterius (Sen. *Con.* 4 pr. 8).

[12] Cf. Cic. *Tusc.* 4. 55 'oratorem vero irasci minime decet, simulare non dedecet' (so also Sen. *De Ira* 2. 17. 1). But note *Orat.* 130–2 as well as *De Orat.* 2. 189f.

[13] Cf. 6. 2. 34 (cited above) on the orator: 'nec agamus rem quasi alienam'. The speaker takes over his client's feelings and transfers them to the judges. One is reminded of the analogy of the magnet and rings in Plato's *Ion*: the rhapsode's tears (535c5), aroused by pity for the Homeric characters, are matched by those of the audience (535e1).

velut rapido flumini obsequitur' (6. 2. 6). The *impetus* of the speech is all-powerful because its counterpart is the *impetus* of the hearer's emotions.

Such a doctrine implies some degree of contempt for the judges thus manipulated. *impetus* was characteristic of children, of youth, of animals, of the Roman mob;[14] and it might have been tactful to the propertied persons who made up Roman juries to represent them as less easily swayed. The ideas were Greek, and perhaps reflected an aristocratic disdain for the large juries of democratic Athens. It was Greeks again who had raised moralizing objections to such methods, as Quintilian well knew: 'fuerunt et clari quidem auctores quibus solum videretur oratoris officium docere, ... primum quia vitium esset omnis animi perturbatio, deinde quia iudicem a veritate depelli misericordia gratia ira similibusque non oporteret' (5 pr. 1). But Quintilian could no more accept so austere a view than Cicero: 'nihil est enim in dicendo' (he makes Antonius say to Catulus) 'maius quam ut faveat oratori is qui audiet, utique ipse sic moveatur ut impetu quodam animi et perturbatione magis quam iudicio aut consilio regatur: plura enim multo homines iudicant odio aut amore aut cupiditate aut iracundia aut dolore aut laetitia aut spe aut timore aut errore aut aliqua permotione mentis quam veritate ... aut legibus' (*De Orat.* 2. 178). It was just a fact that such emotions influenced judgements; and in that case it was essential that an orator should appeal to those emotions. Antonius put very frankly what Plato had found so shocking about the art of rhetoric.

So far we have seen nothing to surprise us in the use of the word *impetus* in the discussion of oratory. The speaker and his speech have *impetus* like the horses and rivers to which they are compared. That onrush corresponds to the onrush of emotions that override the hearer's reason. In this connection too *impetus* is commonly used in Latin.[15] *impetus* and *ratio* make a natural contrast, for 'sunt quidam

---

[14] 1. 3. 10 (boys); Sen. *De Clem.* 1. 1. 3 (youths); 2. 20. 9 (lions); Cic. *Rep.* 1. 9 ('insanos atque indomitos impetus volgi').

[15] Our evidence suggests that Cicero was all-important in extension of the use of *impetus* to mental assaults (from *Inv.* 2. 17 'impulsio est quae sine cogitatione per quandam affectionem animi facere aliquid hortatur, ut amor, iracundia, aegritudo, vinolentia [cf. Dig. 48. 19. 11. 2] et omnino omnia in quibus animus ita videtur affectus fuisse ut rem perspicere cum consilio et cura non potuerit et id quod fecit impetu quodam animi potius quam cogitatione fecerit'; cf. 2. 19, but not thus in *Ad Her.*). The influence of the Stoic ὁρμή is obvious (Ambrose, *De Off.* 1. 228 'appetitus ille qui quasi quodam prorumpit impetu, unde Graece ὁρμή dicitur quod vi quadam serpente proripiat', building on Cic. *Off.* 1. 101; as Harry Hine remarks to me, ὁρμή like *impetus* could get out of hand: πᾶν πάθος ὁρμὴ πλεονάζουσα (*SVF* i.205)). The extension to discussion of oratory comes in *De Orat.*

inrationabiles impetus animorum'.[16] The assault of various strong emotions—grief, love, anger—is regularly called *impetus*.[17] Such onrushes overwhelm the defences of reason. And the most notable case of loss of self-control, madness itself, is described in the same terms.[18] The image of the horse returns in such a passage as Seneca's 'moderare, alumna, mentis effrenae impetus, I animos coerce' (*Phaed.* 255–6).[19] Nor is river imagery found inappropriate for πάθη: 'potius fugientia ripas I flumina detineas...Iquam miseros lugere vetes' (Stat. *Silv.* 5. 5. 62–4).

We come now, however, to a more specialized usage, though one that arises naturally enough from the others.[20]

In 2. 11–12 Quintilian, embarking on the preliminary questions traditionally dealt with in the προλεγόμενα to an *ars rhetorica*, confronts opponents who deny the very need for such an *ars*.[21] These 'naturalists' rely on their own talents and on the ordinary school exercises; they think that eloquence has no need of *praecepta*. They make do, that is, with two of the customary triad, φύσις and ἄσκησις; τέχνη they repudiate. '(2. 11. 3) Igitur impetu dicere se et viribus uti gloriantur: neque enim opus esse probatione aut dispositione in rebus fictis, sed ... sententiis grandibus ... (4) Quin etiam in cogitando nulla ratione adhibita aut tectum intuentes magnum aliquid quod ultro se

---

[16] [Quint.] *Decl. Min.* 325. 13. For the contrast see *TLL* s.v. impetus 609. 23f. Note Cic. *Inv.* 2. 164 'temperantia est rationis in libidinem atque in alios non rectos impetus animi firma et moderata dominatio'.

[17] 6 pr. 14 (grief: contrast 'alia cogitatio'); Sen. *Ep.* 104. 13 (love: see n. 19 below); V. Max 5. 9. 1.

[18] e.g. Cic. *Dom.* 119 'omni impetu furoris in eum civem inruerit'—for madness can lead to physical attack (cf. Sen. *De Ira* 3. 3. 2 *ruat*).

[19] Or (again) Sen. *Ep.* 104. 13 ('cupiditates *refrenavit* ... *indomitos* amoris impetus *fregit*').

[20] For Greek use of ὁρμή (see above, n. 15) in literary criticism, Doreen Innes points out to me e.g. Philostratus, *VS* 568 χολή τε γὰρ ἄπεστι τοῦ λόγου καὶ ὁρμαὶ πρὸς βραχύ ('outbreaks on the spur of the moment' Wright) and, for inspiration, ibid. 533 (Polemo) προοίμιον ποιούμενος τοῦ λόγου τὸ μὴ ἀθεεὶ τὴν περὶ αὐτοῦ ὁρμὴν γενέσθαι οἱ. But, as she remarks, φορά is also relevant: Longinus 2. 2 (φορᾷ καὶ ἀμαθεῖ τόλμῃ), and 20. 2 of πάθος (cf. 21. 2); [Lucian], *Dem. Enc.* 7 (of narrative flow?). The two combine of inspiration in θεοφορήτῳ ὁρμῇ at Philostratus, *VS* 509, cited in n. 31 below.

[21] Cf. Longinus 2. 1. Cf. later Augustine, *De Doctr. Chr.* prol. 4 ('praecepta tractandarum scripturarum' not needed, *divinum munus* enough). We hear of naturalists elsewhere in Quintilian. But whereas in Book 2 they sound like Asian declaimers (epigram, *pravae voluptates*), they later resemble the neo-Atticists: 9. 4. 3 'quosdam ... qui curam omnem compositionis excludant, atque illum horridum sermonem, ut forte fluxerit, ... magis naturalem ... esse contendant'; 11. 3. 10 'sunt ... qui rudem illam et qualem *impetus* cuiusque animi tulit actionem iudicent fortiorem ... sed non alii fere quam qui etiam in dicendo curam et artem et nitorem ... ut adfectata et parum naturalia solent improbare'; 12. 10. 40 'quidam nullam esse naturalem putant eloquentiam nisi quae sit cotidiano sermoni simillima' (and what follows).

offerat pluribus saepe diebus expectant ... (6) Qui plurimum videntur
habere rationis non in causas tamen laborem suum sed in locos intend-
unt ... (7) Unde fit ut dissoluta ... oratio cohaerere non possit ...
Magnas tamen sententias et res bonas (ita enim gloriari solent [*cf. Sen.
Con. 7 pr. 9*]) elidunt; nam et barbari et servi, et, si hoc sat est, nulla est
ratio dicendi.... (2. 12. 9) Verum hi pronuntiatione quoque famam
dicendi fortius quaerunt; nam et clamant ubique et omnia ... emugiunt,
multo discursu anhelitu, iactatione gestus, motu capitis furentes. ...
(11) At illi hanc vim appellant quae est potius violentia: cum interim non
actores[22] modo aliquos invenias sed ... praeceptores etiam qui, brevem
dicendi exercitationem consecuti, omissa ratione ut tulit impetus passim
tumultuentur, eosque qui plus honoris litteris tribuerunt ineptos et
ieiunos et tepidos et infirmos, ut quodque verbum contumeliosissimum
occurrit, appellent. (12) Verum illis quidem gratulemur sine labore, sine
ratione [*cf. 2. 20. 2*], sine disciplina disertis.'

It is clear why Quintilian disliked these people. As teachers they
were rivals who might seem to offer pupils an easier and more
attractive ride than the austere school of Quintilian. As pleaders, they
were a disgrace to the profession, yet might be successful without
deserving to be. If they were right, there was no point in Quintilian
writing the *Institutio* at all. His criticisms are accordingly edged with
satire and irony.

We saw that Quintilian found admirable in Demosthenes his *vis* and
his *impetus* (12. 10. 23). The naturalists seem to be boasting of the
same qualities. As to *vis*, Quintilian argues that in their case it is rather
to be called *violentia*. He devotes a good deal of the passage to denying
that such speakers truly speak *fortius* than the educated.[23] One notices,
particularly, his disapproval of indiscriminate abuse, which may bring
danger to speaker and client alike (2. 12. 4):[24] a warning that coheres
with the already cited advice that the good *altercator* should avoid
anger. The naturalists are represented as lacking self-control as well as
education.

Indeed, the claim to speak *impetu* Quintilian turns back against its
proponents by exploiting the familiar contrast between *impetus* and

---

[22] For naturalists in the courts see my remarks in *JRS* 54 (1964), 90–7.

[23] See 2. 12. 1–3. For *fortiorem* cf. 11. 3. 10 (cited in n. 21). 'Force' went with 'virility'
(9. 4. 3, 11. 3. 10 'solam viris dignam'); compare the Atticist attacks on Cicero as effemin-
ate (12. 10. 12 'viro molliorem'). Note Cic. *De Orat.* 1. 231 'fortem et virilem' (also Sen.
Ep. 114. 22).

[24] Cf. 12. 9. 8–13. Even the naturalists' abuse of people like Quintilian is random: 'ut
quodque verbum contumeliosissimum occurrit' (2. 12. 11, cited above).

reason. It is of course true that the primary sense of *ratio* in these sections—*nulla ratione adhibita, qui plurimum videntur habere rationis, sine ratione disertis*—is 'method'; these people lack the ὁδός which is an integral part of a τέχνη.[25] But there is some hint of the deeper connotation of 'reason'. These shouting and wildly gesticulating speakers are described as *furentes*.[26] Less emotively, Quintilian argues that the uneducated speaker is liable to lack *order*.[27] The speech will not hang together (2. 11. 7), with the result that the speakers *passim tumultuentur* (2. 12. 11); for (7 pr. 3) 'oratio carens hac virtute [*sc.* ordo] tumultuetur necesse est et sine rectore fluitet nec cohaereat sibi'. 'Good things' and 'big epigrams' are, in Quintilian's eyes, no substitute for the basic virtue of organization. So far as the appeal to nature is concerned, Quintilian answers elsewhere that to be an orator it is not enough just to be born (11. 3. 11; cf. Sen. *Ben.* 3. 30. 4). On the contrary, 'id est maxime naturale quod fieri natura optime patitur' (9. 4. 5). Seen in this light, *natura* is a guide to be followed in the pursuit of the highest standards, not a licence to ignore the precepts of one's betters.[28]

To a degree, the naturalists were pressing the claims of extempore oratory. Quintilian describes unsympathetically the disorganized nature of such preparation as they did (2. 11. 4); and when it came to the actual speech 'abrupta quaedam, ut forte ad manum venere, iaculantur' (2. 11. 6). It is illuminating to compare, and contrast, with their procedures what Quintilian will say about extemporization.

At the writing stage, gazing at the ceiling and rousing one's thought processes by humming (cf. 2. 11. 4) will not do; only an orderly consideration of 'quid res poscat, quid personam deceat, quod sit tempus, qui iudicis animus' will enable us to approach composition 'humano[29] quodam modo' (10. 3. 15). Nor is it any better first 'decurrere per

[25] See 2. 17. 41 (Cleanthes) 'ars est potestas via, id est ordine, efficiens'; Dion. Hal. *Comp. Verb.* 206 ὁδοῦ τε καὶ τέχνης.

[26] 3. 8. 59 'cur initio furioso (? -ose) sit exclamandum non intellego'; 11. 3. 45 'ne dicamus omnia clamose, quod insanum est'; Cic. *Brut.* 233 (cf. *De Orat.* 3. 136 'clamore et . . . verborum cursu'). For shouting cf. 4. 2. 37 '*tumultu* et vociferatione'; 7. 1. 44 'pulchre fuerit cum materia *tumultu* et clamore transactum' (associated with 'sententiae praecipites'); Lucian, *Rhet. Praec.* 15.

[27] Cf. Sen. *Con.* 4 pr. 9 (the extemporizer Haterius) 'is illi erat ordo quem impetus dederat' (on the same man Tac. *Ann.* 4. 61 'impetu magis quam cura vigebat').

[28] Typical are 4. 5. 3; 5. 10. 101; 7. 1. 40; 8. 3. 71; 12. 10. 44 'quo quisque plus efficit dicendo, hoc magis secundum naturam eloquentiae dicit'.

[29] A striking adjective: *impetus* is less than human (Sen. *De Ira* 2. 16. 1 'errat qui ea (*sc.* animalia) in exemplum hominis adducit quibus pro ratione est impetus: homini pro impetu ratio est.'

materiam stilo quam velocissimo ... sequentes calorem atque impetum': even the revised version of such effusions leaves traces of the original superficiality (10. 3. 17).

We come to extempore speech in 10. 7. It is praised as an indispensable weapon in an orator's armoury, one which he must be able to use even though he might prefer not to (10. 7. 4). But it is noticeable that Quintilian's account stresses the features that make his ideal of extemporization so different from the practice of the naturalists. In particular, it is not just a gift of nature. An *usus inrationalis*, analogous to the eye's ability to read without conscious thought, is conceivable (11), but it must be preceded by *ars*, 'ut ipsum illud quod in se rationem non habet in ratione versetur' (12).

That *ars* is as learnable as anything else in rhetoric, and it only comes with long practice. And, in a particular case, there is a set method, a *via*, to be followed consciously from start to finish of a speech (5–6). The declaimers criticized in 10. 7. 21 who 'exposita controversia... verbum petant quo incipiant'[30] are the extreme case of the naturalists who 'certa sibi initia priusquam sensum invenerint destinant' (2. 11. 5). All those who do not speak 'disposite ornate copiose' seem to Quintilian to rant (*tumultuari*, 10. 7. 12) just like the naturalists 'all over the place' (*passim*) in 2. 12. 11. As for *impetus*, the word is tamed and found a safe home here. A successful extemporization is explained in terms of well-conceived emotions and fresh images that 'continuo impetu feruntur' (10. 7. 14), like any good passage of oratory, and Quintilian remarks, as he has done before, on the danger of over-anxious search for words. *Impetus* is given its place here subordinate to or hand in hand with art.

The declaimers who sat looking at the ceiling for 'aliquid quod ultro se offerat' (2. 11. 4, cf. 10. 3. 15 'expectaverimus quid obveniat') are in our parlance 'waiting for inspiration'. And there hangs over Quintilian's description of the naturalists a faint air of the mad poet. In 10. 7. 14 Quintilian himself points to an old saying that a god was present when an extempore stroke proved successful.[31] But we have

---

[30] This all goes back to the First Sophistic (Philostratus, *VS* 482: Gorgias' προβάλλετε). For the Second, see Russell (1983), 79–80; an extemporizer might prepare for a short time (cf. Quintilian's advice at 10. 7. 20).

[31] Cf. Philostratus, *VS* 509 τὸ γὰρ θείως (cf. μὴ ἀθεεί in 533, cited in n. 20) λέγειν ... ἀπ' Αἰσχίνου ... ἤρξατο θεοφορήτῳ ὁρμῇ αὐτοσχεδιάζοντος, ὥσπερ οἱ τοὺς χρησμοὺς ἀναπνέοντες (for this verb cf. 515), reminiscent of Longinus 13. 2, cited below (also Sen. *Suas.* 3. 6–7). For *impetus* of divination see Fronto p. 8 Naber (p. 5 van den Hout) (cf. Cic. *Div.* 1. 111).

seen that he explains such success away without recourse to super-natural aid ('ratio (!) manifesta est'). A Plato might be imagined to be inspired (10. 1. 81 'ut mihi non hominis ingenio sed quodam Delphico videatur oraculo instinctus'), but for the rest of us it is *ars* and *studium* that must make up the deficiencies of *ingenium*. A poet, of course, might see things differently.[32] Ovid, in Tomi, felt he could not compose as he had before (*Pont.* 4. 2). That could be put in the language of *ingenium* (15 'nec tamen ingenium nobis respondet ut ante') or of the Muses (27 'vix venit ad partes . . . Musa'); but another way of putting it was that 'impetus ille sacer qui vatum pectora nutrit, | qui prius in nobis esse solebat, abest' (25–6). Or, more obscurely, in the proem of *Fasti* 6: 'est deus in nobis; agitante calescimus illo; | impetus hic sacrae semina mentis habet' (5–6). Is the *impetus* the onrush of the inspiring god, who stirs up the poet to compose, or something internal to the poet that could be thought of as a god? In either case, the connection of *impetus* with the divine remains clear.

impetus in extemporization and inspiration[33] deserved to find some mention in the *Oxford Latin Dictionary*. But the extension of usage is slight. We are still concerned with something to be contrasted with *ratio*, something we can and perhaps should rein in with the help of reason, something which is ultimately alien and mysterious as well as indispensable.

Even the most devoted admirer of Quintilian will concede that for acuteness and eloquence he must bow to Longinus. But the two critics come together interestingly in the matters I have been discussing. If there is an answer to my criticism of Quintilian's admiration of the great orator sweeping his audience away on a flood of emotion, it might be on the same lines as what Donald Russell has written of Longinus: '[He] has a further expectation: he requires that the "emotion" shall be not only vehement but of a certain moral quality. . . . This is why the personality of the writer is important. He cannot be expected either to think grand thoughts or to generate and excite grand emotions if he is ravaged by desire for gain or money, or deaf to

---

[32] Cic. *Fin.* 4. 10 'quod etsi *ingeniis* magnis praediti quidam dicendi copiam *sine ratione* consequuntur, ars tamen est dux certior quam *natura*; aliud est enim poetarum more verba fundere, aliud ea quae dicas *ratione* et arte distinguere' (cf. *Arch.* 18).

[33] Sen. *Nat.* 3. 27. 13 'tantum impetum ingenii' of Ovid, *Met.* 1. 292 (picked up in 14 by *impetus* used of the flood); Petr. 118. 6 'hic impetus' on the civil war (contrasted with *ultimam manum*); Tac. *Dial.* 10. 6 'fortuitae et subitae dictionis impetu'; *Ann.* 14. 16 'impetu et instinctu'; Suet. *Aug.* 85. 2 *magno impetu* opposed to *succedente stilo*.

the calls of honour and posthumous fame.'[34] Quintilian's ideal of the *vir bonus*, whom the *Institutio* aims to train no less than the *vir peritus dicendi*, is reaching in the same direction. As for inspiration, Longinus, like Quintilian, connected it with the Pythia at Delphi: 'she is in contact with the tripod near the cleft in the ground which (so they say) exhales a divine vapour, and she is thereupon made pregnant by the supernatural power and prophesies as one inspired. Similarly, the genius of the ancients acts as a kind of oracular cavern, and effluences flow from it into the minds of their imitators' (13. 2, trans. Russell). But such imitation could only be the product of years of devoted study of the great models. For both Longinus and Quintilian genius was an infinite capacity for taking pains.

[34] Russell (1981*a*), 82.

25

Longinus, Sublimity, and the Low Emotions

DOREEN INNES

Longinus (as I will for convenience term the anonymous author of *On The Sublime*) lists five sources of the sublime: two are innate, from φύσις—greatness of thought (μεγαλοφροσύνη) and 'vehement and inspired emotion' (τὸ σφοδρὸν καὶ ἐνθουσιαστικὸν πάθος)—and three derive from technical skill—figures, diction, and word-arrangement (8. 1). The first is the most important, since its very presence guarantees sublimity (9. 1–2), but it is the inclusion of emotion which provokes immediate justification and polemic.[1] Emotion, Longinus argues, cannot be omitted on the grounds that it is to be identified with the sublime, because (*a*) not all emotions are sublime: 'certain emotions are found which are divorced from the sublime and low, such as cases of pity, grief, and fear' (καὶ γὰρ πάθη τινὰ διεστῶτα ὕψους καὶ ταπεινὰ εὑρίσκεται, καθάπερ οἶκτοι λῦπαι φόβοι), and (*b*) sublimity can be achieved without emotion; emotion is not therefore a necessary source of the sublime (8. 2). It is, however, highly desirable, and when it is noble emotion (8. 4 τὸ γενναῖον πάθος), and therefore compatible with the first source, it is the most effective means of achieving sublimity.

It is important here to distinguish such emotion as a source of sublimity from emotion as the proper impact of the sublime. Longinus almost never uses the vocabulary of πάθος to describe the emotional effect of the sublime (exceptions: 26. 3, 39. 2), presumably in order to avoid confusion of source and impact. In our response to the sublime strong emotion is both crucial and essential, since sublimity evokes surprise and is recognized by a violent response, an ἔκστασις or ἔκπληξις (1. 4).[2] Its whole aim is to stun, not merely please or persuade

---

[1] It is also the most original, since the others have analogues elsewhere in terms of (1) content and (2) the three technical divisions of style, e.g. DH *Isoc.* 3 = Theophr. F 691 Fortenbaugh.

[2] Vocabulary of surprise, τὸ θαυμάσιον esp. 1. 4, 7. 4, 9. 2 and 3, 10. 3, 35. 4 and 5, 36. 1 and 3, 39. 4; ἔκστασις 38. 5; ἔκπληξις 12. 5, 15. 2 and 11, 22. 4, 35. 4.

(1. 4),[3] and it is in short 'a special effect, not a special style'.[4] This emotional impact can, however, be achieved without emotion as a source. Longinus is not, therefore, concerned with the direct transmission of the same emotion in both source and effect, a direct linking of author and audience of the type frequent elsewhere; for example, Aristotle, *Rhetoric* 1408ᵃ23–5 'the listener always shares in the emotion of the speaker who speaks emotionally' (συνομοιοπαθεῖ ὁ ἀκούων ἀεὶ τῷ παθητικῶς λέγοντι), or Horace, *Ars Poetica* 102–3, 'si vis me flere, dolendum est | primum ipsi tibi'.[5] Nor is he concerned with specific, particularized effects, reactions such as pity, grief, and fear, but with a single undifferentiated emotional impact of what startles, an effect which may have as a contributory source individual emotions, provided that they belong to the second source, 'vehement and inspired emotion' (τὸ σφοδρὸν καὶ ἐνθουσιαστικὸν πάθος).

The emotion which does link author and audience is more general, a sense of shared inspiration.[6] The author experiences an overwhelming force of inspiration (e.g. 16. 2), and this evokes a corresponding emotional identification from the audience (32. 4 συνενθουσιᾶν), which is so strong that 'our soul feels as if it has itself created what it hears' (7. 2). In a passage which appropriately illustrates the inspiration of Plato's *Ion* on Longinus himself (13. 2), a chain of inspiration also links the author and the admired predecessor who has stimulated his creative imitation (συνενθουσιῶσι). Emotion might also be thought to form part of the very boldness and willingness to take risks which is intrinsic to greatness of thought (e.g. 33. 2–5); but apparently it is not, since that same boldness appears in the example specifically cited to show lack of emotion in 8. 2, the bold concept of the Aloadae heaping mountain upon mountain to build a path to heaven (Hom. *Od.* 11. 315–17).[7] Emotion as a source seems therefore to cover a rather narrower range: it will be an expression or display of emotion in

---

[3] Cf. 10. 4–6, 15. 9, 33. 5, 39. 1, 44. 1. Compare the three goals or 'officia', to move, delight, and persuade, in e.g. Cic. *Orat.* 69 ff.

[4] Russell (1964), p. xxxvii.

[5] Cf. e.g. Arist. *Po.* 1455ᵃ30 ff., Cic. *De Or.* 2. 189 ff.

[6] For vocabulary of inspiration, e.g. ἐνθουσιασμός and πνεῦμα, cf. 8. 4, 9. 11, 13. 2, 15. 1, 16. 2, 32. 4, 33. 5. False or insincere πάθος will conversely prevent the sublime: 3. 2 and 5, 32. 7.

[7] This boldness of the mind or ψυχή is contrasted with the boldness of these same Aloadae in Ps.-Arist. *De Mund.* 1 (cited by Russell (1964), on 35. 2): the mind can reach heaven, as the body cannot. For the ambiguous relationship with πάθος, cf. Mazzucchi (1990), 148; see also n. 14 below on φορά, and note a similar ambiguity between thought and creative force in 9. 1 παράστημα.

speech, and the examples will show a specific emotion such as anger or the excluded low emotions.

Yet even when he treats emotion as a source Longinus shows little interest in individual emotions. It is true that some discussion of individual emotions may well have occurred in the huge lacuna in 9. 4, the obvious place for an explanation of the wider problem of why emotion, unlike the other four sources, is given no independent analysis.[8] But in our surviving text there is a consistent pattern of emphasis on generalized vocabulary of strong emotion. Anger is prominent in his examples, but Longinus avoids terminology such as ὀργή, preferring the term θυμός, with its convenient associations of heroic spirit and the Platonic θυμός, a generalized type of vigorous, manly emotion.[9]

In view of this focus on generalized emotion, why then is Longinus specific in excluding passages full of pity, grief, and fear, οἶκτοι λῦπαι φόβοι?[10] I shall argue that it is because they are ignoble and unheroic: heroes do not ask for pity, they do not show grief and fear. But in our extant text no justification is offered. We are told merely that they are 'low', a rhetorical manipulation of the polar contrast with ὑψηλός, high/sublime (cf. e.g. 1. 1, 43. 6). But pity, grief, and fear are not a recognized group of 'low emotions', nor are 'low emotions' a recognized group of any specific emotions. On the contrary, Dionysius can without causing confusion contrast Thucydides' exploitation of some πάθη as 'cruel, terrible and deserving piteous laments' (οἴκτων ἄξια) with other πάθη as 'low and trivial' (ταπεινὰ καὶ μικρά), and he means by this that sufferings which can potentially arouse emotion in us are trivialized by a plain and cursory narrative (DH *Thuc.* 15). This is our first clue. The term 'low' (ταπεινός, cf. Lat. 'humilis') is used of what is plain and ordinary, such as low vocabulary (e.g. DH *CV* 3), or trivial objects of everyday life, as in 43. 3. In Longinus it most often describes

---

[8] See Russell (1981*b*), Innes (1995).

[9] Hector (27. 1), Demosthenes (12. 3, 27. 3, 32. 2). In 12. 3 Demosthenes with his greater emotion, παθητικώτερος, has a blazing fieriness of spirit, τὸ διάπυρον . . . θυμικῶς ἐκφλεγόμενον: compare the similar fieriness of the θυμός in Pl. *Tim.* 70c (cited in 32. 5). In 13. 4 παντὶ θυμῷ does not refer to anger but to a whole-hearted competitive enthusiasm, a possible meaning throughout.

[10] The plurals are significant. They suggest concrete examples of the relevant emotion; and at the risk of over-translation I shall use 'piteous laments' for οἶκτοι (cf. 9. 12, 11. 2, and e.g. DH *Thuc.* 15 and Marcellinus, *Vit. Thuc.* 56, both cited later in this chapter; see also n. 28). οἶκτοι are equivalent to ὀλοφύρσεις (as in 9. 12) or ὀδυρμοί, as in Pl. *Rep.* 3. 387d, where Plato scorns such laments by men of distinction, καὶ τοὺς ὀδυρμοὺς ἄρα ἐξαιρήσομεν καὶ τοὺς οἴκτους τοὺς τῶν ἐλλογίμων ἀνδρῶν: the whole passage, as Michael Winterbottom reminds me, may well have influenced Longinus.

the nature of an author,[11] as in 3. 4, 35. 2, 40. 2, and especially 33. 2–4, where 'low and mediocre natures' may be without flaw but are inferior to the necessarily flawed genius of the truly sublime authors, who achieve their top ranking by their very greatness of thought. Low emotions should therefore indicate emotions characteristic of the ordinary man and be incompatible with the first source, greatness of thought.

This last is confirmed by the way in which Longinus consistently pairs low and ignoble, and contrasts low and noble (3. 4, 9. 3, 9. 10, 35. 2). Noble emotion is also, as we have already seen, what Longinus particularly recommends, 'as if with a mad frenzy of inspiration breathing on and as it were inspiring our speech' (8. 4). The question then arises whether only noble emotions qualify for the sublime. But even if all ignoble emotions obstruct the sublime, there may be emotions which are in themselves neither noble or ignoble: these too are presumably a legitimate source, and since the emotion in the second source is 'vehement and *inspired*' (ἐνθουσιαστικόν), madness is the obvious example which Longinus admits and where nobility is not essential.[12]

If Longinus regards pity, grief, and fear as emotions characteristic of ordinary men, we can also explain the curious way in which this group has links with both emotion and *ethos* (πάθος and ἦθος).[13] Longinus gives no formal or independent analysis of emotion as a source, but he shows familiarity with standard ideas in the theory of emotion. Emotion is 'a transporting disturbance of the soul' (20. 2 φορά[14] ψυχῆς καὶ συγκίνησις), and with the loss of vigour (σφοδρότης) in old age the vigorous emotions of the *Iliad* decline into the quiet *ethos* of the *Odyssey* (9. 13–15). In this traditional division of strong and mild emotions, found already in Cicero, *Orator* 128, pity and fear are regular and important examples of πάθος, strong emotion. So for example, Quintilian distinguishes it from *ethos* as 'affectus ...

[11] So also e.g. DH *De Imit.* 2 ἄσεμνον καὶ ἄνανδρον καὶ ταπεινόν, *Ad Pomp.* 5 ἦθος ... ταπεινὸν καὶ μικρολόγον.

[12] I discuss later Sappho's madness of love and Orestes' mad vision of the Furies (10. 1–3, 15. 2 and 8). Note also the madness of inspiration (8. 4), the madness of Homer compared to that of the god of war and a raging mountain fire (9. 11), and the suicide of the mad Cleomenes by chopping his body into pieces (31. 2): this last is not noble but it is an example of extreme behaviour beyond the human norm, what Longinus elsewhere terms τὰ ἐγγὺς ἐκστάσεως ἔργα καὶ πάθη (38. 5).

[13] On the *ethos/pathos* distinction see Gill (1984).

[14] φορά: 20. 2 (bis), 21. 2, 32. 4, 33. 5, and esp. 2. 2 where φύσις needs technical skill, since it is unstable ἐπὶ μόνῃ τῇ φορᾷ καὶ ἀμαθεῖ τόλμῃ. This seems to refer to the wider notion of creative energy I discussed earlier. On this whole topic see Michael Winterbottom's chapter in this volume.

concitatos . . . vehementes motus', it is a temporary passion rather than a permanent disposition (6. 2. 8–10), and examples of individual emotions are anger, hatred, fear, envy, and pity (6. 2. 20 'circa iram, odium, metum, invidiam, miserationem fere tota versatur'); very similar is Anonymus Seguerianus, § 6 (*RG* i. 353 Sp.–H): 'emotion is a temporary disposition of the soul, stirring a more vehement (σφοδρο-τέραν) impulsion or antipathy; for example, pity, anger, fear, hatred, desire'.

Also traditional is the link of *ethos* with comedy and emotion/ πάθος with tragedy: so Quintilian 6. 2. 20, 'illud comoediae, hoc tragoediae magis simile', and Anonymus Seguerianus, § 234 (*RG* i. 394 Sp.–H), linking emotion with tragedy.[15] Similarly in Longinus tragedy and πάθος are linked by Euripides' special success in achieving a tragic effect from the two emotions of madness and love (15. 3), and *ethos* explicitly fits comedy (9. 15). Traditional too is the link Longinus draws between *ethos*, comedy, and ordinary, domestic life when he describes the *Odyssey* as a domestic comedy of manners (9. 15; cf. e.g. Cic. *Pro Rosc. Am.* 47, *Orat.* 128). *Ethos* and pleasure are also linked, especially 29. 2, 'the relationship between sublimity and emotion corresponds to that between pleasure and *ethos*'. Pleasure is not the goal of the sublime;[16] it is too smooth (ἄνθος and τὸ γλαφυρόν are rejected in 10. 4 and 6), and so although Demosthenes may lack Hyperides' *ethos*, charm, wit, and laughter, he triumphs because he has the crucial qualities of sublimity and forcefulness (34. 3–4). But the 'low emotions' disturb this antithesis of sublimity/πάθος and pleasure/*ethos*: they are strong emotions (πάθη), but they also have links with the latter.[17] Thus in addition to charm and *ethos* the *Odyssey* has grievings and piteous laments (9. 12), and Hyperides excels at pity (34. 2). The common link is the ordinary.[18]

Pity and fear are standard examples in lists of emotion, as we have seen in Quintilian and Anonymus Seguerianus above.[19] They also form

---

[15] Cf. Ps.-Apsines, *RG* i. 326–9 Sp.–H (πάθος here has the narrower meaning of pity).

[16] 1. 4, 39. 1, 44. 1 (cf. n. 3).

[17] So does laughter, an emotion of pleasure, πάθος ἐν ἡδονῇ (38. 5).

[18] In Apsines, *RG* i. 324 Sp.–H, Hyperides and Lysias are among the examples of appeals for pity, significantly in speeches of a domestic nature involving family; Simonides has a similar range: plain style, charm, and ability to evoke pity (Quint. 10. 1. 64); and he evokes pity μὴ μεγαλοπρεπῶς ἀλλὰ παθητικῶς (DH *Imit.* 2).

[19] Cf. e.g. Arist. *Rhet.* 1378ª22, Cic. *De Or.* 2. 196, DH *CV* 20—and Longinus himself, 'as in the case of those who really feel anger, fear, indignation, jealousy or any other emotion, for there are innumerable emotions' (22. 1).

a specific group,[20] and as such are often contrasted with anger and indignation. They form, for example, convenient polar opposites to illustrate emotional range in Dionysius of Halicarnassus, *Demosthenes* 54 and Cicero, *Brutus* 322, also of drama in *De Oratore* 2. 193, where Telamon after the death of his son, Ajax, is seen first to rage in anger, 'iratus furere', then in tears and grieving, 'flens ac lugens', or in the contrast of angry Chremes and grieving Telephus and Peleus in Horace, *Ars Poetica* 94–5, a passage I discuss further below.

The division into two groups is formalized in the theory of the epilogue in forensic oratory, where emotional appeals are subdivided into (*a*) pity (ἔλεος/'conquestio') and (*b*) indignation (δείνωσις/ 'indignatio').[21] This division is also applied outside the epilogue, and Apsines distinguishes three types of narrative (*RG* i. 258–9 Sp.–H): (*a*) παθητικαί (emotional = pitiful, cf. e.g. *RG* i. 327–9 Sp.–H), (*b*) σφοδραί (vehement = invective), and (*c*) ἠθικαί (character). Here strong emotion in contrast to quieter *ethos* is subdivided into the two categories of pity and invective, and though both παθητικός and σφοδρός can elsewhere cover all strong emotions (e.g. σφοδρός in the passage of Anonymus Seguerianus quoted above), in this narrower sense of aggressive emotion we can best compare σφοδρός/σφοδρότης in Hermogenes' theory of stylistic qualities (260 ff. Rabe). So there is probably deliberate ambiguity in Longinus' choice of σφοδρός to describe the emotion which is the source of the sublime (8. 1), since σφοδρός also particularly suits the link with angry indignation in 12. 5, where Demosthenic sublimity fits contexts of indignation and vehement emotion (δεινώσεις and σφοδρὰ πάθη). As in the case of θυμός, the terms σφοδρός/σφοδρότης usefully combine wider and narrower associations, both generalized strong emotion (9. 13, of Homer's *Iliad*) and the more specific emotion of anger. Similarly δείνωσις covers both intensification of anger (cf. 11. 2)[22] and the wider

[20] Cf. Gorg. *Helen* 9 '*fear*-encompassing shuddering, much-weeping *pity* and *grief*-loving yearning' (φρίκη περίφοβος καὶ ἔλεος πολύδακρυς καὶ πόθος φιλοπενθής); note also the tears and fear evoked by Homer's epic in Plato, *Ion* 535c, pity and fear as the emotions specific to tragedy in Aristotle's *Poetics* (e.g. 1453ᵇ12), or, to take a later example, the brave rescue of Achilles' corpse in Ovid, *Met.* 13. 282–3 'nec me lacrimae luctusve timorve l tardarunt, quin corpus humo sublime referrem'.

[21] Cf. e.g. Cic. *De Inv.* 1. 98. The division goes back to the sophists, cf. Pl. *Phdr.* 272a. Note also the choice of emotions in the summarizing conclusion to Cicero's analysis of emotion in *De Or.* 2. 196 'ut in dicendo irasci, ut dolere, ut flere possitis' (similarly Arist. *Rhet.* 1378ᵃ22 'e.g. anger, pity, fear').

[22] Note the following exclusion of piteous laments. Amplification in the service of the sublime is suitable for δείνωσις, but not for οἶκτοι.

sense of forcefulness (cf. 3. 1 δεδείνωται), as do δεινός/δεινότης (9. 5, 10. 4 and 6, 12. 4, 34. 4).[23]

In theories of style, advice is often given on emotions as a single undivided group. Emotion, for example, rejects Gorgianic artifices of style since it must appear spontaneous,[24] and for this point critics regularly cite examples of both anger and grief, such as Quintilian 9. 3. 102 'ubi vero atrocitate invidia miseratione pugnandum est, quis ferat contrapositis et pariter cadentibus et consimilibus irascentem flentem rogantem?—cum nimia in his rebus cura verborum deroget adfectibus fidem'. But a plain 'low' style is on occasion explicitly advised for the expression of pity and grief: so Aristotle, *Rhetoric* 1408ᵃ18–19 'and if you express the piteous, speak in a low style' (ταπεινῶς); Hermogenes 363 Rabe (for realism in style follow the recommendations given under σφοδρότης), 'except when you would evoke pity, expressing sorrow: for then you need everything to be simpler' (ἀφελεστέρων); Marcellinus, *Vita Thucydidis* 56 (Thucydides never loses grandeur in style), 'not even in piteous laments' (μηδὲ ἐν τοῖς οἴκτοις); and especially Horace, *Ars Poetica* 93–8:

> interdum tamen et vocem comoedia tollit
> iratusque Chremes tumido delitigat ore
> et tragicus plerumque dolet sermone pedestri,
> Telephus et Peleus cum, pauper et exsul, uterque
> proicit ampullas et sesquipedalia verba.

Here we find (*a*) a contrast of style between high tragic anger and low comic grief, and (*b*) a link between grief and low social status and self-esteem: Telephus and Peleus are poor and in exile. Horace again contrasts anger and grief in 109–10, where Nature 'aut impellit ad iram I aut ad humum maerore gravi deducit et angit.' Here there is open recognition of inferiority in the low bodily posture: the claim to pity and the display of grief are accompanied by a 'low' suppliant position.

This is a commonplace. Compare, for example, Aristotle, *Rhetoric* 1380ᵃ27–8 'those who supplicate and entreat, for they are more lowly' (ταπεινότεροι), and Cicero, *De Inventione* I. 109 (one means of evoking pity is by entreaty) 'humili et supplici oratione ut misereantur'—and Cicero may foreshadow Longinus' contrast of low emotion and the sublime when he contrasts such suppliant lowness, 'humilitas et

---

[23] See Voit (1934).
[24] This goes back in part at least to Theophrastus: see DH *Lys.* 14 = F 692 Fortenbaugh.

obsecratio', with 'virtus et magnificentia'. So in his *Pro Milone* Cicero presents Milo as the *vir fortis*, a heroic figure of *animi magnitudo*—a hero who refuses to weep and make the usual appeals to pity (92 ff.). This strategy was full of risk, as we can see from the criticism of Thucydides' portrayal of Pericles in Dionysius of Halicarnassus, *Thucydides* 45: as a defendant Pericles should not have rebuked the Athenians, a defendant should use countless tears and appeals for pity, using words which are low ($\tau\alpha\pi\epsilon\iota\nu\sigma\iota$) and mollify anger.[25]

It is heroes who spurn fear, grief, and appeals for pity, and these emotions are sometimes termed 'low', as in Statius, *Thebaid* 1. 444–5, where a reaction of anger is appropriate proof that Tydeus and Polynices are 'not low' ('nam vos | haud humilis tanta ira docet'), and 10. 363, where grief is proof of a 'low' mind, 'mens humilis luctu'. In consolation literature excessive grief is weak and unmanly, and the mourner should 'recover the spirit of a brave and noble man' (Plu. *Mor.* 121 f.).[26] In terms of genre too, elegy[27] is a genre of mourning and therefore soft; for example, Horace, *Odes* 2. 9. 17–18 'desine mollium tandem querellarum', whereas epic is of war and heroes, and is brave, 'forte epos' (Hor. *Sat.* 1. 10. 43).

This then is why $\sigma\iota\kappa\tau\sigma\iota$ $\lambda\hat{\upsilon}\pi\alpha\iota$ $\phi\delta\beta\sigma\iota$ are for Longinus 'low' emotions: they are expressions of self-regarding pity, grief, and fear,[28] and such self-regarding emotions are all too human. They may be suitable for the aged Nestor lamenting the death of his son (9. 12, quoting Hom. *Od.* 3. 109–11), but they are incompatible with the heroism of an Ajax (9. 10, quoting Hom. *Il.* 17. 645–7): when darkness prevents Ajax fighting, he prays for light, 'and in light even kill me': a prayer for life would be 'too low for the hero'. The Seven in Aeschylus (*Sept.* 51) show similar heroism when they swear an oath 'without self-pity' (15. 5 $\delta\iota\chi\alpha$ $\sigma\iota\kappa\tau\sigma\upsilon$). So too (14. 3) if an author were in fear ($\epsilon\iota$ . . .

[25] Socrates similarly spurns supplication: so Cic. *De Or.* 1. 231 and *Tusc.* 1. 71 'nec iudicibus supplex fuit adhibuitque liberam contumaciam a magnitudine animi ductam'. Compare the proud Palamedes (Gorg. *Pal.* 33).

[26] Cf. e.g. Pl. *Leg.* 949b $\mu\dot{\eta}\tau\epsilon$ $\dot{\iota}\kappa\epsilon\tau\epsilon\dot{\iota}\alpha\iota\varsigma$ $\chi\rho\dot{\omega}\mu\epsilon\nu\sigma\nu$ $\dot{\alpha}\sigma\chi\dot{\eta}\mu\sigma\sigma\iota\nu$ $\mu\dot{\eta}\tau\epsilon$ $\sigma\dot{\iota}\kappa\tau\sigma\iota\varsigma$ $\gamma\upsilon\nu\alpha\iota\kappa\epsilon\dot{\iota}\sigma\iota\varsigma$, *Rep.* 387e, Hor. *Epod.* 16. 39 'vos, quibus est virtus, muliebrem tollite luctum'.

[27] Compare also the typical 'low' pose of the lover in Roman elegy as a captive suppliant abased before his 'domina' (e.g. Prop. I. 1. 1–4).

[28] It is easier to see the ignobility of fear and grief. Pity is less self-evidently ignoble. But $\sigma\dot{\iota}\kappa\tau\sigma\iota$ are laments (see n. 10): they express self-pity (the type for which Longinus offers examples), or such strong identification with the sufferings of others that the speaker loses objectivity (cf. n. 32). They are not to be identified with pity in the sense of compassion, an emotion which comes from a position of superiority and which might well be compatible with the sublime. This is not a topic which Longinus tackles, and raises wider issues than can be pursued here.

φοβοῖτο), unable to look beyond his own life and times, he will as it were miscarry (ὥσπερ ἀμβλοῦσθαι) and be unable to bring to term what will last through eternity. Nature has created us not as a low and ignoble form of life,[29] but one instinctively drawn to aim high towards greatness and the divine beyond the boundaries of the cosmos (35. 2–3). The sublime transcends the mortal to reach for the immortal, and even 'raises us up to approach the greatness of god's thought' (36. 1).

Homer made his men like gods, his gods like men (9. 7). The former is admirable, as when Demosthenes immortalizes the dead with his powerful Marathon oath (16. 2–3). But the latter is inappropriate, as we see from criticism of Homer in 9. 6–7, where allegorical interpretation defends a passage which is impious and improper, ἄθεα καὶ οὐ σῴζοντα τὸ πρέπον. It lacks propriety, since it shows the god Hades in fear (ἔδδεισεν . . . δείσας)[30] that his kingdom will be ripped apart in the ruin of the universe: the concept of the universe in danger of ruin is sublime, but fear is a low emotion, a reaction appropriate not for a god but for ordinary sailors caught in a storm (10. 5, Hom. *Il.* 15. 624 ff., 'the sailors tremble in fear').

Fear, τὸ φοβερόν, is a legitimate reaction to a sublime passage. Homer's description of the storm which the sailors fear and the dissolution of the universe which Hades fears are sublime precisely because they evoke τὸ φοβερόν in us (10. 4–6, 9. 7), just as it is a sign of the lack of sublimity that no one feels fear, φοβεῖται, in reading Hyperides (34. 4), and the confused images of Boreas are condemned because they evoke scorn rather than fear (3. 1). But in all these cases τὸ φοβερόν is 'the fearsome' and clearly synonymous with τὸ δεινόν, the forceful. The effect on us is not a self-regarding fear (we share no sense that we are ourselves in danger),[31] but is that same sense of τὸ θαυμάσιον and awe which is evoked by great natural phenomena (cf. 35. 4–5), our recognition of the power of the natural force being described. The sublime raises us up and gives us a sense of joy, not abasement (7. 2).

[29] Man is born to look up, not down like the beasts (Pl. *Rep.* 586a, cited in 13. 1). Contrast 44. 8 for failure to look up, failure to reach for the immortal—and hence failure to achieve the sublime.

[30] There are many parallels for this criticism of Homer's gods, but Longinus' list of examples is strikingly adjusted to emphasize the more humiliating ('low') sufferings of the gods: wounds, punishments, tears, chains. Contrast the inclusion of more aggressive emotions and activities in Cic. *De Nat. Deor.* 1. 42 'ira inflammatos et libidine furentes . . . bella . . . odia . . .'; cf. e.g. Pl. *Rep.* 337e–378d, Isoc. *Bus.* 38–40.

[31] For fear and pity as emotions involving expectation of similar suffering, cf. e.g. Arist. *Rhet.* 1382^{b}26–7, 1385^{b}14–16, and Cic. *De Or.* 2. 211 ('ad suas res revocet').

Like fear for oneself, self-pity conflicts with the sublime. Yet it may seem an element in at least one passage which Longinus admires, Heracles' realization that he has killed his own children (40. 3, Eur. *Her.* 1235), 'I am truly full of disasters, and there is no longer any empty place'. Longinus denies any sublimity of thought and recognizes only one source of the sublimity, the word-order, a rare example of sublimity from technique alone, with no contribution from the innate sources. He seems to allow that the situation fits sublimity (the most likely interpretation of the phrase τῇ πλάσει ἀναλογοῦν), and that situation is one of intense emotion. Yet he ignores any contribution from emotion, as he must if it would be self-pity, since he cannot allow a low emotion to contribute to the sublime. Is he therefore inconsistent? Perhaps, but not necessarily or not entirely, if we recognize the very suppression of self-pity in the objectivity with which Heracles analyses his situation.[32] The pity is, as it were, transcended by the objective analysis. The same approach may justify the example in 23. 3, Oedipus' analysis of his family incest (Soph. *OT* 1403ff.): Longinus again identifies the source of sublimity in a technical matter of arrangement, the figure of plurality, which itself pluralizes the misfortunes. As with Heracles, it is the moment of recognition, and again the impact is strongly emotional, but we admire his lack of self-pity. It has been driven out by the extremity of his situation,[33] and Oedipus is not delivering a lament but expressing horror and indignation at what has happened to him.

I would also see a similarity here with Longinus' admiration of Sappho's concentrated, objective analysis of her emotions of love (10. 1–3), a notoriously curious example since love is traditionally an ignoble emotion:[34] but she describes her emotions as if they belonged to someone else (ὡς ἀλλότρια). As in the cases of Oedipus and Heracles, Longinus isolates a feature of arrangement as the source of sublimity: in those the arrangement of a few words, here in Sappho the arrangement of the material of a whole (short) poem. Compression is

[32] The dramatic situation is complex. There is a clear element of self-pity in 1237 (οἰκτρὸς γάρ εἰμι), but Heracles also shows proud defiance in his intention to kill himself (1243 αὔθαδες ὁ θεός, πρὸς δὲ τοὺς θεοὺς ἐγώ). This lack of humility will in context affect our reaction to 1245.

[33] Perhaps compare Arist. *Rhet.* 1386ª19ff., where Amasis as a prisoner weeps over the fate of a friend, but not at the sight of his own son taken off to be killed: the pity is driven out by τὸ δεινόν· τοῦτο μὲν γὰρ ἐλεεινόν, ἐκεῖνο δὲ δεινόν· τὸ γὰρ δεινὸν ἕτερον τοῦ ἐλεεινοῦ καὶ ἐκκρουστικὸν τοῦ ἐλέου καὶ πολλάκις τῷ ἐναντίῳ χρήσιμον.

[34] Cf. 15. 3, where Euripides lacks greatness of thought, but excels in tragic treatment of the two emotions of love and madness, μανίας τε καὶ ἔρωτας ἐκτραγῳδῆσαι.

also explicitly praised in Sappho. We may then compare Apsines, *Rhetores Graeci* i. 316 Sp–H, where Aeschines' concentrated presentation of the destruction of Thebes[35] is said to evoke not pity for the suffering but a stunning impact, ἡ γὰρ ἀθρόα τούτων δήλωσις ἔκπληξιν μᾶλλον ἔχει τῶν ἀκουόντων αὐτὰ ἢ ἔλεον τῶν πεπονθότων. Sappho moreover presents her love as if she is before a god (note how she trembles as nature trembles before the epiphany of Poseidon, 9. 8), her love is a madness, and like Heracles and Oedipus, her suffering is extreme, an example of τὰ ἐγγὺς ἐκστάσεως ἔργα καὶ πάθη (38. 5; cf. n. 12).

Yet Longinus suggests some discomfort with all three examples, Heracles, Oedipus, and Sappho, when in each case he adds a further example which is acceptable in terms of his most important source, greatness of thought: storms in Homer (10. 3ff.), heroes like Hector and Sarpedon (23. 3), and Dirce torn apart by a bull, a noble idea (γενναῖον καὶ τὸ λῆμμα), he says explicitly, whose impact the violent word-order reinforces (40. 4). Similarly the inappropriate idea of Hades' fear is immediately followed by a 'better' example (ἀμείνω) of god as true god, Poseidon in epiphany—and now it is nature which appropriately trembles in recognition of his divinity (9. 8 Hom. *Il.* 13. 18ff.). Euripides may have success in portraying madness and love, despite his lack of greatness of thought (15. 3 ἥκιστά γέ τοι μεγαλοφυὴς ὤν), but the examples of Orestes seeing Furies (15. 2 and 8)[36] are buttressed by further examples where Euripides' thought is also sublime: Phaethon riding a chariot through the stars in heaven, and a whole mountain in ecstasy before the epiphany of Dionysus (15. 4 and 6). Longinus prefers, as elsewhere, examples which have greatness of thought. This greatness is a bigness of idea (an ability to conceptualize mighty storms, for example, or the creation of the universe) rather than a narrowly moral concept, but it is a mind able to despise mundane ambitions like wealth which achieves the sublime (7. 1, 44. 6ff.). It is appropriate that Longinus' exclusion of the low emotions of pity, grief, and fear derives from the image of the hero,[37] who reaches out beyond the ordinary human, and so derives from moral rather than rhetorical criteria.[38]

[35] *Ctes.* 133 Θῆβαι δὲ Θῆβαι . . .

[36] Eur. *Orest.* 255–7 and 264–5. Here again the low emotions are eliminated: Orestes' fear of the Furies is subsumed by his madness, and Longinus derives the sublimity from the vividness with which Orestes visualizes the Furies. On madness see also n. 12 above.

[37] Cf. Segal (1987), 207–17. Compare also Aristotle's μεγαλόψυχος: see Russell (1964) on 3. 4 and 7. 1.

[38] The original stimulus to this chapter was Donald Russell's own query on 8. 2: 'Does not this remark exclude the most characteristic effects of tragedy?' I offer this chapter in less than adequate response to the many years of his generous advice and friendship.

26

'Longinus' and the Grandeur of God

MARTIN WEST

In the famous ninth chapter of Περὶ ὕψους, following the lacuna, we find 'Longinus'—or L, to use Donald Russell's convenient abbreviation—giving examples of sublimity achieved by conceptual power (τὸ περὶ τὰς νοήσεις ἁδρεπήβολον, 8. 1), and initially examples from descriptions of divinities and their doings (9. 5–9). Five illustrations are given, mainly from the *Iliad*. (I leave aside the counter-example from the pseudo-Hesiodic *Scutum*, which illustrates failure.) They are:

1. Eris grown to fill the whole space between earth and heaven (*Il.* 4. 442 f.).
2. The immense stride of the gods' horses (*Il.* 5. 770–2).
3. The terrific noise of the gods' battle, which alarms Hades down below (*Il.* 20. 60a–5).
4. Poseidon's passage from Samothrace to Aegae and his chariot journey across the sea (*Il.* 13. 18–19 + 27–9).
5. The Jewish God's creation of light and of the earth (Gen. 1: 3 + 9).

L did not collect these examples directly from their original sources. Quotations of the Homeric passages in other authors and comments on them in the scholia[1] show that they were current in rhetorical tradition. In the case of the fourth passage L himself acknowledges that it had been discussed by many before him. Perhaps some or all of them had been used in Caecilius' work on sublimity, which L aimed to supersede (1. 1). As for the citation of Genesis, phraseological parallels in L's work with Philo and Josephus[2] indicate his acquaintance with some Jewish Greek writing.[3]

---

[1] See Russell (1964), 90–2; Bühler (1964), 20–33; Mazzucchi (1992), 167–72.

[2] Norden (1954), *passim*; Russell (1964), pp. xxixf., xlf., 72f., 93f., 185, 187f., 191f.; Bühler (1964), 34; Mazzucchi (1992), 173.

[3] There can be no question of his being a Jew himself in view of the detached manner in which he alludes to ὁ τῶν Ἰουδαίων θεσμοθέτης, οὐχ ὁ τυχὼν ἀνήρ, the inaccuracy of his quotation (especially of verse 9), and the limitation of his biblical reference to the first few sentences of the Torah.

On the other hand, he is not mechanically recycling stock material from his predecessors. It is characteristic of him that his own enthusiasm is engaged by it. He personally feels the effects that he ascribes to the passages he quotes, and he does his utmost to define these effects and persuade others to feel them.[4]

What is it that so impresses him about those particular representations of the divine? In his preface he has written (1. 4):

οὐ γὰρ εἰς πειθὼ τοὺς ἀκροωμένους ἀλλ' εἰς ἔκστασιν ἄγει τὰ ὑπερφυᾶ· πάντη δέ γε σὺν ἐκπλήξει τοῦ πιθανοῦ καὶ τοῦ πρὸς χάριν ἀεὶ κρατεῖ τὸ θαυμάσιον, εἴγε τὸ μὲν πιθανὸν ὡς τὰ πολλὰ ἐφ' ἡμῖν, ταῦτα δὲ δυναστείαν καὶ βίαν ἄμαχον προσφέροντα παντὸς ἐπάνω τοῦ ἀκροωμένου καθίσταται.

(For grandeur produces ecstasy rather than persuasion in the hearer; and the combination of wonder and astonishment always proves superior to the merely persuasive and pleasant. This is because persuasion is on the whole something we can control, whereas amazement and wonder exert invincible power and force and get the better of every hearer.)[5]

As Russell succinctly puts it, 'whatever *knocks the reader out* is "sublime"'.[6] This counts for more than realism (τὸ πιθανόν) or charm (τὸ πρὸς χάριν). What sort of things in the natural world knock us out and fill us with awe? Above all, those that are huge and beyond the measure of human things; for (35. 2)

ἡ φύσις . . . εὐθὺς ἄμαχον ἔρωτα ἐνέφυσεν ἡμῶν ταῖς ψυχαῖς παντὸς ἀεὶ τοῦ μεγάλου καὶ ὡς πρὸς ἡμᾶς δαιμονιωτέρου.

(Nature . . . implanted in our minds from the start an irresistible desire for anything which is great and, in relation to ourselves, supernatural.)[7]

Hence we are struck with wonder and astonishment (θαυμάζομεν, ἐκπληττόμεθα) by the sight of mighty rivers such as the Nile, the Danube, or the Rhine, and even more by the Ocean; by the great fires of heaven, and the tremendous ejaculations of Etna (35. 4).

In depictions of the divine, accordingly, it is not surprising to find L being particularly impressed by passages which evoke a sense of vastness. His comments on them underline this.

1. Eris grows heaven-high: this, L suggests, gives us the measure of Homer as much as of the goddess.

---

[4] Cf. the remarks of Gibbon quoted by Russell (1964), 89; Bühler (1964), 24.

[5] Trans. Russell (1965).

[6] Russell (1965), p. xiii. Cf. π. ὕψ. 15. 2 τῆς μὲν ἐν ποιήσει (φαντασίας) τέλος ἐστὶν ἔκπληξις, τῆς δ' ἐν λόγοις ἐνάργεια.

[7] Trans. Russell (1965). 'Irresistible' renders the same Greek word as 'invincible' in 1. 4 quoted above.

2. A single leap of the gods' steeds takes them as far as a man on a cliff-top can see to the misty horizon. L introduces the quotation with the words ὁ δὲ πῶς μεγεθύνει τὰ δαιμόνια; 'How does Homer make the divine *big*?' And he continues: 'He measures their gallop by a cosmic distance. Anyone might reasonably comment, in view of the surpassing scale of the description, that if the divine horses take two such strides in succession they will find no more space in the world.'

3. The theomachy makes Hades afraid that his horrid realm will be torn open to the light of day. L comments as if this were actually happening.[8] The effect, he says, is to involve the whole universe in the battle, πάνθ᾽ ἅμα, οὐρανὸς ᾅδης, τὰ θνητὰ τὰ ἀθάνατα. The enlargement of the picture is certainly awesome (φοβερά, 9. 7), though L has reservations about the propriety of portraying the gods in such turmoil and disunity, unless the battle is to be interpreted allegorically.

4. He approves more of passages that represent divinity as ἄχραντόν τε καὶ μέγα . . . καὶ ἄκρατον, unsullied *and* great, and unadulterated. A new criterion appears here, that of purity, that is, being above the vicissitudes of our mortal world of strife; but *greatness* is still important. The passage quoted in illustration begins with the wooded mountains of Samothrace trembling under Poseidon's mighty tread as he departs; then it jumps a few lines to his driving across the sea from Aegae to Troy, with the creatures of the deep sporting about his chariot and the joyous sea parting before him. There are two interesting things about the text of the quotation. After the first line (*Il.* 13. 18) L has interpolated a verse which actually belongs immediately before his previous excerpt (*Il.* 20. 60). There too Homer had been speaking of Poseidon shaking mountains, and the similarity of contexts has somehow caused L (if not a predecessor who quoted both passages together) to transfer a line from one to the other.[9] Then after 13. 19 he has surprisingly omitted the lines

τρὶς μὲν ὀρέξατ᾽ ἰών, τὸ δὲ τέτρατον ἵκετο τέκμωρ,
Αἰγάς, ἔνθά τέ οἱ κλυτὰ δώματα βένθεσι λίμνης
χρύσεα μαρμαίροντα τετεύχαται, ἄφθιτα αἰεί.

The completion of the god's journey in four giant strides is exactly what we should have expected L to focus on, especially after his

---

[8] Bühler (1964), 26.

[9] The uncanonical line which he quotes before *Il.* 20. 61, on the other hand, should be regarded as a plus-verse of the type familiar in the pre-Aristarchean Homeric tradition; such verses sometimes do appear in quotations in writers of the early Roman period, such as Strabo, who are drawing on Hellenistic sources.

remarks about passage 2, where he may have been influenced by this passage. Did he pass over it because it came too close to the point he had already made? Or has the quotation suffered abridgement in the transmission?

5. The point of the Genesis quotation is once again the colossal, superhuman scale of divine activity and power. The whole element of light comes into being at God's command, and the whole earth.

That, then, is one factor involved in L's response to these passages: the sense of vastness. What else is to be said?

If a literary description (or anything else) is to astonish, it must above all confront us with something out of the ordinary. If the Nile amazes the Greek, it is because he knows no such rivers in his own country. An Egyptian from the Delta would no doubt be more thrilled by a Greek mountain. We can appreciate that L might well be impressed by the Jews' creation story once it had come his way. Here at least was something quite unlike anything to be found in the Greek classics. It was not just a grand conception, but one untarnished by any touch of the conventional or familiar.

The Homeric passages too are out of the ordinary. They go beyond the routine mechanisms of the epic *Götterapparat*; each has its own memorable individuality. They certainly do not reflect normal Greek conceptions of the gods and their workings.

The fact is that they all derive, by whatever means, from Near Eastern poetic tradition.

1. (*Il.* 4. 442 f.) Homer's Eris οὐρανῶι ἐστήριξε κάρη καὶ ἐπὶ χθονὶ βαίνει. It was an ancient motif in Mesopotamian hymns that the extent of a deity's power in heaven and earth was expressed in terms of his or her physical size. A Sumerian hymn to Inanna makes the goddess say:

> When I raise my hand, it encompasses (lit. completes) the heaven.
> I am the queen: my hand has no hand to rival it.
> When I lift my foot, it encompasses the earth.
> I am the queen: my foot has no foot to rival it.[10]

In another she declares:

[10] Haupt (1881), 127f. (+ an unpublished Neo-Babylonian duplicate), kindly translated for me by Dr J. A. Black.

> Heaven placed a crown on my head,
> Earth put a sandal on my foot.[11]

Similarly in an Akkadian hymn to the healing goddess Gula, dating from the late second or early first millennium. She says of her consort Ninurta:

> He wears the heavens on his head, like a tiara,
> He is shod with the earth, as with [san]dals.[12]

The Mesopotamian commonplace no doubt lies behind (pseudo-) Isaiah 66: 1, where Yahweh declares

> The heavens are my throne, and the earth my footstool.

The idea of a divine being stretching all the way from earth to heaven also appears in Ugaritic poetry of the fourteenth century BC. Here it is applied to a god's gaping mouth, which his victim cannot avoid: 'one lip to the earth, one lip to the heavens'.[13] But in some ways the nearest parallel to Homer's verse is to be found in Psalm 73: 9, where it is said of the arrogant:

> They have set their mouth in the heavens,
> and their tongue walks upon the earth.

The structure here is remarkably close to Homer's; even the variation of tenses matches.[14] And as in Homer, the subject is not a deity of cult but the graphic symbol of a human excess. The psalm is of post-exilic date, but no one will suppose the verse in question to derive from Homer rather than from older Hebrew models.

2. (*Il.* 5. 770–2) The huge leap of the gods' horses may be taken together with the similar motif of the god who crosses the sea with three or four giant strides.[15] Again we find a parallel in a recurrent formula of Ugaritic poetry. In the Baal Epic the goddess 'Anat announces her intention of going without delay to visit El, the father of the gods:

> I leave Uġar for the most distant of the gods,
> and Inbab for the most distant of the spirits—

[11] Zimmern (1913), No. 199 iii 17f.; Römer (1989), 647. The translation above has again been supplied by Dr Black.

[12] Foster (1993), 497 (lines 133f.). I have substituted 'earth' for Foster's 'underworld': *erṣetu* can mean the underworld, but it is the ordinary word for the earth, especially as the correlate of *šamû* 'heavens'.

[13] KTU 1. 5 ii 2 (Baal Epic; the voracious god is Môtu, Death); 1. 23. 61f.

[14] The Hebrew is: שַׁתּוּ בַשָּׁמַיִם פִּיהֶם וּלְשׁוֹנָם תִּהֲלַךְ בָּאָרֶץ .

[15] Besides *Il.* 13. 20f. quoted above, we may refer to Hera's peak-hopping progress from Olympus to Lemnos in 14. 225–30, and Apollo's single-stride *démarche* in Pind. *P.* 3. 43. Later imitations in Statius, Claudian, and Nonnus are noted by Bühler (1964), 24.

two footfalls below the earth's springs,
three loping strides.

The divine smith Kothar uses the same expression in responding with
alacrity to a summons from El.[16] The motif may also be found in
several Hittite mythical narratives which are translated from Hurrian
originals. In the text which H. A. Hoffner has entitled *The Song of
Silver*, two gods go on a journey together: 'They went forth, they made
the journey *1-anki*.' The adverb, formed from the numeral 1, normally
means 'once'; in this phrase it is understood to mean 'at one go'. It
appears with the same verb in the story of the serpent Ḫedammu,
when the personified Sea goes in response to a summons from
Kumarbi, the father of the gods; twice again in the *Song of Ullikummi*;
and again in the story of the Sun-god, the Cow, and the Fisherman.[17]

3. (*Il.* 20. 60a–5) The din of the gods' fighting alarms Hades in the
underworld; he is afraid the earth may be broken open and the grim
mansions of decay, which the gods abhor, exposed to view. Beside the
Homeric passage we may put Hesiod, *Theogony* 850–2 (cf. 681, 841),
where Hades and the Titans in Tartarus tremble at the noise of Zeus'
combat with Typhoeus. A series of oriental poetic texts must be
compared:

(i) In the Akkadian *Descent of Ishtar* the goddess Ishtar goes down to
the underworld and demands that the gatekeeper let her in (16–20):

> If you do not open the gate and I do not get in,
> I will strike the door, I will break the bolt,
> I will strike the door-frame, I will overthrow the doors;
> I will bring up the dead, they will devour the living;
> above the living the dead will multiply!

Here as in Homer we have the dangerous potentiality (not realized in
the event) that the hitherto unbroken boundary between the upper
and lower worlds will be breached, and the ghastly realm of death,
which should be sealed away, will spill out into the light. The same
threat by a goddess recurs in a briefer form (without the door-smash-
ing) in two other poems: *Gilgamesh* vi 96–100, and *Nergal and
Ereshkigal* (Standard Babylonian Version) v 9′–12′ and 25′–27′.[18]

---

[16] KTU 1. 3 iv 33–6; 1. 1 iii 20. For 'footfalls' and 'loping strides' I follow the interpretation of Caquot–Sznycer–Herdner, which seems philologically well founded.

[17] Hoffner (1992), 47, 50, 54, 58, 66.

[18] It has been compared with Helios' threat in *Od.* 12. 382f. to go down and shine for
the dead if Zeus does not agree to what he wants—again a reversal of the upper and
lower worlds.

(ii) In another Akkadian poem, *Erra and Ishum*, Marduk, here represented as king of the gods, recalls how he once rose up in his wrath and sent the Flood upon the earth: the heavens trembled, the stars changed their stations, and *the nether world quaked* (1 135).

(iii) In Job 26: 5–13 we find a hymnic recital of Yahweh's accomplishments, including references to the ancient myth of his defeat of the marine serpent Rahab (12–13). It is in the context of this theomachy, probably, that verses 5–6 had their original setting:

> The mighty dead writhe in torment below, the waters and their
> inhabitants ⟨   ⟩:
> Sheol is naked before him, and there is no covering for Abaddon.

Here again we have the motif of the underworld (Sheol, Abaddon) being stripped open and laid bare to the sky.

4. (*Il.* 13. 18–29) We have already dealt with Poseidon's four-stride journey to Aegae, where he has his golden mansion in the depths. It remains to deal with his drive across the sea, with the creatures of the deep coming forth from their lairs to acknowledge their lord:

$$\text{ἄταλλε δὲ κήτε' ὑπ' αὐτοῦ}$$
$$\text{πάντοθεν ἐκ κευθμῶν, οὐδ' ἠγνοίησεν ἄνακτα,}$$
$$\text{γηθοσύνηι δὲ θάλασσα διίστατο.}$$

The god was clad in gold, he held a golden whip, and his steeds' manes were of gold (24–6); probably we should imagine the whole chariot and harness to be of gold, or gold and silver, like Hera's in 5. 724–31. Even if L did not quote lines 24–6 (they are not in the manuscript text), we may assume that the golden equipage was part of the picture in his mind.

In the Ugaritic Baal Epic (KTU 1. 4 iv 1 ff.) the sea-goddess Athirat orders her attendant Qodesh-Amrur to prepare a donkey to take her to El (the Canaanite gods had not learned to manage horses).

> Qodesh-Amrur heard,
> he saddled an ass, he yoked a donkey;
> he put on reins of silver, a harness of gold.

And a Neo-Babylonian text describes the accoutrements of the Sun-god's chariot kept at Sippar, with its gold reins and other equipment of silver and bronze.[19]

---

[19] Pinches (1928), 132 f. The motif was not exclusively Near Eastern; cf. the Vedic hymn quoted in West (1988), 155.

As for the rejoicing sea and sea creatures, a Sumerian hymn supplies the requisite parallel.[20] The poet celebrates the water god Enki's temple at Eridu, where in ancient times the Euphrates broadened out into the Persian Gulf. Built of silver and lapis lazuli, plated with gold, the temple stands on the water's edge with its foundations in the Abzu, the subterranean freshwater ocean; this in itself may make us think of Poseidon's golden palace in the watery depths at Aegae. Now compare Homer's description of the god's journey forth from that palace with the Sumerian account of Enki's excursion from his temple seaward:

> When Enki arises, indeed the fish arise in the waves.
> He steps to the Abzu, a (splendid) sight,
> he brings joy to the Engur.[21]
> In the sea there is numinous awe at him,
> in the mighty river there is terror at him.
> The river Euphrates arises before him (as before) a fierce south wind ...
> As he departs from the temple of Eridu,
> the river responds to (lit. takes counsel with) its master:
> its voice [is ...] the voice of a calf, the voice of a sweet(-natured) cow.

Just as in Homer, the fish greet the god, the sea itself rejoices, the water heaps itself up before 'its king'.[22]

Perhaps L's juxtaposition of Homer and Genesis in this section will now appear a little less strange. These five passages, these choice examples of τὸ περὶ τὰς νοήσεις ἀδρεπήβολον in the portrayal of the grandeur of God, *all* had their sources not in Greek but in Near Eastern inspiration; and however successfully Homer (or some predecessor) accommodated the oriental motifs in the evolving tradition of Greek epic, they continued to stand out as individual and remarkable by contrast with normal Greek ideas about the gods. In valuing ἔκπληξις above τὸ πιθανόν and τὸ πρὸς χάριν, L set a premium on just that element in which oriental poetry sometimes excels, as opposed to those in which Greek poetry nearly always does.

---

[20] Al-Fouadi (1969), 73 f., lines 80–5, 90–2. Dr Black has again provided me with a fresh translation.

[21] Engur is a synonym of Abzu.

[22] Cf. also *Il.* 14. 392, where the sea surges up against the Achaean camp as Poseidon leads the Greeks to battle.

27

Phantasia and *Analogia* in Proclus

ANNE SHEPPARD

Any Platonist is bound to have an ambivalent attitude towards images. On the one hand, images fall short of the reality they represent and are liable to mislead and deceive. On the other, an image can make the beholder think of what lies beyond the image and help him or her to grasp the higher reality reflected in the image. Both views can be found in Plato himself[1] and both recur in the Neoplatonists. Both views have implications for literary criticism and for art in general. Literary and artistic images may be frowned upon, as they often are by Plato, precisely because they distract from the contemplation of philosophical truth. Yet such images may also be valued, not for themselves, but for their power to stimulate the mind towards that contemplation. It is well known that the Neoplatonists valued art more highly than Plato did precisely because they saw artistic images as having a positive value of this kind. I have argued elsewhere that Proclus' theory of literary interpretation combines both views of images. He terms 'good' images *eikones*. They stand in a relationship of *analogia* to the *paradeigma* or model they represent; they resemble the model and can help us to grasp it. 'Bad' images are *eidola*; they are associated with artistic *mimesis* which Proclus condemns just as Plato did in *Republic* 10. There is a further, important aspect to Proclus' theory: higher realities may be revealed not only through *eikones* but also, in a different way, through *symbola*. In symbolism, as distinct from *analogia*, there is no resemblance between the symbol and the object symbolized and indeed a symbol may even be the complete opposite of what it symbolizes.[2] In this chapter I propose to discuss some texts in which Proclus links *phantasia*, 'imagination', with *eikones* as well as

[1] See e.g. *Rep.* 10. 595c–599b, *Plt.* 277–9, *Phd.* 73d–75b and Cassirer (1922–3).

[2] See Sheppard (1980), 196–201 and cf. Dillon (1976). My book originated in a D.Phil. thesis supervised by Donald Russell. I first started to ask questions about Neoplatonic *phantasia* while I was working on my thesis and I offer this chapter as a small return for all his wise advice and support.

some which connect it with *mimesis* and *eidola*. I shall also discuss one passage which brings together *phantasia*, *eikones*, and *symbola*. The inquiry will take us beyond the bounds of literary criticism into other areas of Proclus' philosophy. I shall begin with a brief general account of Proclus' concept of *phantasia*.[3]

In psychology, as in many other areas of philosophy, the Neoplatonists arrived at their views by combining the views of Plato with those of Aristotle and elaborating the resulting synthesis. They accepted Plato's belief in the immortality of the soul and his dualist separation of soul and body as two distinct entities but for the details of psychology they turned to Aristotle, particularly to the *De Anima*. Aristotle's discussion of the different psychological capacities of perception, *phantasia*, and thinking provided a framework for the Neoplatonic division of the soul. At the same time the basic division into an irrational part of the soul, linked to the body, and a rational part, capable of detachment from the body was of fundamental importance. Perception of the physical world clearly belonged with the irrational part; thinking in its various forms with the rational. Where did *phantasia* belong? For Proclus and other late Neoplatonists, *phantasia* has a critical role at the 'joint' of the soul, just where rational and irrational meet. Imagination has a close relationship with perception and much Neoplatonic discussion of *phantasia*, particularly in the Aristotelian commentators, follows Aristotle in examining this relationship. Yet we can call up images of things we cannot see or of things we have never seen and, as Aristotle pointed out, images are used in thinking.[4] *Phantasia* thus has a close relationship with the rational soul too. In Proclus we find different views in different texts of the relationship between *phantasia* and *doxa*, the lowest kind of thinking.[5] We also find, both in Proclus and in some other late Neoplatonists an identification of *phantasia* with *nous pathetikos*, the 'passible intellect' alluded to in only one passage of the *De anima*, but regularly mentioned in Neoplatonist discussions of psychology.[6]

---

[3] I am concerned here only with Proclus' use of the term φαντασία to refer to a faculty of the mind. I am ignoring passages such as *In Cra.* 55. 17 where he uses the word in the related sense of 'image'. In what follows translations from Proclus, *In Euc.* follow Morrow (1970) except that I render λόγοι by 'principles' rather than 'ideas'; translations of other Proclus texts are my own.

[4] Aristotle, *De An.* 431^{a}15–16. Aristotle may not have been right that there is no thinking without images but the Neoplatonists held that some kinds of thinking use images although there are higher kinds which do not.

[5] See Blumenthal (1975) and (1982); also G. Watson (1982).

[6] See Aristotle, *De An.* 430^{a}24–5 and Blumenthal (1991).

One kind of thinking where *phantasia* played a particularly important role was mathematics. In his commentary on Euclid Proclus
develops the idea that when we are doing geometry the figures about
which we are thinking are projections in the imagination of innate intelligible principles. If we are thinking about a circle we are thinking about
a figure with extension and shape. For Proclus the intelligible principle
of circularity has neither extension nor shape since these are attributes
of physical objects. Geometry deals neither with this unextended principle without a shape nor with the extended, imperfectly circular shapes
found in the physical world. The objects of geometry have an intermedi-
ate status which Proclus explains by locating them in the imagination.[7]

'Imagination' is a convenient translation for *phantasia* but, as has
often been pointed out, the Greek word *phantasia* refers to a faculty
which deals with appearances, rather than a faculty which deals with
images. Proclus' most common terms for the objects of *phantasia* are
τύπος ('imprint'), σχῆμα ('figure'), and μορφή ('shape'). σχῆμα and
μορφή, used both in the *Euclid Commentary* and elsewhere, suggest
the mathematical figures and shapes discussed in that commentary.
The term τύπος goes back to Plato, who uses it both at *Theaetetus*
192a, in the 'wax block' analogy, as one of a number of terms for the
'imprint' made by perception on the mind and at *Timaeus* 71b of the
'imprints' made by the mind upon the liver which affect the part of the
soul located there. This part of the soul is capable of divination in sleep
and is clearly related to the imagination although Plato does not
actually label it *phantasia*.[8]

At one point in the *Euclid Commentary* Proclus uses the term
eikones of the figures projected in the imagination:

If someone should inquire how we can introduce motions into immovable
geometrical objects and move things that are without parts—operations that
are altogether impossible—we shall ask that he be not annoyed if we remind
him of what was demonstrated in the Prologue about things in the imagination,
namely, that our ideas inscribe there the images (*eikones*) of all things of which
the understanding has principles. (*In Euc.* 185. 25–186. 5)

This idea that the imagination can reproduce images of higher principles is not confined to mathematics. Proclus also uses it in his

---

[7] *In Euc.* 51. 9–56. 22 and 78. 20–79. 2, discussed by G. Watson (1988), 119–21 and
O'Meara (1989), 166–9. For similar ideas in Syrianus, Proclus' teacher, see Watson
(1988), 118 and O'Meara (1989), 132–4.

[8] See G. Watson (1988), 11–13. τύπος was also a Stoic term: see Verbeke (1966),
pp. LIII–LIV and Charlton (1991), 14.

Commentary on the Cratylus when discussing the power to give names to things. In Proclus' view the names of things reflect their essential nature. When he discusses 'the art of making names', he asserts that there is an εἰκαστικὴ δύναμις, 'an image-making power', in the soul. He remarks in passing that painting is connected with this power which he describes as making inferior things like superior ones. He notes that by this same power the soul can make itself like beings superior to itself, gods, angels, and demons, and continues:

> But by the same power it also makes its inferior products like itself and even like things greater than itself, because it fashions statues of gods and demons. Wanting to bring likenesses of real things into existence from itself, likenesses which are immaterial in a way and products of rational reality alone, and using the linguistic imagination (λεκτικὴ φαντασία) as an assistant, ⟨the soul⟩ produced real names. (*In Cra.* 19. 6–12)[9]

A little later he adds that the true maker of names is Mind (νοῦς), which places in them images of the models (εἰκόνας αὐτοῖς ἐνθεὶς τῶν παραδειγμάτων) (*In Cra.* 19. 22–3). In the Neoplatonic hierarchy of being, Mind comes above Soul and is ultimately responsible for Soul and its products. There is accordingly no inconsistency in Proclus' move here from saying that the soul produces names for things to saying that the true maker of names is Mind. For our purposes the interesting point in this passage is the language of *eikon* and *paradeigma* coupled with the reference to *phantasia*. The image of *phantasia* as the soul's 'assistant' rather than a part of it is initially puzzling. In order to understand it we have to appreciate both that Proclus wants to attribute the making of names to as lofty a power as possible, and that he sometimes uses ψυχή ('soul') to refer to the rational soul alone, regarding irrational psychological powers as outside the soul proper. So while he gives *phantasia* a role to play, he prefers to see the rational soul and ultimately the higher hypostasis of Mind as the true 'legislator' for language. (The parallel with legislation which Proclus develops here is based on *Cratylus* 429a–b; Proclus' mention of painting is no doubt similarly sparked off by *Cratylus* 429a.) In the same way an earlier passage of the *Cratylus Commentary* describes names as products of 'the soul using imagination' (ψυχὴ φανταζομένη) (*In Cra.* 8. 10).

Another aspect of the power of *phantasia* to produce *eikones* derived from models at a higher level appears in the *Commentary on*

[9] The Greek word ὄνομα means both 'word' and 'name' here but since Proclus, following Plato, concentrates on the names of the gods, 'name' seems the best translation.

the Timaeus. There, discussion of Plato's story of the demiurge who forms the world according to an intelligible model naturally leads Proclus to use the language of *eikon* and *paradeigma*. At *Timaeus* 28c–29a Plato makes Timaeus raise the question whether the demiurge formed the world according to an unchanging model or according to one which had come into being. This question prompts Proclus to develop the contrast between those who copy the external world and those who follow models which they find within themselves:

Just as with craftsmen in this world some can copy (μιμήσασθαι) other things accurately, while others have a power of modelling (δύναμις ἀναπλαστική) wonderful shapes and necessary works as required, so the first man to make a ship imaginatively moulded the model of the ship in himself (τὸ παράδειγμα τῆς νεὼς ἐν ἑαυτῷ ἀνέπλασε φανταστικῶς). (*In Ti.* I. 320. 5–10)

Here *phantasia* seems to be going further, producing not just copies but even a model. However, in Neoplatonic terms the model of the first ship is itself bound to be a copy of an intelligible principle. Neoplatonist metaphysics prevents imagination from ever being truly creative; yet this passage does offer the same contrast between the ability just to copy what one sees (*mimesis*) and *phantasia* that is found in a famous passage of Philostratus which regularly appears in discussions of the concept of creative imagination in antiquity. Philostratus in his *Life of Apollonius of Tyana* 6. 19 portrays Apollonius in conversation with an Egyptian called Thespesion. When Apollonius ridicules the animal images of gods found in Egypt, Thespesion asks sarcastically whether such Greek sculptors as Phidias and Praxiteles went up to heaven and copied the forms of the gods there. Apollonius replies that the Greek sculptures were made not by *mimesis* but by *phantasia*, for *phantasia* can fashion even things which it has not seen.[10] Proclus mentioned the power to make statues of the gods in a similar way at *Cratylus Commentary* 19. 7–8. Both Philostratus and Proclus are talking not about an imaginative ability to create something new but about a power which enables the craftsman to portray something which exists in a higher world.

In Proclus' *Timaeus Commentary* an explicit parallel is drawn between the human craftsman and the demiurge of the world. He uses the same parallel in two other passages, *De Providentia* 65. 3 ff. Boese and *In Parmenidem* 4. 958. 36 ff. In all three cases Proclus is primarily concerned to illuminate the activity of the demiurge but he is also

[10] Cf. G. Watson (1988), 59 ff. and Cocking (1991), 43–7.

developing a tradition in which that activity had begun to provide a model for seeing human artists as creative.[11]

In the passages discussed so far *phantasia*, while not creative in the modern sense, is being given a very important role as the power which can project copies of intelligible principles in mathematics, language, and other spheres; these copies can themselves serve as models for products in physical materials. In all these passages the language of *eikon* and *paradeigma* is used in a way which suggests that *phantasia* uses *analogia*. I want now to consider some further passages which complicate this picture.

A passage of the *Euclid Commentary* which has received some discussion presents *phantasia* as dealing with *eidola* rather than *eikones* but clearly sees it in a positive light:

Therefore just as nature stands creatively above the visible figures, so the soul, exercising her capacity to know, projects on the imagination, as on a mirror, the principles of the figures; and the imagination, receiving in pictorial form (ἐν εἰδώλοις) these impressions of the ideas within the soul, by their means affords the soul an opportunity to turn inward from the pictures and attend to herself. It is as if a man looking at himself in a mirror and marvelling at the power of nature and at his own appearance should wish to look upon himself directly and possess such a power as would enable him to become at the same time the seer and the object seen. In the same way when the soul is looking outside herself at the imagination, seeing the figures depicted there (ἐσκιαγραφημένα σχήματα) and being struck by their beauty and orderedness, she is admiring her own principles from which they are derived; and though she adores their beauty, she dismisses it as something reflected (ἐν εἰδώλοις) and seeks her own beauty. (*In Euc.* 141. 2–19)[12]

Here *phantasia* is 'outside' the rational soul, just as it is at *Cratylus Commentary* 19. 6–12, but Proclus stresses that its receipt of intelligible principles is valuable because contemplation of the figures presented in the imagination can turn the soul back towards itself. In Neoplatonism such self-contemplation is the first stage on the way to contemplation of higher reality. Mathematics here is regarded as a means of ascent towards the intelligible, just as it is in Plato's *Republic*. The same idea occurred in the passage of the *Cratylus Commentary* discussed earlier, where at 19. 4–5 Proclus alludes to the 'image-making power' as that by which the soul can make inferior things like superior ones and can make itself like beings superior to itself, gods,

---

[11] Cf. G. Watson (1988), 80–93 and 124.
[12] For other discussions see Charles (1971) and Cocking (1991), 67.

angels, and demons. The use of the term *eidolon* here may be due to the image of the mirror. That image itself goes back to Plato, who uses it not only at *Republic* 10. 596d–e, when scorning the artist's ability to copy what he sees, but also at *Timaeus* 71b, where the liver which receives imprints and images (τύποι καὶ εἴδωλα) from the mind is compared to a mirror. ἐσκιαγραφημένα ('depicted') is another Platonic term, used several times of the shadowy images of reality offered by the physical world. At *Republic* 586b, for example, the 'unreal' pleasures of sensual indulgence are described as εἴδωλα ἐσκιαγραφημένα ('depicted images').

In Plato mirror-images, shadows, and reflections tend to be associated with the derogatory view of images, although the comparison of the divinatory liver to a mirror at *Timaeus* 71b is something of an exception. Modern interpreters may try to explain that strange passage away by talking about the use of myth or suggesting irony but for the Neoplatonists it provided a precedent for sometimes using the image of the mirror in a positive sense. Plotinus at 4. 3. 30. 2–11 describes *phantasia* as like an *eikon* of thought and goes on to say that the verbal expression of a thought 'unfolds' it, brings it into the imagination (τὸ φανταστικόν) and displays it there as though in a mirror.[13] In Proclus *phantasia* is again compared to a mirror at *Euclid Commentary* 121. 2–7:

And thus we must think of the plane as projected and lying before our eyes and the understanding as writing everything upon it, the imagination becoming something like a plane mirror to which the principles of the understanding send down impressions of themselves.

If we think of *phantasia* as a mirror which reflects images from the intelligible, it may be seen positively because although it deals in images these images reflect a higher world. If, however, like Plato in *Republic* 10 we turn the mirror outwards to the external world and think of *phantasia* as reflecting the images given in perception, then it will appear to a Platonist in a much less positive light. Proclus considers *phantasia* in this rather different way in his *Commentary on the Republic* where he combines *Republic* 10 on poetry with *Sophist* 235d ff. and so divides the lowest kind of poetry, imitative poetry, into eikastic poetry which aims at accurate imitation and phantastic poetry which aims only at imitation of things as they appear. This lowly,

---

[13] Cf. also Plotinus 1. 4. 10.

imitative poetry is contrasted with two higher types, inspired poetry
and the poetry of knowledge.[14]

Whether Proclus sees the images with which *phantasia* deals as
good or bad, stimulating or misleading, depends to a considerable
extent on the context within which he is discussing *phantasia*. At the
beginning of this chapter I mentioned that Proclus distinguishes not
only between *analogia*, using *eikones*, and *mimesis*, using *eidola*, but
also between *analogia* and symbolism. This distinction is found in a
number of different works but it is not mentioned consistently
throughout Proclus' works. The *Cratylus Commentary*, although it
distinguishes between *analogia* and the mimetic relationship of an
eidolon to its *idea*, conflates symbolism and *analogia*.[15] It is, I think,
significant that the only passage I have so far found in Proclus which
links *phantasia* with symbolism occurs in this commentary.

My earlier discussion of the passage on the 'image-making power' at
Cratylus Commentary 18. 27 ff. omitted a section at 19. 12–19 in which
Proclus compares the giving of names with theurgy:

> And just as the telestic art makes statues (or pictures—ἀγάλματα) here like the
> gods by means of symbols and secret signs and makes them fitted to receive the
> divine illuminations, so too the legislative art by the same power of producing
> likeness brings names into existence as pictures (ἀγάλματα) of things, making
> them like the nature of reality by means of such and such sounds, and having
> brought them into existence handed them down for men to use.

'The telestic art' is one of Proclus' names for theurgy, the form of religious magic practised by the later Neoplatonists, and the whole
comparison is expressed in Neoplatonic theurgic terminology. Proclus
implies that there is a magical link between a name and what it stands
for just as there was between the 'symbols and secret signs' (σύμβολα
καὶ ἀπόρρητα συνθήματα) which the theurgist would place on statues
of the gods and the gods themselves. The phrase 'making them like the
nature of reality' (ἀπεικονιζομένη τὴν τῶν ὄντων φύσιν) suggests that
Proclus is thinking that names sound like what they stand for but in
fact while some names do, many do not.[16] This may partly explain why
Proclus in the *Cratylus Commentary* assimilates *analogia*, which deals
in likeness, to symbolism, which does not. There is also the point I
mentioned earlier that Proclus wants to claim as lofty an origin as
possible for names, especially the names of the gods on which the

---

[14] See *In Remp.* 177. 7–196. 13 and Sheppard (1980), 162–5 and 187–9.
[15] See *In Cra.* 24. 17–25. 7 and in general Hirschle (1979).
[16] Cf. *In Cra.* 20. 12–21.

Cratylus concentrates. Plato's etymologies there may not be entirely serious but the Neoplatonists took it that they were serious and Proclus' religious outlook made it natural for him to connect naming the gods with other ways of representing them such as statues.

Where Proclus does distinguish between symbolism and *analogia*, symbolism is clearly superior. In the *Republic Commentary* symbolism is associated with inspired poetry, the highest kind of poetry. Such poetry may say apparently shocking things about the gods and represent them as fighting or making love but once interpreted allegorically it can be understood as conveying philosophical truths.[17] The poet who uses symbols employs not *phantasia* but the much higher power of inspiration, associated by Proclus with the 'one in the soul' which he placed right at the top of the rational soul. For Proclus this 'flower of the soul' is not irrational but supra-rational; it corresponds to the One, the highest hypostasis in the Neoplatonic metaphysical system, and is that by which we can come into contact with the divine henads, above Mind, and with the One itself.[18]

My main focus in this chapter has been a collection of passages in which Proclus gives *phantasia* an important role to play in producing mathematical figures, language, and 'blueprints' such as the model of the first ship. He sees *phantasia* as a valuable mediator between the rational and the irrational, the intelligible and the sensible. There is always a danger that *phantasia* will become too involved with the irrational world of sense-perception and sometimes Proclus is very suspicious of it. But when the mirror of *phantasia* is turned upwards, towards intelligible reality, it can help us by reflecting that reality in comprehensible terms. *Phantasia* in Neoplatonism is starting to take on some of the powers later associated with imagination but it never takes on them all.[19] It deals with reflections and likenesses, not with new creation, and when Proclus wishes to describe a non-rational power of directly apprehending truth he follows Plato in talking of inspiration, not of *phantasia*.

---

[17] See esp. *In Remp.* 84. 26ff. and 198. 13–19.

[18] See *In Remp.* 177. 15–23 and 178. 10–179. 3; Grondijs (1960); Beierwaltes (1963) and (1965), 367–82; Rist (1964); Guérard (1987).

[19] Cf. G. Watson (1988), esp. ch. 5, and Cocking (1991), esp. ch. 3.

BIBLIOGRAPHY

ADAMS, J. N. (1995): *Pelagonius, Veterinary Treatises and the Language of Veterinary Medicine in the Roman Empire* (Leiden).

AHERN, C. F. (1989): 'Daedalus and Icarus in the *Ars Amatoria*', *HSCP* 92: 273–96.

ALFÖLDI, A. (1968): 'Die verlorene Enmannsche Kaisergeschichte und die *Caesares* von Iulianus Apostata', *Bonner HA-Colloq. 1966–7*: 1–8.

AL-FOUADI, A.-H. A. (1969): *Enki's Journey to Nippur: The Journeys of the Gods* (diss. Pennsylvania University).

ALPERS, I. (1912): *Hercules in Bivio* (diss. Göttingen).

ALPERS, K. (1984): 'Untersuchungen zum griechischen Physiologus und den Kyraniden', *Vestigia Bibliae: Jahrbuch des deutschen Bibel-Archivs Hamberg*, 6: 13–87.

ANDERSON, G. (1976*a*): *Lucian: Theme and Variation in the Second Sophistic* (Leiden).

—— (1976*b*): 'Lucian's Classics: Some Short Cuts to Culture', *BICS* 23: 59–68.

—— (1977): 'Patterns in Lucian's Prolaliae', *Philologus*, 121: 313–15.

—— (1986): *Philostratus* (London).

ARGYLE, M. (1992): *The Social Psychology of Everyday Life* (London).

ARNIM, H. VON (1898): *Leben und Werke des Dio von Prusa* (Berlin).

ASMIS, E. (1984): *Epicurus' Scientific Method* (Ithaca, NY, and London).

ASTIN, A. E. (1967): *Scipio Aemilianus* (Oxford).

ATHANASSIADI, P. (1992): *Julian: An Intellectual Biography* (London; 1st pub. Oxford, 1981, as *Julian and Hellenism*).

ATKINS, J. W. (1934): *Literary Criticism in Antiquity*, vol. ii (Cambridge).

BABUT, D. (1969): *Plutarque et le Stoicisme* (Paris).

BAIN, D. (1975): 'Audience Address in Greek Tragedy', *CQ* 25: 13–25.

—— (1990): '"Treading Birds": An Unnoticed use of πατέω (Cyranides, 1.10.27, 1.19.9)', in E. M. Craik (ed.), *'Owls to Athens': Essays on Classical Subjects presented to Sir Kenneth Dover* (Oxford), 295–304.

—— (1993): 'Marcianus Graecus 512 (678) and the Text of the Cyranides: Some Preliminary Observations', *RIFC* 121: 427–49.

BAKHTIN, M. (1981): *The Dialogic Imagination*, ed. M. Holquist, trans. C. Emerson and M. Holquist (Austin, Tex.).

BALDWIN, B. (1961): 'Lucian as Social Satirist', *CQ* 11: 199–208.

—— (1973): *Studies in Lucian* (Toronto).

—— (1978): 'The *Caesares* of Julian', *Klio*, 60: 449–66.

BARCHIESI, A. (1991): 'Discordant Muses', *PCPS* 37: 1–21.

BARNES, T. D. (1967): 'Hadrian and Lucius Verus', *JRS* 57: 65–79.

—— (1981): *Constantine and Eusebius* (Cambridge, Mass., and London).

BARSBY, J. A. (1973): *Ovid: Amores Book I* (Oxford).

BARTSCH, S. (1989): *Decoding the Ancient Novel: The Reader and the Role of Description in Heliodorus and Achilles Tatius* (Princeton).

BASSANOFF, V. (1947): *Evocatio: Étude d'un ritual militaire romaine* (Paris).

BEAGON, M. (1992): *Roman Nature: The Thought of Pliny the Elder* (Oxford).

BEAUVOIR PRIAULX, O. de (1860): 'Indian Travels of Apollonius of Tyana', *Journal of the Royal Asiatic Society*, 17: 70–105.

BEHR, C. A. (1968): *Aelius Aristides and the Sacred Tales* (Amsterdam).

—— (1981): *P. Aelius Aristides: The Complete Works*, vol. ii: *Orations XVII– LIII, translated into English* (Leiden).

BEIERWALTES, W. (1963): 'Der Begriff des "unum in nobis" bei Proklos', *Miscellanea Medievalia*, 2: 255–66.

—— (1965): *Proklos: Grundzüge seiner Metaphysik* (Frankfurt).

BETZ, H. D. (1978) (ed.): *Plutarch's Ethical Writings and Early Christian Literature* (Studia ad Corpus Hellenisticum Novi Testamenti, 4; Leiden).

BHATTACHARYA, V. (1943) (ed., trans.): *The Agamasastra of Gaudapada* (Calcutta).

BIRLEY, A. (1987): *Marcus Aurelius* (2nd edn.; London).

BJÖRK, G. (1944): *Apsyrtus, Julius Africanus et l'hippiatrique greque* (Uppsala Universitets Årsskrift 1944. 4; Uppsala).

BLOIS, L. de (1992): 'The Perception of Politics in Plutarch's Lives', *ANRW* ii. 33. 6: 4568–615.

BLUMENTHAL, H. J. (1975): 'Plutarch's Exposition of the *De anima* and the Psychology of Proclus', in *De Jamblique à Proclus* (Entretiens Hardt, 21; Geneva), 123–47.

—— (1982): 'Proclus on Perception', *BICS* 29: 1–11.

—— (1991): '*Nous pathetikos* in Later Greek Philosophy', in H. Blumenthal and H. Robinson (edd.), *Aristotle and the Later Tradition* (Oxford), 191–205.

BLUNDELL, S. (1986): *The Origins of Civilization in Greek and Roman Thought* (London and Sydney).

BOLLACK, J. (1969): 'Les Maximes de l'amitié', *Actes, VIIIème Congrès Budé* (Paris), 221–36.

BOMPAIRE, J. (1958): *Lucien écrivain: Imitation et création* (Paris).

BONIME, F., and ECKARDT, M. H. (1993): 'On Psychoanalysing Literary Characters', in E. Berman (ed.), *Essential Papers on Literature and Psychoanalysis* (New York and London), 202–16.

BONNER, S. F. (1949): *Roman Declamation* (Liverpool).

—— (1977): *Education in Ancient Rome: From the Elder Cato to the Younger Pliny* (London).

BORNECQUE, H. (1902): *Les Déclamations et les déclamateurs d'après Sénèque le Père* (Lille).

BOUFFARTIGUE, J. (1992): *L'Empereur Julien et la culture de son temps* (Paris).

BOULANGER, A. (1968): *Aelius Aristide et la sophistique dans la province d'Asie au IIᵉᵐᵉ siècle de notre ère* (Paris; 1st pub. 1923).

BOWERSOCK, G. W. (1969): *Greek Sophists in the Roman Empire* (Oxford).

—— (1978): *Julian the Apostate* (London).

—— (1982): 'The Emperor Julian on his Predecessors', *YCS* 27: 159–72.

—— (1989): 'Philostratus and the Second Sophistic', in P. E. Easterling and B. M. W. Knox (edd.), *The Cambridge History of Classical Literature*, vol. i.4: *The Hellenistic Period and the Empire* (Cambridge), 95–102.

BOWIE, E. L. (1978): 'Apollonius of Tyana: Tradition and Reality', *ANRW* ii.16.2: 1652–99.

—— (1993): 'Lies, Fiction and Slander in Early Greek Poetry', in C. Gill and T. P. Wiseman (eds.), *Lies and Fiction in the Ancient World* (Exeter), 1–37.

BRADBURY, S. (1987): 'The Date of Julian's Letter to Themistius', *GRBS* 28: 235–51.

BRAMBLE, J. C. (1974): *Persius and the Programmatic Satire* (Cambridge).

BRINK, C. O. (1963): *Horace on Poetry: Prolegomena to the Literary Epistles* (Cambridge).

—— (1971): *Horace on Poetry: The Ars Poetica* (Cambridge).

—— (1982): *Horace on Poetry: Epistles Book 2* (Cambridge).

BRISCOE, J. (1967): 'Rome and the Class Struggle in the Greek States, 200–146 B.C.', *Past and Present*, 36: 3–20; repr. in M. I. Finley (ed.), *Studies in Ancient Society* (London, 1974), 53–73.

BROCK, N. VAN (1961): *Recherches sur le vocabulaire médical du grec ancien: Soins et guérison* (Études et commentaires, 41; Paris).

BROOKS, P. (1984): *Reading for the Plot: Design and Intention in Narrative* (Cambridge, Mass.).

BRUNT, P. A. (1988): '*Amicitia* in the Roman Republic', in *Fall of the Roman Republic* (Oxford), 351–81; repr. and update of *PCPS* 11 (1965), 1–20.

—— (1973): 'Aspects of the Social Thought of Dio Chrysostom and of the Stoics', *PCPS* 19: 9–34.

BUCHER-ISLER, B. (1972): *Norm und Individualität in den Biographien Plutarchs* (Berne and Stuttgart).

BUCHHEIT, V. (1972): *Der Anspruch des Dichters in Vergils Georgika: Dichtertum und Heilsweg* (Darmstadt).

BÜHLER, W. (1964): *Beiträge zur Erklärung der Schrift vom Erhabenen* (Göttingen).

CAIRNS, F. (1972): *Generic Composition in Greek and Roman Poetry* (Edinburgh).

CALBOLI, G. (1978): *Marci Porci Catonis, pro Rhodiensibus* (Bologna).

CALDWELL, R. (1990): 'The Psychoanalytic Interpretation of Greek Myth', in L. Edmunds (ed.), *Approaches to Greek Myth* (Baltimore), 344–89.

CAMPBELL, D. J. (1936): *Naturalis Historia: Liber Secundus* (Aberdeen).

CAQUOT, A., SZNYCER, M., and HERDNER, A. (1974): *Textes ougaritiques*, vol. i: *Mythes et légendes* (Paris).

CARTLEDGE, P. (1981): 'The Politics of Spartan Pederasty', *PCPS* 27: 17–36; repr. in A. K. Siems (ed.), *Sexualität und Erotik in der Antike* (Darmstadt, 1988), 385–415.

CASSIRER, E. (1922–3): *Eidos und Eidolon: Das Problem des Schönen und der Kunst in Platons Dialogen* (Vorträge der Bibliothek Warburg, 1; Leipzig and Berlin), 1–27.

CHADWICK, H. (1957): 'St. Peter and St. Paul in Rome: The Problem of the *Memoria Apostolorum ad Catacumbas*', *JThS*, NS 8: 31–52.

CHARLES, A. (1971): 'L'Imagination, miroir de l'âme selon Proclus', in *Le Néoplatonisme* (Paris), 241–51.

CHARLTON, W. (1991): *Philoponus: On Aristotle on the Intellect* (London).

CHARPENTIER, J. (1934): 'The Indian Travels of Apollonius of Tyana', *Skritt. K. Humanist. Vetenskaps-Samfundet Uppsala*, 29/3: 1–66.

CITRONI MARCHETTI, S. (1977): '"Iuvare mortalem": L'Ideale programmatico della *N. H.* de Plinio nei rapporti con il moralismo stoico-diatribico', *A&R* 27: 124–48.

—— (1992): *Plinio il Vecchio e la tradizione del moralismo romano* (Pisa).

COCKING, J. M. (1991): *Imagination* (London and New York).

CONTE, G. B. (1986): *The Rhetoric of Imitation* (Ithaca, NY).

—— (1992): 'Proem in the Middle', in F. M. Duane and T. Cole (edd.), *Beginnings in Classical Literature* (YCS 29; New Haven), 147–59.

CREWS, F. (1993): 'The Unknown Freud', *New York Review of Books*, 18 Nov.: 55–66.

—— (1994): 'The Unknown Freud: An Exchange', *New York Review of Books*, 3 Feb.: 34–43.

CRISTOFORI, A. (1989): 'Colonia Carthago magnae in vestigiis Carthaginis (Plin. *Nat. Hist.* V.24)', *Antiquités africaines*, 25: 83–93.

CRUM, W. E. (1902): *Coptic Ostraca* (London).

CUGUSI, P. (1983): *Evoluzione e forme dell'epistolografia latina* (Rome).

DAMON, C. (1990): 'Poem Division, Paired Poems, and *Amores* 2.9 and 3.11', *TAPA* 120: 269–90.

de MARTINO, F. (1982): *Omero agonista in Delo* (Antichità Classica e Cristiana, 22; Brescia).

DEICHGRÄBER, K. (1971): *Aretaeus von Kappadozien als medizinischer Schriftsteller* (*ASA W*, phil.-hist. kl. 63/3; Berlin).

DELATTE, L. (1942): *Textes latins et vieux français relatif aux Cyranides* (Liège and Paris).

DESIDERI, P. (1978): *Dione di Prusa: Un intellettuale greco nell'impero romano* (Messina and Florence).

DEUBNER, L. (1907): *Kosmas und Damian* (Leipzig).

DEUTSCH, R. E. (1939): *The Pattern of Sound in Lucretius* (Philadelphia).

DEVIJVER, H., and LIPIŃSKI, E. (1989) (edd.): *Punic Wars* (Studia Phoenicia, 10; Leuven).

DILLON, J. (1976): 'Image, Symbol and Analogy: Three Basic Concepts of Neo-platonic Allegorical Exegesis', in R. Baine Harris (ed.), *The Significance of Neoplatonism* (Norfolk, Va.), 247–62.

DINNAGE, R. (1993): 'Bringing up Raja', *New York Review of Books*, 16 Dec.: 66–8.

DIONIGI, I. (1988): *Lucrezio: Le Parole e le cose* (Bologna).

DIONISOTTI, A. C. (1988): 'Nepos and the Generals', *JRS* 78: 35–49.

DODDS, E. R. (1951): *The Greeks and the Irrational* (Berkeley and Los Angeles).

DOVER, K. J. (1974): *Greek Popular Morality in the Time of Plato and Aristotle* (Oxford).

—— (1978): *Greek Homosexuality* (London).

DOYEN-HIGUET, A.-M. (1984): 'The *Hippiatrica* and Byzantine Veterinary Medicine', *Dumbarton Oaks Papers*, 38; *Symposium on Byzantine Medicine*: 111–20.

DUBEL, S. (1990): 'La Description d'objets d'art dans les Éthiopiques', *Pallas*, 36: 101–15.

DUBUISSON, M. (1989): 'Delenda est Carthago: Remise en question d'un steréo-type', in Devijver and Lipiński (1989), 279–87.

DUFF, J. W. (1966): *A Literary History of Rome in the Silver Age* (London).

DUNCAN, D. (1979): *Ben Jonson and the Lucianic Tradition* (Cambridge).

FABRICIUS, C. (1972): *Galens Exzerpte aus älteren Pharmakologen* (Berlin and New York).

FAIRWEATHER, J. (1981): *Seneca the Elder* (Cambridge).

FARQUHARSON, A. S. L. (1944): *The Meditations of the Emperor Marcus Antoninus* (Oxford).

FEENEY, D. C. (1991): *The Gods in Epic: Poets and Critics of the Classical Tradition* (Oxford).

FELMAN, S. (1982): 'Turning the Screw of Interpretation', in S. Felman (ed.), *Literature and Psychoanalysis: The Question of Reading: Otherwise* (Baltimore), 94–207.

FISH, S. E. (1972): *Self-Consuming Artifacts: The Experience of Seventeenth-Century Literature* (Berkeley).

FITTON BROWN, A. D. (1985): 'The Unreality of Ovid's Tomantian Exile', *LCM* 10: 19–22.

FITZGERALD, J. T., and WHITE, L. M. (1983): *The Tabula of Cebes* (Chico, Calif.).

FLACELIÈRE, R. (1953): *Dialogue sur l'Amour (Eroticos)* (Annales de l'Université de Lyon, 3rd ser. 21; Paris).

FONTAINE, J. (1959): *Isidore de Seville et la culture classique dans l'Espagne Wisigothique* (Paris).

FORD, A. (1991): 'Unity in Greek Criticism and Poetry', *Arion*, 3rd ser. 1: 125–54.

FOSTER, B. R. (1993): *Before the Muses* (Bethesda, Md.).

FOUCAULT, M. (1990): *The History of Sexuality*, vol. iii: *The Care of the Self* (London). (Penguin edn. of the Eng. trans. of *Le Souci de soi*, 1984.)

FOWLER, D. P. (1986): Review of Asmis (1984), *JHS* 106: 227–31.

—— (1989): 'Lucretius and Politics', in M. Griffin and J. Barnes (edd.), *Philosophia Togata* (Oxford), 120–50.

—— (forthcoming): 'The Feminine Principal: Gender in *De rerum natura*', in Proceedings of the 1993 conference *Epicureismo greco e latino* (Naples).

FRAENKEL, E. (1957): *Horace* (Oxford).

—— (1964): 'Kolon und Satz', *Kleine Beiträge*, vol. i (Rome), 73–119.

—— (1965): *Noch einmal Kolon und Satz* (Munich).

FRÄNKEL, H. (1945): *Ovid, a Poet Between Two Worlds* (Berkeley).

FRASER, P. M. (1972): *Ptolemaic Alexandria* (Oxford).

FRÉCAUT, J.-M. (1972): *L'Esprit et l'humour chez Ovide* (Grenoble).

FRIEDLÄNDER, P. (1941): 'The Pattern of Sound and Atomistic Theory in Lucretius', *AJPh* 62: 16–33.

GADAMER, H.-G. (1960): *Wahrheit und Methode: Grundzüge einer philosophischen Hermeneutik* (Tübingen).

GALE, M. (1994): *Myth and Poetry in Lucretius* (Cambridge).

GEEL, J. (1840): *Olympicus* (Leiden).

GELZER, M. (1931): 'Nasicas Widerspruch gegen die Zerstörung Karthagos', *Philologus*, 86: 262–99.

—— (1975): *The Roman Nobility* trans. R. Seager (Oxford).

GILL, C. (1984): 'The *Ethos/Pathos* Distinction in Rhetorical and Literary Criticism', *CQ* 34: 149–66.

GOESSLER, L. (1962): *Plutarchs Gedanken über die Ehe* (Zurich).

GOLDBERG, S. (1986): *Understanding Terence* (Princeton).

GOLDHILL, S. (1986): *Reading Greek Tragedy* (Cambridge).

—— (1994): 'The Failure of Exemplarity', in de Jong and Sullivan (1994), 51–73.

GREEN, R. P. H. (1991): *Ausonius* (Oxford).

GRIFFIN, J. (1985): *Latin Poets and Roman Life* (London).

GRONDIJS, L. H. (1960): *L'Âme, le nous, et les hénades dans la théologie de Proclus* (Amsterdam).

GROSS, N. (1985): *Amatory Persuasion in Antiquity* (Newark, Del.).

GRUBE, G. M. A. (1961): *A Greek Critic: Demetrius On Style* (Phoenix Suppl. 4; Toronto).

GRUEN, E. S. (1976): 'The Origins of the Achaean War', *JHS* 96: 46–69.

GRÜNBAUM, A. (1984): *The Foundations of Psychoanalysis: A Philosophical Critique* (Berkeley and Los Angeles).

—— (1993): *Validation in the Clinical Theory of Psychoanalysis: A Study in the Philosophy of Psychoanalysis* (Madison, Conn.).

GUARDUCCI, M. (1938): 'Le offerti dei conquistatori romani ai santuari della Grecia', *Rendic. Pont. Accad. Arch.* 13: 41–58.

GUÉRARD, C. (1987): 'L'Hyparxis de l'âme et la fleur de l'intellect dans la mystagogie de Proclus', in J. Pépin and H. D. Saffrey (edd.), *Proclus, Lecteur et interprète des anciens* (Paris), 335–49.

HABINEK, T. N. (1985): *The Colometry of Latin Prose* (Berkeley).

HALL, J. (1981): *Lucian's Satire* (New York).

HALLEUX, R., and SCHAMP, J. (1985): *Les Lapidaires grecs: Lapidaire orphique, kérygmes lapidaires d'Orphée, Socrate et Denys, lapidaire nautique, Damigéron-Evax* (Paris).

HALLIWELL, S. (1986): *Aristotle's Poetics* (London and Chapel Hill, NC).

—— (1987): *The Poetics of Aristotle: Translation and Commentary* (London).

—— (1989): Review of M. Heath, *The Poetics of Greek Tragedy* (1987), *JHS* 109: 231.

—— (1992): 'Pleasure, Understanding, and Emotion in Aristotle's *Poetics*', in A. O. Rorty (ed.), *Essays on Aristotle's* Poetics (Princeton), 241–60.

HALM, C. (1863): *Rhetores Latini Minores* (Leipzig).

HALPERIN, D. M. (1990): *One Hundred Years of Homosexuality, and Other Essays on Greek Love* (New York and London).

HANSEN, G. (1992): 'A Stylistic Analysis of Ovid's Elegiac Poetry with a View Towards Determining the Authenticity of Heroides 16–21' (unpub. Toronto diss.).

HARDER, R. (1942): 'Die Meisterung der Schrift durch die Griechen', in H. Berve (ed.), *Das neue Bild der Antike* (Leipzig), 91–108.

HARDIE, P. R. (1986): *Virgil's Aeneid: Cosmos and Imperium* (Oxford).

—— (1991): 'The Janus Episode in Ovid's *Fasti*', *MD* 26: 47–64.

HARRIS, W. V. (1979): *War and Imperialism in Republican Rome* (Oxford).

HARRISON, B. (1991): *Inconvenient Fictions: Literature and the Limits of Theory* (New Haven and London).

HARRISON, S. J. (1988): 'Deflating the Odes: Horace *Epistles* 1. 20', *CQ* 38: 473–6.

HARTLICH, P. (1889): *De exhortationum a Graecis Romanisque scriptorum historia et indole* (Leipziger Studien zur klassischen Philologie, 11; Leipzig).

HAUPT, P. (1881): *Akkadische und sumerische Keilschrifttexte* (Leipzig).

HEATH, M. (1987): *The Poetics of Greek Tragedy* (London).

—— (1989): *Unity in Greek Poetics* (Oxford).

HEINZE, R. (1960): *Vom Geist der Römertums*, ed. E. Burck (Stuttgart).

HENDRIKS, I. H. M., PARSONS, P. J., and WORP, K. A. (1981): 'Papyri from the Groningen Collection, I: Encomium Alexandreae', *ZPE* 41: 71–83.

HERCHER, R. (1871): *Epistolographi Graeci* (Paris).

HERINGTON, C. J. (1982): 'Senecan Prose', in E. J. Kenney and W. V. Clausen (edd.), *The Cambridge History of Classical Literature*, vol. ii: *Latin Literature* (Cambridge), 514–19.

HIGHAM, T. F. (1934): 'Ovid: Some Aspects of his Character and Aims', *CR* 48: 105–16.

—— (1958): 'Ovid and Rhetoric', in N. I. Herescu (ed.), *Ovidiana* (Paris), 33–41.

HINDS, S. (1987): *The Metamorphosis of Persephone* (Cambridge).

HIRIYANNA, M. (1926): 'The First Commentary on the *Mahābhāṣya*', *Indian Historical Quarterly*, 2: 415–16.

HIRSCHLE, M. (1979): *Sprachphilosophie und Namenmagie im Neuplatonismus* (Meisenheim am Glan).

HIRZEL, R. (1912): *Plutarch* (Leipzig).

HOFFMANN, W. (1960): 'Die römische Politik des 2 Jahrhunderts und das Ende Karthagos', *Historia*, 9: 309–44.

HOFFNER, H. A. (1992): *Hittite Myths* (Atlanta).

HOLTZ, L. (1987): 'Pline et les grammariens: Le *Dubius Sermo* dans le haut moyen âge', *Helm.* 38: 233–47.

HOLZBERG, N. (1988): 'Ovid's "Babyloniska" (Met. 4. 55–166)', *Weiner Studien* 101 (1988), 265–77.

HOPKINS, K. (1983): *Death and Renewal* (Cambridge).

HORNBLOWER, J. (1981): *Hieronymus of Cardia* (Oxford).

HOUSMAN, A. E. (1930): *Manilius: Astronomica Book Five* (London).

HOWE, N. P. (1985): 'In Defense of the Encyclopedic Mode: On Pliny's Preface to the *H. N.*', *Latomus*, 44: 561–76.

HUBBARD, M. (1973): 'The *Odes*', in C. D. N. Costa (ed.), *Horace* (London), 1–28.

INNES, D. C. (1979): 'Gigantomachy and Natural Philosophy', *CQ* 29: 167–71.

—— (1995): 'Longinus, Unity and Structure', in J. G. J. Abbens, S. R. Slings, and I. Sluiter (edd.), *Papers on Greek Literary Theory after Aristotle in Honour of Professor D. M. Schenkeveld* (Amsterdam).

ISER, W. (1974): *The Implied Reader* (Baltimore and London; German original, 1972).

—— (1978): *The Act of Reading: A Theory of Aesthetic Response* (Baltimore and London; German original, 1976).

JANSON, T. (1964): *Latin Prose Prefaces* (Stockholm).

JAUSS, H. R. (1983): *Towards an Aesthetic of Reception* (Brighton; German original, 1970).

JONES, C. P. (1971): *Plutarch and Rome* (Oxford).

—— (1978): *The Roman World of Dio Chrysostom* (Cambridge, Mass., and London).

—— (1986): *Culture and Society in Lucian* (Cambridge, Mass.).

JONG, I. J. F. de (1987): *Narrators and Focalizers: The Presentation of the Story in the Iliad* (Amsterdam).

—— and SULLIVAN, J. P. (1994) (edd.), *Modern Critical Theory and Classical Literature* (Leiden).

KAIMAKIS, D. (1976): *Die Kyraniden* (Beiträge zur klassischen Philologie, 76; Meisenheim am Glan).

KARAGEORGHIS, V. (1981): *Ancient Cyprus* (Nicosia).

KENNEDY, D. F. (1984): Review of T. Woodman and D. West (edd.), *Poetry and Politics in the Age of Augustus*, *LCM* 9/10: 157–60.

—— (1993): *The Arts of Love: Five Studies in the Discourse of Roman Love Elegy* (Cambridge).

KENNEDY, G. A. (1972): *The Art of Rhetoric in the Roman World, 300 B.C.–A.D. 300* (Princeton).

—— (1989*a*): 'Ancient Antecedents of Modern Literary Theory', *AJPh* 110: 492–8.

—— (1989*b*): *The Cambridge History of Literary Criticism*, vol. i: *Classical Criticism* (Cambridge).

—— (1991): 'Heath on *Unity* and Daitz's *Living Voice*', *AJPh* 112: 115–18.

KENNEY, E. J. (1969): 'Ovid and the Law', *YCS* 21: 243–63.

—— (1973): 'The Style of the *Metamorphoses*', in J. W. Binns (ed.), *Ovid* (London), 116–53.

KERFERD, G. B. (1978): 'The Origin of Evil in Stoic Thought', *BJRL* 60: 482–94.

KEYES, C. W. (1935): 'The Greek Letter of Introduction', *AJPh* 56: 28–44.

KIESSLING, A., and HEINZE, R. (1915): *Q. Horatius Flaccus: Die Briefe* (Leipzig).

KILPATRICK, R. S. (1986): *The Poetry of Friendship: Horace Epistles I* (Edmonton).

KINDSTRAND, J. F. (1973): *Homer in der zweiten Sophistik* (Uppsala).

—— (1981): *Anacharsis: The Legend and the Apophthegmata* (Uppsala).

KLEVE, K. (1989): 'Lucretius in Herculaneum', *Cron. Erc.* 19: 5–27.

KOLENDO, J. (1970): 'L'Influence de Carthage sur la civilisation matérielle de Rome', *Archaeologia*, 31: 8–22.

KONDOLEON, C. (1995), *Domestic and Divine. Roman Mosaics in the House of Dionysos* (Ithaca and London).

KONSTAN, D. (1973): *Some Aspects of Epicurean Psychology* (Leiden).

KRINGS, V. (1989): 'La Destruction de Carthage: Problèmes d'historiographie ancienne et moderne', in Devijver and Lipiński (1989), 329–44.

KTU: M. Dietrich, O. Loretz, and J. Sanmartín, *Die Keilalphabetischen Texte aus Ugarit*, vol. i (Neukirchen, 1976).

KÜHN, J. H., and FLEISCHER, U. (1989): *Index Hippocraticus* (Göttingen).

LACOMBRADE, C. (1967): 'L'Empereur Julien émule de Marc-Aurèle', *Pallas*, 14: 9–22.

LADA, I. (1993): '"Empathic Understanding": Emotion and Cognition in Classical Dramatic Audience-Response', *PCPS* 39: 94–140.

LÄMMLI, F. (1962): *Vom Chaos zum Kosmos* (Basel).

LANCEL, S. (1989): 'L'Enceinte périurbaine de Carthage lors de la troisième guerre punique: Réalités et hypothèses', in Devijver and Lipiński (1989), 251–78.

LAURSEN, S. (1988): 'Epicurus on Nature xxv (Long–Sedley 10, B, C and j)', *Cron. Erc.* 18: 7–18.

LAUSBERG, M. (1970): *Untersuchungen zu Senecas Fragmenten* (Untersuchungen zur antiken Literatur und Geschichte, 7; Berlin).

LAWRENCE, A. W. (1979): *Greek Aims in Fortification* (Oxford).

LAWSON, E. T., and McCAULEY, R. N. (1990): *Rethinking Religion: Connecting Cognition and Culture* (Cambridge).

Le Corsu, F. (1981): *Plutarque et les femmes dans les Vies parallèles* (Paris).

Levi, D. (1947): *Antioch Mosaic Pavements* (Princeton).

Lieberg, G. (1982): *Poeta Creator* (Amsterdam).

—— (1985): '*Poeta Creator*: Some Religious Aspects', in F. Cairns (ed.), *Papers of the Liverpool Latin Seminar*, 5: 23–32.

Lippmann, E. O. von (1931): *Entstehung und Ausbreitung der Alchemie*, vol. ii (Berlin).

Long, A. A. (1968): 'The Stoic Concept of Evil', *PQ* 18: 329–43.

—— and Sedley, D. N. (1987): *The Hellenistic Philosophers* (2 vols.; Cambridge).

Lotman, J. (1977): *The Structure of the Artistic Text*, trans. G. Lenhoff and R. Vroon (Michigan Slavic Contributions, 7; Ann Arbor).

Lucas, J. (1990): 'Plato's Philosophy of Sex', in E. M. Craik (ed.), *'Owls to Athens': Essays on Classical Subjects presented to Sir Kenneth Dover* (Oxford), 223–31.

Lühr, F.-F. (1969): *Ratio und Fatum, Dichtung und Lehre bei Manilius* (diss. Frankfurt).

Macaulay, Thomas Babington (1898): *Essays and Biographies*, vol. i (Albany edn.; London).

McGann, M. J. (1969): *Studies in Horace's First Book of Epistles* (Collection Latomus, 100; Brussels).

Macintyre, A. (1970): 'The Idea of a Social Science', in B. R. Wilson (ed.), *Rationality* (Oxford), 112–30.

McKeown, J. C. (1987): *Ovid: Amores*, vol. i: *Text and Prolegomena* (Liverpool).

Macleod, C. W. (1979): 'The Poetry of Ethics: Horace *Epistles* 1', *JRS* 69: 16–27 = Macleod (1983), 280–91.

—— (1983): *Collected Essays* (Oxford).

Macleod, M. D. (1991): *Lucian: A Selection* (Warminster).

Marquès-Rivière, J. (1938): *Amulettes, talismans et pentacles* (Paris).

Martin, C. (1985): 'A Reconsideration of Ovid's *Fasti*', *ICS* 10: 261–74.

Martin, H. (1961): 'The Concept of Philanthropia in Plutarch's Lives', *AJPh* 82: 164–75.

Martindale, C. (1993a): *Redeeming the Text: Latin Poetry and the Hermeneutics of Reception* (Cambridge).

—— (1993b): 'Descent into Hell: Reading Ambiguity, or Virgil and the Critics', *PVS* 21: 111–50.

Matthews, J. (1989): *The Roman Empire of Ammianus* (London).

Mayer, R. G. (1986): 'Horace *Epistles* 1 and Philosophy', *AJPh* 107: 55–73.

Mazzucchi, C. M. (1990): 'Come finiva il περὶ ὕψους?', *Aevum Antiquum*, 3: 143–62.

—— (1992): *Dionisio Longino, Del sublime*, Introd., critical text, trans., comm. (Milan).

Mély, F. de (1898): *Les Lapidaires de l'antiquité et du moyen âge*, vol. ii.1: *Les Lapidaires grecs* (Paris).

MÉLY, F. de (1902): *Les Lapidaires de l'antiquité et du moyen âge*, vol. iii (Paris).

MELTZER, F. (1990): 'Unconscious', in F. Lentricchia and T. McLaughlin (edd.), *Critical Terms for Literary Study* (Chicago), 147–62.

MESCHINI, A. (1983): 'Le Ciranidi nel Marc. Gr. 512', *'Atti' dell'Accademia Pontaniana*, NS 31 (Naples), 145–77.

MITSIS, P. (1987): 'Epicurus on Friendship and Altruism', *Oxford Studies in Ancient Philosophy*, 5: 127–53.

MOLES, J. L. (1978): 'The Career and Conversion of Dio Chrysostom', *JHS* 98: 79–100.

—— (1983): 'Dio Chrysostom: Exile, Tarsus, Nero and Domitian', *LCM* 8/9: 130–4.

—— (1985): 'Cynicism in Horace *Epistles* 1', *PLLS* 5: 33–60.

—— (1990): 'The Kingship Orations of Dio Chrysostom', *PLLS* 6: 297–375.

—— (1993): Review of Russell (1992), *CR* 43: 256–8.

MOREAU, J. (1964): *Scripta Minora*, ed. W. Schmitthenner (Heidelberg).

MORGAN, J. R. (1982): 'History, Romance and Realism in Heliodorus', *Class. Ant.* 1: 221–65.

—— (1989): 'The Story of Knemon in Heliodorus' *Aithiopika*', *JHS* 109: 99–113.

—— (1993): 'Make-Believe and Make Believe: The Fictionality of the Greek Novels', in C. Gill and T. P. Wiseman (edd.), *Lies and Fiction in the Ancient World* (Exeter), 175–229.

MORROW, G. R. (1970): *Proclus: A Commentary on the First Book of Euclid's Elements*, trans. with introd. and notes (Princeton).

MORSON, G. S., and EMERSON, C. (1990): *Mikhail Bakhtin: Creation of a Prosaics* (Stanford, Calif.).

MOTTO, A. L., and CLARK, J. R. (1985): 'Seneca e il paradosso dell'avversità', *A&R* 30: 137–53; English version, 'Seneca and the Paradox of Adversity', in A. L. Motto and J. R. Clark, *Essays on Seneca* (Studien zur klassischen Philologie, 79; Frankfurt am Main, 1993), 65–86.

NAUTA, R. R. (1994): 'Historicizing Reading: The Aesthetics of Reception and Horace's "Soracte Ode"', in de Jong and Sullivan (1994), 207–30.

NESSELRATH, H. G. (1990): 'Lucian's Introductions', in D. A. Russell (ed.), *Antonine Literature* (Oxford), 111–40.

—— (1994): 'Menippeisches in der Spätantike: von Lukian zu Julians *Caesares* und zu Claudians *In Rufinum*', *Mus. Helv.* 51: 30–44.

NEWMAN, J. K. (1967): *Augustus and the New Poetry* (Collection Latomus, 88; Brussels).

NICOLL, W. S. (1977): 'Ovid, *Amores* 1. 5', *Mnemosyne*, 30: 40–8.

NIKOLAOU, K. (1963): *Report of the Department of Antiquities, Cyprus, 1963* (Nicosia).

—— (1967): *Report of the Department of Antiquities, Cyprus, 1967* (Nicosia).

NISBET, R. G. M., and HUBBARD, M. (1970): *A Commentary on Horace Odes Book One* (Oxford).

NORDEN, E. (1909): *Die Antike Kunstprosa vom 6. Jahrh. v. Chr. bis in d. Zeit d. Renaissance* (Leipzig and Berlin).

—— (1954): 'Das Genesiszitat in der Schrift vom Erhabenen', *Abh. Ak. Berlin*, Kl. f. Sprachen, Literatur u. Kunst, 1; repr. in *Kleine Schriften* (Berlin, 1966), 286–313.

NUSSBAUM, M. C. (1986): *The Fragility of Goodness: Luck and Ethics in Greek Tragedy and Philosophy* (Cambridge).

—— (1990): *Love's Knowledge: Essays on Philosophy and Literature* (Oxford).

OBBINK, D., and VANDER WAERDT, P. A. (1991): 'Diogenes of Babylon: The Stoic Sage in the City of Fools', *GRBS* 32: 355–96.

O'MEARA, D. J. (1989): *Pythagoras Revived* (Oxford).

OTTO, A. (1890): *Die Sprichwörter und sprichwörtlichen Redensarten der Römer* (Leipzig).

PACK, E. (1986): *Städte und Steuern in der Politik Julians* (Brussels).

PATTERSON, C. (1992): 'Plutarch on Marriage: Traditional Wisdom through a Philosophic Lens', *ANR W* ii.33.6: 4709–23.

PEASE, A. S. (1926): 'Things without Honour', *CP* 21: 27–42.

PELLING, C. B. R. (1986*a*): 'Plutarch and Roman Politics', in I. S. Moxon, J. D. Smart, and A. J. Woodman (edd.), *Past Perspectives: Studies in Greek and Roman Historical Writing* (Cambridge), 159–88.

—— (1986*b*): 'Synkrisis in Plutarch's Lives', in F. Brenk and I. Gallo (edd.), *Miscellanea Plutarchea* (Quaderni del Giornale filologico ferrarese, 8; Ferrara), 83–96.

—— (1988): *Plutarch: Life of Antony* (Cambridge).

—— (1990) (ed.): *Characterization and Individuality in Greek Literature* (Oxford).

PERKELL, C. (1989): *The Poet's Truth: A Study of the Poet in Virgil's Georgics* (Berkeley, Los Angeles, and London).

PFEIFFER, R. (1968): *History of Classical Scholarship* (Oxford).

PICCALUGA, G. (1988): '"Chi" ha sparso il sale sulle rovine di Cartagine?', *Cultura e scuola*, 105: 153–65.

PIETILÄ-CASTRÉN, L. (1991): 'L. Mummius' Contributions to the Agonistic Life in the Mid-Second Century B.C.', *Arctos*, 25: 97–106.

PINCHES, THEOPHILUS G. (1928): 'The Influence of the Heathenism of the Canaanites upon the Hebrews', *Journal of the Transactions of the Victoria Institute*, 60: 122–42.

POHLENZ, M. (1913): 'Eine byzantinische Recension Plutarchischer Schriften', *Gött. Nachr.*: 338–62.

PÖSCHL, V., GÄRTNER, H., and HEYKE, W. (1964): *Bibliographie der antiken Bildersprache* (Heidelberg).

POWELL, J. G. F. (1990*a*): *Cicero on Friendship and the Dream of Scipio* (Warminster).

—— (1990*b*): 'The Tribune Sulpicius', *Historia*, 39: 446–60.

PRATO, C., and FORNARA, A. (1984): *Iuliano, Epistola a Temistio* (Quad. dell'Inst. di Filol. Class. dell'Univ. di Lecce, Studi & testi lat. 2; Lecce).

PRICE, A. W. (1989): *Love and Friendship in Plato and Aristotle* (Oxford).

PRICE, S. R. F. (1990): 'The Future of Dreams: From Freud to Artemidoros', in D. M. Halperin, J. J. Winkler, and F. I. Zeitlin (edd.), *Before Sexuality: The Construction of Erotic Experience in the Ancient Greek World* (Princeton), 365–87.

QUINT, D. (1993): *Epic and Empire: Politics and Generic Form from Virgil to Milton* (Princeton).

RADERMACHER, L. (1897): 'Studien zur Geschichte der griechischen Rhetorik II: Plutarchs Schrift *de se ipso citra invidiam laudando*', *RhM* 52: 419–24.

RAYCHAUDHURI, T. (1988): *Europe Reconsidered: Perceptions of the West in Nineteenth-Century Bengal* (Oxford).

REARDON, B. P. (1989) (ed.): *Collected Ancient Greek Novels* (Berkeley).

REEH, A. (1973): *Interpretationen zu den Astronomica des Manilius* (diss. Marburg).

REHMANN, W. (1969): *Die Beziehungen zwischen Lukrez und Horaz* (diss. Freiburg).

REISKE, J. J. (1784): *Dionis Chrysostomi orationes* (Leipzig).

RELIHAN, J. C. (1993): *Ancient Menippean Satire* (Baltimore).

RIDLEY, R. T. (1986): 'To be Taken with a Pinch of Salt: The Destruction of Carthage', *CP* 80: 140–6.

RIST, J. M. (1964): 'Mysticism and Transcendence in Later Neoplatonism', *Hermes*, 92: 213–25.

—— (1969): *Stoic Philosophy* (Cambridge).

—— (1972): *Epicurus, an Introduction* (Cambridge).

—— (1980): 'Epicurus on Friendship', *CP* 75: 121–9.

ROBERTS, M. (1989): *The Jewelled Style, Poetry and Poetics in Late Antiquity* (Cornell).

RODGER, A. (1972): *Owners and Neighbours in Roman Law* (Oxford).

ROMANO, E. (1979): *Struttura degli Astronomica di Manilio* (Palermo).

RÖMER, W. H. P. (1989) (with K. Hecker): *Hymnen und Gebete* (Texte aus der Umwelt des Alten Testaments, 2; Gütersloh).

ROMILLY, J. de (1979): *La Douceur dans la pensée grecque* (Paris).

ROMM, J. (1990): 'Wax, Stone, and Promethean Clay: Lucian as Plastic Artist', *Classical Antiquity*, 9: 74–98.

ROMMEL, H. (1923): *Die naturwissenschaftlich-paradoxographischen Exkurse bei Philostratos, Heliodoros und Achilleus Tatios* (Stuttgart).

ROSE, H. J. (1966): *A Handbook of Latin Literature* (3rd edn., London and New York).

ROSS, D. O. (1987): *Virgil's Elements: Physics and Poetry in the* Georgics (Princeton).

ROSSETTI, S. (1960): 'La Numidia e Cartagine fra la II e la III guerra punica', *PP* 15: 336–53.

ROSTOVTZEFF, M. (1941): *Social and Economic History of the Hellenistic World* (Oxford).

RUDD, N. (1966): *The Satires of Horace* (Cambridge).

—— (1993): 'Horace as a Moralist', in N. Rudd (ed.), *Horace 2000: A Celebration. Essays for the Bimillennium* (Bristol), 64–88.

RUSSELL, D. A. (1964): *'Longinus' On the Sublime*, ed. with introd. and comm. (Oxford).

—— (1965): *'Longinus' On Sublimity* (trans.) (Oxford).

—— (1966a): 'On Reading Plutarch's Lives', *G&R* 13: 139–54.

—— (1966b): 'Plutarch, *Alcibiades* 1–16', *PCPS* 12: 37–47.

—— (1967): 'Rhetoric and Criticism', *G&R* 14: 130–44.

—— (1972): *Plutarch* (London and New York).

—— (1973): *Ars Poetica*, in C. D. N. Costa (ed.), *Horace* (London), 113–34.

—— (1974): 'Letters to Lucilius', in C. D. N. Costa (ed.), *Seneca* (London), 70–95.

—— (1979): '*De Imitatione*', in D. West and T. Woodman (edd.), *Creative Imitation and Latin Literature* (Cambridge), 1–16.

—— (1981a): *Criticism in Antiquity* (London).

—— (1981b): 'Longinus Revisited', *Mnemosyne*, 34: 143–55.

—— (1983): *Greek Declamation* (Cambridge).

—— (1989): *The Place of Poetry in Ancient Literature* (Oxford).

—— (1990): '*Ethos* in Oratory and Rhetoric', in Pelling (1990), 197–212.

—— (1992): *Dio Chrysostom: Orations VII, XII, XXXVI* (Cambridge).

—— (1993a): *Plutarch, Selected Essays and Dialogues* (Oxford).

—— (1993b): 'Self-Disclosure in Plutarch and Horace', in G. W. Most, H. Petersmann, and A. M. Ritter (edd.), *Philanthropia kai Eusebeia*, Festschrift für A. Dihle (Göttingen), 426–37.

—— and WILSON, N. G. (1981): *Menander Rhetor* (Oxford).

—— and WINTERBOTTOM, M. (1972): *Ancient Literary Criticism: The Principal Texts in New Translations* (Oxford).

RUTHERFORD, R. B. (1989a): *The Meditations of Marcus Aurelius: A Study* (Oxford).

—— (1989b): 'Virgil's Poetic Ambitions in *Eclogue 6*', *G&R* 36: 42–50.

ŞABBAH, G. (1978): *La Méthode d'Ammien Marcellin* (Paris).

SALEMME, C. (1983): *Introduzione agli 'Astronomica' di Manilio* (Naples).

SALLMANN, K. (1986): 'La Responsabilité de l'homme face à la Nature', *Helm.* 37: 251–66.

SANDBACH, F. H. (1985): *Aristotle and the Stoics* (Cambridge Philological Society, suppl. vol. 10; Cambridge).

SANDY, G. (1982): 'Characterisation and Philosophical Décor in Heliodorus' *Aethiopica*', *TAPA* 112: 141–67.

SCHENKEVELD, D. M. (1964): *Studies in Demetrius On Style* (Amsterdam).

SCHEPENS, G. (1980): *L''Autopsie' dans la méthode des historiens grecs du Ve siècle avant J.-C.* (Brussels).

SCHIESARO, A. (forthcoming): in A. Schiesaro and T. N. Habinek (edd.), *The Roman Revolution* (Princeton).

SCHILLING, R. (1978): 'La Place de Pline l'Ancien dans la littérature technique', *RPh* 52: 272–83.

SCHMIDT, V. (1980): 'ὑγιαίνομαι im Corpus Hippocraticum und ein Fragment des Musonius Rufus', *WJhb*, NS 6b: 29–44.

SCHOFIELD, M. (1991): *The Stoic Idea of the City* (Cambridge).

SCHRÖDER, O. (1987): 'Das Odysseusbild des Ailios Aristides', *RhM* 130: 350–6.

SCUDERI, R. (1984): *Commento a Plutarco, 'Vita di Antonio'* (Pavia).

SCULLARD, H. H. (1960): 'Scipio Aemilianus and Roman Politics', *JRS* 50: 59–74.

SEDLEY, D. N. (1989): 'Epicurean Anti-Reductionism', in J. Barnes and M. Mignucci (edd.), *Matter and Metaphysics* (Naples), 297–327.

SEGAL, C. (1987): 'Writer as Hero: The Heroic Ethos in Longinus, On the Sublime', in J. Servais, T. Hackens, and B. Servais-Soyez (edd.), *Stemmata, Mélanges de philologie, d'histoire et d'archéologie grecque offerts à Jules Labarbe* (Louvain), 207–17.

—— (1992): 'Boundaries, Worlds, and Analogical Thinking, or How Lucretius Learned to Love Atomism and Still Write Poetry', in K. Galinsky (ed.), *The Interpretation of Roman Poetry: Empiricism or Hermeneutics?* (Frankfurt), 137–56, with 'Discussion', 170–5.

SHARPLES, R. W. (1993): 'Carneades and Epicurus on the Atomic Swerve', *BICS* 38 (1991–3): 174–90.

SHAW, B. D. (1981): 'The Elder Pliny's African Geography', *Historia*, 30: 424–71.

SHEPPARD, A. D. R. (1980): *Studies on the 5th and 6th Essays of Proclus' Commentary on the Republic* (Göttingen).

SLINGS, S. R. (1981): *A Commentary on the Platonic Clitophon* (Amsterdam).

SMITH, K. F. (1918): 'The Poet Ovid', *Studies in Philology*, 15: 307–32; repr. 1920 in *Martial the Epigrammatist and Other Essays* (Baltimore), 37–74.

SNYDER, J. M. (1980): *Puns and Poetry in Lucretius' De rerum natura* (Amsterdam).

SOUBIRAN, J. (1991): 'Sénèque prosateur et poète: Convergences métriques', in *Sénèque et la prose latine* (Entretiens Hardt, Geneva), 347–77.

STADTER, P. A. (1988): 'The Proems of Plutarch's Lives', *ICS* 13/2: 275–95.

—— (1992): 'Paradoxical Paradigms: Lysander and Sulla', in P. A. Stadter (ed.), *Plutarch and the Historical Tradition* (London), 41–55.

STEPHENS, S., and WINKLER, J. J. (1995): *Ancient Greek Novels: The Fragments* (Princeton).

STERTZ, S. A. (1977): 'Marcus Aurelius as Ideal Emperor in Late-Antique Greek Thought', *Classical World*, 70: 433–9.

STOCK, A. (1911): *De Prolaliarum Usu Rhetorico* (diss. Königsberg).

SULLIVAN, J. P. (1968): *The Satyricon of Petronius: A Literary Study* (London).

—— (1994): 'Introduction', in de Jong and Sullivan (1994), 1–26.

SUSSMAN, L. A. (1978): *The Elder Seneca* (Leiden).

SWAIN, S. (1994): 'Dio and Lucian', in J. R. Morgan and R. Stoneman (edd.), *The Greek Novel in Context* (London), 166–80.

SYME, R. (1939): *The Roman Revolution* (Oxford).
—— (1971): *Emperors and Biography* (Oxford).
—— (1983): *Historia Augusta Papers* (Oxford).
TARRANT, R. J. (1989): 'The Reader as Author', in J. N. Grant (ed.), *Editing Greek and Latin Texts* (New York), 121–62.
TASSEL, R. VAN (1973): 'Bezoars', *Janus*, 60: 241–59.
TEMKIN, O. (1991): *Hippocrates in a World of Pagans and Christians* (Baltimore).
THEILER, W. (1982): *Poseidonios, Die Fragmente* (2 vols.; Texte und Kommentare, 10/1–2; Berlin and New York).
THOMAS, R. F. (1982): *Lands and Peoples in Roman Poetry: The Ethnographical Tradition* (Cambridge Philological Society, suppl. vol. 7; Cambridge).
THOMPSON, E. A. (1947): *The Historical Work of Ammianus Marcellinus* (Cambridge; repr. Groningen, 1969).
THRAEDE, K. (1970): *Grundzüge griechische-römische Brieftopik* (Zetemata, 48; Munich).
TRAPP, M. B. (1990): 'Plato's *Phaedrus* in Second-Century Greek Literature', in D. A. Russell (ed.), *Antonine Literature* (Oxford), 141–73.
TREGGIARI, S. (1991): *Roman Marriage: Iusti Coniuges from the Time of Cicero to the Time of Ulpian* (Oxford).
TROTTER, D. (1992): 'Gesture as language', *London Review of Books*, 30 Jan.: 14–16.
VASALY, A. (1993): *Representations: Images of the World in Ciceronian Oratory* (Berkeley).
VERBEKE, G. (1966): *Jean Philopon: Commentaire sur le De Anima d'Aristote. Traduction de Guillaume de Moerbeke. Édition critique avec une introduction sur la psychologie de Philopon* (Louvain and Paris).
VITTINGHOFF, F. (1951): *Römische Kolonisation und Bürgerrechtspolitik unter Caesar und Augustus* (Wiesbaden).
VOIT, L. (1934): *Δεινότης, ein antiker Stilbegriff* (Leipzig).
WAEGEMAN, M. (1987): *Amulet and Alphabet: Magical Amulets in the First Book of Cyranides* (Amsterdam).
WAITES, M. C. (1912): 'Some Features of the Allegorical Debate in Greek Literature', *HSCP* 23: 1–46.
WALLACE-HADRILL, A. (1983): *Suetonius: The Scholar and his Caesars* (New Haven and London).
—— (1990): 'Pliny the Elder and Man's Unnatural History', *G&R* 37: 80–96.
WARDMAN, A. (1974): *Plutarch's Lives* (London).
WATSON, G. (1982): 'Unfair to Proclus?', *Phronesis*, 27: 101–6.
—— (1988): *Phantasia in Classical Thought* (Galway).
WATSON, P. (1983): 'Mythological Exempla in Ovid's *Ars Amatoria*', *CP* 78: 117–35.
WEBB, R. (1992): 'The Transmission of the Eikones of Philostratos and the Development of the Ekphrasis from Late Antiquity to the Renaissance' (unpub. thesis, Warburg Institute, London).

WEINSTOCK, S. (1971): *Divus Julius* (Oxford).

WEST, D. A. (1967): *Reading Horace* (Edinburgh).

—— (1969): *The Imagery and Poetry of Lucretius* (Edinburgh).

—— (1982): 'Farewell Atomology', Review of J. M. Snyder, *Puns and Poetry in Lucretius'* De Rerum Natura (Amsterdam, 1980), in *CR* 32: 25–7.

WEST, M. L. (1971): *Early Greek Philosophy and the Orient* (Oxford).

—— (1978): *Hesiod: Works and Days* (Oxford).

—— (1988): 'The Rise of the Greek Epic', *JHS* 108: 151–72.

WHITE, M., and EPSTON, D. (1990): *Narrative Means to Therapeutic Ends* (New York and London).

WILKINSON, L. P. (1969): *The Georgics of Virgil* (Cambridge).

WILLIAMS, G. (1968): *Tradition and Originality in Roman Poetry* (Oxford).

—— (1978): *Change and Decline: Roman Literature in the Early Empire* (California).

WINBOLDT, S. E. (1903): *Latin Hexameter Verse* (London).

WINTERBOTTOM, M. (1974): *The Elder Seneca* (2 vols.; Loeb Classical Library).

WOLFF, S. R. (1986): 'Carthage and the Mediterranean', *Cahiers des études anciennes XIX, Carthage IX*, 134–53.

WOODMAN, A. J. (1975): 'Questions of Date, Genre and Style in Velleius: Some Literary Answers', *CQ* 25: 272–306.

ZANKER, P. (1988): *The Power of Images in the Age of Augustus* (Michigan; German original, 1987).

ZIEBARTH, E. (1913): *Aus der Antiken Schule* (Bonn).

ZIMMERN, H. (1913): *Sumerische Kultlieder aus altbabylonischer Zeit*, ii (Vorder-asiatische Schriftdenkmäler, 10; Leipzig).

INDEX OF NAMES

Academy 271
Achaea 136, 143
Achilles Tatius 271
Acragas 142
Acrocorinth 134
Acrotatus of Sparta 226–7
Actium 155–6, 210
Aegae 337, 341–2
Aelian 272, 277
Aemilius Paullus, L. (cos. 182, 168 BC) 220
Aemilius Scaurus, Mamercus (consul under Tiberius) 78
Aeschines 333
Aeschylus 194, 226, 239 n. 8, 264 n. 23, 304, 330–1
Aesop 170, 173, 181
Agathoclea (mistress of Ptolemy IV) 224
Agathon 247
Agesilaus 212–13, 232, 233 n. 51, 235
Agesipolis 231
Agiatis 230–1
Aithiops 273
Alcaeus 311
Alcibiades 213, 224 n. 13, 228 n. 29, 233 n. 49
Alcman 196
Alexander of Pherae 227, 236
Alexander of Seleucia 290
Alexander of Tralles 284
Alexander the Great 73, 86–7, 89–90, 133, 137, 139, 170, 185, 194, 208–9, 228–9, 253, 277, 291–2, 294–5
Alexandria 167–75
Amafinius 17
Ambrose 316 n. 15
Amestris (daughter of Artaxerxes) 225
Ammianus Marcellinus 287–98
Ammonius (commentator on Aristotle) 272 n. 6
Amphis (comic poet) 263 n. 22
Anacharsis 174
Anaxagoras 6
Anaxilas (comic poet) 263 n. 22
Andriscus 139

Anonymus Seguerianus 327–8
Antigonus Gonatas 138
Antioch 274, 291–2, 295, 297 n. 41, 298
Antiochus III 227
Antipater of Sidon 140 n. 41
Antiphanes 269
Antiphon (tragic poet) 103 n. 12
Antoninus Liberalis 276
Antoninus Pius 287
Antony, Mark (M. Antonius) 205–8, 210, 218, 223–4, 233, 235–6
Aphthonius 150 n. 6, 156, 257–9
Apis 173
Apollodorus 263
Apollonius (subject of Philostratus' work) 251–4, 347
Apollonius of Rhodes 13
Appian 133–48
Apsines 327 n. 18, 328, 333
Aratus 22 n. 9
Archias of Thebes 227
Archidamus 215
Arellius Fuscus (declaimer) 63, 77, 79
Aretaeus 281–2
Areus (king of Sparta) 226
Argos 215
Aristaenus of Megalopolis 214, 216 n. 15
Aristarchus 337 n. 9
Aristides (Athenian statesman) 218, 220, 226, 232
Aristides, Aelius 193–204
Aristippus 52, 273
Aristobulus 229 n. 33
Aristogeiton 271 n. 5
Aristophanes 77, 82 n. 34, 263 n. 22, 264 n. 23, 265–6, 301, 306
Aristophon (prosecutor of Iphicrates) 202
Aristotle 22 n. 7, 31–45, 48, 52, 56, 58–60, 76, 98, 101, 104, 199, 231 n. 40, 304–6, 324, 327 n. 19, 328 nn. 20–1, 329, 331 n. 31, 332 n. 33, 333 n. 37, 344
Arrian 229 n. 34, 277 n. 22
Artaxerxes II 224–5

Artemisia I of Caria 256
Artemon (editor of Aristotle's letters) 58
Asclepiades 284
Aspasia (mistress of Pericles) 236 n. 62, 265
Aspasia (Phocian concubine) 225
Asprenas, P. Nonius (declaimer) 80
Assyria 135, 138 n. 27
Athenaeus 139 n. 36, 266 n. 29
Athens 134–5, 138, 140, 146–8, 167–8, 174–5, 180, 214–15, 217, 219, 232, 256, 265, 270–1, 273, 277–8, 316, 330
Ātmabodhendra 252–3
Atossa (daughter of Artaxerxes) 224–5
Atossa (wife of Darius I) 239 n. 8
Atticists 318 n. 23
Augustine 317 n. 21
Augustus 19–20, 24–9, 123, 130, 139–40, 155, 219–20, 291, 294, 311
Aurelius, Marcus 19, 21 n. 5, 287–98
Ausonius 153–9
Avidius Cassius, C. 288, 298
Ayārcya 252–3

Babylon 134, 199, 274–5, 277
Bactria 170
Bagoas 229
Bakhtin, Mikhael 201
Balliol College, Oxford xi
Barsine 229
Basil 239–44
Bias 40
Bibulus, M. Calpurnius (cos. 59 BC) 234
Blossius of Cumae 43
Buñuel, Luis 13
Boeotia 274
Borysthenes 165–7, 175, 184–92
Brahmins 251–4
Brutus, M. Iunius (killer of Caesar) 220, 236
Buddhism 252–3
Byrsa 134, 140
Byzantium 227, 276

Caecilius (author of work on sublimity) 335
Caesar, Julius 42–3, 137, 139–40, 210, 212, 220, 226 n. 23, 233 n. 50, 234, 291, 294
Callias 225
Callimachus 5, 24, 49 n. 10, 127 n. 19, 313 n. 4
Capitol 79, 141

Capua 135, 144
Carneades 77, 146–7
Carthage 133–48
Cassander 215
Cassius Severus (orator) 130 n. 25
Castra Cornelia 137
Catilina, L. Sergius 42
Cato, M. Porcius, the censor 56 n. 33, 77, 83, 98, 121 n. 6, 122, 128 n. 22, 143, 145–6, 225–7, 228 n. 30, 233
Cato Uticensis, M. Porcius 102, 103 n. 12, 215, 229, 234–6
Catullus 4–5, 28, 311 n. 46
Cebes 238 n. 4, 240–2, 247, 249 n. 34
Celsus 55 n. 31, 124 n. 12
Censorinus (grammarian) 139 n. 35
Censorinus, L. Marcius (cos. 149 BC) 134–6, 146
Cestius Pius, L. (rhetor) 87
Chabrias 198
Chaeronea 228
Chariton 271, 275
Chesterfield, Lord 112
Chilon 40–2
Chilonis of Sparta 226–7, 230
Christians 289, 296–7
Chrysippus 31, 37, 76, 99–100, 105
Cicero 3, 17, 20 n. 2, 21 n. 5, 25 n. 14, 26 n. 21, 31–45, 48, 57, 59, 76, 77 n. 13, 82 n. 34, 90–1, 98, 111–12, 121 n. 6, 122, 123 n. 10, 126 n. 17, 127 n. 19, 128 n. 20, 129 n. 23, 131 n. 26, 134 n. 5, 135, 140–2, 145–7, 175 n. 29, 200, 226, 228 n. 30, 310, 313 n. 2, 314–16, 318 n. 23, 319 n. 26, 320 n. 31, 321 n. 32, 324–31
Cilicia 170
Cimon 213, 225, 227–8
Claudius II (Gothicus) 293–6
Claudius Pompeianus, Ti. (friend of Marcus Aurelius) 293
Cleanthes 31, 170 n. 18, 179 n. 11, 319 n. 25
Clearchus 31
Cleitus 208
Clement of Alexandria 239, 241–2
Cleombrotus of Sparta 230
Cleomenes I of Sparta 326 n. 12
Cleomenes III of Sparta 230–1
Cleon 102
Cleonice of Byzantium 227
Cleonymus of Sparta 226–7

Cleopatra VII of Egypt 207–8, 218, 223–4, 231, 235–6
Clitomachus (Carthaginian philosopher) 146
Colchis 258
Columella 121, 124 n. 12, 128 n. 22, 130 n. 24
Commodus 293
Conjeeveram 252
Constantine 291, 293–4, 296–8
Constantius II 288, 293, 295 n. 34, 296
Corinth 133–48, 175, 214, 258, 260–3
Coriolanus 42, 207, 224 n. 13
Cosmas, St. 286
Crassus, L. Licinius (censor 92 BC) 77
Crassus, M. Licinius (cos. 70, 55 BC) 210
Cratinus 193 n. 3
Cremutius Cordus, A. 130 n. 25
Crete 175
Crinagoras 136 n. 18
Crispus (son of Constantine) 296
Critias 263 n. 22
Critolaus (strategos of Achaean League 146–7 BC) 136
Ctesias 225 n. 18
Cynics, Cynicism 112, 170–2, 179–81
Cyprus 213, 276
Cyranides 281–6
Cyrene 36, 227 n. 27, 273
Cyrus I 201 n. 26, 229
Cyrus II 196, 225

Dacia 181–3, 186, 191, 210
Damian, St 286
Damon of Chaeronea 228
Danube 289, 336
Darius (son of Artaxerxes II) 225
Darius III 229 n. 32
Delphi 275, 278 n. 27, 321–2
Demetrius (author of *On Style*) 57–60
Demetrius (freedman) 221, 233
Demetrius Poliorcetes 133, 137, 224, 227–8, 233, 235–6
Democles of Athens 227–8
Democritus 54, 264 n. 23
Demosthenes 90–1, 194, 196, 200–1, 238 n. 4, 249, 313, 318, 325, 327–8, 331
Demylus (tyrant) 103 n. 12
Descent of Ishtar 340
Dicaearchus 97–8
Dikṣita, Rāmabhadra 253

Dio, Cassius 130, 134 n. 4, 143 n. 58, 288 n. 6
Dio Chrysostom 163–92, 196 n. 13, 197 n. 15, 239–46, 249 n. 34, 252
Diocletian 293
Diodorus Siculus 135 n. 10, 140 n. 41, 142 n. 49, 143 n. 62
Diogenes Laertius 35 n. 4, 52, 97, 106, 273 n. 8
Diogenes of Babylon 147–8
Dionysius I of Syracuse 273
Dionysius of Halicarnassus 27 n. 22, 196 n. 13, 313 n. 4, 319 n. 25, 323 n. 1, 325, 327–30
Domitian 183, 251
Domitius Ahenobarbus, Cn. (censor 92 BC) 77
Donatus 8 n. 6
Dyme 136, 145 n. 69

Ecbatana 225
Egypt 270, 272–3, 276–7, 338, 347
Elis 183
Elpinice 225
Empedocles 48
Emporia 135
Epaminondas 196, 198, 201 n. 26, 231
Ephesus 271
Epictetus 31, 38, 99 n. 7, 101 n. 11, 172 n. 21
Epicurus and Epicureanism 6, 8–12, 16–18, 35–6, 38–9, 47–8, 50, 52, 128 n. 22, 182
Erra and Ishum 341
Ethiopia 169–70, 277 n. 24, 279
Etna 336
Euboea 164–5, 175–80
Eubulus (comic poet) 263 n. 22
Euclid 345–9
Euphrates 342
Euripides 26 n. 20, 36, 83, 88, 179 n. 15, 194 n. 8, 256 n. 4, 258–9, 263, 264 n. 23, 304, 327, 332–3
Eurymedon (battle of) 213, 215
Eutropius 137 n. 23, 141 n. 47, 287, 289

Fabianus, Papirius (declaimer-turned-philosopher) 77
Fabius Maximus Aemilianus, Q. (cos. 145 BC) 136, 145 n. 69
Fausta (wife of Constantine) 296
Faustina (wife of Marcus Aurelius) 293
Fenestella 135 n. 13

Festus 142 n. 54
Flamininus, L. Quinctius 228 n. 30
Flamininus, T. Quinctius 136, 212–18
Flora (concubine of Pompey) 221, 223, 233–4
Florus 140 n. 39
Forster, E. M. 43
Foucault, Michel 222, 308
Freud, Sigmund 234, 308–10
Frontinus 131 n. 26
Fronto 21 n. 5, 290, 320 n. 31

Galen 167 n. 10, 238, 281–2, 284
Gargonius (declaimer) 81
Gauḍapāda 252–3
Gaul 210, 287–8, 290, 294
Gellius, Aulus 41, 43, 99–100, 117, 147 n. 75
Geminus (friend of Pompey) 221, 234
Germany 210
Getae 185, 190
Gibbon, Edward 336 n. 4
Gilgamesh 340
Gorgias 320 n. 30, 328–9
Gorgidas of Thebes 231
Gracchus, C. Sempronius 42, 140, 315
Gracchus, Ti. Sempronius 42–3
Gratian 288 n. 7
Gregory of Corinth 200 n. 24

Hadrian 141 n. 46, 208
Hannibal 135–6, 139
Harimiśra 253
Harmodius 271 n. 5
Harpagus 137
Harpalus 215
Hasdrubal 136, 139, 144
Haterius, Q. (cos. 5 BC) 315 n. 11
Helvia 114
Hephaestion 229
Heracles, Hercules 101 n. 11, 102, 139, 170, 210, 231, 237–50, 290–1, 332
Heraclides of Cyme 225 n. 18
Heraclitus 15, 197
Hercules, *see* Heracles
Hermesianax 276
Hermogenes 82 n. 33, 153 n. 12, 156, 256–7, 259–60, 328–9
Herodian 229 n. 34
Herodotus 134, 139, 166, 184, 227, 239 n. 8, 248 n. 30, 277, 281, 286

Hesiod 19, 22 n. 9, 26 n. 21, 31, 182, 246–7, 340
Himalayas 252
Himera 139
Himilco 142
Hippocratic corpus 281–6
Hippolytus 197 n. 15
Homer 11 n. 16, 22 n. 7, 24, 28, 32, 34–5, 130, 138, 163, 165–6, 168, 171–2, 178–9, 182, 185–9, 196, 199, 201–2, 207, 231, 238–9 n. 8, 252, 256, 259, 270, 272–3, 277–9, 295, 305, 324–8, 330, 333, 335–42
Horace 9 n. 10, 19, 21 n. 5, 22 n. 11, 25 n. 14, 39, 47–61, 123, 126, 127 n. 19, 130, 155 n. 19, 256 n. 5, 259, 269, 305, 310–11, 324, 328–30
Hortensius Hortalus, Q. (cos. 69 BC) 234
Hypanis 166
Hyperides 327, 330

Iamblichus 275
Iarchas 251–4
India 170, 251–4, 277
Iphicrates 196, 202
Isocrates 76, 196, 331 n. 30
Isodice (wife of Cimon) 225
Italica 142

Jesus 296; *see also* Christians
Jews and Jewish literature 289, 335, 338–42
Josephus 335
Julia (wife of Pompey) 233–4
Julia Domna 251
Julian 172 n. 21, 287–98
Justin (historical epitomiser) 136 n. 18
Justin Martyr 239–41, 243–4, 247
Juvenal 41 n. 22, 63 n. 3, 73, 82

Kāmakoṭi 252

Labienus, T. (orator and historian) 126 n. 17, 130 n. 25
Lacan, Jacques 309–10
Lactantius 106
Laelius, C. 98, 234
Lais 261–5, 273
Lamia (courtesan) 221 n. 1, 235
Lechaeum 134
Lemnos 339 n. 15
Leonidas (father of Chilonis) 230

Libanius 32, 77 n. 10, 231 n. 40, 255–67, 290, 295 nn. 35–6, 297 n. 41
Licinius, Valerius Licinianus 293
Libya 170
Livy 85, 133–48
'Longinus' 22 n. 7, 192, 317 nn. 20–1, 320 n. 31, 321–2, 323–41
Longus 279–80
Lucan 89–90
Lucian 8 n. 6, 31, 84, 172 n. 21, 237–50, 272, 319 n. 26
Lucilius (satiric poet) 59
Lucilius (addressee of Seneca) 96–7, 107, 109–10, 112
Lucilla (wife of L. Verus) 293
Lucretius 3–18, 19, 26–7, 38, 48, 50, 53–4, 129 n. 23
Lucullus, L. Licinius (cos. 74 BC) 212
Lycophron 264 n. 23
Lycurgus 102, 290
Lysander 212–13, 232 n. 45, 235
Lysias 202, 313, 327 n. 18

Macaulay, Thomas Babington 115, 206
Macedonia and Macedonians 170–1, 173, 229, 235 n. 60
Machanidas of Sparta 213
Macrobius 140
Maecenas 19–20, 48–9, 53, 56–7, 59
Magi 165–6, 188–90
Magnentius, Flavius Magnus 293
Mago (Carthaginian writer) 135
Manilius 11
Marathon 213, 215, 331
Marcellinus 325 n. 10, 329
Marcellus, M. Claudius (cos. 222, 215–14, 210, 208 BC) 212
Marcia (wife of Cato and Hortensius) 234
Marcus Aurelius, *see* Aurelius
Marius, C. 140, 207, 209–10
Marruvium 141 n. 46
Massinissa 135, 137 n. 23
Matius, C. 42
Maximus of Tyre 32, 167 n. 10, 168 n. 12, 170 n. 18, 172 n. 21, 173 n. 24, 239, 241 n. 13, 242
Media 138 n. 27
Megara 36, 175
Megara (Carthage) 140
Meletus 102–3
Memmius, C. 19
Memphis 173

Menander (comic poet) 263 n. 22, 266, 272–3
Menander Rhetor xi–xiii, 168, 172–3
Menemachus of Sardis 215
Metrobates (lover of Sulla) 235
Metrodorus (epigrammatist) 274
Miletus 133, 165, 215, 275
Milo 330
Mithras, Mithraism 188–9
Montaigne 44
Montanus, Votienus (declaimer) 81
Moselle 153–9
Mummius Achaicus, L. (cos. 146 BC) 133–48
Museum of Alexandria 171, 173
Musonius Rufus, C. 32 n. 1, 181
Myron 142
Myrrhine 265

Nea Paphos 274
Neaira 263
Neoplatonism 273, 343–51
Nepos 208–9
Nergal and Ereshkigal 340
Nero 90, 214
Nerva 178, 186, 191
Nicander 22
Nicias 213, 215
Nicolaus of Myra 256 n. 4, 257 n. 8, 259 n. 12, 260 nn. 15–16, 274
Nile 113, 169–70, 197, 336, 338
Nineveh 133
Nonnus 274
Numantia 137, 145 n. 66

Ochus (son of Artaxerxes II) 225
Octavia (wife of Antony) 235 n. 60
Oinanthe (mother of Agathoclea) 224
Olympia 143, 181–4, 271, 339 n. 15
Oropus 146–8
Orosius 137 n. 24
Orpheus 170–3
Ostia 275
Otho (emperor) 205–7
Ovid 5, 8, 12–15, 63–74, 87–9, 126 n. 17, 127 n. 19, 157 n. 27, 239–41, 243 n. 20, 256 n. 5, 314 n. 9, 321, 328 n. 20

Paeon (mythographer) 230 n. 36
Pammenes of Thebes 231
Panteus of Sparta 231
Parmenides 48

Parmenio 229
Parthia 210
Patañjali 252
Pausanias (Spartan general) 227, 236
Pausanias (traveller and geographer)
    135 n. 12, 136 n. 20, 142 n. 55, 143,
    146 n. 74, 271 n. 5
Peisistratus 226 n. 20, 232–3, 256 n. 3
Pelopidas 231
Pergamum 142, 193, 271
Pericles 102, 183, 201 n. 26, 214–15,
    224, 236 n. 62, 330
Peripatos and Peripatetics 35, 39, 45,
    128 n. 20
Persia 135, 138, 141, 165, 170, 228,
    270, 275–7, 287–9, 292, 294
Petronius 8 n. 6, 15, 75, 81 n. 30, 89,
    321 n. 53
Phalaris 102, 142
Pharnabazus 232 n. 44
Phidias 182–3, 347
Philip II of Macedon 85, 228–9, 231
Philip V of Macedon 139
Philo 239–42, 335
Philopoemen 142, 213–18
Philostratus 239–40, 243–4, 251–4, 317
    n. 20, 320 nn. 30–1, 347
Phocion 235
Phocylides 185
Phoenicia 276
Phryne 265
Phrynichus 215
Phyle (deme) 272
Phylarchus 231 n. 37
Picenum 212–13
Pindar 49 n. 10, 196, 339 n. 15
Pittacus 290
Plataea 213, 215
Plato 31–45, 47, 52–5, 76, 86, 98–100,
    102, 111, 134, 165, 168, 172 n. 21,
    178–9, 184–91, 194, 196, 198, 222–3,
    239 n. 8, 248, 273, 281, 291–2, 297
    n. 39, 312, 315–16, 321, 324–5, 328
    nn. 20–1, 330, 331 nn. 29–30, 343–51
Plautus 263 n. 22, 264 n. 23
Pliny the Elder 77 n. 13, 117–32, 139–
    41
Pliny the Younger 154 nn. 14–15, 314
    n. 9
Plotinus 349
Plutarch 27 n. 23, 31, 52, 100, 102–3,
    105, 139, 142 nn. 54 and 56, 199–202,
    205–36, 256, 264 n. 24, 330

Pollux 194 n. 8
Polybius 133–48, 212, 216
Polycrates 195
Polystratus (epigrammatist) 138 n. 28
Pompeii 275
Pompeius Magnus, Cn., *see* Pompey
Pompeius, Q. (cos. 88 BC) 44
Pompeius, Sex. 156
Pompey (Cn. Pompeius Magnus) 42,
    205, 208–9, 212–13, 215, 221–3, 233–
    4, 236
Pomponius Mela 122
Pope, Alexander 304
Porcia (wife of Brutus) 231
Porcius Latro, M. (declaimer) 63, 79, 84
Porphyrio 8 n. 6
Posidonius 93–6, 100, 143 n. 62
Postumius Albinus, A. (cos. 151 BC) 147–
    8
Praxiteles 347
Proclus 343–51
Prodicus 237–50
Propertius 56 n. 32, 65 n. 6, 66 n. 9, 311
    n. 46, 330 n. 27
Prudentius 151–3
Prusa 165–6, 184–92
Ps.-Apsines 327 n. 15
Ps.-Aristides 200–1
Ps.-Aristotle 324 n. 7
Ps.-Diogenes 247
Ps.-Dionysius 200–1
Ps.-Hermogenes 200–1
Ps.-Hesiod 334
Ps.-Lucian 317 n. 20
Ps.-Quintilian 76 n. 9, 90–1, 317 n. 16
Ptolemy IV Philopator 224
Ptolemy XII Auletes 173
Pydna 148
Pyrrhus 85, 138–9, 226–7

Quintilian 20 n. 2, 76, 77 n. 13, 108, 123
    n. 10, 130 n. 24, 150 n. 6, 196 n. 13,
    200, 313–22, 326–7, 329

Rabirius (Epicurean writer) 17
Rhine 336
Rhodes 174–5
Romulus 229–30, 233, 291
Rousseau 206
Roxane 229

Sabines 229–30
Sadāśivabrahmendra 252–3

St John's College, Oxford xii
Salamis 213
Salamis (Cyprus) 276
Sallust 143 n. 61
Samosata 237, 248, 250
Samothrace 337
Sappho 196, 326, 332–3
Sarapis 173, 194
Sardanapallus 102, 247
Sardianus 257–8
Saturnalia 291–2
Sauromatians 189
Scaevola, C. Mucius 97
Scipio Aemilianus, P. Cornelius 133–48
Scipio, Q. Caecilius Metellus (cos. 52 BC) 233 n. 50, 234
Scipio Nasica Corculum, P. Cornelius (cos. 155 BC) 143, 145
Scribonius Largus 55 n. 31, 131 n. 26
Scythia 166, 170, 174, 184, 186
Segesta 141
Sejanus, L. Aelius 130 n. 25
Semiramis 256
Seneca the Elder 63, 74 n. 35, 75–91, 126 n. 17, 130 n. 25, 314 n. 7, 315 n. 11, 318, 319 n. 27, 320 n. 31
Seneca the Younger 31–2, 35–8, 53, 55 n. 30, 93–115, 128 n. 20, 314 nn. 7–8, 315 n. 12, 316 n. 14, 317, 318 n. 23, 319, 321 n. 53
Servilia (mother of Brutus) 226 n. 23
Servius 140 n. 40, 150, 305
Severus Alexander 290 n. 16
Shakespeare 274, 304
Shechem 140
Sicily 141–3
Silius Italicus 239–41, 243–4, 248 n. 32, 249 n. 34
Simmias of Thebes 31
Simonides 196, 327 n. 18
Socrates 33–5, 38, 40, 52, 76–7, 102, 103 n. 12, 168, 179, 185–6, 196, 201, 233 n. 49, 239, 239 n. 8, 273, 292, 306
Solon 40, 196 n. 14, 198, 202, 231 n. 37, 232–3, 236, 290
Song of Silver 340
Song of Ullikummi 340
Sophocles 179 n. 15, 194, 207–8, 261, 264, 304, 332
Sparethra 256
Sparta 86, 148, 174–5, 212, 213–14, 216–17, 226–7, 231–2, 271
Speusippus 31

Sphodrias 232
Spithridates 232
Stateira 229
Statius 330
Stephanus (commentator on [Hippocrates]) 286
Stesichorus 311
Stesilaus (beloved of Aristides and Themistocles) 232
Stesimbrotus 223
Stoics and Stoicism 11, 16, 32, 35–9, 93–106, 111, 118, 128 n. 20, 129 n. 23, 147, 170 n. 18, 179 n. 11, 185–92, 210, 222 n. 7, 316 n. 15, 345 n. 8
Strabo 134 n. 3, 136 n. 18, 139 n. 37, 143 nn. 58 and 61, 167 n. 16, 172 n. 20, 337 n. 9
Suetonius 208–10, 222, 321 n. 33
Suka 252–3
Sulla, L. Cornelius 226, 235–6
Sulpicius, P. (trib. 88 BC) 44
Syria 170, 249
Syrianus (Proclus' teacher) 345 n. 7

Tacitus 27 n. 22, 77 n. 13, 117, 143 n. 59, 199–200, 314 n. 5, 319 n. 27, 321 n. 33
Taxila 252
Tennyson 304
Terence 125
Tetrarchy 295
Theagenes of Rhegium 278 n. 25
Thebes 140, 215, 227, 231–2, 236, 333
Themistius 32, 167 n. 10, 239, 241–2, 246, 248 n. 32, 249 n. 34, 290–1
Themistocles 215, 218, 232
Theodorus of Cyrene 36
Theodote 265
Theognis 31, 40
Theon 150 n. 6, 153 n. 12, 256–8
Theophilus (comic poet) 263 n. 22
Theophrastus 31, 40, 43, 323 n. 1, 329
Thermopylae 86, 213
Theseus 230, 233, 236
Thucydides 22 n. 7, 86, 136, 201 n. 26, 281, 325, 330
Tiber 149–52
Tiberius (emperor) 56
Tibullus 50, 55 n. 28
Timocles (comic poet) 263 n. 22
Timotheus 213
Tiribazus 225
Titus (emperor) 122, 287

Tomi 72, 321
Tomyris 256
Trajan 178, 180, 183, 186, 191–2, 210–11, 287–8, 290 n. 16, 291–2, 294
Triarius (declaimer) 78
Troy 27, 133, 138, 171–2, 259, 337
Tyndaris 142

Valentinian 288
Valeria (wife of Sulla) 235
Valerius Antias 228 n. 30
Valerius Maximus 31, 137 n. 23, 315 n. 11
Varro 121 n. 6, 122
Vedānta 252–3
Velleius Paterculus 139 n. 31, 143 nn. 58 and 61
Verus, L. (joint-emperor with Marcus Aurelius) 288, 293
Victor, C. Iulius (rhetorical theorist) 57 n. 37

Virgil 4–5, 12 n. 20, 19–29, 49 n. 10, 111, 121 n. 6, 128 n. 22, 130 n. 24, 131 n. 26, 149–59
Vitruvius 122–4, 130, 131 n. 26
Vivekananda, Swami 253

Wordsworth 310

Xenarchus (comic poet) 263 n. 22
Xenocrates 31
Xenophon 32, 35, 40, 52, 102, 196, 201 n. 26, 229, 232 n. 43, 237–50, 264 nn. 23–4, 273
Xerxes 86, 133, 138, 239 n. 8

Zeno of Elea 103 n. 12
Zoilus (literary critic) 130
Zonaras 134 n. 4, 135 n. 12, 137 n. 23
Zoroaster 166, 188
Zosimus 296 n. 38, 297 n. 40

INDEX OF ETHICAL, RHETORICAL, AND CRITICAL CONCEPTS

addressees, *see* audience
allegory 183, 237–50, 278 n. 25, 302, 351
anger 328–9
antithesis 109, 112, 114
apostrophe 111
atomology 8–12
audience and addressees 10, 19–29, 66–7, 109–10, 122, 132, 163–5, 177, 179, 190, 192, 205–20, 310, 315–16, 324
autobiography 199–200, 237–8: *see also* self-presentation

balance 5–7, 109, 112
book-division 7, 13
boundaries 3–18

character and characterization, see *ethos*
clausulae 111–12
cognition 3–18, 311–12
colon-division 4–6
controversiae 63, 64 n. 5, 71 n. 25, 75–91
cultural poetics 301–12
culture, see *paideia*

declamation 63, 72–3, 75–91, 255–67
description 113–15, 164–6, 241–4; see also *ekphrasis*
didacticism and didactic style 7–8, 19–29, 68–9, 109, 306; *see also* protreptic
dreams and dreaming 194, 237–50

ekphrasis 77, 113, 149–59, 260, 278–80
emotions 78, 257–60, 266, 313–33
emotive hedonism 305–6
enargeia 149–59; *see also* description
encomium 25, 163, 167–74, 195, 201, 203
enjambement 4–7
epideictic oratory 86, 163–204
epigram, see *sententia*
epistolography and epistolary form 47–61, 73, 109, 132

ethos 37, 78 n. 16, 80–1, 236, 255–67, 269–78, 326–7; *see also* self-presentation
etymology 8–9, 16, 351
exempla 73–4, 84–5, 89–91, 97, 108, 113, 215, 219–20, 265, 287, 295–8

fable 170–1, 173, 181
fear 323–33
forensic language and imagery 125
forgery 251–4
friendship 31–61

grief 258, 323–33

hedonism, *see* emotive hedonism
hexameter, narrative and neoteric 4–6
historicism 301–12
hymns and hymnic style 70 n. 22, 196

iconography 274, 278–80
ideology 117–48, 219–20
images and imagination, *see* forensic language and imagery, medicine and medical analogies, natural images and analogies, *phantasia*, political analogies and images, symbolism
imitatio 237–50, 302
impetus 313–22
indignation 79–81, 84–5, 194, 328–9; *see also* anger
inspiration 24, 197–8, 202–3, 320–1, 324, 326, 351
invective 198
irony 63–74, 181

locus amoenus 149–59, 178

medicine and medical analogies 55–7, 281–6

names and naming 4, 269–78; *see also* etymology

narratology 310
national stereotypes 41, 165–6, 170–1,
    177–8, 181–4, 186–92, 219
natural imagery and analogies 111, 117–
    32, 331

paideia 165–8, 171, 173–4, 207, 237–52
parabasis 194–5
paraphthegma 193–204
paronomasia 195
pathos, see emotion
perception 343–51; *see also* cognition
periodization 303–4
phantasia 343–51
pity 315, 323–33
political analogies and imagery 11–12,
    14, 28–9
post-structuralism 309–10
praise, *see* encomium
proems 21
progymnasmata 150, 255–67
propaganda 133–48, 219–20; *see also*
    ideology
protreptic 47–60, 107–13, 167–74, 205–
    20, 237–50
proverbs 52, 59–60; see also *sententiae*
psychoanalysis 222, 308–9
psychology 16, 16 n. 19, 222, 236; *see
    also* psychoanalysis

reader-response 218–20, 310–11
realism 178–9, 336

reciprocity 34–5, 39
repetition 109, 114, 157
rhetorical questions 111, 257
rhythm 111
ring-composition 110

scepticism 307
segmentation 3–18
self-control 221–36, 262, 323–33
self-praise 27, 193–204
self-presentation 19–29, 47–61, 67, 69,
    73, 109–10, 193–204, 206–7, 237–50,
    287–98
self-sufficiency 31–45, 52, 178
semiotics 307–8, 312, 343–51
sense-units 4
sententiae 51–2, 56–7, 60, 75–91, 109,
    112, 114, 319
sexuality 191, 221–36, 261–3, 270, 273–
    4, 308–9
soliloquy 71, 89, 258–9
Sperrung 5
sublimity 192, 323–42
suasoriae 63–91
symbolism 237–50, 350–1; *see also*
    allegory *and entries listed under* images
    and imagination

theatre-imagery 280

usefulness of work 24–5, 118, 131, 208–
    17